HEINEMANN
AVCE

ADVANCED

Business

Dave Needham • Rob Dransfield

B, L & T – Amersham

Ewelina Chyzyona

Edexcel
Success through qualifications

Heinemann Educational Publishers,
Halley Court, Jordan Hill, Oxford OX2 8EJ
A division of Reed Educational & Professional Publishing Ltd

Heinemann is a registered trademark of Reed Educational & Professional Publishing Limited

OXFORD MELBOURNE AUCKLAND JOHANNESBURG BLANTYRE GABORONE
IBADAN PORTSMOUTH NH (USA) CHICAGO

© Rob Dransfield, Dave Needham 2000

First published 2000
2004 2003 2002 2001 2000
10 9 8 7 6 5 4 3 2 1

A catalogue record for this book is available from the British Library on request.

ISBN 0 435 45316 5

All rights reserved.

Apart from any fair dealing for the purposes of research or private study, or criticism or review
as permitted under the terms of the UK Copyright, Designs and Patents Act, 1988, this
publication may not be reproduced, stored or transmitted, in any form or by any means, without
the prior permission in writing of the publishers, or in the case of reprographic reproduction only
in accordance with the terms of the licences issued by the Copyright Licensing Agency in the
UK, or in accordance with the terms of licenses issued by the appropriate Reproduction Rights
Organization outside the UK. Enquiries concerning reproduction outside the terms stated here
should be sent to the publishers at the United Kingdom address printed on this page.

Typeset by TechType, Abingdon, Oxfordshire

Printed and bound in Great Britain

Tel: 01865 888058 www.heinemann.co.uk

Contents

Acknowledgements

The authors would like to thank Christine Bullock of Edexcel for her constructive suggestions on the text, Anna Fabrizio, our editor at Heinemann, for all her sterling efforts in getting this book published, and our publisher Margaret Berriman, also of Heinemann, for her encouragement and enthusiasm. Thanks also to Margaret Dewsbury, Paul Plumridge and Anne Griffin.

The authors and publishers would also like to thank the following individuals and organisations for permission to reproduce photographs and other copyright material:

p. 7 Nottingham Forest Football Club; p. 38, 100, 126 Photodisc; p. 42 Co-Operative Wholesale Society (CWS); p. 104 Iceland.co.uk; p. 177, 206 Corbis; p. 347 CACI Information Solutions; p. 375 Asda Wal-Mart; p. 402 Sally and Richard Greenhill; p. 432 Nestlé; p. 435 Investors in People; p. 659 Studentnet.com.

Every effort has been made to contact copyright holders of material published in this book. We would be glad to hear from unacknowledged sources at the first opportunity.

Rob Dransfield and Dave Needham
August 2000

Introduction

Self-managed learning

Now that you are studying at Advanced level you will need to take more responsibility for your own learning.

This will involve:

- identifying what you need to learn

- developing a plan of action to learn what is required (including consideration of time management)

- researching materials, and finding information from relevant sources

- turning you research into a well-structured piece of work which is clearly and appropriately presented.

1 Identifying what you need to learn

Each unit and chapter contains an introductory section which sets out clearly what you need to learn. Read carefully through these sections so that you are clear about what you will need to understand.

You will also need to examine the **assessment** section for the relevant unit (there are 6 units in all).

The assessments in this book outline the evidence you will need to provide to show that you know, understand and can perform required activities. The assessment brief specifies the sorts of information that you will need to produce, e.g. a business report illustrated with photographs, charts and diagrams.

The assessment sections also explain the sort of evidence which would count as given levels of performance, e.g. what you need to do to get a Grade E, a Grade C, and a Grade A.

In order to help you build up ongoing evidence of what you know, understand and can do we have also signposted the book with a number of short activities which are labelled 'Check your understanding':

Check your understanding

By carrying out these activities you will be building up evidence which you may want to use as part of your assessment, where appropriate.

2 Developing a plan of action to learn

An action plan is a very simple planning tool. You should be able to quickly construct an action plan for carrying out an assignment. The action plan will enable you to work to deadlines.

The action plan will contain the following components:

- task to be completed, and series of sub-tasks that make up the overall task

- a timeline for completing the various components

- allocation of responsibilities for each component

- resources that will be needed for each component
- a way of checking that each component has been successfully completed.

For example, imagine that a group of four students has been given the responsibility of finding out how many businesses in a shopping precinct use e-commerce and what benefits these businesses see in this approach to buying and selling. The students have four weeks to carry out the work and must then present their findings to the class.

They split the task up into:

1 Identifying names, addresses, telephone numbers, email addresses of local businesses, and identifying a contact in each business.

2 Interviewing the named business contact.

3 Collating the data.

4 Producing material for the presentation.

5 Delivering the presentation at the end of week 4.

The group choose Ajay as their team leader for the work and together set out the following action plan:

3 Researching materials and finding information

Developing research skills and being able to find out information for yourself is very important in your development as a learner. In order to research materials you will need to decide what you are looking for and where best to find this information.

Some information will need to be collected by primary research. This will involve devising questionnaires which you will then use in the field. It is always helpful to first pilot test your questionnaires on a small sample of people to find out whether the questions you ask are suitable. Sometimes you will find that they are ambiguous and are not fully understood. Piloting a questionnaire therefore gives you the opportunity to restructure your questionnaire before you use it with a larger group of people.

Today, students are able to gather large quantities of what we call secondary information (it is called secondary because someone else has already gathered it) by using the Internet. The Internet gives you access to up-to-the-minute information

Task	Who is responsible (and resources required)	Checked by	Time completed by
1 Identifying	Sally & Raj (clipboards, telephone directories)	Ajay	Friday 6 Oct 2000
2 Interviewing	Ajay & Liam (clipboard, voice recorder)	Sally & Raj	Friday 13 Oct 2000
3 Collating	Sally & Raj (PC with database package)	Ajay	Tuesday 17 Oct 2000
4 Producing material	Ajay & Liam (PC, with graphics package, Powerpoint package, coloured paper, acetates, access to photocopier)	Sally & Raj	Friday 20 Oct 2000
5 Practising presentation	All (Computer with Powerpoint, and screen, empty room)	All	Tuesday 24 Oct 2000
6 Giving presentation	All (Computer with Powerpoint and screen, 20 copies of all handouts)	All	Friday 27 Oct 2000

which will enable you to carry out many of the research activities suggested in this book. Please read through the section below about using the Internet – and then freely use the Internet sources which are suggested in the text.

4 Turning your research into a final piece of work which is carefully presented

Sifting through information to find out what is relevant is a skill that develops over time. Practised researchers can often quickly sort out what is relevant from the irrelevant. One problem today is that the Internet provides us with a wealth of information produced by a range of people. Some of the information is very useful while other sources are of very dubious quality. One problem of using websites is that they have often been constructed for public relations purposes and just provide one side of the story. You therefore need to be very careful about using websites. Ask yourself the following questions: Who has put together this information?; What was their purpose in constructing the website?; Can I find a counterbalancing view somewhere else?

You then need to piece together your information into a form that is suitable for presentation.

For many writers the problem is where to start. You may have reams and reams of information but are not sure how to break it down. How can you structure it in a logical form? Making a plan is always useful. Work through your information, noting important areas under headings and subheadings. Then try to put these in a logical sequence. If you put your headings

and sub-headings into a word processing file, you will be able to juggle them around later on.

The following outline may be helpful to your work:

1 Title page to help display

2 List of contents

3 Main body of work

4 Bibliography

5 References

6 Appendix

7 Index.

The reference section should list all the books, magazines and journals that you have referred to directly in your work.

For example, in your work you might state that Patel, P. (2001) defines marketing as 'anticipating and meeting customer requirements'. In your references you would then list Patel in the following way:

Patel, P., *Marketing in the new millennium*, Heinemann, 2001.

The bibliography is different to the reference section. The bibliography should list books, journals etc. that you have used as part of your research but have not directly referred to in your text.

The appendix is a section at the end of a study which contains additional useful information. It might contain copies of letters you have written which illustrate the depth of your investigations, tables and figures which can be referred to and any other useful information. If you have anything else which you think would improve the study and which would indicate the extent of your investigations, put it in the appendix.

Report writing

Many people, when they hear the word report, immediately think of a school report, others think of a news report.

In business, a report commonly refers to a written statement from someone who has made a study of something (such as an event, the cause of some occurrence, or the performance of a person or organisation), which is then sent or passed on to someone else to be used for a particular purpose. Often the conclusions stemming from a business report will provide the basis for business decisions.

A written report is an important form of business communication and a perfectly acceptable and businesslike way of presenting your work.

A suggested form of presentation for a written report is:

1 Title page

2 List of contents

3 Terms of reference

4 Procedure

5 Findings

6 Conclusion

7 Recommendations

8 Signature.

The **terms of reference** explain the reasons for the report by referring to the group or persons asking you to produce it. This brief section should explain why you are writing the report. For example:

'This report is being produced in response to a request from ASDA Head Office to assess the potential market for developing a new supermarket in Midtown.'

Or,

'This report is being produced to fulfil the criteria required for Unit 1 of the Advanced VCE course in Business.'

The **procedure** section will refer to the stages that have taken place in the build-up of your report. What letters have you sent? Which people have you interviewed? What types of secondary sources have you consulted? What else did you have to do?

The **findings** will indicate what you have discovered as a result of your investigations.

Your **conclusion** will contain a summary of your findings. For example:

* The population of Midtown is expanding by 3% per annum.

* There is full employment in the town, and consumers' incomes are 10% higher than the national average.

* The chosen location is ideal for passing trade.

* The existing competition is not strong in ASDA's segment of the market.

* The potential for sales is 20% higher than in comparable ASDA stores nationwide.

Recommendations are only necessary where appropriate. For example, if you are trying to look at ways of resolving a problem through your investigation, then the likelihood is that, as a result of your report, you will be suggesting some form of action: e.g., there seems to be a strong case for ASDA to build a new supermarket in Midtown given the current market conditions.

Making presentations

Making presentations is an important area of communication skills. Most students enjoy making presentations once they have overcome their early nerves.

You will usually work together as a group to make a presentation. This will involve jointly planning work and then deciding on how you are going to structure your presentation.

A key rule is not to leave things to the last minute. You should run through your presentation in advance. The more you practise, the easier the words will come to you on the day. Remember that all the students in your class will also need to make presentations. They too will be nervous. Students should therefore seek to support each other. Indeed, students will be judged partly on the way they support each other. Students should therefore not:

- seek the limelight, taking it upon themselves to do all the presentation

- refuse to be involved in making presentations.

In this course in Business the most able communicators and group members will be those who help others to make a success of presentations.

In preparing a presentation you will benefit from using the following checklist to prepare your presentation:

To plan and organise the presentation
Aim to:
- set out your objectives
- set out a main idea and a clear conclusion
- set out your introduction clearly
- think about your audience, their interests and their level
- brainstorm some main ideas
- plan handouts and overheads
- keep a clear thread linking main points.

To prepare for the presentation
Make sure you:
- practise
- check the equipment
- arrange your notes and handouts in the order you're going to use them.

To develop the visual aids
Make sure you:
- make them clear and easy to look at
- choose the correct type of chart
- use computer graphics packages (like Powerpoint)
- use 18-point or 24-point font sizes on overhead projectors
- have clear titles
- talk to the audience, not to the visual
- place yourself in the centre of the stage
- use a pointer, but not too often.

To stop being nervous
Plan to:
- take deep breaths
- move during the presentation
- establish eye contact.

Delivering the presentation
Plan to:
- be aware of what you say and how you say it
- speak with a strong clear voice, and don't speak too quickly
- be animated, clear and enthusiastic
- use eye contact to make the presentation conversational and personal.

Questions and answers
Plan to:
- prepare for questions and practise the answers
- ask for questions by stepping forward with hand raised
- watch the questioner and listen carefully
- repeat the question to make sure everybody has heard it

- Stand when you make your presentation.
- Do not just read from your work or from a prepared report. Make notes to guide you but talk freely through your presentation (refer to notes using a series of headings or a system of small cards).
- Use slides, handouts, overhead projector transparencies, flipcharts, computer generated images e.g. Powerpoint, posters, or any other form of visual aid to support your talk.
- Make sure that you keep to the point. Try to make your talk interesting, and sound cheerful.
- Do not gabble, or talk too slowly.
- Start your talk by making it clear what your subject is and how you propose to present your ideas.
- Finish your talk with an appropriate ending which leaves an impression.

- keep the same bearing as in your presentation
- use eye contact and look at the whole audience.

A guide to using the Internet

How to get on the Internet

From home

You first need an Internet provider (there is a huge variety to choose from, but a few examples are BT, Virgin and Cable & Wireless). The provider will supply you with the software to enable you to connect to the provider. Most software will automatically install the software needed, leaving you very little to configure, but if in doubt there are help lines, but watch out for the charges (£1 per minute!!!). Then follow the instructions.

From college

Once you have logged onto the university network click on either the Netscape icon or the Internet Explorer icon and you will be taken to the college home page. From there, type in the address (this is called a URL, and we will learn more about URLs below) of the website you want to go to in the address bar at the top of the page. If you are not sure where you want to go, try using a search engine (see below).

From school

Although there are variations depending on your school, the age of your computer network and the way the computers have been configured, the most common way to get onto the web is as above – a user name and password are generally required.

What happens now?

Home page: this is the first page you see when you are connected to the Internet, at work or in an academic institution (e.g. the home page of The Nottingham Trent University is www.ntu.ac.uk). If you are accessing the web at home, your home page can be any page you choose, such as your favourite website or even your own website. See the user guides in your browser for information on how to do this.

General navigation

Whenever you move the mouse over an area and the image changes to a hand, this means that there is a link to another part of a document, or a different site entirely. Click on the area to follow the link. Also, the area you move the mouse over may change colour, or there may be a different picture entirely.

URLs

A URL (Uniform Resource Location) is the actual address or location of a website and it will look like this: http://www.ntu.ac.uk. If you are having difficulty getting to the site, double check the address and if it is a long address try going to the main page first e.g. www.blest.net rather than the exact location **ww.blest.net/nemesislive.html**.

Remember that the Internet sometimes runs quite slowly and it can take a while to connect to the page you want. If it seems to be taking a longer time than usual, try pressing the reload/refresh (depending on your browser) button.

Information

You will see various extensions at the end of addresses. The main ones are:

.com = commercial organisation
.org = non-commercial organisation (usually)
.ac = academic institution
.gov = government
.co.uk = UK site.

Due to the increasing popularity of the web the range of extensions which are available is growing – http://register-names.co.uk is the place to look at the different extensions which are now available, and it is particularly useful if you want to register your own donation name.

Downloads

At home You will need a program like winzip (www.winzip.com) (free for thirty days) for compressed files and acrobat (free) http://www.adobe.com/products/acrobat/readstep.html for files with a .pdf extension. Once you have these you should have no problem with downloading as most download automatically. Just remember the name of the file and where it is stored. Before downloading, always make sure that you have an up-do-date virus checker, you have checked the file and you trust the source of the file.

At college or school Do not download any programs. Files which you want to refer to later can be saved by clicking on the file menu, choosing 'Save as' and then saving to a local hard drive or a floppy disk. As a general rule, pictures are not saved with these files. Any pictures or graphics should be saved separately by right-clicking on the picture and choosing 'Save picture as'.

For a list of terms you might come across while surfing, you could have a look at the following site: http://www.matisse.net/files/glossary.html.

What's good about the Net?

- The information available, the free stuff, movies, games, music and programs, chat rooms and lots more.

- You can find out anything about almost anything with very little effort.

- The Net gives a medium to people who otherwise would not be able to get their message out to a global audience.

- Global communication; you can make friends with people from anywhere in the world.

What's bad about the Net?

- The information available – sometimes you have too much information. The information can be out of date; the site may no longer be active. Also, because because most of the sites are American and many are provided for PR purposes you can get a one-sided view.

- The weird stuff. Because the Internet is not regulated, it is up to the individual to ensure that minors cannot gain access to websites containing any inappropriate content. Software is available (e.g. Net Nanny, Cyber patrol) which can help to protect you from these sites, but this only goes part of the way towards stopping these sites from being displayed on your screen. It is up to you as an individual to make sure that you do not view sites with unsuitable content. A word of warning: while prosecutions are rare, they do happen.

Search engines

A search engine is the best way of finding sites on the Internet. The basic principle is that you enter a word or words of interest in the box at the top of the page. The engine then goes and searches through the index of Internet pages and the results are returned in a list. However, as with most things there are many different types of engine and they all look for things in different ways. This is because of the way the search engine is programmed. Search engines look for key words, phrases or the number of times a certain word is used, or a combination of these approaches. For instance a search on Lycos UK for Pentium returned 39,562 responses whereas the same search on Yahoo returned just 166!

A single search engine such as Lycos (www.lycos.com) will only look through a limited range of pages. A meta search engine such as Ask Jeeves (www.aj.com) or Savvysearch (www.savvysearch.com) searches several engines at once. You can have UK-specific engines (e.g. www.yahoo.co.uk, or www.lycos.co.uk).

So which search engine should you choose? There is no easy answer – it depends on what you are looking for. One suggestion is that you could try using meta search engines for general topics and then try out a few of the single search engines to find one or two that suit you.

Site of interest

In this book we outline a number of relevant web sites that you might want to look at which relate to business topics at appropriate points in the text. Here are some other sites of general interest that might appeal to you:

News

www.bbc.co.uk
www.channel4.com

Newspapers – Today's news and past issues

www.the-times.co.uk
www.electronictelegraph.co.uk
www.ft.com
www.pa.press.net Press Association web site.

General

www.beeb.com
www.student-net.co.uk
www.gameplay.com
www.downloadsafari.com
www.classicgaming.com
http://www.coolhomepages.com
www.cannondale.com

Films

www.realplay.com Watch movie clips and get the latest movie news

Internet authors

Here are a few simple rules for budding Internet authors. Do not include very large graphic images in your html documents. It is preferable to have postage sized images that the user can click on to 'enlarge' a picture. Some users with access to the Web are viewing documents using slow speed modems and downloading these images can take a great deal of time.

It is not a requirement to ask permission to link to another's site, though out of respect for the individual and their efforts, a simple email message stating that you have made a link to their site would be appropriate.

When including video or voice files, include next to the description a file size, i.e. (10KB or 2MB), so the user can see how long it might take to download the file. Keep naming standards for URLs simple and don't keep changing the case (changing from capitals to small letters). Some users do not realise that sites are case sensitive or they might receive a URL verbally where the case sensitivity is not easily recognisable.

When in doubt about a URL, try accessing the domain address first, then navigate through the site to locate the specific URL. Most URLs begin with the node address of WWW followed by the site address – e.g.

http://www.cern.ch
http://www.fau.edu
http://www.ibm.com
http://www.cpsr.org

Business at work

Anyone thinking of starting his or her own business or joining an existing business needs to have at his or her fingertips knowledge about what makes business work successfully and know how to apply that knowledge to a particular business. For instance, imagine a salesperson who doesn't know what his or her business is trying to achieve or what makes it different from its competitors. Imagine a production manager who is unable to explain to his or her staff what quality means, or doesn't understand what they mean when they call him or her an autocratic manager.

This unit is about exploring real business. You will evaluate information provided by businesses and gather your own information from at least one business. A good way of doing this might be to imagine yourself as someone thinking of joining that business or competing with it. You will need to decide what information you need and what questions to ask.

In this unit you will find out about different types of businesses, their objectives, structures and cultures, and how these affect the way businesses work. You will also explore how all these different aspects of a business interact with the business. You will learn about the different functional areas within businesses and how these operate together to allow businesses to make products or offer services that contribute to the wealth of the economy. You will also learn about the variety of processes by which products and services are created and how and why businesses try to assure the quality of their products or services.

This unit will give you knowledge and skills you will draw on when you are working on advanced Unit 2 The competitive business environment and Unit 4 Human resources. There are also links with Unit 3 Marketing, Unit 5 Business finance and Unit 6 Business planning.

This unit is assessed through your portfolio work. The grade on that assessment will be your grade for the unit.

Chapter 1 Business objectives

Businesses exist to provide goods and services. All businesses, whether they aim to make a profit or not, have to make products and/or provide services that satisfy customers' wants or needs. Businesses set themselves objectives that govern the way they operate. You need to be able to identify and explain different objectives for businesses, including:

- making a profit (or surplus)
- increasing sales or market share
- surviving
- providing services to the community
- offering charitable or non-profit services, such as caring for the environment
- developing staff skills
- producing high-quality products or offering high-quality service.

All businesses have particular attitudes, values and beliefs that make up their culture.

You need to be able to identify and describe the economic, social, environmental and ethical influences that contribute to a business's culture and describe different business cultures. You should also be able to explain how the culture of a business may affect its objectives and structure, and help or hinder the success of the business.

Introducing business objectives

Having a focused objective gives you a clear idea of the direction you are heading in. It should also help you to judge how successful you have been in meeting your objectives.

You need to have the underpinning knowledge of what business objectives mean

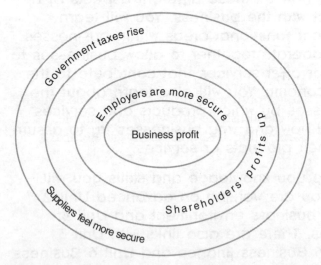
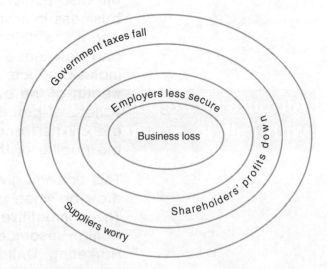

Figure 1.1 The ripple effect of profits or losses

in practice. You should then be able to apply this underpinning knowledge in examining the way in which businesses operate in the real world.

The most frequently mentioned business objective is making a profit. Profit is the difference between the total revenue of a business (what it takes in receipts) and its total cost. Failure to make such a profit leads to a loss of confidence in the business, particularly among the shareholders (people who have bought shares). But, it is not just the shareholders whose livelihoods are threatened; there is a ripple effect as employees start to worry about their jobs, people who have supplied the business with goods on credit worry if they will be paid back, the government may receive less in tax from the business, etc.

Taking a real-world example, on 15 July 2000 shares in Airtours, the UK's biggest tour operator, fell more than 17% on the announcement that the company's profits were less than expected. Share prices fell from 307p a share to 253p a share.

Daily News

15 JULY 2000

Airtours share prices tumble with fall in profits warning

A major cause of the fall in profits was a downturn in bookings. England's early failure in the Euro 2000 competition led to a fall in bookings in Belgium, Holland and France. In Scandinavia there were fewer bookings because Airtours had increased its brochure prices to offset higher fuel costs and the

abolition of duty free. Airtours were also selling fewer holidays in the United States.

In simple terms the company was offering too many holidays for sale relative to customer demand for such holidays – leaving half-empty planes and hotels.

This meant that while Airtours' sales revenues were greater than costs – yielding a profit, the profit would have been much larger if demand had been greater. The sensible business decision would therefore be for Airtours to cut back on the number of holidays it offers.

It is not surprising that making a profit is such an important business objective – the Airtours example shows how in just one day 17% can be wiped off the share value of a company because of worries about profits.

For many companies the objectives of increasing sales and/or market share are closely associated with that of profitability. As a general rule, companies with high sales levels or which have a large share of a particular market are best placed to make high profits (although this is not always the case).

A business likes to have a high market share because this enhances the image of the organisation and places the business in a strong position compared with rivals. Again, we can illustrate this with an example. Glaxo is a leading UK pharmaceutical company. On 14 July 2000 the price of Glaxo shares fell by 63p following a report presented at an International Aids Conference in South Africa. The report showed that a study in Uganda found that babies treated with Viramune, a drug being trialled by Germany's Boehringer, were 39% less likely to become infected with Aids.

Daily News

14 JULY 2000

Boehringer may gain market share at expense of Glaxo

The implications of this announcement were that it was expected that Boehringer's sales, and share of the drugs market to fight Aids would increase, while Glaxo's would fall. This would lead to increasing profits for Boehringer at the expense of Glaxo.

Sales, market share and profits are very important. Shareholders want to put their money where they can make most profit. The most profitable companies thus attract most funds. They grow and prosper.

At the same time there are many other businesses that are just concerned with survival. Examine the shop premises on the High Street of your local town. While many are thriving, others will be struggling along, others still will have closed down. In the longer term all businesses are faced with the problem of survival. For example, in 1999/2000 Marks & Spencer, one of the most famous names of British retailing, found themselves struggling to change their image in order to pick up from a situation of falling profits and sales – ten years ago it would have been unthinkable. Marks & Spencer were faced with the business reality of survival.

While profit is the essential driving force behind business it is not necessarily the most important objective of an organisation. Some organisations exist to provide a service to the community or because they offer charitable or non-profit services. For example, the principal aim of Talking Newspapers for the Blind is not to make a profit – it exists to provide talking newspapers and magazines for blind and partially sighted people. Oxfam sets out its 'purpose' as:

- 'Oxfam works with others to overcome poverty and suffering'.

Oxfam sets out its 'beliefs' in the following way.

- The lives of all human beings are of equal value.

- In a world rich in resources, poverty is an injustice which must be overcome.

- Poverty makes people more vulnerable to conflict and natural calamity; much of this suffering can be prevented and must be relieved.

- People's vulnerability to poverty and suffering is increased by unequal power relations based on, for example, gender, race, class, caste and disability; women who make up a majority of the world's poor are especially disadvantaged.

- Working together we can build a just and safer world, in which people take control over their own lives and enjoy their basic rights.

- To overcome poverty and suffering involves changing unjust policies and practices, nationally and internationally, as well as working closely with people in poverty.

As a result, Oxfam's 'identity' can be described as follows.

- Oxfam works internationally as part of a world-wide movement to build a just and safer world.

- Oxfam is an independent British organisation, registered as a charity, affiliated to Oxfam international, with partners, volunteers, supporters, and staff of many nationalities.

- Oxfam is accountable both to those who support it and to those whom it seeks to benefit by its efforts.

You can see that Oxfam is an example of a radically different way of going about organising an organisation. Oxfam sees itself as being accountable to the people that provide it with money voluntarily, and to people suffering from poverty – this is quite different from the profit-oriented objectives of a company driven by shareholders.

In the modern world we are increasingly seeing the development of a number of new companies which are committed to new objectives of fairness. For example, for many years chocolate manufacturers have been accused of profiting at the expense of suppliers of cocoa in poorer parts of the world.

However, chocolate lovers who have suffered years of guilt over their cravings can now hold their heads up high. The Day Chocolate Company does not claim to cut calorie intake, but it does say that those who eat its Divine bar can feel better because of the way the sweet is produced. The Day Chocolate Company is a 'fair trade' business – part of the Fairtrade group of firms that takes into consideration the interests of suppliers in the developing world. By owning a third of the business and having seats on the Day Chocolate Company board, the 35,000 farmers in the Kuapa Kokoo cocoa co-operative in Ghana have a large say in how the chocolate bar is produced and sold. The company was set up to help improve the lives of cocoa bean growers at survival level because the market price for their produce was below production costs of the crop.

Other examples of successful companies that have operated with a community perspective include Café Direct, the well-known coffee label.

Daily News

16 JULY 2000

The Day Chocolate Company wins Business in the Community's Award for Excellence

Business does not therefore have to be just about profit, it can be concerned with other objectives such as social fairness and protection of the environment.

Another business objective that has increasingly gained prominence in recent times is that of developing the skills of the staff who work for an organisation. While the early 20th century was characterised by companies that sought to create systems of production that enabled mass production with little thought for the human side of work, today there is far more emphasis in business on developing people and their skills. In the modern business world of .com organisations and Information and Communications Technology, people are very important to business success. It is the people who work for the organisation that come up with many of the new ideas, and it is the organisation's personnel who deal directly with customers. It therefore makes good business sense to develop the skills of your people.

Finally, it is important to mention the objective of producing high-quality products or offering high-quality services. As you will see in Chapter 6, 'Quality is in the eye of the beholder'. 'Quality' in business means providing a good or service which is 'fit' for the purpose that the consumer intends to use it for. A Friday night drinker who buys a pie and chips from a fish and chip shop after closing time may be totally satisfied with the product – he or she may feel that it is 'a top-quality meal'. At the same time someone else may be disappointed with the expensive meal that he or she has shared with friends at a local French restaurant because it does not quite live up to expectations. Providing quality should mean that the punter will be inclined to buy the product or service again . . . and again.

Daily News

18 JULY 2000

Quality Award for Black Pudding Producer

David Hirst's of Barnsley have won another prestigious quality award for their finest Barnsley Black Pudding.

In the sections that follow you will build up your underpinning knowledge of business objectives, while having the opportunity to show your understanding through working on a number of case studies.

Objective 1: Making a profit (or surplus)

Ask most people what they think is the main objective of a business and they will almost certainly say 'to make a profit'. The reason businesses seek to make a profit is that, without profit, a business is unable to do all the things it wants to do.

Without profit the business cannot keep its shareholders happy, it cannot pay higher wages to its employees, it cannot invest in better technology to improve its products and so on.

Nowhere is this more true than in the modern world of football, in which the most profitable clubs are able to buy the star players, enabling them to play the attractive football that keeps the spectators happy.

One of the most important objectives of a business is to make a profit. A company that does not make a profit will find it difficult to plough back money into research and development, it will find it difficult to invest in new technologies, it will not have money available to give to charities and to carry out 'good works', and it will not be able to increase the rewards to its employees. Of course, if you make a loss it is possible to borrow – but lenders will look very carefully at your profit potential before parting with their funds.

It is a basic fact of business life, therefore, that profit is important. Nottingham Forest are a public company. They are owned by their shareholders. Of course, these shareholders want Forest to do well, but they also want to receive a return on their shares in the form of dividends (money paid at regular intervals to shareholders as a reward for the sacrifice they are making in buying shares). If Nottingham Forest continue to make a loss, the shareholders will lose confidence and many would sell their shares.

Case Study: Nottingham Forest in March 1998

	P	W	D	L	F	A	Pts
Nottingham Forest	34	20	8	6	56	29	68
Middlesborough	34	20	8	6	55	31	68
Charlton	35	18	8	9	62	43	62
Sunderland	33	18	8	7	59	36	62
Sheffield United	34	15	13	6	50	37	58
Ipswich	35	14	13	8	56	37	55

Figure 1.2 League Table for top of Division One, Wednesday 4 March 1998

Nottingham Forest FC, 2000–2001

Nottingham Forest will start the season 2000–2001 in the First Division. They are one of those clubs that in recent years have yo-yoed between the Premier Division and the First Division. These clubs are faced with the reality that most of the financial advantages go to those clubs in the Premier Division: sponsorship, television revenues, merchandising revenues, etc. For example, from 2001 television revenues alone for the Premier Division will be in excess of £500 million.

This case study looks back to 1998 when Nottingham Forest were seeking promotion to the Premier Division; it shows why it is so important to be successful in business. (The reader may be interested to note that while Forest won promotion in 1998, they were relegated again in 1999.)

At the time when the league table in Figure 1.1 was published, it was widely reported in the press that Nottingham Forest (http://www.nottinghamforest.co.uk/) would have to sell star players and slash costs if their gamble to win promotion had failed.

The club, which was relegated from the Premiership in 1997, was clocking up huge losses by keeping on expensive players in a make-or-break effort to get back to the top (in March 1998). Nottingham Forest was faced with the stark choice of having to cut back dramatically on expenses to make up for lost millions of TV revenues if they stayed in the lower division. As a public limited company, over the long term the club's cost base has got to be in line with its revenues. No club can carry on losing money.

At the time, the average Premier League club received £8 million from BSkyB, the satellite broadcaster, to screen live games (in 1999 Manchester United, Arsenal and Chelsea each received over £10 million each). First Division clubs, in contrast, typically received just £800,000. Over the next few years the gap was likely to widen, with top-flight clubs getting more than £10 million.

Nottingham Forest made a loss of £6.5 million in the six months to November 1997. The players and staff bill of £4.7 million meant they made a loss of £2.4 million on their operations. In addition, they also spent £4 million on transfer fees.

1 Why might it be easier for some Premier League clubs to make a profit than First Division ones?
2 Why might some Premier clubs not be able to make a profit?
3 Why were Nottingham Forest prepared to make a loss to gain promotion?
4 Why would they have to sell players if they fail to be promoted? What other costs might they be able to 'slash'?
5 What do you think is meant by the following terms mentioned in the case study: 'expenses', 'cost base', 'revenues', 'loss', 'operations'.
6 Were Nottingham Forest promoted at the end of the 1998 season?
7 How would their success in that year have affected their ability to make profits in the following season?
8 How can a business organisation make a profit? Why is it so important to make a profit?

We can illustrate the importance of making a profit to a business by taking the example of a small fictional non-league football team – Melchester Rovers. Melchester have a ground capacity of 5,000 and in May 2000 they are in a very strong position to win promotion to the National Conference League. Their only source of revenue (money earned) is through gate receipts.

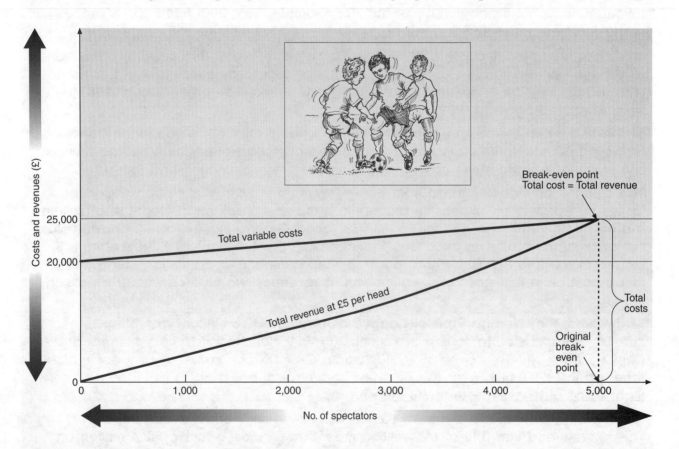

Figure 1.3 Breaking even at Melchester Rovers

This year they have spent a lot on ground improvements to enable them to qualify to play in the Conference League.

Figure 1.3 shows that with their current scale of charges of £5 per spectator, they are just able to break even (cover their total costs) with 5,000 spectators watching each game. This is because Melchester Rovers' costs consist of £20,000 of fixed costs per game (mainly consisting of wages for players and interest payments on money borrowed for the ground improvements). Melchester Rovers have variable costs of £1 per spectator, consisting of the costs involved in supervising the crowd (the bigger the crowd, the more stewards who have to be paid).

What Melchester Rovers are banking on is promotion to the Conference League, which will enable them to charge £7.50 per spectator.

Check your understanding

Can you calculate how much profit per match Melchester Rovers would make in the Conference League, assuming they continue to play before crowds of 5,000? Why might Melchester Rovers' costs rise if they are promoted to the Conference League? How might Melchester Rovers' revenues increase if they are promoted to the Conference League?

In the world of football it is profitability that usually separates the success stories from the also-rans. In the last ten years we have seen clubs like Manchester United, Chelsea and Arsenal gain a leading edge in the Premier Division based on their ability to buy top-class footballers from around the world and to develop commercial interests that go well beyond the football field (e.g.

merchandising of replica shirts, gifts and a range of associated products). Today, clubs such as Arsenal have financial offshoots using the Arsenal brand to sell insurance.

The Premier clubs have been able to soak up much of the revenues coming into the game and, in the season starting in September 2001, the Premier clubs are estimated to take over £1 billion – a figure that has been increased by the development of pay-per-view watching of matches.

At the same time, clubs in the lower divisions are suffering. In the spring of 2000, Delia Smith's Norwich City announced losses of £7 million and QPR £9.5 million. In April 2000, Charlton (the champions of the First Division) found themselves in exactly the same position as Nottingham Forest (as described in the case study). Despite being clear winners of the First Division and having sold out at every home match for two seasons, they were still in a loss-making position. Their profits, it is hoped, will return now they are back in the Premier Division.

Thus the nature of business is that while everyone seeks to make a profit, a considerable number make a loss. The year 1999 was heralded the rise of the new .com companies – the ones that would make their fortune through the Internet. Many did, but more have gone under.

In March 2000 everyone was getting excited by Lastminute.Com (http://www.lastminute.com/), the new Internet site that would trade a range of products (airline tickets, holidays, theatre tickets, stays in hotels) people wanted to buy and sell at the last minute.

However, within days the glow went from the launch as people began to question whether buying shares in the .com companies would yield the massive returns everyone had come to believe would be there.

By April 2000, the experts were predicting that 'seven out of ten British dot.com new businesses wouldn't last a year'. The dot.com companies that appeared to be most at risk were those that wouldn't be able to compete with high-street stores or ones where products could be ordered with a simple telephone call (such as chocolates, flowers and wine).

While profit will continue to be the driving objective behind many businesses, for most it is likely to be an elusive objective in the medium to long term.

Making a surplus

While business organisations seek to make a profit from their activities, there are many 'not-for-profit' organisations that do not set out to make profits. For example, an organisation such as Oxfam, which is a charitable organisation, will seek to provide a surplus from its trading activities in its charity shops, which can be put to charitable purposes (e.g. in providing famine relief to less developed countries).

Of course, in the modern world many charities operate along strictly business-like lines because they want to make best use of the resources available to them. However, it is still important to use the term 'surplus' because this recognises that 'not-for-profit' organisations are not driven by the need to make profits primarily for shareholders.

Check your understanding

Find a story from a broadsheet newspaper (*The Times*, *The Independent* or the *Guardian*) showing what is happening to the profit, loss (or surplus) of a well-known organisation.

Write a brief newspaper column (only 200 words) setting out how large or small the surplus/profit or loss is, what has caused it and who is affected by it.

Case study: Laura Ashley to shut clothes factory

In 1999, Laura Ashley, the British retailer best known for their floral skirts and home furnishings, cut their 45-year tie to the garment manufacturing business by announcing they were closing their last clothing factory, cutting 150 jobs. The news came as the group's first-half financial results showed mounting losses. Pre-tax losses grew to £8.1 million from £7.9 million in 1998.

The group decided to pull out of manufacturing after making heavy losses in this area. The company's clothing needs will now be met by overseas suppliers, mostly in Asia.

1 What factors are likely to cause a company to make a loss?

2 How are shareholders likely to react to a company making a loss?

3 Apart from shareholders, who else is likely to suffer from a company making a loss?

Discussion point

The well-known American business writer and economist Milton Friedman once said, 'The business of business is business'. The implication is that businesses should focus on using resources to make a profit rather than having broader social objectives. Do you agree with Friedman's view?

Objective 2: Increasing sales or market share

Another well-known American business writer, Michael Porter, has suggested to business organisations that 'If you can gain the lion's share of the market then the profits will follow'. The logic behind this is quite straightforward. The organisation that sells the most products is best placed to benefit from the cost savings that arise from producing on a larger scale.

It is easy to see why. For example, you can bake 24 cupcakes in an oven using the same amount of gas or electricity as when you produce 12. In the same way, a large company can benefit from using a production line 24 hours a day to mass produce items. The large company will be best placed to buy products and materials at a discount from suppliers. The large-scale producer is best able to spread its advertising costs over a larger output and so on.

Case study: Increasing the market share of BSkyB

In early 1998, BskyB (http://www.sky.com/home/GeneralIndex) set out its intentions (objective) to boost the satellite broadcaster's presence from 25 to 75 per cent of British homes within five years. During the 1990s BSkyB was able to grow very rapidly. Its principal weapon was to buy and dominate sports coverage, particularly live Premiership football. In 1998 it was the first company to launch a digital television service in this country. It went on to offer free set-top boxes in an attempt to beat off competition in the digital television market. However, by the late 1990s this growth was slowing down, and BSkyB was having to investigate other areas for expanding market share (e.g. by developing made-for-TV movies).

Increasingly, BSkyB has also had to face competition from cable and digital terrestrial television, with new companies and channels providing an alternative to BSkyB.

1 Why have BSkyB been so successful in winning a large market share?

2 Why is it important for BSkyB to be able to increase this market share?

3 What are the dangers to BSkyB of losing market share to rivals?

Many firms seek to be market leaders. They are all too aware of the importance of market share and will fight tooth and nail to gain supremacy. And when they succeed in gaining the lion's share, they will broadcast their success far and wide. You can immediately identify major market leaders: once they have acquired an edge, they are often able to hang on to it by ploughing money into investment, product improvement, and advertising and promotion. Coca-Cola is an obvious example of a market leader.

Researchers in the USA came up with a theory that supports the importance of gaining market share. The study was called 'Profit Impact of Marketing Strategies', more usually referred to as PIMS. This attempted to analyse the marketing factors that had the biggest influence on profits. One important finding of the study was that there was a close relationship between market share and profits. This comes out

Check your understanding

Find out who is the market leader in particular markets, such as disposable nappies, washing powder, lawn mowers and tabloid newspapers.

What advantages do they have over competitors? How do they seek to protect their market leadership?

clearly in Figure 1.4. The PIMS research showed clearly that organisations with a

Market share (%)	Profitability (%)
Under 7	9.6
7 – 14	12.0
14 – 22	13.5
22 – 36	17.9
Over 36	30.2

Figure 1.4 The link between market share and profits (%)

Case study: Supermarket wars

One of the most rapidly changing marketplaces in the UK in the first decade of the twenty-first century is supermarkets. The late 1990s saw the increasing jostling for position between the UK's major supermarket chains, with Tesco taking over from Sainsbury's as the market leader. However, in June 1999 the American giant Wal-Mart took over Asda and showed it wanted to expand still further by gaining a bigger market share.

Wal-Mart typifies the modern trend towards market domination by giant companies. Wal-Mart benefits from buying in great quantities and thus being able to win large discounts from suppliers. In addition, the company uses a very sophisticated information technology system which enables it to control stock and re-ordering patterns in their shops to best meet customer needs.

1 What do you see as being the benefits to a business of dominating the market in the supermarket sector?

2 How might a firm that has the biggest market share be further able to increase its market share while rivals lose market share?

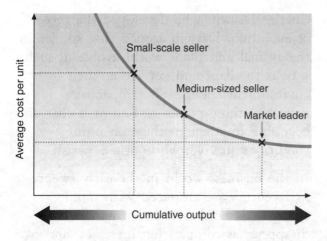

Figure 1.5 The experience curve

large market share were more likely to be profitable.

The Boston Consultancy Group have shown how, through an 'experience curve', market share leads to falling costs (see Figure 1.5.)

The cost of producing each unit will fall as the total output that has been produced increases over time. This makes sense. The more you do something the more experience you have of doing it, and the more likely you are to do it better because you can highlight faults and cut them out. Gains in efficiency stem from greater experience. The Boston Consultancy Group argued that this is a general principle and that, as a rough rule, average cost per unit fell by 20% with each doubling of experience.

Greater experience stems from the following:

• Economies of scale (i.e. the cost advantages stemming from doing things on a larger scale rather than a smaller scale).

• Cutting out the use of less efficient factors of production and production methods.

• Increased productivity stemming from technical changes and learning effects. For example, a large firm can often afford to carry out more detailed market research than a smaller one.

• Improvements in product design.

The key lesson to be learnt is that the benefits of experience do not just arise – they need to be worked at. Companies must take steps to ensure these benefits are reaped, through deliberate management policies.

Companies that have a high market share should be able to accumulate more experience. Therefore companies should strive for a high market share. The best indicator of market share is relative – that is, the ratio of a company's market share to that of its largest competitor:

$$\text{Relative market share of company A} = \frac{\text{Market share of company A}}{\text{Market share of nearest competitor}}$$

This indicator gives a clear measure of competitive strengths. The Boston Consultancy Group used statistical evidence to argue that a ratio of 2:1 would give a 20% cost advantage.

Objective 3: Surviving

According to the business writer Peter Drucker:

It is the first duty of a business to survive. The guiding principle of business economics, in other words, is not the maximisation of profits; it is the avoidance of loss. Business enterprise must produce the premium to cover the risks inevitably involved in its operation. And there is only one source for this risk premium: profits.

What Drucker meant by this statement was that the survival of a business depends on making enough profit to make it worthwhile continuing with that business. Many businesses fold because the people running them eventually feel they are not making enough profit to cover the efforts they are making and the risk they are taking.

A classic example of this emphasis on survival was provided in April 2000 when Barclays announced they were cutting out 171 branches in villages and rural communities 'in order to survive'. Unmoved by petitions signed by thousands of branch users, and from protests in many parts of the country, Barclays stated that these branches were uneconomic to run. The bank stressed it was important to make a profit.

Increasingly in recent years business writers have identified 'survival' as being one of the main objectives of business. In some ways their ideas draw a parallel with the work of Charles Darwin who developed the theory of evolution. Darwin argued that species in the animal and plant world evolve in such a way as to adapt and survive as their environment changes. If temperature increases, those plants and animals that are best able to adapt to these changing conditions survive, while others perish.

In the business world in the early twenty-first century we are faced with rapid changes, as borders between nations disappear, as competition increases, and so on. To survive, the intelligent organisation adapts to this changing world. For example, in recent years as environmental legislation has become tougher, many companies have adopted greener approaches. Some of the companies that have not done so have lost favour with consumers and governments and have disappeared or been swallowed up by other companies.

Survival is about continuing to exist today, tomorrow and into the foreseeable future.

Case study: ICI – a chameleon company

ICI (http://www.ici.com/index/html), the chemicals company, is one of the UK's major business organisations. At the end of the twentieth century the company made dramatic changes in order to survive into the twenty-first century. Traditionally, the company had a poor record for environmental pollution and had been associated with an old 'smokestack' image. What the company did in 1999, therefore, was to buy a number of businesses that were concerned with a more modern approach to chemical manufacture – making popular consumer chemicals (e.g. ingredients going into eye liners, lip glosses, etc.). To raise the money to make this shift ICI sold off some of their old businesses that produced bulk industrial chemicals.

Like a chameleon that changes its colour to adapt to its environment, ICI changed their business in order to survive and grow in the new greener age of the twenty-first century.

1   Why do you think ICI set 'survival' as being a major objective?

2   Can you find other examples in the newspapers of companies that have changed what they do in order to survive into the twenty-first century?

You may not be the most profitable company today, but at least you will be there to compete into the future.

Check your understanding

Explain in one paragraph why survival might be a more realistic business objective in the twenty-first century than going all out to maximise company profits.

Objective 4: Providing services to the community

If the business of business was simply business, we wouldn't find the many organisations that operate in this country whose key objective is to provide a service to the community. Such services are an important part of the function of organisations such as the Post Office and the BBC. While these organisations run many of their activities in a profit-orientated way, this is not their sole concern. In addition, they seek to meet a responsibility to provide a service to the community.

For example, if the Post Office was purely concerned with profit-making it would not offer a service to out-of-the-way places. If the BBC was just concerned with making a profit, it would not run some of its programmes for which there is a very small audience.

The objectives of these organisations, therefore, include elements of public service. For example, the objectives of the BBC include the following. To:

- Nurture and cherish the rich diversity of the UK's heritage, identity and cultural life; bringing people together for moments of celebration, common experience and in times of crisis.

- Enable all sides to join the debate on issues of national, regional and local significance through providing the most comprehensive news service, of range and depth, rooted in experience.

- Help people broaden their horizons through learning, and by enriching their skills to provide something of particular value to all UK licence payers, exposing audiences to new ideas, to scientific discovery, to great art, music and writing, to the spiritual and uplifting.

- Create programmes and services of real cultural value, offering the most gifted individuals in every area the opportunity to create fresh and pioneering television, radio and online services.

- Ensure no one is excluded from access to new kinds of service made possible by new technology.

- Use its ability to reach into every home to engage audiences in new experiences and to act as a trusted guide in a world of abundance.

You can see from this list of objectives that the BBC has a far-reaching responsibility to provide services to the community.

Case study: Barclays and the New Economy

Read the following newspaper article and answer the questions that follow:

Like many other large companies Barclays Bank have been embracing the so-called 'new economy' based on the Information and Communications Technology revolution. In the new economy ICT and e-commerce lie at the heart of the way in which many organisations are and will run. More and more B2B (Barclays to business) and B2C (Barclays to ordinary customers like you and me) links will be carried through computer networked links and telephone lines.

In the Spring of 2000, Matthew Barrett, the new chief executive of Barclays, set out plans to reduce the company's costs by £1bn by 2003. A new e-commerce unit has been set up, to speed up the technological transformation of Barclays. This means not merely using the Internet and information technology as a sales channel but using it as a way of transforming every aspect of the way the organisation runs. By the spring of 2000 Barclays was claiming to be the UK's leading e-commerce bank, with 640,000 online customers and new ones signing up at the rate of 100,000 a month.

As Matthew Barrett explained to a press conference: 'With 300 years of staying power and a customer base that a dot.com company would die for, we are uniquely placed for the new economy. Five years from now there will be no distinct e-business or dot.com companies, only companies that have learnt to change their businesses or those that have fallen by the wayside.'

However, there is a downside to these changes. Part of the transformation involved axing 7,500 jobs, about 10% of the payroll, and closing 200 branches.

Increasingly, as people do business with Barclays through computers and telephones, the branches in small communities have become uneconomic. Many village communities may only have had one bank – Barclays – which provided local jobs and a key financial centre for the poor and elderly who are less likely to have access to the Internet. There was a storm of protest in many rural areas where branches were closed down. There was a feeling that Barclays were employing double standards. While their mission statement, claimed to 'put customers first' and 'to support the communities in which they serve', they were not meeting the needs of many of these customers. This raises the whole issue of business responsibility to the wider community. Some people argue that businesses should consider all their stakeholders – including rural customers – rather than simply trying to make large profits for shareholders.

1 The article above quotes Barclays' mission statement which says that the company has a duty to support the communities in which it serves. Do you think that Barclays are doing this? Is Barclays failing in its responsibilities to serve local communities?

2 What might Barclays' response to any criticism regarding their responsibility to local communities be?

3 Who do you think Barclays should be serving? Local communities or shareholders? Who else is involved and what is their stake in decision-making at Barclays?

Check your understanding

Give five examples of situations in which business activity is driven more by community service than by profit maximisation. For example, there is a subsidised service which provides talking newspapers for the blind, which is supported by volunteer workers and charitable donations.

Objective 5: Offering charitable or non-profit services

There are many organisations in this country that can be seen as comprising the charitable or 'not-for-profit' sector of the economy. Here the organisation's objectives are widely different from those of the 'for-profit' organisation.

The 'not-for-profit' organisation will measure its success in terms of meeting its other objectives. For example:

- War Child might measure their success in providing aid and assistance to children in war-torn regions of the world.

- Shelter would measure their success in terms of helping to find accommodation for homeless people.

- Oxfam would measure their success in providing famine relief.

Of course, these organisations will also need to operate in a business-like way. They will seek, for example, to cut out any wasteful use of resources to drive down costs. They will seek to optimise the success of their trading activities to maximise revenues, etc. However, the key difference between them and other organisations is that their primary objectives will always focus on charitable, socially committed, not-for-profit ends.

Case study: The objectives of War Child

War Child (http://www.warchild.org.uk) is an international charity dedicated to improving the lives of children caught up in areas of conflict and war around the world. War Child take essential medical and food aid into war zones, targeted especially at children and families, as well as providing a variety of aid to long-term refugee and rehabilitation projects They also support and run therapeutic projects after wars have ended.

War Child have set out their objectives in the following way. To:

- Alleviate the suffering of children by bringing material aid into war zones.

- Support those children who have been evacuated into refugee camps.

- Initiate rehabilitation programmes once children return safely to their homes. This includes identifying needs for capital reconstruction projects.

- Be instrumental in healing the psychological damage caused to children by their experience of war.

- Focus public attention on the plight of children in war zones.

War Child established these objectives after numerous visits by their founders to war zones and areas of conflict. The charity set out to prioritise and identify the greatest needs of children in areas of conflict and how best to help them.

War Child raise the money for their activities by running a small number of high-profile concerts.

The charity is bound by the laws of the land requiring that charities should not make investment involving anything other than very small risks when fund-raising. People do not give their cash to War Child for speculative purposes; rather, they expect the donation to be used directly to help children in war zones.

At any one time War Child have a clearly defined budget to spend. The criteria for spending the budget are determined by the objectives of the organisation.

So far, key achievements of the charity have been to create the Pavarotti Music Centre in Mostar (in the former Yugoslavia) and the Liberian Children's Village in West Africa. For example, in 1996–97 Pavarotti and Friends concerts' associated media rights and ticket sales raised a total of approximately £3 million for War Child, which was spent on the Pavarotti Music Centre in Mostar.

1 How do the objectives of 'not-for-profit' organisations differ from those of 'for-profit' organisations?

2 Why is it just as important to establish clear and precise objectives for not-for-profit organisations?

3 How can not-for-profit organisations judge their success?

One of the most important areas of not-for-profit work is in caring for the environment. Organisations such as Greenpeace set out directly to protect the world's environmental resources from exploitation by humanity. Greenpeace take direct action (e.g. in setting out to save whales using voluntary contributions). Other environmental charities include The National Trust, which seeks to protect and enhance our natural heritage, and the Woodland Trust, which sets out to preserve green spaces and woodlands and which engages heavily in tree-planting activities.

Check your understanding

Carry out some research to find out the objectives of an environmental charity of your choice. Show how these objectives differ from those of a for-profit organisation.

Objective 6: Developing staff skills

Today, most organisations include objectives related to developing people at work in their list of objectives. For example, Bass Breweries set out in their objectives that:

We will attract, develop and motivate a team of people of outstanding quality who will share in the success they generate.

The importance of people in organisations is widely recognised. In the last decade of the twentieth century, many business writers realised that 'intelligence' lay at the heart of modern business success. 'Intelligent employees' are able to add millions/billions of pounds to the value of a corporation – people who use the latest information technologies, and who interact either face to face or through some other form of communication with customers. The UK government is all too aware of the importance of intelligence. For example, Gordon Brown in his 1999 budget address stated that:

Those who are left out of the knowledge revolution will be left behind in the new knowledge economy. The more individual talent we nurture, the more economic growth we will achieve.

Just as the government has created a series of objectives at national level for developing the intelligence of people, so too have individual business organisations set about creating their own objectives for knowledge and skill development.

The intelligent worker requires a range of skills and aptitudes that enables him or her independently to make decisions on behalf of the organisation. The sorts of decisions the intelligent employee makes require good communication skills, good interpersonal skills, the ability to work with numbers and information technology, and the ability to work effectively in problem-solving situations.

Most successful organisations, therefore, have developed detailed training and development programmes that seek to create a skilled workforce. We will examine the process of training and development in Unit 4, which focuses on human resources in the organisation.

The student on an Advanced Business course should be aware of how he or she fits into the knowledge revolution. Successfully gaining an Advanced qualification in Business will prepare you for a wide range of jobs in the business sector, or for further study at university. While doing your Advanced course you will not only be becoming more knowledgeable about business but you will also be developing the key skills that will enable you to make a better contribution to organisations and to the wider economy.

Check your understanding

Identify a local organisation that has gained the Investors in People award. Produce a short desk-top published newspaper article (200 words) explaining how and when the organisation received the award and what the award tells us about the way the organisation develops a skilled workforce.

Objective 7: Producing high-quality products or offering high-quality services

The term 'high quality' is often mistakenly confused with 'most expensive'. Yet frequently the most expensive items are not the best quality.

Today we use the term 'quality' to mean 'producing a good or service to customer requirements'. Another way of defining quality is 'fitness for purpose'. A high-quality product or service is therefore one that gives the customers what they expect – or even more than they expect. Leading businesses often talk about 'delighting' the customer. It is not surprising, therefore, that the provision of quality products and services has become a leading objective of modern business organisations.

We live in a world in which the customer has considerable power. Customers can choose to visit one hairdresser or another, to buy one model of car or another and which college or university to take a course at. The customer will choose which organisation to do business with on the basis of their ability to satisfy customer requirements. Hence the importance of quality. We can see this emphasis on quality by studying the key objectives of most business organisations.

For example, The Body Shop (://www.bodyshop.co.uk/index.html) have set out that:

*The Body Shop International's business is the manufacture and retailing of skin and hair care products. **We want to do things better than they have ever been done before**, and we want to include our staff, franchisees and suppliers in making that happen.*

Case study: How IKEA aims to give people high-quality products

IKEA (www.ikea.com/) are one of the best examples of an organisation that sets out to give consumers what they want. IKEA are a Swedish company set up by Ingvar Kamprad to incorporate what he referred to as 'Swedish values'.

Kamprad states that:

> *Once upon a time, a long time ago we decided that, instead of making furniture for people with fat wallets we would side with the majority of people instead and offer them a better everyday life. We decided to offer a wide range of home furnishing items of good design and function, at prices so low the majority of people could afford to buy them.*

Ingvar Kamprad wanted to help create a better everyday life for the ordinary people in the area of Sweden where he lived. He was brought up in a farming community in an area were people were struggling to make a living out of stony fields and limited resources. Nothing could be taken for granted, and surviving meant hard work, ingenuity and trust in (and co-operation with) one's neighbours. The combination of IKEA's roots and Ingvar Kamprad's vision, founded on the basis of a strong company culture, has helped to make IKEA so successful.

In a recent IKEA publication *Democratic Design*, this concept of giving everyone the same opportunity is set out in the following way:

> *everyone who has grown up in Sweden has learnt – either from their Dad, or from society in general – people who are not all that well off should still be given the same opportunities as people who are. It's hardly surprising that, as a Swedish company, IKEA espouses Swedish values.*

To realise the aims of the business idea, Kamprad needed a way of designing that would make it possible to maintain high-quality standards while, at the same time, making reductions in price. The solution he came up with was based on common sense and a respect for the customer. He carried out detailed research into the different life stages and the needs of customers at each of these stages (e.g. setting up home for the first time, raising a young family, retirement, etc.). He was able to calculate what customers would be able to afford while still having some money over. Then he sourced the right materials and the production units with the expertise and capacity to produce economically. In many cases these were producers who concentrated on items that were not a mainstream part of furniture manufacture. For example, a shirt manufacturer may well be suited to producing loose covers. Finally, the designer was called in and given a brief that started with the finished price.

IKEA built large stores on the outskirts of towns where rates were cheaper and people could park easily. The furniture was sold in flat packages, which saved space and allowed for ease of handling and transport.

Finally, Ingvar Kamprad built his business on the philosophy 'We do a little, you do a little, together we save money', which meant that the customer became part of the production process. The DIY idea was refined and put into operation on a large scale. All this allowed for long production runs, which provided economies of scale and growth while maintaining the quality of the finished product.

Today IKEA set out their business idea in the following way:

To offer a wide range of home decorating articles with good form and function, at prices so low that as many people as possible will be able to afford them.

1 How can IKEA be said to have the objective of providing a high-quality product?

2 Who benefits from this focus on quality?

Of course, this notion of high quality is just as relevant for services as it is for products. For example, in recent years we have seen a rapid rise in the buying of insurance and banking services directly over the phone. This is because many consumers prefer the convenience of buying these services directly from home. In the first decade of the twenty-first century we are also seeing an explosion in e-commerce, particularly in the field of retailing were consumers are increasingly able to buy goods over the Internet.

Check your understanding

Define the term 'high quality' in three sentences. Give examples of high-quality products and high-quality services. What makes these goods and services 'high quality'?

Organisational culture

We have seen that organisations work towards different objectives. Some organisations are very profit centred while others have a much clearer concern for the people who work in the organisation and the customers or clients they serve.

Given these differing objectives, it is not surprising that the way different organisations operate varies widely. It is not difficult to sense this difference. In some of the organisations where you might work or where you are a customer, you may get the impression the organisation and its people do not care about you. In others you may feel very important.

We use the term 'culture' to describe the typical approach within an organisation. Culture refers to the personality of an organisation, the shared beliefs and the written and unwritten policies and procedures that determine the ways in which the organisation and its people behave and solve business problems. You can quickly get a feel for the culture of an organisation just by looking around an organisation and talking to the people who work for it. For example, some organisations are very dynamic and its people are encouraged to take risks. Others are backward-looking and rarely take risks.

Different organisations have different cultures that are expressed in their

Case study: BT staff to strike over 'dictatorial' management

We can contrast IKEA's culture with that of BT in November 1999, when it was widely reported through the news media that a number of BT staff were not happy with the culture of the organisation. Staff at BT call centres were threatening to take industrial action over their management's 'Big Brother attitude'.

More than 4,000 staff at 37 BT sites who deal with domestic telephone customers voted in favour of a series of day-long stoppages because the company allegedly monitored their every move, including time spent in the lavatory. Representatives of these employees reported they had become increasingly angry over the company's dictatorial approach. Each member of staff is allowed 4 minutes 40 seconds to deal with a call, and people are disciplined if they go over the limit. One union representative stated that: 'Sometimes we have to deal with a call from an elderly person who may not have talked to somebody for a week so we feel we ought to chat. But management says we've got to learn to be hard.'

Staff who dealt with queries over bills and repairs were also angry over the fact that time away from work stations was strictly monitored. It was alleged that 'sometimes, pregnant women have been told that they to go the toilet too often'.

1 How do the attitudes, beliefs and values of BT, as illustrated in this case study, differ from those of IKEA?

attitudes, values and beliefs. For example, IKEA have a very democratic culture, as being: 'A community of professionals, constantly developing the skills necessary to create a better everyday life at home for the many people.' This is translated down to a personal vision for all IKEA's employees: 'I, as an employee at IKEA, can make a difference. I am able to help to create something for the benefit of everybody, a better everyday life at home.'

People who work for IKEA are therefore encouraged to participate in the life of the company. They work in teams and they meet frequently to discuss all sorts of work issues. IKEA seek to produce products for ordinary people, but they also seek to look after their employees while still making a profit. However, not all organisations are so good at managing their cultures, as the BT case study shows.

Cultures are very important. American textbooks often define culture as 'the way we do things around here'. It does not take long to get a feel for the culture of an organisation. For example, it can be gauged in terms of the extent to which people are encouraged to be involved in decision-making (e.g. the IKEA experience), or whether people are told what to do (the BT call centre experience).

Types of organisational culture

Cultures are founded and built over the years by the dominant groups in an organisation, although in the modern business world organisations can be rapidly transformed by a process of managing change. Here we shall consider the four main types of culture (see Figure 1.6).

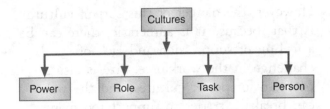

Figure 1.6 Types of organisational culture

Power culture

The centralisation of power is the key feature of a power culture. It is frequently found in small organisations where control rests with a single individual or small group of individuals. Its structure is best pictured as a web (see Figure 1.7). There is a central power source (the spider) and the rays of influence spread out from that central figure. In this type of organisation the emphasis is on individuals rather than group decision-making, enabling it to move quickly to make decisions and to react well to threat or danger.

Figure 1.7 The power culture

However, the danger of this sort of culture is that, because it is autocratic, there can be a feeling of suppression and lack of challenge in the workforce. Size is also a problem for power cultures, and the web can break if it tries to support too many activities. Power cultures tend to suffer from low morale and high staff turnover in the middle management layers.

The power culture can also exist in large organisations. The best-known example of a power culture was the Ford organisation in the first part of the last century when it was dominated by Henry Ford. He was like a giant colossus sitting astride the Ford organisation, which turned out millions of standardised black Model T Fords for the mass market. The industrial system he created came to be called 'Fordism' and involved the mass production of standardised motor cars. Ford was a great industrialist but he was also a tyrant. He insisted everything was done to his instructions. One day arriving at his car plant he found a hole being dug. 'Why is that hole being dug?' he asked. 'I didn't order it, fill it in again'.

Check your understanding

What do you see as being the main strengths and weaknesses of a power culture? Is the power culture effective in enabling the organisation to meet its objectives?

Role culture

The role culture is typical of bureaucracies. Bureaucracies are large organisations in which all members have a defined job or role to carry out. The bureaucracy became increasingly common in the nineteenth century in government departments such as the civil service, as well as in such organisations as the army and, in some ways, the Church.

During the twentieth century, as companies became bigger, they increasingly took on a bureaucratic form (e.g. major public companies such as the oil companies and, of course, the state-owned nationalised industries). A bureaucracy is normally split up into a number of functions that are then organised in a hierarchical way. For example, the army may be divided into The Royal Engineers, The Scots Guards, etc. Each of these regiments would then be organised in a hierarchical way – Field Marshal, General, Colonel, Captain, etc.

Businesses would be divided into various functions (e.g. accounts, marketing, production, etc.). These would then have a hierarchical ordering of offices (e.g. Production Director, Production Managers, Supervisors, Technicians, Operatives, etc.).

This culture works by logic and rationality, and a simple diagram depicting this type of culture bears a resemblance to the temple of Apollo, the Greek god of reason (see Figure 1.8).

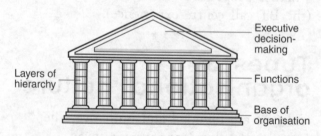

Figure 1.8 The role culture

Power is hierarchical and derived from the employee's position in the organisation. The organisation's strength lies in its pillars or functions. Within the functions, what people do at different levels is determined by job descriptions (which are clearly written down) and defined communication procedures. In this culture the job description is just as important as the person who fills it, and performance over and above the role is not required. 'Position' is the main source of power, and 'rules and procedures' are the main source of influence.

> ### Check your understanding
>
> Have you been a member of an organisation that approximates to the role culture?
>
> How did the role culture help the organisation to meet its objectives?

Task culture

Task cultures have become very important in business in the first decade of the twenty first century. Today, many people work in teams together, combining to complete projects together. Teams may work together for a short or long time to complete a task. Particular individuals may work on more than one task at a time. In the task culture there is a strong emphasis on building the team. Team members will need to share values and aspirations. They will also need to feel valued by the organisation they work for.

Increasingly, employees are being encouraged to take on more power and responsibility rather than waiting to be told what to do. The term for this process of handling down power and responsibility is 'empowerment'.

In a task culture, teams will often have considerable input in determining how a particular job will be done. Their views and opinions will be listened to.

> ### Check your understanding
>
> How does a modern task culture help an organisation meet its objectives?

Person culture

In a person culture, individuals are central. The organisation exists only to serve the interests of those within it. Not surprisingly, person cultures are more likely to be found in co-operatives and not-for-profit organisations, such as charity and voluntary organisations, rather than in profit-motivated enterprises.

In a person culture, hierarchies are impossible except by mutual consent. An individual may leave the group but the organisation does not have the power to evict the individual. In this sort of culture, the individual has almost complete freedom to adopt any direction and to do as he or she pleases. Some educational establishments have been set up on these lines, whereby the individual student is free to follow his or her own lines of interest rather than work to a prescribed curriculum.

Backward-facing and forward-looking cultures

Another distinction that is frequently made is between backward-facing cultures, which are based on what has gone on before in an organisation, and forward-looking cultures, which enable rapid change into the future.

One important aspect of organisational culture is the emphasis on tradition. Some organisations are heavily influenced by previous practice, legends and ways of doing things. Other organisations are innovative and entrepreneurial, with little respect for previous patterns or methods.

For example, Anita Roddick has stated that being prepared to run in the opposite direction to convention and to be prepared to break the rules is part of the culture of The Body Shop.

A company with a backward-facing culture is likely to be:

- Procedure led.

- Controlled by traditional managers who have been in the organisation for a long time.

- Conservative in attitude.

- Resistant to change.

- Inward looking.

- A risk avoider.

A company with a forward-looking culture is likely to:

- Look at what its customers want.

- Look outside itself at the world around it and what its competitors are doing.

- Be keen to introduce new managers and people with new ideas.

- Seek change.

- Be prepared to take risks.

Check your understanding

Contrast two organisations you are familiar with, one with a backward-facing culture and the other with a forward-looking culture. What are the key differences between these two organisations?

Influences on culture

Economic, social, environmental and ethical influences contribute to a business's culture.

The culture is also likely to affect the objectives and structures of the business – which will help or hinder the success of the business.

For example, Oxfam describe their culture in the following way...it:

'reflects a passionate commitment to overcoming the injustice of poverty and suffering. We seek to be:

- making a difference,

- innovative,

- collaborative,

- accountable,

- cost-effective.'

This description of Oxfam's culture gives a fairly clear picture of how people in the organisation would operate ('the way we do things around here') and what the priorities of the organisation would be. The emphasis would be very much on raising money for the poor and campaigning against social injustice. Oxfam employees would seek to take actions that make a genuine difference, working collaboratively with each other, with the general public and with relevant agencies.

However, we can also see the business emphasis in the way Oxfam operates. This stems from operating in a competitive environment – people do not have to give donations to Oxfam – they could give their donations to other organisations which might use the donations more effectively. Oxfam therefore needs to be accountable to people such as donors. Oxfam needs to be cost-effective, cutting out waste and unnecessary expenditure. Like other organisations they also need to be innovative, to come up with new ideas to match changes in the business environment.

In this chapter we have examined a range of different organisations, each of which will have its own distinctive culture. The culture of an organisation like Glaxo, the pharmaceutical company, will be concerned with coming up with new ideas, paying detailed attention to quality and safety standards, and matching or exceeding the product offerings of competitors. In contrast, IKEA emphasises competitiveness and good business practice, but also places strong importance on meeting the needs of the ordinary family. IKEA prides itself on the democratic way in which the organisation is run, encouraging individual contributions of ideas from employees.

Alternative organisations such as the Day Chocolate Company which was set up to help cocoa growers to make a decent living also emphasise democratic thinking and ways of working whereby everyone in the organisation makes a contribution. The Day Chocolate Company places a strong emphasis on fair and ethical trading practice and fair dealings within the organisation. Such an organisation can be contrasted with a major chocolate manufacturer such as Nestlé or Cadbury Schweppes where decision-making would be far more top down.

These differences in culture can be illustrated in chart form:

Organisation	Objectives	Aspects of culture	Impact of culture on organisation
Oxfam	To overcome poverty and suffering.	Passionate commitment to overcoming poverty. Emphasis on: • Making a difference • Innovative • Collaborative • Accountable • Cost-effective	Collaborative patterns of working. Respect for all individuals within and outside the organisation. Democratic ways of working. Encourages people to think think for themselves.
IKEA	To create a better home life for ordinary people. To make a profit.	Community of professionals working together to create quality products for the general public.	Participative form of working. Members of organisation encouraged to make decisions – rather than being told what to do.
Glaxo	To be the market leader in pharmaceuticals, to make a profit and to develop new products.	Emphasis on research and development, strong emphasis on quality standards and safety.	Emphasis on encouraging employees to be innovative, while at the same time operating in such a way as as to guarantee safety of products, and quality image of brand.

The culture of the organisation is very important to the success of the business. The culture should reflect the environment in which the organisation operates. For example, in a highly competitive and dynamic market, the culture needs to be flexible and adjustable. In markets where the emphasis is on the highest standards of ethics, the organisational culture needs to be one of high moral standards. Where the organisation is operating in an environmentally sensitive market, the way of working within the organisation must strongly emphasise protection and improvement of the environment, etc.

Organisations which fail to keep in touch with their environment will rapidly fall back. For example, organisations which engage in 'shady dealing' will quickly be in the spotlight of public scrutiny through the media, leading to shareholders selling up their shares, customers not wanting to buy products, suppliers not wanting to supply the company. It is thus essential for organisations to be forward, rather than backward, looking. For example, an organisation which was a heavy polluter in the 1970s and 1980s will not survive in the post-millennium world in which people are so environmentally conscious.

Cultural change

Organisations can and do change their cultures. Today, managers have learnt how to change the culture of the organisations they work for in order to enable the organisation to meet its objectives.

Increasingly, organisations are operating in a more dynamic world in which change is frequent. In a world of change there is less scope for the role culture. Organisations are having to operate with task cultures based on team work. This means the people who

work in the organisations need to develop team skills, such as interpersonal skills, communications, the ability to work with information technology and decision-making skills. Managers need to learn to listen and to encourage teams, rather than to tell people what to do.

Changing the culture of an organisation requires a great deal of skill. Change management is always most successful when the participants in the change process feel involved. Changing the culture of an organisation, therefore, is best achieved by involving everyone in the organisation and listening to their ideas. In this way they will feel committed to the change rather than seeking to resist it.

Check your understanding

Can you identify a major change that has recently been made in an organisation you are familiar with? How was the change brought about? Was the change forced on people, or were they encouraged to participate in the change process? How was the change managed? Did the way in which the change was managed contribute to the success of the process?

The environment of change

There are a number of key influences that affect the culture of an organisation. A key economic factor is the nature of the competitive environment in which the organisation is operating. In the cut-throat world of competitive business, the organisation may be very concerned with making a profit. The drive to profitability will help to shape the attitudes, values and beliefs in the organisation. Members of the organisation may go all out to win business for the organisation, perhaps because they are paid a commission according to their successes in selling.

Such an organisation may have a very entrepreneurial risk-taking culture, in which the value of hard work and enterprise is strongly emphasised. In contrast some organisations have different motivations. For example, a not-for-profit organisation may be more concerned with helping people and providing a service to the community than going all out for profits.

Social influences also play an important part in shaping the culture of an organisation. For example, some organisations are set up and run by people who have particular beliefs (e.g. a business organisation set up by people with strong social or religious beliefs). Many of the early entrepreneurs in this country were Quakers (e.g. Cadburys and Rowntrees of York). These people believed in supporting the community as well as making profits in the business. There was a strong emphasis in the business on looking after employees rather than treating them as part of the machinery.

Today, companies that are social innovators seek to empower their workforces rather than to talk down to them and tell them what to do. The socially innovative company will emphasise empowerment and teamwork.

Concern for the *environment* has also become a key ingredient of the way in which a number of organisations think. The Body Shop, for example, is an organisation that has pioneered new practices, such as campaigning against testing cosmetics on animals, against exploiting indigenous peoples in countries where raw materials are extracted and campaigning against the exploitation of child labour. The Body Shop have developed a culture in which their staff (and their customers) are very aware of issues such as recycling and the minimisation of waste.

Finally, *ethics* have increasingly played an important part in shaping organisational culture. Ethics are sets of moral principles that are generally accepted and recognised in a particular society. Ethical behaviour covers a vast range of business behaviours – being transparent (open to scrutiny) in all business dealing, treating customers and suppliers equally and fairly, not being involved in double standards or shady business practice, etc. Ethical organisations are most likely to involve task or individual cultures, because these are the ones that involve the greatest openness, internal and external discussion and debate.

Check your understanding

With reference to an organisation you are familiar with, show how:

1 Environmental concern influences the culture of that organisation.

2 Social issues influence the culture of that organisation.

Culture, objectives and the structure of the organisation

Organisations that have power cultures will have a top-down structure and their objectives will be determined by the individual or individuals who dominate the organisation. In business, such organisations are likely to be profit motivated or may have objectives related to building up the power or ego of the individual at the heart of the spider's web.

Organisations with role cultures will be structured in a hierarchical way, and will be divided into a number of functions. Such organisations tend to be backward-facing (with their ideas shaped by the past), with their objectives being related to some overarching purpose (e.g. protection of the public and the prevention, detection and arrest of criminals, in the case of the police force; processing passport applications and issuing new passports in the case of the Passport Office, etc.). In business, organisations with role cultures may have a range of objectives, from being market leaders to maximising sales and/or profits. Because of the bureaucracy that exists in such organisations, they will not always be particularly effective in meeting their objectives.

Organisations with task cultures tend to be organised into teamworking structures, and often involve considerable flexibility, with people working in one or more teams and moving between tasks as and when appropriate. The objectives of the organisation will be related to the tasks the teams are performing. Such organisations are generally effective in the modern dynamic business world.

Organisations with individual cultures have a range of fluid structures. Their objectives tend to be related to meeting the needs of the individuals who make up the organisations.

Check your understanding

Show how the structure and objectives of two organisations you are familiar with are influenced by the organisations' cultures.

Chapter 2 Types of business

Businesses can be classified in different ways. You need to know whether a business is in the voluntary, private or public sector. You need to understand the differences between the following types of business:

- sole trader
- partnership
- private limited company
- public limited company
- co-operative
- not-for-profit or a charity
- franchise.

You need to understand when each type of business organisation is likely to be appropriate. You will also learn that the type of business appropriate will be, to some extent, related to the size of the business. These are usually categorised as small, medium and large businesses. This will require you to consider businesses operating internationally and globally, as well as those operating in national, regional or local markets.

You need to recognise that businesses can change their types of ownership and identify the reasons for such changes. You also need to understand the implications of changes in business ownership in terms of:

- limited and unlimited liability
- access to different sources of finance

- control
- use of profits
- legal liabilities.

There are all sorts of businesses – small ones, medium-sized ones and large ones; businesses owned by one or two people, and those owned by thousands of shareholders; businesses that make things and others that sell things; businesses that are just starting

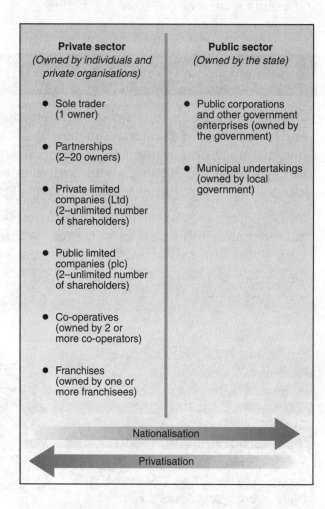

Figure 2.1 The different types of private and public sector enterprises

out and ones that have been in existence for hundreds of years. The type of business is, in some ways, related to size. For example, a simple one- or two-person business will have a very simple structure when contrasted with a corporation such as the Anglo-Dutch company Unilever, which sell their famous 'power brands' (such as PG Tips, Persil, Dove soaps and Calvin Klein fragrances) across the globe.

In this chapter we will be examining the basic structure of organisations in the private and public sectors of the economy. Figure 2.1 (see page 31) shows the broad range of businesses that appear in these two sectors.

Sole traders

This is the most common form of business ownership and the easiest to set up. A sole trader is a business owned by one person though, of course, this business might employ several people. Examples of sole traders might include a freelance Internet web page designer, a mobile hairdresser, a gardener, a small retailer, an electrician or a plumber.

Case Study: Jenny's Sandwich Bar

Jennifer McSweegan set up a small sandwich bar supplying the lunchtime trade in her home town of Midport. She saw there was little competition and that many office and shop workers wanted to buy good-quality sandwiches with a range of fillings. Jenny set up the business with capital she had been able to save from her previous job as a secretary in a solicitor's business.

Jenny enjoys her work and finds it is much more enjoyable making decisions for herself rather than having to be told what to do. Of course, she is worried about the long hours she has to work and the fact she has no one to turn to if she gets into difficulties. Should the business go bust, she will have to pay all the debts herself.

Sole traders are a form of business in which the owner has what is termed in law 'unlimited liability'. This means that, should the business get into debt, then not only will Jenny have to sell off the business to pay off the debts but also, if there is not enough capital in the business to meet the debts, she will have to sell some or all of her private possessions to meet debts.

Jenny also suffers in that she has to be a 'Jack-of-all-trades' – she has to open the bar in the

morning, serve customers, supervise staff, arrange all the advertising and promotion for the bar, do the bookwork and accounts for the business and many other tasks. However, because she spends so much time in the business she has got to know local people really well and is able to provide sandwiches specially for her customers, like the group of employees from a small local factory who regularly ask her for tuna and banana sandwiches.

One thing that worries Jenny is what might happen if she were sick. So far she has had a clean bill of health but she is worried about whether she would be able to trust her existing staff to get on with things if she had to ring in sick one day.

A problem Jenny had in setting up her business was that, because it was a sole trader business, she had to raise all the finance herself. She wonders whether it might have been better to take on a partner to help her raise the capital for the business. However, she feels that being able to keep all the profits for herself more than compensates for the benefits a partner would have brought to the business.

Of course, Jenny's business is very small. This means she is not able to gain substantial discounts from suppliers, such as the local bakery or greengrocer. It also means she has to charge slightly higher prices than those charged for sandwiches in the local supermarket. She hopes her friendly approach will continue to attract customers despite the higher prices.

Another thing Jenny really appreciates about being a sole trader is that she doesn't have to publish the affairs of her business in any form of written report as would be the case if she were a company. She simply provides an annual set of accounts for the Inland Revenue to work out her tax liability.

1 Set out a table outlining all the advantages and all the disadvantages to Jenny of being a sole trader.

2 What do you see as being the prime benefits to Jenny of being a sole trader?

Check your understanding

Interview a local sole trader. What does he or she see as being the principal advantages and disadvantages of adopting the sole trader form of business?

Partnerships

An ordinary partnership can have between two and 20 partners. People in business partnerships can share skills and the workload, and it may be easier to raise the needed capital. A group of vets is able to pool knowledge of different diseases and groups of animals, and two or three vets working together may be able to operate a 24-hour service. When one of the vets is ill or goes on holiday, the business can cope. Partnerships are particularly common in professional services (think also of doctors, solicitors, accountants). A small business such as a corner shop may take the form of a husband-and-wife partnership.

There are disadvantages in partnerships. People can fall out (he doesn't work as hard as me!). Ordinary partnerships do not have limited liability, and partners can rarely borrow or raise large amounts of capital. Business decisions may be more difficult to make (and slower) because of the need to consult the partners. There may be disagreements about how things should be done. A further disadvantage is that profits will be shared (but so are losses).

Partnerships are usually set up by writing out a 'deed of partnership', which is witnessed by a solicitor. This deed sets out important details, such as how much each partner should put into the business, how the profits and losses will be shared and the responsibilities of each partner. There is also a special form called a 'limited partnership'. Limited partners (sometimes called 'sleeping partners') can put money into the business and have the protection of limited liability, but they play no part in the running of the business. It must be run by at least one non-limited partner.

Check your understanding

Find one business in your locality that runs as a partnership. Who owns it? What is the relationship like between the partners? What are the advantages and disadvantages of this form of organisation to the partners?

Compare your results with other students' work.

Companies

A company set up to run a business has to be registered before it can start to operate but, once all the paperwork is completed and approved, the company becomes

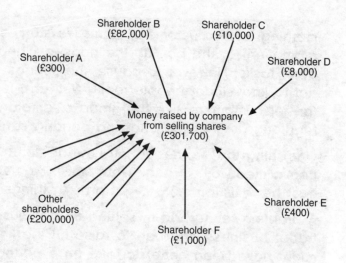

Figure 2.2 A company raises money from its shareholders

recognised as a legal body. The owners of a company are its shareholders. However, other individuals and businesses do not deal with the shareholders – they deal with 'the company'.

Shareholders put funds into the company by buying shares. New shares are often sold in face values of £1 per share, but this is not always the case. Some shareholders will have only a few hundred pounds' worth of shares, whereas others may have thousands of pounds' worth (see Figure 2.2).

The promoter or directors of the company can apply to the Registrar of Companies for permission to issue new shares. The amount the registrar agrees to is called the authorised capital. The issued capital is the value of the shares that are actually sold to shareholders. A company may choose not to issue the full value of its authorised capital: it may hold back a certain amount for future issue.

Shares can be issued for payment in stages over a period of time. Each stage is then termed a 'call'. There may be three or four calls before the full price is finally paid. The paid-up capital is the money that has been received for these partly paid shares.

Private companies

Private companies tend to be smaller than public ones (discussed below), and are often family businesses. There must be at least two shareholders, but there is no maximum

Check your understanding

Obtain the prospectus of a new company. This will show details of the offer of shares for sale.

What is the value of the authorised capital? How much capital is actually being sought? What arrangements are being made for the payment of the shares?

Case study: Patak's

Patak Ltd are the leading supplier of authentic Indian foodstuffs worldwide. By the year 2000, Patak's held the dominant share of the UK's Indian pastes market, with over two-thirds of the market.

Patak's were set up by the father of the current Chairman and Chief Executive, Kirit Pathak, in the late 1950s. On his arrival in the UK from Kenya, L.G. Pathak began by selling samosas from home to raise sufficient capital to buy his first small shop in north London. The business expanded with the introduction of other products, including pickles and chutneys, as orders from small shops, housewives and students flooded in and Patak's fame spread. Kirit Pathak joined his father's expanding business in 1970 and his wife, Meena, who is a qualified chef and expert on Indian cuisine, also takes personal responsibility for overseeing all recipe development.

Today, the business operates as a private company. The company's capital mainly comes from family members, who are the principal shareholders, and a few other prominent shareholders. Having company status means the shareholders have limited liability. The maximum liability of the shareholders is the money they have put into the business. The company employs specialist managers and now has a number of factories at key locations in the UK.

1 Why do you think Patak's moved on from being a sole trader to becoming a company?

2 List three advantages of taking on company status.

3 Explain one disadvantage of being a company rather than continuing to operate as a sole trader.

number. Shares in private companies cannot be traded on the Stock Exchange, and often shares can be bought only with the permission of the board of directors.

The board of directors is a committee set up to protect the shareholders' interests. The members of the board choose the managing director, who is responsible for the day-to-day running of the business (see Figure 2.3). The rules of the business set out when shareholders' meetings will take place and the rights of shareholders.

Figure 2.3 Choosing the management in a private company

Private companies may find it possible to raise more cash (by selling shares) than unlimited liability businesses. The shareholders can also have the protection of limited liability.

The main disadvantages compared with unlimited liability businesses are that they have to share out profits among shareholders, and they cannot make decisions so quickly. They cost more to set up.

Check your understanding

Study a local private company. Who owns it and who controls it? How much share capital does it have? What are the advantages and disadvantages of this organisational form for this particular company?

Public companies

A public company has its shares bought and sold on the Stock Exchange. Companies can go to the expense of having a 'full quotation' on the Stock Exchange so their share prices appear on the dealers' visual display screens.

The main advantage of selling shares through the Stock Exchange is that large amounts of capital can be raised very quickly. One disadvantage is that control of a business can be lost by the original shareholders if large quantities of shares are purchased as part of a 'take-over bid. It is also costly to have shares quoted on the Stock Exchange.

To create a public company, the directors must apply to the Stock Exchange Council, which will carefully check the accounts. A business wanting to 'go public' will then arrange for one of the merchant banks to handle the paperwork. Selling new shares is quite a risky business. The Stock Exchange has 'good days' (when a great many people want to buy shares) and 'bad days' (when a great many people want to sell). If the issue of new shares coincides with a bad day, a company can find itself in difficulties.

For example, if it hopes to sell a million new shares at £1 each and all goes well, it will raise £1 million; but on a bad day it might be able to sell only half its shares at this price. There is quite a deal of luck involved, therefore, in getting the day just right to launch new shares because the date has to be chosen well in advance. Some companies are very unlucky, launching their shares on a day when people are gloomy about prospects in the economy.

One way around this problem is to arrange a 'placing' with a merchant bank. The merchant bank recommends the company's shares to some of the share-buying institutions with which it deals (pension funds and insurance companies, for example), who may then agree to buy, say, one-tenth of the new shares. In this way the merchant bank makes sure the shares are placed with large investors before the actual date of issue comes round. Then, even if it is a bad day on the Stock Exchange when the shares are issued, the company's money is secure.

Case study: Reading share prices in a national newspaper

Have you ever wanted to understand the share price page of a national newspaper? Here's your chance. The shares appear in the paper under a number of categories (major headings) – e.g. mining, health care, household and textiles, etc.

Figure 2.4 gives details of share prices over the previous year (i.e. 52 weeks). The high shows the highest price the share has been traded for in that year (248p for Care UK shares). The low shows the lowest price during the year (190p for Care UK). The name of the stock is listed under the heading 'Stock' (stock is another word for a share).

High	Low	Stock	Price	Change	Yield	P/E
Health care						
248	190	Care UK	210	0	0.9	20.8
Household and textiles						
114	68	Black Arrow	68	+1	8.3	6.0
Mining						
662	303	Lonmin	580	−25	3.2	33.3

Figure 2.4 Share prices for the previous year

The column 'Price' shows the price at which you would be able to buy shares on the previous day at the Stock Exchange (Monday 8 November). The symbol +/- denotes changes up or down in price from the close of trading the previous day.

The yield is the rate of return to shareholders paid in the form of dividends; the higher the yield, the more money a shareholder earns.

P/E is the price/earnings ratio, which is calculated by dividing the share price by the earnings per share. P/E shows roughly how many years it would take the company to earn an amount equal to its market value.

1 Which share has gone up by most since the previous day?

2 Which share has fallen by most since the previous day?

3 Which share would give the highest yield to the shareholder?

4 Why might a prospective shareholder: a) be keen on investing in Lonmin; and b) be wary of buying shares in Lonmin, given the information presented above?

Case study: The London Stock Exchange

The London Stock Exchange plays a vital role in maintaining London's position as one of the world's leading financial centres, as well as providing finance for UK public companies. The origins of the Exchange go back to the coffee houses of seventeenth-century London, where entrepreneurs who wished to invest or raise money bought and sold shares in joint-stock companies to fund journeys to the unexplored Far East.

The Stock Exchange now provides an essential marketplace, where companies large and small can raise finance for expansion, and investors can share in their growth. Offering companies the opportunity to grow by raising capital is one of the principal roles of the exchange. Companies wishing to raise money can issue new shares, which are sold to investors through the exchange. This is commonly done when the company joins the market (also known as a 'flotation'). Companies wishing to float on the London Stock Exchange have a choice of two markets, the Official List or Alternative Investment Market (AIM).

The Official List, or main market, is for established companies. There are now nearly 3,000 companies whose shares are traded on the Official List, and over 500 of these are non-UK based. Companies seeking to join the Official List must meet tough conditions to give investors confidence.

The Alternative Investment Market is a market for smaller companies that was established in 1995 to allow younger and growing businesses to raise capital to fund their growth. There are fewer rules for AIM but companies whose shares are quoted here are required to retain the assistance of a firm providing market expertise (known as the nominated adviser) at all times.

Investors can participate in the stock market either when a company issues new securities or subsequently when the shares are traded on an ongoing basis. There are all sorts of securities available to buy and sell on the exchange, including UK and foreign equities (i.e. shares in companies) and UK gilts (issued by the UK government).

The key benefits to a company of seeking a flotation on the exchange are as follows:

- Access to funds from the widest range of UK and international, institutional and private investors.
- The ability to raise money to fund future projects at a later stage.
- A higher profile for the company's business, nationally and internationally.
- 'A stamp of approval'.

Another common method by which public companies raise share capital is by offering new shares for sale to the general public. The company's shares are advertised in leading newspapers and the public invited to apply.

When a company is up and running, a cheaper way of selling is to write to existing shareholders inviting them to buy new shares. This is a rights issue.

A stockbroking firm acts as an investor's professional eyes and ears. It is the investor's link with the stock market and its role is to obtain the best price available for the investor's shares, whether they are buying or selling. A stockbroker can also deal with all the paperwork involved in transactions in stocks, such as gilt-edged securities and shares, which leaves the investor free to concentrate on his or her investment strategy.

Many people find their stockbroker by word of mouth alone (through friends, colleagues or acquaintances who recommend their own stockbroker). There are, however, a number of other ways in which to find a good stockbroker. It is possible to find a list of stockbrokers in *Yellow Pages*. There is also a national directory of private client stockbrokers issued by the Association of Private Client Investment Managers and Stockbrokers. It starts with an explanation of the main features of the membership, then lists the type of service offered by them, followed by the range of available products.

Case study: Welcome to Webvan

Webvan (http://www15.webvan.com/default.asp) provide us with a good example of the launch of a post-millennium public company based on a futuristic way of thinking. Webvan came into being in 1996 as an online grocery start-up based in Foster City in northern California. They had a customer base of less than 20,000. In June 1999 they set up a delivery service that originally extended no further than the San Francisco Bay area and, in 1999, it made losses of $73 million on sales of $11.9 million.

However, the company is expected to do very well in the future and has some of the leading IT brains behind it.

The company went public in the USA in early November 1999. On the night before its launch, Goldman Sachs the lead underwriter of the share issues, raised the estimated price range from $11 to $13 per share, a price that would give the company a capital start of $475 million. On the first day of trading, the price rose to $34 and finished the day at nearly $25 – 65 % above the offer price.

One reason for the public confidence in Webvan derives from the prominence of their backers and the strength of their management team. Another is the sheer scale and apparent solidity of the company's ambitions – to automate and expand in ways more sophisticated and grander than anyone has tried. The list of board members is impressive.

Founder and Chairman is Louis Borders, 51, who is also the founder and President of Borders, one of the biggest US bookstore chains. Mr Borders worked for years tying to automate the 'back end' of the grocery business, calculating how customers' orders could be assembled, stored and delivered most efficiently.

His vision for Webvan was of supermarket shopping without the supermarket. He once said: 'I knew I'd have a real financial model if I could eliminate store costs.' Other board members include Christos Costakos, Chief Executive of E-trade, the Internet online share-trading company, and Tim Koogle, chief executive of the Internet company Yahoo!

The underlying concept, and the one that convinced such high-powered investors to part with their cash, is the belief that all the costs involved in the food trade – buying, marketing, storage and delivery – can be cut drastically through advanced automation.

Webvan will not have conventional supermarkets. So far, they have one distribution centre, in Oakland near San Francisco. The floorspace is 350,000 ft^2, equivalent to 18 average American supermarkets. The plans are for many more.

The company wants to deliver 300,000 lines, including hand-cut meats, fresh fruit and vegetables and fine wines, breakfast cereal, cosmetics and toilet paper. Fresh fish, including live lobster and semi-prepared meals, are on their list. Same-day delivery is promised for an agreed 30-minute 'window' convenient to the customer.

1 Why have Webvan had to become a public company?

2 Why have their shares been so successful despite the fact the company was making a loss in 1999 and 2000?

3 How does the company provide a revolutionary leap forward in business thinking?

The importance of multinational corporations

Today, many large companies have become multinationals. Multinationals are mainly plcs. Examples are car manufacturers, such as Peugeot, soft drink and confectionery manufacturers, such as Cadbury Schweppes, computer manufacturers, such as Microsoft, and household product giants such as Unilever. Some multinationals are still private companies (the best known example being Mars, which is still in the hands of the Mars family).

A multinational enterprise (MNE) is a company with its headquarters in one country but with operations in other countries. Today there are over 12,000 MNEs. However, the largest 50 of these account for over 80% of the world's foreign direct investment (i.e. investment that takes place across country borders). Some 434 of the world's top 500 multinationals are from what is referred to as the triad blocs of the European Union, Japan and the USA (see Figure 2.5).

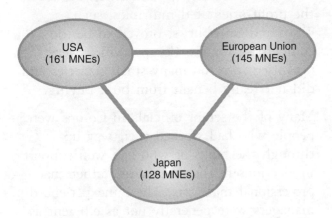

Figure 2.5 The triad 'bloc' of multinational companies

An MNE has two major areas of concern: the home country of its headquarters and the host countries in which it operates. An important characteristic of a multinational is that it is able to draw on a common pool of resources, including assets, patents, trademarks, information and people. These resources can be shared within the organisation (e.g. the pooling of information through organisation-wide databases and the use of patents and technologies on a global scale).

There are a number of advantages to operating as a multinational:

- To spread risks, so that the company is able to protect itself from a downturn of sales in its own home market – it can cushion the fall through its successes abroad.

- To benefit from the growing world market for goods and services. This is part of the process of globalisation (the rapid growth of similar goods and services produced and distributed by MNEs on a world scale).

- As a response to foreign competition and to protect the MNE's world market share. When other foreign multinationals start to compete in a particular MNE's market, it is time to expand into new markets. Attack is the best form of defence.

- In order to reduce costs. By setting up operating units close to foreign customers, it is possible to reduce transport costs (e.g. setting up soft drinks bottling, and confectionery-manufacturing plants in other countries).

- To overcome tariff walls by serving a foreign market from within. This is a major reason why so many Japanese car manufacturers have set up in the UK. This enables them to get inside the European Union.

- To take advantage of technological expertise by making goods directly rather than allowing others to do so under licence. A typical licensing contract lasts for about seven years and gives the licensee access to patents, trade marks, etc., in exchange for a fee or royalty. However, if instead the multinational produces goods directly, then the company will be closer to emerging technological development, enabling it to adapt new ideas itself.

Co-operatives

Co-operatives are a form of business organisation that has become more popular in the UK but that are unlikely to make a major impact in the early years of the twenty-first century. At one time they were to be found only in agriculture and retailing, but in recent years the biggest growth areas have been in service occupations and in small-scale manufacturing.

The basic idea behind a co-operative is that people join together to make decisions, to work and to share profits. There are many different types of co-operative. We consider here the three most commonly found in business.

Retail co-operatives

CWS is Britain's best known co-operative business

The first successful co-operative in this country was set up in the northern town of Rochdale in the nineteenth century. Twenty-eight weavers clubbed together to start their own retail shop, selling a few basic grocery items. The profits were to be shared according to the amount spent, and everyone would have an equal say in how the shop was run.

Since then Co-ops have spread and there are many retail outlets in Britain. To become a co-operator you need only buy a £1 share, and this entitles you to vote at meetings to choose the president and other officers of the local Co-op Society.

In the latter part of the nineteenth century, the Co-ops flourished and societies sprang up all over Britain. It was the Co-ops that introduced the first supermarkets. However, the profit-orientated multiples, such as Tesco and Sainsbury's, proved to be too competitive for the Co-ops, which were organised into too many small societies and did not really benefit from bulk buying.

Many of the senior officials in Co-ops were people who had worked their way up through the ranks or who had won support in elections in the local areas, rather than professional managers. These inexperienced managers were generally not as efficient as those managing the new multiples, or as cut-throat. They also clung to their social conscience.

During the 1970s and 1980s the Co-ops increasingly lost market share. They came to be associated with a rather dowdy image and downmarket products. The Co-ops have continued to suffer with the development of hypermarkets.

To fight back, small societies have merged together, closing hundreds of small shops and branches. During the 1980s, the Co-op began to build its own Leo hypermarkets. It increasingly employed specialist managers with good qualifications and retailing experience. It began to develop a new, slicker image. Co-ops still continue to be located in many traditional working-class areas as well as having high-street stores, which are often indistinguishable from those of other retailers. The Co-op has had to project a similar image to that of most other retailers – hi-tech check-outs, wide variety, clean and bright shops, and value for money.

The Co-op continues to serve the local community (e.g. by sponsoring community projects and by offering customers a square deal). In the late 1990s the Co-op decided to get back to some of its first principles by focusing on ethical trading. Today, it makes sure all the products it purchases are produced and supplied under fair trading conditions that do not involve exploitation. In addition, it makes sure the products it sells are produced in such a way as to give maximum consideration to environmental values. The question is whether this emphasis on an ethical approach will convince enough extra customers to shop at the Co-op.

Retail co-operatives are usually registered as limited liability companies.

Producer co-operatives

Producer co-operatives are usually registered as companies 'limited by guarantee', which means each member undertakes to fund any losses up to a certain amount. There are many types. A workers' co-operative, for example, is one that employs all or most of its members. In a workers' co-operative members:

- share responsibility for the success or failure of the business

- work together

- take decisions together

- share the profits.

Other examples of producer co-operatives are groups to grow agricultural products (such as tomatoes, celery, onions, etc.) and to make furniture or to organise child minding.

In agriculture, a producers' co-operative will normally have a president and full-time or part-time staff responsible for the marketing activities and administration of the co-operative. These officials will also take responsibility for quality control and for making sure the product reaches the market in an appropriate state. Co-operators will have to abide by the regulations of the co-operative (e.g. in regards to ensuring the quality of their products).

The main problems such co-operatives face are finance and organisation. Some co-operatives find it difficult to raise capital from banks and other bodies. This is not the case with profitable co-operatives, but where the co-op has been set up for 'not-for-profit' reasons, raising capital is more difficult. A number of co-operatives raise capital by selling shares, while others set up detailed management structures for decision-making.

Marketing co-operatives

Marketing co-operatives are set up exclusively to help groups of co-operators to market their products jointly (e.g. art and craft co-operatives). With this arrangement, most co-operators can focus on what they do best (e.g. making things), while specialists arrange the publicity and the selling of the work.

Marketing co-operatives are also popular in farming, where the co-operative will take responsibility for grading, packing, distributing, advertising, selling and other activities.

Check your understanding

Find an example of a co-operative in your local area. How is the co-operative run and managed? Who makes the decisions in the co-operative? Does the co-operative seek to make a profit? What happens to profits? What are the benefits of this form of business organisation to the co-operators?

Franchising

In America, over 40% of all retail sales are made through firms operating under the franchise system. It is a form of business organisation that has also become very popular in the UK.

Franchising is really the 'hiring out' or licensing of the use of 'good ideas' to other companies. A franchise grants permission to sell a product and trade under a certain name in a particular area. If I have a good idea, I can sell you a licence to trade and carry out a business using my idea in your area. The person taking out the franchise puts down a sum of money as capital and is issued with the equipment by the franchising company. The firm selling the franchise is called the franchisor and a person paying for the franchise is called the franchisee. The franchisee usually has the sole right of operating in a particular area.

This type of trading is common in the fast-food industry (examples being Spud-U-Like and Pizza Hut). Further examples are Dyno-Rod (in the plumbing business), Tumbletots, The Body Shop and Prontaprint.

Where materials are an important part of the business (e.g. hamburgers, confectionery, hair conditioners), the franchisee must buy an agreed percentage of supplies from the franchisor, who thus makes a profit on these supplies. The franchisor also takes a percentage of the profits of the business, without having to risk capital or become involved in the day-to-day management.

The franchisee benefits from trading under a well-known name and enjoys a local monopoly. Training is usually arranged by the franchisor. The franchisee is his or her own boss and takes most of the profits.

In 1999, the British Franchise Association's (www.british.franchise.org.uk) Franchisee of the Year was Huw Smith, who operates the carpet and upholstery care franchise Rainbow International in Lantrisant, South Wales. Five years before joining Rainbow, Huw Smith was a man with a van and a turnover of less than £20,000. By 1999 he had 25 staff and in the year 2000 had taken his business worldwide to reach an annual turnover of £1 million.

Check your understanding

McDonald's is an example of brand franchising. McDonald's, the franchisor, 'sells' the right to sell its branded goods to someone wishing to set up a McDonald's franchise. The licence agreement allows McDonald's to insist on manufacturing or operating methods and the quality of the product. Under a McDonald's franchise, McDonald's own or lease the site and the actual restaurant building. The franchisee buys the fittings, the equipment and the right to operate the franchise for 20 years. To ensure uniformity throughout the world, all franchisees have to use standardised McDondald's branding, menus, design layouts and administration systems.

Interview your local McDonald's manager to find out what are the benefits and drawbacks of operating the franchise outlined above.

Case study: Taking out a delivery franchise

If you enjoy driving, why not take out a delivery franchise? There are many opportunities to take out a franchise that involves driving, usually to deliver goods to customers. In some cases the vehicle is supplied by the franchisor, but after you have to buy or lease it yourself, though franchisors may help with the arrangements.

Clearly such a franchise will suit only people who enjoy driving for a living. It could be for hours every day of the week and may have an effect on your health. Some franchises also require you to pick up heavy loads when making deliveries.

Delivery franchises seeking new franchisees include Trophy Petfoods, where you deliver pet foods, accessories and an advice service. In early 2000, it was seeking 50 new franchisees.

The overall start-up fee is about £10,000–£12,000 including working capital, but you also need to buy a van. It does not need to be new but must be in good order and be capable of coping with the level of business you anticipate. Expect to pay £6,000–£15,000 for the van. Livery is included in the fee to the franchisor and deliveries are local.

A Chemical Express franchise involves the delivery and sale of cleaning and hygiene chemicals to commercial users. In 2000, it was looking for another ten people with full driving licences and a will to succeed, but no experience is necessary. Cost is £17,000 plus working capital and you pay £450 a month to lease a Mercedes van, which the firm will convert into a mobile showroom.

1 What would be the benefits of taking out a franchise that involved delivering goods?

2 What might be the drawbacks of taking out such a franchise?

3 What sorts of people would be most suitable for taking out the franchises outlined above?

In 1999 the award for Franchisor of the Year went to Perfect Pizza, the UK's largest pizza and delivery take-away company, with 130 franchisees, 200 outlets and a turnover of £42 million.

'Not for profit' or 'charity' organisations

A charity is an organisation set up to raise funds and support other people or a cause. The objectives of charities are to raise enough funds, or a surplus, for use in helping others. A surplus is a balance from the income of a charity after all costs have been paid. This contrasts with the profit-based objective of a private sector organisation. The management of charity work is overseen by a group of trustees – volunteers with a reputation as responsible citizens. Many will have a variety of experience in both charity and business activities. Charities have to register as such and must produce annual accounts that are available for anyone to see.

Most charity organisations start out as good ideas. Someone recognises the need for such an organisation and acts accordingly. For example, Shelter was set up in 1966 to help the many homeless people on the streets. The Toybox Charity was founded in 1991 by the Dyason family, who were horrified by a television documentary showing the plight of some of the 250,000 children orphaned by civil war in Guatemala. The charity has grown into a comprehensive rescue strategy for children who live on the streets of Guatemala City.

Charities employ paid managers and workers (unlike voluntary organisations, which rely on the goodwill of their staff). Many large charities employ resources on a large scale in the same way as private business organisations. These resources need to be managed effectively and efficiently to ensure they are used in the optimum way to meet the needs of various stakeholder groupings. Today, therefore, charities employ professional business managers who are accountable for using resources in the best possible way to meet the charity's objectives.

A voluntary organisation is another radical alternative to the 'for-profit organisation'. It is a not-for-profit organisation. It is set up, organised, staffed and run by people who are working purely on a voluntary basis, usually for a 'good cause'. However, just because an organisation is run as a voluntary activity does not mean it should not operate in a professional way.

Voluntary organisations (like any other) use scarce resources. These need to be used to optimal effect or else money and time will be wasted. Examples of voluntary organisations are the Women's Royal Voluntary Service (WRVS) (http://www.wrvs.org.uk/index.html) and Voluntary Service Overseas (VSO).

Check your understanding

Identify one well-known not-for-profit organisation. Find out what the key objectives of the organisation are. Identify the main sources of revenue for the organisation. Identify the main sources of expenditure of the organisation.

Explain how the organisation operates differently from a for-profit organisation.

The appropriate type of business organisation

Most big businesses have been through several forms of organisation on the way to attaining large-scale status. For example, Marks & Spencer started off as a one-man business. Michael Marks arrived in this country as an emigrant from Russia. He

A new concept in retailing

spoke hardly any English and travelled as a sole trading pedlar from door to door, selling household items such as needles and thread. He had a sign which he carried that said: 'Don't ask the price, it's a penny.' Later he opened up market stalls and worked with a partner, Tom Spencer, who had a better command of the English language. While Spencer did the administration for the business, Marks concentrated on the buying and selling and on running the stalls. Later, Michael Marks' son visited America, from where he took the idea of opening up a chain of stores throughout the UK. The time was right to go public to raise more capital. Today, M&S is an international company with stores in such European capitals as Paris.

The form of business you adopt depends very much on your objectives and the scale of your operations. Typically, large-scale businesses will be public companies because of their access to capital through the stock exchange.

Small businesses will take the form of the sole trader, the partnership or the private limited company. We have also seen that franchising is becoming the most rapidly expanding form of new business, with

benefits for both the franchisee and the franchisor.

Some businesses have more idealistic objectives and they will, therefore, go for an alternative form, such as a co-operative, charitable or voluntary form of organisation.

Today, many large organisations are going for an international or global reach. No longer are they happy to work within the local, regional or national market – they want to operate in Preston, Paris and Pittsburgh at the same time. For example, companies such as the Italian Benetton (which generally operate under the franchise scheme) have stores throughout North America, Europe and southeast Asia.

As businesses change their types of ownership, this will have implications for:

- limited and unlimited liability
- access to different sources of finance
- control
- use of profits
- legal liabilities.

Limited and unlimited liability

Shareholders in companies and co-operatives have the legal protection of limited liability. Sole traders and ordinary partners cannot have limited liability. Limited liability means that, if the business goes bankrupt because it is unable to meet its debts, the shareholders/owners will not be liable (responsible by law) to lose their possessions to pay the money that is owed. The maximum amount they could lose is the amount they have put into their shares.

People in business will think carefully about this question of limited liability. When the risk of running their business is high, they will often feel it is important to change the status of the business to one that gives them limited liability. This is why even some very small businesses with only a few shareholders will be formed into private companies.

When a business expands to become very large, it will feel limited liability is essential because it will be asking a great many shareholders to risk their capital in the business. Without limited liability status, large numbers of people will not be prepared to sink their capital into a business. For similar reasons co-operators need the protection of limited liability in order to commit themselves to co-operate.

Check your understanding

List three types of business in which the owners have limited liability. List two types of business in which the owners do not have limited liability.

Access to sources of finance

As an organisation becomes larger and takes on more sophisticated forms of business ownership (such as company status), it has access to a wider range of sources of finance.

When Michael Marks was a sole trader, he would have to provide capital from his own savings or could take out a loan or overdraft from a bank or other type of institution. He could also take out a mortgage. When he took on Tom Spencer as his partner, their joint capital went into the business. However, there are restrictions on the number of partners allowed in an ordinary partnership. The number is 20. There is also a special type of partnership called a 'limited partnership' in which the partnership can obtain additional capital from so-called 'sleeping partners'. The sleeping partner can put capital into the business but can have no say in the running of the business. The sleeping partner is protected by limited liability.

When an organisation moves on to corporate status (i.e. it becomes a company), it is able to draw on a much wider range of sources of finance. Not only does it have access to more sources of finance but it will also find it easier to raise finance because it is seen as being more financially secure. When M&S (http://www.marks-and-spencer.co.uk) became a company, a great many people were prepared to buy shares. The shareholders knew they were not risking their personal assets. Initially, M&S were a private company with shareholders being made up largely of family members. Later on, they went for a full Stock Exchange listing as they became a public limited company. Plcs are able to raise capital through shares, bank loans, overdrafts, mortgages and many other sources. Generally speaking, large companies will be able to borrow money more cheaply (i.e. at lower rates of interest) than smaller companies.

Co-operatives raise finance from co-operators by selling shares and from the usual means of loans and borrowed money. Not-for-profit co-operatives will find it difficult to raise finance from the commercial financial sector, which generally looks for a higher return on investment. However, in recent years they have benefited from the increasing number of investors who are looking for ethical sources of saving and investment, rather than a pure financial return.

An individual taking out a franchise will usually need to provide the start-up capital of setting up the franchise – generally more than £10,000. An individual who is already in a particular line of business (e.g. someone in the transport business) can benefit from converting from a sole trader (or partnership) to a franchise, as a result of the image and reputation the franchising company provides.

Charitable and voluntary organisations will raise much of their capital from fund-raising activities. Their ability to borrow is often restricted by the legal terms and conditions under which they are set up and allowed to operate.

> ### Check your understanding
> Why is a plc able to raise more finance than a sole trader or co-operative?

Control

Control is a key consideration in deciding on what type of business to form. The great thing about being a sole trader is that it is your business and you make the decisions. In other words, you have more or less total control. When you take a partner into your business, you have to share control. The relationships between partners are generally determined by a deed of partnership. Where no deed exists, the provisions of the Partnership Act 1980 will specify the relationship between partners. Deeds normally cover areas such as capital, profit shares, responsibilities, salaries and procedures for dissolution (breaking up the partnership). One problem of a partnership is that partners can, and often do, fall out. A major source of disagreement is over control – one partner wanting to do something other partners disagree with.

Many business people prefer private to public companies because it is easier to control a private company. In a private company, shares can be sold only with the permission of the board of directors. By keeping shares in a small number of hands, the key shareholders are able to control the activities of the business. For example, they would not sell shares to someone who might want to interfere with the way the business has been run. Hence, family companies often take the form of private companies.

The danger of losing control really comes to the fore when you become a public limited company. Now the shares can be traded on the Stock Exchange, and individuals or groups of individuals can take over other companies by buying up 51% of the shares (a controlling interest). In the real world, companies are bought and sold all too frequently. Existing shareholders are often tempted to sell by an attractive offer to buy shares at an inflated price by another business or interest group.

All too often we see successful private companies becoming public companies only to be bought up, with their original owners (directors) losing their jobs and their interest in the business. In the world of multinational enterprise and global business, even the most successful businesses make good targets for a take-over. One complaint frequently voiced by shareholders in public companies is that there has been a split between the ownership and control of their organisations. The shareholders own the business but professional managers make the decisions (i.e. the managers control the business).

However, the professional manager does have to be careful because, if shareholders are not happy at the annual general meeting of the company, they are in a position to sack the directors. In the early part of the twenty-first century we are increasingly seeing shareholders winning back a share in controlling their companies by increasingly putting over their viewpoint to boards of directors.

Co-operatives tend to be controlled by the co-operators although, when the co-operative sets up a management committee, it is the managers who will start to make the major decisions in the co-operative.

In a franchise operation, activities are controlled by both the franchisor and the franchisee. For example, we have seen that McDonald's licence agreement enables McDonald's to insist on manufacturing and operating methods and the quality of their product, as well as controlling branding, menus and design layouts. Generally, most franchisees do feel they have quite a lot of control of their own businesses – in particular, of how much of their own effort and hard work they put into making their business a success.

Case study: Trouble at Somerfield

During 1999, it was widely reported by the press that Somerfield, the struggling supermarket group, were under financial pressure, with trading in their stores poor and profits falling. The trading results led to the resignation of Somerfield's beleaguered Chief Executive, David Simons. At this time, shares in Britain's fifth-ranking supermarket operator had plunged nearly 20% to a new low of 94p. In 1998 the shares had stood at 458p before the collapse in confidence and competition from companies such as Wal-Mart.

The new Chief Executive of Somerfield is Alan Smith. He has the mammoth task of turning round the fortunes of the company. He admits that, 'Buying Kwiksave and trying to turn it into a Somerfield proved disastrous'. The two stores are just too different. One of his first jobs was to visit stores to reassure the 67,000 staff that they faced a brighter future. But now that the American supermarket giant Wal-Mart has opened its first UK store in Bristol, he feels that Somerfield can compete by avoiding direct competition, by offering the right services to customers. The immediate priority is to improve the trading performance of the business. One of the ways the company intends to do this is by making deliveries of groceries and fresh produce to rural stores. Somerfield believes that unlike large superstores that operate on out-of-town sites, it has the advantage of operating in inner city and suburban convenience stores in the notorious 'fresh food deserts'. Although the food may be more expensive than in the main supermarkets, the convenience involved will more than cut down the costs and travelling time involved.

1 Describe why the price of Somerfield shares has fallen.

2 How might a new Chief Executive make a difference?

3 Describe the new strategy for Somerfield.

4 Working in groups, think of other ideas that would make this company more successful. Discuss your responses.

Charity and voluntary organisations are not faced with the take-over problem of the cut-and-thrust world of for-profit organisations. However, as many charities have grown, they have increasingly been professionalised. Instead of the organisations being controlled by the people who originally set up the organisations, they are controlled by professional managers.

Use of profits

The great benefit of being a sole trader is that all the profits belong to you – the owner. However, so do the losses! A large number of sole traders go out of business each year.

As we have seen, partners will have to share profits. When deciding on whether to form a partnership you should think about whether the benefits (such as being able to draw on your partner's time and expertise) more than outweigh the cost of having to share your hard-earned profits with the partner.

In companies, shareholders may receive a benefit from owning shares in two ways. First, they may be paid a dividend upon the shareholding, which is expressed as a return on the par (face) value of the shares. Secondly, they may receive income by selling their shareholding at a value above that which they originally paid for it. In recent years we have seen many examples of people setting up companies and then quickly amassing personal fortunes as the value of their companies soared (e.g. Richard Branson and Anita Roddick).

Traditionally, retail co-operatives distributed profits as dividends that related to purchases made by each member of the society. Thus profits were shared amongst customers. Some co-operative retail stores distribute their profits in the form of discounts to shoppers while others give trading stamps. Producer co-operatives and marketing co-operative share profits between the co-operators.

In a franchise operation, the franchisee will often pay a given percentage of his or her sales or profits to the franchisor. The remainder franchisees can plough back into the business or draw on for their personal use. One problem of many franchises is that the franchisee will have to pay a royalty to the franchisor, even if he or she makes a loss.

Not-for-profit organisations make surpluses rather than profits. The surplus can then be allocated to the further good work of the organisation.

> ### Check your understanding
> How might the motivation to make a profit differ for someone setting up a co-operative from someone setting up a private company?

Legal liabilities

Different forms of business are faced with different legal requirements. The more complex the legal requirements, the more the business will need to operate on a larger and more sophisticated basis. Large companies have the resources to employ specialist lawyers and legal departments. Small businesses are likely to find legal liabilities to be a time-consuming hassle.

Sole traders and partnerships require much less paperwork than companies. For example, a sole trader or partner can fill in a tax return fairly easily (perhaps with the help of an accountant). The large multinational plc will need dedicated accountants to work out its tax liabilities.

The sole trader business does not have a separate legal identify from that of the individual. The individual trades under his or her own name. If the sole trader breaches a contract, he or she will be held personally responsible in law. Sole traders have the advantage of being self-employed, which enables them, for tax purposes, to offset legitimate business expenses against income tax. Income tax liability is assessed in arrears; although self-employed people will pay a balance estimated on their previous year's earnings.

Like sole traders, partnerships in England and Wales are not recognised in law as being separate from the partners. It is the partners who will therefore be taken to court rather than the business. Partners are also responsible for the business debts of other partners. Partnerships may limit the flexibility of partners to sell or transfer their ownership as no partner may be able to transfer ownership without the consent of the other partners.

As a result of a law case (Saloman v. Salomon & Co. (1897)), a company exists as a separate legal identity from that of its owners. Assets (such as property) as well as debts belong to the company and not to individual members. To set up a limited company it is necessary to go through a number of legal procedures in order to gain recognition. This mainly involves the presentation of various documents and records to the Registrar of Companies. These documents are open to scrutiny.

All limited companies must present a memorandum of association and articles of association in order to receive a certificate of incorporation (Figure 2.6). The memorandum spells out the nature of the company when viewed from the outside. Someone reading the memorandum would

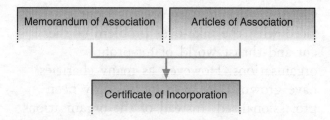

Figure 2.6 The documents required to set up a company

be able to obtain a general idea of what the company is and the business with which it is concerned. The memorandum sets out the company's:

- name
- registered address
- objectives
- capital.

Most companies will produce a fairly vague list of objectives in their memorandum. This will give them the opportunity to alter their activities if market opportunities arise.

The articles of association set out the rules that govern the inside working of a company. They include the following:

- The rights attached to the holding of the various types of shares offered by the company.
- The rules and procedures for issuing and transferring shares.
- The procedures and timing of company meetings.
- The details of how accounts will be kept and recorded.
- The powers and responsibilities of directors.
- The details of how company officers will be appointed.

Once these documents have been accepted, the private company will be granted a certificate of incorporation and can start to trade. The certificate of incorporation sets up the company as a legal body in its own right. The company (not individual shareholders) enters into contracts and can sue or be sued in a court of law.

In setting up co-operatives, detailed paperwork is involved to ensure the co-op is being run on a sound and secure footing in order to qualify for limited liability status.

Franchise agreements involve detailed legal arrangements between the franchisor and the franchisee that set out each party's legal

Check your understanding

Give examples of ways in which the legal burden of setting up a plc are considerably less than for setting up as a sole trader business.

Carry out an investigation to find out about what is included in the contractual agreement between a local franchisee and their franchisor.

responsibilities. By tying the franchisee down to tried and established patterns, the franchisor is able to ensure the work is carried out in the most appropriate and safe way.

Chapter 3 Organisational functions

All businesses combine 'factors of production' to produce their products and/or services. You need to understand how a business uses factors of production – labour (people), capital (machinery and equipment) and land or buildings.

Combining these factors means the business has to carry out a range of functions. These include:

- finance
- production
- human resources
- marketing
- administration
- research and development.

You need to understand the activities and characteristics of each function and how each functional area contributes to the running of a business. You will need to see how well these functions are carried out, as this affects the success and efficiency of the business and helps it to meet its objectives. You also need to understand the connections between the different functional areas.

Factors of production

Imagine you are visiting a modern crisps factory. What would you see? The first and most obvious sight would be large areas of land and building. Inside, you would find machinery and equipment (a production line) and the employees working on the line. For the machines to work, they need to use energy, raw materials and packaging.

A business unit is therefore a unit of production that sets out to bring together and to organise factors of production to produce goods and services. The factors of production are the ingredients that make an enterprise work. These factors are labour, capital, energy, materials and information:

- *Labour* is the effort (both physical and mental) provided by employees. Work carried out takes a number of forms, such as handling information, sorting information, communication, decision-making and control, as well as more obvious manual tasks. In a Walker's crisps factory (http://walkers.co.uk) the most obvious example of labour would be the workers on the production line – however, they are also supported by a range of technicians, marketing specialists, packaging designers and many others.

- *Capital* is represented by the machines and tools, without which there would be no production. In a Walker's crisps factory, this would be represented in the plant and equipment, such as the automated production line. This is the physical capital of the firm (which would be financed by financial capital – often money borrowed from banks to purchase the physical capital).

- *Energy* is provided by some of the raw materials – the fossil fuels, gas, steam and solar power that make the machines work and that provide heat and light for the factory.

- *Materials* are needed to make any product. In a crisps factory these might include the potato (or potato substitute materials) and the flavourings, as well as the packaging material.

- *Information* is the know-how (all the accumulated experience of members of an organisation) that provides a driving force behind the enterprise. For example, there would be an accumulated wisdom of recipes and marketing ideas.

Another more traditional way of looking at factors of production is to divide them into land, labour, capital and enterprise.

Enterprise is regarded as the factor that brings the other factors together to produce goods in order to make profits. Land is considered to be all the resources of nature (e.g. water, coal, farm land). Using this alternative classification, the rewards accruing to the factors of production are as shown in Figure 3.1.

Factor	Reward
Land	Rent
Labour	Wages
Capital	Interest
Enterprise	Profits

Figure 3.1 The rewards accruing to factors of production

The entrepreneur is the risk-taker in the business and, in a small business, would be the individual owner/s. In a larger business the risk-takers are the shareholders.

Check your understanding

Classify the following factors of production as land, labour, capital or enterprise:

- The fish in the sea available for catching by a fishing business.
- The buildings and machinery in a factory.
- The shareholders of a business.
- The brainpower of intelligent workers.
- The interpersonal skills possessed by modern service employees.
- The maintenance equipment owned by a company.
- Anita Roddicks's initiative in bringing the various elements of The Body Shop into a successful organisation.
- The area where a factory is located.

Case study: Harry Ramsden's

Harry Ramsden's (http://www.harryramsdens. co.uk) started out as a popular fish and chip restaurant in West Yorkshire. Today, the company is widely known for its fish and chips and holds the world record for the largest fish and chip shop. The company is very famous and has franchises as far away as Jeddah, Singapore and Melbourne. It has a total of 33 outlets.

Harry Ramsden's first 'hut' was opened in 1928 and, since then, new outlets have all been modelled on that first fish and chip shop plus the provision of a large car park. The company has also entered into licensing agreements in over 2,000 supermarkets with various fish and chip complementary products (mushy peas and pickled onions are the best-selling items). In the early days, as you might imagine, the enterprise behind the company came from the owner, Harry Ramsden himself, but in the 1980s as the organisation expanded the business was sold on by the Ramsden family, although it still trades under the original name.

Today, Harry Ramsden's is a public company. In recent times it has borrowed money to finance its expansion. Harry Ramsden's employ a range of people, including waiters and waitresses, cooks and food specialists, as well as a back-up staff of accountants, administrators and marketing specialists. In recent years the company has borrowed extensively from financial institutions to provide the momentum for its expansion.

From the case study, identify the land, labour, capital and enterprise that make up the Harry Ramsden company.

Business functions

It is helpful to view a business as a system or, more specifically, as an overall system that can be viewed as a series of subsystems. A system processes inputs to produce output. For example, in a crisps factory the ingredients and other inputs are processed by the production system to produce crisps.

The production process takes place within defined boundaries, which are usually fairly obvious. The inputs flow into this system. Some of the resources used will be current resources – for example, potatoes (or potato substitute), additives, salt, energy, etc. What actually goes into the production process will be 'filtered' to ensure only desirable inputs are accepted. For example, quality control ensures no fragments of glass enter the production system. Current resources then 'combine' with elements (or fixed assets), such as machinery and buildings, and flow from one element to another element across links between the

elements (see Figure 3.2). For example, the potatoes for crisps flow from the ingredient mixing element, through rollers and into heating ovens.

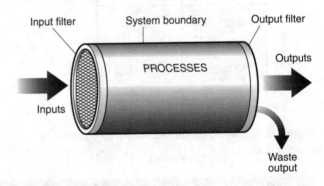

Figure 3.2 A production system: the input/processes/output method

The system is controlled by a user, who puts in the primary inputs and the secondary inputs. The primary inputs are the settings (control parameters) that control the operation of the system (e.g. the speed of the line, the temperature, the

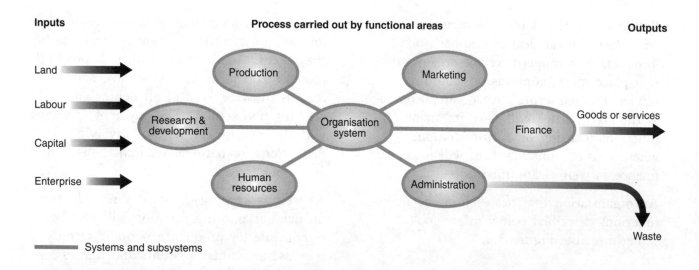

Figure 3.3 An organisation's functions work together harmoniously to process the resources

quality standards, the hours worked and so on). The secondary inputs are the current resources.

In order to carry out its operations involving the use of factors of production to produce finished goods and services, an organisation will need to be structured into a series of functions. Each of the functions of an organisation should work in harmony

to process resources successfully into final outputs, as shown in Figure 3.3.

Search the Internet using the heading Organigram or Organogram and you will find thousands of examples of the ways in which organisations across the world are structured on functional lines. The types of functions a company/organisation has depend on the nature of its objectives.

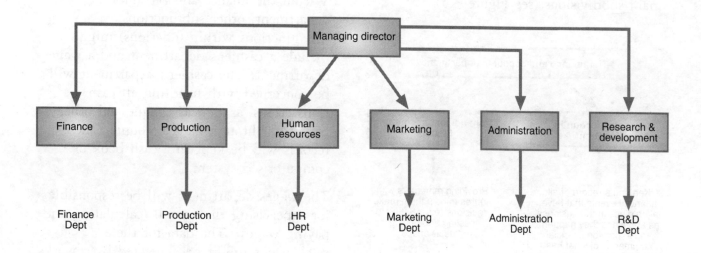

Figure 3.4 An organisation structured along functional lines

While a traditional manufacturing company will place a great deal of emphasis on 'production' a modern service organisation will place more emphasis on 'consumer service' or 'marketing'. An organisation such as the civil service will have its major functions focusing on administration, whereas an accountancy firm will focus on finance as well as administration.

An organisation that has each of the major functions described below might look something like Figure 3.4.

Finance and accounts

The chief accountant is responsible for supervising the accounts and finance department. The accounts section must keep a detailed record of all money paid in and out and present the final balance sheet, sources and use of funds, profit and loss account, and other financial records at regular intervals. Modern accounts are stored on computer files, and accounting procedures are greatly simplified by the use of specialised software. Within the finance and accounts department there will be two main subdivisions (see Figure 3.5).

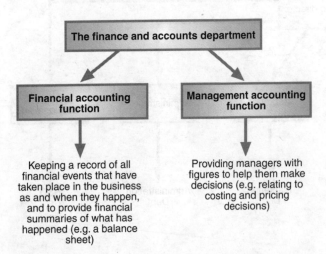

Figure 3.5 The finance and accounts department

The *financial accounting function* is responsible for keeping records of financial events as they occur. Accounts need to be kept of all moneys paid to or by a company, and records must be kept of all debtor and creditor transactions. The payment of wages will also require calculations involving deductions for national insurance, pensions and other factors.

As well as keeping day-to-day records, the financial accounting function will also be responsible for producing periodic records such as the annual accounts and figures for discussion at meetings of directors.

The *management accounting function* has the responsibility for nudging the company in certain directions, based on analysis of figures for the present and predictions for the future. Management accounts will break down figures, to extract information about a company's present performance and about what sorts of improvements can be made in the future. Using systems of budgetary control, it will set targets for achievement and limits for spending for the various parts of the business.

Within the finance and accounts department, other subfunctions (i.e. functions within functions) might include a cashier's department and a wages department. The cashier's department will be concerned with handling all cash transactions, as well as cheque and other payments through bank accounts. These records will be kept in a cash book or computerised system.

The wages department will be responsible for supervising the payroll (calculating and paying wages). The data for these calculations might be generated by a works department or other department responsible for recording the amount of work carried out by employees.

subordinates. As we move across the continuum we see a range of other positions. For example, the manager decides what will happen and then 'sells' it (i.e. explains to the people who carry out the decision why it will be done). We also see greater opportunities for others within the organisation to contribute to the decision-making process.

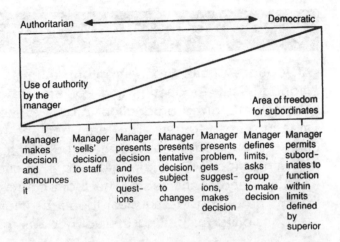

Figure 4.14 The continuum of management styles

Check your understanding

Are there situations in which an autocratic style of management will be most suitable?

What situations are likely to be best suited to the democratic style of management?

The managerial grid is a matrix model of management that instead of concentrating on autocratic versus democratic styles, looks at 'concern for people' and 'concern for production'. This is easiest to understand in diagrammatic form (see Figure 4.15).

Of the five styles of management shown in the grid, only 'Team' is the ideal style because it combines concern for people with

concern for production, gets things done and keeps everybody happy. Looking at the others:

- 'Country Club' is too concerned with people and gets very little done.

- 'Task' is too concerned with production and creates an atmosphere of low morale.

- 'Impoverished' has no concern for people or output.

- 'Middle-of-the-road' shows some concern for people and some concern for production.

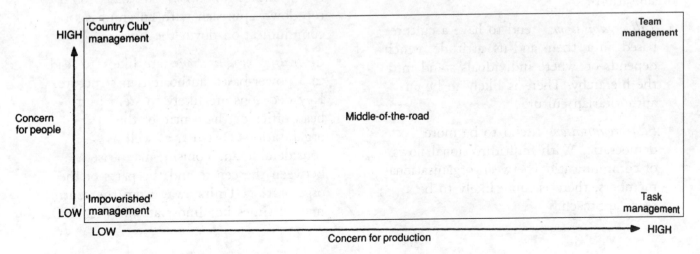

Figure 4.15 The management grid

Case study: Teamworking at Jaguar

At Jaguar's Castle Bromwich plant, there is a strong emphasis on democratic management. Production line workers are grouped into teams with a team leader. The team is given production targets to meet but then decides how it will go about meeting these targets. The team decides how it will organise work in its own area (i.e. the physical layout of the area). Alongside the production line are team meeting areas with chairs grouped in a circle. In this area are charts showing the performance of the team. The team meets to discuss what is going well and what is going badly, and to suggest ideas for improvement. The team then has the responsibility for putting their own ideas into practice.

1 How does the Jaguar model fit in with the continuum of leadership styles?

2 What do you see as being the principal advantages of this approach?

3 Are there any drawbacks?

A manager can study the grid, assess where his or her leadership style lies and consider where improvements are possible.

The relationship between culture and structure

There is a clear relationship between the structure and the culture of many organisations:

- *Tall organisations* tend to have a culture based on a 'them and us' attitude, which depends on where individuals stand in the hierarchy. There is likely to be an authoritarian culture.

- *Flat organisations* tend to be more democratic. With multidirectional flows of communication between organisational members, there is more likely to be a team approach.

- *Matrix structures* tend to be more democratic than tall organisations. In the matrix, people will mix with people from more than one functional area, so there is less likely to be a situation in which departments become very defensive about their territories. Where the matrix involves process teams, this can create a bonding between members of these teams and a cross-fertilisation of ideas.

- *Hierarchical organisations* are based on a top-down approach with an emphasis on communication down the line.

- *Centralised organisations* are likely to lead to a power-based authoritarian structure. Key decisions are likely to stem from head office or the centre of the organisation. Distrust, as well as considerable antagonism, may arise between the centre and the parts of the organisation. Units away from the centre may at times be almost at war with HQ, perhaps 'failing to understand' instructions and carrying out other sabotaging activities.

- *Decentralised organisations* are most likely to be based on democratic structures/ teamwork/empowerment, etc.

Check your understanding

In two organisations that you are familiar with, identify the relationships between the structures of an organisation and their cultures.

Chapter 5 Communication

Businesses need to communicate with a range of individuals and organizations, including their customers, their competitors and their suppliers, as well as their own employees. Good communication within a business is essential if that business is to operate effectively. You need to be able to identify the communication channels that exist within businesses and the effect these have on the quality of communication. You should be able to compare different channels of communication, including:

- internal and external
- formal and informal
- upward and downward
- open and restricted.

It is important you understand the relationship between effective communication and the achievement of business objectives.

Information and communication technology (ICT) has had a dramatic effect on the way communication takes place in business. You need to be able to identify and understand where ICT has changed the means of communicating within a business, and analyse the strengths and weaknesses of current development in ICT for business.

What is communication?

To communicate means to impart knowledge or to express ideas in words or other symbols. The previous sentence, it is hoped, will have communicated to you clearly what is meant by communication. It may not have done because the ideas are poorly expressed, because the vocabulary is too complex, because you weren't concentrating when you read it and so on.

All organisations need to have good, clear paths of communication so that:

- Everyone is clear about objectives.

- There is smooth and accurate communication both within the organisation (internal communication) and between the organisation and other individuals, bodies and groups (external communication).

- Everyone in the organisation is kept informed of developments and changes.

- Ideas and views are clearly heard.

- New ideas can bubble up through the organisation.

- People don't feel frustrated – 'nobody listens to me'.

- The organisation and its members can respond quickly to new developments, etc.

The communication process

The process of communication involves a transmitter (or sender) sending messages to receivers. A transmitter should put information into a form the receivers can understand, and this might involve oral, written or visual messages. This process is known as encoding. The transmitter chooses a particular medium to use to send messages to the receivers – letter, report, fax, phone call, email, web site, etc. The receivers then interpret the messages through a process of decoding (see Figure 5.1).

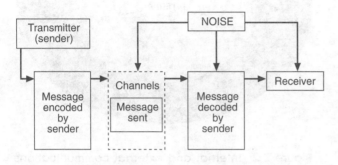

Figure 5.1 The communication process

The leaky bucket theory

The communication of information and ideas can be likened to transferring water by bucket from the tap in your kitchen to parched plants in your garden. A 'good' bucket will not let any of the water escape, so you can carry out the job in an efficient way. However, many of us rely on leaky buckets. The more holes in the bucket and the further the distance from tap to flower

bed, the less efficient the system will be. The greater the need the plants have for water and the more holes there are in the bucket, the greater will our frustration be in the process.

Though a message flows from the sender to receivers, there is no guarantee the receivers will either receive the full message or even understand it. This is because the process may involve communication problems. These communication problems are known as 'noise', and this may weaken or destroy the message being sent.

The following are a few examples of 'noise':

* *Language problems*. The language used may not be fully understood, particularly if a receiver comes from a different background from the sender or has considerably less knowledge (technical or otherwise).

* *Jumping to conclusions*. The receiver might read into the message what he or she expects to see rather than what is really there.

* *Lack of interest*. The receiver may not be prepared to listen to the message. The message has to be designed to appeal to the listener.

* *Competing environment*. Background sounds (real noise) or interference from other activities in the work environment may influence the message, particularly if it is long or complicated and requires concentration by the receiver.

* *Channels of communication*. Effective communication will be hampered if the means chosen to pass on the message is poor.

* *Cultural differences*. We all have different perceptions of the world according to our backgrounds and experiences, and this

may result in our interpreting a message in different ways.

- *Steps in the message.* If there are too many stages in the message (i.e. if it is too complicated), it may not be properly understood.

Internal and external communication

Internal communication is communication that takes place within an organization, while external communication takes place between the organisation and the outside world. Figure 5.2 shows typical examples of internal and external communications.

Both internal and external communications have been transformed by rapid developments in information and communications technology. The modern organisation may have:

- A linked internal communication system – an internal network.

- Links with customers – a system for e-commerce (B2C – see below)

- Links with other businesses – e-business. (B2B – see below)

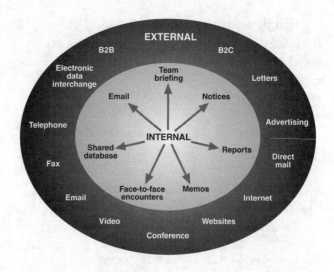

Figure 5.2 Internal and external communications

Together, these links create what is called the networked economy, which vastly increases the potential of business to connect with employees, customers, other businesses, shareholders, etc. We live in exciting times in which the potential for new business is enormous, and in which start-up businesses can, literally, become worth millions of pounds overnight. The new networked economy enables businesses to cut costs and to increase efficiencies.

Case study: E-business

Not only has information and communications technology transformed what is referred to as 'the new economy' made up of ICT companies such as web page designers and the .com companies focusing on e-commerce, but ICT has also helped companies in 'the old economy' (the old manufacturers) to transform their businesses.

For example, in the aerospace industry, four of the world's biggest aerospace and defence companies (BAe Systems, Boeing, Lockheed Martin and Reytheon) joined together in April 2000 to launch an online trading exchange that will open up an electronic marketplace worth £71 billion to manufacturers, components suppliers and end customers.

This trading exchange replicates similar e-business marketplaces that have also been launched by suppliers, distributors and the retailers themselves. Now the big battalions of industry (the equipment manufacturers) are getting in on the act, principally as a means of cutting their procurement (buying in of parts) bills. In March 2000, 40 of the world's largest food manufacturers got together with the Grocery Manufactures Association of the United States to form an exchange aimed at simplifying the buying processes – including Coca-Cola, Colgate-Palmolive, Gillette, Heinz, Kellogg's, Procter & Gamble and PepsiCo. Similar ventures have been introduced by major manufacturers in the car, oil and retailing sectors.

Riding on the wave of the Internet, these so-called business-to-business (or B2B) ventures are booming. In early 2000 there were estimated to be at least 50 online business-to-business transactions underlying each business-to-consumer (B2C) transaction. In other words, every time a customer clicks his or her mouse to order a book or CD from Amazon.com, a great deal of trading will be going on behind the scenes to make this possible. That is why B2B revenues were forecast to grow from less than $100 billion in 1999 to $800 billion by 2002 – more than four times the predicted level of B2C revenues.

It is easy to see how B2B transactions using the new electronic trading exchange will cut costs in the aircraft industry. For example, all six million components that go into a commercial aircraft could be ordered online. Research indicates that, for every 1% saved on procurement costs, the aerospace industry could increase profits by 7%.

Costs could be cut in three ways:

- Cutting the time to conduct a transaction and the paperwork involved.

- The companies doing the buying could buy in bulk together to obtain larger discounts from sellers.

- They could use e-auctions, where suppliers are invited to tender for business via the Internet to encourage greater transparency and lower prices.

1 Why are large firms so keen to club together to benefit from networking economies?

2 How has ICT made this improvement in communication systems possible?

3 Do large organisations have any choice in deciding whether or not to improve their communication systems?

Networking

Networking involves linking together two or more computers to allow facilities and information to be shared. This has the effect of decentralising information and communications so that managers have more information upon which to base their decisions. A computer network may be specifically developed for almost any type of organisation or application. Terminals may be just a few metres apart or they may exist in completely different parts of the world.

A local area network (LAN) may be used to connect computers within a single room, building or a group of buildings on the same site, without the use of telecommunications links. LANs may be linked to a file server, which is a permanent data store that provides files and software for other PCs and also acts as a storage base (Figure 5.3).

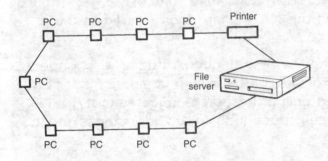

Figure 5.3 Examples of a local area network (LAN)

A wide area network (WAN) may be used to connect computers on different sites by making use of telecommunications. The great benefit is that WAN networks extend the use of the computer beyond the office by using a modem (modulator/ demodulator), which converts computer signals for transmission over the telephone lines before reconverting them again.

Modems are used because telephone lines are primarily for speech transmissions and not for use by computers. Waves travelling along lines are analogue waves, where sound and images are converted into corresponding

variations in electrical voltages or currents. However, the digital revolution has seen the creation of new formats that enable the transmission of video and voice signals. Information transfer is much faster under the new digital systems.

The uses for networks include the following:

- *Electronic mail (email).* Here computers linked through a LAN or WAN send mail between terminals. Each user has his or her own mailbox for storing messages.

- *Teleconferencing.* Meetings may take place with individuals widely dispersed, using a number of terminals.

- *Remote databases.* These include the sorts of services you can pick up on your television, such as Teletext, which provides users with vast amounts of information that is updated constantly.

- *Electronic data interchange (EDI)* This allows users to exchange business documents and information (such as orders and invoices) directly through the telephone network and other, more sophisticated, electronic communication systems.

Internal communications

Before examining the sorts of communications that need to take place within the organisation, it is helpful to look at two popular forms of internal computer networks in organisations that are at the heart of modern internal communication systems – peer-to-peer and client/server networks.

Peer-to-peer networks are networks designed to serve employees with a similar status in an organisation. These are often found in organisations in which there is a considerable blurring of the hierarchy and in which there is a teamwork approach to work.

In a peer-to-peer network, file storage and printing facilities do not come from a single server but from any computer connected to the network. Each work station can use the resources of another work station (e.g. CD-Rom drives, hard disks, fax, printers, graph plotters, etc.). Peer-to-peer networks are easy to set up and economical to run, as an expensive central server is not required.

The weaknesses of the peer-to-peer system are that it is difficult to administer if there are a great many people networked together, and the system might slow down if people are using the same facility at the same time. They are best suited for networks involving fewer than 20 computers.

Client/server networks involve the use of one, more powerful computer (the server) which is responsible for printing, the maintenance of files and any other peripherals connected to the network. The less powerful computers connected to the server are called 'clients'. Large organisations often prefer to use the client/server system because each of the computer terminals can access all the network facilities without losing any of its own processing power.

The weakness of this system is that clients are dependent on the server and, therefore, the server needs to be administered properly and looked after to make sure there are no problems with the system.

Many organisations use an intranet system, which is an organization-wide system of communications that runs over the Internet.

Common forms of internal communication

The three main ways of communicating information inside an organisation are verbal, written and electronic.

Verbal information is communicated in 'face-to-face' interactions, through telephone messages or recorded messages using answering machines and voice mail. Although verbal information can be obtained quickly, it often needs backing up in written form. For example, when you communicate an important message to a work colleague he or she might also say 'could you email me about that', or 'please can I have that in writing?'

Written information will cover a range of paper documents that are exchanged within an organisation (including memos, letters, brochures, etc.). Written information takes time to process and often requires extensive filing and distribution systems.

Electronic information is rapidly replacing other forms of communication. For example, a stock list can be transferred electronically from a supermarket to its head office. Most large organisations use an internal networking system. Nearly all networks have an email facility, and this is used to send documents in electronic form around a company.

Giving instructions

There are a number of ways of giving instructions inside an organization, in written or spoken form. Written instructions can be passed on by means of a memorandum (memo). Memos are the most widely used form of written communication in an organisation because they are brief and to the point. Most large organisations print their own memo pads for this purpose. Today, most memos will be sent electronically using email. The emailed memo can be sent to a group of employees who are part of a mailing list. Using emails for memos saves paper and storage space and is quicker. The main disadvantage is that if recipients do not check their email frequently, they may miss an important message. The amount of unsolicited emails are sent sometimes means important messages are inadvertently 'junked'.

An organisation's name does not normally appear on a memo for internal use, and it is not necessary to have a salutation or complementary ending. Memos should be kept as short as possible and, ideally, should deal with item only. Copies of the same memo are often distributed to a number of recipients.

The style of memoranda varies considerably (see Figure 5.4). Instructions from senior management are likely to be written in relatively impersonal language, while a quickly scribbled message on a memo sheet to a close colleague may be in conversational English. It is often necessary to be more careful and diplomatic when writing memos up the seniority ladder rather than down the seniority ladder.

Another form of written internal communication is in the form of guidebooks, manuals and operating instructions. This form of communication

Memorandum	
To:	Recipient's name
From:	Sender's name
Date:	12 November 2000
Subject:	Subject

Figure 5.4 Templates like this for a memo will be included in most word processing applications

needs to be very precise and clear, and will often use diagrams, flow charts, bullet points and numbered instructions. This is so that people carrying out the instructions have clear guidelines to follow. This sort of information will typically be stored for use on an organisation's central database so it can be shared by organisation members.

Many instructions in an organisation are given verbally. This is why managers and others using managerial skills need to have excellent communication skills.

Check your understanding

Either:

Set out a clear set of instructions written for a group of people to carry out an operation or set of operations in an organization

Or:

Practise giving oral instructions to a group of fellow students outlining the ways in which they should communicate with each other in carrying out a given task or project.

Case study: Setting out clear instructions at Fenland Foods

Fenland Foods specialise in making cook-chill meals for Marks & Spencer. These are ready-prepared restaurant menu dishes that are:

- assembled from ingredients (such as vegetables and meat)
- cooked on a large scale
- packed
- chilled and stored
- transported to Marks & Spencer stores
- sold to shoppers
- reheated ready for eating.

Hygiene and cleanliness are of great importance in the food industry, and staff must be trained in safe working practices. Figure 5.5 is a list of the official rules for changing for work.

1 Why do you think the instructions outlined in Figure 5.5 are numbered and put in a flow chart form?

2 Are the instructions given clear and easy to follow?

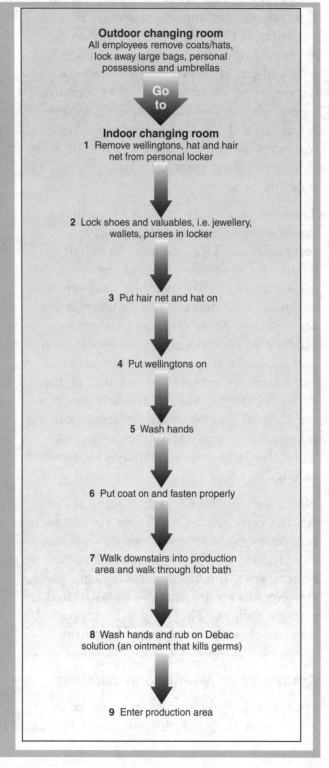

Figure 5.5 Fenland Foods: rules for changing for work

Passing on information

There are a number of ways of passing on information in an organisation. The most common form of passing on information is through word-of-mouth messages. In organisations dominated by a teamwork approach, this form of communication is part-and-parcel of everyday interactions between team members. A more formalised way of passing on information in such as organisation is 'team briefing', in which managers and others with information to share brief their team on a daily, weekly or monthly basis.

There are a number of ways of passing on information in writing. Many large companies produce employee newsletters, detailing the achievements of the organization and its members, and setting out plans and changes taking place in the organisation. Some large organisations produce an official employees' report each year which is all part of the process of encouraging employees to feel part of the decision-making process. House magazines are a useful way of communicating policies, information, events and other activities. They also help to give employees a sense of belonging.

Notices are another common form of written communication. These are placed in prominent positions and used to publicise any changes in policy, dates to be remembered, functions, events taking place, etc. Notices are usually short and related to a single subject. They might be supported by artwork to catch the staff's attention.

Reporting on events and meetings

It is often helpful to have a report of an event or meeting for the purpose of keeping accurate records or to inform future decision-making processes. Particular individuals may be asked to give a verbal report (e.g. if they have attended an important conference or when they need to report an issue of major consequence – for example, the impact of a meeting with a client or an account of a breach of health and safety regulations).

Written reports are a key feature of organisational life. Informal reports may be most suitably written or typed in memo form. It is important to start with a title, and possible, a brief introduction before going on to the body of the report. Recommendations for action should be clearly identified if these have been requested.

Formal reports will have many of the following features:

- Title page (subject matter, name and position of writer, date, etc.).

- Contents page.

- Terms of reference (explaining the reason for the report).

- Procedure (how the task was completed).

- Findings.

- Conclusions and/or recommendations.

When preparing a formal report, decisions have to be made on aspects such as language and style, circulation and the presentation (including whether the report should have a cover and binding).

Other aspects of reporting on meetings are dealt with in the case study that follows.

Case study: Meetings

Nearly all employees at all levels in an organisation will spend some time attending meetings. Meetings are held to deal with issues, problems and areas of concern for an organisation. They provide an opportunity for a group of people to use their specialist backgrounds, experiences and knowledge to contribute to a range of matters.

Meetings can be called for a variety of purposes:

- To generate ideas by drawing on the knowledge and skills of a range of specialists.
- To arrive at collective decisions. Sometimes, an individual does not have the authority to make a decision so he or she might call a meeting in order that, jointly, a group can make decisions.
- For investigative reasons (e.g. to find out what has gone wrong in a company's sales strategy, or why important procedures have not been put in place in relation to health and safety).

Some meetings are simply informal gatherings in which no formal records are kept. In contrast, a formal meeting may involve lots of procedures and set ways of doing things.

The features of a formal meeting are as follows:

- The meeting is called by a notice or agenda.
- Conduct in the meeting depends on the organisation's formal rules.
- Decisions are often reached by voting.
- There are formal terms and expressions used in the meeting.
- The proceedings are recorded in 'minutes'.

Formal meetings must be conducted according to legal requirements or to a written constitution. It is usual to give notice of the meeting to every person entitled to attend, according to the rules and regulations. The notice should be signed by the issuer and should specify the date, time and place of the meeting (see Figure 5.6).

A notice of a meeting will be accompanied or followed by an agenda, which is a list of topics to be discussed at the meeting. It will normally be sent to all those entitled to attend the meeting so they can consider the topics in advance of the meeting (see Figure 5.7).

NOTICE OF MEETING
Melchester Hockey Club

The Annual General Meeting of the Club will be held at Melchester Hockey Club on the 14 February 2000 at 7.30 pm. Any items for inclusion in the agenda should reach me no later than 16 January 2000.

Sally Brown

Club Secretary

Figure 5.6   Notice of a meeting

A chairperson has certain duties and powers in a meeting. He or she makes sure the meeting is properly constituted, keeps order, works through the agenda (preventing irrelevant discussion) and ascertains the views of the meeting by putting motions and amendments to those attending.

Often, a chairperson will have a special copy of the agenda (known as the chairperson's agenda). On this, further information is provided for the chairperson's guidance, and space is left on the right-hand side for notes to be made.

Shortly before the time a meeting starts, the chairperson makes sure there is a quorum. This is the minimum number of people required for the meeting to go ahead, according to the rules. The chairperson will make sure everyone has an agenda and that all new members are introduced.

The secretary then states whether any apologies have been received for absence, and reads through the official record (the minutes of the last meeting). If the minutes have already been circulated, it will be assumed they have been read! Members are asked to approve them as a correct record of the last meeting and, if necessary, the secretary will amend them before they are signed by the chairperson.

At this stage any matters arising from the minutes will be discussed. For example, if the last meeting suggested certain individuals undertake certain actions, these may be mentioned.

The chairperson then works through the business of the meeting, according to the agenda. If reports are to be read (again, circulated reports are assumed to have been read), the writers of the report may be asked to speak briefly. If a motion is proposed, the chairperson will ask for a proposer and a seconder, this will allow for discussion of the motion and will make sure all sides are heard. The chairperson will then call for a vote. The chairperson usually has a casting vote if the voting is tied.

Any other business is normally limited to non-controversial issues because, if it is felt something deserves further attention, it must be put on the agenda for the next meeting. At the end of the meeting a decision may be made about the date, time and place of the next meeting.

AGENDA
Melchester Hockey Club

Annual Meeting of the Selection Committee to be held on 14 February 2000 at 7.30 pm at Melchester Hockey Club.

1 Apologies for absence.
2 Minutes of the last meeting.
3 Matters arising from meeting.
4 Reports: Treasurer's report
              Team secretary's report
              Chairperson's report.
5 Proposal to redecorate clubhouse.
6 Proposal to increase match fees.
7 Any other business.
8 Date of next meeting.

Sally Brown

Club Secretary

Figure 5.7 An agenda for a meeting

While a meeting is taking place, the secretary records the proceedings with a series of notes (the minutes). These should provide an accurate and clear record of what has taken place at the meeting. They are usually written up immediately after a meeting and are in the past tense:

- Narrative minutes include details of discussion and the decisions reached.
- Resolution minutes record only details of the decisions agreed.
- Action minutes have a column that indicates who is to follow up and take action upon any decisions made.

The secretary will usually have a folder containing agendas and minutes from previous meetings. It is important such documents be kept, as they provide a permanent record of issues that have been discussed and decisions that have been sanctioned (see Figure 5.8).

1 What tense are the minutes presented in?

2 Why has an extraordinary general meeting been called?

3 Who ran the meeting?

4 How will the minutes be of use to the ongoing running of the club?

MINUTES OF A MEETING
Melchester Hockey Club

Minutes of the Annual General Meeting of the Club held on 14 February 2000 at the Melchester Hockey Club.

Present: Jane Hopkins (President), Pritham Patel (Vice President), Basil Burge (Honorary Life President), Dorothy Perkins (Team Secretary), Pulvi Shah (First Team Captain), Sally Evans (Second Team Captain), Sally Brown (Club Secretary), Duncan Roberts (Treasurer), John Griffiths, Nick Curtis, Dawn Young, Louise White, Lindsay McNish.

1 Apologies	Apologies for absence were received from Paul Smith and Gerry Denston.
2 Minutes	Minutes for the last meeting were taken as read, approved and signed.
3 Matters arising	Nick Curtis reported that, since last season, he has taken on the task of writing the press releases and match reports that had regularly appeared in local newspapers.
4 Reports	Duncan Roberts presented the Treasurer's report. Subscriptions had been falling, leading to a shortfall. There was also a discrepancy in the amount taken over the bar, suggesting some mismanagement. A copy of the audited accounts was distributed.
	Dorothy Perkins presented the Team Secretary's report. The first team was strong and had a good season. However, the second team had struggled with numbers and had not been able to meet some of their fixtures.
	Jane Hopkins thanked everyone for their hard work last season. However, she felt an emergency general meeting would need to be called to look into the alleged malpractice/mismanagement in the upper bar.
5 Clubhouse redecoration	Jane Hopkins said this was long overdue and was conveying a poor image of the club to visiting teams and supporters. After detailed discussion it was agreed to look into this further and Pritham Patel agreed to seek quotes from decorating firms for the refurbishment of the clubhouse. These would be presented after the exraordinary general meeting.
6 Match fees	Duncan Roberts pointed out that match fees had not increased over the last three years. It was decided that these would increase by 20% starting in September 2000.
7 Any other business	Dorothy Perkins proposed a plaque should be put up in the clubhouse to commemorate the 25th anniversary of the club in 2000. The motion was carried unanimously.
8 Date of next meeting	It was agreed that an extraordinary general meeting of all club members would be held on 3 March 2001.

Jane Hopkins

14 February 2000

Figure 5.8 The minutes of a meeting

At the majority of meetings you attend you will be a participant rather than the chairperson, secretary or treasurer. In such circumstances, the sort of contribution you wish to make will be up to you. Raising a point at a meeting is something many people do not feel comfortable about doing. The following might be a useful guide:

- Scrutinise agenda items before you attend the meeting to see if there are any areas that may be of interest to you.

- Research such areas of interest and obtain any associated reading materials.

- Plan out, either in your mind or by making notes, what you might wish to say.

- Listen to what others have to say before speaking yourself.

- Timing is important. Make sure the point you make fits into the discussion.

- Do not ramble on.

- Be tactful, and do not deliberately upset someone.

- Be assertive.

- Make your contribution coherent.

- Be ready for some sort of opposition by trying to anticipate the response you might receive to the points you are making.

Organisational databases

A database is a store of facts that can be called upon to provide information.
A database may be used, for instance, in a bank or building society to store information on the state of all accounts.
A database may be kept by a church to keep a record of all members of the congregation and their addresses. One may be used by a football club to keep a record of all tickets sold for various matches and so on.

For example, a supplier might have a record of the account of Amin Stores. It would store the information in a number of fields (such as address, value of goods supplied, payments received and balance of the account). If Mr Amin rings up asking for the state of his account, the supplier can simply order the computer to produce the appropriate information and display it on the screen.

Organisations use databases for internal communication so that members of the organisation can quickly access records and information about all aspects of the business. Databases are also used for external communication (in making orders and payments to suppliers, sending out promotional material to customers, mailing information to clients, etc.). Successful large organisations are very dependent on running an effective database. Indeed, one of the reasons why Wal-Mart has come to dominate in the retailing field is because their database system is far more elaborate and sophisticated than those of major rivals.

In the world of banking, the most successful banks have been those that have the best database systems. In the past, organisations such as banks depended heavily on their physical capital (e.g. bank buildings and equipment). Today they are far more reliant on the quality of their information technology communications systems.

Modern organisations recognise that, if they have the best systems and that these are applied appropriately to their communication needs, they are strongly placed to gain competitive advantage.

Check your understanding

What are the main forms of internal communication available in an organization? List one strength and one weakness of each of these forms of communication.

External communications

Organisations need to communicate with a range of stakeholders, including shareholders, customers, government officials, suppliers and the community. A range of different external communications media can be employed to communicate with these groups (Figure 5.9).

Shareholders*
Company reports, notification of meetings

Customers
Advertising materials, offers, warnings about faulty products, etc.

Suppliers
Enquiries, orders, payments, etc.

The organisation

Government
Statistics about the organisation, PR materials

The community
PR materials, environmental audits, etc.

* Shareholders are really part of the organisation – they are the owners.

Figure 5.9 Examples of external communications

Organisations are continually communicating with groups outside the organisation. These communications perform a number of functions:

- A *public relations function* To present a good image of the company (e.g. company reports and advertising materials).

- An *informative function* To provide various groupings with essential information about the company (e.g. tax records to the Inland Revenue, hours of opening for customers, details of supply arrangements to suppliers, etc.).

- A *day-to-day trading function* To transact the business's daily commercial relationships (e.g. making orders, buying goods, making enquiries about goods being offered, etc.).

- A *transparency function* Today, it is often important that outsiders can see what is happening inside the organisation so they know the company is carrying out its business in a true and fair way (e.g. by providing environmental reports and audits, ethical reports, etc.).

Case study: Making an art form of external communications

Jim Moran who died in June 2000 was one of the most effective exponents of the art of external communications for a business. He managed to do everything that PR specialists are doing in the post-millennial world back in the 1940s and 1950s, at the time when television was just starting to take off.

It was Moran who sat on an ostrich egg for 19 days, 4 hours and 32 minutes before hatching it to publicise the novel *The Egg and I.* He searched for a needle in a haystack for 10 days to promote a property that he was going to sell. He also climbed from one horse to another in a Nevada river to urge voters to vote Republican after the Democrats had urged voters not to 'change horses in mid-stream'.

It was also Moran who created the greatest soundbite the world had yet known. To publicise some bizarre product, Moran engaged an extermely short man to go up into the air over Manhattan's Central Park on a vast kite. Inevitably, the New York cops intervened and banned his behaviour.

An outraged Moran gave a press conference where he said:

> 'It's a sad day for American capitalism when a man can't fly a midget on a kite over Central Park.'

PR specialists like Moran knew how to gain the public attention. Today, we see similar attempts to capture public interest – e.g. the actress Joely Richardson baring her back to promote the film *Maybe Baby*, and Benetton advertising.

1 Give examples of recent PR campaigns carried out to gain attention for a particular organisation or product. How successful were they?

2 Can you think of examples of PR activities where the external communications of an organisation have backfired to create negative publicity?

3 Can you think of an idea for a PR stunt which would have an immediate impact in enhancing the external image of an organisation of your choice?

Types of external communications

(Most of the methods outlined below can also be used for internal communications.)

The telephone

The most frequently used form of external verbal communication is the telephone. Its great benefit is that it is fast and allows people who would find it difficult to meet to converse.

A telephone call may be the first point of contact an outsider has with an organisation. If a bad impression is created through this first call, it may be difficult to correct. Developing a telephone technique that makes the caller feel at ease and that creates the impression of efficiency is always very important. There are, therefore, basic rules for answering the telephone (see Figure 5.10).

- Answer calls promptly.
- Greet the caller with 'Good morning' or 'Good afternoon'.
- Be courteous – your tone of voice is crucial.
- Be brief but not abrupt.
- Speak clearly and slowly.
- Be resourceful and think of ways you might be able to help.
- Remain calm, even when under pressure.
- Have pencil and paper handy in case you have to take a message (don't forget to record the date and time of the call).

Figure 5.10 How to answer the telephone

If you have to make a telephone call, make sure you:

- have all the necessary information to hand

- know whom you want to talk to

- are prepared to leave a message on an answering machine, if necessary

- speak clearly.

Interviews

Another form of external verbal communication is an interview with someone from outside the organisation who may be interested in something the organisation has done (e.g. press, radio or television). Part of a public relations strategy in such circumstances is to build up a positive perception and image of the organisation. The response should, therefore, be designed to improve public understanding of the organisation's actions.

Business letters

The business letter is still the most widely used form of external communication. It may be used, for example, to:

- Make arrangements without the need for parties to meet.

- Provide both parties with a permanent record of such arrangements.

- Confirm verbal arrangements.

A well-written business letter conveys its message while maintaining goodwill. If a letter is sent promptly, is well set out and conveys its message accurately, the person who receives it will develop a favourable impression of that organisation and is more likely to want to have further dealings than if the letter is late and inaccurate.

The layout, style and appearance of business letters – and even the envelope – vary from organisation to organisation. Most will try to create a good impression, particularly by going for an eye-catching heading and layout. Organisations often have a house style they encourage all administrative staff to follow. Business letters are usually typed on A4 or A5 paper, and a fully blocked, open-punctuated style is now the most common form of display. Business letters

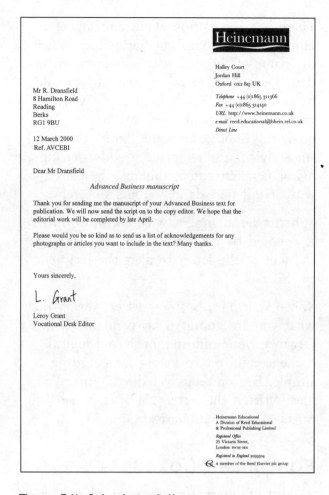

Figure 5.11 A business letter

will usually have the following features (see Figure 5.11):

- A heading or letterhead (Heinemann in Figure 5.11).

- A reference, enabling the letter to be filed and traced later.

- A date.

- The inside address – which is that of the person who will receive the letter.

- The salutation (Dear Mr Dransfield).

- The subject heading ('*Advanced VCE Business manuscript*')

- The body of the letter.

- The complimentary close (Yours sincerely . . .).

There is a convention about pairings of salutation and complimentary close. When the name of the recipient is not known, so that 'Dear Sir/Madam' is used, this should be paired with 'Yours faithfully'. When the name is known and 'Dear Mr/Mrs . . .' is used, this should be paired with 'Yours sincerely'. If the recipient is addressed by his or her first name, this may be paired with 'Kind regards . . . Yours sincerely'.

When a letter is sent with enclosures, this is denoted by the letters 'Enc' or 'Encs' at the foot of the letter to alert the recipient to this fact.

When writing a business letter, always plan what you are going to say beforehand. Organise your information into a logical sequence and try to keep your language simple. Be courteous yet direct. After you have written the letter, check it for spelling mistakes and grammatical errors.

Fascimiles (faxes)

A form of external communication that has experienced massive expansion over recent years and that is capable of sending both written and visual information is the facsimile ('fax'). Fax machines send information electronically over telephone lines.

Electronic mail

As an alternative to writing letters, organisations widely use electronic mail (email). With email sent through a service provider (e.g. CompuServe), the sender forwards the document to the receiver's email address (which is actually a small area on the service provider's computer), not directly to the recipient. When the receiver logs on to his or her computer system, he or she can see on screen there is a message waiting which he or she can either read while logged on to the system or store on the hard drive to read later. Anyone who is connected to the Internet and has a modem can use email.

The key advantages of email are that:

- It is faster than ordinary mail ('snail mail').

- You don't have to bother to print the message, put it in an envelope with a stamp, etc.

- It is more environmentally friendly as less paper and energy (in the delivery process) are used.

Disadvantages are that people may not read their email regularly, and not everyone has access to email facilities.

Videos and CDs

Corporate videotapes and corporate CDs have become increasingly popular over recent years as methods of providing a variety of interested parties with visual information about an organisation's activities.

File transfers

While electronic mail transfers text between computers, it is quite slow at transferring very large files. Another specialist system (known as file transfer) is therefore better for sending files such as computer programs, graphics and so on, using a method that bunches the data into packages. The receiving computer will check each bunch to make sure no errors have been made. If everything is fine, it will confirm this and wait for the next bunch.

Electronic data interchange (EDI)

Increasingly, the world's giant food manufacturers and retailers are setting up large-scale systems for the electronic purchasing of goods. Manufacturers such as Coca-Cola and Heinz have joined together with retailers such as Sainsbury's and Carrefour (of France) to create a company known as GlobalNetExchange. EDI is a network link that allows retailers to pay suppliers electronically without the need for invoices and cheques, thus dramatically reducing time, paperwork and costs.

Video conferencing

Video conferencing has improved out of all recognition as a result of the development of digital systems. Video conferencing makes possible face-to-face meetings with people who are geographically separated. Desktop systems make it possible for participants in a conference to communicate with each other without leaving their desks.

Desktop video conferencing requires a powerful PC, a sound card, a video camera and a video compression card.

The advantages of video conferencing are as follows:

- Savings in time and travel expenses (including expensive hotel bills).

- Ready access to supplementary sources of information (e.g. pulling down and transmitting files from a computer for discussion).

- Enabling people who work from home to communicate with others (e.g. at head office).

Web sites

Perhaps the most dramatic increase in the use of electronic media for the purpose of external communication is the creation of Internet websites. Most companies have an Internet web site they use for all forms of external communications purposes and for public relations activities.

Check your understanding

Figure 5.12 shows the statistics for current and anticipated online spending over the next few years.

Take one of the sectors that have been identified to experience a mass increase in online shopping over the next few years. What methods of external communication are going to be most important to a business in this sector in winning a good share of this market?

How do these methods of external communication differ from those used by organisations in this sector in the past?

	1997	1998	1999	2004 (est.)
Computer software	77	100	122	934
Books	25	60	106	430
Music and video	19	42	85	175
Grocery	5	12	165	2,295
Clothing and footwear	3	4	5	1,210
Other	67	79	98	1,951
Total	196	297	581	6,995

Figure 5.12 Spending on the Internet in the UK (million)

Case study: Iceland.co.uk

Iceland (html://www.iceland.co.uk), the supermarket group, threw themselves into the digital age with a radical decision to rebrand their shops with their Internet name. In April 2000, Iceland's 760 high-street stores have been rebranded 'Iceland.co.uk'. The redesign is costing £8 million and, by 2002, the group's vans, advertising and carrier bags will carry the new name.

Iceland's chairman, Malcolm Walker, believes the change will help establish Iceland's online grocery shopping operation as a leader in the sector: 'The new name says we are in the 21st century. It's our website address and everyone in Britain will know it.' Research carried out with customers showed that the rebranding would be popular. The move will help support Iceland's Internet shopping business, which saw orders doubling to 5,000 a week following an advertising campaign.

1 How successful do you think Iceland.co.uk's new name will be in developing communications with customers?

2 Might the change of name lead to any problems of external communication?

Formal and informal communications

Formal communication in an organisation is communication that takes place through the recognised channels (e.g. official meetings, memos, newsletters, etc.). Informal communications are ones that take place that are not part of the 'officially' recognised networks of the organisation. This does not mean informal communications are necessarily negative or anti-organisational. Indeed, much of the good work in organisations is carried out by organisational members taking initiative into their own hands and coming up with ideas that directly benefit the organisation. Informal communications can also serve as motivating forces because they are based on individual initiative.

Research into the nature of communications in organisations indicates it is important to have both formal and informal communications. For example, management may break information to employees through team briefings, but the full understanding of what management has had to say may come about only through informal discussions between team members. Unofficial discussions and conversations have an educative impact within an organization, and most managers recognise the importance of informal communications networks.

However, there is a danger of misinformation being spread along 'the grapevine'. This is particularly the case when changes are being planned within an organisation. Individuals involved in the informal communications networks may deliberately distort messages or, through lack of understanding of what is going on, may give out confusing messages.

Check your understanding

Give examples of formal and informal communication in an organisation you are familiar with. Do the patterns of informal communication support the formal channels or work against them?

Upward and downward communication

Much of the communication in old-fashioned, traditional industries was carried out in a downward direction. Managers created the systems, the rules and the work programmes and communicated these down the line to junior employees.

There are clear advantages to such an approach:

- Senior managers are able to set targets and objectives, and then give the instructions to make sure they are carried out.

- Because there is a clear line of command, instructions can be clear and consistent.

- Costs can be cut by operating with an efficient system in which fewer errors are made.

However, in recent years, there has been more of an emphasis on upward communication. This is felt to be important because:

- Good ideas can bubble up from below from people who deal with 'nuts and bolts' decisions on a day-to-day basis.

- Many people at the bottom of an organisation are very talented and have good ideas that are worth listening to.

- Managers can be made aware of likely problems before they occur.

- It provides feedback on the decisions being made by senior managers.

- People lower down an organisation are more likely to know what is practical in a working setting than those higher up.

- Being asked to be involved in the communication process motivates those lower down in the organisation.

Check your understanding

Using your own experience of working for a particular organization:

What examples of downward communications can you think of? What examples of upward communication can you think of? How does the organisation benefit from such upward communication? Does the organisation rely more on upward or downward communications? Could it benefit from changing its communication patterns?

Case study: Communication networks

Bavelas identified a number of communication networks, each with its own strengths and weaknesses. The wheel network (Figure 5.13) places a particular individual or department in an organisation at the centre of the wheel.

All communications flow through the individual or department that is at the centre of the wheel (and which thus acts as a gatekeeper). For example, in a company there may be a department that processes all order forms whatever their nature. This process is used at the Nottingham Trent University and can be very frustrating when orders are held up, e.g. because the processing department is waiting for an official signature.

In examining Information and Communications Technology networks in an organisation we saw that the client/server network was most like the 'wheel'. Client/server systems employ one more powerful computer – the server – to look after the printing, file maintenance and any other peripherals connected to the network. The less powerful computers are called clients.

The chain network (Figure 5.14) allows two-way information, but this information ultimately stems from or is sent back to the individual who is the linchpin in the chain. The chain network typifies the formal approach often associated with government departments or bureaucracies, such as the army. The 'buck stops' with the person at the head of the chain.

The circle network (Figure 5.15) consists of individuals, sections or departments that communicate with only two others. For example, this might occur when middle managers in an organisation deal directly only with other departments at the same level in the organisation.

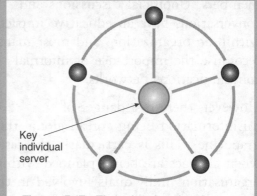

Key individual server

Figure 5.13 The wheel network

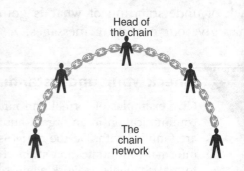

Head of the chain

The chain network

Figure 5.14 The chain network

The circle network

Figure 5.15 The circle network

Finally, the completely connected network (Figure 5.16) is based on an 'all channel' communication system (e.g. in teamwork situations). Each member of the team is in direct and regular contact with all other team members. Modern computer networks increasingly make possible the development of the completely connected network system, in which organisation members are able to share common communication systems and have common access to communication applications and databases.

1 Where have you come across these sorts of communication networks in organisations that you are familiar with?

2 What do you see as being the strengths and weaknesses of each network? (Use your experience of these networks to give your answers.)

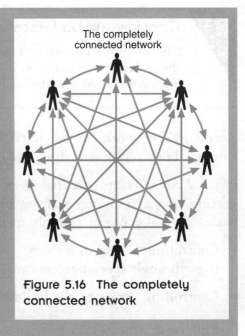

Figure 5.16 The completely connected network

Open or restricted channels

With any form of communication it is important to identify the purpose of the message as well as the people at whom the message is to be targeted. If the message is targeted at everyone within the organisation or groups outside and does not contain confidential materials, then the message is open for anyone to see or interpret (e.g. notice-boards, memos to all staff, staff magazines, etc.). On the other hand, if the message contains confidential materials, the likelihood is it will be targeted at only a few groups of users, either within a particular department or at certain levels of seniority, so that its use is restricted. For example, in a school or college a staff briefing will normally take place behind closed doors, where no students are allowed (restricted channels). In contrast, a students' consultative committee might be open to a range of students and/or their representatives as well as staff (open channels).

It is important to build a communications network that provides a system whereby restricted messages can be sent. For example, management information systems (MIS) ensure certain information goes to specified people only, and this can contribute to the control, confidentiality and security of information (Figure 5.17).

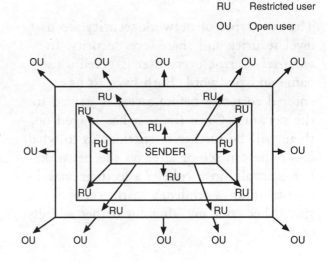

Figure 5.17 Open and restricted users

Check your understanding

Give examples of open and restricted channels of communication in an organisation you are familiar with.

Access to a network can be controlled through both physical and logical methods.

Physical controls stop potential users from getting near a computer or from making it work. Typical physical controls include:

- Controlling access to a room (e.g. through special access cards).

- Controlling access to the building.

- Putting locks on computers.

- Storing computers where they cannot be accessed.

Logical controls are used to prevent users, once they have logged on, from accessing or changing information. For example, you may want to stop unauthorised people from changing customer records. At the same time, an organisation will want to stop people from accessing particular information (e.g. a subordinate finding out how much his or her boss is earning).

The two types of network security are user-level security and share-level security. In *user-level security*, every user is given a user name and password. Both have to be entered correctly before access is gained to the network. Once the user has logged on, there will be further restrictions as to what he or she can see or alter on the network. For example, in a college a lecturer may be able to input a student's marks on a spreadsheet but not alter his or her address or age.

Share-level security means every resource available on the network has its own password, rather than each user. There may be two passwords — one for full access and the other for read-only access. Of course, a problem here is that it might require users to know lots of different passwords. If they write them down somewhere, they can always be copied by someone who should not have access.

Communication and the achievement of business objectives

An organisation needs to create the communication channels that most effectively enable it to achieve its business objectives. Clearly, in some instances downwards communications channels may be most effective — particularly where clear instructions need to be carried out that must to be followed to the letter.

However, it is widely recognised that upwards communications are also helpful. The American business writer, Rosabeth Moss Kanter, argues strongly that empowerment of people at the base of the organisation enables good ideas to bubble up. People at the base of the organisation are used to making all sorts of responsible decisions in their daily lives (e.g. buying a house, raising a family, organising family holidays, etc.). They are the sorts of people who should be trusted by the organisation to come up with ideas. Many organizations, therefore, give greater emphasis to open channel, multidirectional communications in the organization, based on self-managing teams.

This makes sense in meeting a range of organisational objectives (e.g. building strong relationships with customers, becoming a market leader, developing a reputation for excellence, being able to adapt in flexible markets, to maximise sales and revenues, etc.).

Check your understanding

Using the example of a service organisation you are familiar with, show how open channel communications systems can enable that organisation best to meet its objectives.

Information and communications technology (ICT)

In the first decade of the twenty-first century, we can see that ICT has totally transformed ways of communicating within business. Examples are as follows:

- The use of email to replace many communications that previously were carried out by letters, faxes and phone calls.

- The use of networked databases to replace organisations' traditional systems of filing and storing information.

- The use of computers to replace a range of standardised operations involving the interface between an organisation and its customers (e.g. registering an order, requesting items from stores, maintaining stock levels, organising delivery, preparing invoices, controlling credit and recording payment).

- Enabling the contracting out of work previously carried out within an organisation so that communications are now with the external contractor rather

than an internal department of the organisation.

- The use of an Internet web site to create a communications link between the organisation and its global market.

- The use of the Internet to find out about all the current developments that are taking place in the field in which the organisation is operating.

- The use of digital methods for much faster communications, involving a range of visual, sound, and other forms of communications that enable face-to-face contact between an organisation and people in far-flung places. For example, the organisation in London can interview candidates for a post in Australia or New York almost as easily as in its own head office.

Traditional businesses were often organised into functional specialisms. Each person in the organisation carried out one step before passing the job on to someone else. Often, a job was passed on from one department to another. Figure 5.18 shows this sort of flow.

For example, market research is carried out by a few people in the marketing

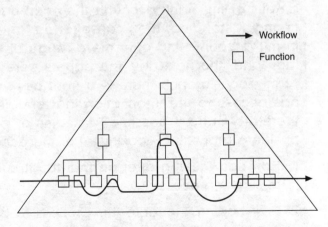

Figure 5.18 In a functional organisation, the work flows step by step

department, who pass on the results to the technology department. The technology department comes up with some proposals that are passed on to production . . . and so on. The departments shown in Figure 5.18 have worked together in a flow on a particular 'business process', which is simply a set of work activities arranged logically to realise a business objective.

Case study: Working on a customer's account

Today, teams of people service our bank accounts for us. For example, I have a bank account at Grantham (see Figure 5.19). I am able to go into the bank and withdraw money from my account, request my bank balance, arrange to receive foreign currency, etc. This simply involves me in communicating with counter staff at my local branch. They are able to do this because they are part of a team working to process my account. They simply call up the details on their computer terminals.

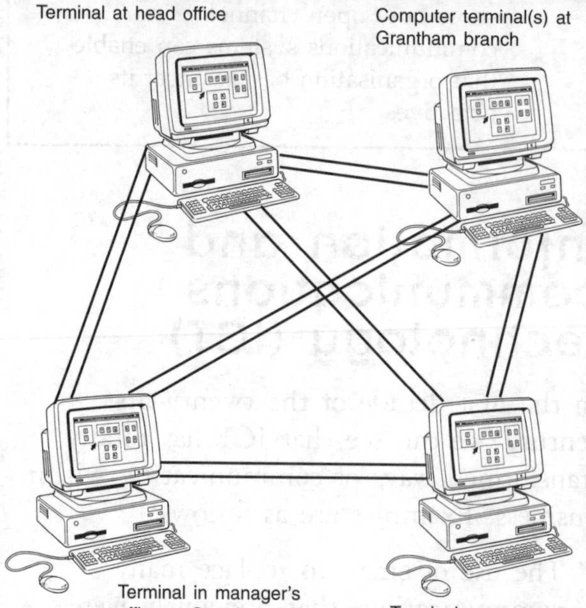

However, there are other people also working to process my account. I have access to a 24-hour banking system whereby I can ring my bank's head office. Again, because they are networked to a set of computers with details of my bank account, they can call up my details. On the basis of my financial standing, they can offer me an overdraft or loan, tell me how much I have in my account, and offer me a range of banking services. Recently I took out a loan and, the next day, the papers were there for me to sign at my local branch. At my local branch there is a front desk with a customer services officer. She too has access to the information that enables her to process my account. ICT has therefore made it possible for teams of people to work together efficiently on the business process of looking after my account.

Figure 5.19 An information network

1 How can looking after an individual customer's account be seen as being a business process?

2 How does ICT enable this process to be carried out in an efficient and cost-effective way?

3 Who benefits from the efficiency of ICT networks as outlined in this case study?

Transformed businesses

Today, many business writers use the term 'transformed business'. Such an organisation is run according to business processes rather than functional specialisms. The business processes are handled by teams of people from different functions, working together to achieve the aim of the process.

In a transformed business, people involved in particular processes are given more freedom to make decisions and have more information at their finger-tips by virtue of information and communications technology. Instead of having to get permission from their line manager, they are allowed to make more important decisions. Senior managers then become more concerned with external matters than with running the internal system.

Organisations based on business processes put a high premium on information and on sharing ICT facilities. ICT has a very important role to play. Groups working together in a team will need to share information, and computer terminals of different specialists are linked, so that information is available to all.

One major benefit is a cost reduction as a result of simplifying the work flow. A job stays with one individual or team instead of passing in batches from specialist to specialist. The team is given authority to make decisions, as well as to the information and tools needed.

Another benefit is the improved responsiveness to customer needs. Front-line staff are given powers to act rather than passing problems up to line managers. Improved job satisfaction can result.

Case study: The development of the Internet

The Internet came into being in the last quarter of the twentieth century. It was born in 1969, the year of the Apollo moon landings. For a number of years it was used mainly by computer buffs or 'Netties' who wallowed in their own brand of computer jargon but, today, it has become widely accessible to a broader group of users and, every day, more people are joining the Internet. In 1998, the number of computers connected to the Internet was 36 million; ten years earlier it was 100,000. One of the major criticisms of the Internet today is that it is dominated by white, male, upper-income groups in the world's richest countries.

The Internet began life as a defence network that linked the computers of a few thousand researchers and military personnel. Today the Net might carry almost anything: the late-night ramblings of a *Star Trek* fan, the plight of a third-world refugee, and computer games software. No matter how obscure the information, it will probably exist on the Internet.

In the first decade of the twenty-first century, the Internet is proving a magnet for most of the world's major businesses, who have spotted the opportunities for advertising and communications to open up a whole new world of e-commerce. Net shopping is becoming increasingly important across a wide range of areas of buying and selling.

The World Wide Web is a form of software that makes it easy for people with limited IT skills to use the Internet. Users have no difficulty in employing a range of search engines to find what they are looking for in just a few minutes.

1 Why do you think the Internet has been so successful as a form of business communication?

2 What sorts of businesses are most likely to benefit from using the Internet for communications purpose?

3 What dangers does the Internet pose for organisations?

Case study: Demise of the print industry in the USA

A report in the *San Jose Mercury News* in November 1999 pointed out that, in Silicon Valley, printers were in their second straight year of double-digit decline. The same source also pointed to the record number of sales, mergers and failures of printing companies. The reason is that many people in Silicon Valley do not write letters on stationery; they send email. They put up web sites instead of mailing catalogues. When they do print, it tends to be short-run, custom jobs on digital presses or colour printers close to the point of sale.

Emailers often sign their missives with their contact information (name, address, phone number, etc.), reducing the need for business cards. Personal digital assistant (PDA) users can beam their business cards to each other via infrared ports, and many email packages support an electronic business card feature that plugs automatically into contact databases. Gone are the days of big runs of printed matter. One computer maker stopped printing brochures because its products were often off the shelf by the time the printed matter came back from the printers.

The New York Times reported that American magazines have, on average, lost half of their advertising pages in the last 10 years. There are many viable magazines, but the loss of ads means they've cut back on pages (another source of declining demand for print).

Of course, while Silicon Valley leads the way, we must remember that only 2% of the world's population has access to the Internet.

1 Do you see the trends to increasing use of the Internet affecting UK business in the same way it has affected business in Silicon Valley?

2 Why do you think there has been such a dramatic fall in demand for printed materials? Is it likely to continue?

Strengths and weaknesses of ICT

Moore's Law states that computer power doubles every 18 months. The price of computer power has already fallen 10,000 fold within a single generation. Growth of 35% in computer power dwarfs the 5% a year power growth delivered by steam engines and their successor, electric engines between 1869 and 1939. At the same time, the expansion of computer use has been extraordinary. Use of the Internet is growing literally exponentially. It took radio 37 years to reach a global audience of 50 million, and television 15 years. Yet it took the World Wide Web just three years after the development of the web browser in 1994.

It seems likely that in this new century the impact of the ICT revolution will hit us with more and more force as its influence begins to strike home. The economic historian, Paul David, showed how it took US industry 40 years to reorganise to exploit the electric dynamo efficiently. Once US industry made full use of this new technology, the impact was staggering, leading to mass production and mass consumption.

It seems likely that ICT will have the same sort of impact in transforming production systems on a worldwide scale. As the Internet expansion increases, so too will the knowledge revolution – leading to knock-on effects that have the potential to transform businesses in new and unforeseen ways.

Information and communications processing systems and their applications influence the ways in which business organisations operate and compete at all levels of decision-making. Given this vital role it is essential constantly to appraise the effectiveness of the systems to ensure they provide the maximum possible benefits for the organisation.

One way of analysing the effectiveness of an information and communications processing system is to look at a simple operating application. Imagine that a customer puts in an order. Now consider what happens. What if the organisation takes a long time to process the order? Having processed the order, they then make mistakes with the transaction and deliver the wrong goods. From the customer's point of view, he or she will be less than satisfied with the way the organisation has dealt with the order. The limitation of the information processing system has influenced a customer, who will not come back for repeat business. The system has, therefore, strategic and competitive implications.

It is imperative to create user-friendly communication systems that deliver what they promise. All too often we see the development of new communication systems that fail to deliver. For example, on 22 November 1999, Amy Vickers, the media correspondent of *The Independent* newspaper, reported on 'Smile' (the Co-op's online bank) as being 'enough to make you weep'. She had tried unsuccessfully to open a bank account with them and had failed on account of their mystifying web pages.

An efficient system would, on the other hand, have meant the customer was satisfied and would probably return for more business. Because information and communications processing affects the ways in which an organisation competes, an effective system should create genuine competitive advantage.

There are a number of ways in which the effectiveness of an information and communications processing system can be analysed.

Fitness for purpose

Information and communications processing systems must be developed that best support the organisation in meeting its objectives. By being fit for the purposes intended, the information and communications system should help to provide solutions and not create problems. A system that is fit for its purpose should reap results – an organisation should be able quickly to point to ways (measures) in which it is meeting its objectives more effectively.

To ensure a system does meet the required objectives, it is important to provide feedback on its activities and to control its output (see Figure 5.20).

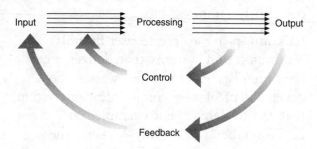

Figure 5.20 The feedback and control of a system

Cost

Cost has a clear influence upon the design of an information and communications processing system. For example, a manager may have a budget constraint that determines how much can be spent upon its introduction. One danger of a tight budgetary constraint is that it can be too restrictive and can make it difficult to develop a system that undertakes activities as efficiently as originally required.

Value for money

The most important element in any system design is that it should eventually result in the maximisation of benefit relative to cost. There are two ways of assessing whether or not a new system might provide value for money. Quantitative analysis identifies clear savings that have been made through the introduction of the new system e.g. fewer staff, less paperwork and reductions in other costs).

Qualitative evaluation is more difficult as this identifies the ways in which a series of activities and services have improved as a result of spending on the new system. Though difficult to quantify, these are very important and may include higher morale, work that is less tedious and improved customer satisfaction.

Effects upon the efficiency of the user

Information and communications processing systems must be developed to meet the needs of a number of users. The overall aim should be to reduce the time taken to carry out activities, to increase the speed with which output is generated, to undertake a larger volume of work and to make it easier for the user to access and operate the system. It is important, therefore, when developing a system to consider the user's needs.

Capacity to retain and use information

The most important element in any system is its capacity to generate output. A good information system will have the right information available when required and in the form specified by the user.

Meeting legal and other requirements

Any system must take into account the requirements of the Data Protection Act and other legal requirements (e.g. concerning health and safety).

Improving security

If data or program security is important, a system must ensure unauthorised people do not access it. Security features may include electronic controls (such as passwords and data encryption) to ensure that the system is kept secure.

Check your understanding

Examine the application of Information and Communications Technology in one organisation. Outline all the ways that ICT has been used to improve communications. To what extent has the use of ICT:

a) improved communications,

b) led to a deterioration in communications? Do the strengths of ICT outweigh the weaknesses?

Chapter 6 Production and quality

Businesses change inputs (such as people and materials) into outputs to produce goods and services that meet the needs of their customers. You need to be able to track the production process in order to understand the physical transformations and activities that lead to the finished product or delivery of a service.

From observing the product process you will understand how value is added to a product throughout. You will need to be able to distinguish between the following main ways of adding value:

- combining inputs to create a physical change
- combining inputs to create a service
- meeting customer requirements.

Quality is an important factor in the production process. You need to be able to distinguish between quality control and quality assurance (QA). Quality control means inspecting or testing quality at various points in the manufacture of a product or delivery of a service. It is usually applied during or after production. However, many businesses use organisation-wide approaches to quality, making quality the responsibility of everyone at all stages of the production of the goods or services. This is quality assurance.

There are numerous quality control and assurance systems, including:

- total quality management (TQM)
- quality circles
- self-checking or inspection
- ISO 9000
- benchmarking
- training and development.

You need to know in which circumstances different quality control and assurance systems might be appropriate. You need to be able to describe their relative advantages and disadvantages and understand how one system works in detail.

Adding value in the process of production

One of the prime concerns of any business is to convert inputs into outputs (finished goods and services) to satisfy the needs of consumers. Figure 6.1 shows the various

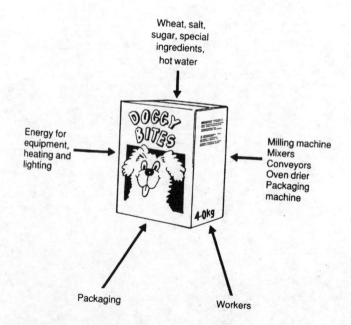

Figure 6.1 Adding value in the process of dog biscuit manufacture

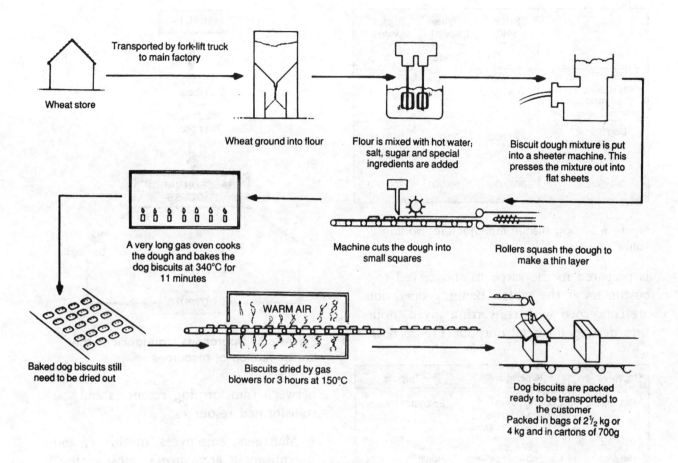

Figure 6.2 Inputs needed to manufacture dog biscuits

processes involved in adding value in the process of dog biscuit manufacture. You can see there are many processes involved in the manufacture of dog biscuits.

There are also a number of inputs required, and these are shown in Figure 6.2.

Adding value to a product simply means making it more desirable to the final customer (so the customer is willing to buy more products, at higher prices). We can measure the value added to a product at each stage of production. For example. The dog biscuit manufacturer buys in each month £100,000 of ingredients from suppliers (e.g. wheat from farmers). The

manufacturer then produces and sells £250,000 worth of biscuits to retailers. The retailers sell all these biscuits to end customers for £300,000. We can set this out in a diagram (see Figure 6.3). The column we really need to look at is the middle one, which shows the value added at each stage of production.

We use the term 'operations' to describe all those processes and methods by which an organisation uses its resources to produce something or to provide a service. For example, in a factory, operations are the processes used to turn raw materials and other inputs into finished products. In a restaurant, operations take place when food

	Price sold at	Value added at each stage	Total value added
Suppliers of raw materials	100,000	100,000	100,000
Dog biscuit manufacturers	250,000	150,000	250,000
Retailers	300,000	50,000	300,000

Figure 6.3 Dog biscuit manufacture: adding value

is prepared in the kitchens and served to customers at the tables. Banking operations are concerned with converting given inputs into desired financial outputs (Figure 6.4).

Organisation	Operations	Outputs
Restaurant	Cooking meals Serving at tables Entertaining customers	Enjoyable meals
Hospital	Looking after patients Operating on patients Giving medicine to patients	Healthier patients Care

Figure 6.4 Operations and outputs

In any type of organization, operations managers will be responsible for controlling and co-ordinating the organisation's resources, such as finance, capital equipment, labour, materials and other factors. Timetables and schedules are needed to show how these resources will be used in production.

Figure 6.5 shows how operations management involves successfully transforming inputs into desired goods and services. Note we can make a distinction

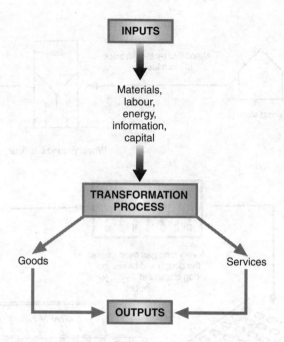

Figure 6.5 Operations management: the transformation of resources

between transforming resources and transformed resources:

- Managers, employees, machinery and equipment are a firm's transforming resources.

- The transformed resources are the materials and information they process.

Check your understanding

List the transforming resources and the transformed resources in each of the following:

- a bank
- a shoe factory
- a public house.

Case study: Adding value to products

Businesses recognise that the secret of their ongoing success is in adding value to products. Businesses have always had some awareness of this but, today, it is a fine art.

There are many classic examples of adding value to products:

- Whoever thought of putting messages on Lovehearts, such as 'Kiss me Quick' and 'Bad Boy' was on to a winner. These little messages turned a sweet that would have been largely ignored to one that nearly all children in this country have bought at one time or another.

- Another example from the world of sweets is the sherbet dab. Simply by bringing together a tube of sherbet and a hollow stick of liquorice or a lollipop, the sweet's creator had added a world of value to a product children would find irresistible.

- More recently, we have seen Mars convert their chocolate bars into Mars ice-cream – creating a new market for the product.

1 How is value added by the changes outlined in each of the examples given above.

2 Can you think of other examples from the sweet and confectionery world in recent years, where value has been added by simple pieces of ingenuity?

Combining inputs to create a physical change

Different business organisations convert inputs to outputs in different ways. It is possible to classify production methods into a number of headings.

Most businesses use one of the following methods of production:

- Project production.

- Job production.

- Batch production.

- Line production

- Continuous flow production.

Project production

A project may involve bringing together a number of people and resources to complete one product (e.g. building a new hotel or motorway, making a Bollywood movie, developing a new CD-ROM, etc.). When you do a coursework assignment, you will look at it as a 'one-off' project. You will need to carry out operations in a set order. For example, you will:

- Write down the assignment title and assessment objectives.

- Decide how to collect information.

- Start collecting information by interviewing and writing letters.

- Start to assemble and make sense of information.

- Design a front cover for the project.

- Write up the introduction, etc.

Project production works in exactly the same way. For example, a project may be to produce a film for a television company. There will be a sequence of steps that need to be followed. The success of the operation depends on:

- Planning the tasks.

- Carrying them out in a logical sequence.

- Making sure all the steps in the project fit closely together.

- Making sure the steps are successfully carried out.

- The term we use to describe this is 'project management'.

Job production

Job production is the term we use to describe a situation where an organisation produces one or a small number of items and where the product is smaller than in a project – for example, a designer dress or hand-made suit. The product would normally be made on the producer's premises and then transported to the purchaser.

The producer might work on several jobs at the same time for different groups of customers. Firms operating in this way need to make sure they keep having orders for new jobs to replace the ones that are nearly completed.

Batch production

This is where a number of identical or similar items are produced in a set or batch. The items need not be for any specific customer but are made at regular intervals in specific quantities. Batch production involves work being passed from one stage to another. Each stage of production is highly planned.

A simple example would be the production of loaves of bread in a bakery. Every day, 200 brown loaves, 100 white loaves and 500 small buns are produced. First, the dough is made for the brown loaves. While this rises, the dough is made for the white loaves. While this is rising, the dough for the brown loaves is kneaded and so on.

A key feature of batch production is that, every now and then you have to stop the production process and reset it for a different product. Most manufacturing companies work in this way, as do most service organisations. For example, a cinema attendant at a multiplex cinema checks the tickets of a batch of cinema-goers waiting to see *Charlie's Angels*; he or she then checks the tickets of a batch going to see *Tomb Raider* and so on.

Line production

This involves products or services passing down a line of production. The production process is a repeating one, with identical products going through the same sequence of operations. Car assembly lines are a classic example of line production. The work comes down the line to the worker, who carries out a set operation. Nowadays, humans have been replaced by robots on many production lines. Examples of line production can also be found in fast-food outlets.

Check your understanding

Which type of production is shown in each of the illustrations in Figure 6.6?

Figure 6.6 Which type of production?

Line production produces identical products. The disadvantage of this is that many customers (e.g. car buyers) want their purchase to be made different or distinctive in some way.

Continous flow production

Continuous flow production takes line production one step further. Today, it is an advantage to be able to mass produce

Case study: Coca-Cola

The creation of the Coca-Cola drink provides us with a classic example of adding value to products through the physical transformation of inputs. At the end of the day, the individual ingredients that go into a can of Coca-Cola are not particularly special. The bulk of the drink is made up of water and sugar, as well as caramel and other flavourings. These inputs are not expensive to grow, harvest, extract or process. However, the secret behind the value added in Coca-Cola rests in the product's branding and advertising. Coca-Cola (html://www.coca-cola.com) are able to add the largest part of the value to their product by creating an image through advertising and the distinctive logo.

It is this that creates the exclusivity and the appeal of the drink so that Coca-Cola is the second best known expression globally after 'OK'.

1 What do you understand by the term 'adding value' in the context of Coca-Cola?

2 Why is it that rival organisations are not able to create value in the same way Coca-Cola can?

standard items such as Mars bars and cans of beer. Continuous flow involves producing for 24 hours a day, using automatic equipment in a standardised way.

An oil refinery, for example, works on a continuous flow basis, with petrol being refined around the clock. Modern breweries, paper mills and chocolate factories also use the continuous flow method.

In continuous flow, the whole operation is handled by machinery controlled by computers. Human labour does not touch the product. Continuous flow, therefore, does not apply in the service industries, which depend more on human labour.

Design as a key aspect of the adding value process

Today, design is one of the greatest values added to a product. A well-designed product will stand out from rivals and will win customer loyalty – and sometimes even a 'fan club' as in the case of classic cars such as the MG sports car and the Volkswagen 'Beetle'. In Victorian times, ordinary people dreamed of owning a Dursley-Pederson bicycle, and modern-day consumer icons include the Renault Twingo car and the Dyson Dual Cyclone vacuum cleaner.

The concept of good design involves a number of attributes, including aesthetics (appealing to the senses through the colour, size, appearance, shape, smell and taste of a product), reliability, safety, maintenance requirements, impact on the environment, convenience and efficiency, ease of manufacture and commercial viability.

Some products are regarded as representing good design because of their functionality: they do what they are required to do in an efficient manner (e.g. a modern tin-opener, a ring-pull on a soft drinks can, the Ford Ka, etc.).

Other products are said to represent good design because they offer style and visual impact (e.g. a gourmet restaurant dish, an expensive designer dress or a Jaguar car).

Volvo cars are said to be well designed because of the safety features that are built in to them, while IKEA furniture is known for its durability, simplicity and usefulness.

Check your understanding

Give four examples of products you are familiar with where design has been the prime factor in adding value to the products.

Case study: Sony's Art Couture range of personal cinema entertainment

Over the years our TVs and video recorders have brought us an increasingly wide choice of entertainment yet, on an aesthetic level, they have left a great deal to be desired. Now Sony (html://www.sony.co), who revolutionised the ways we listen to music and play games, have turned their attention to our TVs, video and DVD players. The result is their new Art Couture range, which uses pure geometric forms and constructional connectivity as design principles to create an entertainment system that is exciting as well as elegant.

Sony has just launched its new Art Couture entertainment centre which epitomises the move towards good-looking, high-performance consumer goods. Incorporating TV, video recorder and DVD player on a matching stand, it encases state-of-the-art technology in a shimmering pearl exterior and is, quite simply, gorgeous to look at. The pearl white colour is perfect for an entertainment system: it is calm and cool, blending subtly with any decor, and its iridescence reflects the surrounding lights and colours. Enhanced by a classic design and slim lines, the system looks good anywhere in the room.

The boom in home entertainment shows no sign of ending, and the trend-spotters say that 'staying in is the new going out'. After putting in the longest working days in Europe, we don't want to compromise when we retreat to our personal space for privacy and recreation. Home entertainment is part of our reward, and we're becoming increasingly discriminating about both style and quality. Only the most beautiful objects deserve to be part of our environment. (Taken from a Sony advert in late 1999.)

1 Why is there a demand for new home entertainment systems such as the one described above?

2 How have Sony been able to gain a competitive advantage in this field?

3 What is the relationship between design and value added in this example?

Just-in-time production

Just-in-time production became an increasingly popular part of the British industrial scene in the last decade of the twentieth century, and is one that is likely to continue this century. Just-in-time (JIT) manufacturing is one of the strengths of the Japanese production system and is one that has enabled Japan to have a highly productive economy.

Just-in-time production is a very simple idea:

- Finished goods are produced just in time for them to be sold, rather than weeks or months ahead.

- The parts that go into a finished product arrive just in time to be put together to make the final product, rather than being stored (at some cost) in a warehouse.

The idea is to run a company with the smallest possible levels of stock and work-in-progress. Clearly, this needs careful planning:

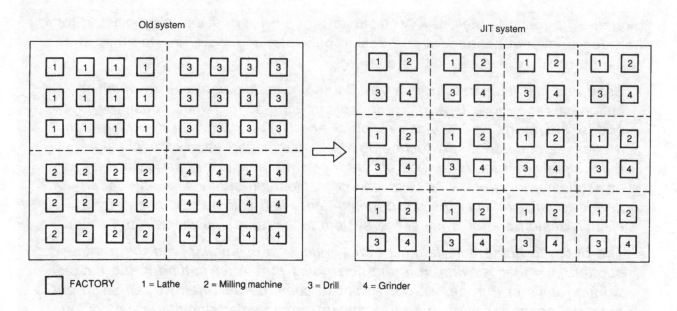

FACTORY   1 = Lathe   2 = Milling machine   3 = Drill   4 = Grinder

Figure 6.7 Changing to the JIT system

- All sources of uncertainty must be removed from the manufacturing process. There must be absolute reliability of production targets, supplies and levels of output achieved.

- The time to set up machines must be reduced to a minimum so that components and finished products can be produced in small batches as and when required.

- Bottlenecks must be eliminated.

Using a JIT system requires a complete reorganisation of the traditional factory. Factories have usually been organised into 'shops', each working on a particular stage in producing a final product. With a JIT system the factory is reorganised so people are grouped together around the products they produce. They may need to have access to a family of machines (e.g. a lathe, a milling machine, a drill and a grinder, as in Figure 6.7).

Case study: JIT at Jaguar

The Jaguar plant at Castle Bromwich on the outskirts of Birmingham has adopted JIT and lean production systems. The speed at which the plant operates is determined by the demand from customers for Jaguar cars. If demand goes up, so does the speed of production. If demand goes down, the production line slows down so that there is no need for extra parts, and there are no cars standing around unsold in the car parks.

The rate at which cars pass along the production line is therefore carefully timed to correspond to demand which, because a great many Jaguars are sold abroad, is determined by the price of the pound against the dollar and other currencies, as well as other demand factors.

In the plant people work together in teams known as 'production cells'. These employees take a great deal of responsibility for managing their own work areas, for creating improvements to the way they tackle work and for managing their own affairs. The site where a cell works is clean and uncluttered – they do not have spare parts and stores lying around. If they want new parts, they press a cord, signal the parts they want and these will be delivered by a fork-lift driver just in time for the parts to be used. In this way Jaguar do not need masses of storage space, and they do not have to order parts from suppliers until they need them.

Employees are encouraged to work smarter (i.e. to come up with better ways of carrying out production). Because employees are involved in the decision-making process, they feel more motivated and work harder for Jaguar and for themselves.

1   What do you see as being the principal benefits of the JIT system employed by Jaguar?

2   What do you understand by: a) cell production; and b) lean production?

3   How can these ideas, which have been borrowed from such Japanese companies as Toyota, be more widely applied in UK industry?

Automation

The first decade of the twenty-first century is likely to see the most rapid development in production capacity ever witnessed, fuelled by the breakthroughs that took place at the end of the last century. In the USA and Western Europe, there was a considerable investment in ICT software and hardware dating from the economic recovery of 1992.

The microchip and its more recent variants lie everywhere in modern production systems, and this has led to a massive fall in production costs, as reflected in Figure 6.8, which shows the fall in price of Intel chips.

Mechanisation involves the use of machinery. The machine is, however, controlled directly by the operator.

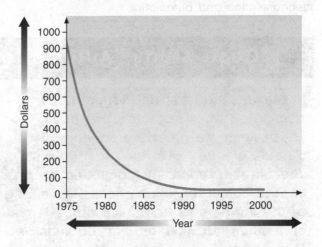

Figure 6.8 The price of computer chips as expressed in dollars per million computer instructions per second

Automation, on the other hand, involves the creation of a unit to control the machine. Instructions are fed into the control unit, which then controls operations.

Machines are at work in our homes. Examples of machines controlled directly by the operator include food mixers, hair driers and vacuum cleaners. Automatic machines, however, are under automatic control. These machines are able to control themselves once they have been fed instructions. Examples include washing machines, central heating systems, burglar alarms and video recorders (see Figure 6.9).

An automatic machine needs to have some method of controlling itself. It must be able to sense and measure when and when not to take action. An example of the way this operates is the central heating system of a house. Generally, this system will be triggered by one of two mechanisms – the timer or the thermostat. The system can be programmed to switch on and off at set times, or to come on whenever the temperature in the house falls below a certain level.

Today, many industrial and commercial processes are automated and, clearly, this facilitates high levels of production at low unit costs. Organisations that fail to automate their processes will be at substantial cost disadvantages.

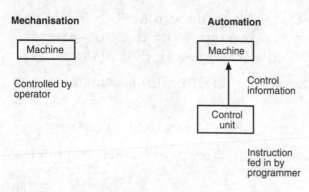

Figure 6.9   The differences between mechanisation and automation

Case study: Automation in a modern brewery

In the UK, the beer and lager market is dominated by a few large breweries. These firms are able to produce high outputs at a low average cost per unit. The brewing process is controlled by a central computer which checks the mixing of the ingredients has taken place correctly, and takes regular readings on temperatures and fermentation.

Bottles returned from public houses and other outlets are on pallets containing several crates. Each crate is lifted off the pallet automatically and a machine picks up the bottles to pass them down a line into a washing machine. The bottles are then checked for faults by an electronic device that examines the bottle's structure.

The bottles are automatically filled and an electronic eye checks that the contents reach a certain level. The machine line will then label and cap the bottles. They are placed in crates and the crates are automatically placed on a pallet, which is stacked on an out-going lorry.

The whole process is predesigned to eliminate the need for labour in the main line of production. Labour is required only to supervise the computer, to maintain the machinery and to keep an eye on it in case it breaks down.

1 Why is the beer and lager market suitable for mass production?

2 What other production lines can you think of that are suitable for automated production?

3 What types of production might be unsuitable for automation?

4 Who benefits from automation?

5 Who loses out as a result of automation?

The word 'control' means the ability to direct or restrain. A controller carries out a function automatically. For example, in a washing machine, once a program has been set the controller takes over, switching the heater on and off, regulating the water supply and outlet, and switching the motor that rotates the drum.

Robotics

Robots are really an application of automatic control. They are of special benefit for jobs that are repetitive and where human manipulative skills are not required. Another application is in dangerous or unpleasant work areas.

Robots vary in the method of programming. Some are programmed by keying in instructions, but this is laborious and liable to error. In other cases the robot can learn to copy movements carried out by a human operator. As robots become more 'intelligent' they increasingly have some system for checking progress (e.g. an electronic eye or camera).

The benefits of using robots are, therefore, as follows:

- People can be replaced by robots in mundane jobs where human intelligence is not required (e.g. routine assembly work).

- Robots can be used where working conditions are difficult or dangerous (materials may be heavy, hot or radioactive, or deep underground or under water).

The disadvantages of using robots are as follows:

- Further erosion of craft skills may result.

- Greater levels of capital investment increase the pressure for shift working.

- A new physical danger is introduced into the workplace. Fatalities have already occurred as a result of using robots at work.

Case study: Micro-subs may soon tour our bodies to kill bugs

The prospect of miniature robots being let loose inside the body to perform minor surgery has come a step closer with the invention of prototype 'molecular motors'. Microscopic engines, powered by chemical fuel or light, could be used to drive the propellers of tiny submarines for repairing internal organs or unclogging blocked blood vessels. Two teams of scientists have independently devised motors from complex molecules, which can be manipulated to move or rotate in a watery solution.

One engine, built at Boston College in Massachusetts, uses chemical fuel to rotate a carbon-based molecule through an angle of 120 degrees. The other, devised at the University of Groningen in The Netherlands, shows how light energy can rotate a molecular motor through 360 degrees.

Both engines provide important evidence that it is possible to build small-scale engines to manipulate or move molecular-sized tools or instruments. One future application for the light-sensitive device could be to place it on the side of a microscopic particle or instrument that can be moved around using the rotating molecule as a propeller. The molecular engine could be the first device to go through blood vessels to strip them of cholesterol.

Computer-aided design (CAD)

Forty years ago, designers spent a great deal of time at drawing boards. The skills brought to the job included:

- creativity (thinking up ideas, styling, etc.)
- analysis (calculating strengths, quantities, etc.)
- mechanical drawing (putting the ideas on paper).

Although the central role of the designer was to carry out creative and analytical work, much of the time was spent on drawing and redrawing. Today, with the development of sophisticated computers, it is possible to use a computer screen instead of a drawing board. This saves considerable time.

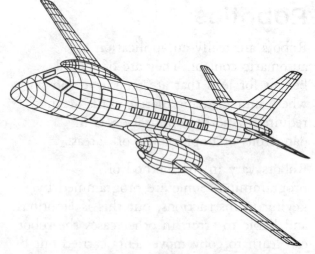

CAD has revolutionised almost every area of industrial design

A designer using a CAD program uses a keyboard (or mouse), a screen and a graphics pad. The designer is able to program the computer to perform many quick calculations of angles, volumes, dimensions, etc.

Having drafted the design, the designer can view the item on the screen as if from different positions, and view it as a solid object instead of just a series of lines. The computer can then be asked to calculate all the important features of the design, and to show how these change when, for example, one dimension is altered.

CAD has revolutionised almost every area of industrial design, from wedding dresses to supertankers.

Computer-aided manufacturing (CAM)

In addition to CAD, developments have also taken place in the use of machine tools. Many are now controlled numerically by a computer (computer numerical control – CNC).

Other developments have taken place in robotics. With CADCAM (computer-aided design/computer-aided manufacturing), data from the CAD system is used to drive machines, making the CAD system part of the manufacturing process. With CAM, computers play a key role in organising and supervising the manufacturing process, making sure that production is carried out according to specified standards.

Computers may be able to check standards, alter production runs and processes and carry out other operations far more quickly and with a much greater degree of accuracy than human operators. Computer-aided manufacturing has been one of the driving forces behind just-in-time manufacturing because of its high level of quality control.

Check your understanding

Show how an organisation in your locality has used one or all of the following as part of the manufacturing process:

- automation
- CAD
- robotics
- CAM.

Combining inputs to create a service

It is in the service industries that we have seen some of the greatest increases in value added in recent years. Here are some examples:

- Digital television, where the viewer can select from a much wider range of choice of entertainment than ever before.

- Multiplex cinemas, where the cinema goer has a choice of screens and can drive in and out of the cinema area, with films showing for several viewings a day.

- Personalised banking, where the customer can carry out financial transactions over the telephone.

- Internet and television shopping, where the customer can order groceries over his or her TV or computer keypad.

In service industries the customer is king or queen, and service organisations are continually jumping to provide additional services to meet customer requirements. For example, in supermarket retailing we are not only seeing the supermarket chains lowering prices to offer us better value for money but they are also creating much more value in the shopping experience – greeters to welcome us into the shops, a much wider selection of items to choose from, shorter queues, in-house banking facilities, etc.

Today, the service sector dominates the economy and, therefore, there is often intense competition between rival suppliers. The only way they can gain competitive edge is by offering the customer more than rival offerings.

The two major inputs of service industries are:

1 people

2 information and communications technology.

Service industries generally involve a great deal of face-to-face interaction between customers and the front-line employees of the organisation. These-front line employees are the people who operate the telephone switchboard, who deal with customer complaints, who serve customers and so on. Thus it is through people that service organisations add much of their value. This is why these organisations have to spend a great deal of time and money training employees in customer service and customer relations.

Moreover, these front-line troops need to be motivated to work for the organisation. When you are greeted by an Asda official greeter when you enter the supermarket you want to feel the greeting is sincere (if the greeter is pleased to work for Asda, this is likely to be the case).

There are three major reasons service businesses usually cite when investing in information and communications technology. To:

• Achieve improvements in productivity.

• Achieve a competitive advantage.

• Improve the flexibility of the organisation so it that can respond more readily to changes in the marketplace.

For example, when BT first introduced digital telephone exchanges (a long time ago), a frequently quoted joke was that the new exchanges needed only a man and a dog to run them; the man was needed to feed the dog and the dog to keep the man away from the equipment.

Today we are seeing many large organisations increase their investments in information and communications technology in order to speed up operations, to cut out waste and to improve accuracy and quality control while reducing costs. Particular examples are banking and retailing operations. Of course, an organisation's ability to raise productivity depends on the careful application of information and communications technology to create effective solutions. One of the reasons why the giant US supermarket chain, which took over Asda in late 1999, has been so successful is because of the sophistication and extent of its ICT system, which enables it to drive down unit costs much lower than rivals.

Information technology can be used by an organisation to give it a competitive advantage by using improved systems to carry out existing operations. For example, airlines can adopt an electronic booking system that is accessible to all travel agents. Of course, the reality is that all its rivals will purchase and operate similar systems. However, the point is that the business that stays still while all its rivals are moving forward will quickly encounter problems.

Finally, organisations can become more responsive to customers by adopting an ICT system. For example, the financial services industry has been revolutionised by ICT. In particular, we have seen the rise of telephone banking, which has slashed the cost of personal banking and has forced all the major banks to develop personal banking systems whereby consumers can be provided with online information about the current state of their accounts, the availability and cost of new financial services, etc.

> ### Check your understanding
>
> Explain how a supermarket, bank or other major service organisation in your area uses its people and information and communications technology to add value to product.

Meeting customer requirements

Peter Drucker wrote 'there is only one valid definition of business purpose – to create a customer'. Having created customers, the next step is to satisfy them: 'Customer satisfaction' has become the great watchword of business in the early twenty-first century. External pressures have played a major part in bringing about this change.

The first reason for this change is that of oversupply. Historically, this was created by overexpansion in boom time and disappeared after slumps. More recently, abundance has become chronic, partly because of the globalisation of markets. When the supply of everything from micro-circuits to motor cars can come from anywhere, efforts to control that supply are futile. The recent sensational collapse in memory chip prices is one result.

An equally profound cause is the revolution in manufacturing processes. The same old plant, using new methods, becomes far more productive. Moreover, new technologies allow smaller producers to compete with high effectiveness, often with brilliant innovations that reinforce another decisive factor. Innovators have helped to fragment markets into multiple segments. So economies of massive scale have ceased to be reliable barriers to entry. The new entrants not only add to supply but also intensify competition as they seek customers.

The customer is an active participant in this process of change. Across the world, customers have become more demanding. In part this reflects the rise in disposable incomes fuelled by economic growth. Customers are also responding with a will to the increase in the quantity, sources and variety of supply. Rising affluence and education have bred a race of highly active consumers. Today, therefore, production must be tied in closely with what consumers want. We explore this concept in greater depth in Unit 3 ('Marketing').

> ### Check your understanding
>
> Give an example of:
>
> - A company whose product is highly focused on meeting customer requirements.
>
> - A company that has recently had to become far more customer focused because it was losing customers.

Case study: Xerox

Xerox (html://www.Xerox.com) are a major document processing firm many people will associate with photocopying. They are based in Marlow in Buckinghamshire. In the 1980s they survived a crisis that took them to the verge of bankruptcy and then prospered again by leading the introduction of quality management ideas in the West.

Xerox recovered from their setbacks in the 1980s by prioritising quality and concentrating on large customers who were prepared to pay a premium for more versatile and reliable copiers. In 1991 they introduced a 'total satisfaction guarantee', pledging to change or replace equipment less than three years old at no extra cost and with no questions asked. Since then, they have steadily raised the stakes by continually encouraging higher expectations in the market. Customer satisfaction levels in 2000 are rated at higher than 90%.

A guide for staff outlining the company's vision, values and goals for 2005 sets a target of doubling the number of customers. It states: 'Xerox's productivity flows from knowing where the customers need to be next and what solutions they will need to get there.'

1   Why do you think Xerox have become so customer focused?

2   What do you see as being the benefits of such a customer focus?

Adding value through quality

In his widely acclaimed book *Thriving on Chaos*, Tom Peters argued that consumers' perception of the quality of a product or service is the most important factor in determining its success. Quality as defined by the consumer, he argued, is more important than price in determining demand for most goods and services. Consumers will be prepared to pay for the best quality. Value is thus added by creating those quality standards required by consumers. Figure 6.10 highlights what is meant by quality standards from the consumer's point of view.

Figure 6.10 Customer quality standards

An interesting quotation is worth remembering as it gives us a useful indicator of the importance of quality:

We judge ourselves mostly by our intentions, but others judge us mostly by our actions.

In the context of quality, consumers judge a good or service in terms of what they actually get, not by what the producer hopes to provide.

Peters emphasises the importance of total quality management, which involves taking quality to new heights. Peters identifies three stages in the development of quality:

1 Quality control.

2 Quality assurance (QA).

3 Total quality management (TQM).

Quality control is an old idea. It is concerned with detecting and cutting out components or products that fall below set standards. This process takes place after these products have been produced. It may involve considerable waste as defective products are scrapped. Quality control is carried out by quality control inspectors. Inspection and testing are the most common methods of carrying out quality control.

Quality assurance (QA) occurs both during and after the event, and is concerned with trying to stop faults from happening in the first place. Quality assurance is concerned to make sure products are produced to predetermined standards. The aim is to produce with 'zero defects'.

Quality assurance is the responsibility of the workforce, working in cells or teams, rather than an inspector (although inspection will take place). Quality standards should be maintained by following steps set out in a QA system.

(Total quality management TQM) goes beyond quality assurance. It is concerned with creating a quality culture so that every employee will seek to delight customers.

The customer is at the centre of the production process.

Companies such as Marks & Spencer and Tesco have been following this policy for a long time. It involves providing customers with what they want, when they want it and how they want it. It involves moving with changing customer requirements and fashions to design products and services that meet and exceed their requirements. Delighted customers will pass the message on to their friends (see Figure 6.11).

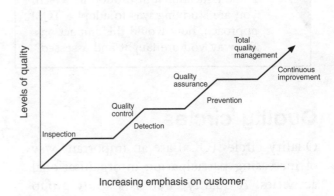

Figure 6.11 Moving to total quality management

Customer preferences will constantly change. The organization, therefore, has to provide new ways of responding to changing tastes, needs and wants. For example the third edition of this book has been produced even though the first two editions were highly successful. This is because it is recognised that you, the students of the twenty-first century, want case studies, materials and approaches that are bang up to date, you want a text that meets the new Advanced VCE specifications, and you want a text with lighter paper so it is not so heavy for you to carry around in your bags.

Total quality management

Total quality management (TQM) is the most complete form of operations management. It is concerned with encouraging everyone in the workplace to think about quality in everything he or she does. Every employee sets out to satisfy customers, placing them at the heart of the production process.

> **Check your understanding**
>
> If the educational institution in which you are studying was to adopt a TQM approach, how would this impact on the way you are taught and assessed?

Quality circles

Quality circles (QCs) are an important way of increasing participation in organisational activities. A quality circle is a study group of volunteers (5–15 people) who meet regularly to work on a variety of operational and employee problems. The quality circle will be made up of ordinary working employees and their immediate supervisors and managers. One supervisor or manager will usually operate as the circle's leader.

Quality circles do not deal with theoretical problems. They are concerned with putting ideas into action. This involves in-depth analysis, proposals for action and presentations to management on what could be or ought to be done. There are four main components of a quality circle framework:

1 A steering committee (one per organisation), staffed by senior managers, will make general policy and set up the framework and resources for the circles to operate within.

2 The facilitator is there to support the process in each of the circles, as well as to provide an operational framework and guidance, if required.

3 The circles' leaders will often be the unit supervisors, and they will stimulate discussion within their circle without dominating it. Leaders need to be familiar with problem-solving techniques and group dynamics.

4 The members of the circle.

The circles meet during company time, perhaps for one hour a week. Problem-solving techniques employed will include brainstorming graphs showing the frequency of problems, randomised sampling of product units produced, and cause-and-effect diagrams.

> **Check your understanding**
>
> What do you see as being the main strengths of the quality circle approach? Why might this approach not work?

Self-checking or inspection

Should quality be a continual process in which employees monitor and check their own performance and that of the processes they are working on against given standards, or should these be subject to outside inspection?

By developing a quality culture there should be no need to inspect. In schools, colleges and universities, for example, national standards have been created, and some people argue that educational institutions should be able to inspect themselves. They know what the standards are and thus can develop the systems to ensure quality is effectively guaranteed. There are is a lot to be said for this. If people (lecturers, teachers, etc.) understand the required quality standards, they can make sure they are met. Failure to ensure quality would be the responsibility of the managers of schools and colleges, because they create the quality systems. It is then up to individual staff to implement these systems.

The staff are the best people to implement the systems because they know what is going well and what is going badly at grass-roots level.

Involving ground-level staff in ensuring quality means they are more motivated – because they are involved in decision-making and because they have a better understanding of the objectives of the organisations they work for.

Another major advantage of self-checking is that it is cheaper to carry out. Improvement is a continuous process, and you do not have to wait for the problems to come to light at the end of the process.

Of course, inspection is also important to check standards are being met. However, perhaps the inspection should be just to check quality standards have been implemented effectively.

> ### Check your understanding
>
> Find out from your college or school tutor whether he or she is in favour of self-checking or inspection. What does he or she see as being the strengths and weaknesses of these approaches?

ISO 9000

Reliable quality is a prime concern when deciding which supplier of a good or service to use. Retail organisations such as Marks & Spencer have, for many years, extended their own quality control procedures into their suppliers' organisation to ensure reliability. A reputation for quality is important, but it can be established only over time. This presents problems for organisations tendering for orders from new customers. The International Standard ISO 9000 certificate indicates to potential customers that the quality procedures of the certificate holders are reliable and, by implication, they are capable of delivering consistently the promised quality product or service.

> ### Check your understanding
>
> Carry out an in-depth study of how an organisation uses ISO 9000 both to guarantee its own quality and to ensure it only buys in from quality organisations.

Benchmarking

Best practice benchmarking (BPB) is a method many organisations use to help them to discover the 'best' methods of carrying out processes available and then using them in their own organisations. An organisation can benchmark internally to find out best practice within the organisation, or externally by looking at other organisations. Many organisations will set themselves the objective of becoming 'the benchmark for the industry'.

BPB involves:

- What customers consider 'excellent' practice to be.

- Setting standards for business processes based on best practice.

- Finding out how the best companies create best practice.

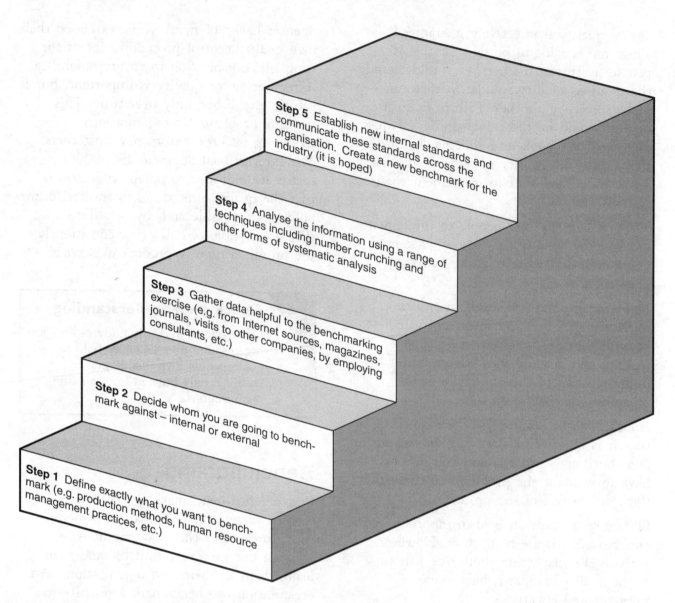

Step 5 Establish new internal standards and communicate these standards across the organisation. Create a new benchmark for the industry (it is hoped)

Step 4 Analyse the information using a range of techniques including number crunching and other forms of systematic analysis

Step 3 Gather data helpful to the benchmarking exercise (e.g. from Internet sources, magazines, journals, visits to other companies, by employing consultants, etc.)

Step 2 Decide whom you are going to benchmark against – internal or external

Step 1 Define exactly what you want to benchmark (e.g. production methods, human resource management practices, etc.)

Figure 6.12 The benchmarking process

- Creating standards within an organisation that meet or exceed the best currently available.

Benchmarking can be seen as a stepped process, as shown in Figure 6.12. Recent research has shown that over two-thirds of major companies in the UK use benchmarking, and that 90% of these use benchmarking regularly.

Check your understanding

Benchmarking has been defined as 'the continuous process of measuring products, services and practices against the toughest competitors of those companies recognised as industry leaders'.

Can you identify a firm that is a leader in retailing? Which of its practices do you feel provide the benchmarks?

Training and development

Because quality is all about continuous improvement in an organisation, it necessarily involves ongoing training and development for all staff. Employees of modern organisations need to be trained in approaches to quality such as total quality management and benchmarking.

If individuals are going to be best able to contribute to helping the organisation continually to improve, they need to be fully in tune with the organization's

Check your understanding

Show how an organisation you are familiar with encourages and supports its employees in training and development activities related to improvements in quality.

objectives. At the same time, the organisation needs to understand the development objectives of the people who work for it.

Case study: Xerox and training

During the 1990s, Xerox moved from being a top-down organisation to one that is based on a teamworking approach. To make the change, they had to replace a number of managers who were unable to make the change to such an approach.

In 2000, they are spending nearly £2,000 per head on training their employees.

1 Why do you think an organisation such as Xerox spends so much on training?

2 Why do you think some of their managers would not have been able to adjust to the new ways of working in the company?

Unit 1 Assessment

You need to produce a detailed business report on one medium-sized or large business. Your business report will consider the objectives, organisation, structure, culture and communication channels within the business and will examine how these factors inter-relate to the success of the business. Your report needs to explain how quality assurance and control systems help the business to add value to its products. You will also need to consider alternative methods and quality assurance and control. You will need to consider how well the business is meeting its objectives and explain the impact of information and communications technology upon the internal and external communications of the business.

You will need to examine the notes about writing a business report set out in the Introduction (page viii).

To gather information for this assignment, you will need to have direct access to an organisation and to speak to people who work for the organisation. Some of the information, such as a description of what the business does and the business's objectives, can be acquired through examining official company literature (such as the company report you can acquire through writing to the company's head office or by examining the web site of that company). However, other aspects, such as details of the informal structure of the organisation, its culture and communication channels, are best found by interviewing people who work for the company or, more easily, by direct work experience.

Your course co-ordinator, it is hoped, will have arranged for you a short work experience placement in an organisation specifically to carry out this assignment.

Many of you will also be able to use your job experience. One of the best sources of information for this assignment would be work in a supermarket environment. Supermarkets are organisations with distinct cultures, structures and communications channels.

Students carrying out first-hand research should show a copy of this assessment brief to a supervisor in an employing/work experience placement. Ideally, you would show the supervisor the criteria for a Grade A so that he or she can best support you in collecting information for the assignment. If possible, you should ask your work placement supervisor to sit down for three-quarters of an hour with you at some stage during the placement, at which time you would tape record an interview with the supervisor outlining key aspects of the business's appropriate features.

Your business report should be illustrated with photographs, charts and diagrams.

To achieve a Grade E you must show you can:

- Classify the business according to its ownership, and explain the benefits and constraints of the type of ownership.

- Clearly describe and explain the objectives of the business.

- Describe the functional areas that exist in the business, and explain how they help the business to meet its objectives.

- Describe the management style and culture of the business.

- Describe the use of ICT for internal and external business communication.

- Clearly explain how the production process and quality assurance/control system used by the business helps it to add value to its product or service.

To achieve a Grade C you must also show you can:

- Make judgements about how successfully the business is meeting its objectives.

- Analyse how the organisational structure, culture and management style of the business affects its performance and operation and helps it to meet its objectives.

- Provide a detailed analysis of the impact of ICT on internal and external business communications.

To achieve a Grade A you must also show you can:

- Explain how the organisational structure, culture and management style inter-relate in the business and evaluate their impact and that of ICT on the business's performance.

- Evaluate an alternative approach to quality control or quality assurance and the effects it could have on the functions of the business and how it achieves its objectives.

Opportunities to develop key skills

As a natural part of carrying out this unit and doing the work set out in the text and through your assessment you will be developing your key skills. Here's how.

Communication, Level 3

When you are:	*You should be able to develop the following key skills evidence*:
• Discussing the management style and culture of the business	*C3.1a* Contribute to a group discussion about a complex subject.
• Describing the functional areas in a group before submitting the report	*C3.1b* Make a presentation about a complex subject, using at least one image to illustrate complex points.
• Researching information for the report	*C3.2* Read and synthesise information from two extended documents about a complex subject. One document should include at least one image.
• Producing the report	*C3.3* Write two documents about complex subjects. One piece of writing should be an extended document and include at least one image.

Information technology, Level 3

When you are: | *You should be able to develop the following key skills evidence:*

- Planning to collect appropriate information, perhaps from the Internet

  IT3.1 Plan and use different sources to search for, and select, information required for two different purposes.

- Planning to collect appropriate information, perhaps from the Internet

  IT3.2 Explore, develop and exchange information and derive new information to meet two different purposes.

- Describing the organisational structure

  IT3.3 Present information from different sources for two different purposes and audiences.

  Your work must include at least one example of text, one example of images and one example of numbers.

Improving own learning and performance, Level 3

When you are: | *You should be able to develop the following key skills evidence:*

- Liaising with your tutor and with the organisation in the development of the plan

  LP3.2 Use your plan, seeking feedback and support from relevant sources to help meet your targets, and use different ways of learning to meet new demands.

- Liaising with your tutor to develop the plan

  LP3.3 Review progress establishing evidence of achievements, and agree action for improving performance.

Working with others, Level 3

When you are: | *You should be able to develop the following key skills evidence:*

- Beginning to plan objectives, your investigation and liaising with members of the organisation

  WO3.1 Plan the activity with others, agreeing responsibilities and working arrangements.

- Developing your report and liaising with the organisation and your tutor

  WO3.2 Work towards achieving the agreed objectives, seeking to establish and maintain co-operative working relationships in meeting your responsibilities.

- Judging whether your plan was carried out effectively

  WO3.3 Review the activity with others against the agreed objectives and agree ways of enhancing collaborative work.

The competitive business environment

If you want to be successful in business, you need to have a 'feel' for the business environment in which you operate: tracking the moves of your competitors in the UK and overseas; anticipating how governments will react to changes in prices, employment and output; judging when to buy and sell and at what price; and looking after the stakeholders of the business – these are just some of the key elements of what it means to have a 'feel' for business. They are also the key elements of what it means to be competitive. Without awareness of these key elements, the chances of your business surviving and meeting its objectives are slim.

In this unit you will explore why being competitive is important to business. You will also learn what is meant by 'a market' and you will find out how and why both businesses and the government try to influence markets. You will look at how businesses work in national and international markets.

This unit links to your understanding of how individual businesses operate, developed in Unit 1 Business at work.

This unit is assessed through an external assessment. The grade on that assessment will be your grade for the unit.

Chapter 7 How competition in the market affects business

An understanding of the markets in which businesses operate is central to your appreciation of the business environment. You need to be able to identify the different types of markets in which businesses operate:

- commodity
- consumer
- capital goods
- industrial
- services.

You should also learn to identify, analyse and evaluate the range of factors that influence how markets operate. You also need to understand how businesses seek to shape and influence these markets.

The main market factors show how:

- Demand-side and supply-side factors for a product or service interact to generate price.

- Supply is affected by costs, technology, physical conditions, taxation and subsidies.

- The amount of competition in markets varies according to different factors, for example, the number of buyers and sellers.

- Competition in markets is influenced by the globalisation of economics.

- The influence any one business has over its products and services varies

significantly between different products in different markets and regulatory frameworks.

- Changes take place in markets and many market factors accelerate this pace of change.

- Businesses seek to become more competitive by using a range of strategies, such as adding value, improving quality, product differentiation, advertising and pricing policies.

- Businesses seek to manage the competitiveness of the markets within which they operate by using a range of strategies (such as mergers, take-overs and product differentiation).

- Competition affects stakeholders in the market – consumers, employees, creditors, shareholders, suppliers and the community.

- Consumer demand is affected by income, age distribution, tastes, advertising and other products.

You need to be able to identify, analyse and evaluate this range of factors and explain how they combine to determine the market conditions within which a business operates. You will need to identify the implications for businesses operating at the UK national level.

The effect of the competitive market can be seen in the changing pattern of industry. You need to be able to classify businesses into the primary, secondary and tertiary industrial sectors and know how to interpret trends within and across these sectors as a consequence of market changes.

The marketplace

Business activity takes place in the marketplace. The key features of this marketplace are buyers (and their buying actions), sellers (and their selling actions), an exchange (between the buyers and sellers) and the price (at which the exchange is agreed). Another key ingredient of the marketplace is the existence of competitors and other buyers who will have an influence on prices in the marketplace, as well as on the terms under which buyers and sellers can make an exchange (see Figure 7.1).

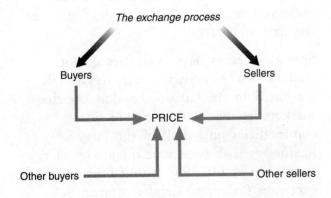

Figure 7.1   The ingredients of the marketplace

The price at which items are bought and sold in the marketplace depends upon the relative strength of two forces – demand and supply (see Figure 7.2).

Demand is the quantity of anything people will be willing to buy at a particular price.

Demand	Supply
The quantity that buyers will be prepared to buy at different prices	*The quantity that suppliers will be prepared to supply to the market at different prices*
● The higher the price the lower the demand	● The higher the price the higher the supply
● Increases in demand lead to rises in price	● Increases in supply lead to falls in price
● Falls in demand lead to falls in prices	● Falls in supply lead to rises in price

Figure 7.2   The effects of demand and supply on prices

The lower the price, the greater quantity buyers will want to buy. (Common sense tells you that when the price of something falls (e.g. a CD), the more inclined you will be to buy it.) When demand increases this will push up prices. It is easy to see why. Take the example of Manchester United Football Club – the more people are prepared to buy season tickets (demand), the easier it is for the club to push up their prices.

Supply is the quantity of anything suppliers will be prepared to supply to the market at a particular price. The higher the price, the greater will be the quantity suppliers are willing to supply to the market. If the supply of a product increases, prices will fall – simply because there is more available for consumers to purchase.

For example, if Manchester United Merchandising produced only 1,000 club strips to sell to the general public in a given year, the price of these strips would be very high because of their rarity value. However, if Manchester United produced 100,000 the price they sold for would be much lower (although some would probably think the price is still too high!).

Different types of markets

There are many types of markets: 'flea markets', antiques markets, the market for stocks and shares, second-hand markets, art markets, animal markets and so on.

However, for the sake of simplicity and usefulness for business, we will examine the most important types of markets for the business organisation.

Commodity markets

Commodities lie at the heart of modern industrial society and include a wide range of primary products ranging from foodstuffs (such as rice, grain and coffee) to industrial raw materials (such as oil and iron ore).

Our daily lives are built around the consumption of products that originally started as raw commodities. Think, for example, of the food on our tables:

- Do you drink orange juice? Where do you think the concentrates and blends came from?

- Do you drink coffee or cocoa? Where did the beans come from?

- Do you eat toast, buns or croissants? What was the origin of the grain that went into these products?

- Do you use low-fat margarine? Where did the sunflower seeds that were crushed to make the oil come from?

The answer to these and many other questions is they all started as raw commodities grown by farmers and were usually bought in bulk by a business that processed the raw commodities (crushed the sunflower seeds, processed the beans and so on). And it is not just food products that modern society is based on; there are all sorts of other commodities – iron ore, oil and gas, diamonds, etc.

Commodities are subject to price fluctuations over time as a result of changing supply and demand conditions in the marketplace. Demand and buying patterns can change – for example, more oil than normal may be consumed during a particularly cold winter and so demand increases. The supply of commodities can also vary considerably for a variety of reasons – frosts may destroy olive trees in southern Italy, potato blight may wipe out a crop in the east of England, political upheavals in the Middle East may prevent the free flow of oil.

Special markets have been created for trading in commodities that, in the UK, are based in the City of London. At these markets 'traders' will buy and sell commodities on behalf of the large businesses that need vast quantities of raw commodities for their manufacturing processes (food and drinks companies, engineering companies, construction companies, etc.).

Case study: Agricultural prices in June 2000

Figure 7.3 shows the prices of a number of agricultural commodities on the London Exchange on 14 June 2000.

1 Which commodity is most expensive per tonne, and which is the cheapest per tonne? Why do you think these differences exist?

2 What is happening to the prices of these commodities as we move further into the future from 14 June? Why do you think this is?

Cocoa		Coffee		Barley		Potatoes	
Jul 00	629.00	Jul 00	890.00	Sep 00	65.25	Nov 00	84.55
Sep 00	650.00	Sep 00	908.00	Nov 00	67.25	Mar 01	90.50
Dec 00	683.00	Nov 00	920.00	Jan 01	68.75	Apr 01	99.00

Figure 7.3 Prices of agricultural commodities on the London Exchange, 14 June 2000 (£/tonne)

Commodity exchanges have been developed over a long period of time to enable contracts to be made for the purchase of these commodities. So, for example, a manufacturer of soft drinks that needs a great deal of sugar will not buy sugar only for today's and next week's needs will also buy sugar for three months ahead, six months ahead and even longer. It therefore makes what is called a 'futures contract' – an agreement to purchase at some date in the future. Generally speaking, the further into the future you are buying for the more you will have to pay because of the increased risk of uncertainty about whether prices will rise or fall.

Check your understanding

Using a website browser, look up www.bloomberg.com/uk. Choose the option 'Stock Market Update' and click on 'Commodities', and then 'Most active futures'. Using the data provided, work out which commodity prices have risen, and which have fallen, most recently. What factors might account for these price changes?

Consumer markets

The market we are most familiar with is the market for consumer goods. Most production in this country focuses on the consumer goods section. Just think about what you had for breakfast this morning: orange juice, cereals, tea, milk and sugar are all consumer goods. We can think of them as being 'consumer *consumables*' – we buy them and then consume them (use them up) very quickly.

We buy consumer goods because of the satisfaction we get from them. Value for money can be thought of as the satisfaction we receive from goods relative to the price we pay for them. Generally speaking, we will buy more of good A (say, for example, a favourite brand of chocolate biscuits) if it gives us more satisfaction per pence than good B (say, for example, another kind of biscuit).

Many of us are skilful calculators of value for money. You will see people going round supermarkets with calculators working out exactly how much they have spent on a particular shopping trip. Often they have only a limited budget to spend, so they may take some items out of their baskets and put others in to ensure what they leave the supermarket with are those items that give them the best value for money.

Many of the consumables you buy in a supermarket will contain ingredients that were originally traded on the commodity markets. So when commodity prices go up, this will quite quickly filter through to create increases in prices in supermarkets.

The demand for consumables depends on their price. Some consumables can be classified as luxuries while others are necessities. Necessary items might include bread, milk, heating and lighting. People have to have these items and so will continue to buy almost the same quantity of these items when prices rise. In contrast, consumers do not 'have' to purchase luxury items so, when their prices rise, consumers may choose to buy fewer of them (e.g. boxes of chocolates, cakes, grapes, etc.). Of course, one person's luxury is another's necessity. Some people argue that items like cigarettes, cream buns and whisky are necessities.

The other type of consumer good is the consumer *durable*. Consumer durables are goods that give us streams of satisfaction over a lengthy period of time (e.g. washing machines, spin dryers, video recorders, computers, cars, etc.). Because consumer durables are more expensive, people can postpone their purchase for a while if prices rise or incomes fall. Again, this depends on the individual. For some people, to have a new car every year is seen as being a 'necessity'; for others, being able to afford a cake is a 'luxury'.

Check your understanding

Make lists of the following:

1 Ten different items you could buy in a supermarket where key ingredients would originally have been traded on the commodity markets.

2 Ten items you regard to be luxuries and ten you see as being necessities. How do you make the distinction?

3 The four most recent consumer durables purchased in your household. To what extent was price a major factor in determining which product to buy?

Capital goods markets

In business, a capital good is an item that is used to produce other goods. For example, a spanner or a machine tool is an example of a capital good. The most obvious examples of capital goods are the machines that go into the production process (Figure 7.4 shows the capital goods employed in two different businesses).

Businesses will often borrow money to buy their capital goods. Capital goods are very important in that they are used to make the consumer goods (and other capital goods) at the heart of the economy.

Businesses will demand more capital goods when the demand for the consumer (or capital) goods that they produce is increasing. They will also demand capital goods to replace existing capital goods that have worn out or gone out of date. The demand by businesses for capital goods is commonly called *investment*.

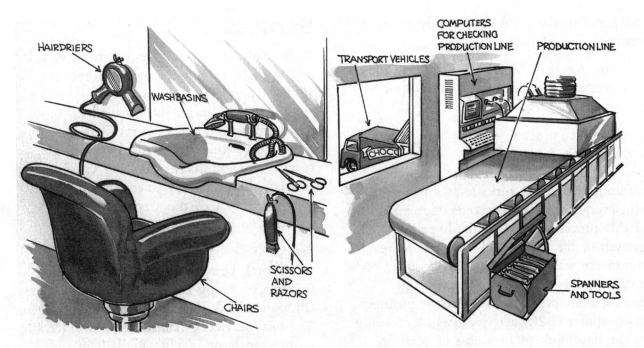

Figure 7.4   Capital goods employed in business

Check your understanding

Choose a business organisation you can quickly visit or gain access to (e.g. a retailing organisation). What are the principal capital goods the organisation employs?

See if you can interview someone from the organisation to find out what factors determine the amount the organisation spends on capital/investment goods.

Industrial markets

Business organisations buy in a range of products (usually in the form of semi-manufactured goods, supplies and spare parts) as well as machinery (investment goods) and services. The buying and selling of these goods and services takes place in an industrial as opposed to a consumer market.

Take the example of a complex modern product, such as a computer. It is made up of several hundred individual components

(a glass screen, internal circuit boards, plastic casings and coatings, electric wiring, etc.). Each of these components will be bought in from a range of suppliers from across the globe. The suppliers of many of the parts will have sub-suppliers as well.

In industrial markets, buying and selling to the end-user does not usually take place in shops (as you would typically expect in many consumer markets). Instead, trading tends to be carried out through sales staff (of the supplying firm) and buyers (from the firm needing industrial goods) meeting together to examine catalogues, to be given demonstrations of how parts, materials and machinery work, etc. In some cases, the seller will go to the buyer's premises; sometimes it will be the other way round.

Of course, once an order has been won it tends to lead to repeat business, but sellers will continually need to communicate with buyers about new offers, new products, etc. As in many other areas of commerce industrial markets are increasingly Internet trading – e-commerce.

E-commerce is the buying and selling of products and services by businesses and consumers over the Internet.

Electronic commerce is not a new phenomenon. Companies have exchanged business data over a variety of communication networks for many years. However, there is now accelerated expansion of this process driven by the hyperfast growth of the Internet. Until recently, e-commerce was concentrated on business-to-business activity (B2B). However, the development of the web has made business-to-consumer (B2C) activity possible, leading to the development of a host of what are termed .com businesses, as well as existing businesses developing e-commerce e.g. banks, bookshops, food retailers, sportswear sellers, etc.

Advantages of e-commerce include:

- access to new markets
- reduced advertising costs
- reduced manufacturing and design costs
- reduced delivery costs for many products
- improved market research information
- more opportunities for niche marketing
- a general reduction in costs per customer, and per sale made.

Check your understanding

If you live in an area where there are a number of manufacturing firms, see if you can make a contact to interview a buyer or a salesperson who works for a company. Find out how he or she goes about buying and selling the products that are used in the production process.

Services

Today, service markets are an extensive part of the economy. Every day we purchase services. Services are intangibles – you cannot physically touch or see them, but you may be able to see parts of the equipment which are used to provide the service. For example, when you visit a dentist, you are likely to feel the drill she uses, even though the service being provided is dental care.

Services to people include riding on a bus (transport), being covered by insurance (insurance), being able to make transactions through a bank (banking), having a hair cut (personal services), swimming at the local leisure centre or playing football in the local park (leisure), etc.

Business services include all the services businesses are able to benefit from – postal services, telecommunications, banking, insurance, etc.

What increasingly distinguishes services provision from the production of manufactured goods are the inter-relationships between the customer and those involved in producing the service. In manufacturing, many of the intermediate processes take place in factories out of sight. However, with a service, most of the provision of the service is highly visible and involves interpersonal dealings between the service provider and the customer. For example:

- Telephone contacts with an insurer when buying insurance.
- In-store advice, and dealings over the check-out in retailing.
- The personal service of a masseur/se.
- Interpersonal contact with a personal trainer at a fitness club, etc.

In the twenty-first century it is the quality of relationships in these service markets that will determine which firms are the most successful. Even where the links involve e-commerce, as they increasingly do, it is the quality of the interface between the web site and the consumer that will determine success (what we term 'user friendliness').

Check your understanding

Identify three service markets you are familiar with. Show how these markets involve personal contact between service providers and their customers.

Factors that influence markets and how businesses seek to influence these markets

This section is concerned with identifying, analysing and evaluating the range of factors that influence how markets operate. It also explores how businesses seek to shape and influence these markets.

Demand and supply

Demand

The demand for a product is a *want* backed up by *money* to make the *purchase*. If everyone starts demanding a particular item of fashion clothing, producers will rush to make that item.

Each year millions of students attend schools and colleges following a range of courses. One of the most popular is business. All young people and many adult returners to education are entitled to follow courses that meet their needs. The government is keen to support Vocational

A Level courses in business because of the important part they play in preparing students both for the world of work and for life in modern society. Colleges receive funds from the government for each student place (up to a certain number). We can therefore say there is a substantial demand for places on such courses. The students' wants are backed up by money.

We can illustrate the demand for a good in the marketplace by drawing what is known as a 'demand curve'. Imagine Wimbledon Tennis Club have decided to sell off some of their very old and worn-out tennis balls at reduced prices to tennis fans. They have carried out some market research which produced the figures given in Figure 7.5. This information can then be set out in the form of a demand curve (Figure 7.6). Note that the demand curve typically slopes down from left to right.

Price of balls (£)	Quantity demanded per month
2.50	200
2.00	400
1.50	600
1.00	800
0.50	1,000

Figure 7.5 Wimbledon Tennis Club: sale of old tennis balls

The demand curve slopes down because:

* People will be able to afford fewer items at higher prices.

* The higher the price, the greater the opportunity cost to the buyer. The opportunity cost is the next best alternative sacrificed in making a decision. As prices go up, the greater the sacrifice the consumer will need to make to purchase an item.

As the price of the tennis balls falls, they will become more affordable.

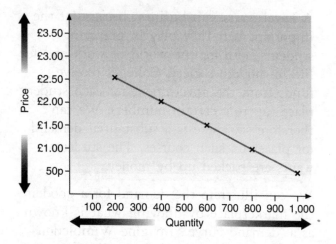

Figure 7.6 Demand for old tennis balls per month

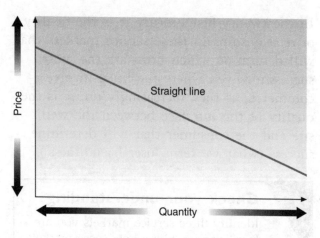

Figure 7.8 A straight line showing demand

It is convenient to think of demand as fitting a nicely drawn demand curve but, of course, in the real world, demand patterns are not so simple. The demand for products varies considerably with fresh price changes. Some price rises will have little effect on quantities bought, whilst other quite small price rises may be critical. Typically, however, we shall represent demand curves as neat curves or as straight lines (see Figures 7.7 and 7.8).

Supply

The profit from selling a good or service is the difference between the price at which it is sold and the cost of producing it. The quantities of the good the company offers will, therefore, depend on the price it receives for each unit sold relative to the cost of producing each unit.

As price rises (other things remaining the same), the company will at first make a large profit on each item it sells. This will encourage it to make and sell more. However, the company may face rising costs as it expands (for example, the cost of paying employees at overtime rates will increase). For these reasons we should expect that companies will offer more for sale at higher prices and, as they increase their output, they will ask for higher prices.

We can draw either a supply curve for an individual company or a market supply curve by adding together all the individual supply curves. A typical supply curve will slope upwards from left to right.

Imagine the managers of Wimbledon Tennis Club are pleased at the response from the public to their idea of selling tennis balls.

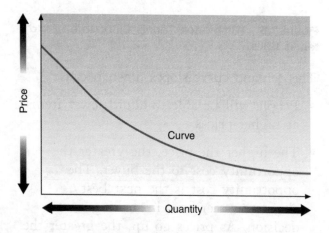

Figure 7.7 A curve showing demand

They have a large stock of these balls and have decided to control the number they sell to the market depending on the price they receive for them. They will supply more at higher prices than at lower prices. (If prices were too low it would not be worth the administration costs of supplying more than a few. However, if they can sell a great many, it will be worth the administration costs.) They have set out a graph showing how much they would be prepared to supply at different prices per month (see Figure 7.9).

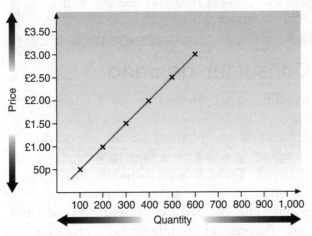

Figure 7.9 Supply of old tennis balls per month

A supply curve shows the relationship between the price at which a good will be sold and the quantity producers will be prepared to supply to the market at this price. A steeply rising curve would indicate that producers would want to see relatively large increases in price before they expanded output.

In contrast, a shallow curve would indicate that producers would be prepared to increase their supply considerably in response to relatively small increases in price.

The concept of market price

Figure 7.10 sets out side by side the demand and supply curves for old balls at Wimbledon in a typical month. We can combine these two curves on a single drawing to illustrate how prices are determined in the marketplace. The point at which the two curves cross is where the wishes of both consumers and producers are met (see Figure 7.11).

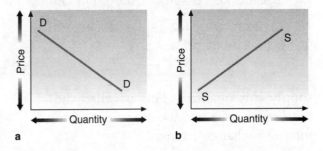

a   b

Figure 7.10 Old tennis balls: a) demand curve in a typical month; b) supply curve in a typical month

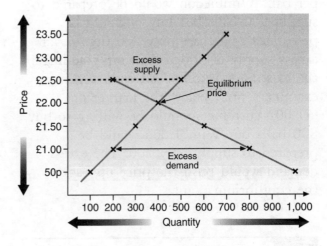

Figure 7.11 Old tennis balls: market equilibrium

We can now see that, at a price of £2.00 per ball, 400 would be bought each month. At this price consumers are happy to buy 400 balls and Wimbledon are happy to

Case study: Demand and supply for 'Sweet Pastilles'

Figure 7.12 sets out the demand and supply schedules for a particular make of sweets called 'Sweet Pastilles'.

1 Set the table out in the form of a graph.

2 What is the equilibrium price? Why is this the equilibrium price? What volume of goods will be supplied to the market at the equilibrium price?

3 Explain why 10p and 40p are not the equilibrium price.

Price per packet (pence)	Demand (million packets per annum)	Supply (million packets per annum)
0	400	0
10	320	0
20	240	80
30	160	160
40	80	240
50	0	320
60	0	400
70	0	480

Figure 7.12 'Sweet Pastilles': demand and supply schedules

supply this quantity. This is called the *equilibrium price* because there is nothing forcing a change from it.

We can see why this point is an equilibrium one by considering non-equilibrium points. For example, at £2.50 per ball, Wimbledon would be prepared to supply 500 balls but buyers would be prepared to purchase only 200 (leaving an excess supply of 300 balls, simply adding to the existing stockpile). Alternatively, if we examine a price below the market one (£1.00), customers would be willing to buy 800 balls but Wimbledon would be prepared to supply only 200. The excess demand would push the price up back to the equilibrium point.

Check your understanding

With reference to a market of your choice, explain who are the suppliers and who are the main customers in the market. Also explain how demand in this marketplace might increase over time.

Consumer demand

In addition to price, there are a number of factors that influence the demand for a product. If one of these factors alters, the *conditions of demand* are said to have changed. These factors include tastes, income, the age distribution of the population, the price of substitute products and the price of complementary products.

Changes in one (or a combination) of these factors will cause a shift in the demand curve. The demand curve can shift either in a leftward or in a rightward direction. A shift to the left indicates smaller quantities are wanted than before at given prices. A shift to the right indicates larger quantities are wanted than before at given prices. These changes are illustrated in Figure 7.13.

The illustration shows that in the original situation, a quantity of 600 highlighter pens would be bought at 80p. When the conditions of demand move in favour of the product, more will be required at all prices so that, for example, at 80p perhaps 800 would be bought each week. Alternatively,

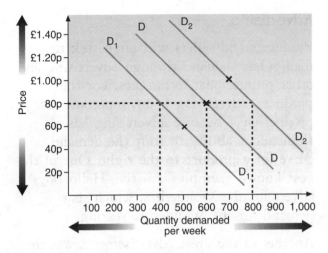

Figure 7.13   Demand for highlighter pens

if conditions of demand move against a product, fewer will be bought at all prices so that, for example, at 80p perhaps 400 highlighter pens would now be demanded.

Factors that can cause these shifts in demand are outlined below.

Income

The more money people have, the easier it is for them to buy products. The amount of income people have to spend on goods is known as their *disposable* income (their pay minus taxes and other essential deductions).

Average incomes tend to rise over time, and this will lead to a general increase in the level of demand for goods. The demand for individual items will, however, be related more to the changes in incomes earned by different groups, such as teenagers (for teenage magazines and fashions), pensioners (for retirement homes, winter-sun holidays, etc.) and so on.

An increase in incomes will lead to a shift in the demand curve to the right. Rising incomes will tend to result from improving job opportunities, the increased use of cost-cutting technology and increases in demand for products.

Some products may become less popular as incomes rise. These are products that come to be regarded as being inferior as people's spending power increases. The consumer who was once happy to rent accommodation, wear scruffy clothes and drive a second-hand, low-powered car may switch to buying a house, wearing designer labels and driving a status symbol car when his or her income increases.

So, for most products, demand will shift to the right when incomes increase, and to the left when incomes fall. In the case of inferior items, however, demand would shift to the left when incomes rise.

Check your understanding

Fred Jones is a self-made man who has made his way up from being a warehouseman to owning his own company. Which of the following do you think Fred might see as inferior goods, and which as normal goods?

- A holiday to Skegness?
- A multimedia digital sound system?
- A black and white television set?
- An Armani suit?
- A boiler suit?
- A world cruise?
- A Ford Ka?
- A Rolls-Royce?

Age distribution

Many products appeal to some age groups more than others. A clear example of this is in tastes in popular music. During the 1990s, pop music entrepreneurs realised that popular music was increasingly being bought by younger and younger age groups – with the bulk of purchases being made by 11–15-year-old girls. Increasingly, the popular music market was re-targeted to appeal to this group (e.g. by the creation of teenage boy and girl bands specifically packaged to sell records and fashions to 11–15-year-olds).

Business needs to be keenly aware of the changes taking place in the numbers in different age segments so as to know where the best opportunities lie. For example, in recent years we have experienced a phenomenon known as the 'greying' of the population – with more and more older people. As this age group has expanded, so too has demand for products bought by these 'third agers', e.g. an increased demand for gardening products, for medical aids, for retirement homes, etc. – see Figure 7.14).

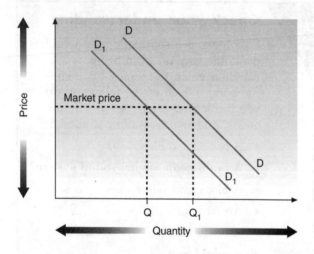

Figure 7.14 Demand for gardening products as the numbers of 'third agers' increase

Tastes

The most obvious cause of an increase in demand for a product is a change in tastes in favour of that product. We see this all the time: new goods become popular and old-fashioned ones lose favour. In fashion, the winter's colour may be black, the autumn's brown, and the summer's pastel shades. Last season's fashions quickly become sale items.

Advertising

Producers and sellers will often seek to manipulate demand through advertising and other promotional techniques. For the producer, advertising is an important cost of production – because advertising has a tremendous ability to shift the demand curve for a product to the right. One of the best known examples was the 'Hello Boys' advert for the Wonderbra, which sent demand for the Wonderbra soaring.

Another of the great advertisements was the 1985 Levi's launderette advert produced by the advertising agency Bartle Bogle Hegarty. The advertisement showed Nick Kamen strip to his boxer shorts to wash his Levi 501s in a launderette. The advertisement not only led to a massive increase in the sale of Levi's but it also increased the demand for all forms of jeans, and even created a massive demand for boxers!

Price of other products

The demand for products that have close substitutes will often be strongly influenced by the price of substitutes. This would be the case, for example, with different brands of tinned fruit or different brands of petrol, because there are many different brand names from which to choose.

The demand curve for a product is likely to shift to the right if a substitute product rises in price. The demand for a product is likely to shift to the left if a substitute product falls in price.

Some products are used together so that the demand for one is linked to the price of another. An example of this might be cars and car CD-players. If the price of cars falls, this is likely to lead to an increase in demand for car CD-players.

Check your understanding

Choose a particular product or service (e.g. a brand of chocolate, a type of consumer durable good, cinema attendance, etc.). Show how the demand for this product has been influenced by changes in incomes, age distribution, tastes, advertising and the appearance of other products in recent times.

Draw illustrations (demand and supply diagrams) to show each of these changes.

Supply

The cost of producing an item is made up of the price of the various inputs, including raw materials and the machinery used to make it. Rises in the prices of some of these factors will increase production costs, and this results in a reduction in supply at each and every price (see Figure 7.15).

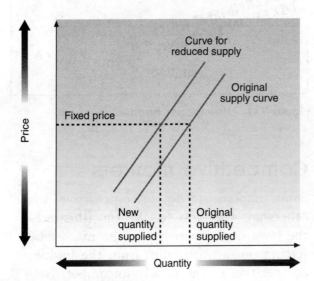

Figure 7.15 Shifts in the supply curve

The supply curve shifts to the left: at any given price, fewer items will be produced and offered for sale than before. For example, when the Bank of England's Monetary Policy Committee raises interest rates (i.e. the cost of borrowing money), this will increase the cost of production of many goods.

Production costs

A rise in production costs pushes the supply curve to the left (it will cost more to produce each level of output than before), and a fall in production costs will push the supply curve to the right.

Production is based on the combination of inputs of factors of production, e.g. combining a worker (labour) with a machine (capital equipment) to produce an output, e.g. a finished car. If the cost of a factor input rises, it will become more expensive to produce outputs. Factors of production will be used in the long term only if the value of their output is greater than their cost of hire. As factor prices rise, fewer factors will be used in production and, hence, the supply of a product will fall.

For example, let us assume an agricultural crop requires three main inputs – land, labour and chemical fertiliser. If the cost of one of these inputs (or a combination of them) were to rise, farmers might cut back on the acreage committed to this particular crop. Conversely, when the price of factors of production falls, it becomes less costly to supply a product, which encourages producers to supply more, leading to a shift in the supply curve to the right.

Changes in technology

The first decade of the twenty-first century is seeing an unparalleled level of technological development. Each new development that is incorporated into production processes has the impact of slashing production costs and, hence, of shifting the supply curve to the right.

Physical conditions

Changes in physical conditions can have a major impact on supply (here we mean changes in the weather, changes in the quality of the soil and changes in other natural phenomena). For example, in 1999 the earthquake in Honduras in South America had such a dramatic impact it knocked back the productive capacity of the whole economy by at least 20 years. More commonly, weather conditions (such as drought or torrential rain) can quickly destroy the supply capacity of agriculture.

Taxation and subsidies

Taxation and subsidies pull in opposite directions in their impact on the supply curve. A production tax of 10p per unit on a good would increase the cost of production of that good by 10p per unit. In contrast, a subsidy would have the effect of

lowering the costs of production. Supply will therefore shift to the left as a result of taxes on a product, and to the right as a result of a subsidy (see Figure 7.16).

Check your understanding

The headlines in Figure 7.17 all appeared in the national press in early 2000. State in each case what the likely impact would have been on supply in the relevant industries.

PRICES OF COMPUTER CHIPS TO TEMPORARILY RISE

WAGES TO FALL IN THE PRINTING INDUSTRY

GOOD GROWING CONDITIONS FOR FRENCH WINES

NEW SUBSIDIES FOR START-UP BUSINESS IN HIGH-TECH INDUSTRIES

BAD COFFEE HARVEST IN BRAZIL

GOVERNMENT RAISES TAXES ON SMOKING

EARTHQUAKE IN SOUTH-EAST ASIA

Figure 7.17 Newspaper headlines

Competitive markets

Some markets are highly competitive, while others are a lot less so. We can illustrate the level of competition in the market by setting out a continuum from the highly competitive to the totally uncompetitive (see Figure 7.18).

Competitive markets

A good example of a competitive market in which there are many buyers and sellers is

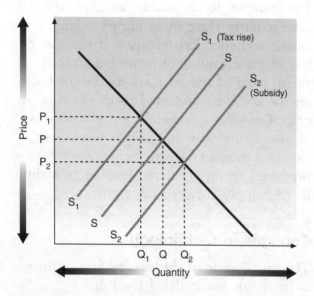

Figure 7.16 Impact of taxes and subsidies on the supply of a product

Extremely competitve	Some competition	Little or no competition
Either: a. Many small sellers and buyers or b. Small number of highly competitive firms and many buyers	Often a small number of sellers and many buyers	One (monopoly) or two (duopoly) firms and a number of buyers

Figure 7.18   Market competition

that of petrol stations, particularly in urban areas. A recent government report showed

that, in urban areas, there are 75 petrol stations in every 10 km^2 with 14 different brands on offer.

This market is so competitive because, in addition to the three majors in petrol retailing (Shell, BP and Esso), there are many smaller retailers (e.g. JET, Q8, etc.) as well as all the major supermarket chains. The result of this intense competition is that the profit margin is virtually non-existent in this market segment. The petrol retailers

Case study: Retailing in the UK

In late 1999 the retailing sector of the economy was hit by story after story in the press of one big high-street name after another showing disappointing profits and sales results.

Figure 7.19 shows the value of retailing shares compared with the price of all other shares expressed as 100%. Some of the biggest names had the worst results, led by Marks & Spencer and Sainsbury's.

Each suffering store group had succumbed to a unique combination of problems management had failed to resolve. But the sector's troubles were not just the accumulation of a series of special circumstances. It is in retailing that competition had intensified fastest and fiercest as a result of e-commerce and the Internet – coming as it did on top of over-capacity (there were just too many competitors producing too much in retailing).

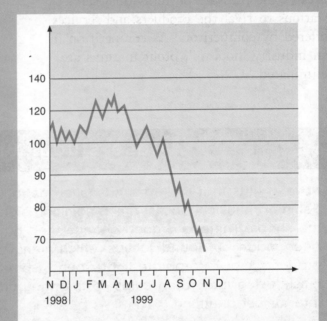

Figure 7.19   The retailing share index compared to all other shares (November 1998 = 100%)

Whenever competition intensifies, there is a fall in profitability. In the USA, which is further along the path of introducing new technologies in retailing, there has been an even more dramatic reduction in profits.

1 Why do you think profit potential in retailing has been falling?
2 Why has e-commerce been so significant in this change?
3 Apart from retailing, can you think of other industries where competition is intensifying, leading to a squeeze on profits?

compete in a range of areas in addition to price, including the following:

- A similar range of petrols, diesel and other fuels.

- A similar range of customer services (e.g. fast service, paper towels to wipe hands on after filling up, toilets, etc.) and a range of extra products (such as cut flowers, comics, newspapers, etc.).

- Light, flexible hoses.

- A place to check air pressure, vacuum the car, etc.

The higher the level of competition, the greater the pressure on individual service stations to rival the products and services offered by competitors. As competition in an industry 'hots up', profit margins are eliminated.

Non-competitive markets

Competition occurs where two or more organisations act independently to supply their products to the same group of consumers. Some markets are characterised by an abundance of products and services so that customers have a considerable amount of choice (e.g. modern retailing and banking). In other markets there may be little (if any) competition, and consumers may be able to make only a limited choice from the range of goods and services on offer.

Direct competition exists where organisations produce similar products that appeal to the same group of consumers. For example, this book is in direct competition with other books written for the AVCE in Business.

Even when an organisation provides a unique end-product with no direct competition, it

Case study: Singing socks

Novelty gifts that make sounds (such as talking T-shirts or musical socks) are a common sight in the shops. There is a good chance they have been made by Sound Tactics, which manufactures products that incorporate light, sound, speech or music using integrated chips so tiny they can fit into almost anything.

Company founder Don Hockman has seen turnover rise from £70,000 in 1995 to £500,000 in 2000. There are also football socks that play the Match of the Day theme. In the early 1990s Don researched the development of music, sound, light and speech in retail and promotional products and discovered that the music in greeting cards came from an integrated chip. Developing the product so that it could be used in a range of other consumer products required a great deal of further research, particularly in the area of quality control and safety standards. Sound Tactics was set up in 1994 to concentrate on products that incorporate sound and, today, most of the products are made in the UK, while the electronic components are imported from Taiwan.

Sound Tactics sell their items through shops such as Marks & Spencer, Boots and Asda. The order books are long and profit forecasts are excellent for 2000 and 2001.

1   Why are Sound Tactics able to make such healthy profits?

2   Why might these profits be competed away in the longer period?

will still have to consider indirect competition. This occurs where potential customers examine slightly different ways of meeting the same needs. For example, instead of going on holiday to Bath or Bournemouth, they go to Barbados or Benidorm; instead of buying a tabloid newspaper they may buy a 'quality' broadsheet.

The degree of competition in a market is likely to influence the level of sales and profits. The firm that is first to the market with a new product may be able to make large sales and profits. However, in the course of time other firms will enter the market, so that sales will be shared among a larger number of producers. Each of these producers will be competing for market share and so price wars may result, leading to falling profits.

Monopoly

A highly competitive market exists when firms compete vigorously with each other. The features of intense competition might include the following:

- Producers supplying highly similar products (e.g. packets of salt and vinegar crisps).

- Consumers having detailed knowledge of the offers being made by different suppliers (e.g. a shopper in a large supermarket who can check the prices of different brands of such products as soap powders).

- Ease for producers and suppliers to enter a market (e.g. if there are good prices and profits to be made from selling musical socks, new manufacturers might enter the market to take advantage of this situation).

A monopoly situation does not include these competitive conditions. A pure monopoly exists if there is only one producer or seller. Because there is only one firm in the market it has considerable powers. For example, if you are not happy with the prices, quality of service, conditions of sale, etc. offered by the monopolist, you cannot switch to a rival product because there aren't any.

A business that does not have direct competition is said to be a monopoly. It does not face outside pressure to be competitive. We must be careful, however, not to assume that monopolies are inefficient. Where one firm (a monopoly), rather than several, dominates a market, there is no need to duplicate systems of administration, services and other processes (there needs to be only the one system in the one firm). Successful monopolists can also put a great deal of money into product development and research in order to maintain a long-term competitive edge. Coca-Cola, for example, ploughs back a high percentage of its profits into new marketing and product development.

In the real world there are unlikely to be many examples of pure monopolies because most manufactured goods can be copied. Some minerals, however, are restricted to a few geographical areas (for example, a large concentration of world's gold reserves are found in the Russian republics and southern Africa). This situation will lead, naturally, to monopolies. Similarly, when a new product is invented, the firm that supplied it will, initially, have a monopoly. However, very soon other people will copy the product and provide close imitations (singing socks!). An understanding of monopoly, however, is very important in business. Monopoly powers help to explain how firms are able to make more than a normal amount of profit.

When a firm can restrict competition it is in a position to raise prices and, perhaps, to exploit consumers. For example, if you desperately needed a loaf of bread when the shops were closed, you might be forced to buy an over-priced loaf of not-too-fresh bread from a service station which has a monopoly when other shops are closed. Another example is that Harrods is able to exploit the monopoly it has over toilet facilities within its own shop by charging shoppers £1 to use the loo!

Oligopoly

Whereas monopoly means there is one seller, oligopoly means there are a few sellers. Oligopoly is typical of many markets in the UK, where there are a few major sellers in national and local markets (although there may be additional smaller sellers).

Examples of oligopoly markets are as follows:

- Quality newspapers (e.g. *The Times*, *The Independent*).

- Tabloid newspapers (e.g. the *Mirror*, the *Sun*).

- Contraceptive manufacturers (e.g. Mates (Virgin), Durex (London Rubber)).

- Soap powders (e.g. Unilever, Procter & Gamble).

Case study: Restricting access to the Internet

In November 1999, a federal judge in Washington issued an initial 'finding-of-fact' ruling in the Justice Department's 1997 anti-monopoly case against Microsoft, saying that the software company had abused its dominant position in the personal computer industry to stifle its competitors.

In the same month we saw the launch of a new spoof monopoly game on the web. This remake of the classic board game featured, instead of streets and properties, various companies and ventures in which Microsoft have an interest – Hotmail, Apple, WebTv and so on – with visitors able to submit new squares and descriptions. The cards showed the kind of 'dastardly deeds a software monopolist might be tempted to do to thwart the competition'.

1 What arguments might a company like Microsoft put forward for seeking to stifle competition?

2 What arguments could you make against these restrictions?

- Confectionery (e.g. Cadbury, Nestlé).

- Petrol (e.g. Shell, BP, Esso).

Oligopoly markets have the potential for intense competition as well as the potential to restrict competition and to act as monopolists.

Oligopolists could agree to share a market and to avoid potentially damaging competition (e.g. they could agree: 'Company A can dominate the north, company B the south, company C the west and company D the east'). However, they would be unlikely to do this because:

- Business organisations tend to have a natural desire to expand and dominate. For example, company A may also want to be the major player in the south, east and west.

- It is against the law to carry out uncompetitive practices. Companies that collude are using their powers to exploit less powerful groups and individuals. In this country this will lead to investigation by the Competition Commission, often leading to legal penalties.

Oligopoly markets are, therefore, often characterised by extensive competition. Competition acts as a spur, encouraging individual firms to improve their performance in order to increase their market share, sales, receipts and profits.

Check your understanding

Show how the level of competition varies between two markets – one in which there are a great many competitors in the market, and one in which there are only a few competitors.

Globalisation

The nature of competition has been transformed by the process known as globalisation. There are many aspects of globalisation. Some of the most important are as follows:

- Many large firms have changed their focus from the national market to the global market. Companies such as Heinz and Unilever have decided to focus their efforts and resources only into those lines where they can be 'the best' (i.e. the most competitive in the international economy). For example, for Heinz this includes baby foods, sauces and canned fish, as well as other lines.

- Products are now designed to appeal to a global rather than a narrow local audience. For example, in 1999 Heinz spent several billion dollars relaunching their Heinz tomato ketchup bottle and on advertising so they would give the same message and image across the globe. Mars changed the name of its Marathon Bar to Snickers because they felt this name was easier to communicate across international languages and cultures.

- Firms have set up globally integrated production systems so that raw materials and parts for products (such as cars and computers) can be bought in from across the globe for final assembly. Factories can be located in many parts of the globe – usually where production and transport costs are lowest. This has been made possible by revolutions in communications, transportation and information processing technologies.

- Many people today work for giant multinational corporations whose range of interests will be spread over several continents.

When UK firms sell their goods in the UK they are selling to a market which, at most, contains 60 million people. When the same firm extends its horizon to the European market, immediately the opportunities are far greater (e.g. 80 million people in Germany, 56 million in France, etc.). The opening up of the Single European Market on 1 January 1993 created golden opportunities for capitalising on a huge 'domestic' market of 340 million customers, and this number is growing as new members join. Today, the frontiers have been pushed out to global markets, with UK-based firms targeting customers in China, Australia and USA, among other nations.

The global marketplace is dominated by three major areas: Japan (and the coastal areas of Southeast Asia), North America and the European Union.

There are benefits to business from thinking globally. On the demand side, the company is faced with a much bigger target market; on the supply side, it has the opportunity of reducing the costs of production through producing very large outputs of standardised products – e.g. millions of bottles of tomato sauce and packets of soap powder, etc. These cost reductions are termed economies of large-scale production.

At the same time, the UK market is under competitive attack from global competitors – for example, from Japanese firms in consumer electronics, from European food producers, from Southeast Asian and Eastern European textile manufacturers, from computer data processing specialists in India, etc.

Nowhere had this impact been felt more dramatically than in late 1999, when Wal-Mart entered the UK retailing market through its take-over of Asda. Immediately, Wal-Mart stated that prices of thousands of goods sold in the UK would fall.

Check your understanding

Cut out a story from the national press showing how the globalisation process is affecting a UK industry or a particular business firm. Summarise the major factors affecting competition as a result of the globalisation process identified.

Business influence on products and services

The amount of competition varies depending upon the market under discussion. The amount of competition in the consumer market is different from the amount in the commodity market or in an internal market. There are many different influences on the amount of competition, such as the extent to which the goods and services can be differentiated and the tendency for customers to make repeat purchases.

In some markets the individual business can be powerful. In other situations the business has little power. We can show this difference by making a comparison between price-makers and price-takers.

The firm that makes a unique product is best placed to be a price-maker – by exercising monopoly powers. It is able to dictate to the market – setting standards and prices. Because it is likely to make a profit it can plough back profits into making its good better and more appealing to customers. Bill Gates' Microsoft is a classic example of a firm that led the marketplace, coming to dominate the industry that characterised the closing decade of the twentieth century. Microsoft became the most highly valued stock on Wall Street. Making very large profits enabled Microsoft to explore new product areas and to keep ahead of the field.

We can contrast Microsoft with firms that were being left behind by technological developments. For example, travel agents have increasingly become obsolete as 'wired up' consumers turn to the Internet to book their own holidays direct from the holiday companies. As competition has intensified, the profit margins the travel agents are able to make have been cut, giving them less scope for innovation and for building up their businesses. The travel agents that remain are becoming price-takers in an ever more competitive market. The prices they take are barely enough to keep them in business.

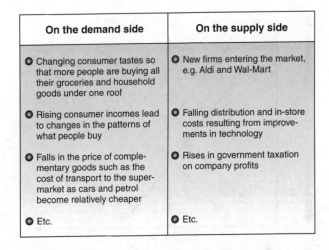

On the demand side	On the supply side
● Changing consumer tastes so that more people are buying all their groceries and household goods under one roof	● New firms entering the market, e.g. Aldi and Wal-Mart
● Rising consumer incomes lead to changes in the patterns of what people buy	● Falling distribution and in-store costs resulting from improvements in technology
● Falls in the price of complementary goods such as the cost of transport to the supermarket as cars and petrol become relatively cheaper	● Rises in government taxation on company profits
● Etc.	● Etc.

Figure 7.20 Changes in the supermarket sector

Check your understanding

Give examples of two businesses:

1 One that exerts considerable influence over its products and services (because of its market domination).

2 One that exerts very little influence over its products and services.

Acceleration in the pace of change

Businesses do not operate in static markets: they operate in dynamic markets. We can illustrate this by taking the example of a particular market – supermarkets. Recently, there have been many factors causing changes in this market (see Figure 7.20). These dynamic factors lead to an environment of change which impacts on businesses and on their prices and on what they are able to offer consumers.

Markets are constantly in motion, and combinations of factors cause shifts in demand and supply. For example, we can see that in Figure 7.21 a shift to the right in the demand curve for a new type of hockey boot

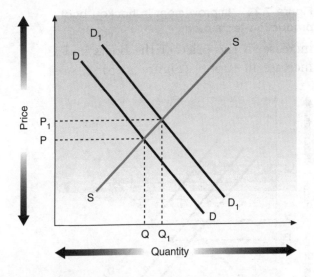

Figure 7.21 Increasing demand for hockey boots

has increased the equilibrium price and the equilibrium quantity in the market.

At the same time, an improvement in the technology used to manufacture such shoes has led to a shift in the supply curve to the right, leading to an increase in the quantity being supplied to the market and the opportunity to lower prices (Figure 7.22). The improved technology used in the production of the hockey boots leads to a fresh injection of demand as the boots become even more popular, leading to an

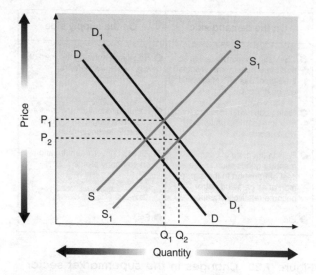

Figure 7.22 Improvement in hockey boot production technology

increase in the price of the boots and an increase in supply (Figure 7.23).

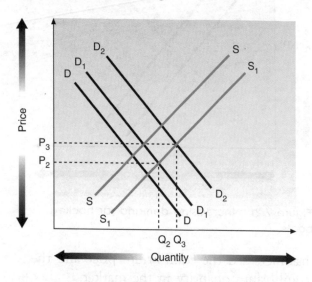

Figure 7.23 Further increase in demand for hockey boots

This is what happens in dynamic markets. The successful business will be the one that is best able to predict the dynamics of the marketplace and to lead the process of change in the market.

Check your understanding

Draw diagrams to illustrate the following dynamic market situations:

1 The demand for cigarettes falls as a result of a ban on cigarette advertising in January 2000.

2 Cigarette manufacturers develop new technologies that improve production processes in March 2000.

3 The number of teenagers smoking cigarettes falls in the summer of 2000 because of an increased fashion for healthy lifestyles.

Increasing business competitiveness

Businesses continually seek competitive advantage (i.e. being better than the competition). There are a number of ways they can achieve this.

Adding value

As we have seen, adding value involves continually seeking to provide a 'little bit extra' to what the customer is looking for in a product (e.g. a computerised route-finding facility in a car, a more convenient way of opening a tin can, etc.).

Improving quality

Improving the quality of a product is very similar to adding value. Quality involves making sure a good or service is 'fit for the purpose' for which it is intended. Quality, therefore, needs to be viewed from the customer's perspective. The individual will feel he or she is receiving quality if the good or service he or she purchases does everything expected of it (and more).

When you visit the hairdresser, he or she will ask you 'how would you like it'? The

Case study: Tesco and Sainsbury's battle for the home-shopping market

Britain's two leading supermarket groups expanded their online shopping services in 2000 as the e-commerce grocery battle got more intense.

Sainsbury's (http://www.sainsburys.co.uk) chose Park Royal in northwest London for its first home delivery 'picking centre'. The 120,000 ft^2 warehouse stocks 15,000 lines and is used for Sainsbury's Orderline service, through which shoppers order by phone, fax or Internet and pay £5 for delivery. The £7 million centre opened in the summer of 2000. Sainsbury's believe the home shopping market within the M25 area around London is underdeveloped and that it has excellent potential.

At the same time, Tesco Direct home-shopping service is on track to become the world's largest Internet grocery business in 2000 (http://www.tesco.co.uk). In February 2000, Tesco Direct was offered from 120 stores with a nationwide service planned for late 2000. By 2000, Tesco had added books, gifts and personal finance to its Internet offer.

During late 1999, Tesco group sales figures outperformed industry averages and enabled Tesco to expand their market share – in which they were already the dominant player.

1 How does providing a direct home-shopping service add value to Sainsbury's and Tesco's existing product line?

2 How is such a process of adding value likely to increase competitive advantage?

hairdresser who meets your specifications because he or she has the skill, the commitment to detail and the understanding of exactly what you require will get your repeat business. The hairdresser who fails to deliver to your specifications may get your money, but once only!

Businesses will, therefore, seek continually to improve the quality of their product so that their quality is ahead of the field.

Product differentiation

Differentiation involves creating products that are different (better) than rival offerings. A Rolls-Royce is clearly differentiated from other cars, as is the Ford Ka or the new Mini. In these cases, the total product concept is differentiated – the Mini is not just any car it is a Mini.

As well as differentiating the total product, it is also possible to differentiate various features of a product from rival offerings. For example, some cars have stylish interiors that set them apart, and some overcoats have exclusive linings and really useful extras (such as hidden pockets). Some cameras and watches are differentiated by being waterproof or shockproof.

Being able to differentiate a product often relies on the ingenuity of the design team. For example, what makes this book better than rival Advanced Business books is not just the content but the way the product has been designed to look attractive and special.

Businesses are finding it more and more difficult to demonstrate product differentiation over competitors. Customer service, on the other hand, offers almost endless opportunities for superiority and differentiation. It covers the way a customer is treated by the sales staff (on the telephone, in the shop, at the check-out), the way queries and complaints are handled and the use of the latest communication technology to personalise even the most large-scale promotional campaign letters. All these contribute to the ideal one-to-one relationship.

Advertising

Advertising is a prime way of gaining competitive advantage. Advertising not only enables the firm to present and describe the key features of a product to potential customers but it also has the power to transform the product by creating subtle associations between the product and lifestyles (and sex appeal, fashionability and a range of other aspects). In the modern world competitive advantage often rests just as much in the advertising message as in the product itself.

Check your understanding

Think of four well-known adverts.

How did each of the adverts enable the company that produced the product to gain competitive advantage?

Pricing policies

The American writer Michael Porter argues that there are two main ways to gain competitive advantage. One of these is through differentiation and the other is through price. He argues that a company can seek to dominate a market by charging low prices and by *not* offering much in the way of differentiation – for example, a cut-price supermarket, a cheap tub of margarine, a supermarket's own brand of beans, etc. The low-price producer will aim to sell in very large quantities using all the economies of low-cost production that are available. Alternatively, a firm can charge a higher price and produce a more differentiated product. The higher price enables the firm to cover the higher costs of production involved with differentiation.

Interestingly, when Tesco first entered retailing they went for the low-price strategy. The motto of Tesco's founder, Jack Cohen, was 'pile them high and sell them cheap'. He bought in bulk and sold at a low price. As time moved on, Tesco moved more and more up-market, moving away from low price to differentiation strategies. Tesco did this because they realised UK consumers were becoming better off and many of them were changing in their tastes away from cheap groceries (see Figure 7.24).

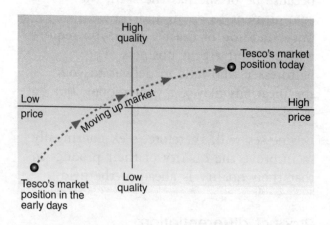

Figure 7.24   Tesco moves up market

Check your understanding

For a market for consumer goods of your choice, show how two (or more) firms have sought to become more competitive by adding value, improving quality, product differentiating, advertising and through pricing policies.

Managing competition

Business organisations can respond to the competition in the marketplace in which they operate by joining together with competitors or by moving apart from competitors through product differentiation (see Figure 7.25). For example, for much of the 1980s (until 1988) we saw a tendency for a number of business organisations to engage in merger activity in order to gain scale economies (such as buying in greater bulk, cutting down on the use of inefficient units of machinery) and other advantages. During the 1990s we saw fewer mergers as firms started to downsize. Downsizing means breaking up into smaller core units, and selling off non-core activities which are not essential to the business. For example, companies such as Shell reduced their own advertising and photography divisions, and

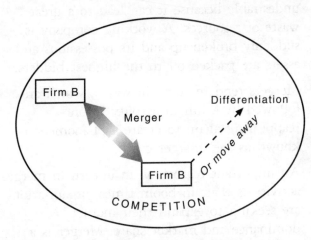

Figure 7.25 Responses to competition

bought these services from other firms instead.

However, in the first decade of the twenty-first century we are seeing (and will continue to see) mergers and take-overs taking place as multinational organisations seek to control particular product markets based on their size and the advantages this brings.

Mark Cook and Craig Meredith have defined a merger as a situation in which two or more enterprises 'cease to be distinct'. This can occur in two ways:

1 When they are brought under common ownership and control.

2 There is an agreement between the enterprises so that one of them ceases to operate. For example, company X may agree with company Y that the latter will close down operations that compete with those of company X.

A take-over is a kind of merger and occurs where one company buys a majority shareholding in another company.

It is possible to distinguish, at a general level, between full legal mergers and mergers involving only changes in the ownership of the companies concerned. A legal merger transfers the assets and liabilities of two or more companies to a single new or existing company. The companies whose assets are merged may all disappear into one new company (companies X and Y merge to form a new company Z, or one of the companies involved may absorb the other, e.g. X takes over Y).

A number of explanations have been put forward for the increasing merger activity in the UK and Europe in recent times:

• The spread of companies' global activities. For example, in the global car market there was considerable pressure for French car company Renault to take over Nissan in March 1999 in order to gain a stronger foothold in a very competitive market. Market share usually leads to competitive advantage. For a global corporation like Renault, this involves taking on giants like Ford and BMW.

- The intense pressure on organisations by shareholders to increase earnings per share. Today, shareholders (often in the form of giant financial institutions) are all too aware of the relative earnings on the different parts of their share portfolios. They will switch finance to successful organisations and divert finance away from those that are less successful.

- When the market undervalues the real value of a company and there are high real interest rates, this means profits are heavily discounted. It is therefore cheaper to buy existing companies than to expand new ones.

- Acquisitions allow established companies to change quickly and to reposition themselves. For example, when ICI wanted to move out of heavily polluting chemical plant in the late 1990s, they sold off their old 'smokestack' chemical plants and used the cash to buy new consumer chemical plants that were a lot less harmful to the environment.

- Acquisitions help companies to plug an existing gap in their current portfolio of assets (e.g. a car company may not produce a sports car but it can *buy* a sports car manufacturing company).

- Mergers can help to integrate organisations with converging technologies (i.e. bringing together two firms who are starting to use the same sorts of automated production lines).

- Acquistions help organisations to spread their sphere of influence (e.g. a UK cement producer buying companies that produce cement in Poland and France).

- To acquire the benefits of synergy. Synergy is usually explained through simple mathematics in the form of $2 + 2 = 5$. In other words, the sum of the parts working together in an effective merger are greater than the individual components involved in the merger.

Cook and Meredith argue convincingly that the motives behind mergers can be divided into four main categories:

1 Diversification.

2 The addition of new and profitable products.

3 The acquisition of management or technical personnel to overcome poor operating performance in the main business.

4 The acquisition of business that can be turned round into a profitable venture.

They also argue that opportunism is a fifth factor (i.e. when companies purchase others at a knock-down price and sell off their assets for a profit). This is called *asset stripping*. Asset stripping is particularly undesirable because it can lead to a great waste of resources. A working company is suddenly broken up and its possessions and assets are packed off to the highest bidders.

Mergers tend to come in waves, which are followed by a lull in activity before reappearing again to create a phenomenon known as the 'merger cycle'.

An important reason for an upturn in merger activity is that, in boom times, organisations are seeking to expand their market dominance and market share. Merger is a quick way to achieve market growth. In a

Case study: Demerger

November 1999 saw Tomkins (http://www.tomkins.co.uk), the diversified engineering and food conglomerate, demerge its food manufacturing division in a move that signalled the end of Britain's last remaining major conglomerate that was built up during the 1980s. (Tomkins was known in the 1980s as the 'guns to buns' group.)

The demerger followed similar moves by major conglomerates – Hanson, Williams Holdings and BTR, which split into smaller parts. During the 1970s and 1980s, a number of major business people argued that it didn't matter what business a company was in: a good management team ought to be able to get the best out of it. During this period the major conglomerates were able to buy many different companies which were underperforming at the time. It was felt that an advantage of building a conglomerate was that companies that made large profits could transfer their cash surpluses to others that needed cash for expansion but which were strapped for cash at the time.

However, business thinking changed in the second half of the 1990s and into 2000 and beyond. Now people feel businesses should be focused on what they do best. When shareholders want to buy shares in a food company, they look for a dedicated food company that is putting all its efforts into leading the food market. The old notion of guns to buns has lost its popularity.

The Chair of Tomkins explained why the move to demerger took place: . . . business is a dynamic thing. You've got to change with the times. We always follow industry developments and have decided that the time is right to focus on our industrial businesses.

1 Why has there been a recent trend to focus businesses, rather than to build conglomerates?

2 Can you think of exceptions to this rule? Why do they exist?

downturn, organisations are more concerned with cutting costs (although an effective way to do this is to merge with another organisation and to rationalise products, processes and services).

In a merger boom shareholders receive a relatively good return on capital, giving managers more funds to play around with to expand the business sphere of influence. A further explanation put forward to explain the merger cycle is that, at a time when there is a bull market for shares (there is a rush to buy), companies tend to be overvalued. The managers of companies are aware that they are overvalued on paper and they therefore seek to acquire more physical assets to justify the paper valuation of their companies.

The logic of focusing on your best lines rather than building a big conglomerate is to become the best at what you do. So in a very real sense the alternative to merger/take-over is to differentiate your product. Differentiation will be achieved by making sure you understand your market, and by meeting the requirements of the market by providing something that is better than anything rivals can offer.

Check your understanding

Study the business pages of a quality newspaper to find two examples of recent mergers. Show how these mergers have been aimed at enabling the organisations involved to manage the competitiveness of the industry in which they operate.

Looking at the same industry, choose one company not involved in the merger activity that has chosen to differentiate in order to manage the competitiveness of the industry. Explain which of these strategies you feel will be the more effective.

The effects of competition on stakeholders

The prime responsibility for an organisation is to serve its stakeholders. These are individuals and groups who have a stake in the running of the organisation and in the consequences of the organisation's activities (see Figure 7.26). stakeholder expectations will influence and shape the way in which the organisation competes in the marketplace, and the nature of competition in the marketplace will affect the organisation's stakeholders.

Figure 7.26 Stakeholders in an organisation's activities

Take the example of a company that is able to outcompete the competition in the marketplace. Figure 7.27 shows how this may affect each of the key stakeholder groupings.

High sales figures and profits enable the organisation to	pay high dividends to shareholders and the share price will rise
The achievement of profit targets and organisational objectives enables the organisation to	give profit-related pay awards to directors and managers – and managers get a great deal of personal satisfaction
Because the company is flourishing and has high order books and profits, it can	employ more workers and give higher rewards to existing workers
Because the company (it is hoped) has a good cash and profit flow	it increases orders to suppliers
Because the company has cash flowing in and a healthy profit position	it can pay creditors on time
Because the company has excess profits available for distribution	it can inject money into community projects, such as sponsorship arrangements. It is able to pay more to the government in taxes
Because the company is flourishing it has the funds available	to invest in projects that aid the wider public (e.g. better environmental management projects
Because the company is successful it	is best placed to give consumers what they want through extensive market and product research

Figure 7.27 Responses to competition

Check your understanding

Hazlewood Foods, which make sandwiches, pizzas and quiches for supermarkets, found their share price fell from 240p in late 1998 to 95p in late 1999. The problem for Hazlewood was pressure from the supermarkets, which were funding a price war by pressing their suppliers for better terms. Sales to the top-five supermarkets account for 60% of Hazlewood's turnover, with the bulk in pizzas, sandwiches and ready-made meals. The problem for Hazlewood was that, while they were able to sell more, they had to do so at lower prices – leading to a loss for the company.

How might the increased competition in the supermarket sector have affected each of the stakeholder groupings involved with Hazlewood Foods?

The changing patterns of industry

Industrial activity is often broken down into three sectors:

1 Primary extractive.

2 Secondary manufacturing and construction.

3 Tertiary services.

Primary industries are concerned with using natural resources. These include farming, mining and oil drilling. Farmers grow and harvest crops and farm livestock, while miners take out fuel and minerals from the ground.

Secondary industries are concerned with making and assembling products. Manufacturers use raw materials and parts from other industries. A semi-manufactured good is one that is only partly made. Most products go through several stages of production. Examples of manufactured products are furniture, cars, chocolate and oil rigs.

Tertiary (service) industries are particularly important in Britain today. Services give something of value to people but are not physical goods. You can physically touch or see a sandwich, a car or a television set but you cannot touch or hold in your hand life insurance or the protection offered by the police.

Many experts talk about three waves of industrial development. In the first wave, countries are dominated by agriculture and farming. This was the case in Britain until the Industrial Revolution of the late eighteenth and early nineteenth centuries.

In the second wave, countries are dominated by manufacturing (when industries such as coal, steel, car manufacture and shipbuilding become important). In the third wave (sometimes called postindustrial society), services become the most important sector of the economy, with many people working in insurance, banking, office administration, leisure and similar industries. Today, services produce more than 70% of the value of all goods in the USA, Britain and France, and just over 60% in Germany and Japan.

The last 100 years have seen a reduction in jobs requiring physical strength and stamina, with increasing mechanisation and decreasing employment in agriculture, manufacturing and mining. This has led to more opportunities for women. Therefore, the last 100 years have seen a steady increase in women at work, leading to nearly 50% of the workforce currently being female. It is predicted that the next 100 years will see the skills women bring to the workforce (i.e. flexibility, creativity and intuition) becoming increasingly important.

The growth in women at work should level off rather than increase dramatically over the next 100 years. Predictions possibly overestimate the attraction of work for women as a personal liberator and do not take account of the likelihood that childcare arrangements will not be able to keep pace with what would be needed to maximise female participation.

As we move into the twenty-first century we find that predictions that clerical and secretarial jobs would have disappeared as a result of the advance of ICT have proved false. In reality, these jobs are only just beginning to level off. The advent of computers has meant that people can concentrate on being more human, developing and using caring and creative skills now they have been released from more mechanical functions.

New industry sectors appeared in the last century, including the media and airline industries. The last 100 years have also seen the creation of many new jobs, including:

- TV/radio presenters
- Market researchers
- PR consultants
- Management consultants
- Airline pilots
- Computer programmers.

The skills required up to the year 2100 will probably fit into the following categories:

- The managers, who will sit at the heart of virtual organisations providing the driving force and the vision.

- The knowledge workers with applied scientific and technical knowledge and good information management skills.

- The tutors. Whilst many of the additional educational requirements of the next 100 years may be met by virtual reality and tele-presence, we will still need those who excel at teaching, especially teaching people how to learn as well as simply imparting knowledge.

- The service workers for those jobs that will always require a human interface and for jobs that facilitate the lives of knowledge workers and managers, many of which may equate to the domestic service jobs of the turn of the last century.

- The care workers – the sector where most growth is predicted to occur.

Check your understanding

Explain why each of the industries listed in Figure 7.28 has grown by the figures shown.

Industry	Change (%)
Agriculture	−15
Mining, etc.	−35
Utilities	−26
Metal, minerals, etc.	−17
Engineering	−18
Chemicals	−6
Motor vehicles	−5
Food, drink and tobacco	−25
Textiles and clothing	−23
Other manufacturing	−10
Construction	+5
Distribution, etc.	+6
Transport and communication	−5
Banking, insurance and business services	+10
Miscellaneous services	+31
Health and education	+21
Public administration	+5

Figure 7.28 Changes in industry growth, 1991–2001

Explain how the figures shown illustrate the process of moving to a postindustrial society.

Chapter 8 How business is affected by government policy

Competition has both positive and negative effects on the stakeholders of a business – for example, the customers, employees, shareholders, suppliers and the community. You need to understand how and why the government intervenes to influence the effects of business activity on the market. You need to know about the work of the Competition Commission and understand the ways in which the government acts to protect consumers. You also need to understand how and why the government becomes involved in environmental, social and ethical issues.

You will need to explain the role the European Union plays in social and environmental policy.

The government plays a key role in establishing economic policy. It also tries to manage the economy to control the effects of market changes on stakeholders. You need to be able to analyse the impact on businesses of government policies for controlling inflation, unemployment and growth, and to evaluate the responses of businesses to those policies. You also need to be able to explain how businesses are affected by policies towards:

- taxation
- benefits, subsidies and grants
- exchange rates
- public sector services
- changes in interest rates (under the control of the Bank of England).

You need to be able to describe the extent to which businesses can be affected by these policies (for example, the extent to which increases in taxes are passed on from businesses to consumers).

The need for government

If societies are to work as groups of people co-operating together, they will be best placed to create common solutions to common problems. We can illustrate the need for co-operation in the following way. Imagine there are two cars heading for each other on a collision course. Each driver can veer to the left or to the right. If both veer to the right or both veer to the left, a collision is avoided. Therefore there needs to be some form of co-ordination of the decisions of the two drivers if the worst possible situation is to be avoided.

Co-operation can be made effective by establishing social institutions, in this case, rules and conventions about driving on the left- or right-hand side of the road. The *Highway Code* 'codifies' UK driving rules and regulations. The co-operation that results from all UK drivers obeying the *Highway Code* leads to benefits for all.

If people concentrate on just looking after their own interests, this may be harmful to society as a whole. What is best for me alone might not be best for the whole community. Fisherfolk who consider no interests but their own may quickly deplete an essential national and international resource by overfishing, so that the stocks of fish dwindle.

To achieve the benefits of co-operation it is essential to have a referee or umpire who makes sure all parties in society keep to rules that are of benefit to the whole community. Societies, therefore, create laws to govern dealings between people. An important role of government is to make new laws to help smooth the relationships between members of society.

Check your understanding

Give three examples of the anti-social behaviour of businesses that need to be controlled by government legislation (law-making).

The ways governments are chosen and operate

This section provides you with an introduction to the way governments are chosen and operate in the UK. It is important to have this sort of background before going on to look more closely at the reasons for government intervention in markets, and the means by which governments can influence markets.

The electoral system

In this country citizens are able to choose people to represent them at a number of levels. At a national level, they can choose Members of Parliament. MPs represent people who live in a particular area (a constituency). Who is your local MP? What is your local constituency? What political party does your local MP belong to?

At a European Union level, electors can choose Euro-MPs. The European Parliament is one of the three major union institutions. It is the only directly elected institution, so it is particularly important that all European citizens exercise their right to vote. (The Maastricht Treaty gave the European Parliament more powers, as we shall see in Chapter 9.) Who is your Euro-MP? What party does he or she belong to? What is your Euro-constituency?

At a local level, you can vote for local councillors. The local council is concerned with affairs in your locality. What is your local council area? Who is your local councillor? What party does he or she belong to?

The electoral system for national government

In the British electoral system, the country is divided into 651 single-member constituencies. Representatives are elected to Parliament by the first-past-the-post (simple majority) method, which awards seats in the House of Commons to candidates with the largest number of votes in each constituency. The boundaries of the constituencies are reviewed every 10–15 years to take account of population movements or other changes.

The government is said to have the electorate's mandate – the right to govern based on legal or moral force. This is because:

- Electors choose between parties at least in part on the basis of their programmes, i.e., their policies and plans for what they will do if they get into government.

- Such programmes are distinguishable from each other, so they offer electors a basis for choice.

- The party or parties that form the next government have the responsibility to carry out their programme (this is a major basis on which they have been elected).

- They also have the authority to carry out their programme in government, as it has been selected by at least a sizeable number of electors as the best short-term programme for the country.

- Parties do, in the main, carry through the main components of their programmes when in government.

Forming a government

The party that wins most seats at a general election, or that has the support of a majority of members in the House of Commons, is usually invited by the Sovereign to form a government. The party with the next largest number of seats is officially recognised as 'Her Majesty's Opposition'. This party has its own leader (who is paid a salary from public funds) and its own 'shadow Cabinet'. Members of both parties, or any independent MPs who have been elected, support or oppose the government according to their party or their own view of the policy being debated at any given time. Because the official Opposition is a minority party, it seldom succeeds in introducing or changing legislation. However, its statements and policies are important, since it is considered to be a potential government – and would

become so if successful at the next general election.

The law

Parliament is responsible for creating new laws. These can affect the ways in which markets operate and so can affect businesses. If the government raises income tax, for example, people have less money to spend, which affects sales. Government actions bring into play a wide range of changes to taxes. These changes then become law through a Finance Bill, which becomes an Act of Parliament (a new law).

Over the years a complex system of laws has developed. Some laws have not come from Parliament but have arisen through common practice. It is often impossible to find out when these laws first came into being (this is called 'common law'). An example of this is the right of people to walk on a particular village green. Other laws are new laws passed by Parliament (this is called 'statute law').

The law courts play an important role in protecting the rights of individuals and groups. When the law of the land has been broken, cases are taken to the criminal courts; when there is a disagreement between groups or individuals, the case may be taken before a civil court.

Government intervention in markets
Market failure

Markets working on their own are unlikely to create economic efficiency. There will be a tendency for too much of some goods to be produced and too little of others. In the extreme case of complete market failure, the market will fail to exist so that certain goods will not be produced at all. The chief cause of market failure is the inability of individuals to work co-operatively.

The causes of market failure include the following.

Poor information

Buyers and sellers are not clear about what goods are available in the marketplace and at what prices. The government often plays a role in helping to inform consumers about what is available to them – particularly in the case of those in greatest need who may not be taking up entitlements required for healthy living because they do not know what is available to them.

The government also creates laws that protect consumers against exploitation by producers (e.g. where sellers give false information to buyers).

Externalities

The act of producing some goods and services has knock-on harmful effects, such as noise, waste, dereliction, etc. Externalities exist when the actions of consumers and producers also affect third parties. In a free market, how could we make people pay for the costs created by externalities? The government, therefore, often intervenes to tax and fine business organisations for creating such externalities as pollution and other forms of waste.

Public goods

Public goods are goods for which, at any output, consumption by extra consumers does not reduce the quantity available for consumption by existing consumers. For example, when you listen to the BBC news on the radio, you are not preventing anyone

else from listening to the same programme. (Contrast this with a sandwich which you buy and eat – no one else can eat the same sandwich!) Examples of pure public goods include the peace and security of a community; national defence; the law; air pollution control; fire protection; street lighting; weather forecasts; and public television. If we take the example of peace and security, it would be very difficult to make people pay privately for a police service everyone benefits from – hence the need for provision by the government (or at least by government funding).

Imperfect competition

Competition in the marketplace does not take place on equal terms between competitors. Some firms are much larger than others and are able to sell goods in bulk at lower prices. Because of their size, they are often able to 'see off' competitors. Once they are in a position of power, they can start to exploit the consumers. Hence there is a role for government in creating fair competitive conditions.

Uncertainty

In the marketplace, consumers and producers may be unwilling to make products or to carry out transactions when they cannot see into the future. The government often takes a long-term view – for example, investing in major infrastructural projects which private business may be reluctant to touch.

A historical view of government intervention

In the nineteenth century, the UK government played only a small part in the control of the economy. Today, the proper role of the government is open to debate, but most people accept it should at least try to influence economic activity. Why has this change in attitude taken place? We shall look at some of the more important reasons.

Widespread unemployment in the 1920s and 1930s

March of the Unemployed, London, 1930

In some towns in the 1920s, over half the potential labour force were unemployed. Many people felt, in the light of the terrible suffering during this period, that the government should play a central role in creating and sustaining employment. Preventing mass unemployment became the priority of the years after the Second World War. Between 1945 and 1979, there was a much stronger emphasis on the government taking more and more decisions about the economy.

Rapid inflation in the 1970s

The 1970s was a period of rapid increases in prices. People felt the effect of inflation in different ways depending, amongst other things, on how much power they had to raise their own incomes to cope with price rises.

The general effect of price rises is to distort the working of the price system. Trading, ideally, needs to take place in settled conditions. If you expected to be paid £100 in three months' time you would be very disappointed if you found that, when you received payment you could purchase only half the goods you would have been able to afford those three months earlier.

If people become reluctant to trade, fewer goods will be produced for sale. If fewer goods are made, fewer people are employed in production. Price disturbances can therefore cause the whole economy to stagnate.

From 1979 (when Margaret Thatcher came into government), the emphasis in government policy switched very much from worrying about unemployment to trying to cut out inflation.

The privatisation years

The years of Conservative rule (1979–1997) were ones in which the government sought to reduce the role of the state in the economy (i.e. to reduce government taxation and spending). One of the main ways of removing government interference was through the policy of privatisation – selling back government-owned industries to private shareholders.

This was a good way for the government to raise finance without having to tax people.

The new economy

At the beginning of the new century, some economists are talking about the arrival of a 'new economy'. The new economy is one of mass production resulting from the widespread use of new technologies across nearly every industry. The microchip has revolutionised the ways in which businesses are run. By creating great increases in the production of goods, it has become possible to cut down inflation to very low levels. At the same time (early 2000), we have seen an increase in the job creation ability of the economy, particularly in the new hi-tech industries, as well as lots of part-time jobs across the economy generally.

So far the policy of the Blair government has been to seek to keep inflation down while, at the same time, to encourage people to take up new jobs. The Blair government does not believe in widespread government interference in the economy in the way that Labour administrations since the Second World War did. The current government is, however, seeking to switch resources in particular directions (e.g. to get more money for education and for the public transport system by, for example, heavy taxes on car users).

Government involvement in the marketplace

In this section we look at reasons why government involves itself in ensuring competitive conditions in the marketplace.

To increase competition

Competition is seen by many as a major driving force behind the market system. Competition between producers in the marketplace keeps prices down and ensures goods are produced in line with consumer requirements. If a baker tried to charge more than competitors, trade would disappear; or if employees asked for more than the going wage, they would not be able to find work. If landlords sought to exact a higher rent than others with property of the same quality, they would get no tenants.

Governments should ensure competition can take place freely between competitors. The

more competition the better, because this will lead to better-quality products and lower prices, and acts as an incentive for producers to be better than their rivals.

Regulating competition

Whilst many people argue that competition is a good thing, they might also argue that there need to be guidelines and rules within which the competitive framework can operate. For example, whilst it may be beneficial to encourage competition between taxi firms, it is essential they abide by health and safety regulations (e.g. concerning the number of people allowed in a cab at any one time or the maximum length of time a driver can drive without having a break).

National government and EU regulations provide a framework for competition in many markets. For example, while recent EU policies have encouraged competition between airlines on European routes, there are given standards airlines must meet before they are allowed to carry passengers.

In recent years we have seen an increase in competition in industries such as gas, water and electricity. Regulators have been appointed to oversee the way in which new companies operate in these markets.

The large City of London markets such as Lloyd's of London and the Stock Exchange need to be carefully regulated to ensure fair trading practices are in operation.

Counteracting anti-competitive activities

Anti-competitive activities come in a variety of forms. Examples include:

- Firms jointly agreeing to fix prices.

- Firms jointly agreeing who they will be prepared to supply goods and services to.

- Selling goods at one price to a particular group of customers, and at a higher price to another group.

- Limiting supply in order to raise price.

- Forcing rivals out of business by ensuring their supplies are cut off.

All these practices and many others involve the abuse of power in the marketplace and run counter to the principles of competition.

Ensuring fair and honest trading

In business dealings it is important that all transactions are carried out in a fair and honest manner. Parties to bargains need to be clear about what they are committing themselves to and the consequences of making a deal or exchange. The government is responsible for establishing the legal framework within which trade takes place.

Protecting consumers

Any product or services that are provided to the marketplace must meet certain standards. Some of these standards are established by law, some by voluntary codes of practice within an industry and others by individual businesses.

Check your understanding

In which of the following instances might the government be expected to intervene to increase competition, to encourage fair trading or to protect consumers? Explain why the government is likely to be involved.

1 A supplier agrees to provide a retailer with a given product for three months at a set price.

2 Suppliers agree to stop supplying a particular retailer who is cutting prices below those of other retailers.

3 Textile businesses engaged in cut-throat competition start employing child labour at very low wage rates.

4 Electrical suppliers sell cheaply produced, faulty goods to buyers.

5 Market traders use weighing scales they have designed themselves to measure out quantities of fruit and vegetables.

6 One firm is the sole supplier of goods in a considerable area of the country.

7 Two firms agree to split up a region so that one firm will sell goods in half the towns and the other will sell in the other half.

Case study: Drug firms to face price probe

In November 1999, the Office of Fair Trading (html//:www.oft.gov) was asked by the government to find out why the cost of some drugs had soared over the previous year. Examples included the antibiotic amoxycillin, up from 21p in 1998 to £1.26 in 1999. Rocketing prices like this were estimated to be costing the NHS £200 million a year.

Genuine supply problems had initially caused shortages of some of the tablets, but government ministers want trading watchdogs to investigate whether 'middlemen', such as traders and wholesalers, could have jumped on the bandwagon to hoard supplies, forcing up the price and driving doctors to use ever more expensive alternatives.

Pharmaceutical firms vehemently denied inflating prices. However, government health ministers asked the OFT to investigate the price explosion in generic drugs. Generics are established medicines that can be produced by any firm. They are cheaper than new branded drugs, which are licensed only to the firms that developed them.

Competition between rival firms usually keeps generic prices down, so doctors are urged by the Department of Health to use them wherever possible, to save money. When a generic drug becomes difficult to obtain, the government puts it on a list alerting doctors and pharmacists they may use the more expensive branded version. The number of drugs on this list rose from 30 in the autumn of 1998 to 190 in November 1999.

1   What evidence is given that the market for generic drugs was becoming less competitive?

2   How might this have come about?

3   What might be the dangers of such a development?

4   What is the role of government in this case?

Before the 1960s, consumers had very little protection under the law. They had to rely on their own common sense. The Latin expression *caveat emptor* (let the buyer beware) applied.

Businesses supply goods or services for consumers in return for payment. The legal system exists to provide a framework within which transactions can take place, and to provide a means of settling disputes. Large or well-developed organisations often deal with relatively small consumers, so there is a need for the law to make sure that this inequality in bargaining power is not abused.

Environmental, ethical and social interests

In recent times we have become increasingly conscious of our shared responsibilities for the environment.

Gro Brundtland (*Our Common Future*, 1987) defined sustainability as 'development which meets the need of the present without compromising the ability of future generations to meet their own needs'. In *The Pearce Report*, David Pearce argued that 'sustainability ought to mean that a given stock of natural resources – trees, soil quality, water and so on – should not decline'. Many people believe that, left to its own drives and forces, the market might fail to take account of the need for sustainability.

As the environment tends to be seen as a free good because it is often not priced, it tends to be used up without consideration of the implications. For example, businesses and individuals in pursuit of their own private ends may exploit resources too quickly. A famous quotation from Mahatma Gandhi (*Young India*) is relevant here:

God forbid that India should ever take to industrialisation after the manner of the West. The economic imperialism of a single tiny island kingdom [Britain] is today keeping the world in chains. If an entire nation of 300 million took to similar economic exploitation, it would strip the world bare like locusts.

Government therefore has a key role to play in helping the market to create a sustainable future by taking measures to protect the environment, as well as to look after social interests (such as protecting the poor and needy from exploitation by the powerful).

Case study: Driving out road congestion

In 1999–2000, the government became more serious about intervening in the market in its attempts to stop traffic congestion by taxing motorists more heavily. We can illustrate how this works by taking the example of London.

London is the most densely populated city in the UK, or indeed (excluding Brussels) in Europe. For two hours a day the city more or less seizes up as Underground and road systems operate at or beyond capacity. London clogs up with frazzled commuters from outside, and the statistics show that even London dwellers themselves take longer to get to work than people living in any other part of the country.

The solution to the problem has been for government bodies to penalise car users. The dynamic of congestion charging, provided for in the Greater London Authority Act and in various Transport Bills, works like this. Drivers are dissuaded from using their cars by the charging of fees for entering crowded areas. Those who go on driving provide the revenue to improve public transport.

In addition, there might be increasing use of workplace parking taxes.

Of course, major critics of this scheme argue that the public transport scheme in London should be improved first. Taxes act as a 'push' factor on travellers. It would be better to work on them through the 'pull' factor of better public transport.

1 Why might these new taxes on motorists be imposed in London?
2 Do you think this is a good idea?
3 What should come first – push or pull?

In addition to environmental concerns the government can – and should – play an important part in ensuring appropriate social and ethical requirements are met by business. For example, from 1997 onwards we saw the Labour government introduce a raft of new measures to protect employees in the workplace in line with European Union requirements. In 1999 the government introduced minimum wage legislation and applied the Working Time Directive, which guaranteed all employees a maximum working week of 48 hours and also guaranteed everyone, including part-time workers, an annual four weeks' holiday.

Ethics are sets of moral principles, that are generally agreed by members of a society at a particular moment in time. Ethical concerns include not exploiting suppliers in developing countries or the use of child labour.

Case study: Child labour

The Labour Secretary of State for International Development, Clare Short, made the following remarks about the employment of child labour in a speech in December 1999:

There are national and international laws on child labour agreed by the International Labour Organisation [ILO] in Geneva. This represents governments, business and trade unions from all the countries of the world.

The problem is that in the poorest countries these laws are not implemented. The ILO needs to do more to ensure these are put into practice and stuck to.

We must also encourage governments of poor countries to devote more energy to getting children into school and improving the job opportunities of their parents.

So what can be done to help solve the problem? In Sialkot, Pakistan, we are working with Save The Children on tackling child labour in the football stitching industry.

It's a ground-breaking project, involving business, the ILO and local charities. It helps children to stop working and get an education, while money-earning schemes ensure their families can survive without their children's earnings.

In Bangladesh – where the problem of child labour is appalling – we are working with the Bangladeshi Government and UNICEF to provide basic education for working children.

Through the Ethical Trading initiative we are supporting many of Britain's biggest retailers in ensuring their suppliers are not exploiting children. These firms are committed to ensuring children's lives are improved, not to throwing them into poverty in order to clean up the companies' images.

Trade sanctions punish the poor because they prevent poor countries from selling their goods abroad. Instead, we would prefer there to be closer co-operation between the ILO, the World Bank and other agencies to get children into school and their parents into work.

If we are to help the 150 million children in Asia and the 100 million in Africa and elsewhere in the world, we must make sure that everyone understands the reality of the situation.

Trade sanctions and boycotts will not end child labour, they will make life worse for the poorest children of the world.

1 Why is the issue of employing child labour an 'ethical one'?

2 What role do you think the government should have in relation to business practice involving the use of child labour?

3 Do you agree with Clare Short's view that resorting to trade sanctions is not the appropriate solution to this problem?

The government and competition policy

Competition policy exists to encourage and improve the competitive process and it shows no favours to individual firms. Instead, it sets out to intervene to protect individuals and organisations against unfair practices. The law provides a number of ways of helping to create more effective competition, to punish those who act unfairly and to protect those who have been wronged.

A case-by-case approach

Competition policy is there to protect the 'public interest'. Individual incidents are examined using a 'case-by-case' approach to decide whether public interest is threatened or not.

Competition is not regarded as an end in itself. In most cases the law makes no pre-judgement that actions which reduce competition are wrong in themselves. It must be found out whether it would be against the public interest to reduce competition in a specific case (see Figure 8.1).

The Competition Commission

The Competition Commission is a public body established by the Competition Act 1998. It replaced the Monopolies and Mergers Commission (MMC) on 1 April 1999.

The commission has two sides to its work: a reporting side that has taken on the former MMC role, and an appeals side that

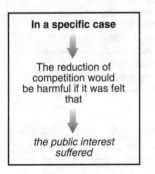

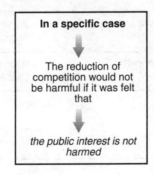

Figure 8.1 A case-by-case approach to competition

The Secretary of State is a government minister with a particular area of responsibility – e.g. the Secretary of State for Trade and Industry (who, in this case, has overall responsibility for competition policy – among other things). The minister will be a key figure in government, sitting in on Cabinet meetings with the Prime Minister and other senior ministers to make key policy decisions in the economy.

The Director General of Fair Trading (DGFT) is appointed by the Secretary of State for Industry to take overall responsibility for creating a climate of competition in this country. The Director General heads the Office of Fair Trading, which is a government department. This is a non-political (independent) post.

Public Utility Regulators When a number of formerly nationalised industries were privatised, independent regulators were created to make sure that the new private firms controlling these industries do so in a way that creates a competitive climate and one where consumers are protected. Examples of regulatory bodies are OFWAT (water services), and OFTEL (telecommunications).

Figure 8.2 The Competition Commission: useful terms

will hear appeals against decisions made under the prohibition provisions of the new Competition Act.

Reporting side

The MMC's role was to investigate and report on matters referred to it relating to mergers, monopolies, anti-competitive practices, the regulation of utilities and the performance of public sector bodies. The MMC could not initiate its own inquiries. Most referrals were made by the Director General of Fair Trading (DGFT), the Secretary of State for Trade and Industry, and the regulators of utilities (see Figure 8.2). In almost all cases, the MMC was asked to

decide whether the matter referred was against the public interest (see Figure 8.3).

Appeals side

The prohibitions set out in the Competition Act 1998 are modelled on European Community competition law. Essentially, there is a prohibition on agreements or joint practices that prevent, restrict or distort competition in the UK. However, the Director General of Fair Trading and the utility regulators will be able to grant exemptions in individual cases and the Secretary of State will be able to grant exemptions of general application. There is also a prohibition on conduct that amounts

Type of inquiry	Governing legislation/referral made by	Type of inquiry	Governing legislation/referral made by
Monopoly	*Fair Trading Act 1973* Director General of Fair Trading, Secretary of State or certain utility regulators	**Utility references** Telecommunications	*Telecommunications Act 1984* Director General of Telecommunications
Merger	*Fair Trading Act 1973* Director General of Fair Trading, Secretary of State or certain utility regulators	Gas	*Gas Acts 1986 and 1995* Director General of Gas Supply
Newspaper merger	*Fair Trading Act 1973* Secretary of State	Water	*Water Industry Act 1991* Director General of Water Services
Anti-competitive practices	*Competition Act 1980* Director General of Fair Trading or certain utility regulators	Electricity	*Electricity Act 1989* Director General of Electricity Supply
Public sector references	*Competition Act 1980* Secretary of State	Railways	*Railways Act 1994* Rail Regulator
General references	*Fair Trading Act 1973* Secretary of State	Water merger	*Water Industry Act 1991* Secretary of State
Restrictive labour practices	*Fair Trading Act 1973* Secretary of State	Airports	*Airports Act 1986* Civil Aviation Authority
Broadcasting	*Broadcasting Act 1980* Independent Television Commission or holder of regional channel 3 licence		

Figure 8.3   Possible sources of investigations

to abuse of a dominant position in the UK. These prohibitions came into effect from 1 March 2000 and are enforced by the DFGT and the utility regulators. If it is found that a company has breached a prohibition, it may be required to pay a penalty of up to 10% of UK turnover (of that company).

An appeal can be made to the commission against certain decisions made under the prohibition provisions. While the detailed provisions are complex, they essentially include appeals against decisions on whether a prohibition has been breached, the amount of a penalty and whether an individual exemption should be granted or cancelled. In most cases, an appeal can be made not only by the party directly affected by the decision but also by anyone with a sufficient interest, such as competitors and customers.

European Community competition law

The main European Community (EC) competition law of relevance to the Competition Commission's work comprises Articles 81 and 82 of the Treaty of Rome and regulation on the control of mergers.

Article 81 (1) prohibits all agreements and concerted practices that might affect trade between member states and that have as their object or effect the prevention, restriction or distortion of competition within the Common Market.

Article 82 prohibits any undertaking from abusing a dominant position it enjoys in so far as it may affect trade between member states.

The EC adopted a regulation on the control of mergers in 1989 that came into force on 21 September 1990. Under the regulation, mergers with a Community dimension are subject to the exclusive jurisdiction of the European Commission.

Broadly, this means that mergers involving parties with a combined worldwide turnover of more than 5 billion ecu (around £4.2 billion) are subject to the control of the authorities within the European Union, provided that the EC turnover of each of at least two undertakings involved exceeds 250 million ecu (around £210 million) and the undertakings concerned do not have at least two-thirds of their EC turnover from the same member state.

Mergers which are not caught by the EC merger regulation remain subject to national competition law.

Some mergers with a Community dimension may be reviewed by the national authorities. Under Article 9 of the regulation, a member state can ask the European Commission to refer a merger back to its national competition authorities for investigation. In these cases, the member state must demonstrate to the European Commission that the merger threatens to create, or strengthen, a dominant position as a result of which effective competition would be significantly impeded in a distinct market in the member state.

After preliminary inquiries, it is decided whether to deal with the matter at a European level or to refer the case to the authorities of the member state concerned with a view to the application of national competition law. For example, the proposed joint venture between Steetley PLC and Tarmac PLC in March 1992, and also the proposed acquisition of Lloyds Chemist PLC by GEHE AG, were referred back to the UK in March 1996.

Article 21 (3) of the regulation allows member states to take appropriate measures to protect legitimate interests, other than those taken into consideration by the regulation, such as public security, plurality of the media or prudential controls.

Organisation and structure of the Competition Commission

The commission is made up of members and staff, headed by a chairperson. A President of the Appeal Tribunals, who is also a member of the commission, is responsible for the commission's appeal functions. The chair and members of the commission are appointed by the Secretary of State for Trade and Industry following open competition. With the exception of the chair, members are part time (see Figure 8.4).

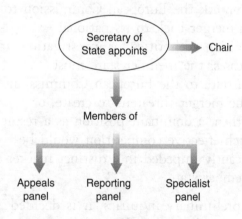

Figure 8.4   The structure of the Competition Commission

The commission represents a wealth of experience as members are drawn from many walks of life, including business, the professions, trade unions and the academic world. Members are appointed for their diversity of background, individual experience and ability, and not as representatives of particular organisations, interests or political parties. They are normally appointed for an initial term of three years and are eligible for re-appointment.

The commission is made up of an appeals panel, a reporting panel and specialist panels. Members of the appeal panel hear appeals against prohibition decisions, and members of the reporting panel will assist in some of the regulatory enquiries. A member can be appointed to all three panels.

How the reporting panel operates

The commission chair appoints a group of members for individual reporting enquiries. A group will typically be made up of five members. Inquiries by the reporting panel of the Competition Commission will essentially adopt the working procedures of the MMC. Merger inquiries will usually take three months; others take six months to a year.

The commission submits a report (to the secretary of state or the regulator) that sets out the background to the inquiry, a detailed analysis of the industry and fully reasoned conclusions and recommendations. The consequence of a commission report will depend on the legislation under which the reference was made. If the commission decides a matter does not operate against the public interest, that decision is normally final. If, however, the commission finds a matter is against the public interest, its recommendations are, in most cases, not binding on the secretary of state or regulator.

How the appeals panel operates

The President of the Appeal Tribunals appoints members of the appeals panel to tribunals. Each tribunal consists of a legally qualified Chair and two other members.

An appeals tribunal may uphold or quash the decision or fine against which the appeal had been made, may vary them or, in some circumstances, may refer the matter back to the DGFT or the regulator concerned.

The Competition Commission has a staff of about 90, the most senior of whom is the Secretary to the Competition Commission. The staff include administrators and specialists (such as accountants, economists, industrial advisers and lawyers) as well as those engaged in support services. About two-thirds are direct employees, most of the remainder being on loan from government departments.

Check your understanding

1 What major new function has been added to the Competition Commission that did not exist under the former Monopolies and Mergers Commission?

2 What is prohibited by Article 81 (1) of the Treaty of Rome?

3 What scale of merger activity is EC competition law concerned with?

4 Who deals with mergers that are not of a sufficient scale to be dealt with at EC level?

5 Who appoints members of the Competition Commission?

6 Study the press to find a report relating to the work of the Competition Commission. How has the commission been involved in the issue reported?

Consumer protection

Any product or service that is provided to the marketplace must meet certain standards. Some of these standards are established by law, some by voluntary codes of practice within an industry and others are set by individual businesses.

Businesses supply goods or services for consumers in return for payment. The legal system exists to provide a framework within which transactions can take place, and to provide a means of settling disputes.

How do disputes arise?

(See Figure 8.5.)

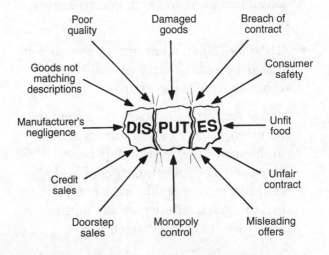

Figure 8.5   Some causes of disputes

- *Damaged or poor-quality goods*. It quite often happens that purchased goods do not function properly. They may have been damaged in transit or they may be of a poor standard and not suitable for the purpose for which they are intended.

- *Goods not matching descriptions*. Goods may not be as described on the packaging or in an advertisement.

- *Manufacturer's negligence*. Faulty manufacturing processes or bad design might lead to the personal injury of the consumer or damage to other goods. For example, a faulty electrical component might cause fire.

- *Breach of contract*. This could include the failure of the supplier to supply, a failure to meet the required quality or a failure to supply by a given date. For example, a shop selling bridal gowns might fail to supply the dress by the agreed date.

- *Consumer safety*. Goods may not be safe and could cause injury to customers.

- *Unfit food*. Eating unfit food can have particularly unpleasant consequences and consumers need to be protected against this.

- *Misleading offers*. Consumers can easily be misled by offers, bargains and their rights concerning sales items.

- *Unfair contracts*. Contracts may contain exclusion clauses or disclaimers that might make the relationship between the buyer and the seller unreasonable. It would be unacceptable for a company to disclaim responsibility for an injury caused by its own negligence.

- *Doorstep sales*. There need to be guidelines to protect clients who might have been intimidated into buying goods from doorstep salespeople, particularly if these goods are expensive and have been bought on credit.

- *Credit sales*. Customers 'buying now and paying later' over an extended period leave themselves open to abuse. They could well be charged excessive interest rates, pay large administration costs or be tied to an expensive maintenance agreement.

Legal processes in consumer protection

Consumers may need help to ensure they get a fair deal when making a transaction with an organisation. Various Acts of Parliament set out to ensure organisations honour their responsibilities.

The criminal justice system deals with cases where the laws of the country have been broken. These laws attempt to protect members of society and to punish offenders whose actions have been harmful to the community. Cases might, for example, be brought to court for dishonesty or for selling unhygienic foodstuffs. Punishment could be fines, imprisonment or both.

Civil law is concerned with disputes between individuals and groups (see Figure 8.6). Civil laws have been built up over the years, dealing with buying and selling activities. Laws related to contracts set out the obligations individuals have to each other every time they enter into an agreement. The law of torts, on the other hand, protects individuals and groups from others' actions, particularly if an individual or group suffers injury as a result of these actions. Individuals and groups enforce their rights by suing in the civil courts.

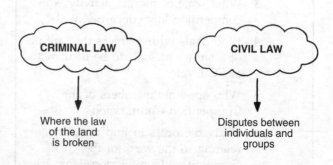

Figure 8.6 Criminal and civil law

Case study: Acts of Parliament covering the quality of goods or services

There are a number of Acts of Parliament drawn up to protect you – the buyer.

The Sale of Goods Act 1893 and 1979

This Act states that goods must be:

- 'Of merchantable quality' – i.e. free from significant faults, excepting faults that are drawn to your attention by the seller (for instance, if goods are declared to be 'shop soiled').

- 'Fit for the purpose' – including any particular purpose mentioned by you to the seller. For example, if you ask for a jumper that is machine-washable, you should not be sold one that has to be hand-washed.

Figure 8.7 Unfit for its purpose?

- 'As described' – i.e. on the package or sales literature, or verbally by the seller. If you are told a shirt is 100% cotton, it should not turn out to be a mixture of cotton and polyester.

Any good you buy from any sort of trader (e.g. shop, street market, mail order, or door-to-door salesperson) should meet these basic requirements. They also apply to food and goods bought in sales (see Figure 8.7).

What to do if things go wrong

If there is something wrong with what you buy, you should tell the seller as soon as possible. Exactly what you are entitled to depends on how serious the fault is and how soon the goods are returned.

If you return faulty goods straight away, you should be able to get your money back. You have not legally 'accepted' the goods, and this means you can 'reject' them (i.e. refuse to accept them). You can still reject goods even if you have taken them home, provided you examine and try them out as soon as possible, and then take them back at once (or within a few days of purchase).

What is acceptance?

When you take faulty goods back to the seller, you may be offered a replacement or a free repair. You do not have to agree to this. You can insist on having your money back. If you agree to a repair, you may have problems getting all your money back later if the fault is not sorted out, because, in law, you will have accepted the goods. If you accept a credit note, you will not usually be able to exchange it for cash later on.

Once you have 'accepted goods' in the legal sense, you lose your right to a full refund. You can claim only compensation.

'Acceptance' normally happens when you have kept the goods beyond a reasonable time. The law does not lay down any fixed periods for what is considered 'reasonable' – it depends on the goods and the circumstances. But you would generally be expected to make it clear to the seller you are rejecting the goods as soon as possible after purchase.

Buyers' rights

Buyers should not be put off by traders trying to talk their way out of their legal responsibilities. The law says it is up to the seller to deal with complaints about defective goods, so the seller should not try to lay the blame on the manufacturer.

As a buyer, you have the same rights even if you lose your receipt. A receipt, however, is useful evidence of where and when you bought the goods.

You may be able to claim compensation if you suffer loss because of faulty goods – for example, if a faulty iron ruins your blouse or trousers.

Buying a service

When you pay for a service (for example, from a dry cleaner, travel agent, car mechanic, hairdresser or builder), you are entitled to certain standards.

A service should be carried out:

- *With reasonable care and skill*. The job should be done to a proper standard of workmanship. If you have a dress made for a special occasion, it should not fray or come apart at the seams for no reason.

- *Within a reasonable time*. If you have to have your hi-fi system repaired, it should not take weeks and weeks. You can always agree upon a definite completion time with the supplier of the service.

- *At a reasonable charge, if no price has been fixed in advance*. However, if the price is fixed at the outset, or you have agreed some other way of working out the charge, you cannot complain later it was unreasonable.

Other Acts of Parliament

Other consumer laws established by the government to protect the consumer include the following:

- *The Trade Descriptions Act 1968*, which prohibits false or misleading descriptions of a product's contents, effects or price. It affects packaging, advertising and promotional materials.

- *The Weights and Measures Act 1963 and 1985*, which sets out to ensure consumers receive the actual quantity of a product they believe they are buying. For example, prepacked items must have a declaration of the quantity contained within the pack.

- *The Food and Drugs Act*, which covers the contents of food and medicines.

- *The Food Safety Act*, which governs activities in the food sector. Food sources, including farmers and growers, are subject to food safety legislation. It is an offence to sell food which is not of the 'nature or substance or quality' demanded by the purchaser. In recent times this has led to a number of disputes about foods where it was not made clear that they contained genetically modified ingredients.

From a business perspective, consumer protection has supported businesses in better catering for customer needs and requirements. Consumers are increasingly aware of their rights and of the importance of receiving goods in the form that they expect. Businesses that fall foul of the law are likely to rapidly lose customer support.

Another impact has been increasing pressure on businesses to put in place better quality standards at every stage of production to ensure compliance with legal requirements.

Consumer protection has also raised costs for businesses. Improving standards always has a cost implication. However, provided competitors too are forced to comply with the law then the costs should be incurred by all businesses. Falling foul of consumer protection legislation will incur penalty costs on business.

Managing the economy: growth, inflation and unemployment

One of the government's most important jobs is to manage the economy. To understand how the government is able to do this we first need to know something about aggregate monetary demand (AMD) and aggregate monetary supply (AMS):

- *AMD* Aggregate demand is the total level of demand in the whole economy.

- *AMS* Aggregate supply is the total level of supply in the whole economy.

We can show the relationship between total demand and supply in the economy by means of a simple circular flow diagram. To draw this we assume the economy is divided into two sectors – the firms sector and the household sector (see Figure 8.8).

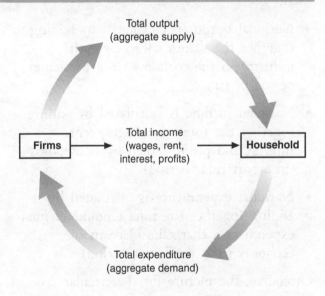

Figure 8.8 The relationship between total demand and supply

Firms produce output (goods and services) which they will sell to households. We could measure the value of this output by adding together the value created by all the industries in the economy.

At the same time, households provide services for firms in a number of ways. I may sell my labour to an employer for a wage, rent out my land to a farmer, invest in a public company as a shareholder (receiving a profit) and also put some money into a bank account for which I receive interest. The total income received by households should therefore add up to the same figure as that for total output.

Households that receive income will then spend it on the goods that are available in the economy.

Thus we have three ways of adding up the same thing:

Output = Income = Expenditure

We use the terms 'national income' or 'gross domestic product' to refer to this total:

- National output is calculated by adding together the values added by each industry in the economy (in a particular period of time).

- National income is calculated by adding together the totals for wages, rent, interest and profit earned by households (in a particular period).

- National expenditure is calculated by adding together the total amount of final expenditures that take place in the economy (in a particular period).

Of course, the picture for the circular flow of income is more complex in the real world because, in addition to firms and households, we need to take account of the government, the foreign trade sector and the financial sectors (see Figure 8.9).

Money leaves the circular flow in three ways:

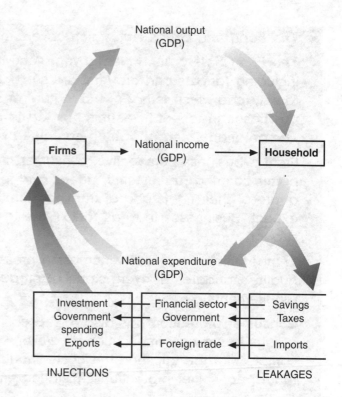

Figure 8.9 The circular flow of income

1 *Savings* Consumers don't spend all their money. However, it is hoped this will be channelled through the financial sector back into the economy in the form of *investment*.

2 *Taxes* The government will deduct taxes from households. However, the government, it is hoped, will then channel this money back to firms in the form of *government expenditure*.

3 *Imports* UK citizens will spend some of their incomes on foreign goods. However, foreigners, it is hoped, will also buy our *exports* to bring spending back into the system.

Savings, taxes and imports are referred to as leakages from the circular flow. Investment, government spending and exports are referred to as injections.

Aggregate demand

Aggregate demand is the total level of demand in the whole economy. Aggregate demand is made up of:

- Demand by consumers for goods and services (call this C).

- Demand by producers for goods that go into further production (call this I, for investment demand).

- Government demand for goods and services (call this G).

Furthermore, we need to add the demand from foreigners for our goods and services (exports, X) and subtract the demand (M) by our citizens for foreign goods and services, because money leaves the country. A useful measure of aggregate money demand is, therefore:

Aggregate money demand =
$$C + I + G + X - M$$

This is shown in Figure 8.10.

We have said that the amount people spend in an economy will be received by the providers of goods and services. If we want to be absolutely accurate, however, we should also account for indirect taxes and subsidies.

If I buy a packet of sandwiches in a bakery, the owner of the bakery will not be able to use all this money in his or her business. Some of this revenue will be paid over to the government in VAT (Value Added Tax) and other indirect taxes. Furthermore, some sellers will receive more than the sales price of their goods, probably as a result of government subsidies. A subsidy should therefore be seen as an addition to

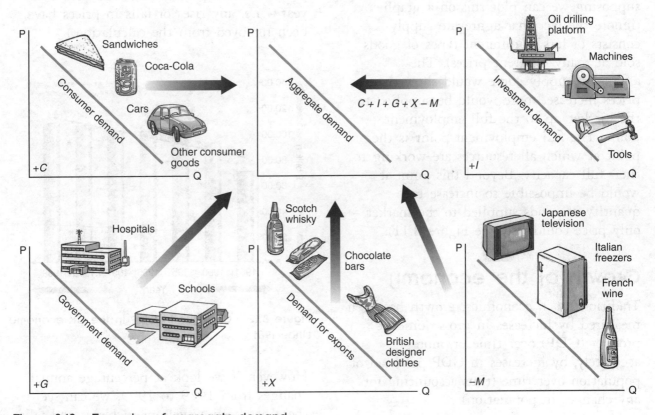

Figure 8.10 Examples of aggregate demand

consumer demand, provided by the government. A more comprehensive definition of aggregate money demand (AMD) is, therefore:

$$AMD = C + I + G + X - M - \text{Indirect taxes} + \text{Subsidies}$$

Aggregate monetary demand goes into purchasing all the goods produced in a country (i.e. the national output). National output is another way of describing total supply (aggregate monetary supply).

When aggregate monetary demand (AMD) in the economy equals aggregate monetary supply (AMS), the economy is in balance.

Aggregate supply

Aggregate supply is made up of all the goods in the economy that can be supplied at a particular moment in time. Just supposing we can plot this on a graph (ignore the fact that aggregate supply consists of lots of different types of goods sold at many different prices). The aggregate supply curve would show that, as prices increase, more would be supplied to the market up to the full employment point. The full employment point is the point at which all resources are working to their full capacity. Beyond this point it would be impossible to increase the quantity of goods supplied to the market – only price could rise (see Figure 8.11).

Growth of the economy

Traditionally in economics, growth has been measured by increases in gross domestic product (GDP) over time or, more accurately, by increases in GDP per head of population over time (thus accounting for any changes in population).

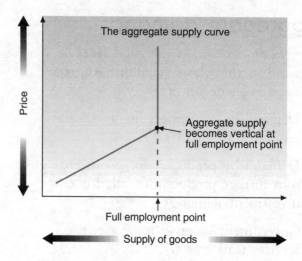

Figure 8.11 Aggregate supply

Figure 8.12 shows changes in GDP in the UK economy since 1981. It shows that, over time, there has been a steady rise in GDP as shown by the trend line. (Note that GDP is measured at constant market prices and compared with 1995 as a base year – i.e. any rises or falls in prices have been removed from the calculation.)

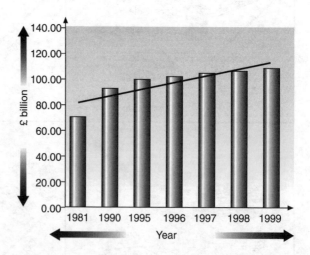

Figure 8.12   Changes in GDP in the UK economy since 1981

However, if we look at percentage annual changes from 1979 to 1999, we can see there has been a cycle of increases and falls.

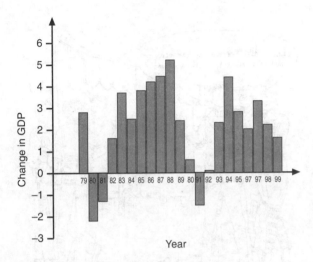

Figure 8.13 The business cycle

We call this the business (or trade) cycle (see Figure 8.13).

We can see that the economy goes through periods of rising output, incomes and expenditure, followed by periods in which this rate of increase falls. Traditionally, economists have measured growth in terms of these changes in NO (National Output), NI (National Income) and NE (National Expenditure).

> ### Check your understanding
>
> Monitor changes in GDP over a one-year period by taking information from the web site for the Office of National Statistics (www.statistics.gov.uk).

The business cycle

There are four parts to the traditional business cycle:

1 A boom occurs when an economy is at a peak. During a boom, a number of economic indicators related to demand all tend to increase. The main indicators are:

- production
- employment
- sales
- interest rates
- investment.

2 A boom is usually followed by a recession, when we see falling rates of increase of GDP as the economy slows down.

3 A slump occurs when there is a real fall in GDP so that output, incomes and expenditure start to fall and firms lay off workers, and prices and interest rates drop.

4 Recovery is the period in which there are, once again, real increases in GDP so that firms start to take on more employees, and expenditure starts to pick up again (see Figure 8.14).

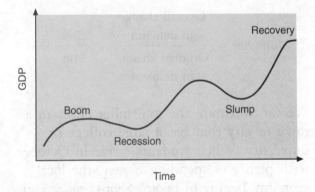

Figure 8.14 Economic recovery

Government can play a major role in stimulating demand in the economy. The problem is that, once a recession starts, it tends to be self-perpetuating over two or three years (and sometimes longer).

Once demand falls from a peak, business people become pessimistic about the future and start to make cutbacks in production. Because they are making cutbacks in production, they will invest less in capital equipment. This means people earn less and

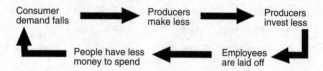

Figure 8.15 The vicious circle of recession

spend less. The whole process is a vicious circle (see Figure 8.15).

A small fall in consumer demand can, therefore, lead to a much bigger overall change in incomes and spending. We call this a 'multiplier effect' because the original fall in demand is multiplied. For example, if consumers reduce spending by £1 million and this leads eventually to an overall fall in demand of £3 million, we can see that the multiplier is 3:

$$\text{Multiplier} = \frac{\text{Overall change in demand}}{\text{Original change in demand}} = \frac{£3m}{£1m} = 3$$

We can illustrate the multiplier effect in a town or city that has a large college or university. When students arrive in October with plenty of spending money, the local economy begins to boom. Shops, cafés, and bookshops take on more part-time staff, who receive wages for their work. These wages are then spent in the town or city and the multiplier effect continues. The original increase in spending by students is multiplied around the local economy. However, in the summer holidays, the reverse happens as students leave town and a great many part-time jobs disappear, leading to a localised recession.

The government operates in an environment in which the economy goes through this

cycle of recession and recovery. It plays a major role in trying to ensure a recession does not lead to a slump (i.e. falls in national output). The government, therefore, may want to take measures to stimulate demand when demand in the country is falling.

An ideal situation? Demand and supply both increasing

In an ideal world we would have increases in supply and demand matching each other in the macro-economy, leading to economic growth with no inflation. Figure 8.16 shows how this could happen.

Imagine we start from a situation of full employment where demand = supply (D = S). In the next time period, supply increases to S_1 and demand increases to D_1 so that, once again, we have full employment and prices have not risen. The only thing that has increased in the economy is the level of national output so that people are better off.

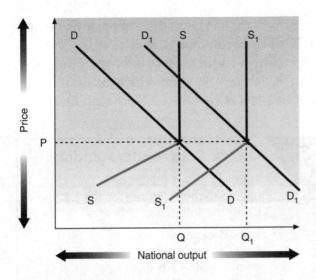

Figure 8.16 Increases in demand match increases in supply

Unemployment

In the real world, however, we are often faced by situations in which unemployment exists. In other words demand and supply in the economy meet at a point below the full employment point (see Figure 8.17).

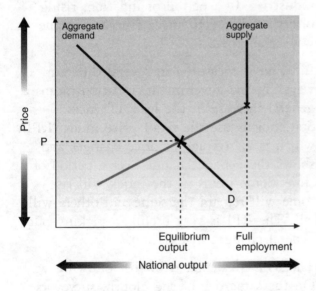

Figure 8.17 Unemployment in the economy

In the early 1990s, many commentators were pessimistic about the possibilities of returning to full employment because, during the first half of the 1990s, many large (and smaller) businesses downsized by getting rid of a great many full-time employees.

Commentators felt the days of mass employment were behind us and that companies would increasingly be staffed by fewer employees doing more than before.

However, at the dawn of the new millennium it appears this pessimistic scenario may not necessarily be the case. In 2000 we had lower levels of unemployment than we have had since 1979. It may be that it took time for the economy to adjust to the new realities of the hi-tech revolution. As low-tech industries and companies shed jobs, it has taken time for the new hi-tech employers and the leisure industries that have been developing to absorb labour in the same way.

We use the term 'structural unemployment' to refer to a situation in which major restructuring is taking place in the economy – because some industries are going into decline while new ones develop. It takes time to restructure.

'Cyclical unemployment' refers to situations where unemployment rises because of a recession or slump. 'Technological unemployment' refers to situations where unemployment rises because of the development of labour-saving technologies. Hence, technological and structural unemployment are closely related.

There are currently two official methods of calculating unemployment in the UK:

1 *The Claimant Count*, whereby the number of unemployed is calculated on the basis of the number of people claiming benefit. These figures are calculated by the Office of National Statistics, and is the method favoured by the government.

2 *The Labour Force Survey*, carried out by the International Labour Office (ILO), which includes people without a job who were available to start work in the two weeks following their interview, and had either looked for work in the four weeks prior to the interview or were waiting to start a job they had already obtained. The Labour Force Survey gives a higher figure for unemployment than the Claimant Count.

There are many problems associated with getting an accurate figure for unemployment.

Be wary, because governments tend to favour methods that show them in the best light.

Figure 8.18 shows the figures for unemployment using the Claimant Count method. There were a number of reasons why unemployment was falling up to 2000, including the low levels of inflation that increased economic stability, government job

creation schemes and the strength of many UK hi-tech companies in a new international order, as well as the flexibility of UK labour markets, which made it easy for employers to take on new employees.

Check your understanding

Find out about the latest unemployment figures for the UK by using the following web sites:

www.dss.gov.uk
www.dfee.gov.uk
www.treasury.gov.uk
www.incomesdata.co.uk
www.statistics.gov.uk

Inflation

Unemployment and inflation are economic problems that have repercussions for a large number of individuals and organisations. When unemployment is at a high level, the population as a whole has less money to spend, and this affects many firms and industries. In a period of inflation, rising prices are likely to affect everyone in one way or another.

Inflation is measured in several different ways. To the government, inflation means a general increase in the level of prices. Statisticians use the retail price index (RPI), which is an average of price changes and shows the general change over a period of time. Some items in the index will rise, some will remain the same and others will fall. The RPI is very useful in picking out general changes in inflation.

The RPI is calculated in the following way. On the same day of the month, surveyors are sent out to record 150,000 prices for 600 items. Prices are recorded in different areas of the country as well as in different

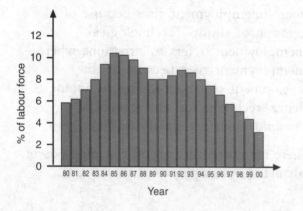

Figure 8.18   Unemployment: Claimant Count

types of retail outlets, such as corner shops and supermarkets. These results are averaged out to find the average price of goods, and this figure is converted into an index number form (i.e. comparing it with 100 for a chosen base year).

Using these data the average inflation rate can be calculated. Each individual price change is given a 'weight' which depends on how important it is in the typical household's spending pattern. For example, food makes up about one-fifth of a typical household's spending so that a 10% rise in the price of food would raise average prices by one-fifth of this (2%).

Price changes are measured over a definite period of time so that it is possible to compare the changes from one period to another. The choice of a starting (or 'base') date is very important, the aim being to choose a time that is 'normal' – that is, when nothing abnormal or unusual is happening to prices.

The base date is given an index of 100. We can then say, for example, that if in 1995

the RPI stood at 100 and today it is 112, prices on average have risen by 12% over the period covered.

Suppose in an imaginary country, Averageland, the family Average spend half their income on food, three-tenths on clothing and the remaining two-tenths on entertainment. We can give these items 'weightings' out of 10: food 5, clothing 3, entertainment 2. In 1995 (the base year) food cost on average £1 per unit, clothing £5 per unit and entertainment £2 per unit. In 2001, food in Averageland cost £1.01 per unit, clothing £5.05 per unit and entertainment had fallen to £1.90 per unit. We can analyse these changes in prices as in Figure 8.19.

	Original index	New index	Expenditure weighting	New index × weighting
Food	100	101	5	505
Clothing	100	101	3	303
Entertainment	100	95	2	190
Total				998

Figure 8.19 Averageland: the retail price index

The total of the last column is 998. In order to find out the new RPI in Averageland we must divide this total by the total number of weights (10). So:

$$\text{New RPI} = \frac{998}{10} = 99.8$$

This shows that, on average, prices fell by 0.2%. While entertainment fell by 5% in price, the rises in food prices and clothing had a greater impact on consumers (even though they had risen by only 1%).

Check your understanding

1 In Redland, the average consumer spends seven-tenths of his or her income on wine, two-tenths on bread and one-tenth on cheese. In 1995 (the base year), the price of all these items was £1 per unit. By 2001 wine had fallen to 50p per unit, bread had gone up to £2 per unit and cheese had risen to £4 per unit.

   • What is the new index for 2001?
   • Has it risen, fallen or remained the same?
   • Give at least three reasons why the weighting may need to be altered in 2001.

2 In Blueland, the public buy four items – eggs, cheese, bread and salt. Four-tenths of their income is spent on cheese and two-tenths on each of the other three items. Between 1995 (the base year) and 2001, eggs doubled in price, cheese went up by 50%, bread remained the same and salt went down by 10%. Calculate the new index relative to the base year.

Case study: An error that makes us better off than we thought

Millions of people are better off than they should be because of a persistent miscalculation in the rate of inflation over the 1980s and 1990s, research has revealed. Over a 23-year period, the RPI overstated the actual increase in the cost of living by between 1% and 3%. This means that pensioners and welfare claimants (whose annual payments are increased in line with inflation) have received extra cash. The same is true for the millions of workers whose pay rises are dictated by the rate of inflation.

The miscalculation of the RPI was highlighted in an investigation carried out by the Institute for Fiscal Studies in November 1999. Its researchers examined data from 50,000 households set out in the *Family Expenditure Survey*.

They found that the true inflation figure was distorted by the introduction of new goods, improving quality in existing products and the use of a fixed basket of 77 different items, regardless of changing trends.

The National Lottery was cited as an example of the introduction of new goods. Launched in 1994, it accounts for 1% of all consumer expenditure, which makes it a more important part of the nation's shopping than 42 of the 77 items in the RPI 'shopping basket'. Yet the lottery was not included in calculations for the RPI. It is now!

The improved quality in existing goods is highlighted by audio-visual equipment. The survey found the quality of these goods had increased so much over the 23-year period that it was the equivalent of their price dropping by more than 60% but that was not taken into account in the RPI calculation.

The study also questioned the use of a fixed basked of items, saying it failed to take account of the fact that consumers tend to change their shopping habits partly because of price changes. This usually means there is an upward bias in the fixed-weight price index compared to the true change in the cost of living.

1 What do you see as being the main criticisms of the RPI as set out in the case study?

2 How could these be remedied to give a more accurate measure?

3 Who benefited from the miscalculation of the index?

We can illustrate how too much demand can cause inflation by means of the graph in Figure 8.20. If demand continues to rise (from D to D^1 and D^2) beyond the full employment point, this can lead only to increases in price (from P to P^1 and P^2).

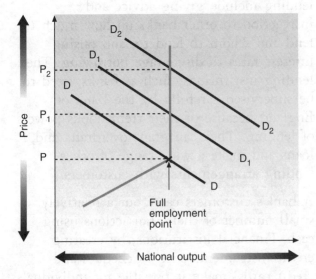

Figure 8.20 Too much demand causes inflation

Of course there is considerable discussion as to whether inflation is caused by failures in supply or the existence of too much demand. If the fault lies with supply, the supply curve will not shift (or not shift very much) to the right in response to increases in demand. This may be because business people do not have very much confidence about the future of the economy.

Government policy instruments

We now need to examine the nature of government policy instruments before going on to examine the impact these have on businesses in the marketplace. The principal instruments government has available to it are:

- monetary policy
- fiscal policy.

The government will use these instruments to try to control the levels of growth, unemployment and inflation in the economy.

The government plays a major part in trying to smooth out economic cycles so that businesses can operate in a predictable environment based on ongoing economic growth. We can think of this in terms of a set of traffic lights – the government having green light and red light policies (see Figure 8.21).

Monetary policy

The government plays a key role in the economy in controlling the availability of money for spending. Monetary policy is concerned with controlling:

- the quantity of money in the economy
- the price of money in the economy.

Monetary policy is felt to be important today. Most people now feel there is a strong link between the amount of money in the economy and inflation. The view is that, if people start spending money at a faster rate than new goods appear on the market, prices will rise.

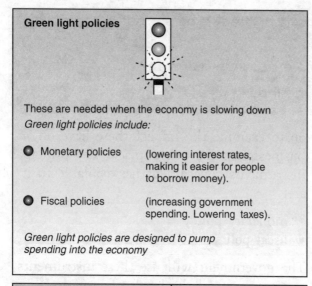

Green light policies

These are needed when the economy is slowing down
Green light policies include:

- Monetary policies   (lowering interest rates, making it easier for people to borrow money).

- Fiscal policies   (increasing government spending. Lowering taxes).

Green light policies are designed to pump spending into the economy

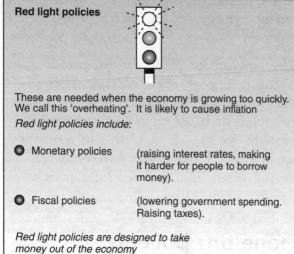

Red light policies

These are needed when the economy is growing too quickly. We call this 'overheating'. It is likely to cause inflation
Red light policies include:

- Monetary policies   (raising interest rates, making it harder for people to borrow money).

- Fiscal policies   (lowering government spending. Raising taxes).

Red light policies are designed to take money out of the economy

Figure 8.21   Government green light and red light policies

Monetarists believe it is essential to eliminate general price rises because of the way they destabilise industry and the economy. Uncertainty about prices means industry cannot concentrate on its main task – producing goods. People become dissatisfied and the whole economic order starts to crumble. People fail to pay up on time, businesses are reluctant to invest, there is more industrial unrest and so on.

The amount of money in the economy depends on how much lenders are prepared to lend. The more cash I have available to me and the more I am able to borrow, the more money I am able to spend. As a general rule, therefore, we can say that the more easy credit there is in the economy, the more money is available to spend.

The Bank of England has an important part to play in controlling the lending of banks and other lenders. The measures available to the bank for limiting increases in cash and lending include giving advice and instruction to other banks on how much to lend and whom to lend to, and raising interest rates to discourage borrowing. The lending institutions, such as banks, need to be supervised carefully by the Bank of England because of their tremendous powers of lending. They can grant overdrafts and loans and make a wide range of other lending arrangements with customers.

A bank's customers carry out a relatively small number of their transactions using cash. Financial institutions, by creating credit instruments such as cheques and credit cards, make it possible for individuals and organisations to borrow money and make payments by means other than cash. The more these credit instruments are expanded, the more purchasing power there is in the economy. It is essential the government does not let this spending get out of hand. It therefore sets targets and builds up a framework for controlling the financial system.

The Bank of England plays an important part in policing this system – it licenses financial institutions and keeps a watchful eye on their lending practices. This policing is very important. If a bank collapses it creates a loss of confidence in an economy, as well as leading to losses for depositors. In 1995, for example, Barings Bank (one of the oldest merchant banks in this country) collapsed. The bank had not controlled the speculations of one of its dealers, Nick Leeson. He had been speculating with billions of pounds of bank assets. When his speculations were unsuccessful, he gambled on the 'double or quits' principle. The bank collapsed and was sold for £1 to a Dutch bank. The Bank of England was criticised for not exercising enough control.

As well as controlling the quantity of money in the economy, the government can control the price of money – the interest rate. Today, the Bank of England establishes a base rate at which it is prepared to lend money. This base rate determines all the other rates of interest in the economy. The base rate is set by a group of experts known as the Monetary Policy Committee, which meets regularly. Their job is to decide whether to raise or lower the base rate. Their prime consideration will be the level of inflation in the economy. If inflation is rising, they will raise interest rates to dampen down demand in the economy. If inflation is falling, they will lower interest rates (see Figure 8.22).

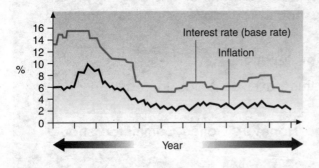

Figure 8.22   UK interest and inflation rates

Monetary policy has a big impact on business. When the Bank of England reduces the quantity of money available in the economy and raises interest rates, this will cut back demand. With high interest rates consumers will borrow less and savers will save more. If businesses have borrowed money, they will have to pay it back at higher rates of interest. So when the supply of money falls and interest rates rise, businesses will cut back on their investment plans and be generally gloomy.

Check your understanding

Study the business pages of a broadsheet newspaper to find out what has been happening recently to the rate of interest and the quantity of money in the economy.

What impact is this having on businesses? Give examples of the ways in which particular businesses have been affected.

Fiscal policy

Fiscal policy is the government's policy with regard to public spending, taxes and borrowing. The government can try to influence the level of demand in the economy through directly altering the amount of its own spending in relation to its total tax revenues.

A *deficit budget* (see Figure 8.23) arises when the government spends more than it takes in taxes. The government can then borrow money from banks and other sources or sell stock in order to carry out its expenditure policies. The difference between government spending and tax revenue is known as the public sector borrowing requirement (PSBR).

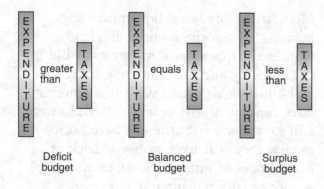

Figure 8.23 Fiscal policy: types of budgets

The logic of the deficit budget is simple – if there is not sufficient spending in the economy to create enough demand for goods to give everyone a job who wants one, the government can itself boost spending. However, as we have seen earlier, this may have inflationary effects.

In a *balanced budget* (see Figure 8.23), the government matches its spending with taxes. The idea behind the balanced budget is that the government should not encourage price increases. There is also a belief that the government itself should spend as little as possible, because private individuals and groups are in a better position to make their own spending decisions.

A *surplus budget* (see Figure 8.23) arises when the government takes in more revenue than it spends. A government would typically run a budget surplus if the economy was stagnating or had been going

Case study: A low-inflation economy?

In late 1999, the National Institute for Economic and Social Research (NIESR) (www.niesr.ac.uk) predicted that the British economy was on course for a strong recovery with low inflation. It said that public finances were remarkable and that the budget surplus will inevitably create expectations of increased spending. However, it also said that accelerating pay claims were making the tight jobs market a worry, and urged the Monetary Policy Committee to raise interest rates.

The report calculated that the strength of tax revenues gave Gordon Brown, the Chancellor, plenty of scope to raise public spending or cut taxes without breaching his rules for prudent fiscal policy. However, it advised against this, saying growth was picking up without the need for an extra boost from government tax and spending policy.

1 What is meant by a strong recovery with low inflation?

2 What is a budget surplus, and why might this have led to an increase in spending?

3 Why was the NIESR recommending that the Monetary Policy Committee should raise interest rates?

4 Why do you think that the NIESR recommended the government should not lower taxes and raise spending?

5 How do you think businesses would have felt about the NIESR report? How might this have influenced their actions?

through a period of recession. In such a situation, the government would lower taxes and perhaps raise its spending. Businesses would welcome such a budget because it is likely to inject fresh demand into the economy – thus fuelling business optimism about an upturn in the economy. Of course, businesses may not be totally optimistic because they may fear increases in government spending could fuel inflation; so, while they may be keen to make short-term investments, they may be more cautious about long-term ones.

Governments would seek to get their budgets more into balance when they want to deflate the economy, perhaps because inflation levels are at an unacceptable level. In such a situation businesses may be pessimistic because they will feel the pinch of government cutbacks, particularly because such a fiscal policy is usually tied in with a rise in interest rates. Since 1994 the UK government has announced its plans for expenditure and revenue raising – at the same time – in the autumn.

Check your understanding

Study newspaper accounts of the most recent UK autumn budget. What were the main things the government was trying to achieve in its fiscal policy? What would be the major impacts on business?

What the economists say about how the economy should be run

Every student completing an AVCE Business course should know something about the key differences in opinion as to how the government should intervene in the market place. We therefore need to look briefly at the history of economic ideas (see Figure 8.24).

Laissez-faire policy

The French expression *laissez-faire* means 'leave it alone'. It therefore signifies government non-interference in the economy. The theory behind laissez-faire is that free markets will lead to the best use of resources. If people want goods they will choose them by voting (with their money) for them to be produced. They will also make themselves available for work so that they can earn money to buy goods. Employers will employ labour so long as they can make a profit.

This theory was applied throughout the nineteenth century. The economy grew rapidly and many new products were invented and developed.

When some goods become old-fashioned they are replaced by new goods. Wages fall

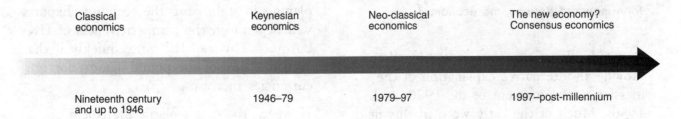

Figure 8.24   The development of economic theories

in some industries and rise in other industries. Some people will be temporarily unemployed, but they will be taken up in the newer industries. The natural state of affairs for the economy is thus one of full employment.

The mass unemployment of the 1920s could be explained by the fact that trade unions and other groups did not allow wages to fall in a period of recession. If wages and other prices had fallen, employers would have been prepared to employ labour in the new growing industries.

Demand-side economics

John maynard Keynes, the economist

Demand-side economics was developed to provide an alternative explanation of the massive unemployment of the 1920s and 1930s. Much of the early work in this field was carried out by the economist, John Maynard Keynes. Keynes argued that full

employment was just one possible state for the economy. Keynes maintained that the factors that create supply do not always lead to demand for goods. Earners of money do not always spend it. This can lead to a fall in national expenditure and to a reduction in output as suppliers are not able to sell stocks of goods. The problem is that aggregate demand is composed of a number of different types of demand, and that the demanders in each case have different motivations (see Figure 8.25).

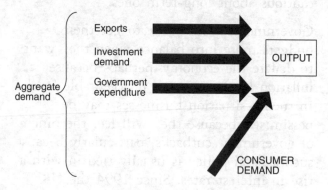

Figure 8.25   The demand for goods and services

Consumer demand is likely to be affected largely by the level of people's incomes but, in a recession, many households will start saving because they are worried about losing their jobs (and for other reasons), which leads to an increased fall in consumer demand.

Government spending will largely be determined by political factors as well as the role the government sees itself as playing in stabilising the economy. Exports will depend on the competitiveness of UK business. This can fall quite quickly if the exchange rate of the pound against foreign currencies increases.

However, the most volatile ingredient of aggregate demand is business investment. If business people are confident the economy will boom for a period of time, they will be keen to invest. However, when they are gloomy they will cut back heavily on investment projects. If you watch business news programmes, you will frequently hear references to 'business confidence'.

Check your understanding

What is the current state of business confidence in the economy? What are the likely effects on investment?

Changes in demand factors can have a dramatic impact. For example, when a building contractor loses a contract to build a new plant, he or she may have to lay off workers. These workers then do not earn wages. They buy less in local shops. The local shops then 'feel the pinch'. They buy in fewer stocks and reduce staff overtime. In turn, these people have smaller incomes and they spend less. We have already seen that this is called the multiplier effect.

We can set out a simple rule that relates to the multiplier effect:

- The greater the percentage of any fresh increase in demand that is leaked away, the smaller the multiplier effect will be.

- The smaller the percentage of any fresh increase in demand that is leaked away, the larger the multiplier effect will be.

Supply-side economics

From 1979 onwards, when Margaret Thatcher's Conservatives came to power, there was a big switch in economic policy away from demand-side to supply-side theories. Whilst demand management had worked very well after 1945, the policy eventually ran into trouble. After the war, most governments used Keynesian policies (i.e. the ideas of Keynes). To counteract unemployment, the government would use its own spending to pump up demand in the economy.

However, a major fault of this policy was that outdated industries were artificially supported. Instead of inefficient units being cut they continued to survive on government subsidies. This meant the UK was lowering its competitive edge in world markets.

The supply of goods in the economy rose very slowly in the 1960s and 1970s. Because supply was rising slowly, an increase in demand tended to lead to both rising prices and an increased reliance on foreign imports. Too many imports led to an increasing national debt, and the government was forced to cut back on spending to reduce imports. Britain experienced 'stagflation' – a stagnant economy that was not growing, coupled with inflation. Demand management did not seem to be working.

The possible cure came with new policies the Conservative government began to introduce in 1979. These policies concentrated on increasing supply rather than increasing demand. A whole host of measures were introduced to get supply going. These included the following:

- Reducing income tax to encourage people to work longer hours.

- Reducing taxes on profits made by companies.

- Reducing benefits to those out of work.

- Reducing subsidies to loss-making industries.

- Privatising rather than nationalising industries.

- Reducing the size of the civil service.

- Reducing government spending.

- Passing laws to reduce trade union powers.

- Measures against monopolies and restrictive practices.

- Encouraging competition amongst groups such as solicitors and opticians, and even in the health sector and schools.

The emphasis of the policy was to use supply as the means to drive the way forward.

The new economy

At the end of the twentieth century, people began to talk about the 'new economy'. This was an economy that had been transformed not by the deliberate actions of governments but by the actions of the new high-tech sectors of the economy and by the breakthroughs in science and technology that had led to a new computer-based network economy driven by rapid communications. In particular, the US economy experienced a continuous boom throughout the 1990s, which was fuelled by the US giants in the new technology fields. Statistics show it was these new high-tech industries that fuelled much of the growth in GDP in the USA (see Figure 8.26).

An interesting aspect of the leap forward in GDP was shown by the fact that, in the USA, recorded figures for national income rose much faster than similar figures for output. The statisticians could easily calculate the incomes people took away in their pockets. However, rises in productivity were much more difficult to measure

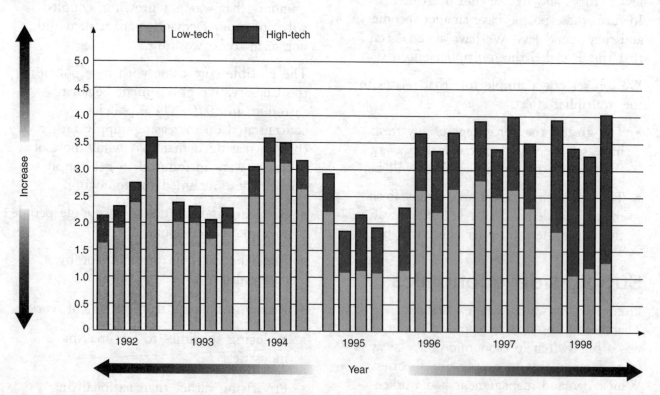

Figure 8.26 US income in terms of real GDP, 1992–98

because there were so many new products hitting the markets it was difficult to record increases in productivity. And, of course, with any revolution in industry, it takes time for industry to reorganise itself around the innovations. Today, in the twenty-first century, we are seeing the impacts strike home at an accelerating rate, leading to a new economy whose characteristics are:

- low inflation rates
- high increases in productivity
- falling unemployment levels.

These impacts are clearly apparent in the UK economy and are likely to continue (although with economic forecasting you can never tell what sorts of downturns lie just around the corner).

The Labour government has been fortunate to take over the reins of office at the time of the development of the new economy. However, they have developed intelligent sets of policies to make sure they capitalise on these opportunities.

New Labour under Tony Blair has followed through an agenda of modernisation, involving the development of close links with business to generate new jobs in the economy. In particular, the government has been successful through its monetary policy in keeping inflation down, and this is essential for business confidence.

The government has also put a strong emphasis on the unemployed to take responsibility for themselves in the labour market, while working with business to create a 'New Deal' policy that provides work for young and other unemployed workers through the creation of subsidised jobs. New Labour has continued with the previous government's policy of privatisation

while taking measures to increase competition in the marketplace.

Check your understanding

To what extent does the 'new economy' continue to drive down unemployment and lead to increases in GDP? What are the latest UK statistics?

Business and taxation

Governments tax households and business organisations to:

- raise revenue
- discourage certain activities (e.g. a tax on pollution).

Taxes on households affect business because they divert money away from expenditure. The two types of taxes on households are:

1 Direct taxes, taken directly away from individuals (e.g. taxes on income).

2 Indirect taxes, taken indirectly from individuals, for example VAT is collected by businesses for the government before being passed on in higher prices to the end consumer.

Taxation	£bn
Income tax	88
National insurance contributions	56
Corporation tax	30
Value Added Tax	54
Excise duties	36
Council tax	13
Business rates	16
Other receipts	56

Figure 8.27 Government taxation, 1999–2000

Figure 8.27 shows government taxation for the years 1999–2000.

Businesses will worry if the overall level of taxation increases to such an extent that it exerts deflationary pressures on the economy. However, at the same time business will favour a taxation policy that prevents inflation because of the way in which inflation creates instability in the economy.

We will briefly mention the immediate impact of each of the taxes shown in Figure 8.27 on business.

Income tax

Income tax is generally deducted by a firm's wages department directly from an employee's salary and paid to the government. For the employees it is a direct tax because they have no choice – they are taxed on incomes above a certain level. Rises in income tax are used as part of fiscal policy to dampen down the general level of spending in the economy.

National insurance

National insurance contributions consist of two major elements, an employee's contribution and an employer's contribution. The wages department of a company will pay both elements to the government. National insurance is a compulsory insurance paid to fund key parts of the social security system, such as state pensions. The employer's part of national insurance can be seen as a tax on business. When national insurance contributions are increased, this will increase costs of production to a firm.

Corporation tax

Corporation tax is a tax on company profits.

Businesses that make over a certain level of profits may pay corporate taxes to the government. Of course, there are many items that can be offset against tax, such as money ploughed into investment projects. Businesses argue that corporate taxes should be kept to a minimum if business is to survive and to invest in future production.

Value Added Tax

Value Added Tax (VAT) is levied on selling prices and is calculated at each stage of production. For example, if a retailer buys a box of goods for £500 and sells them for £800, £300 has been added to the value of the goods. The retailer will be responsible only for the £300 worth of value that has been added to the goods when it comes to tax liability.

One criticism of indirect taxes such as VAT is they tend to be regressive (i.e. they take a larger percentage of the income of the lower paid). In contrast, direct taxes such as income tax, are more likely to be progressive (taking a greater percentage of income from the rich than the poor).

Under the Conservative government (1979–97), the emphasis was on indirect taxes because the government believed this gave people freedom of choice (they could choose to buy goods with VAT on them or they could choose not to buy them). Under Labour the emphasis is switching more towards direct taxes again. Many small businesses find VAT a nuisance because of the amount of paperwork it involves.

Excise duty

Excise duties are taxes on particular goods that are levied for revenue-raising purposes (e.g. a tax on whisky and cigarettes). Excise duties are often levied on goods that are regarded as luxuries and/or harmful to health. Businesses that have excise duties levied on them are often quite hostile to these taxes because they feel the tax burden is too high.

Council tax

Council tax is a tax paid by householders to the local council to help fund local expenditure. A rise in council tax will have very much the same impact as a rise in income tax by reducing the money in people's pockets, thus leading to a reduction in expenditure on other things.

Business rate

Business rates are levied on local businesses to pay for local council services. Again, they are seen by businesses as a cost that discourages their efforts.

Case study : Taxes and the supply curve

Figure 8.28 shows the impact of placing a £5 tax on a bottle of Scotch whisky. Originally the price of the whisky was £20 (where demand and supply cut in the marketplace). You can see the impact of the tax is to shift the supply curve to the left because the producer would see the tax as a cost of production.

Originally, the supplier was prepared to supply 4,000 bottles at £20. The supplier is now prepared to supply only 3,000 bottles at this price.

Figure 8.29 shows how the supply curve shifts to the left.

1   As a result of the tax, the supply curve has shifted to the left. How much would be supplied at £25?

2   What is the new equilibrium price?

3   How much has the price risen by?

4   Has the price risen by as much as the tax? If it has risen by less than the tax, how much of the tax has been paid out of the producer's profits and how much have consumers had to pay?

5   Why are producers able to pass some of the tax on to consumers?

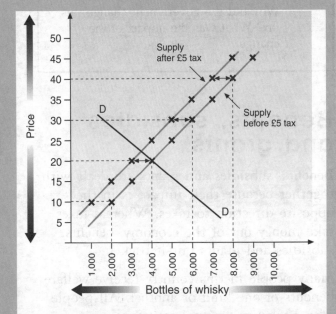

Figure 8.28 The impact of a £5 tax on a bottle of Scotch whisky

Price (£)	Original supply	New supply (after tax)
£10	2,000	1,000
£20	4,000	3,000
£30	6,000	5,000
£40	8,000	7,000

Figure 8.29 Taxing a bottle of Scotch whisky

Your answers to the previous case study will show that, when taxes on products increase, not all the tax is paid by the supplier. The supplier is able to pass some of the tax increase on to the consumer – because when consumers have a sufficiently intense demand for a product, they are still willing to buy the product when its price rises (although some people will buy less).

Check your understanding

Carry out some research into one business tax that was altered at the last budget (use the Internet).

Why did the government change this tax? What was the impact of the change?

Benefits, subsidies and grants

Benefits, subsidies and grants are dealt with together because their impact is in the opposite direction to taxes. Whereas taxes take money out of the economy, benefits, subsidies and grants put it back in.

Many people in this country receive welfare benefits of one kind or another. All people who work pay national insurance contributions provided they receive more than a given minimum income. There are a range of benefits, including pensions, sickness benefits, invalidity benefits, etc.

In times of recession, more people are made unemployed and have to rely on the state safety net. Fortunately this has a positive impact of redistributing income from the state to benefit earners – thus pumping some demand back into the economy in a recessionary period. Benefit earners are

likely to spend most (if not all) of what they receive.

Subsidies are moneys paid by the state to encourage certain business activities. Subsidies have the same effect on business as a fall in production costs and thus push the supply curve to the right. So, for example, if the government subsidises agriculture, this enables farmers to produce cheaper food (see Figure 8.30).

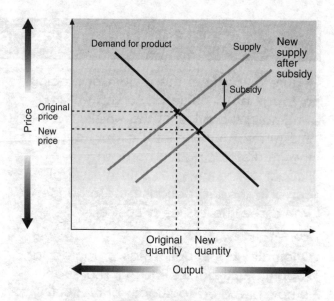

Figure 8.30 The impact of a government subsidy on production

The government will subsidise businesses that are starting up, ones that face intense foreign competition and essential services (e.g. a ferry service to a remote Scottish island). Subsidies are also given for activities that are regarded as being important to society (e.g. ones that preserve jobs and communities in remote areas). Subsidies are given by both the UK government and by the European Union's social fund (e.g. subsidies to hill farmers for sheep farming, etc.).

Grants are sums of money provided by the government to support particular business activities, e.g. grants for small business set-ups, grants to finance specific research projects, etc.).

Check your understanding

Identify grants or subsidies that are given to businesses in your area (e.g. specific subsidies to farmers and/or grants by the local council to entrepreneurs).

Exchange rates

The exchange rate is the rate at which one currency will exchange against other currencies. When your currency rises in value against other currencies, this makes your goods more expensive when you export them.

It is important your currency exchanges at a high enough rate to bring in good revenues from selling goods overseas. However, if the value rises too much, foreigners will become reluctant to buy your products. On the other hand, if the value of your currency falls too much, it will be easy to sell products abroad – but it may not be worth doing so if each product does not yield much revenue.

The importance of exchange rates in the competitiveness equation cannot be overestimated. Business people often suffer from an ongoing fall in competitiveness caused by exchange rate changes, either because the pound sterling is too strong or because it is too weak. The key is to secure just the right balance that makes goods competitive without being too cheap. It is important that exchange rates remain stable over a period of time so that traders know what to expect when they exchange goods.

Government plays a key role in helping to determine exchange rates. In the modern world, the price of the pound is determined by the demand for and supply of pounds. When foreigners have confidence in the UK government's handling of economic policy, they will be keen to invest in the UK. They look for strong government that has a tight control over fiscal and monetary policy. A strong UK government will lead to confidence in the pound, which tends to be good for business. A weak government leads to a volatile pound, which is bad for business decision-making.

Check your understanding

What is the current rate of exchange between the pound and the franc and the pound and the dollar?

Are these rates of exchange good for business generally?

Follow reports in a broadsheet newspaper and summarise your findings.

Public sector services

A number of key services are provided in the public sector, including the postal service, and, at a local level, services such as education and recreation, housing, environmental and conservation services, some bus services, fire, police, ambulance and local justice and social services.

Before the privatisation years (starting in 1979), many of these services were controlled far more directly by the hand of government. However, as the impetus to privatisation gained momentum, more and more services, or aspects of these services, were contracted out to private companies. So, for example, today the rubbish produced by a business may be collected by a private firm that has a contract with the local council.

Increasingly, the management of business aspects of a service, such as the police, has been put in the hands of specialist managers working within and for the police service itself.

There have been two reasons for this:

1 To ensure business responsibility lies in the hands of those directly responsible for running and managing a service. So, for example, those responsible for running the police service should directly take the decisions about how best to manage the resources available and to use those resources to maximum effect.

2 The notion that decision-making should increasingly be moved away from central bureaucrats to local managers who are responsive to the needs of the local community.

Central government funds much local public service activity through a direct grant. In addition, such services are also funded through local taxes and by making the public pay for the services they use (e.g. charges for using a swimming pool).

It is often argued that the needs of local communities are best met by running services at a local level by people who are most sympathetic and responsive to the needs of the local community (e.g. through the self-management of budgets in schools). Running public services at a local level also enables smooth and direct communications rather than the problems of poor communications that were characteristic of large central government organisations in the past.

Public sector services are of great benefit to business – for example, the provision of security of premises by the police, safe road provision by the highways department, refuse disposal and pollution control by the environment and conservation departments, etc. By being able to draw on these services, businesses are able to keep their costs down and their efficiency up. While they have to pay for these services in taxes to central and local government, the benefits will generally outweigh the costs.

The government in this country has traditionally been able to keep much tighter control of wage levels in the public sector than in the private sector because, in the public sector, they pay the wages. The government has, therefore, controlled wages tightly in this sector in order to pursue anti-inflationary policies.

Check your understanding

Give two examples of public sector services local businesses are able to benefit from. How are these services funded?

How does business contribute to the funding of these services? How does business benefit from these services?

Privatisation

Privatisation in the UK was associated particularly with the last quarter of the twentieth century. In the first decade of this new century, there is very little left to privatise.

The government influences the market in a major way through its policies of public ownership and privatisations. For example, during the Second World War, huge swathes of industry were taken over by the government in order to co-ordinate production to meet the war effort. Immediately after the war a number of industries were nationalised (taken over by the government by Act of Parliament) – for example, coal, steel and the railways. The Labour Party was in government at the time.

Later, the Conservative Party denationalised many of these industries so that, once again, they were owned by shareholders.

During the 1960s and 1970s the Labour Party renationalised a number of industries.

In 1979 Margaret Thatcher's government came into power and this government pursued an extensive policy of mass privatisation. The new Labour government has continued with this policy of privatisation into the new millennium, in the belief the market is the most efficient way of making economic decisions.

Case study: Rail privatisation

With the privatisation of rail in the mid-1990s, the government split responsibility for rail infrastructure (e.g. track, signalling and equipment) from the operation of train services. Previously, both had been the responsibility of the public corporation (nationalised industry) British Rail. Privately owned Railtrack is now responsible for owning and looking after track, signalling, bridges, viaducts, tunnels, stations and other property.

Train services are now run by privately owned train companies who have a franchise to operate in a particular area of the country. To gain a franchise, a train company has to be licensed by the rail regulator.

British Rail were well known for inefficiency – late trains and poor service. However, many of the new train-operating companies have met with the same criticism, although others have been investing in new trains and better services.

There continues to be heated debate about the extent to which the government should be involved with the industry. Accidents such as the Paddington rail disaster of 1999 led some people to argue that Railtrack was cutting corners, particularly in the area of safety, and that safety was being sacrificed to profitability. However, against this, those in favour of privatisation have shown that services are far more reliable and that, taken as a whole, the railways have had an excellent record of safety in recent years.

1 Do you think the railways should have been privatised? Set out the arguments for and against this move.

2 Why do you think Railtrack was split from the operation of train services?

A study carried out into privatisation in the UK and the USA indicated that privatised organisations go through five stages as they move from being state monopolies:

1 *Stage 1: equilibrium*. These organisations initially fit into a set of guidelines established for them by the regulators. They set out to provide a universal (generally available) service. They subsidise consumers who cost more to serve (e.g. people in out-of-the-way places). Customers are passive.

2 *Stage 2: rumblings in the provinces*. The development of substitute products, and changes in technology and in public policy, mean competitors begin to develop at the periphery of the industry.

3 *Stage 3: identity crisis*. Stage 2 does not last long. Often the new competitors start to attract some of the most lucrative contracts, where the largest profits are made. Market dominance begins to crumble as more firms start to take away business. Existing concerns now become reluctant to subsidise consumers in the market.

The privatised concerns appeal for support from the regulator. When this fails they start to cut prices and to use other competitive strategies.

4 *Stage 4: refocus*. In stage 3 a number of bankruptcies occur as competition steps up. In stage 4 companies begin to focus on particular segments of the market where they are strongest. Mergers take place between organisations carrying out similar activities in the market.

5 *Stage 5: dynamic competition*. This stage represents the full adjustment of the industry to competitive conditions. The success of an organisation in the market depends on how smoothly it can adjust to changes in demand and supply conditions.

Check your understanding

One of the post-millennium privatisation issues is the extent to which the government reduces the monopoly of the Royal Mail in handling postal business.

How far has the government moved down this track? What have been the implications for the Royal Mail of these changes?

Changes in interest rates

Interest rates represent the price of borrowing money. Generally speaking, the Bank of England will lower its base rate (the rate around which other interest rates are determined) when it wants to stimulate the economy. If you lower the price of borrowing, people will borrow more – and spend more (Figure 8.31).

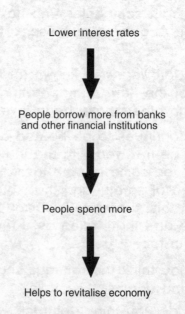

Figure 8.31 Lowering the price of borrowing

The Monetary Policy Committee will raise interest rates if spending is getting out of control. Higher interest rates discourage spending and dampen down business activity.

Check your understanding

Interview a local business person to find out the extent to which changes in interest rates affect his or her business.

The European Union
Social policy

The European Union establishes regulations that directly affect businesses in the UK because we have signed up to agreements.

In particular, the Amsterdam Treaty of 1998 bound us to abide by a series of social measures related to entitling employees to:

- Freedom of movement.
- Employment and remuneration.
- Improvements in living and working conditions.
- Social protection.
- Freedom of association and collective bargaining (trade union rights).
- Vocational training.
- Equal treatment for men and women.
- Information, consultation and participation at work.
- Health protection and safety in the workplace.

Case study: The EU directive on parental leave

An example of one type of social protection at work is the EU directive on parental leave.

The main points of this directive are that:

- Employees must have completed one year's service before being entitled to parental leave.
- Employees are entitled to 13 weeks' parental leave to care for each child born or adopted after 15 December 1999. This applies equally to mothers and fathers.
- Leave can be taken at any time up until the child's fifth birthday or five years after adoption date.
- Parents of disabled children can take leave up until a child's 18th birthday.
- The employee is guaranteed the right to return to the same job or a similar one with the same level or greater pay and benefits.
- If less than four weeks are taken, the employee is entitled to the same job on return to work.

1 What do you see as being the main advantages to employees of this directive?

2 How do you think employers might view this directive?

The European Social Chapter is designed to give maximum protection to employees and, clearly, can be seen as a step forward to creating better working conditions. Of course, some employers will have seen it as a burden that adds to their costs, and hence, cause them to make reductions elsewhere (e.g. by cutting back on the labour force).

Environmental policy

From the beginning of the 1980s, the European Union has been one of the principal forces operating on the British system of environmental protection. Apart from agriculture, the environment has been the area of policy most affected by European Union regulations and directives.

The EU has sought to create common environmental standards for member states so that there is a harmonisation of standards – for example, with regards to vehicle emissions. The EU has responded to public concerns about environmental issues by seeking to act in a co-ordinated way. Environmental regulation officially became part of EU responsibility with the Single European Act 1987.

From the mid-1980s, Germany played a prominent part in pushing other European Union states to impose higher environmental standards on products and manufacturing processes (e.g. stringent controls on sulphur dioxide emissions, tighter controls on water pollution, reductions in packaging and waste, and higher standards on vehicle emissions).

During the late 1980s the UK developed a record of opposing higher standards on environmental control and became known as 'the dirty man of Europe'. More recently, however, the UK has undergone a sea change in attitudes and has developed leading ideas (such as the introduction of integrated pollution control, through which emissions to air, water and soil are controlled as a whole).

In recent times, the Labour government has had to deal with the issue of taxes on pollution. Many experts believe the only way to deal with environmental problems is to broaden the base of taxation, particularly by extending it to activities that create pollution (e.g. through the use of pesticides or energy use). In the 1999 Budget, the government began to introduce new measures to charge people for parking at work and for entering congested city areas.

Post-millennium Britain is one in which the UK is increasingly having to take environmental measures that conform to European requirements. Of course, these are not always popular with business because they are seen to raise costs. However, by adopting strong environmental policies, businesses should be able to develop competitive advantage over rivals that have poorer records.

Check your understanding

Study the press to find an example of the way in which European Union social or environmental policy has had an impact on UK business.

Chapter 9 How businesses are affected by international competitors

Although you will have gained an understanding of the national markets, the developing global economy means you need to find out how businesses aim to be competitive internationally. You should understand the meaning of international competitiveness and how multinationals and other businesses operating in international markets try to be competitive. It is also important that you can explain how the following factors can affect the competitiveness of an international business:

- The trend towards increased freedom of trade and the role of the World Trade Organisation.
- The effects of barriers to trade – trading blocks, tariffs, quotas.
- The European Union, European Monetary Union and the Single Market.

You will learn to analyse the extent of the influence of these factors on a business and how business responds to them. You will also gain a basic understanding of how the use of the Internet is 'breaking down' international barriers.

The developing global economy and its impact on business

Until the 1980s, the world economy did not really exist. The former USSR and its East European satellites opted out because

of communism. So did China. India closed its doors to international trade on a large scale. The same was true of many other smaller countries. Altogether, more than half the world's population was outside the market economy.

Today many of these countries (totalling 3 billion people) have returned or are returning to the international economy. They are doing so at different speeds, are faced by differing problems and have differing chances of success. The potential gains from the process are enormous. Trade and investment have the ability to revitalise the world economy in an extended period of growth.

In the last 20 years of the twentieth century we saw the dynamic growth of the Asia–Pacific–Japan region, and the Asian 'tigers' of South Korea, Hong Kong, Singapore and Taiwan, which became prosperous through their trading with America and Europe. In the twenty-first century we have seen the development of open market economies in India and the cities and coastal areas of China. These are huge markets that, because of their close proximity to the Asian 'tigers', the west coast of America and Australasia have the potential to create a new dynamic economic growth area (see Figure 9.1).

The closing years of the twentieth century also saw the creation of major trade blocs – groupings of countries for trade purposes, such as NAFTA (the North American Free Trade Area) and the European Union. It became increasingly important to develop strategic alliances between groups of countries for trading purposes. Typically the

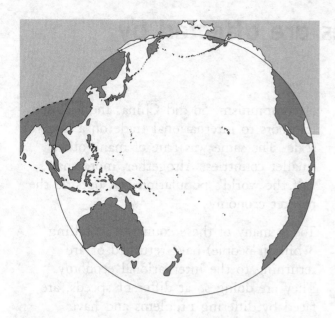

Figure 9.1 The Pacific Rim trading area and India

bulk of trade has been focused on three main areas of the globe, known as the triad (Figure 9.2).

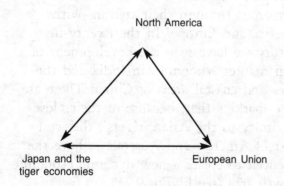

North America

Japan and the tiger economies

European Union

Figure 9.2 The triad of world trade

Globalisation: an opportunity or threat?

The global economy is characterised by the breakdown and, in some cases, the disappearance of boundaries between one nation and another, and one continent and another. Globalisation can be defined as 'the increasing international integration of markets for goods, services, and capital'. The key characteristics of globalisation are as follows (see also Figure 9.3).

Rapid communications   Free flow of capital

Transnational corporations   Globalisation   Global products and global marketing

Free trade   Development of global media systems

Figure 9.3 The characteristics of globalisation

- Rapid and sometimes instantaneous communications between one part of the globe and another. This has become possible through the Internet, through ultra-fast telecommunications and through the development of very quick air and sea transport systems.

- The ease with which capital can move from one country to another. Finance can move very quickly between countries, and large companies can set up new factories and plant almost anywhere in the world.

- The development of transnational corporations – businesses that are international in flavour, with shareholders from across the globe, and employing people across the globe.

- The development of global products and global marketing. For example, Coca-Cola products are identical across the globe, and the advertising and marketing used to promote these products are almost identical – allowing economies of scale.

- The development of a free trading regime between countries in which restrictions on trade have been progressively cut back by the World Trade Organisation (WTO).

- The development of global media systems so that, for example, American, British and French television programmes are broadcast in nearly all countries – spreading what many commentators believe to be an international pro-market consumerist culture.

Globalisation has thus the ability to bring to the planet unprecedented levels of economic growth, as costs of production are slashed and the variety of products available increases.

Since the 1950s, world trade has grown faster than world gross domestic product (GDP), indicating that increases in trade are an engine for growth in the world economy. Figure 9.4 shows how the ratio of merchandise trade to GDP has grown for the G5 (Group of 5) countries between 1890 and 1990. Merchandise trade is the average of imports and exports of merchandise goods (mainly agriculture, mining and manufacturing).

It is interesting to note that, for countries like the UK, trade is only now beginning to return to the importance it had at the end of the nineteenth century. Of course, an economy such as the USA is able to generate the bulk of its GDP within its own huge marketplace. The statistics shown in Figure 9.4 also underestimate the trend towards the growth of trade because they exclude the service sector, which has fuelled growth in so many advanced economies in recent times.

	1890	1913	1960	1970	1980	1990
France	14.2	15.5	9.9	11.9	16.7	17.1
Germany	15.9	19.9	14.5	16.5	21.6	24.0
Japan	5.1	12.5	8.8	8.3	11.8	8.4
UK	27.3	29.8	15.3	16.5	20.3	20.6
USA	5.6	6.1	3.4	4.1	8.8	8.0

Figure 9.4   The ratio of merchandise trade to GDP of the Group 5 countries (%)

Case study: The impact of the information revolution on costs

There can be no doubt that the information and communications technology revolution has been at the heart of the new global economy we are seeing in the first few years of the twenty-first century.

As the Internet plays a more central role in the international economy, we are seeing the displacement of materials by information. Cars weigh less than they used to while performing better (see Figure 9.5). Many industrial materials have been replaced by near weightless high-tech know how in the form of plastics and composite fibre materials. Because of improved materials, high-tech construction methods and smarter office equipment, new buildings today weigh less than similar ones built in the 1950s.

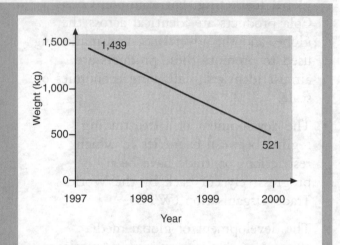

Figure 9.5   The fall in the average weight of a car, 1997–2000

Many products are losing weight, leading to a fall in transport and distribution costs. For example, the weight of this text is substantially less than the two previous editions as we use more sophisticated paper and binding techniques, while the quality of the words continues to improve (partly because the authors have access to more information through the Internet).

Even when mass is conserved, information increases. An average piece of steel manufactured in 2001 is vastly different from an average piece of steel made in the 1970s. Both pieces weigh the same, but today's piece is far superior in performance because of the research and knowledge that went into creating it. Its superior value is not due to extra weight but due to extra information. Today, every industry has a knowledge component (media, retailing, shoe manufacture, catering, etc.) and that knowledge element is increasing, leading us towards the 'weightless economy'.

1 What do you understand by the 'weightless economy'?

2 How does the weightless economy support the trend towards globalisation?

For business, the opportunity to ride the waves of the new global economy provides lots of opportunities to steal a march on competitors and to create extra value for shareholders. It is not surprising that the share prices of high-tech companies saw the biggest rises in the FTSE top companies as the curtain came down on the twentieth century (see Figure 9.6).

Top 10 companies (FTSE 100)			
Company	Value at 1/1/99	Value at 6/12/99	Actual % change
Sage Group	1570	5265	235.35
Logica	523	1480	183.25
Colt Telecom	897	2493	178.08
Biliton	120	323	170.08
WPP Group	366	985	169.31
Marconi	441	1020	131.37
Anglo American	1680	3686	119.41
Telewest comms	171	359	110.10
Sema Group	591	1205	103.89
Hays	528	998	89.19

Best sectors (FTSE Allshare)			
Company	Value at 1/1/99	Value at 6/12/99	Actual % change
IT Hardware	1053	8020	661.39
Info Tech	1402	3883	178.95
Software	1443	3340	131.49
Electronics	2837	5737	102.19
Mining	2629	5144	95.68
Forest & Paper	4001	7588	89.66
Steel	1677	3159	88.36
Telecom	5313	8613	62.13
Services	3545	5289	49.20
Distributors	1853	2761	48.99

Figure 9.6   The top ten companies and the best-performing sectors at the end of the twentieth century

However, we must be careful about being over-optimistic about the potential of the global economy to do good and to be good to everyone. The countries that have experienced the fastest rates of growth and that have been leaders in the technological revolution are characterised by extensive inequalities in incomes between the rich and the poor. You only have to take a walk up the Strand in London to observe the differences between the ultra-rich and those living on the streets.

At the same time, we see growing differences in the wealth of rich and poor nations.

The tenth anniversary edition of the *United Nations Human Development Report*, which ranks countries according to their level of economic and social development (published in July 1999), described the growing gap between the rich and the poor as grotesque, and called for urgent action to make the world a fairer place.

A special message from Ted Turner, the media mogul who donated $1 billion (£602 million) to the United Nations in 1998, echoed the report's demand for poverty reduction. 'It is as if globalisation is in fast forward and the world's ability to react to it is in slow motion,' he wrote. Average income in the world's five richest countries is 74 times the level in the poorest five, the widest the inequality gap has ever been.

Other figures showed that the world's richest 200 people had more than doubled their wealth in the four years to 1998, to more than one trillion dollars (£602 billion). The 20% of the world's population that lives in developed countries enjoy 86% of the income.

A chapter in the report on technology highlights the unequal spread of such new technologies as the Internet and biotechnology. Only in the richest countries is Internet access widespread, and even there it is mainly a white, male, upper-income group phenomenon. Basic phone connections are rare outside big cities in the developing world, and can be poor in the rainy season.

The report reveals some startling differences between the rich and the poor. For example:

- A Bangladeshi would have to save all of his wages for eight years to buy a computer; an American needs only one month's salary.

- The number of telephones per 100 people in Cambodia is one; in Monaco it is 99.

- Tanzania spends nine times more on repaying debts than on health care, and four times more than it spends on education.

These statistics are important to remember. The danger of getting too excited about the process of globalisation is that we often forget its benefits are not evenly spread.

Developing a global business strategy

For businesses, there are also profound impacts resulting from the move to globalisation. Increasingly, large multinational corporations are developing strategies for globalisation. Generally speaking, these strategies have involved identifying those things they are particularly good at and then focusing on these lines in order to seek international competitive advantage.

In the past many large businesses looked to the national market as the prime source of their activities and revenues. Today, most realise they can no longer do this: they have to rely on global networks.

The company that continued to rely on its domestic (national) market would find its market share fell as large overseas companies entered this market as part of their growth strategies. Companies, therefore, while continuing to seek competitive advantage in their home markets, must go on the attack and move into markets overseas. Increasingly, companies have therefore had to identify their best lines, and then develop a global strategy for these lines.

Case study: Heinz' Project Millennia

Like many global producers today the Heinz Corporation (www.heinz.co.uk) started off on a small-scale, localised basis. The first product produced by Henry John Heinz in 1869 was horse-radish, followed by pickles, sauerkraut and vinegar, all delivered by horse-drawn wagons to grocers in and around Pittsburgh, Pennsylvania. In 1875 a new product was introduced, one that flourishes today – tomato ketchup.

As Heinz' markets have grown from local to national to global, from one product to a dozen, to several thousand today, the ideal of quality has been at the heart of Heinz' thinking. Heinz' revenues have climbed from the thousands in 1869, through the millions, tens and hundreds of millions, now billions and edging towards the tens of billions.

As the years passed, Heinz expanded in the USA and around the world, at first through internal growth (by ploughing back profits into investment in new plant and equipment) but, since the 1960s, largely by acquisition and brand building (by taking over and buying up well-known producers of products and brands that complement Heinz' existing ones). In 2000 Heinz had an operational presence in more than 150 separate locations in scores of countries across six continents.

In the new global economy it makes sense to concentrate on what you do best – your best lines. All organizations, therefore, need to build organisational structures that make it easy to:

- Concentrate on the best lines (i.e. the ones in which they have the greatest competitive advantage).

- Identify new opportunities arising in these areas.

- Channel resources and initiatives into these lines and opportunities.

- Manage effectively these best lines and opportunities.

Heinz have identified the six product categories they will focus on in the early twenty-first century:

- food service
- ketchup and condiments
- tuna

- instant feeding
- weight control
- petfoods.

Heinz, therefore, have reorganised their organisation to concentrate on these lines. This has involved buying other producers, for example of tuna and petfoods, to gain an increased market share in these areas. The firm that sells most is best placed to take advantage of the latest advances in technology, to spread its marketing and advertising costs over a wider output, to buy components and ingredients in bulk, to distribute products at lower unit costs, and to gain many other economies of scale.

Heinz, therefore, have concentrated on producing many standardised products and selling them across the globe. For example, in 1999 they relaunched their Heinz tomato ketchup bottle so that the shape of the bottle, its look and labelling are the same across the globe.

1 How have Heinz set about improving their global presence?

2 Why have they focused on six product categories?

3 How can they build competitive advantage in these categories?

Check your understanding

What do you understand by the term 'globalisation'? Do you think globalisation is a good thing or not?

The multinational company

What examples do you think of when you hear the term 'multinational company'? Obvious examples are:

- Coca-Cola – selling soft drinks in nearly every country on the globe.

- Nestlé – which have set out to become 'the world food company'.

- Nike – marketing their designer trainers everywhere there are consumers with disposable incomes.

A multinational enterprise (MNE) is a company with its headquarters in one country but with operations in other countries.

You will often read in the literature about transnational corporations (TNCs). Often writers use these terms to refer to the same companies. However, sometimes a distinction is made between an MNE and a TNC, in which the shareholders and operations of the company are so spread across the globe that it is difficult to identify the home base of the company with any particular country.

A multinational enterprise has two major areas of concern – the home country of its headquarters, and the host countries in which it operates. The MNE will operate in a changing environment in which there are a range of influences, including the actions of competitors, customers, suppliers, financial institutions and governments.

Another important characteristic of a multinational is that it is able to draw on a common pool of resources, including assets, patents, trademarks, information and human resources. These resources can be shared within the organisation (e.g. the pooling of information through organization-wide databases, and the use of patents and technologies on a global scale).

A short history of multinationals

Stage 1

Even before the industrial revolution, giant trading multinationals were involved in trading in a range of commodities (e.g. the British East India Company).

Stage 2

In the period 1870–1910, giant vertically integrated corporations emerged in many branches of primary production, such as mining, bananas, rubber and oil. These multinationals often built strong ties with governments in the countries where they operated. A number of these countries were virtually mono-exporters, producing one or a small number of products for export which they were able to do through the multinational organisation that set up in their country.

Stage 3

After the Second World War, many developing countries wanted to break away from their reliance on basic commodities. They felt they needed to industrialise. Many set up their own industries which were heavily protected (through tariffs and quotas) against foreign competition. This process was known as import substitution industrialisation (ISI), i.e. replacing foreign imports with domestically produced goods. The ISI approach effectively locked out of the domestic market the products of many manufacturing companies of the advanced industrial nations.

In response, many large manufacturing multinationals, particularly those based in the USA, reacted (where they could) by 'jumping the tariff walls' and setting up 'standalone' branch plants in less developed nations outwith large enough domestic markets.

Stage 4

From the late 1960s and continuing throughout the twentieth century, global factories began to emerge, sparked by revolutions in communications, information processing and transportation. The multinationals were not primarily investing overseas to win the domestic markets where they set up; rather, they were looking to benefit from cheap labour, the near absence of environmental restrictions relating to production activities, the absence of trade unions and other factors that would help the multinationals to lower their costs of production.

At a time when international tariff barriers were falling, it was becoming easier to set up in a country such as Brazil or Mexico and to transport your products to wherever there was a market. We thus saw the development of truly global factories. The east Asian 'tigers' developed during this period. The new era was one of 'globally integrated production' and it has helped to bring in post-millennium prosperity in the triad economies (in a world of incredible contrasts between the rich and the poor worlds).

Global production makes sense because of the rapid fall in costs of distribution and communications (e.g. transport costs and telephone calls, etc.). It also makes sense for firms to exploit their know-how, technologies, patents, etc., on as wide a basis as possible. Another reason for global

production is that may of the processes of modern production have been deskilled, so that they can be carried out by anyone anywhere but, of course, supported by a group of core, highly skilled technicians and managers.

Step 5

A variation on step 4 that is popular today is the setting up by multinationals of joint ventures in countries that are only starting to come round to free market principles. For example, Nestlé has created joint ventures in China, Western oil companies have set up joint ventures in Vietnam, and many companies have set up joint ventures in the former Eastern bloc. Typically, the joint venture will be based on an injection of capital and know-how by the triad-based multinational, and an injection of manpower, resources and local connections by the company with which the joint venture is being established. Multinationals recognise that to be successful in these new markets, they need to know the right people with the right connections.

We can thus see that multinationals lie at the heart of the new global economy:

- Injecting vast sums of capital.
- Setting up new production systems.
- Processing goods into finished goods on an international scale.
- Producing mass market goods (for the global economy).
- Developing globalised marketing systems.
- Injecting new ideas and systems across the globe.
- Developing information and communications technology networks.

Why individual businesses become involved in international operations

There are a number of reasons why business organisations typically move from a national to an international presence.

Opportunistic developments

A UK-based company may start off by distributing products within the UK, producing sales literature to support the sales programme. Perhaps some of this material is read by people overseas, who then start to put in orders. Most large international companies originally developed many of their overseas leads through opportunistic developments.

Following customers abroad

Many businesses move into new international markets to follow their customers. For example, suppliers of car parts move abroad when the company they supply develops new factories and plant in new countries.

Geographic diversification

A number of businesses deliberately set out to spread their risks by moving into new overseas markets. This is particularly the case when you have saturated your home market, and where there are large markets overseas in which you can quickly build up a competitive advantage.

To increase profits

It makes sense to move abroad to make the best use of existing resources. For example, a company that spends a great deal of money on research and development will find it can then spread the R&D cost over a much larger output by selling in wider markets – thus leading to higher profits.

To exploit different growth rates in different countries

Different countries grow at different rates. In particular periods, economies experience very fast growth rates. At other times, particularly in a mature economy, growth rates may slow. The intelligent multinational will therefore seek to match its capabilities to opportunities that arise in areas of fast growth.

To exploit differences in the product life-cycle

While the product life-cycle for some products might be coming to a halt in this country, it may be in an early stage in another country. Once the product life-cycle has matured or is in decline in one country, it will be sensible to seek other markets where there are better opportunities in the product life-cycle. For example, such companies as Coca-Cola are moving into new markets where the demand for their products is only just starting to take off.

The hugeness of overseas markets

While we tend to think of the US and European markets as being large, they are actually very small when compared with the potential of such huge markets as China and India.

Internationalising for defensive reasons

Sometimes companies are not interested in pursuing new growth or potential abroad but decide to enter international business for largely defensive reasons. When a domestic company sees its markets invaded by foreign firms, that company may react by entering the foreign competitor's home market in return.

Pursuing a global logic

The term 'global logic' identifies a condition in the market that requires a company to adopt a global strategy. The nature of the market makes it the only sensible thing to do, to go global. Again, Coca-Cola have to go global because Coca-Cola is an international product. By going global they can spread all their costs over billions of consumers. We have seen with the Heinz case study (above) that more and more companies are pursuing this global logic, which applies to nearly all mass-produced consumer goods.

Case study: Unilever swallows up French mustard maker

In November 1999, Unilever (the Persil to Oxo group) (www.unilever.co.uk) increased their food portfolio by acquiring the French mustard maker, Amora-Maille, for £460 million. The Anglo-Dutch consumer product group bought the Dijon-based company that produces the gourmet Maille mustard brand, as well as ketchup, sauces and salad dressings, under its Maille and Amora labels. The group holds the top spot in the French condiments market and Unilever intend to position Maille as their global delicatessen brand.

These new products will sit alongside existing ones, such as Colman's mustard and Chicken Tonight ready-made cooking sauce, in Unilever's European food and beverage unit. The company hopes the acquisitions will boost its share of the European culinary market from 9% to 12%. The deal was well received among UK investors, driving Unilever shares up 22p.

The deal was Unilever's third culinary products purchase in 1999, and this deal was seen as part of an ongoing process of consolidation.

In October 1999, Unilever took over Sweden's Slotts and Kockens, which make mustard, ketchup and seasonings. In April, the group had bought Melissa Pumaro's Greek tomato products business.

1 Why do you think Unilever purchased these companies in 1999?

2 How would these acquisitions serve to give Unilever greater competitive advantage?

3 Get hold of a Unilever company report to find out if they have made any more recent acquisitions to this portfolio.

The advantages of being a multinational

There are a number of advantages to organisations of being a multinational:

- To protect themselves from the risks and uncertainties of the trade cycle within their own economy. By spreading their sphere of influence, they are thus able to spread risks.

- To benefit from the growing world market for goods and services. This is part of the process of globalisation (the rapid growth of similar goods and services produced and distributed by MNEs on a world scale).

- As a response to increased foreign competition and to protect their world market share. When other foreign multinationals start to compete in a particular MNE's market, then it is time to expand into new markets.

- In order to reduce costs. By setting up operating units close to foreign customers, it is possible to reduce transport costs (e.g. setting up soft drinks bottling and confectionery manufacturing plants in other countries).

- To overcome tariff walls by serving a foreign market from within. This is major reason why so many Japanese car manufacturers have set up in the UK. This enabled them to get inside the European Union.

- To take advantage of technological expertise by making goods directly rather than allowing others to do so under licence. A typical licensing contract lasts for about seven years and gives the licensee access to patents, trade marks, etc., in exchange for a fee or royalty. However, if instead the multinational produces goods directly, the company will be closer to emerging technological development, enabling it to adapt new ideas itself.

The benefits of multinationals to an economy

There is considerable debate as to whether multinationals and their activities are good or bad for economies and their people.

Job creation and employment

One argument put forward in favour of multinationals is that they create jobs. For example, the establishment of the Toyota plant near Derby created a great many local jobs and was welcomed by many people in the area.

The reverse of this is that some people argue that multinationals can just as easily pull out of a country as stay in. If they feel it is more advantageous to set up elsewhere, they can close down large plants at a moment's notice.

The balance of payments

The UK has benefited from having a number of Japanese, American and European car manufacturers operating in this country. Clearly, the finished goods they produce can be sold abroad, thus creating exports for the UK. However, on the downside this may mean having to import a great many raw materials, parts, etc., which go into the finished products.

Technology and expertise

Foreign multinationals may introduce new technology, production methods and ways of working into an economy and thus help it to move forward. For example, in recent years we have come to talk about the 'Japanisation' of UK industry (i.e. the wide-scale adoption of factory robots, just-in-time working practices, teamwork and quality management, to name just a few initiatives). It is widely recognised that the adoption of such practices has helped to improve the competitive edge of organisations in this country.

The process whereby technology is taken up in one country from another is called 'technology transfer'. This process is particularly effective in bringing foward less developed countries.

Social responsibility

Multinationals have received the most scathing criticism for the social costs of some of their activities (e.g. in destroying local communities, pollution, etc.). In particular, a major criticism levelled at MNEs is that of employing 'double standards'. They may transfer their manufacturing operations to economies that do not have such tight environmental standards, and thus effectively 'export' pollution from richer to poorer countries. Economies desperate for income may be susceptible to the advances of unscrupulous multinationals.

Government control

The size and financial power of multinationals may make it difficult for governments to control them. For example, MNEs may be able to win concessions as a result of their size and influence. Some corporations evade taxation by transferring profits from one country to another (i.e. declaring high profits in low-tax countries, and low profits in high-tax countries).

Some commentators argue that, increasingly, global trade and global business operations have become far more important than national governments. They argue that the important decision-makers in the world today are the multinationals.

> ### Check your understanding
>
> Obtain the most recent copy of a company report for a well-known multinational (e.g. Coca-Cola, Pepsi-Cola, Unilever, Mars, Nestlé). Find out what countries the multinational is based in and how it seeks to standardise its products across the globe.
>
> What new markets is the company moving into, and what markets is it exiting? Why?

What is international competitiveness?

Competitive advantage tends to stem from two main sources – charging lower prices than rival products or by offering better quality (i.e. the sort of differentiated product the consumer is looking for). With rapid increases in technology in recent years and the development of the Internet, it seems consumers are going to be able to enjoy lower prices and more differentiated products as we enter an age of innovation. A huge multinational organisation such as the American retailer Wal-Mart is able to benefit from charging low prices (because it benefits so extensively from economies of scale) and from differentiation (because it offers so many products and such a quality service).

There are two contrasting views as to how an organisation should gain international competitiveness. One view is that the organisation should look at the competition and then beat the competition. The other is that the organisation should focus on its own strengths and core competences and build these up. The best answer probably contains both elements.

The American business writer Michael Porter argues that competitive advantage comes from positioning your organisation or product relative to competitors in such a way that you out-perform them. For example, Parker pens have a reputation for superior quality while, at the same time, being affordable. Many aspects of the pen and its presentation (packaging, magazine advertising, etc.). support this differentiation.

The Jaguar car for many years was seen as an exclusive up-market luxury. However, as modern production techniques associated with Japanisation were applied to more and more cars, the advantages of superior engineering associated with the Jaguar were eroded. More recently, Jaguar have gone through their own Japanisation process to improve quality and performance while, at the same time, new, more affordable models of the car have been produced to ensure a new type of competitive advantage (see Figure 9.7).

International competitiveness stems from a number of sources:

- A particular company's reputation. Some products have the sort of reputation that make them different. For example, we still use the term a 'Rolls-Royce' of a product to indicate its status and superiority. Other UK products and businesses that continue to have a strong international reputation are Marks & Spencer, Manchester United, Harrods and *Vogue* magazine.

- The research and development basis of a company. Some UK companies have invested considerably in research and development to give them a scientific and technical edge over competitors (e.g. Glaxo in the pharmaceuticals world, ICI in chemicals and Dyson in household cleaning equipment).

- The reputation for style and excitement associated with products and companies (e.g. Virgin Airways have a reputation for exciting new ideas about air travel, and many British designers and fashion labels lead the field, e.g. Paul Smith Jeans).

- The attention given to customer service (e.g. some London hotels have an international reputation for the way they treat visitors).

- Distinctiveness of a particular product. For example, many British manufacturers are able to trade on their distinctive Britishness (e.g. Twinings tea and Oxford marmalade).

- The excellence of particular products. For example, Wilkinson Sword razors are known for the quality of the steel and the engineering processes that go into making them. Scotch whisky is famous throughout the world.

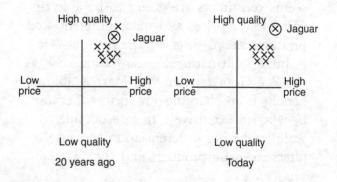

× = competitors

Figure 9.7   The Japanisation of Jaguar

- The quality of the human resources that go into a particular product (e.g. 'made by the finest craftspeople': products of the Scottish woollen industry).

- The low prices associated with a product, enabling the customers to feel they are getting 'value for money'.

The importance of doing things well

If a business organisation is to be successful, it needs to do things well. People often make the mistake of just looking at the firm's end-products to see what it is doing well. However, top-quality products result from top-quality processes at every stage in production. International competitiveness really stems from the value chain through which an organisation adds value at each stage in production. For example, part of this value chain is the way in which the firm builds good links with its suppliers; another part is the way in which the firm builds up relationships with its employees.

Products that are superior to rival offerings on international markets are the sum of the various processes and value-adding activities that have gone into making that product so successful. Guinness is successful as a drink, but it is also successful because Guinness is a company that knows how to do business at every stage along the value chain.

By doing things well, the organisation will gain visible advantages in terms of:

- The firm's products, which are competitively priced.

- The firm's technological orientation (i.e. technologically superior processes and products).

- Product quality.

- Delivery.

- Flexibility of service, etc.

Technology and international competitive advantage

In the modern economy it pays to be at the forefront of technological development. Some commentators argue that it is technology that drives much of economic growth in modern society. For example, the influential writer Kevin Kelly argues that:

each actualisation of a desire – that is, each new service or product – forms a platform from which other possible activities can be imagined and desired. Once technology satisfies the opportunity to fly, for instance, flying produces new desires: to eat while flying, to fly by oneself to work each day, to fly faster than sound, to fly to the moon, to watch TV while flying. Once technology satisfies the desire to watch TV while flying, our insatiable imagination hungers to be able to watch a video of our own choosing, and not see what others watch. That dream, too, can be actualised by technical knowledge. Each actualisation of an idea supplies room for more technology, and each new technology supplies room for more ideas. They feed on each other, rounding faster and faster.

The clear message is that, if organisations can come up with the new ideas, and can produce the products associated with these ideas, they will generate the demand not only for the product but also for the next one, and the next after that. This is one reason why Japanese companies were so successful in the last quarter of the twentieth century, because of the range of new ideas they were able to bring to the marketplace. Robert Solow, an American economist, suggested that technology is responsible for about 80% of growth in the economy.

Research and development should be seen as a considerable investment in competitive advantage and in future profitability. In a survey of products developed in the latter half of the twentieth century, Japan's Ministry of International Trade and Industry (MITI) found that Britain was responsible for 52% of revolutionary ideas; America came up with 22%, while Japan produced only 6%. But when it came to product development this order was reversed. So Britain was losing competitive advantage by not delivering new ideas to the marketplace.

A number of UK commentators have pointed out that industry is not spending enough on research and development to bring new products and processes to market. Research and development in the UK accounts for about 2.5% of national income.

Technological development is the process of using new techniques to improve and enhance industrial performance. In an increasingly hi-tech world, it is necessary to be at the leading edge of development. Competitors will certainly make use of this edge.

At any one time, society has a given stock of knowledge about the ways in which goods can be made. Technical advance can come through:

- *Invention* – the discovery of new knowledge.

- *Innovation* – building new knowledge into production techniques.

Invention can lead to spectacular increases in technical knowledge, and successful inventors are always at a premium in society because they help us to leap forward – for example, the creation of crisps, followed by putting flavourings into crisps, followed by being able to produce crisps in a variety of shapes.

Innovation will usually require investment in new machinery and other capital items. This is an area where Britain is sometimes criticised as being slow. The Japanese MITI, in comparison, is very good at making sure government money is available to convert new inventions and ideas into developed products.

Major new inventions can lead to periods of investment and innovation as these ideas are put into practice. Today we are seeing a

Check your understanding

Outline the ways in which one major UK company has been able to gain competitive advantage in international markets. In addition to the product or service the company makes, what aspects of the business and its relationships have enabled the company to be so successful?

wave of new products replacing old ones as new technologies sweep away old ideas. If we allow innovations to take place, we can benefit from an ongoing process of change.

Freedom of trade and the World Trade Organisation

Many people believe that free trade is a desirable end in itself. Free trade exists when there are no barriers to trade. With free trade, individuals, organisations and countries will specialise in the things they do best and will then sell the products of their labour. Free trade is based on the principle of comparative advantage, which states that 'factors of production should concentrate on their best lines'. The authors of this book concentrate on writing and let accountants look after their accounts for them. This is because we are better at writing books than keeping accounts, although we could do both tasks.

Some of the products we import into this country could be produced here (indeed, we might be better able to produce these goods than the countries we buy them from). However, it is far more sensible if we concentrate on producing those things we are best at doing – like producing Scotch whisky or Jaguar cars.

Under free trade, the argument goes that there is room for everyone to specialise in something. Developing countries can specialise in growing the things their climate suits them for (e.g. sugar cane, tea, coffee and other products).

This sounds fair, but is it? There are many people who feel free trade is not fair trade. Under free trade there is no guaranteed income to people in less developed countries. Because a crop such as sugar can be grown in many parts of the world, it does not command a very high price. So countries that produce it and trade it 'freely' do not receive a very high income from it. International trade therefore, tends to favour those countries that produce the high value-added products, those countries that own the patent to produce Coca-Cola, that produce Johnny Walker whisky and so on.

Fair trade is the idea that some countries and people will sink rather than swim in free trade conditions, because they are exploited by large multinational companies.

The World Trade Organisation

The World Trade Organisation (WTO) really hit the headlines only in December 1999, when the Seattle Conference led to demonstrations in America and other countries on a scale not seen since the 1960s.

The World Trade Organisation is an extension of the General Agreement on Tariffs and Trade (GATT), which was created in 1947 and which operates on three levels as:

- A set of trading rules ('the rules of the road for trade').

- An international agency for helping to resolve trade disputes between countries and groups of countries.

- A means for countries to get together to create freer trade and to cut down existing barriers.

In 2000, the World Trade Organisation is a 135-member body that sets the rules for global commerce. Fans of free trade say the

WTO helps keep the arteries of world commerce clear and makes sure trade is conducted fairly. Opponents say it over-rides national sovereignty (the control of a nation over its own affairs) in the interests of multinational companies, ignores the environment and tramples on human rights.

The 1999 Seattle Conference was a gathering of (mainly) trade ministers to kick off a new round of world trade talks. It lasted a week but started a round of negotiations that will last at least three years and that will produce a treaty each national delegation will sign and ratify. The Europeans who attended the conference had a big agenda for reductions in trade and called it the Millennium Round, while the Americans (who wanted a smaller-scale effort) called it the Seattle Round. The fundamental aim of the Millennium Round was to improve market access for all products. Market access is the general openness of an economy to goods and services from outside.

The most basic form of trade barrier is a tariff – a government tax on particular goods as they enter the country. One of the main efforts in Seattle was to reduce tariffs on most goods. One of the major parts of the Round was concerned with cutting/removing direct support and subsidies to farmers.

The wealthy WTO members have cut back on payments to farmers who support domestic production by 20% between 1995 and 2001. Poorer countries have made smaller or no cuts. The developing countries (led by India) wanted to speed up access for their textiles to the EU and the USA, partly because they think that Washington and Brussels are going too slowly, and partly because of the worry that, because

China is entering the WTO, it will take over large shares of existing markets.

China, the world's most populous country, is now joining WTO. This will have a considerable effect for trade, both because China is a mass producer of items such as textiles and electrical goods, and it is a huge potential market itself.

The World Trade Organisation and its deliberations have profound effects for many UK businesses and particular sectors. For example, the progressive freeing of trade on a world scale has led to the decimation of the UK textile industry because it has been impossible to compete with the low costs of developing countries. A symbol of this was that Marks & Spencer, which had previously relied on buying many of their garments in the UK, were forced to change their policy in late 1999 because they could not compete with rivals.

The freeing of trade generally has meant that UK companies have to be internationally competitive in their own domestic market. At the same time, the freeing of trade has provided UK firms with many opportunities throughout the globe. The development of much freer trade in the world has been one of the most important factors in creating the global economy.

Check your understanding

Identify a local business that has been affected by the freeing of world trade resulting from the rounds of talks of the WTO.

Identify a manager at the business to find out how freer trade has affected his or her business.

Case study: Different interest groups at the Seattle Conference

Some of the differing views that were raised at the Seattle Conference are listed in Figure 9.8.

1 Why are there so many different viewpoints about the direction forward for the WTO?

2 Which of the arguments put forward do you sympathises with most? Why?

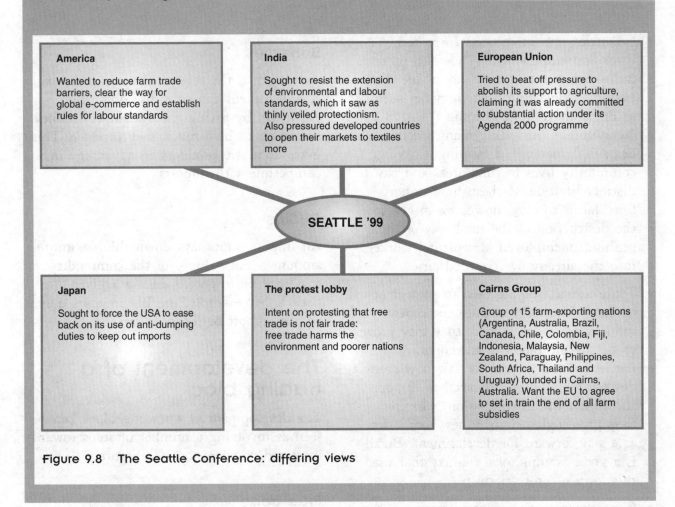

America

Wanted to reduce farm trade barriers, clear the way for global e-commerce and establish rules for labour standards

India

Sought to resist the extension of environmental and labour standards, which it saw as thinly veiled protectionism. Also pressured developed countries to open their markets to textiles more

European Union

Tried to beat off pressure to abolish its support to agriculture, claiming it was already committed to substantial action under its Agenda 2000 programme

SEATTLE '99

Japan

Sought to force the USA to ease back on its use of anti-dumping duties to keep out imports

The protest lobby

Intent on protesting that free trade is not fair trade: free trade harms the environment and poorer nations

Cairns Group

Group of 15 farm-exporting nations (Argentina, Australia, Brazil, Canada, Chile, Colombia, Fiji, Indonesia, Malaysia, New Zealand, Paraguay, Philippines, South Africa, Thailand and Uruguay) founded in Cairns, Australia. Want the EU to agree to set in train the end of all farm subsidies

Figure 9.8   The Seattle Conference: differing views

The effects of barriers to trade

Often, individual countries or groups of countries (trading blocs) restrict imports from other countries. They do this for a number of reasons:

- Countries protect their own industries. Industries develop over time and involve considerable investment. Specialist machinery needs to be bought, and the labour force needs to build up the skills to run these industries. Countries are therefore reluctant to see their domestic industries destroyed by cheaper foreign imports. Japan, for example, is well known for the way in which it has protected its domestic market from foreign competition while, at the same time, exporting widely to the rest of the world.

- Countries restrict imports to protect firms and employment. They also protect industries to maintain a way of life. For example, some European countries such as France have large farming communities (including many smaller peasant farmers). The farming community lives in rural areas and has a distinct lifestyle. If cheap food imports force farms to close down, we might see the destruction of the rural way of life, pushing unemployed agricultural workers into the already overcrowded cities.

- Trade restrictions are used to protect new or 'infant' industries. Once these new industries are established, they may prove to be the life blood of an economy. Earlier in this chapter we saw how many developing countries resorted to import substitution industrialisation, whereby they protected their own new industries as a way forward for development. Brazil is a good example of a country that used this form of protectionism.

- Countries may also want to restrict the import of strategic goods (e.g. basic sources of energy, fuel, materials and defence goods).

Types of barriers

There are a number of methods of restricting imports from other countries (or groups of countries).

Import duties (tariffs)

An import duty is a tax. The price of the taxed commodity will be higher as a result of the tax.

Subsidies

A subsidy is the reverse of an import tax. A government can subsidise domestic producers by giving them a sum of money according to how much they produce. This gives domestic products an advantage in competing with imports.

Quotas

An import quota lays down the maximum amount – not value – of the commodity that may be imported during a given period. For example, the EU imposes quotas on the import of Japanese cars.

The development of a trading bloc

The development of a trading block can be seen as involving a number of steps towards increased co-operation (see Figure 9.9).

Free trade

Developing a free trade area involves getting rid of some of the barriers to free trade in a particular area (e.g. the removal of quotas and tariffs between members of the trading community).

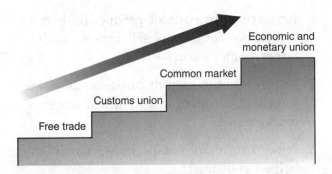

Figure 9.9   The steps in the creation of a trading bloc

Customs union

In addition to a free trade area, member states operate a common external tariff. This means that an import to the European Union from a non-member country (e.g. Venezuela) would carry the same tariff whether it entered France, Germany, Italy or any other member of the bloc. Within the customs union, the member states develop common trading policies and move towards equal conditions for businesses to compete in.

Common market

A common market involves the free movement of factors of production (land, labour, capital and enterprise) and the free movement of goods. For example, the European Union is characterised by the four freedoms:

1 The free movement of goods.

2 The free movement of services.

3 The free movement of people.

4 The free movement of capital.

Economic and monetary union

This occurs when countries operate with a single currency and with a single central bank, and when they start to harmonise many other aspects of economic management, such as taxes.

Check your understanding

Identify goods where UK firms are faced by quotas and tariffs when exporting to foreign countries. What is the impact of these restrictions on the companies concerned?

Identify goods where UK firms are protected by quotas and tariffs. What is the impact of these restrictions on the companies concerned?

The European Union, European Monetary Union and the Single Market

The European Union (EU) we know today is the product of an ongoing process of economic, social and political union between member states. The member states are shown in Figure 9.10.

Member states	Date of entry
France, Germany, Belgium, Luxembourg, The Netherlands, Italy	1960
UK, Ireland, Denmark	1973
Greece	1981
Spain, Portugal	1986
East Germany	1990
Austria, Finland, Sweden	1995
Czech Republic, Hungary, Poland, Slovakia	Early 21st century?

Figure 9.10   Member states of the European Union

In 1951 we saw the creation of the European Coal and Steel Community, involving the linking together of the coal and steel industries of the six founding member states.

The Treaty of Rome

The next step in the evolution of the EU came in 1956, with the creation of the European Economic Community as a result of the signing of the Treaty of Rome. This involved the six countries giving up some of their decision-making powers to the European Economic Community (EEC) in relation to a number of areas of the economy. A common customs union was created with a common external tariff to the rest of the world.

Key dates in the development of the European Union:

- 1957 (the signing of the Treaty of Rome).
- 1992 (the creation of the Single Market).
- 1993 (the Maastricht Treaty).
- 1999 (the creation of the euro).

The creation of the Single Market

In 1992, the Single European Act created a European common market protected by a customs union and a common external tariff barrier. For member countries the Single Market area now became their 'home market'.

The four main advantages of the creation of the common market were as follows:

1 Reductions in costs of production because companies could now sell into a much larger home market.

2 Improved efficiency of business, as it was forced to compete in this much larger marketplace.

3 New patterns of competition, which helped consumers.

4 New innovations, processes and products coming on to the market as a result of increased business efficiency and competitiveness.

The Maastricht Treaty

Over the years there has been increasing co-operation between member states with, for example, the creation of a common fisheries policy and a joint environmental policy. Finally, in 1993, we saw the signing of the Maastricht Treaty, which heralded the creation of a European Union (i.e. moving the range of co-operation on from simple economic relationships to new political and social relationships). Decision-making in the European Union is divided between supra-national European institutions (the European Commission and the European Parliament) and governments of the member states, which send ministers to the Council of Ministers. The Court of Justice serves as the final decider in legal matters or disputes among EU institutions or between EU institutions and member states.

The new areas added to existing treaties by Maastricht included a common foreign and security policy and a justice and home affairs policy.

In 2000, the development of a joint security force was prompted by the European Union's perceived failure to take action quickly enough, and on a sufficient enough scale, in the Kosovo crisis of 1999. Increasingly, the European Parliament is beginning to take on more responsibility and this is likely to continue. The Social Chapter of the Maastricht Treaty is now beginning to have an increasing impact on business in this country – with the development of minimum wage legislation and a working time directive limiting the numbers of hours people are allowed to work.

The key institutions of the EU are as follows.

The European Commission

The European Commission makes policy proposals and presents them to the Council of Ministers. The European Commission also represents the EU in economic relations with other countries or international organisations. The Commission also manages EC funds and programmes.

The Council of Ministers:

This is the main law-making body of the EU and is composed of a single representative from each of the member states. The Council cannot draft laws but it can accept, reject or request proposals from the Commission.

The European Council

Summit meetings among the top leaders of the member states are called at least once every six months by the country holding the presidency of the Council of Ministers.

The European Parliament

The European Parliament is the only body of the EU whose members are directly elected by the citizens of its member states. Seats are allocated according to the population of each member state. The Parliament may veto a proposal after it reaches the Council of Ministers if it disagrees with the Council's position. The European Parliament also works with the Council of Ministers on the EU budget and can reject a budget plan if agreement cannot be reached within the Council.

In 1999, the Parliament was not happy with the way in which many European Commissioners were conducting their affairs, with huge waste and corruption evident in the community. It managed to have the President and most of the commissioners replaced.

Creation of the euro

Another new development that will have a profound impact on business is the development of the single currency – the euro. European Monetary Union refers to the section of the Maastricht Treaty that provides for the creation of a 'monetary union' between EU members. Individual currencies (such as the pound, the franc, the mark and the lira) have, in effect, ceased to exist and will be replaced (in 2000) by a single currency known as the euro.

On 1 January 1999, 11 sovereign nations handed over control of their currencies to a committee of bankers. Currency (notes and coins) will appear in 2002. Up to 2002, francs, lire and other currencies will remain in circulation. In 1999, the value of the currencies of the 11 euro nations was locked against the euro.

Now, all decisions affecting the euro (on interest rates or monetary flows) are taken by the European Central Bank in Frankfurt. So far the euro has not been very successful, and it has fallen steadily against other major currencies, including the pound (as at early 2000).

Figure 9.11 summarises the arguments for and against the euro.

Check your understanding

Interview the owners/managers of two businesses that import and export a considerable quantity of goods. How do they feel the euro will affect their business?

How the Internet is breaking down international barriers

The Internet has had a massive effect on international business in recent years. International companies that have failed to realise the power and influence of the Internet have rapidly lost competitive advantage to those that have grasped the opportunity.

Advances in computer technology have transformed the structure, functioning, and rules of the economy creating what is termed the 'Network' or 'New Economy'.

For	Against
A fixed exchange rate will end currency instability in Europe	National government will have less control over monetary policy
Unstable markets have caused economic crises in the past, forcing governments to choose between high interest rates (leading to unemployment) and currency devaluation (leading to high inflation)	Global economic shocks are likely to affect member states in different ways
Low interest rates and a fixed exchange rate will encourage more progressive and long-term government domestic policies and boost trade and investment	Unemployment could increase, at least in the short term, if a government comes under pressure to cut public expenditure owing to restrictions relating to the requirement to limit its deficit
No one member of the EU will be able to dictate monetary policy	Critics fear that the German central bank (the Bundesbank) will dominate proceedings
The euro should be strong enough to compete against the dollar and the yen on world markets	The European Monetary Institute and European Central Bank might not look beyond the issue of price stability and might ignore the knock-on social and political effects of monetary policy

Figure 9.11 Arguments for and against the euro

The 'Internet' and the subsequent development of the 'World Wide Web' are principal drivers in this transformation. The Internet is a worldwide computer network. It was originally planned by military and educational institutions in the United States during the 1960s and has actively developed in the 1970s. The World Wide Web is a further development of the Internet, which took off in the early 1990s. It uses special transmission protocols to deliver text, graphics, and audio materials over the Internet. These materials are linked to other materials by 'hyper-text links'. The way in which the information that is available over the Web through the use of these links is completely in the hands of the computer user. Thus, the World Wide Web is a highly powerful mechanism for the exchange of information.

By improving the flow of information between buyers and sellers the Internet and the World Wide Web have caused changes in the business world: a new marketplace, a new form of communication, a new means of distribution and a new information system. Commerce can now be conducted using the Internet and the World Wide Web. Internet-enabled commerce has variously been called 'e-commerce', 'electronic commerce', 'Internet commerce', 'e-trade' or 'e-business'. Arguably, however, the Internet's most dramatic impact on organisations is the cutting of costs.

Today, the Internet companies can build new brand names very quickly. An example is Amazon.Com, the book retailer. Awareness of Amazon was developed very quickly through Internet links.

The success of Amazon is representative of the way in which transactions can now be made from one part of the world to another, very quickly and efficiently. Private and business consumers are quickly able to access information about the availability of goods in different parts of the world – they can select goods and have them delivered from other countries rather than from close to home.

The Internet provides a means through which capital transfers can take place almost instantaneously, with the development of investment opportunities in other countries, and the means of making electronic transmission of payment.

Increasingly, large business organisations are responding to the challenge of the Internet by focusing on a range of powerbrands, which they can promote and market globally, using the Internet as the international form of communication.

Large companies like the US retailing giant Wal-Mart are using the Internet to make bulk purchases across continents in order to minimise their costs of purchasing and distribution.

More and more large multinational corporations are using the Internet as a global marketing tool – to promote and advertise their goods and services on a global basis, to develop a database of relationships with customers on an international scale, and to develop a more refined understanding of global purchasing patterns.

While the Internet operates in a variety of languages, the predominant language is English. Internet users mainly communicate in English which has become a global means of communication, to the advantage of American and British companies.

A key impact of the Internet has been the creation of instant communications. It seems that there is very little in the modern world that can be hidden from those with access to the Internet. This has forced businesses to develop more ethical images and more ethical practices. If a business is involved in a scandal in one part of the world, it will rapidly be publicised through the Internet to billions of potential consumers.

Check your understanding

1 Explain how the demand for one product that you are familiar with has increased as a result of the successful exploitation of the Internet by the firm which makes that product.

2 Show how the Internet has made it possible to improve the supply of a product that you are familiar with, by reducing the costs of producing and supplying that product.

3 Explain one other way in which the Internet is breaking down international barriers.

Unit 2 Assessment

This unit is assessed through an external assessment. The grade on that assessment will be your grade for the unit.

In your external assessment you will be expected to answer questions about a business/businesses operating within an international market.

This will involve identifying the following:

- The market sectors in which businesses operate.

- The characteristics of the market within which the business operates.

- The market conditions that affect the way businesses operate.

- The ways in which competition affects different stakeholders in business.

- The methods of government intervention and their effects on businesses.

- The factors affecting the competitiveness of international markets.

To achieve a Grade E you must show you can:

- Correctly identify the market and sector of industry within which businesses operate.

- Recognise and describe the characteristics of the market within which businesses operate.

- Understand market conditions that affect the way businesses operate.

- Identify how and why businesses seek to influence market conditions.

- Explain the different ways in which competition affects different stakeholders in business.

- Identify methods of government intervention and describe how this intervention affects business.

- Identify and describe the factors affecting the competitiveness of international markets and how businesses operating in international markets are affected by these factors.

To achieve a Grade C you must also show you can:

- Analyse how businesses are affected by the type(s) of market within which they operate.

- Analyse how changes in market conditions might affect businesses and stakeholders.

- Explain why businesses seek to influence market conditions.

- Analyse the reasons why governments intervene to manage the economy and businesses.

- Explain how businesses adapt to international competition and to the conditions found in international markets.

To achieve a Grade A you must also show you can:

- Evaluate the benefits and drawbacks to businesses of operating in specific markets.

- Present proposals and justify appropriate actions businesses could take when faced with changes in market conditions.

- Evaluate the effects of government policy on businesses and the responses of businesses to changes in policy.

- Evaluate the impact of international competition on businesses and the effectiveness of their responses to changing conditions in international markets.

UNIT 2 ASSESSMENT

Key skills in this unit

Because this unit is externally assessed, there will be fewer opportunities to demonstrate/provide evidence of using key skills while following this unit. However, there will be a number of appropriate opportunities as signalled below.

Opportunities to develop key skills

As a natural part of carrying out this unit and doing the work set out in the text you will be developing your key skills. Here's how:

Application of number, Level 3

When you are:	You should be able to develop the following key skills evidence:
• Investigating market trends and analysing data about demand and supply for goods and services	N3.1 Plan and interpret information from two different types of sources, including a large data set.

Information technology, Level 3

When you are:	You should be able to develop the following key skills evidence:
• Extracting information to explain changes in the market and describing the markets in which businesses operate	IT3.1 Plan and use different sources to search for, and select, information required for two different purposes.

Communication, Level 3

When you are:	You should be able to develop the following key skills evidence:
• Describing market characteristics	C3.1a Contribute to a group discussion about a complex subject.
• Analysing the impact of government economic policy	C3.2 Read and synthesise information from two extended documents about a complex subject. One document should include at least one image to illustrate complex points.

Marketing

If you have been stopped in the shopping mall 'just to answer a few questions' or heard a TV advertisement which says 'nine out of ten customers preferred', you have seen some aspects of marketing. You may have wondered how a supermarket decides which products to promote or place on the top or bottom shelf. These are all very visible parts of a highly skilled and sophisticated marketing process which interacts with all the other functions of a business.

Marketing is about understanding the customer and ensuring that products and services match existing and potential customer needs. Marketing is also about looking at ways of influencing the behaviour of customers. This unit focuses on the marketing process, from initial research into a market through to the success or otherwise of a strategy. You will investigate the principles and functions of marketing and the way in which they contribute to the generation of income and/or profit in business. The learning activities will give you hands-on experience of the process and the opportunity to devise your own marketing strategy.

The unit relates to the understanding of markets in Unit 2 The competitive business environment (Advanced), the functions of marketing in Unit 1 Business at work (Advanced), and provides knowledge and understanding for Unit 6 Business planning (Advanced). The marketing strategy can contribute to evidence for Unit 6 Business planning (Advanced), and it also provides a basis for study of Unit 7 Marketing and promotional strategy (Advanced), Unit 8 Marketing research (Advanced), Unit 9 Sales (Advanced), Unit 10 Customer service (Advanced) and Unit 20 International trade (Advanced)

This unit will be assessed through your portfolio work only. The grade awarded will be your grade for the unit.

Chapter 10 The principles of marketing

Marketing is essential to the success of any business. Its primary aim is to enable businesses to meet the needs of their actual and potential customers, whether for profit or not. You need to understand that, if a business's marketing is to be successful, it must:

- understand customer needs

- understand and keep ahead of the competition

- communicate effectively with its customers to satisfy customer expectations

- co-ordinate its functions to achieve marketing aims

- be aware of constraints on marketing activities.

You need to understand how these criteria for successful marketing are related to the central aim of marketing – meeting actual and potential customer needs. You should also understand the importance to many businesses of developing and maintaining a relationship with the actual and potential customers and other stakeholders.

How easy it is to take all we have for granted! Wherever we look there are advertising messages bombarding us with images of goods or services designed to provide us with more choices and a better lifestyle. Shops, mail-order services and even the Internet provide us with the opportunity to buy almost anything we want, as long as we have the 'filthy lucre'. It was only in 1942 that Joseph Schumpeter, the great Austrian economist, wrote:

Queen Elizabeth I owned silk stockings. The capitalist achievement does not typically consist of providing more silk stockings for queens, but in bringing them within the reach of factory girls in return for steadily decreasing amounts of effort.

Today we live in a *market economy*, in which many consumers have been able to enjoy the range of goods and services that were previously afforded by kings and queens only. The existence of a market makes it

possible for consumers to express their preferences for the goods and services they would like, and prices act as signals to suppliers informing them which goods are in most demand.

In this marketplace, today's consumers indicate to suppliers through their purchases what should or should not be produced for the market. In effect they have become king or queen.

Case study: Shopping without stress for fun

You need to go back only a few thousand years to find that humans were hunter-gatherers. While men killed creatures with bows and arrows or spears, women cultivated the ground and made clothing, etc. from parts of these animals. Although today our hand and eye co-ordination may be improving as we use our mouse to follow the adventures of Lara Croft or alternative cyber toys, our clothing has become off the peg and our food chilled. Clothes are now so full of labels they have become haute couture and our food is nouvelle cuisine. And the shopping we do to obtain them need only be fun!

Recent research has shown that shopping helps people to feel better about themselves. For example, it helps them to fantasise about who they would be if they had all the wonderful goods they see. Cutting-edge shopping involves going into heightened shopping environments, with good-looking shop assistants, cool muzak, three-dimensional wares and trendy clothes. Having made a purchase the customer is provided with a trendy carrier bag which helps him or her feel he or she has not simply bought a product but also a lifestyle.

Today, you can even shop without leaving your home. Internet shopping provides an opening into a shopping environment unrestricted by geographical or cultural boundaries. The Internet puts buyers and sellers in touch with each other, wherever they are, simply by pointing and clicking a mouse. As well as providing increased choice, the Internet also provides shoppers with the ability to compare prices and products. However, with the Internet you are not using as many of your senses as when you go out to buy a product. You cannot touch and feel a product or try it on. You also have to wait for it to be delivered. Though far less exhausting than trekking around the high street, the Internet does provide users with the opportunity to browse in their leisure time. For example, try the following web sites:

- www.bigsave.com – where you can visit a department store with sections that include electronics, home and garden, toys and designer goods.
- www.supermarketsuk.co.uk – where you can gain up-to-date information on special offers available at the four main UK supermarkets.
- www.richclickings.co.uk/shopping.shopnews.html – which brings together 170 shops and keeps browsers up to date with special offers.

1 How has shopping changed in recent years?

2 In what ways have the changes been focused on meeting more closely customer needs?

3 Provide a personal example of a very customer-focused experience you have had when shopping, as well as one that was not very customer focused.

This case study helps to highlight that, now that *market orientation* has arrived on the scene, modern organisations that use it will meet the needs of their customers better than other businesses, and are therefore likely to be more successful.

The Chartered Institute of Marketing defines marketing as:

The management process responsible for identifying, anticipating and satisfying customer requirements profitably.

This definition provides an important starting point to help you gain a clear picture of the major issues facing a market-focused organisation.

There are a number of key words in the above definition:

- *Management process* – the use of this term indicates the level of importance of marketing decisions. Successful marketing needs managerial input because it requires constant information gathering, as well as data analysis, in order for decisions to be made.

- *Identifying* involves answering questions such as 'how do we find out what the consumers' requirements are?' and 'how do we keep in touch with their thoughts and perceptions about our goods or service?'

- *Anticipating* takes into account that consumer requirements change all the time. For example, as people become richer they may seek a greater variety of goods and services. Anticipation involves looking at the future as well as at the present. What will be the Next Best Thing people will require tomorrow?

- *Satisfying* involves meeting consumer requirements. Customers seek particular benefits. They want the right goods, at the right price, at the right time and in the right place.

- *Profitability* is the margin of profit that *motivates* organisations to supply goods to consumers in a market. Of course, profit may be simply one motive for supplying goods to a market. Others may include market share or market leadership.

A recent major study of some 1,700

companies showed that marketing-orientated firms have enhanced profitability. In other words, good marketing helps managers to improve the performance of their part of the business and to meet the most basic of business objectives – profit.

One of the key components of marketing, therefore, is anticipating market needs and opportunities.

Marketing is, therefore, the process through which Jaguar is able to identify the kinds of cars people will want to buy in the near future and the features that should be built into those cars; it helps Reebok anticipate changes in consumers' preferences for trainers, and Sky Television to identify the types of channels viewers will want to watch in the future.

In a relatively short period of time organisations have moved forward from *production orientation* to *sales orientation,* and, more recently, to *marketing orientation* (see Figure 10.1).

In a market dominated by production orientation, manufacturers feel they know what is best for customers. When there is little competition (for example, where there is only one supplier of telecommunications services in a particular geographical area or where there is only one producer of motor vehicles), organisations may not have to pay close attention to customer needs.

As consumer incomes began to rise after the Second World War, standards of living began to improve. During the 1950s and 1960s, emphasis was upon sales orientation. Harold Macmillan claimed that 'You've never had it so good!', and the focus was upon trying to persuade customers they needed the goods rather than attempting to find out about buyers' needs.

Marketing orientation is all about focusing the activities or organisations on meeting the needs of consumers. It means the consumer is the driving force behind everything an organisation does. No longer is marketing something that is simply added on to a number of company functions. Today, the customer drives all the activities of a market-focused organisation.

> **Discussion point** Starbucks (www.starbucks.com) have 15,000 coffee bars throughout the USA. Look at the organisational chart in Figure 10.2. What does it tell you about their orientation?

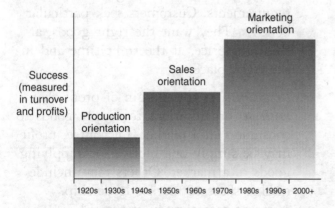

Figure 10.1 Business orientation

Figure 10.2 Starbucks organisation chart

Case study: Virgin Holidays

One of the key ingredients of the success of Virgin has been its managers' ability to anticipate market needs. Their successes include high-street record stores in the 1970s and cheap flights across the Atlantic during the 1980s, followed by contraceptives and Virgin Cola.

A more recent venture for Virgin has been into online holidays. It is now possible to book a holiday with a couple of clicks of a mouse. Before making a booking decision, it is possible for these shoppers to experience aspects of their holidays from their armchairs. This could include descending a piste in the Alps or looking at a 360° view from a campsite on the French Riviera.

Virgin started doing this by providing CD-Roms of their skiing holidays. More than 10,000 of these were distributed each year. The Internet has, however, provided even better opportunities to reach potential customers. The Virgin site at www.virginholidays.co.uk offers panoramic views of the slopes and resorts and interactive piste maps, along with details of off-piste activities as well as a hotel search. It is now also possible to use a number of relatively easy steps to book holidays.

1   Why have many of the business strategies adopted by Virgin been successful?

2   What customer needs do online holidays meet?

Check your understanding

Use an example of an organisation known to you to describe how it anticipates market needs and opportunities.

Understanding customer needs

In order to anticipate change, organisations need to have an antenna that is highly sensitive to changes taking place in the buying population. For example, what is happening to:

• the age structure of the population?
• tastes and preferences?
• incomes?

Market research is the antenna of an organisation and is far more complicated

then simply asking 100 people if they like a product. This is the stage where market research starts, and this is something we look at in detail in the next chapter.

Pedigree Petfoods, one of the leading producers of pet foods in this country, have stated that:

We work constantly towards identifying and satisfying customer needs. It is the activity from which all else springs. We never forget that we cannot influence millions of consumer choices until we have convinced first one, then a second and a third customer that our product is worthy of purchase. Our success is based on thorough research of the wide range of needs for pet animals and their owners. The knowledge which we gain is translated into our range of quality products which satisfy these needs better than any of our competitors.

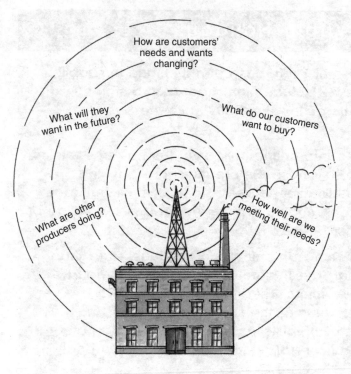

How are customers' needs and wants changing?

What will they want in the future?

What do our customers want to buy?

What are other producers doing?

How well are we meeting their needs?

why some supermarkets have people crowding the aisles whereas others are practically empty.

It is, therefore, the ability to satisfy customers that marks the difference between a successful and unsuccessful organisation. This is why some schools are oversubscribed and have a huge demand for places while others have falling roles. It is the reason

Discussion point

What is the purpose of marketing? Discuss the following statement:

Marketing, therefore, is concerned with attempting to reduce risk by applying formal techniques systematically to assess the situation and develop the company's response to it.

Check your understanding

Figure 10.3 shows percentage participation in selected sporting activities by females in Great Britain during 1999. Look at the figures. What do these indicate about the sorts of products females might require when engaged in these activities? How might manufacturers use this information?

	15–19 years	20–24 years	25–34 years	35–44 years	45–54 years	55–64 years	65+ years
Aerobics	33.4	32.4	24.7	18.6	12.2	7.8	4.2
Badminton	20.2	7.2	6.0	4.4	3.8	1.4	0.8
Cycling	16.2	8.9	9.9	8.6	6.0	3.1	1.4
Golf	2.0	1.9	1.9	1.9	3.1	2.6	1.3
Horse-riding	9.9	7.5	4.3	3.5	2.7	0.6	0.4
Snooker	6.3	4.8	1.0	1.2	1.1	0.5	0.7
Swimming	35.0	28.1	28.8	26.6	18.1	13.7	7.4
Tennis	16.0	6.6	3.8	4.2	3.2	1.1	0.8

Figure 10.3   Participation in selected sporting activities, females, Great Britain, 1999 (%)

Being human, all customers are different! But only a few businesses (a tailor, for example, or a firm of architects) can provide products specifically designed for each individual customer. Most marketing activities are therefore designed to meet the needs of groups of customers within a market.

A market is made up of actual or potential buyers of a product and the sellers who offer goods to meet buyers' needs. The market for computers is composed of existing owners and prospective buyers of computers, as well as companies such as Apple Macintosh who manufacture them, Microsoft who develop software and Time who distribute them within the marketplace. A market requires a process of exchange between buyers and sellers – the *marketing mix* (see Figure 10.4).

Figure 10.4 The marketing mix

The first challenge for any organisation is to find a set of customers and to identify their needs so that appropriate goods and services can be developed. The first element in the marketing mix is the *product*. Once organisations have a product, then all the other elements in this marketing mix can be engaged to meet customer needs. These

may include developing the *pricing* for the product or service provided, working out how to *distribute (place)* goods to the customers, as well as how to *promote* them.

When Shell UK (www.shell.co.uk/nonflash/main index.htm) identified a large group of potential customers known as 'top-up shoppers', they realised their service stations could be transformed into mini supermarkets to provide consumers with a range of top-up items, such as magazines, drinks, biscuits, sweets and many other items as well as petrol and oil. When First Direct (www.firstdirect.co.uk/Pages/home/html) identified a large number of people who were too busy to visit their high-street bank, they developed telephone banking.

In recent years we have seen increasing efforts to meet the individual wants and needs of customers – a process known as *customisation*. This has been particularly noticeable in service industries. Services such as delivering parcels, guarding property or maintaining equipment can be designed to suit a particular customer.

ACTIVITIES

A focus group is a small panel of people who are brought together by an interviewer for the purpose of talking about a product, service or organisation. The interviewer focuses the group discussion upon important issues.

Form focus groups of around six to eight people to discuss how M&S can improve the ways in which they meet the needs of their customers. Each focus group should have a chairperson and someone taking notes.

Spend at least half an hour discussing this issue and then report your findings back to your class.

Case study: Falling behind the needs of the customer

For many years, Marks & Spencer (www.marks-and-spencer.co.uk) had been a British institution, supported by the blind faith of their customers. Their products were the fruits of endless compromises between buyers, managers and suppliers. The products were a benchmark of British quality – dependable and decent – and stood as a British emblem. But people increasingly came to think that much of this merchandise was dull, and was out of touch with changing fashions. However, at the heart of these products' success was a strong bond between M&S and the British public.

During the 1980s, M&S were probably propped up by good fortune. Men's and women's fashions in the 1980s were based on the older styles of the 1940s and, as more women entered the workforce the ready-made meal became accepted as a comfort food. At the time the alternatives to M&S were probably not attractive enough, but then George at Asda and designers at Debenhams, Zara, IKEA and Gap changed the fashion world, with new merchandise every three weeks instead of M&S's twice-yearly collections. Fashion was also blown apart the moment Next arrived on the scene. Niche-ing, sub-branding and product clustering became the new buzz words. The most fashion conscious of women suddenly became those women in their thirties and forties. They had money, knew about fashion and wanted to make an effort.

During the 1990s M&S emphasised 'value' rather then price, and this provided them with an enviable position in the high street. However, it was during this time they also got so hung up on quality they forgot about style and fashion. With inappropriate styles, sales fell and even their food halls lost customers. The unthinkable had happened . . . perhaps M&S was not so great after all. The disaffected customers went elsewhere.

Today, M&S is ripe for acquisition. Valued at more than £9 billion, they have many sites that would be a valuable catch for a predator.

The future of M&S largely depends upon how well their designers are able to push through improvements to core products and win back the confidence of the British public. It is argued today that M&S's biggest problem is public perception. Former customers are cross with them, in a way they would probably not have been with any other store.

1   What problems have M&S encountered in recent years?

2   Describe how marketers within M&S failed to keep up with customer needs.

3   What were the consequences for M&S?

Understanding and keeping ahead of the competition

One of the key factors in any market is the existence and strength of competition. In a competitive environment organisations are forced to be on their toes. They cannot allow rivals to gain advantages by offering lower prices or goods customers perceive to be substantially better.

In order to be successful, organisations will gear their activities to being better than their competitors, and to keeping up with any improvements competitors make. For example, in the UK newspaper industry we find that newspapers in a similar market segment, such as 'tabloids', tend to have similar prices. They also have similar stories, offers and promotions (such as scratch-card games). In fact, the tabloid press is known for the 'spoil up' – a process whereby one newspaper tries to spoil another's excusive by creating a similar story of its own.

You have only to walk down the aisle of your local supermarket to appreciate the large number of competing brands of products. From time to time a new product will arrive, which is subtly different from existing brands. If the new product is successful this will lead to a flurry of business activity as existing producers try to come up with rival versions. For example,

Case study: An online rival to Dixons

Jeff Bezos, the billionaire founder of Amazon.com (www.amazon.co.uk), the world's best-known Internet company, is planning to launch an online consumer electronics shop that will compete directly with Dixons (www.dixons.co.uk).

The 35-year-old entrepreneur, with an Amazon stake at more than £10 billion, aims to break up the dominance of Britain's biggest electrical retail chain by stocking a much wider range of goods at lower prices. He also aims to undermine the reputation of many electrical retailers for employing poor staff who have little product knowledge. Amazon have already launched an electronic retailer in the USA through Amazon.com, which is proving successful.

Dixons already sells a wide range of goods on the Internet. They also sell goods electronically through Open, the interactive television service owned by a consortium that includes BSkyB, the satellite broadcaster. Dixons own The Link and PC World as well as 80% of Freeserve, Britain's largest quoted Internet media company.

1   How do most consumers of electrical products currently purchase goods?

2   What types of customers might an electronic retailer appeal to?

3   Describe the sorts of strategies Dixons will have to undertake to remain the biggest electrical retailer within the UK.

4   What might happen if Dixons fail to respond to this competitive threat?

255

the introduction of 'I Can't Believe It's Not Butter' by Van der Bergh Foods led to the development of numerous products that not only looked the same but also had similar brand names.

Marketing in any organisation must constantly seek to enable the organisation to manage the effects of change and competition – by coming up with new products, advertising promotions, price alternations and special offers.

As competitor activity is one of the biggest threats to a business organisation, many marketers spend a lot of time finding out what their competitors are doing. In fact, it has been argued that most companies react to competitors' responses. *Competition* orientation, therefore, sits alongside *marketing* orientation – they are the driving forces that constantly encourage firms to make sure their offerings provide more value for money than those of rivals. Indeed, competitor orientation is in many ways another form of customer orientation: rivals prove a threat only if they have a better understanding of customer wants and needs than the managers of another business.

Finding out about competitors involves a considerable amount of research. This will start with finding out as much as possible about competitors' products and other elements of their marketing mix (product, price, place, distribution and promotion). It is necessary to identify points of difference between an organisation and its competitors, as well as areas of competitive advantage. This process is often referred to as the *competitive audit*. The term 'audit' means a review or appraisal of an activity.
A business should then evaluate this information and integrate it into its planning process on a regular basis.

Check your understanding

Identify two market-leading products. These may be in markets such as tomato sauce, chilled ready meals, packet soups, pet food or sectors of confectionery. The purpose of this activity is to undertake a competitive audit. Use a matrix like the one in Figure 10.5 to make comparisons.

	Product A	Product B
Product	• Features • Benefits • Design • Brand • Other elements	• Features • Benefits • Design • Brand • Other elements
Price	• High price • Market price • Low price	• High price • Market price • Low price
Place/distribution	• Availability • Types of outlet	• Availability • Types of outlet
Promotion	• Advertising • Sales promotion • Publicity and image	• Advertising • Sales promotion • Publicity and image

Figure 10.5   A competitive audit matrix

Few organisations today operate in a static world: we live in a global marketplace for many goods and services in which technology, purchasing power, tastes and many other factors are all changing at the same time. In adapting to many of these changes, good marketing is a key factor.

Unfortunately, over the course of time, many organisations develop a product orientation rather than a market orientation. Marketing orientation is based on the belief that, if organisations do not satisfy the needs of customers, they will not survive. It is therefore essential to match the production and development of goods and services with the identification and anticipation of customers' desires and requirements.

It is important, then, for organisations not just to look at their competitors' products but also at how they deal with their customers. Customer needs and requirements are identified in every area of organisational activity, from the original idea and design right up until the final sale and after-sales support.

Marketing orientation can be contrasted with production and sales orientations. A production-orientated company holds the view that products will tend to find their own markets if they can be produced cheaply and are of good quality. Such companies spend relatively little time investigating consumers' wishes. As a result, they often come to grief because, although their products are good in a technical sense, they do not provide the benefits consumers require.

A sales-orientated company holds the view that success depends on effective advertising, selling and promotion rather than on achieving a real difference between the product it is selling and those offered by its competitors. This philosophy will be easily seen, such a company argues, if consumers shop around.

The real distinction between marketing orientation and sales orientation is that selling tries to get the customer to want what the company produces; marketing, on the other hand, tries to get the company to produce what the customer wants.

Check your understanding

Identify organisations and/or products in similar markets that appear to be:

- product orientated
- market orientated
- sales orientated.

Which of the products and/or organisations are likely to be more successful?

Communicating effectively with customers to satisfy their expectations

From the very beginning, human beings have used hand signals, vocal patterns, symbolic drawings and facial expressions for the purpose of communicating some form of message to one another. Today, the exchange of information is a sophisticated process that produces subtle messages and that uses emerging technologies, such as the Internet and digital television.

An effective network of communications is essential for any form of promotional activity. It enables an organisation not only to communicate with its customers and satisfy their expectations but also to build an image with the world at large. Such an image will help others to form a judgement about what the organisation stands for, and will influence their dealings with it.

For marketing purposes, communication of products and services contributes to the persuasion process, which encourages consumers to avail themselves of whatever is on offer. The various tools used to communicate effectively with customers to satisfy their expectations fall within what is known as the *promotional mix*.

Check your understanding

Visit the World Advertising Research Center on www.WARC.com. It is open 24 hours a day, 365 days a year. Think about how you would use some of the information you discover. Discuss your findings with other members of your group.

The promotional mix comprises all the marketing and promotional communications methods used to achieve the promotional objectives. These methods can be broken down into two distinct areas:

1 controllable and

2 non-controllable.

Non-controllable communication consists of marketing messages that occur as a result of word of mouth, personal recommendation or a consumer's overall perception of a particular product or service. For example, consumers' opinions are influenced by a number of factors, such as whether the family has regularly used the product. Consumers today are increasingly influenced by the power of brands and designer labels. A brand is a particular good or characteristic that identifies a particular product. A brand heritage, character, colour and image will also help to create brand loyalty and will promote regular purchasing patterns.

Controllable communication consists of marketing messages that are carefully directed to achieve an organisation's promotional objectives. These may include the following:

* *Advertisements* – messages sent via the media which are intended to inform or influence the people who receive them.

* *Direct mail* – personally addressed advertising sent through the post.

* *Public relations* – non-personal communication using the media. Unlike advertising, the success of public relations is not measured by the product's popularity. It is used to develop favourable relationships between an organisation and its public.

* *Sales promotions* – techniques designed to increase sales, such as money-off coupons, free samples and competitions.

* *Sponsorship* – the financing or partial funding of an event, personality, activity or programme in order to gain consumer awareness or media coverage.

* *Product presentation* – improving a brand's visibility through packaging, the use of labels, merchandising and branding.

* *Direct selling* – making sales with an emphasis on the importance of salesmanship.

An organisation needs to appraise the communication process carefully. It must have a clear idea of what a message should be, to whom it should be sent and the expected outcome of sending it. Promotional requirements will vary with geographical size, demographic dispersion and the nature of market segmentation. The more clearly an organisation can define its target audience, the more relevant the promotional mix.

Check your understanding

The lists in Figures 10.6 and 10.7 show the top radio stations by breakfast-time advertising revenue as well as the top advertisers on breakfast radio during 1999. Explain why advertisers target breakfast radio.

Looking at the independent radio stations, what does this say about the sort of audiences they are looking for? Use an example to comment upon the effectiveness of this kind of advertising. Try to match some of the advertisers with the sorts of radio stations they might like to advertise on.

Position	Radio station
1	Capital 95.8 FM
2	Virgin 1215 AM
3	Classic FM
4	Clyde 1 FM
5	Virgin 105.8 FM
6	96.4 FM BRMB
7	Capital Cold 548
8	Key 103 FM
9	City 96.7 FM
10	Heart London FM

Figure 10.6 The top radio stations as measured by breakfast-time advertising revenue

Position	Advertiser
1	BT – British Telecom
2	Carphone Warehouse
3	COI – Central Office of Information
4	Coldseal
5	Camelot
6	Renault
7	One 2 One Communications
8	News International
9	Vodaphone Retail
10	Vauxhall

Figure 10.7 The top advertisers on breakfast radio, 1999

To achieve its promotional objectives, an organisation has to set its promotional strategy. A common mnemonic used to describe a promotional strategy designed to persuade a customer to make a purchase is 'AIDA':

A A customer's *attention* is captured and he or she is made *aware* of the product.

I The *impact* of the promotion stimulates the customer's *interest*.

D The customer is persuaded he or she is *deprived* by not having the product, and this helps to stimulate a *desire* for it.

A *Action* involves the purchase of the product.

Case study: Interactive advertising

Two-way TV has arrived. The year 2000 sees the introduction of the UK's first interactive television commercials offered to cable subscribers and Sky Digital (www.sky.co.uk/home) customers. The services will be offered in two distinct areas:

1 Real-time interactive advertising. This means that an interactive advertisement is contained within the time frames of the commercial. For example, an advertisement from MFI takes the viewer through a sequence of interactive messages. The first proposition asks the viewer if he or she wants £50 off his or her next kitchen purchase. The viewer has to click OK to respond. After that, the viewer is given the opportunity to receive further information on kitchens, bedrooms or cabinets. Another interactive message is a quantification question, asking when viewers think they will be changing their kitchens. Given the choices made by the viewer MFI can then target the viewer with appropriate literature at the appropriate time.

2 Non-real-time advertising. With this form of advertising the viewer is provided with an icon on his or her television screen. If the viewer wants to, he or she can

then interact with the advertisement when it finishes. For example, British Airways (www.britishairways.com) have introduced this sort of advertisement. By clicking the icon at the end of the ad, the viewer is taken through a series of transaction-based screens where he or she can find out further information about flights – and even make bookings.

As interactive TV develops, consumers will be able to experience one-to-one services without having to move away from their TV screens. The great advantage for advertisers is that they can have individual leads from a mass communications platform.

1 What is interactive advertising?

2 To what sort of target groups may this sort of advertising appeal?

3 What sort of product categories might use this form of advertising?

4 Describe the difference between real-time and non-real-time advertising.

5 List the advantages and disadvantages of this medium for:

   a) the TV viewer; and
   b) the advertiser.

Co-ordinating marketing functions to achieve marketing aims

Business strategy is concerned with the big decisions organisations make. This may have substantial implications for the whole organisation and influence the future of a business for a long time to come. For example, a strategic decision for a car manufacturer might be to produce a new model of a car. This may involve channelling resources into building a new factory, re-financing the business as well as employing new workers and developing awareness of this new model.

An organisation with a strategy knows where it is going because it is planning ahead. Marketing strategy is concerned with identifying and meeting the requirements of customers successfully so that the organisation can meet a range of objectives (see Figure 10.8).

Because modern organisations focus so much attention on the customer, marketing today has come to be seen as a *strategic discipline*. Marketing strategies are the means by which organisations attempt to find out exactly what their customers want, and then

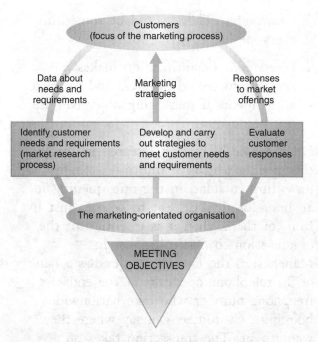

Figure 10.8 The strategic process

to influence customers in a way that is favourable to the organisation.

Marketing strategies require detailed research to find out about:

- customer requirements
- the right products to develop to meet customer needs
- how to position the product or service in relation to other products and services
- the right marketing mix.

Check your understanding

You have recently developed a computer mouse that does not use a ball and has no moving parts. Your new mouse will not 'fluff-up' and will have a longer life than the traditional mouse. At the moment, your ideas need to be developed further, and you have not as yet created a user-friendly design for your new mouse.

Working in groups, comment upon the sort of research you need to undertake before making a major investment in this product.

It is important to be able to differentiate between marketing strategy and marketing tactics. The terms 'strategy' and 'tactics' are of military origin. Military *strategy* is a general overview that involves the creation of clear aims and objectives and then deciding the key means to achieve these. Military *tactics* are the means used to win a particular campaign or battle.

Having established the marketing strategy, it is possible to decide on the tactics and tools to be used to make the strategy work. For example, this may involve carrying out some detailed market research, developing a product, working out the best price to charge, developing a distribution strategy, running an appropriate advertising campaign or engaging in sales promotional activity (see Figure 10.9).

Figure 10.9 Marketing strategy and tactics

Planning is at the heart of marketing. It enables decision-makers within an organisation to plan for the present and for the future, and to learn from the past. The three main reasons for planning are to:

1 assess how well the organisation is doing in the various markets in which it operates

2 identify the strengths and weaknesses of the organisation in each of these markets

3 establish goals and objectives, so that resources can be used appropriately.

Assael defines a *marketing plan* as:

a document developed by marketing managers that:

1. *identifies marketing opportunities;*

2. *defines the target market that represents that opportunity;*

3. *develops a mix of strategies directed at this target;*

4. *guides the evaluation of the marketing effort*

Marketing objectives are an essential part of the marketing plan as they provide direction for the activities to follow. Without clear objectives it is difficult to evaluate what a marketing plan is trying to achieve or whether a plan has been successful. It is usual to translate marketing objectives into quantifiable 'result areas', such as market share, market penetration or growth rate of sales. Some of these may be further broken down into specific sales volumes, value goals or geographical targets. Marketing objectives may have a time frame and direction. They also provide a basis for evaluation. Marketing must ensure that organisational activities are co-ordinated in such a way that marketing objectives are met.

Marketing objectives should therefore be:

1 *Achievable.* They should be based on a practical analysis of an organisation's capabilities.

2 *Understandable.* They need to be clear so that everyone knows what they are trying to achieve.

3 *Challenging.* They should be something everyone has to strive for.

4 *Measurable.* Quantification makes it possible to record progress and to make adjustments if marketing objectives are not being met.

For example, if market research indicates that people who visit multiplex cinemas are unwilling to stand in the rain queuing for an hour for the last seat to be sold just in front of them, then it is essential for the organisation to find solutions. In Manchester, the UCI multiplex has a bank of 90 telephone operators at the end of a freephone number who take nationwide bookings. Customers can say where they want to sit. The transaction takes on average 64 seconds. Marketing thus has a responsibility to ensure all aspects of the way in which an organisation operates are geared to meeting consumer requirements.

Figure 10.10 The cycle of marketing activities

Check your understanding

One of the oldest products around is the umbrella. Though people still use them, and many are branded, there have been few improvements to the product over the years.

Talk to umbrella users and find out if there is anything else they would like from their brolly, such as warm handles or any other product features. Find out if there are any marketing opportunities. Decide upon the type of customer who might be attracted to any new features you identify. Think about how you would develop both the umbrella and other elements of the marketing mix for this market. Identify some specific marketing objectives for the first year.

Constraints on marketing activities

Every organisation involved in marketing activity is faced with a number of constraints that may limit their activity. They then need to work within these constraints.

Internal constraints relate to the resource capabilities of an organisation. For example, an organisation might identify potential customers, but how capable is it of meeting their needs? It might not have the resources to do so. In recent years Coca-Cola (www.cocacola.com/home.html) has developed a global presence. It has been able to do this by ploughing money into long-term investment. Coca-Cola invests 70% of its profits and achieves a staggering rate of growth.

When a company wants to develop new products or services, it needs the resources to finance expansion. The bigger the scale of the development projects, the more resources are required. Sometimes companies finance expansion by selling off existing assets – for example, ICI have moved into higher value-added chemical products, such as chemicals for lip-glosses and eye shadow. To finance this move, ICI sold off a number of their existing heavy chemical plants, which had low long-term profit potential.

In addition to financial resources, business organisations need the skills and know-how for a range of marketing activities. Increasingly, companies rely on buying in expertise from outside the organisation.

External constraints involve a series of factors within the business environment in which an organisation operates that limit, in one way or another, the organisation's activities. These will include the following:

- *Consumers.* If an organisation is not market focused or if consumers are not interested in a product, then it will be difficult to market.

- *Competitors.* It may be difficult to market a product for which a competitor already has an advantage.

- *Economy.* In a period of economic recession when consumers have falling incomes, it may be difficult to market a luxury product.

- *The law.* There may be a number of laws constraining the activities of a business, which may make it difficult for the business to do well.

The market-focused company will research all these constraints fully and will try to find solutions that enable it to turn weaknesses into strengths and threats into opportunities.

Case study: Becoming millionaires!

Dan and his younger brother Ron are experienced market traders, flitting from one market to another across southeast London. They are self-motivated entrepreneurs whose main aim in life is to become millionaires. As small businessmen, they do not always find life easy!

Dan was recently offered the opportunity to buy some of the latest videos, which were claimed to be 'kosher'. These are a big opportunity to expand the business, with an up-to-date consumer product that will bring the punters in. The great benefit is that, if customers are interested in the videos, Dan knows he can do a deal with some quick-boiling kettles he bought a few months ago that he has had trouble getting rid of. The kettles look smart but take 15 minutes to boil.

Dan's real problem is that he has not got the 'readies' to buy the videos. Ron is always 'skint' and cannot help. He is wondering about whether to sell off the van to provide him with the capital. The problem then would be they would have to buy an alternative form of transport, such as 'company mopeds', but this might have the benefit of allowing them to start some courier work.

Another idea Dan has to expand the business is to use Ron's expertise in information technology to set up training courses. Though Ron was very good with computers, he has not used one for five years and feels that, if Dan is going to do this, they need to buy in help from another person.

1   Identify two internal and two external constraints on Dan and Ron's business.

2   Describe how these constraints limit their activities.

3   Explain how they could/should deal with these constraints.

Maintaining a relationship with other stakeholders

The notion of stakeholders in an organisation has been a popular one for at least twenty years. Recently, the notion of 'stakeholders' was taken up by Tony Blair's New Labour and used to emphasise the idea of a one-nation society in which the views of all relevant groups are taken into account in decision-making.

Stakeholders are individuals, groups or organisations who are affected by, or have some level of involvement in, particular decisions or sets of decisions.

As individuals, groups or organisations are affected by what an organisation does, they are said to have a stake or interest in the decisions the organisation makes.

A company's stakeholders, therefore, include not only its customers and owners but also its workforce, its suppliers (and their families), those living near to its sites, special interest groups and, of course, society as a whole, including the environment (see Figure 10.11).

Figure 10.11 Stakeholders

Check your understanding

Identify each of the stakeholder groups for your school or college. Briefly explain how each of these groups is affected by the actions of the school or college.

Could the performance of the school or college be improved by focusing more upon these stakeholders?

The concept of stakeholders marks a radical shift from the way in which organisations operated in the past. Managers used to talk about having 'the right to manage' and to make decisions within an organisation. Owners often felt that, because the organisation was theirs, they had the right to ride 'rough-shod' over everybody else. After all, it was their organisation. In marketing terms, this type of management is associated with *product orientation*.

There are a number of reasons for today's change in emphasis:

1 The growth of *international competition*. In the more complex, integrated global economy in which we operate today, business organisations are more likely to be successful if they employ 'best practice'. There is little scope for dinosaur organisations that use out-of-date methods. It is recognised today that success is more likely to be generated by those organisations whose operations are based on values shared by all stakeholders in the organisation.

2 The growing *importance of the customer*. Modern organisations are market focused. They recognise that it is the customers who ultimately make the choice of whether or not to spend their money on a particular product.

3 The *Japanese economy*. One of the reasons for the success of Japanese businesses was their more 'consensual' view of business practice. This included reducing divisions between managers and workers, placing more emphasis on the customer and building stronger links in the supply chain.

4 The growing importance of the *media*. As the media can show an organisation

either in a bad or a good light, stakeholder groups may use media coverage to air their views and to give them more prominence.

In meeting the needs of its stakeholders, a responsible organisation will have a number of distinguishing characteristics:

- It meets its marketing objectives by supplying products or services people want to buy.

- It contributes to its own and the community's long-term prosperity by making the best possible use of resources.

- It minimises waste of every kind and, where possible, promotes reuse or recycling.

- It respects the environment locally, nationally and globally.

- It sets performance standards for its suppliers – and helps in their achievement.

- It offers its employees worthwhile career prospects, professional training, job satisfaction and a safe working environment.

- It expects the best from its employees and rewards them accordingly.

- It acts at all times as a good citizen, aware of its influence on the rest of society, including the communities near its plant and offices.

Modern organisations recognise that marketing orientation involves treating customers as stakeholders and stakeholders as customers. The organisation that simply sets out to maximise its return to shareholders would quickly alienate other stakeholders. For example, recent studies on changes in share prices before and after incidents of environmental damage show this clearly. Suppliers and financiers typically have a choice as to whom they do business with, and they are more likely to offer the best terms to organisations with strongly positive public images.

Check your understanding

It is not easy to satisfy all stakeholder groups all the time. For example, a group of innovative and creative employees may want to influence the decisions of senior managers, but might be dominated by an autocratic and repressive manager. Some decision-makers within an organisation may want to develop products that serve the wider community, while others are more concerned with maximising profits.

Identify four other situations over which stakeholders might disagree.

Case study: Stakeholder interests

- Barmac, which make rigs for offshore oil and gas operations, are to make redundant more than 3,300 employees at their yards near Inverness. The cuts are a blow to the local economy because Barmac are the biggest industrial employer in the Highlands.

- The Halifax recently suspended its online share dealing service after a security lapse allowed people to trade on investors' accounts. They may have allowed a number of their customers to view the personal details of other investors.

- Microsoft have faced a number of lawsuits from computing industry competitors who feel their operation as a monopoly has damaged their interests. Microsoft are currently appealing against a court ruling that the company should be divided up.

- Protests are growing over government plans to implement European regulations relating to part-time workers. Advisers are warning that, if applied with vigour, They could stifle small businesses with more red tape.

- Rival service providers of BT allege that the telecoms giant is waging a dirty-tricks campaign against them in a bid to retain and win back customers.

- Officials at the Department of Trade and Industry claim that the Post Office could make its first loss in almost 25 years as a result of the government's decision to switch benefit payments to banks.

1 Identify the stakeholders in each of the above instances.

2 How many of these issues are capable of being resolved?

3 Chose one instance and explain what action you would take to try to reach an agreement between the different stakeholder groups.

Chapter 11   Establishing customer needs

A business has to explore the needs of its customers and the activities of its competitors before it can develop a marketing strategy. To gain an understanding of the market for a product or service, you will need to understand the use of different research methods and data.

You need to know how primary research is carried out, and how to interpret primary research data for use in developing marketing strategies. Primary research methods you should be able to use and understand include:

- discussions with people (for example, interviews, focus groups and panel discussions)

- questionnaires and surveys

- sampling

- testing through pilots and field trials.

You need to know the uses and sources of secondary research data. You will need to understand the purposes of marketing databases and how these are used to provide information about:

- customer behaviour, such as customer preferences and buying patterns, sales trends for new and existing products, product substitution

- the market, such as market share, market segments, competitor activities.

You need to be able to use these methods and to interpret their findings.

You also need to understand why particular market research techniques are suitable for different products and businesses, and how this is related to the cost of conducting the market research, the accessibility of data, and the validity and reliability of the data gathered.

Business activities, by their very nature, are competitive. Within a dynamic business environment producers may be constantly entering and leaving the market. At the same time, changing consumer preferences may provide signals for them to develop new strategies with different products and services. Whereas some organisations will succeed and achieve or surpass their marketing objectives, others will inevitably not perform as well.

In the last chapter we learnt how market orientation was about 'identifying, anticipating and satisfying customer requirements'. The key issue is: how do organisations do this? Market research is that vital link in the chain between buyers and suppliers. And it fulfils this function by enabling those who provide goods and services to keep in touch with the needs and wants of those who buy the services.

The American Market Research Association defines market research as:

The systematic gathering, recording and analysis of data about problems related to the marketing of goods and services.

We can break this definition down into its various ingredients:

- *Systematic* – in other words, using an organised and clear method or system.

- *Gathering* – knowing what you are looking for, and collecting appropriate information.

- *Recording* – keeping clear and organised records of what you find out.

- *Analysing* – ordering and making sense of your information in order to draw out relevant trends and conclusions.

- *Problems related to marketing* – finding out the answers to questions that will help you understand better both your customers and other details about the marketplace.

Discussion point	It has been said that 'a problem well defined is a problem half solved'. How might this relate to the context of market research?

All organisational activities take place in an environment where there is some element of risk. For example, last year a firm might have sold 40,000 fridges to a market in Italy. Who is to say they will sell the 50,000 they planned to sell this year? They may suddenly find new competitors in this market with a much better product than they currently produce, which is being sold at a lower price. Italy may go through a cold spell. There may be problems in the economy that reduce the likelihood people will change their fridges. To reduce risk, market research provides an invaluable source of information to help organisations make decisions and develop strategies for products. For example, it could help them to:

- identify their competitors

- improve their knowledge of consumers and competitors so that changing trends can be identified

- use trends to forecast activities

- monitor their market position and develop plans and strategies

- improve their competitive advantage.

Case study: Connecting the washer to the web

Ariston have developed a washing machine that can communicate with the Internet using its own mobile phone. The margherita2000.com washing machine will be able to send breakdown reports for repair and download new washing cycles from its own web site. The householder will also be able to control his or her washing machine remotely, either by using a mobile phone or by logging on to the machine's own web site.

The key achievement of this machine is that it is the first of a range of web-connected devices in the home that will be able to talk to each other, using a new open communications system called WRAP (WebReady Appliances Protocol). In the first years of this new century, Ariston hope to follow up the launch of the washing machine with dishwasher, fridge and then an oven.

These will be joined by Leon@rdo, a touch-screen computer in the kitchen. This will download recipes, act as a diary, email box and shopping list, as well as program the oven and diagnose faults. All these machines will communicate through the house's ring main and to the web through the washing machine's cellphone. Web sites to explore are:

• www.merloni.com

• www.aristonchannel.com

• www.margherita.com

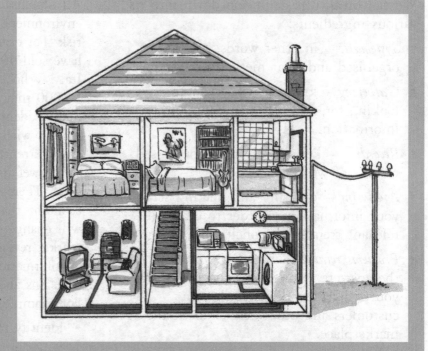

The launch of the washing machine and the peripheral gadgets represents the beginning of a new era. Having gone through the market research stage, Ariston are now ready to face the market. The main obstacle, however, is the price. The washing machine will be launched on to the market at between £800 and £1,000.

1   Explain why it was important for product developers at Ariston to link their product research to their market research.

2   What would their market research aim to find out?

3   Comment upon the new range of products developed by Ariston, as well as their market-entry price.

All organisations require answers to key questions. Answers help decision-makers to understand the nature of the decisions they have to make about the products they provide and the markets in which they operate.

Questions may include the following:

• *How do we define the market?* What are its features, such as size and character, and what is the nature of the competition?

• *What do customers require?* At the heart of marketing should be the ongoing activities of satisfying the needs and aspirations of customers.

• *Who are the target groups and how do we reach them?* The market may be made up of different groups and segments. Different distribution channels may be used to reach different groups of customers.

• *What strategies are used by our competitors?* It is important to know and understand how the actions of competitors might influence the market.

- *How do we measure our performance?* Market performance may be measured according to a number of key criteria, such as the value of volume of sales as well as brand or market share.

- *Where is our competitive position?* An important feature of marketing analysis is an ongoing review of where the organisation is within the market, its competitive advantage and how changes in its actions might influence market shape and market share.

In short, the purpose of market research is to make the process of business scientific, by cutting out unsubstantiated guesswork and hunches!

One	Research brief	Define the problem to be investigated
Two	Plan of work	Specify the data to be collected, the method of collection and the timings
Three	Collection of data	The efficiency of each stage should be checked
Four	Analysis and evaluation of data	Data storage and retrieval using a marketing information system
Five	Presentation of findings	This should be made to management groups and decision-makers, together with conclusions and recommendations

Figure 11.1 The five phases of a market research programme

Check your understanding

Imagine that your school or college wanted to develop two new courses that would either encourage new students to enter or persuade existing students to stay longer.

What information would be helpful before any decisions are made? How might they go about collecting this information?

The process of market research should not be a 'one-off' activity that takes place as part of new product development. It should be ongoing, so marketers should constantly be collecting and analysing information and feeding it through for planning and decision-making purposes. There are five identifiable stages in the setting up of a market research programme (see Figure 11.1).

Some organisations are creative in their outlook to planning and research. These businesses may anticipate developments in markets and introduce new ideas and new

methods to exploit opportunities or minimise problems. In doing this they may take risks to develop new ideas. In contrast, other businesses will wait to see what their competitors do before reacting.

Some businesses, therefore, use market research to move ahead of the competition while others simply see it as a way of keeping up with their competitors. The first type of firm we would describe as being *proactive*, while the second we would describe as *reactive*.

The proactive business will be the first to come up with new ideas and, consequently, will be well placed to exploit its ideas in meeting adventurous marketing objectives such as brand leadership in a new market. Sony are famous for breaking new ground and taking risks through proactive planning and research.

The reactive business does not put itself at the mercy of such risk and can never be in a position to make the same sort of impact as a proactive firm. Equally, it does not fall foul of the mistakes made by proactive firms.

Check your understanding

Working in small groups, make a list of:

• five proactive organisations, together with some of their products

• five reactive organisations and their products.

One of the most important things to remember is that what comes out of market research is only as good as what goes in. Identifying the information required, successfully choosing the most suitable research method, and then the type and nature of questioning should all be carefully considered before any project proceeds.

The information gathered through market research may be described as either *qualitative* or *quantitative* in nature. Qualitative information informs the organisation about the opinions and preferences of individuals and cannot always be interpreted statistically. For example, in response to a qualitative interview about cakes, one person might feel the cake is too moist and rich, while another might think it has a good taste. Qualitative research is therefore about descriptions. This type of information is difficult to categorise and

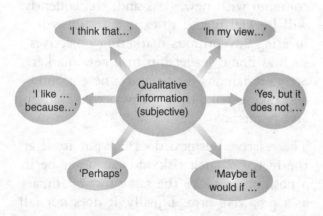

Figure 11.2 Qualitative information

measure because it is based upon personal views deemed to be subjective (see Figure 11.2).

On the other hand, quantitative information is research that produces figures that can be examined statistically. For example, 15 out of 20 people might prefer one brand to another. As this information is considered to be based upon hard facts, it is considered to be objective (see Figure 11.3).

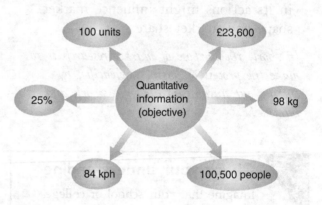

Figure 11.3 Quantitative information

Many research methods supply both qualitative and quantitative information, and the two are closely interlinked. Qualitative information provides the context within which quantitative facts operate. The 'What do you think about . . .?' approach gives people the opportunity to offer a variety of opinions, reasons, motivations and influencing factors. A group discussion, for example, allows different opinions to be offered, which will frequently lead to a *consensus* (an idea of the popular view). People enjoy offering their opinions on subjects as diverse as the current political climate and the taste of a particular margarine, and what this gives the researcher is an overall view of that particular audience's reaction to a proposition.

Quantitative data helps to produce an idea of the size and overall shape of markets and the effects of strategies on the demand for goods and services. Qualitative data helps to take this process further to show how goods and services have met the needs of current and potential customers (Figure 11.4).

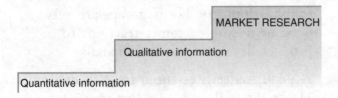

Figure 11.4 Supporting quantitative data with qualitative information

There are two broad areas in which market research can take place. If information does not already exist in an identifiable form, it will have to be collected first hand. This is known as *primary research*. Any information that is already published outside an organisation is known as *secondary research data* (Figure 11.5).

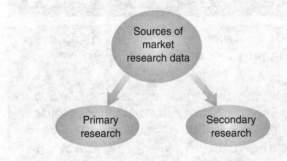

Figure 11.5 Sources of research data

Primary research methods

Any information that is original and is obtained outside an organisation is referred to as primary data. It is obtained by research conducted by or on behalf of the organisation, is specific to its needs and will involve a range of methods, such as discussions, questionnaires and surveys, and testing through pilots and field trials.

Discussions with people

It has been said that 'good decisions require good data'. One of the best ways of finding out about people's knowledge, feelings, preferences or thoughts is by asking them directly through discussion. Discussion is widely used as the basis for primary data collection. There are a number of research methods that involve discussions with respondents (people asked to answer questions).

Face-to-face interviews

Face-to-face interviews may be conducted by freelance market researchers. Sometimes, however, the employees of market research companies undertake them. Face-to-face interviews may include the following:

- *Street surveys.* These are sometimes referred to as 'clipboard surveys'. People are approached in the street, often in busy town centres, and are asked to complete a survey immediately. This can, however, be a problem if a respondent is busy or in a hurry. As a result, it is important that such surveys are brief and do not require too much concentration from the interviewee.

- *Shop surveys.* These take place in shops, often in the entrance, and shoppers are asked to take part in the survey as they leave the store.

- *Household surveys.* This involves interviewers going from door to door asking questions. Such interviews might also inconvenience respondents and need to be brief.

- *Hall surveys.* These involve booking a hall and inviting respondents to attend, or bringing them in from the street. Respondents are often offered free gifts or food to encourage them to take part. This can be useful if the researcher wants to show the respondents mock-ups or displays.

- *Home interviews.* These are normally prearranged with specific appointment times, and they take place in the respondent's home. As respondents are on their own territory they may feel more confident and be prepared to divulge more information.

- *Business surveys.* These are the business version of the home interview. They are prearranged and will take place on business premises.

Focus groups

Focus groups are an inexpensive method of obtaining useful qualitative information from consumers. For example, under the guidance of a chairperson, a group of users of the same product may be invited to provide opinions on its use. Participants in a focus group might be members of the public who have opinions on certain products and services. They may also be drawn from a particular market segment or from an industry. Focus groups are very good at testing customer reactions to product developments or proposals.

A good leader is essential for a focus group. He or she will introduce key topics for discussion, keep order and ensure every group member has the opportunity to make a contribution. The main benefit of such groups is that new ideas and opinions can be 'bounced off' each group member to refine them and prompt further creative thought. A focus group requires a note-taker. It may also be audio- or video-taped.

Case study: Using focus groups in the car industry

Like other manufacturers, Vauxhall (www.vauxhall.co.uk) has to cope with a rapidly changing world and, to keep pace, it begins planning the next model even as the wraps are coming off a new launch.

This begins with a series of 'clinics' where the reaction to a new shape is tested out on a number of preselected motorists. These motorists are recruited by an outside agency from owners of cars in the target group, together with a small number positioned above the group (who may be persuaded to trade down) and below the group (who may be persuaded to trade up). These will be people who have no connection with the motor or advertising industries.

Confidentiality is very important at this stage, so the cars are not given badges and the respondents are not told which manufacturer is conducting the clinic. This also avoids any personal prejudices coming into play about a particular marque.

1   Why do Vauxhall use focus groups or clinics?

2   What sort of issues are likely to arise at such groups?

3   Who might be targeted to attend such groups?

4   How might Vauxhall use this information?

There are a number of advantages of face-to-face interviews:

- Skilled interviewers would argue they are able to gauge the truthfulness of the response from facial expressions and other body language signals.

- Face-to-face interviews usually achieve a good response rate.

- Because it is conducted personally, the risk of inaccurate data is reduced. It is possible for the interviewer to give better explanations if the respondent has difficulty understanding. For example, the interviewer could show a diagram, draw a picture or show a prompt card.

- The interviewer is able to judge the respondent's mood and to alter the approach accordingly to keep him or her interested, or to calm down a person who is becoming agitated.

The disadvantages of face-to-face interviews are as follows:

- Interviewing is costly because not only must you cover the cost of paying researchers but you may also pay their travelling expenses and the cost of training and/or briefing them.

- They are more difficult to organise than some of the other methods.

- Supervisors must be appointed (and paid) to ensure the survey goes according to instructions.

- You rely on the professionalism of your interviewers and on their honesty – e.g. not to fill out any bogus responses in order to meet their interview quotas.

- It is a fairly time-consuming process.

Panels

Another market research method is to set up panels of consumers, which consist of groups of consumers who agree to provide information about their attitudes or buying habits.

A consumer on a *home audit* panel will discuss consumer issues during a series of personal visits by a researcher. The great advantage is that this type of panel will supply information over a long period of time from a willing participant, who may agree to sample, test or use a range of products or who is simply asked to respond to questions on consumer issues.

Another type of panel is a *diary* panel. With this type of panel, consumers record their purchases and/or media habits, usually in a diary. The purpose of this diary is not just to record purchases but also to provide research information that relates to demographic details and neighbourhood.

For example, the Broadcasters' Audience Research Board (BARB) (www.dganet.co.uk/barbinfo.htm) analyse the various television programmes people are watching at different times of the day. They do this by using 'a peoplemeter system' which polls carefully selected panel homes in order to create a sample from which national, regional and cable/satellite audience figures are derived. The total panel is some 4,500 homes, which is about 12,500 people. BARB measure audiences for a total of over 40 channels. As advertisers want value for money, this is a scientific business. For every programme transmitted, audience figures are calculated for a range of target age and social groups.

Check your understanding

Set up your own consumer discussion panel. Provide respondents with a suitable form and then ask five people to monitor their purchases over a fortnight. Think of some appropriate questions and then interview each person to discuss his or her purchases. Record your results.

Case study: Waving the wand

A.C. Nielsen's electronic consumer panel is known as Homescan. This brings a new dimension to consumer analysis, providing a powerful insight into the behaviour of customers. In a sophisticated and competitive marketing environment, this type of panel provides instant and precise data using barcode technology. Launched in June 1989, Homescan became the first panel in Europe to use in-home scanning.

Households are chosen to mirror the demographics within regions so that they provide accurate representations of purchasing across the country. Each household is equipped with a small hand-held scanner, referred to as a 'wand'. After each shopping trip they record the date, the items bought, any promotional offers that applied, the price, the quantity and the store used.

The wand asks a series of questions to prompt the panellist. Scanning each product's barcode enables its 'fingerprint' to be recorded and provides A.C. Nielsen with a precise record of consumer purchasing. The information is then transferred directly, via telephone modem links, to Nielsen's host computer. Collecting daily purchasing data gives marketing speed and precision.

Homescan includes all grocery purchases brought into the home from any outlet. The panel includes 10,500 households throughout the UK, including Northern Ireland.

For organisations that buy this information from Nielsen, there is the opportunity to understand exactly who their customers are. They find out about what products customers are buying day by day so that they can tailor this knowledge to develop promotions and their advertising for the days when the right customers come into store. They can assess a new product launch. By using Homescan they can evaluate the retail distribution of a new product and understand the factors behind its build in volume and market share. It also provides an opportunity to track products to find out the factors that might be undermining their performance.

This all helps to measure the tactical and strategic objectives of a marketing campaign, and this information can be used to refine and develop the precise elements of marketing strategies. For example, it might help to address questions such as the following:

- Has the relaunch succeeded in regaining lapsed buyers?

- What is the best way to target mailing activity?

- How does advertising expenditure help which brands?

- Where do consumers buy?

- How loyal are consumers?

1   What would being a member of a Homescan panel involve?

2   Why is this information considered valuable?

3   Who would purchase this information and how would they use it?

Telephone interviews

Surveys conducted over the telephone are increasingly popular as they are both convenient for both the interviewer and the respondent. The interviewer can conduct the interview without leaving the office or from home, and the respondent can similarly reply from an armchair. There is a ready supply of respondents to contact – you need only look in a telephone directory. It is also possible to sample wide geographical areas – even abroad – very easily. However, this method is often regarded as intrusive as it catches people unawares. This means the respondent may start the interview with a negative viewpoint, which questioning will not necessarily overcome.

With more businesses today being involved in telephone interviewing, people have become increasingly tired of being called at home and asked questions. The number of people refusing to take part is on the increase. However, it is a cost-effective way of reaching people, and the replies received are likely to be truthful.

Postal interviews

Postal surveys (Figure 11.6) are a cheap method of interviewing, which is why almost a quarter of all surveys carried out use this method. They do, however, have a low response rate. Often fewer than 10% of questionnaires sent out are returned, usually because people simply put them in the bin along with all the other mail they consider to be 'junk'.

To improve response rates, organisations often include incentives, such as shopping vouchers or free pens, or a promise the respondent will be placed in a prize draw. As respondents can answer in their own time and at their own convenience, it is possible to ask a large number of questions. This is also a good way of asking personal questions as no personal contact takes place.

Multi-media computer-assisted personal interviewing (CAPI)

This is a relatively recent method of data collection that is increasing in popularity. The object of CAPI is to allow the

WIN OUR EXCLUSIVE PRIZE DRAW
BY PARTICIPATING IN A NATIONAL MOTORING SURVEY

Dear Motorist,

Your opinions really CAN make a difference. Manufacturers and Motoring organisations need to understand who today's motorists are and what they want.

The information you provide will be held by ABC Ltd and safeguarded under the Data Protection Act. ABC uses your answers for market research and analysis purposes which will determine the offers you receive. ABC may make your responses available to other reputable companies who may wish to contact you with offers of goods and services. You can choose not to receive special offers by ticking the box on page 3.

As a thank you for completing and returning your survey you will be automatically entered into our motoring prize draw. If you don't want to answer some of the questions that's OK - just skip to the next question!

Thank you for your valued help.

Kate Ellison

Kate Ellison, Research Director

PLEASE REPLY WITHIN 14 DAYS

EXAMPLE: Do you watch TV?   1 ☑ Yes   9 ☐ No

| PLEASE PRINT | 1 ☐ Mr.   2 ☐ Mrs.   3 ☐ Miss   4 ☐ Ms. |

Your Surname:

First Name: Partner's First Name:

Address:

Town:

County:

Post Code:

Moisten this pink strip and stick to page 4

This questionnaire is divided into two main sections. The first section is specifically about Motoring and the second section relates to you and your lifestyle. All of this information will enable leading companies to produce a full picture of today's motorist.

1 Why do you drive? (Tick all that apply)
1 ☐ To get to work   4 ☐ To get to shops
2 ☐ For leisure   5 ☐ Take children to school
3 ☐ For work   6 ☐ Other

2 Where do you do most of your driving? (Tick all that apply)
1 ☐ On Motorway   3 ☐ In the Country
2 ☐ In Town/Village   4 ☐ In Cities

3 Do you think the current motorway speed limit (70mph) is:
1 ☐ Too high   3 ☐ Acceptable
2 ☐ Too low

4 Do you agree that Motorway Tolls should be introduced in the UK?
1 ☐ Yes   9 ☐ No

5 When choosing a new car what are the most important factors you look for? (Tick all that apply)
01 ☐ Price   06 ☐ Style
02 ☐ Safety features 07 ☐ Environmentally friendly
03 ☐ Power   08 ☐ Extras
04 ☐ Economy (MPG)   09 ☐ Performance
05 ☐ Insurance Group 10 ☐ Others

6 If you could afford to buy and run any car what car would you choose?

Make   Model

7 Which petrol stations do you use most often?
01 ☐ BP   06 ☐ Jet   10 ☐ Shell
02 ☐ Esso   07 ☐ Mobil   11 ☐ Burmah
03 ☐ Fina   08 ☐ Q8   12 ☐ Texaco
04 ☐ Elf   09 ☐ Gulf   13 ☐ Other
05 ☐ Supermarket/Hypermarket

8 If you collect tokens/points please write the number of the company from Q.7

9 What is the reason for choosing the petrol station you visit most often:-
1 ☐ It's on my regular route   5 ☐ Collect tokens
2 ☐ It's close to home   6 ☐ Friendly services
3 ☐ Price of petrol   7 ☐ Car wash
4 ☐ Shop facilities

10 When visiting your petrol station which of the following do you use:-
1 ☐ Car wash   4 ☐ Car Vac
2 ☐ Shop   5 ☐ Air
3 ☐ Water   6 ☐ Other

1

---

11 Besides cost what do you believe is the most important thing manufacturers need to do to improve their cars?

12 In your opinion what is the most important Act the government should pass to relieve congestion on the roads?

13 If you have a company car, can you:
Choose the make/model   1 ☐ Yes   3 ☐ No
Choose a Vauxhall   2 ☐ Yes   4 ☐ No

The following questions are all about your lifestyle. Both sections will be used together to enable leading companies to produce a full picture of today's motorist. If you don't want to answer some of the questions that's OK – just skip to the next question!

You & Your Car(s)

MAIN CAR

15 Make of Car?
e.g. Ford
16 Model & Type
e.g. Focus   MAKE   MODEL   TYPE

17 Registration Letter e.g. X   CC:
18 Who is the main driver?   1 ☐ You   2 ☐ Partner
19 Is the car owned?   1 ☐ Privately   2 ☐ By Company
20 Its yearly mileage?   ,000
21 Bought: 1 ☐ New   2 ☐ Used   in 20
22 Plan to change it: 1 ☐ 0-6mths
2 ☐ 7-12mths   3 ☐ 1-2yrs
23 Is the car: 1 ☐ Diesel   2 ☐ Automatic
24 Body type:
1 ☐ Saloon   4 ☐ Hatch
2 ☐ Coupe   5 ☐ Convertible
3 ☐ Off Road 6 ☐ Estate

25 Number of cars in your household:
1 ☐ 1   2 ☐ 2   3 ☐ 3+   9 ☐ None

26 When does your current car insurance expire? (If not sure of exact month, tick nearest)

Main Car:	01 Jan	05 May	09 Sep
	02 Feb	06 June	10 Oct
	03 Mar	07 July	11 Nov
	04 April	08 Aug	12 Dec

Second Car:	01 Jan	05 May	09 Sep
	02 Feb	06 June	10 Oct
	03 Mar	07 July	11 Nov
	04 April	08 Aug	12 Dec

---

14 What in your opinion are the most key motoring safety issues the Government/manufacturers need to address? (Please tick a maximum of three)
1 ☐ A more rigorous test (including, M-way driving)
2 ☐ Retests for banned drivers/dangerous driving convictions
3 ☐ Increase the legal driving age from 17 to 19
4 ☐ Mandatory safety devices on new cars eg ABS/airbags/side impact bars
5 ☐ Mandatory seat belts in all coaches, mini buses etc
6 ☐ Heavier fines for speeding in 30/40 mph areas
7 ☐ More use of speed cameras
8 ☐ More use of "sleeping policemen" in residential areas
9 ☐ Better road safety education for children

SECOND CAR

MAKE   MODEL   TYPE

Reg. Letter   CC:
1 ☐ You   2 ☐ Partner
1 ☐ Privately   2 ☐ By Company
Its yearly mileage?   ,000
Bought: 1 ☐ New   2 ☐ Used   in 20
Plan to change it: 1 ☐ 0-6mths
2 ☐ 7-12mths   3 ☐ 1-2yrs
Is the car: 1 ☐ Diesel   2 ☐ Automatic
Body type:
1 ☐ Saloon   4 ☐ Hatch
2 ☐ Coupe   5 ☐ Convertible
3 ☐ Off Road 6 ☐ Estate

27 How many years No Claims do you have?
You: 0 ☐ 0   2 ☐ 2   4 ☐ 4   ☐ 4+
         1 ☐ 1   3 ☐ 3   5 ☐ 5   ☐ Unsure
Partner: 0 ☐ 0   2 ☐ 2   4 ☐ 4   ☐ 4+
         1 ☐ 1   3 ☐ 3   5 ☐ 5   ☐ Unsure

28 Where do you keep your car(s)?
Main Car: 1 ☐ Garage   2 ☐ Driveway   3 ☐ Road
Second Car: 1 ☐ Garage   2 ☐ Driveway   3 ☐ Road

29 What do you use your car(s) for?
Main Car   **Second Car**
1 ☐ Social/Domestic/Pleasure   4 ☐ Social/Domestic/Pleasure
2 ☐ Travel to work   5 ☐ Travel to work
3 ☐ Business   6 ☐ Business

2

Figure 11.6   A postal survey

Your Interests

49 Please tick ALL the leisure interests and activities you and your partner enjoy regularly:

01 Coin/Stamp Collecting	12 Home Computing		
02 Collectables	13 Active Sport/Exercise		
03 Crossword/Puzzles	14 Pets		
04 Do-It-Yourself/DIY	15 Playing Golf		
05 Eating Out	16 Photography		
06 Fine Art/Antiques	17 Record/Tape/CDs		
07 Fishing	18 Snow Skiing		
08 Foreign Travel	19 Theatre/Cultural/ Art Events		
09 Gourmet Foods/ Wines	20 Wildlife/Environment		
10 Grandchildren	21 Wines by Mail Order		
11 Gardening			

50 Please write the numbers of your three favourite activities from the list above:

You: Partner:

51 Do either of you bet on: (Tick all that apply)
1 Pools   3 Horseracing
2 Bingo   4 Other

52 Where have you been on holiday in the last 3 years? (Tick all that apply)
1 UK   3 USA
2 Europe   4 Rest of the world

53 How many times in the last year have you bought goods/services via the mail?
1 1   3 4-5
2 2-3   4 6 plus   None

54 Please tick all the newspapers that are REGULARLY read by your family: 99 None

	Daily	Sunday
Express	01	14
Independent	02	15
Mail	03	16
Mirror	04	17
Sport	05	18
Telegraph	06	19
Times	07	20
Other/Local	08	21
Guardian	09	
Star	10	
Sun	11	
Today	12	
Daily Record	13	
News of the World		22
Observer		23
People		24
Post		25
Sunday Mail (Scotland)		26

55 What causes have you contributed to in the past year? 9 None   5 Helping the elderly
1 Wildlife   6 Childrens' Welfare
2 Environmental   7 Disaster Relief
3 Health Research   8 Animal Welfare
4 Third World Causes   0 Other

56 How do you contribute? (Tick all that apply)
1 By covenant   3 By post
2 In street/at door

IMPORTANT

If you or your partner smoke, each person must sign below so they can receive special tobacco offers.

Please sign that you are a smoker aged 18 or over:

PARTNER'S SIGNATURE

Now please indicate for each tobacco product category which ONE brand you and/or your partner smoke most often.

57 CIGARETTES You / Partner

	You	Partner
B&H	01	51
B&H Superkings	02	52
Berkeley	03	53
Craven A	04	54
Dorchester	05	55
Dunhill	06	56
Regal	07	57
JP Special	08	58
Kensitas	09	59
Lambert & Butler	10	60
Marlboro	11	61

	You	Partner
Raffles	12	62
Red Band	13	63
Embassy	14	64
Rothmans	15	65
Rothmans Royals	16	66
Silk Cut	17	67
Stuyvesant	18	68
Superkings	19	69
Other: Under £4.50	20	70
Other: Over £4.50	21	71

58 Please tick if your brand is light/mild: 22 / 72
59 Please tick if your brand is menthol: 23 / 73

60 HANDROLLING You / Partner

	You	Partner
Golden Virginia	24	74
Old Holborn	25	75
Other Handroll	26	76

61 PIPE You / Partner
	You	Partner
Clan	27	77
Condor	28	78

62 CIGARS You / Partner

	You	Partner
Café Crème	33	83
Classic	34	84
Castella Panatella	35	85
Hamlet	36	86
Hamlet Miniature	37	87
Hamlet Reserve	38	88
Henri Wintermans	39	89
King Edward Coronets	40	90
King Six	41	91
Panama	42	92
Other Cigars	43	93

	You	Partner
Dutch Blend	29	79
Gold Block	30	80
St. Bruno	31	81
Other Pipe	32	82

63 How often do you/your partner smoke cigars? You / Partner
	You	Partner
Occasionally	44	94
1 pack per week	45	95
2-4 packs per wk	46	96
1 pack per day	47	97

4

---

30 Has anyone who drives your car had: Yes / No
An accident in the last three years? 1 / 3
A licence endorsement in the last 5 years? (not parking/speeding) 2 / 4

You & Your Home

31 Is your home a:
1 Flat   4 Semi-Detached
2 Maisonette   5 Detached
3 Terraced   6 Bungalow

32 When did you move to this address?
Year: 19   Month:

33 How many bedrooms do you have?
2   3   4   5   5+

34 Do you:
1 Own   3 Rent (Private)
2 Rent (Council)

35 When does your Home Contents insurance expire?
01 Jan   04 April   07 July   10 Oct
02 Feb   05 May   08 Aug   11 Nov
03 Mar   06 June   09 Sep   12 Dec

36 When does your Buildings insurance expire?
01 Jan   04 April   07 July   10 Oct
02 Feb   05 May   08 Aug   11 Nov
03 Mar   06 June   09 Sep   12 Dec

37 What are you and your partner's occupations?

	You	Partner
Craftsman/Tradesman	01	11
Education/Medical Services	02	12
Housewife	03	13
Manual/Factory Worker	04	14
Middle Management	05	15
Office/Clerical	06	16
Professional/Sen. Management	07	17
Retired	08	18
Shopworker	09	19
Student	10	20

38 Are you/your partner: You / Partner
	You	Partner
Self-Employed/Business Owner	1	3
Running own in home business	2	4

39 Which cards do you or your partner have?
(Please tick all that apply)
1 Access/Mastercard   3 Visa/Barclaycard
2 American Express/Diners Club   4 Store/Shop Cards   5 Other

40 Do you or your Partner have:
You: 1 Hearing Difficulties   3 A Hearing Aid
Partner: 2 Hearing Difficulties   4 A Hearing Aid

41 What are the dates of birth for:

You: Day / Month / 19 Year
Partner: Day / Month / 19 Year

42 Are you:
1 Married   3 Divorced/Separated
2 Single   4 Widowed

43 Please tell us the age of all your children living at home: 99 None at home

00 0-12 Mths	07 7 Yrs	14 14 Yrs	
01 1 Yr	08 8 Yrs	15 15 Yrs	
02 2 Yrs	09 9 Yrs	16 16 Yrs	
03 3 Yrs	10 10 Yrs	17 17 Yrs	
04 4 Yrs	11 11 Yrs	18 18 Yrs	
05 5 Yrs	12 12 Yrs	19 19 Yrs	
06 6 Yrs	13 13 Yrs	20 20 Yrs	

44 Are you or your Partner considering changing your bank or building society current account?
You: 1 Yes   3 Possibly
Partner: 2 Yes   4 Possibly

45 Which group best describes your COMBINED annual household income?
1 Up to £5,000   5 £20,000-£24,999
2 £5,000-£9,999   6 £25,000-£29,999
3 £10,000-£14,999   7 £30,000-£34,999
4 £15,000-£19,999   8 £35,000 plus

46 How many prize draws, competitions or lotteries did you enter in the last year excluding the National Lottery? 9 None
1 1-3   3 7-10
2 4-6   4 11 plus

47 Do you forsee the need for a personal loan?
1 In the near future   3 In 12 months
2 In 6 months   9 No

48 Do you/your partner have any of the following? (Please tick all that apply)
1 Pension Plan - Private
2 Health Care (BUPA, etc)
3 Stocks and Shares
4 High Interest Investments & Unit Trusts
5 Savings Plan
6 Cheque Guarantee Card

3

Figure 11.6   A postal survey (continued)

researcher to conduct (in the respondent's home) the type of research that would normally have to be undertaken in a hotel room or other large venue. The interviewer arrives equipped with a laptop computer that has full multi-media capability, which not only records the respondent's views but is also able to display pictures, video, TV and cinema advertisements. It can show the same product with different packaging designs superimposed, and can run in various languages. Answers from the respondent may be recorded via a microphone into the laptop for analysis later.

This method has proved particularly useful when prompting respondents to identify TV advertisements they have seen recently, especially those using abstract images and/or musical content. Field staff away from base can send the data back to the office using email, where the task of analysis can begin.

Check your understanding

Suggers are interviewers who are not truly doing research but are selling whilst pretending to do market research. Fuggers are involved in fund raising under the guise of market research.

How do consumers distinguish between suggers and fuggers and real market researchers?

Internet questionnaires

Perhaps the cheapest way of obtaining information today is by placing a questionnaire on a web site using the Internet (see www.CustomerSat.com/rtr/). Respondents answer questions, directly on to a web page, and the information is logged by computer at the host site.

Individual organisations may put questionnaires on their home pages. Some universities conduct such surveys.

The Centre for Public Opinion (CFPO) provides polling and survey services for corporate customers. Volunteer respondents register with the centre and are then contacted via email to say a survey has been made available and their opinions are requested. Participation is voluntary. The participant sends an email ID, and organisations may elect to send respondents coupons or discount offers by way of thanks for their co-operation.

With more people owning PCs and higher numbers connected to the Net, there are a number of ways in which Internet marketing and research are likely to develop over the next few years. Is it possible to envisage days or weekends spent with market researchers, organisational managers and their customers, discussing product details and developments using web-cams?

Discussion point	How in the future might market research over the Internet change the relationship between us as consumers and the organisations from which we buy?

Phone-in polls

A magazine, newspaper or television programme may ask its readers or viewers to telephone to express their views on a particular topic, normally one of current interest or perhaps to make a choice between alternatives. Respondents use different telephone numbers to register different responses. This method has been used for television awards. It has been criticised, however, because it:

- represents only those interested in the particular area under discussion

- is used only by those respondents who have the money to make a call

- is used only by those respondents who want to express their views. Those who are impartial are unlikely to call.

Observation

This involves looking at how consumers behave in the shopping environment. Information like this can help marketers make decisions about packaging or influence the choice of point-of-sale materials designed to attract the attention of shoppers. It may also help to make decisions about where to place particular products in a shop.

The process of putting products in a store in the right place at the right time is known as *merchandising*. This is particularly important in the retail trade. Today, a number of electronic devices can be used to monitor individual responses. For example:

- A psycho-galvanometer measures perspiration, and this may be used for a variety of forms of testing.

- An eye camera may record reactions, such as visual stimulation.

- A tachistocope exposes material for a short period and then measures responses.

Check your understanding

Find out about the hobbies or leisure pursuits of four members of your group by interviewing each of them. Present your results.

Did you encounter any problems conducting the interview? Describe what these were.

Look further at the other market research methods discussed in this book. Would any of these have been more suitable for obtaining the information you required?

Accompanied shopping

With this method a qualitative researcher accompanies a shopper around a supermarket or on a shopping trip, and observes and questions the respondent as he or she makes each purchase. The researcher tries to determine why the shopper chose one brand in preference to another. Such research is time consuming and expensive.

Mystery shopping

Although mystery shopping has been around for some time, it has only recently been accepted as a valuable tool for market research. In principle, it is simple – a researcher will pose as a customer and go into a branch of a retail outlet in order to report on the level of service provided. They may comment upon the following:

- How they are greeted by staff.

- How promptly they are dealt with.

- The knowledge of the staff.

- The staff's selling skills.

- The appearance of the branch.

- The quality of facilities, such as toilets.

- Hygiene standards, where appropriate.

Mystery shopping may help to assess levels of customer service, the effectiveness of staff training and staff motivation.

Discussion point	Remember the classic Basil Fawlty episode entitled 'The Hotel Inspectors'? It showed that someone involved in providing customer service could be influenced by an inspector who was assessing the facilities of an outlet and the behaviour of its staff.
	Could it ever be argued that the process of mystery shopping infringes the rights of staff by 'spying' upon them?

Questionnaires

Many of the market research methods described above depend on the use of a questionnaire. A questionnaire is a systematic list of questions designed to obtain information from people about:

- specific events

- their attitudes

- their values

- their beliefs.

The quality of the information obtained via the questionnaire is inextricably linked with the survey. A good questionnaire will result in a smooth interview, giving the interviewer a precise format to follow and ensuring he or she obtains exactly the information required in a format that is easy for the researcher to analyse later.

Questionnaire design is critical. Although it is easy to make up questions, it is very difficult to produce a good questionnaire – and a badly designed questionnaire may lead to biased results.

Another problem may arise if very few completed forms are returned, or if those returned are only partially completed. In addition, if the questionnaire is being administered by a number of interviewers, there is always the danger that some may misinterpret questions and introduce their own personal bias in a way that prompts certain answers from respondents.

If you were asked to write a questionnaire, where would you start? The starting point would be to think about the focus of your questions. For example, what information do you require and why do you need it? You would also need to think about the target audience you wish to examine. It would be important to question all the people who are likely to have relevant opinions or information.

When people give up their own time to answer the questions on a questionnaire, it is useful to tell them who you are and why you are undertaking this research. This is not only polite but will also put the respondent at ease and may facilitate co-operation. The language used and the number of prompts and examples to support the points made within the questionnaire need to be considered.

A good questionnaire will do the following:

- Ask questions that relate directly to information needs.

- Not ask too many questions.

- Not ask leading or intimate questions.

- Fit questions into a logical sequence.

- Use language appropriate to the target group.

- Not use questions that are confusing or ambiguous.

- Avoid questions relating to sexuality, politics and religion unless they are very relevant.

Sequencing the questions logically is very important. It may be useful to start with a few factual questions that are easy to respond to. Some form of multiple-choice questions may follow these, before introducing questions that require the respondent to think about some of the issues being researched. The questionnaire may be closed with 'filter questions' about the respondents' backgrounds, which help to locate them in the sampling frame.

There is no point including questions that do not relate to the main purposes of the research. The questionnaire should be kept as short as practically possible. More than 40 questions could put respondents off or cause them to provide hasty replies.

The questions in a questionnaire may be 'open' or 'closed'. *Open* questions allow the person answering to give an opinion and may encourage him or her to talk at length. You have to be careful, though. Asking questions such as 'What type of music do you listen to?' could lead to such a variety of answers that analysing them would be very difficult. *Closed* questions usually require an answer picked from a range of options (which may be simply yes/no).

Most questionnaires, use closed questions so they can be answered quickly and efficiently, and answers to these questions are easier to analyse (see Figure 11.7).

Please indicate with a tick which types of music you listen to regularly (tick all that apply):

☐ Classical
☐ Easy listening
☐ Jazz
☐ Blues
☐ Golden oldies
☐ Popular
☐ Heavy metal
☐ Punk
☐ Indie
☐ Rap
☐ Dance
☐ Swing
☐ Hip hop
☐ Other (please specify) ....

Figure 11.7 A closed question

Sometimes it is necessary to judge the degree of the respondent's feelings on a subject. The best way to do this is to use a rating or response scale. There are various types. *Likert scales* show how strongly the respondent agrees or disagrees with a statement (see Figure 11.8). *Rank order scale* questions ask the respondent to put a number beside various items in order to put them in some sort of order of preference, as in Figure 11.9.

An *intention-to-buy* asks respondents to indicate by ticking a box, how likely it is they will buy some items in the future (Figure 11.10). *Semantic differential scales* use two words describing the opposite ends of a

Put a cross in the box that shows how strongly you agree or disagree with each of the following statements:

	Strongly agree	Agree	Neither agree nor disagree	Disagree	Strongly disagree
The AVCE course has prepared me well for work		X			
The lecturers at college are well prepared			X		
The lecturers at college are interesting	X				
I was well prepared for my assignments				X	

Figure 11.8 A Likert scale

These are all considerations when choosing where to buy a new computer. Put them in rank order with 1 by the most important, 2 by the second most important and so on down to 5 against the least important.

Wide choice	2
Helpful sales staff	3
Value for money	1
After-sales service	4
Quick delivery	5

Figure 11.9 A rank order scale

If a textbook were available covering this unit/module, I would:

Definitely buy	Probably buy	Not sure	Probably not buy	Definitely not buy
1 ☐	2 ☐	3 ☐	4 ☐	5 ☐

Figure 11. 10 An intention-to-buy question

Place a cross on the scale below to show what feelings you have about Frosty's ice creams:

Frosty's ice creams are:

Good value	│ │ │ │ │ │ │	Poor value
Tasty	│ │ │ │ │ │ │	Tasteless
Well packaged	│ │ │ │ │ │ │	Poorly packaged
Satisfying	│ │ │ │ │ │ │	Unsatisfying

Figure 11.11 A semantic differential scale

scale, with a series of points highlighted between. The respondents are asked to indicate where on the scale their opinion lies (see Figure 11.11). Once the respondent has completed such a question, the points can be joined up to produce a profile of that product. Comparing replies from a number of respondents provides a useful profile of how the product is viewed by customers (see Figure 11.12). It is then possible to compare products or brands by superimposing two or more profiles on one scale to identify the strengths and weaknesses of each (Figure 11.13).

Frosty's ice creams are:

1 2 3 4 5 6 7 8 9 10

Good value	X	Poor value
Tasty	X	Tasteless
Well packaged	X	Poorly packaged
Satisfying	X	Unsatisfying

Figure 11.12 Comparing respondent replies

The purpose of a closed question is to get people to commit themselves to a concrete answer. The problem with open questions is they are difficult to analyse. Closed questions tie respondents down so they have to make a decision within a range of choices.

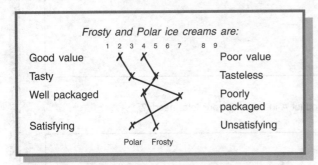

Figure 11.13 Comparing product strengths and weaknesses

Check your understanding

Think back to any questionnaire or form you have filled in recently. (If necessary, use your course enrolment form as an example.)

What was the purpose of the form or questionnaire? Was it easy or difficult to understand? Do you feel it was well designed? If not, why not?

To help interviewers operate a questionnaire, a *prompt card* is sometimes used. This means that, if several or all of the questions in the questionnaire have the same range or set of

answers, these can be numbered and the respondents' answers can, hence, be recorded as numbers (see Figure 11.14).

Dolland & Aitchison	01
Specsavers Optical Superstores	02
Boots Opticians	03
Vision Express	04
Rayner & Keeler	05
Optical Express	06
G.C. Bateman	07
Co-op	08
Scrivens	09
Others	10

Figure 11.14 A prompt card

Some questionnaires are designed so that respondents can concentrate on the questions that are relevant and skip over the questions that do not relate to them (see Figure 11.15).

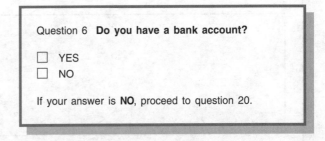

Figure 11.15 A question that permits a respondent to skip to the next relevant part of a questionnaire

Case study: Your opinion about the performance of a product you regularly purchase

Using the questionnaire in Figure 11.16, discuss your feelings about one product you regularly purchase (Product A).

Total performance of Product A (including product, sales, support, price, etc.):

Dissatisfied ☐ ☐ ☐ ☐ ☐ ☐ ☐ ☐ ☐ ☐ Very satisfied

1   2   3   4   5   6   7   8   9   10

Compared to one year earlier, is Product A's total performance:

☐ Better   ☐ Worse   ☐ Same

Why?

What one thing can ——— do to improve the performance of Product A in meeting your total needs?

Figure 11.16   A simple questionnaire

1 Explain how the answers you have provided for this brief questionnaire might be used.

2 What information has it provided?

3 Comment on the structure of the questions.

4 How easy would it be to analyse and interpret the information it provided?

Surveys and sampling

Surveys are one of the most common ways used to collect market research information. They use market research methods, such as various types of interviews, to find out how respondents react to a range of issues often contained within a questionnaire.

There are two types of survey: a census and a sample. A *census* involves questioning every supplier or customer within a particular market. However, unless the market is very small (such as an organisational market), this is unlikely to be practicable. Taking a *sample* involves questioning a selection of respondents from the target market. To ensure the results of a sample survey are accurate, the market research process must identify a representative group of customers. If the selection is fair and accurate, the information should be *statistically reliable*. If the sample is incomplete and does not accurately represent a group of consumers, misleading data is obtained and the sample is said to be *biased*.

There are a number of different ways of choosing a sample.

Random sampling

With this method, individuals and organisations are selected from a 'sampling frame', which is simply a list (usually numbered) of all the members of the market or population to be surveyed. There are three main forms of random sampling:

1 *Simple random sampling* allows the researcher to choose the size of the sample required and then to pick the sample on a purely random basis. The sample must be selected in such a way that every item in the sampling frame has an equal chance of being selected.

One way of doing this is to use a computer to draw names and numbers from a list at random.

2 Another way is to use *systematic sampling*, which involves selecting items from the list at regular intervals after choosing a random starting point. For example, if it is decided to select a sample of 20 names from 1,000, then every 50th name (1,000 divided by 20) should be selected, after a random start in the first 50. If 18 is chosen as the starting point (possibly by using a table of random numbers), then the sample series would be 18, 68, 118, 168, etc.

3 *Stratified random sampling* takes into account that some customers are more important than others. It therefore weights the sample on the basis of the importance of each group of customers in the market.

For example, if an organisation has 5,000 small users of products accounting for sales of £1 million, 4,000 medium users accounting for £1 million, and 1,000 big users accounting for £2 million, a random sample of 200 would not be representative of the whole market. To make the sample more representative would involve allocating the big users half the sample because they make up half the sales, with a quarter of the sample being allocated to medium users and a quarter to small users. The stratified random sample would then include 100 big users, 50 medium users and 50 small users, all randomly chosen from their respective categories.

Cluster sampling

With this method, the population/customers are divided into small areas but, instead of sampling from a random selection of these areas, sampling is carried out in a few areas that are considered to be typical of the market in question. For example, you might divide the city of Newcastle into 200 segments and then, because of the nature of your survey, decide you will sample only from a segment that contains at least one school, one church and one shopping centre; any segments without these facilities are avoided.

Quota sampling

Although random sampling, if properly conducted, produces the best results, it can be expensive and time consuming and, in some situations, it is not possible to identify a random sample. In these circumstances quota sampling may be used. With quota sampling interviewers are given instructions as to the number of people to interview with certain characteristics – such as sex, age, socioeconomic group or other demographic detail.

For example, if the interviewers are asked to investigate housewives aged 30–50 years, they will quiz every housewife 'fitting the bill' (possibly in the high street) up to their maximum quota. The problem is that there is no assurance the housewives interviewed are typical of housewives in that band, and the statistical accuracy of such sampling is questionable.

Convenience sampling

This involves gathering information from anyone available for the interviewer to survey, no matter what his or her background.

Judgement sampling

This involves the interviewer selecting respondents using his or her own judgement that they seemed to be, and looked representative of, the group of customers in the market being researched.

A good sample will be representative. Good sampling will, therefore, save time and effort, and is normally as accurate as a census. In order to be as accurate as possible, researchers should, therefore, do the following.

1 Ensure they have an accurate target population or sampling frame. Sampling frames are lists of people's names, census or electoral role details, details from surveys carried out previously, or simply maps of areas. It is important that:

   a the population sampled are truly potential customers. Doing this may involve checking sales records, trade journals, lists of customers, maps or directories

   b the person who buys the products is identified. The customer and consumer are not always the same person

   c individual items do not appear more than once

   d the sampling frame is complete.

2 Select a sampling frame that best meets their needs in identifying a representative group.

3 Choose a suitable sample size. This may be dictated by cost considerations. However, larger surveys are likely to be more accurate.

> You wish to find out more about the use of one product of your choice – for example, a magazine, some make-up or perhaps an event.
>
> Is a sampling frame available? Which sampling method would you use? Discuss your answers.

Pilots

A pilot 'is a small-scale experiment which is undertaken before something is introduced on a larger scale'. If time and cost constraints allow, a questionnaire should be piloted by trying it out on test respondents. This may not involve a great many respondents, perhaps 10 or 12 at most. A pilot is useful in identifying any major problems with the questionnaire. It will help to identify errors in the order of the questions or in the questionnaires themselves. It will also include whether the questionnaire will meet the research objectives, so a pilot is time and money well spent if it ensures the final questionnaire provides accurate and reliable information.

Prior to the national launch of a product, many organisations pilot a product within part of the market. For example, AVCEs, the new Advanced GNVQs for the year 2000, were piloted in a number of colleges. The purpose of such an exercise was to obtain feedback from the partial launch so that any fine-tuning or adjustments could be made to the product.

Field trials

Selected consumers may be asked to test a product prior to its launch. The purpose of this is to ensure the product performs according to expectations in the home environment, and it provides an opportunity for problems to be ironed out.

Check your understanding

Make a list of some of the products you would expect to have gone through extensive field trials before launch.

Secondary research methods

Secondary marketing information can be obtained from both *internal* and *external* sources.

Internal sources

Internal information is information already held within the organisation, more often than not in databases. A database is a large amount of information stored in such a way that it can easily be found, processed and updated. Users across an organisation may access the database.

Information on existing customers will form the core of the database, with sales invoices probably being the most valued source of data. The invoice is created for financial purposes but it contains a considerable amount of customer data that can be made immediately available for others. For example, it might contain information such as the following:

- *Customer title:* gender, job description, other forms of identification.

- *Customer surname:* ethnic coding.

- *Customer address:* geographical coding.

- *Date of sale:* tracking purchase rates and repurchasing patterns.

- *Items ordered:* product category interests.

- *Quantities ordered:* heavy/medium/light users.

- *Price:* value of customer.

- *Terms and conditions:* customer service needs.

Case study: The Electricity Generating Company

We can understand how one type of database works as a source of market research by looking at the activities of an electricity distribution company. Customers are provided with a customer reference number (CRN). To the CRN the electricity company attaches a vast array of information that tells it about the consumer:

- Tariff type. The price a customer pays for electricity can vary according to whether the customer is a home or a business or a large or small customer.

- Consumption. The company can then track the amount of electricity a customer uses, and when.

- Method of payment. Some customers prefer prepayment rather than credit, while others prefer to pay monthly rather than quarterly.

- Change of tenancy. The company knows when customers move out of and into a property.

- New buildings. The company knows when and where new buildings that use electricity are being erected, because an electricity supply is applied for.

From such information it is possible to obtain answers to an almost endless list of questions, such as the following:

- What is the size of the market?

- What type of user uses the most/least electricity?

- How do customers prefer to pay?

- What is the average credit period?

- How many new users are coming on-stream?

- How many users are the company losing?

- What is the average consumption per user?

- What is the profitability of each type of customer?

- How does the use of electricity vary during the day?

- Where is the market expanding/contracting?

1 How will the answers to these questions improve the way the electricity company manages its business?

2 What other questions might be answered from this type of database?

External sources

External data exists in the form of published materials, collected by someone else. It can give a broader dimension to data previously collected.

For example, external information can be used to enhance existing knowledge. For instance, postcodes may help to group customers geographically. By identifying and labelling certain characteristics of customers, a company may be able to make assumptions about their needs. Two examples of useful external sources are as follows:

- *Domestic socioeconomic data.* Customers are classified according to their house type, the assumption being that a certain lifestyle is associated with that type of house.

- *Industrial classification.* Organisational customers can be classified according to the nature of their activities. Certain types of organisations can then be expected to have predictable demands for services.

External information can complement an organisation's own information by permitting direct comparison with competitors, by putting the organisation's performance within the context of the economy as a whole, and by identifying markets that offer potential.

> ### Check your understanding
> Imagine you are the owner or manager of a small shop selling sports equipment in your local neighbourhood.
>
> What sort of information might give you a better understanding of the decisions you have to make?

> **Discussion point**
> The population projections in Figure 11.17 would be of value to those marketing consumer products and services. Explain why.
>
> What further demographic information might they require?

	1996	2001	2011	2021	2031	2041
0–14 years	11,358	11,289	10,507	10,368	10,277	9,851
15–29 years	11,903	11,197	11,717	11,221	10,723	10,757
30–44 years	12,935	13,747	12,170	11,687	11,907	11,149
45–59 years	10,582	11,228	12,660	13,033	11,243	11,766
60–74 years	7,831	7,752	9,272	10,574	12,032	10,665
75+ years	4,193	4,406	4,602	5,361	6,640	8,066
Males	28,856	29,377	30,206	30,916	31,153	30,813
Females	29,946	30,241	30,723	31,328	31,669	31,443
TOTAL	**58,801**	**59,618**	**60,929**	**62,244**	**62,822**	**62,256**

Figure 11.17 Population projections (thousands)

Government statistics

These are principally supplied by the ONS (Office for National Statistics – www.ons.gov.uk/), the DTI (Department of Trade and Industry – www.2.dti.gov.uk), the DfEE (Department for Education and Employment – www.dfee.gov.uk/), the GSS (Government Statistical Service – www.statistics.gov.uk/) and the OECD (Organisation for Economic Development and Co-operation – www.oecd.org/). Some of the key government publications include the following:

- *Monthly Digest of Statistics* – summary information on many economic trends.

- *Regional Trends* – regional profiles, households, work, living standards, etc.

- *Labour Market Trends* – topical articles, hours worked, sickness, training, vacancies, disputes, earnings and unemployment.

- *Social Trends* – trends in labour markets and incomes, and spending by item and by region.

- *Family Spending* – details on who earns and spends what.

- *New Earnings Survey* – earnings listed by industry, area, occupation, etc.

- *National Food Survey* – expenditure on, and consumption of, food by income group and region.

- *Population Trends* – family statistics, including births, marriages, deaths, etc., in the regions.

- *Annual Abstract of Statistics* – population, social conditions, production, prices, employment.

- *Bank of England Quarterly Bulletin* – articles on financial trends.

- *General Household Survey* – social and socioeconomic issues.

- *Retail Prices Index* – changes in prices across the country.

- *Census of Production* – data about production by firms in all industries.

- *Eurostat Publications* – a variety of publications covering economic, industrial and demographic changes across Europe.

- *Indicators of Industrial Activity* – production, employment and prices across a variety of industries and compared worldwide.

- *Business Monitors* – statistics concerning output in different business sectors. The *Retailing Monitor* is of particular interest, covering (by region) what is being bought.

The media

Another useful source of information are the media. Whilst unlikely to yield detailed data, the media may present a series of stories about key market sectors or larger organisations. Media sources normally include the following:

- *Newspapers* – broadsheets such as *The Times* and *The Financial Times* are both authoritative sources. However, they do not take into account the value of local papers and local circumstances.

- *Magazines and trade journals* – the obvious ones are *The Economist* (www.economist.com/) and *The Grocer*.

- *TV and radio* – these include specialist news and current affairs programmes.

- *Teletext* – this provides a wide variety of current information covering many topics.

Check your understanding

Choose a product market or industry to research. Visit the reference section and the periodicals section of either your school or college library or your local public library. Identify which sources would help you with this research and produce a short report. Use the Internet to support your final analysis.

Directories

There are many business directories that provide general information about industries and markets. These include *Kompass Register* (www.Kompass.co.uk), *Who Owns Whom* and *Key British Enterprises*.

Trade associations

Trade associations publish information for their members concerning their particular fields, and there are associations for almost all trades.

The Internet

The Internet has rapidly become an invaluable research tool, providing a rich resource for information from a multitude of sources. As a resource it is predicted to continue to grow rapidly and to become much more central to the workings of organisations, not just in terms of 'Internet marketing' but also as a business resource. Try visiting MORI at www.mori.com/. Many organisations such as Boots (www.boots-plc.com/) or Nestlé (www.nestle.co.uk) have their own *intranet*. Unlike the Internet which is available to all, an intranet is a data-sharing facility within an organisation.

Market research companies

There are a number of commercial market research companies offering a range of services and selling data they acquire from a variety of sources. For example, Mintel (www.mintel.co.uk/) is a commercial research organisation which, in return for a fee, provides a monthly journal containing reports on consumer markets – for example, bread, alcoholic drinks and financial services. Information includes such areas as market size, main competitors, projected growth, the market share of main competitors, the advertising spend of main competitors and other trends. Mintel also produces in-depth reports on certain markets.

The types of reports produced by agencies include the following:

- *Retail Business Market Surveys.* These are published monthly and each carries details of certain industries. It is important for those involved in market research to be able to access those surveys relevant to their particular field. Each copy carries an index of the industries investigated. For example, there will be details on market size, market distribution, branding and prospects for the industry.

- *Key Note Reports.* These carry even more information, with specific information on each industry.

- *Retail Audits.* Some organisations, such as Retail Audits, collect data of retail sales through supermarkets and larger chains and then sell the information to organisations wishing to buy it. These figures enable producers to work out the market shares of their markets, the sales of different products and the effects of any recent strategy, such as a price change or a promotional campaign.

Case study: Applying to be a market researcher

Market researchers organise the collection of public and business opinion about products, services or organisations. They may also conduct market research interviews and test new questionnaires.

Tasks and duties

If you apply to be a market researcher, you may be asked to do the following:

- Discuss information with clients.
- Design surveys and questionnaires.
- Organise and manage surveys.
- Liaise with field workers and their supervisors.
- Supervise survey staff.
- Conduct interviews.
- Undertake comprehensive secondary research and generally develop an understanding of how such knowledge could be used to support decision-making processes.

Skills

Market researchers need good research skills and the ability to think logically, so that they can design good surveys and questionnaires. They need mathematical and statistical ability and computer skills to analyse and interpret their data. Organisational and time management skills are important in this work. Market researchers should also have good written and oral communication skills, and they should be good listeners. It is also important to have creative thinking ability so as to be able to find solutions to problems.

Knowledge

Market researchers should know about questionnaire design, survey methods and marketing techniques. They should also know how to interpret statistics. They should understand how humans behave and think, and they need to be aware of different sampling and interview methods. It is important for market researchers to have some knowledge and understanding of the businesses or industries they research. Market researchers need an understanding of marketing, business and research methods.

Personal qualities

Market researchers need to be able to work well under pressure and to be able to juggle many tasks at once while undertaking a project. Accuracy is important, and they should be culturally sensitive when designing questionnaires and managing survey projects. They should be team players, and honesty and the ability to manage tasks and take responsibility are important. Market researchers must also be able to keep information private and confidential.

Appearance

As market researchers spend a great deal of time dealing with people such as clients, respondents and other professionals outside the organisation, their appearance is important.

1 Using this case study, draft a person specification for a market research post.

2 Look at the above requirements for market researchers. Think about how you might or might not fit the bill for such a post. Draft a letter of application for the post of a market researcher at an organisation you have some knowledge of or interest in.

Marketing databases

Having generated information through market research techniques, it is important that the data is managed correctly. For example, in the area of sales, information may be collected about past and current customers, together with future prospects. Building accurate and up-to-date profiles of existing customers enables an organisation to stay close to them. Keeping an electronic database of customers and prospects, and of all the communications and commercial contacts made, also helps to improve future contacts.

A database is a large number of files or a large file structured in such a way that the data can be processed by different users in a large number of different ways. A database is a computer file, and the collection of programs written to process data on the file in many different ways is referred to as a database management system.

These systems provide managers with support for their decision-making. For example, they:

- Enable data to be entered easily.
- Enable records to be sorted into any sequence.

- Control user passwords.
- Accept user-written programs for enhancing the system.
- Validate the data.

Databases may be used to meet a variety of objectives. For example, this may include:

- Focusing upon prime prospects.
- Evaluating new products and business opportunities.
- Cross-selling related products.
- Launching new products to potential customers.
- Identifying new distribution channels.
- Making comparisons with the products of competitors.
- Building and fostering customer loyalty.
- Converting occasional users to regular users.
- Generating enquiries and sales.
- Providing a basis for predicting demand for forthcoming periods.

The list is endless. Databases may help managers to make the following decisions:

Product decisions

Databases may help managers to:

- Analyse the market for existing products.

- Forecast demand for new and existing products.

- Identify market shares.

- Compare the features of competing products (types, brands, packaging).

- Analyse consumer preferences.

- Test product concepts and features.

Pricing decisions

They may also help to:

- Analyse the elasticity of demand to show the effect of changes in price on demand.

- Analyse the views of consumers about price levels.

- Identify customer perceptions of price.

- Evaluate the role of price in relation to other ingredients in the mix.

- Compare competing prices.

- Identify opportunities for the use of price as a strategic tool.

Distribution decisions

Market research databases may:

- Provide information that helps with the evaluation of different distribution alternatives.

- Emphasise the importance of different aspects of the distribution mix.

- Enable the organisation to cut distribution costs, such as inventory and transport.

- Identify a more efficient way of reaching customers.

- Compare channels used by competitors.

- Provide information about technologies that could improve the efficiency of distribution.

Promotional decisions

Market research databases may:

- Analyse the effectiveness of advertising.

- Provide feedback on the effectiveness of sales techniques.

- Help with the development of a promotional policy.

- Analyse customer responses to promotional techniques.

- Provide data that helps with the targeting of groups of customers.

- Help to identify the most appropriate and efficient forms of the media to use.

With so much information available from market research sources, it is important to keep the database up to date. For example, whenever new mailing lists are purchased, they should be purged to prevent duplicated names and addresses from being kept on file.

Discussion point	In these days of freedom of information, why should access to such databases be limited to certain users?

Most databases have access controls aimed at preventing unauthorised entry. The mechanisms may prevent access totally or allow individuals to access only the portion of the database relevant to their work role. It is common for users to be given log-in codes or user identifications such as passwords.

Desktop mapping

Computer programs are now available from market research and data-handling companies that are aimed at helping firms to understand and analyse their markets. Desktop mapping enables individuals to view and analyse data geographically, superimposed in layers on digital maps. Example of such services are MapInfo (www.mapinfo.com/) and Illumine Programs (www.datasets.com/datasets/pages/reports. htm), both of which can display and create maps, zoom in or out to any scale, find addresses, postcodes and sales areas, display and analyse customer records, shade or colour boundaries or points to highlight differences, undertake census demographic analysis and display details of competitors.

For example, a desktop mapping program may help with:

- the siting of new premises
- geographical areas to target
- analysis of sales
- competitor analysis
- evaluation of sales territories
- mailing list response analysis
- store layout
- customer analysis
- demographic analysis
- customer profiling
- market penetration
- customer targeting
- arranging deliveries or collections
- creating sales territories.

Check your understanding

Identify a product market you feel has potential for growth.

Explain briefly what sort of information would help you to analyse the changes taking place within that market. Present this in the form of a short report.

Using market research information to make decisions

The real benefit of market research information is determined by how much it improves the marketer's ability to make decisions. Good-quality information will enable decisions to be made that satisfy the needs of the target market and also help the organisation to achieve its goals.

The use of market research represents a change from problem-solving by intuition to decision-making based on scientific gathering and the analysis of information. The great advantage is that market research provides information systematically upon which managers may base product decisions.

Market analysis may, therefore, be used to identify the following.

Changes in the markets for different products and businesses

The size and potential of any market must be constantly monitored for change. Analysis of sales trends as well as the size and potential of any market must be considered important. If the total size of the market is known, an organisation can work out what percentage of the market it has (market share) and then develop a strategy that helps it increase its proportion of the market.

Market analysis may also be used to predict changes in the potential of the market, both in the short and the long term. Few markets are static and, as changes take place, it is important to understand about potential buyers as well as existing buyers. See Figure 11.18.

For example, there are three digital platforms (ways in which digital TV is made available for consumers) of digital television. These are Terrestrial (DTT) with OnDigital, Digital Satellite Television currently served by BSkyB, and Digital Cable Television. Digital television currently has 9% penetration of UK homes. For the marketers of digital television, it is important to know about the numbers of households who do not have digital set-top boxes as well as those who have them. They need to think about how long it will take to reach buyers who do not have digital services. (Find out more about current developments in television from the Independent Television Commission on www.itc.org.uk).

In high-growth markets, it is usually easier

Figure 11.18 Market growth

to meet growth objectives, and these markets are often considered to be more profitable. Low-growth markets, by their very nature, are more static and may even be declining. As the market size approaches market potential, growth slows and competition usually intensifies.

Profit opportunities

As products go through their product life-cycle (see page 327) the profitability of different products changes. Marketing analysis helps to direct an organisation towards those activities where profitability and other business objectives can best be satisfied.

The need to make changes to the product mix

The product mix comprises all the products an organisation provides for its customers. Research will help managers to understand the sort of decisions they have to make about the product mix (see Figure 11.19). For example, it might help them with the following:

- Identifying opportunities for growth and development for new and existing products.

- Showing how new products could replace existing products. This is known as *product substitution.*

- Showing how some products are in decline – by modifying a product it may be possible to slow down its decline and sustain its profitability.

- Highlighting that, because a product is no longer satisfying a number of customers, it ought to be deleted.

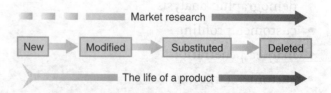

Figure 11.19 Using research during a product's life in order to make key decisions

Changes in consumer behaviour

The process of buying a good or service is not as simple as it might appear. A customer does not usually make a purchase without thinking carefully about his or her requirements. Wherever there is choice, decisions are made and these are influenced by complex motives.

Market research will help an organisation to understand why customers make particular decisions, especially through the analysis of buying patterns – who buys, what they buy, how they develop preferences and how they buy. Analysing these changes will help an organisation cater more closely to customers' needs.

Changes in the activities of competitors

An organisation must at all times be aware of its competitors and the nature of what they are doing. Competition exists when two or more organisations act independently to sell their products to the same group of consumers. In some markets there may be a great deal of competition, signified by an abundance of products and services so that consumers have a massive choice. These markets are characterised by promotional activities and price competition.

In other markets competition is limited, and consumers are able to choose from only a limited range of products and services. In these circumstances consumers may feel that prices are too high – they are not getting value for money.

Direct competition exists where organisations produce similar products that appeal to the same group of consumers. The *Daily Star* competes directly with the *Sun*;

and if you want to have a wall built, all the builders in your area looking for this type of work are in direct competition.

Even an organisation with no direct competition may face indirect competition as potential customers may consider different ways of meeting the same need. Instead of buying a motor car, they might buy a moped; instead of buying a box of chocolates on Mother's Day, they could buy a bunch of flowers . . . or send their mothers a lottery ticket! (www.nlcb.org.uk).

Changes in the effectiveness of other marketing mix ingredients

Market research will also provide valuable information about the use of other marketing mix ingredients. For example, what are customers' perceptions of price? How effective is the advertising? Do distribution systems cater for customer requirements? What would be the effect on demand of changes in pricing policies?

Check your understanding

Look at the market for one particular type of product. For example, it could be cars, electricity, confectionery or even beer. Comment upon how organisations within this market behave.

What sorts of decisions have some of them recently made? What type of information would they have had available before they made these decisions?

Validity and reliability of data

Planning and data collection processes help to ensure data is reliable. In *primary research* it is important to think about what you are trying to achieve from the survey. If you are unclear about what you are trying to achieve, the results will be equally unclear. It is also important with this type of research to beware of vague objectives. Choosing the correct sampling method and research technique is particularly important.

Although there may be a ready availability of *secondary research* data, it has to be remembered that the information has been collected by someone else and will not be specific to the needs of a particular organisation. It may also be dated.

Whatever technique is used for collecting data, it is important to ensure the research is both reliable and of value. A research technique is considered reliable if it produces almost identical results in successive or repeated trials. To have validity a research technique must measure what it is supposed to measure and not

something else! A valid market research method provides data that can be used to test what is being sought.

As market research takes place, it provides a wealth of data that has to be collected, processed and analysed. Data may be collected by the organisation's own market research staff from an agency. Alternatively, secondary data may be bought in the form of reports. Clearly, primary collection of data is likely to cost more than simply buying data. Data collection is not only expensive but also subject to error. The process, therefore, has to be carefully monitored and managed.

The final stage in the market research process is to interpret the findings and draw conclusions. These are then reported back to managers and other decision-makers. Many different statistical techniques may be used to support this process. Clearly, if managers are to make decisions based upon the data, they will want to know that the research process was carried out properly and that they can rely on the data before deciding what action to take.

Chapter 12 Methods of analysing marketing opportunities

As part of developing your marketing strategy, you need to be able to use market information to analyse the competitiveness of your product or service and to gain an understanding of the environment within which the business is operating. You will need to be familiar with the PEST and SWOT models for generating information on the business environment. It will be important to consider the following constraints on marketing activities:

- Industry-based constraints, such as the Advertising Standards Authority and the Code of Advertising Practice Committee.

- Ethical, environmental and social constraints, such as business stakeholders and pressure groups.

- Legal constraints, such as the Trades Description Act and the Monopolies and Mergers Act.

You need to understand how businesses will develop different marketing strategies depending on their circumstances. You need to be able to distinguish between the following strategies:

- marketing penetration

- new product development

- entering new markets

- diversification.

Using appropriate models such as the Ansoff matrix, you should be able to identify the circumstances in which the above strategies may be appropriate. You need to understand the importance of innovation, creativity and insight when identifying strategies for changing market position and for new product development. You need to understand how an analysis of product life-cycle might help to evaluate the current and potential position of a product or service. You also need to know how to use the Boston matrix to make judgements about the portfolio of products marketed by a business.

All businesses operate within an environment of change. Some of these may be relatively slow, for example, a steady change in the population, which is predictable. Other changes may be rapid and dramatic, such as the sudden development of new technological processes, the entry of new competitors into a market or simply the fickleness of consumer demand.

If a business wants to succeed, it needs to be able to anticipate and be ready for all types of change. Of course, it is the rapid shocks that are sometimes the most difficult to prepare for. The key is to build a flexible organisation that can adjust quickly to changes.

Check your understanding

Make a list of five rapid changes and five relatively slow changes that are taking place in the environment of a business with which you are familiar.

What can an organisation do to anticipate and respond to these changes?

Appreciation
(Marketing audit)

Reviewing the business environment in order to analyse problem areas, strengths, weaknesses, changes, competitors and opportunities

Plan
(Marketing plan)

Constructing a plan of action involving a number of strategies designed to improve performance

Implementation

Figure 12.1 Implementing the audit

In this world of change it is imperative that organisations think and plan ahead. In order to do this they need to understand the environment in which they operate and be able to make strategic decisions based upon their own capabilities. This is at the core of the process of marketing planning. According to Henry Assael, a marketing plan is 'a corporate "game plan" that will map out where the company should be going over the next five years and how to get there.'

Marketing is therefore used for assessing past performance (its traditional function), for analysing its business environment and for evaluating future courses of action.

Discussion point	How true is the statement that 'A business is only as good as its next product'?

Case study: Washing clothes

A good example of change within an industry is that of detergents. In the immediate period after the Second World War, only 3% of households had any form of washing machine, and these were not automatic. Today, over 80% have a washing machine, and automatic washing machines account for more than four out of five machines bought. Many people today also buy washer-dryers. Sales of low-suds powders and liquids necessary for automatic washing machines grew for several years at a rate of around 20% per year.

There have also been rapid changes in the social patterns that affect the clothes-washing task. Today's variations in family size, occupation, leisure pursuits and so on are considerable. Sophisticated research techniques are required to build up an accurate picture of washing habits.

Over the last 25 years the cotton content of fabrics has halved, and today artificial fibres account for over half of fabrics sold. Around 80% of articles washed are coloured. In response, washing products, such as tablets, liquids, mixed powders, conditioners and stain removers, have been developed that do not eventually bleach out colour and that wash as well or better at lower temperatures.

All these different consumer needs have to be met by products which, though highly sophisticated and chemically complex, are easy and quick to use and relatively inexpensive. Only 20p of every £100 of household expenditure goes on washing products.

1 In what ways have organisations that develop washing products had to change in recent years?

2 Describe some of the strategies they have developed for this process.

3 What would have happened to the business of an organisation that had failed to move as quickly as its competitors?

Good marketing involves looking:

- *outwards,* in order to respond to changes in markets, business conditions and competition

- *inwards,* in order to develop the organisation so that it can meet all those consumer needs that have been identified by the marketing process (Figure 12.2).

Figure 12.2   Ensuring a good fit between the external environment and an organisation's resources

A widely used model for strategic marketing is based upon the three elements of strategic analysis, strategic choice and strategic implementation. The auditing process is primarily concerned with the first stage, i.e. *strategic analysis* (see Figure 12.3).

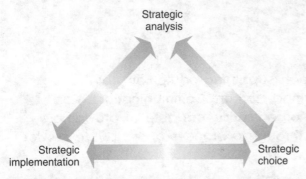

Figure 12.3   A three-phase model for marketing activity

Strategic analysis is concerned with understanding the strategic position of an organisation. For example, what sorts of environments are we operating in? What is the scope of our operations? How can we match our activities to our environment and our resource capability? Do we have marketing systems, policies and activities that will enable us to meet our objectives?

These questions are really about matching what an organisation intends to do with the reality of the marketing environment. The strategic reality for the organisation is shaped by the nature of the environment in which it operates. Strategic intentions are concerned with plans and proposals for the future. These intentions must be based upon a thorough knowledge of the environment if they are to be realistic.

If managers within an organisation are to be able to make good business decisions, they need both an understanding of the external business environment in which the organisation is operating as well as a detailed understanding of the organisation itself and its capabilities. A key part of marketing is examining the internal resources and capabilities of the organisation and then matching this to strategic intentions and plans.

Strategic choice involves:

- setting out a menu of strategic options

- comparing the options provided by the menu

- choosing the best option from the menu.

Strategic implementation involves putting the chosen marketing strategy into action.

Remember, this model should be viewed by an organisation as an ongoing process based on continuous analysis of the business environment through which information and data filter to help evaluate performance and influence business strategies.

Case study: Rapid change in an expanding marketplace

In recent years few industries have been faced with more challenges than the telecom industry. In fact, although the industry has been around for more than one hundred years, it has changed more in the past few years than at any other time in its history! Three key features of the modern business environment are technological change, competitive rivalry and global communications. The ability to make sense of these influences is particularly important for managers because, on the one hand, they signal opportunities, and on the other, they warn of threats.

Marconi Communications (www.marconicomms.com) is a GEC company developing telecoms equipment for industrial markets. Until 1984, BT was the primary telecoms operator within the UK. This period was characterised by lack of consumer choice and a one-price service. The privatisation of BT and deregulation of the telecoms sector increased competition at a time of rapidly developing broadband technologies.

As a result there has been a rapid growth in telecommunication services, such as call waiting, call identification, conference calls and voice mail. A larger development has been in the world of data rather than voice. The development of the Internet has, however, provided the most significant increase in demand for telecom services, particularly the development of email traffic. Other applications also evolving are video telephony, video on demand and home-working.

As business became dependent upon this changing technology, they wanted to ensure that the quality and integrity of such data would not be interrupted. Marconi set about developing technology that built upon its core competencies of:

- speed of response
- technological scale
- global reach
- highly skilled and well-motivated people.

Whereas in the past emphasis was simply upon supplying equipment for telecommunication companies, the newly formed Marconi Communications was concerned with becoming a market-sensitive organisation capable of providing business solutions for each of its customers through a process of worldwide service support. Its role is to:

- understand the challenges of its customers

- propose solutions that can help to meet those challenges

- deliver what is promised

- help customers to use its networks and create value.

Massive investment by Marconi was made in transmission technology so that today, in this rapidly expanding marketplace, Marconi is the world's leading supplier of broadband transmission equipment. Being a first-time mover in this industry has enabled Marconi to develop rapidly in fast-growing markets in the face of established and well-developed competitors.

1 What has happened to the telecoms industry in recent years?

2 How has Marconi responded to the challenges facing it?

Understanding the business environment

The process of 'knowing the other' is often referred to as 'scanning the environment'. A key part of this is understanding the nature of rivalry in the field and the threat of new entrants. The scanning process may highlight changes an organisation needs to take. For example, Sainsbury's acquired Texas to gain a major share of the DIY market. Similarly, Coca-Cola and McDonald's moved into Russia in order to take control of market shares ahead of the opposition.

Examining the business environment helps an organisation develop appropriate marketing strategies, including the marketing mix. Important external forces that influence marketing include the following:

- *The customer* – the buying behaviour of customers, including why they buy, their buying habits and the size of the market.

- *The industry* – the behaviour of organisations within the industry,

e.g. retailers and wholesalers, their motivations, and the structure and performance of organisations within the industry.

- *Competitors* – their position and behaviour.

- *The government and regulatory bodies* – their influence over marketing and competitive policies.

Selection of an appropriate marketing mix involves creating the best possible match between the external environment and the internal capabilities of the organisation. Though the elements of the marketing mix are largely controllable by marketing managers within an organisation, many of the changes and forces within the business environment are not.

The success of the marketing programme therefore, depends upon how well an organisation can match its marketing strategies and marketing mix to the external business environment in which that business is operating.

Developing an appropriate marketing strategy involves creating the best possible match between the external environment and the internal capabilities of the organisation.

PEST model

One useful way of analysing an organisation's external environment is by grouping external forces neatly into four areas using a PEST analysis. PEST stands for Political, Economic, Social and Technological influences, all of which are external (see Figure 12.4).

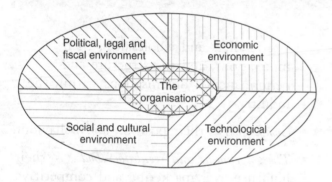

Figure 12.4 The wider business environment: PEST analysis

Carrying out a PEST analysis involves identifying the key factors external to an organisation that are in a state of flux and that are likely to have an influence on the organisation in the coming months and years.

Whereas identifying these factors is relatively easy, assessing their ongoing impact and effect is more difficult. An effective PEST analysis will be based on detailed research using all the latest journals and publications. For example, if certain taxes are likely to be lowered, how much are they likely to be lowered by? What will be the impact on the sales of each product?

Figures need to be as accurate as possible – if interest rates are expected to go up, how much will they go up? How long will they be raised for? What will be their impact upon sales and costs?

Political, legal and fiscal factors

Business decisions are influenced by political, fiscal (taxation) and legal decisions. For example, although in recent years many people have been encouraged to become self-employed, there has been a feeling among many of these people that they are over-regulated.

Influences might include:

- changes in the tax structure

- privatisation

- trade unions

- changes in the availability of raw materials

- duties and levies

- regulatory constraints, such as labelling, quality, safety.

Economic factors

Though the economic environment is influenced by domestic economic policies, it is also dependent upon world economic trends. Rates of economic growth, inflation, consumption patterns, income distribution and many other economic trends determine the nature of products and services required by consumers, as well as how difficult it becomes to supply them!

Influences might include:

- inflation

- unemployment

- energy prices
- price volatility.

Social/cultural factors

To understand the social and cultural environment involves a close analysis of society. Demographic changes, such as population growth, movements and age distribution, will be important, as will changes in cultural values and social trends, such as family size and social behaviour.

Factors might include:

- consumer lifestyles
- environmental issues
- demographic issues
- education
- immigration/emigration
- religion.

Technological factors

In marketing goods and services, organisations must become aware of new materials as well as developments in manufacturing and business processes. At the same time, organisations have to look at the nature of their products and, in particular, their cost-effectiveness, as well as their performance in relation to the competition.

Factors might include:

- new technological processes
- energy-saving techniques
- new materials and substitutes for existing materials.
- better equipment
- new product developments.

Forces external to the organisation are rarely stable and many of these forces can alter quickly and dramatically. It is important to recognise that, while some of these forces will be harmful to marketing efforts, others will create new opportunities.

Check your understanding

This activity is best undertaken when working in a small group. The starting point is to identify an organisation you are going to use as the centrepiece for a PEST analysis. It would be useful if you know someone who works for the organisation who will be able to provide you with some of the information you require. Meet the person to discuss each of the PEST forces influencing his or her business. This is the starting point for your analysis.

Use the Internet and a reference library to find out more to support the points made during the interview. Present your findings to your group and discuss the impact all these external forces have had upon the strategic decisions made by the organisation over recent years.

SWOT model

A particularly useful approach to examining the relationship between an organisation and its marketing environment is a SWOT analysis. A SWOT analysis sets out to focus upon the Strengths, Weaknesses, Opportunities and Threats facing a business or its products at a given moment. It includes both an *internal* and an *external* element. The internal element looks at current strengths and weaknesses of the organisation. The external element looks at the opportunities and threats present in the environment in which the organisation operates (see Figure 12.5).

Inside the organisation (internal)	Outside the organisation (external)
Strengths (positive)	*Opportunities* (positive)
Weaknesses (negative)	*Threats* (Negative)

Figure 12.5   SWOT analysis

Carrying out a SWOT analysis requires research into an organisation's current and future position. The analysis is used to match an organisation's strengths and weaknesses with the external market forces in the business environment.

As a result of carrying out a SWOT analysis, an organisation should go on to develop policies and practices that will enable it to build upon its strengths, minimise its weaknesses, seize its opportunities and take measures that will cancel out or minimise threats. The SWOT is thus sometimes called 'the planning balance sheet' (see Figure 12.6).

Inside the organisation	The external environment
Strengths +	Opportunities +
Weaknesses –	Threats –

Figure 12.6   The planning balance sheet

A simplified SWOT analysis might show, for example, that a business organisation has the following:

(Strengths)
- good product
- good relationship with customers
- good management team.

(Weaknesses)
- operates on a small scale
- regular cash-flow problems
- deals in a limited market.

(Opportunities)
- new and rapidly growing markets
- changing tastes of consumers
- could diversify into a number of product lines.

(Threats)
- growing competition from rivals
- recession leading to poor demand in the economy
- development of foreign competitors.

Case study: Developing the portable DVD player

DVD is in the process of transforming the electronic entertainment industry. This case study involves undertaking a SWOT analysis to study changes in the marketing environment in which a business operates and then going on to develop marketing activities that will take an organisation forward.

In recent years we have heard about the 'convergence' of technologies. Today this is becoming a reality. Your role is as a marketer/product developer for an electronics

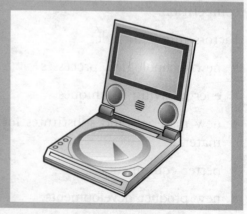

company that has the capability of bringing the latest technologies into the marketplace. As part of your role, you have been considering integrating various technologies into a portable communications and entertainment centre people can carry and use wherever they are. This is to include DVD technologies, email and telecommunication capability and computer compatibility.

Working in groups, discuss how you would like to use these technologies and the sort of product you could develop. You may wish to produce a product design. Undertake a SWOT analysis listing at least three strengths, three weaknesses, three opportunities and three threats for your product proposition. Use a SWOT analysis sheet to do this (see Figure 12.7).

Product description

Strengths	Weaknesses
Opportunities	Threats

Figure 12.7 A SWOT analysis sheet

You have to consider whom you are selling to and must identify your target market. This is the group of people you think will be interested in your product and who may have the money to spend on it.

- Try to identify the target audience for your chosen product. You will probably target two or three groups to concentrate on. An example of a target group might be single women in the 18–24 age-group on high incomes. Clearly, you will be best placed to target an appropriate group if you do some original research of your own to find out which age-group primarily makes the buying decisions for these products.

- What type of media would be most suitable for reaching the target audience you have chosen?

To help you choose the most effective media for your promotions, consider the following guidelines. You will have detailed costs of these media outlets and you should make a sensible selection to suit your chosen product. This will be your media plan. (Use the 'Target customers' sheet and 'Media plan' sheet in Figure 12.8 when making your decisions.)

Considerations when choosing appropriate media:

- Television. In order to have a meaningful TV campaign, you need at least 10 on-peak and 20 off-peak spots in any one month. Some months are cheaper than others. Do you feel that spots during particular programmes are more desirable (e.g. Coronation Street, Emmerdale)?

TARGET CUSTOMERS
PRODUCT _____

STATUS	AGE	INCOME H – HIGH L – LOW	TARGET AUDIENCE	SUITABLE MEDIA
MALE (MARRIED) NO CHILDREN	18–24	H / L		
	25–45	H / L		
	OVER 45	H / L		
FEMALE (MARRIED) NO CHILDREN	18–24	H / L		
	25–45	H / L		
	OVER 45	H / L		
MALE (MARRIED) + CHILDREN	18–24	H / L		
	25–45	H / L		
	OVER 45	H / L		
FEMALE (MARRIED) + CHILDREN	18–24	H / L		
	25–45	H / L		
	OVER 45	H / L		
MALE SINGLE	18–24	H / L		
	25–45	H / L		
	OVER 45	H / L		
FEMALE SINGLE	18–24	H / L		
	25–45	H / L		
	OVER 45	H / L		

MEDIA PLAN
PRODUCT _____

MEDIA		£COST	JAN	FEB	MAR	APR	MAY	JUN	JUL	AUG	SEP	OCT	NOV	DEC	SUB-TOTAL COSTS	COMMENTS
TELEVISION (CENTRAL AREA)	30 SECOND TV COMMERCIAL OFF PEAK (OCT, NOV, DEC, MAR, APR, MAY)	1,200														
	30 SECOND TV COMMERCIAL ON PEAK	8,000														
	30 SECOND TV COMMERCIAL OFF PEAK (JAN, FEB, JUN, JUL, AUG, SEP)	800														
	30 SECOND TV COMMERCIAL ON PEAK	6,000														
LOCAL RADIO	30 SECOND SPOT	200														
NATIONAL PRESS	ONE INSERTION PER NEWSPAPER	10,000														
LOCAL PRESS	ONE INSERTION PER NEWSPAPER	1,000														
FREE TRADE PRESS	ONE INSERTION PER NEWSPAPER	400														
ELECTRICITY ACCOUNT INSERTS	ONE FOR EACH DOMESTIC CUSTOMER PER QUARTER	60,000														
DIRECT MAILING	1000 PACKAGES DELIVERED BY THE POST OFFICE (SELECTED AREAS)	900														
	1000 PACKAGES HAND-DELIVERED (SELECTED AREAS)	600														
TELEPHONE SALES	PER HUNDRED CALLS	20														
EXHIBITIONS	SMALL	500														
	MEDIUM	3,000														
	LARGE	8,000														
LEAFLETS	PER THOUSAND	500														
SHOP DISPLAYS	76 SHOPS	20,000														

Figure 12.8 Target sheet and media plan

- Local radio. For maximum effectiveness you need 50 spots per month. This medium is particularly effective with the 16–25 age-group and has high listening ratings during drive-time.

- Press. Which newspapers and magazines are the most suitable for your target customers?

- Electricity account inserts. Each quarter of the year, millions of electricity company customers receive an electricity bill. You have been offered the opportunity to include a mailshot/promotional literature with these bills. Electricity companies are keen to participate because they feel these high-tech products are complementary to their own business.

- Direct mailing. This is an excellent means of communicating with small customer groups (e.g. recent purchasers of cars, computers and phones) whose addresses can be readily obtained from existing sources. Direct mail can be hand delivered.

- Telephone sales. A member of staff can be employed to phone prospective customers directly.

- Shop display. Adverts could be placed in shops selling these goods.

- Exhibitions. The company may take part in local or national exhibitions, building its own stands that are staffed by trained advisers who can promote the products.

- Leaflets. These are a very useful promotional aid a potential customer can take home to help him or her decide whether to buy the product after visiting a shop or an exhibition.

1 As a group, produce an advertisement for a newspaper or magazine.

2 Now that you have a clear idea about who your customers are, you should prepare a media plan for the next 12 months. You can do this either on a copy of the media plan or set out your media plan on a spreadsheet. Here are your media guidelines:

- You have a budget of £750,000 to spend over 12 months.

- If the campaign is going to be a success you will need to use several different types of promotion. You would almost certainly use the power of television as part of your campaign.

- On your chart or spreadsheet, show during which months you would spend your money, as well as how much you would spend.

- Remember to put in your subtotals. Your total spending should not exceed £750,000.

3 To finish off this activity, prepare a presentation for the rest of your class. A creative advertisement, a poster, a video, a PowerPoint presentation or some other creative element should support this. The presentation should be divided up as follows:

- Two minutes to set up.

- Two minutes to explain your SWOT analysis and to discuss your media plan, explaining how you intend to communicate effectively with your targeted customers.

- Four minutes to present your creative execution in any way, shape or form, using your chosen media.

- Two minutes to pack away.

During your four-minute presentation you should explain how you expect to maximise the product's strengths and overcome the weaknesses you identified in your SWOT analysis

Gap analysis

Another tool for analysing what is happening in the business environment is gap analysis. Gap analysis helps by comparing recent variations between forecast and achieved figures. The gap is the difference between a product's or market's actual performance and its predicted performance (see Figure 12.9). By analysing the gap, managers can seek reasons for the variation and, where required, take corrective action.

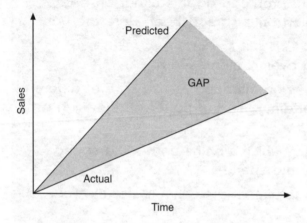

Figure 12.9   Gap analysis

Where there is an unfavourable gap (i.e. performance is not what it was expected to be), gap analysis helps to diagnose the problem and offer solutions, which might include the following:

- Analysing the marketing mix in order to improve sales – for example, by adjusting price or making product improvements.

- Attempting to increase market penetration. This involves making more sales in the present market without making any big changes to existing products.

- Entering new segments to extend the market.

- Implementing diversification strategies.

- Reducing costs.

Position audit

This incorporates features of the environmental review (such as markets) but includes a review of an organisation's *internal* advantages and disadvantages. Issues such as financial soundness, skill levels and operating efficiency can show how ready the organisation is to face the challenges of the marketplace.

Constraints upon marketing activities

In Chapter 10 we saw there are a number of constraints upon marketing activities that limit the sort of activities in which organisations engage. For example, internal constraints refer to the limiting factors that make it difficult for organisations to do everything they intend to do. External constraints are those within the business environment designed to limit and regulate business activities to ensure everything they engage in is acceptable and in the interests of all concerned.

There are a number of reasons for the need for constraints upon marketing activities. Before the 1960s, consumers had few rights and very little say in the bargaining process. They often had to rely upon their own common sense. The Latin expression *caveat emptor* – 'Let the buyer beware' – held true. Hence, *consumerism* came into being. Consumerism aims to break down this vast inequality in bargaining power and so provide consumers with more rights and enable them to obtain greater value for money.

The need for consumers to be better protected and therefore insured against the actions of the organisation they bought from arose because of such problems as the following:

- Poor-quality services or damaged goods.

- Goods or services that failed to match the descriptions applied to them.

- Manufacturer's or supplier's negligence affecting the safety of the product or service.

- Breach of contract.

- Misleading offers, information, advertising or labelling.

- Unfair terms in contracts.

- Monopoly control or lack of competition that limited the quantity and/or quality of a product and that resulted in artificially high prices.

Check your understanding

Based upon your own experiences, provide a range of examples of situations where you or a relative has purchased products and needed protection and support.

Greater equality, freedom of speech, improved educational standards, increased government regulation and vastly improved communications are all factors that have encouraged greater consumer power. Consumers today *expect* a product to be safe and to perform and function well. They also feel it is important to be protected against questionable products and practices. Producers are expected to behave in a socially responsible manner. The newspapers and the consumer organisations are there to bring wrong-doers to the public attention,

and the law courts are there to punish offenders when necessary.

Voluntary and statutory control (as well as the formation of active pressure groups that often gain popular support from the media) have helped to develop a changing climate for marketing activity. Organisations today can no longer disregard groups of consumers or wider issues in which they should be involved, and have to show increased sensitivity to their many publics.

Industry-based constraints

The *Advertising Standards Authority* (ASA) was set up in 1962. This is an independent body that exercises control over all advertising except that on radio and television. This control includes the following:

- *Press* – national and regional magazines and newspapers.

- *Outdoor advertising* – posters, transport and aerial announcements.

- *Direct marketing* – including direct mail, leaflets, brochures, catalogues, circulars, inserts and facsimiles.

- *Screen promotions* – including cinema commercials and advertisements in electronic media, such as computer games, video, CD-Rom and the Internet.

- *Sales promotions* – such as on-pack promotions, front-page promotions, reader offers, competitions and prize draws.

The authority draws up its own codes which it uses to ensure advertisements are 'legal, decent, honest and truthful'. Advertisements should be prepared with a sense of responsibility to both consumers and society, and conform to the principles of fair competition. The ASA has no statutory powers to force companies to comply with its rulings but replies on consensus, persuasion and an effective network of sanctions which stems from its own authorship of the codes.

The ASA identifies a number of advantages of self-regulation over a legislative process. The ASA process is accessible – with complainants needing only to write a letter to initiate action – and fast, with no complex legal procedures to undergo. This means the ASA can secure the withdrawal of misleading or offensive advertisements within a very short time. The process is free, with complaints investigated at no cost to complainants and incurring no legal fees.

It is argued that, in many instances, the ASA's codes go further than the law requires and, while the ASA does not enforce the law, it will refer complaints that fall directly under legislation to the appropriate law enforcement body. Should an advertiser refuse to remove an advertisement, the ASA could use a number of sanctions to enforce its decisions, such as:

- Adverse publicity generated by monthly reports of adjudications.
- Refusal of media space.
- Withdrawal of privileges, such as discounts and incentives resulting from membership of advertising bodies.
- Legal proceedings against persistent offenders.

Case study: Toyota (GB) Ltd

Complaints were made about a national press advertisement for the Lexus GS300 car headlined 'HEAR LOTS OF OPINIONS. LISTEN TO YOUR OWN'. The advertisement pictured the car apparently being driven on a deserted beach. The complainant objected that the car was shown in an illegal location and believed it would encourage drivers to act illegally.

The complaint was not upheld as the advertisers said the purpose of the advertisement was to show the car in an interesting and aspirational setting. They added that the photograph was not taken on a beach but on the plains of southern Spain. The ASA considered the complainant's interpretation of the advertisement was not likely to be widely shared. The advertisement was accepted.

1 Explain why advertisers should take account of the sensitivities of groups and individuals who view their adverts.

2 Why was the complainant unhappy with the Lexus advert?

3 Comment upon the decision made by the ASA.

Check your understanding

Over the period of a month, look at the various types of advertisements by surveying magazines and periodicals.

Make a list of advertisements (if any) you feel are not altogether 'legal, decent, honest and truthful'. Explain why in each instance.

Advertisers, agencies and the media whose representatives make up the *Code of Advertising Practice Committee* support the *British Code of Advertising Practice*. This code sets out rules which those in the advertising industry agree to follow. It also indicates to those outside advertising that there are regulations designed to ensure advertisements can be trusted.

The *Chartered Institute of Marketing* has its own code of practice to which members are required to adhere. The code refers to professional standards of behaviour in securing and developing business, and demands honesty and integrity of conduct.

Voluntary subscriptions and government grants finance the *British Standards Institution* (BSI). Its primary concern is with setting up standards that are acceptable to both manufacturers and consumers. Goods of a certain standard are allowed to bear the BSI Kitemark, showing consumers the product has passed the appropriate tests.

Professional and trade associations promote the interests of their members as well as the development of a particular product or service area. In order to protect consumers, their members will often set up funds to safeguard consumers' money. For example, the Association of British Travel Agents (ABTA) will refund money to holiday-makers should a member company fail.

Ethical, environmental and social constraints

Ethics are moral principles or rules of conduct generally accepted by most members of society. Most organisations today believe it is necessary to take up a stance that shows the public they operate in an ethical manner. Emphasis on the interests of the consumer is a key aspect of many organisations. Some ethics are reinforced through the legal system and thus provide a mandatory constraint upon business activities, while others are the result of social pressure to conform to a particular standard.

Potential areas of concern for organisations include product ethics, where issues such as genetically modified foodstuffs or contaminated food may seriously and quickly affect short-term demand. For example, complaints about the marketing of various baby milk products in developing countries resulted in widespread criticism and boycotts of powdered milk manufacturers.

Another area of concern relates to business practices, where restrictive practices and poor treatment of employees have been highlighted in the media, and businesses have faced criticism from the public. The trading policies of companies who buy cheap imports from overseas organisations involved in 'sweat-shop labour', or who trade with businesses employing young children in unacceptable conditions, have

Discussion point

'In the new millennium consumers simply want low prices and high-quality goods. Consumerism was simply a fad of the 1980s and 1990s!' Is consumerism dead or has the process just begun?

also faced critical scrutiny from both the media and the public.

In recent years environmental issues have been highlighted by accidents at chemical plants or at sea with oil tankers. Such accidents can not only damage wildlife and the environment but also the image of the organisation concerned.

With many companies' *environmental performance* becoming central to their competitiveness and survival, a range of new tools for environmental management have been developed. These include *environmental impact assessments,* which assess the likely impact of major projects, and environmental audits or *eco-audits*, which involve carrying out an audit of current activities to measure their environmental impact. Alternatively, by looking at the environmental impact of a product through its life-cycle, from the sourcing of raw materials to the final disposal of waste products, a *product-life-cycle analysis* can be established.

Organisations face many potential dangers with regard to ethics and public opinion, and no organisation is capable of satisfying all stakeholders but, by becoming good corporate citizens and being socially responsible, they can generate considerable goodwill. This strategy can be developed as a marketing advantage.

The idea of organisations working in and for the community is not new. Companies like Boots and Marks & Spencer have long advocated and contributed to community programmes, with involvement in areas as diverse as health care projects, education and training, arts and sport.

This movement towards responsible marketing is an acceptance by most organisations that they have a responsibility to serve their stakeholders. As we have

Case study: Eating GM convenience foods

Green pressure groups have dubbed genetically modified products 'Franken foods', arguing they are unsafe and that their development is ecologically unsound. During their early introduction into the UK, genetically modified foods faced little resistance. However, increasing knowledge about such foods has resulted in offensives being mounted by some consumer and green pressure groups against companies such as Unilever, who became one of the first manufacturers to put their weight behind genetically modified foods when they launched their Beanfeast brand.

With the European Union about to rule upon whether these products should be specially labelled, Unilever have accepted consumer concerns. Their food labels inform customers about the presence of genetically modified foods. They have also undertaken a campaign to tell customers more about genetic modification.

1 What are the arguments for informing consumers about specific details of the products they are consuming?

2 Is it possible to change negative perceptions of GM foods into positive ones?

3 Can you think of another instance where food labelling should be changed?

already seen in Chapter 10, stakeholders are individuals and groups who have a stake in the successful running of an organisation or who may be affected by its actions. Frequently, they will have shared expectations based on the well-being of the organisation. For example, the stakeholders in a large public company might include shareholders, managers, banks, unions, etc. (see Figure 12.10).

Figure 12.10 The stakeholders in a large public company

> ### Check your understanding
>
> Make a list of the stakeholders for your school or college. (Remember, this will include any individual or group affected by the actions of the school or college.)

While most stakeholders will share common expectations, there will be other areas over which disputes arise. Furthermore, expectations may change with time. Within an organisation, coalitions may develop between groups of stakeholders, such as managers and shareholders. Most people who work for an organisation will be members of more than one coalition.

For example, there might be a coalition between departments in an organisation, between individuals at the same level in the management structure, etc. In an organisation that operates in international markets, these coalitions of stakeholders may be complex.

Discussion point	If an organisation wanted to downsize, which groups of stakeholders would be most likely to: **a** support the proposition; and **b** protest against it?

There is no doubt that, in a world of increasingly articulate consumers, we shall see more *social marketing*, linking the actions of organisations to the interests of consumers in social, ethical and environmental issues. If consumers are unhappy with the actions of certain organisations, they can either set up or join pressure groups.

Protection pressure groups may be set up to fight a specific issue, such as the closure of a plant or the increased traffic on a road as a result of a local business. *Promotional pressure groups* are usually more formal and would be set up to fight highly organised campaigns across a range of issues. They would have clearly defined long-term objectives related to a particular concern. *Political pressure* might come from political parties unhappy with the actions of an organisation. Support for politicians and their actions would come from the electorate.

There are also a number of independent consumer groups. For example *The Consumers' Association* examines goods and services offered to the public and publishes the results of its research in *Which?* This magazine was founded in 1957 and has developed a circulation of more than half a million. It has become an invaluable source of information for consumers.

The National Federation of Consumer Groups is a co-ordinating body for voluntary and local consumer groups. Local groups survey local goods and services, publish reports and campaign for changes.

There is no doubt that, when consumers' rights and obligations are abused or when dangerous goods are brought into the marketplace, feelings run high. The media – newspapers, television and radio – increasingly become involved in campaigns.

Check your understanding

Set up your own consumer group to monitor the standards of products and services you regularly use. For example, you might set up a consumer group that monitors whether the cost of visiting your local football Premiership side is worth the money. You might set one up to look at the social facilities for young people in your district or perhaps a group that provides feedback to your course leader on the quality of your AVCE course.

Legal constraints

In the UK, the regulation of television is undertaken by the *Independent Television Commission* (ITC). The ITC licenses and regulates commercial television and undertakes to protect viewers' interests by setting and maintaining standards for programmes and advertising. The powers of the ITC are derived from the Broadcasting Acts of 1990 and 1996. The ITC issues licences that allow commercial television companies to broadcast in and from the UK. It then regulates these services by monitoring broadcasters' performance against the requirements of published codes and guidelines on programming content, advertising, sponsorship and technical performance, and has the power to issue a range of penalties for failure to comply.

Discussion point	It is unfair to restrict the advertising of specific products, such as cigarettes, on television. Discuss.

The *ITC Code of Advertising Standards and Practice* has four general principles to which advertisers are expected to adhere. These are that:

- Television advertising should be legal, decent, honest and truthful.

- Advertisements should comply in every respect with the law, common or statute, and licensees must make it a condition of acceptance that advertisements do so.

- The detailed rules set out are intended to be applied in the spirit as well as the letter.

- The standards in this code apply to any item of publicity inserted in breaks in or between programmes, whether in return for payment or not.

Check your understanding

Monitor advertisements you watch on television over a two-day period. Do these advertisements meet the guidelines of the ITC code of practice?

The purpose of *The Sale of Goods Act* is to ensure that sellers provide goods that are of 'merchantable quality' – that is, they must not be damaged or broken. Goods sold must be fit for the purpose intended. If you bought a pair of shoes and they fell apart at the seams within a week, they would not have been fit for the purposes for which they were sold – serving as footwear. Under this law you can ask for replacements if goods do not meet the requirements you specified to the seller.

The Trade Descriptions Act attempts to ensure that the description given of the goods forms part of the contract the buyer makes with the seller. This Act makes it a criminal offence for a trader to describe goods falsely. One type of case frequently prosecuted under this Act is the turning back of odometers on used cars to make them appear as if they have covered fewer miles than they really have. The main objective of the Trade Descriptions Act is quite straightforward – descriptions of goods and services must be really accurate. Articles described as 'waterproof' or 'shrinkproof' must be exactly that.

The Weights and Measures Act ensures that consumers receive the actual quantity of a product they believe they are buying. For example, prepaid items must have a declaration of the quantity contained within the pack. It is an offence to give 'short measure'.

The Food and Drugs Act is concerned with the contents of foodstuffs and medicines. The government needs to control this area of trading so that the public is not led into buying harmful substances. Some items have to carry warnings – packets of dried kidney beans, for example, must carry clear instructions that they need to be boiled for a certain length of time before they can be eaten. The contents of medicines are strictly controlled by this Act. Certain substances such as mercury are not allowed at all!

There are numerous sources of help and advice for consumers, providing opportunities for people to follow up complaints and grievances. For the consumer it is important to consider carefully the circumstances of each grievance before deciding on the most appropriate way forward.

The government protects consumers through a number of official bodies. The *Office of Fair Trading* (OFT – www.oft.gov.uk/), a government body, was set up to look after the interests of consumers and traders. It publishes a wide variety of information and encourages businesses to issue codes of practice to raise the standards of their service. Traders who persist in breaking the law must provide an assurance they will 'mend their ways'. The OFT also keeps an eye on anti-competitive practices, monopolies and mergers and might suggest changes in the law.

The *Competition Act 1998* replaced the Monopolies and Mergers Commission (MMC) on 1 April 1999 with the *Competition Commission* (www.mmc.gov.uk/quest1.htm). The Competition Commission has two functions. It has taken on the role of the former MMC, investigating and reporting on matters referred to it by the Director General of Fair Trading, such as monopolies, mergers and regulatory disputes. It now also hears appeals against decisions make under the new Competition Act.

Local authorities and *trading standards departments* investigate a range of issues such as misleading offers or prices, inaccurate weights and measures, and consumer credit.

Environmental health departments enforce legislation covering health aspects of food – for example, unfit food or unhygienic storage, and the preparation and serving of food.

Developing marketing strategies

In developing marketing strategies a range of options will always be available to decision-takers. This is why the process of marketing audit, environmental analysis, SWOT analysis, setting objectives and understanding all the constraints upon marketing activities is so important.

The most appropriate strategy for an organisation will depend upon the nature of the organisation, the type of market in which it competes and the actions of its competitors, and upon what sorts of risks an organisation is willing to undertake. This will depend on an analysis of the opportunities within the marketplace, as well as the uncertainty in the environment in which the organisation is operating.

Remember that the simplest and most important principle of marketing is that *marketing and its related activities should be designed to serve the customers.* Serving customers' needs with goods and services that do so more precisely than those of competitors in a market-orientated society has today become more important than ever. Whereas in the past, in many markets, all customers were treated to a similar diet of goods and services, organisations now recognise that groups of consumers have different needs, wants and tastes.

Customers have different needs, wants, likes and dislikes. Not every person likes the same make of motor car or has the same taste in clothes. Equally, if cost and production time were of no importance, manufacturers would make products to the exact specifications of each buyer. On the other hand, neither can they serve all customers successfully if they group all their customers' needs and wants together.

Instead of trying to serve all customers equally, an organisation may focus its efforts on different parts of the total marketplace. Within the total marketplace it is possible to group customers with similar characteristics and divide the market into parts. This is known as *market segmentation*. Market segments are groups of customers with similar needs and characteristics. The task is to produce and supply different products to suit these segments.

> Market segmentation is therefore a process of separating a total market into parts so that different strategies can be used for different sets of customers.

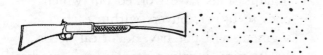

Figure 12.11 Marketing by blunderbuss

If you attempt to market a single product to the whole population, this is sometimes said to be like using a blunderbuss, firing shots to pepper the whole marketplace (see Figure 12.11). This is sometimes called *undifferentiated* or *mass marketing*. A single marketing mix is offered to the whole marketplace. In other words, all potential customers are treated as if they have similar characteristics. This may be a relatively cheap way of tackling marketing, but its weakness is that it ignores individual differences (see Figure 12.12).

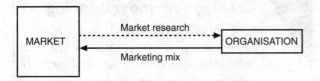

Figure 12.12 Undifferentiated marketing

Discussion point	Does any market today exist where segmentation does not take place?

When it is not possible to satisfy all its customers' needs with a uniform product, an organisation will use market segmentation to divide consumers into smaller segments consisting of buyers with similar needs or characteristics so that marketing becomes like firing a rifle instead of a blunderbuss. A rifle with an accurate sight will hit the target more efficiently without wasting ammunition (see Figure 12.13).

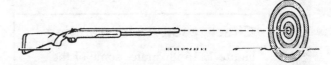

Figure 12.13 Marketing by rifle – hitting the target segment

Market segmentation using *differentiated marketing strategies* tailors separate products and market strategies to different sectors of the market. For example, the market for cars has many segments, such as economy, off-road, MPV, luxury, high performance, etc. This approach recognises that, in order to be successful and hit consumer needs, it is necessary to recognise the needs of different groups of consumers and meet them in different ways (see Figure 12.14).

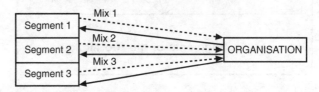

Figure 12.14 Differentiated marketing

In fact, some organisations simply exist to serve highly specialised market segments. They deliberately choose to compete in one segment and develop the most effective mix for that market. This is known as *concentrated marketing*. For example, Morgan serves the specific and highly esoteric needs of customers who like a car from the past. Jaguar cars are associated with luxury market segments. Similarly, quality fashion retailers today increasingly use brand names to position themselves in particular parts of a market. This is sometimes called *niche marketing*. A disadvantage is that, if sales of a product decline in that segment, the lack of diversification means this may affect the performance of the organisation.

Check your understanding

Figure 12.15 illustrates some of the main segments of the tea market, showing examples of teas sold in each segment.

Choose two of the segments and explain how you might use a slightly different marketing mix to appeal to consumers in these segments.

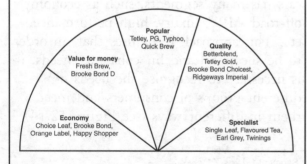

Figure 12.15   Segments of the tea market

There are three elements to segmentation:

1 *Market segments.* Market segments are groups of customers with similar needs and characteristics. The task is to produce and supply different products to suit these segments.

2 *Targeting.* Once segments have been identified, organisations have to identify one or more segments that have a need that can best be met by the organisation. This is known as targeting and may involve mass, undifferentiated marketing or concentrated marketing.

3 *Positioning.* Even though parts of the market are divided into segments, and organisations have worked out which ones to target, buyers within each segment will not have identical needs. Positioning involves developing a market strategy through the marketing mix that takes into account the thoughts and perceptions of customers about a product relative to other products and brands. The position is how the product is perceived in the minds of customers.

Repositioning involves moving the product away from its current position in the market to another part of the market, where it might compete more effectively. Perhaps the most famous repositioning strategy in recent years is Skoda, who have moved away from a low-cost, low-reliability position in the market to become a well-respected, high-value brand.

Check your understanding

Look at two similar products. Comment upon the similarities and differences of their marketing mixes. To what extent are these due to positioning strategy?

Case study: Is the replica football shirt dead?

The last few years have seen the sales of replica shirts plunge as football fans shun them for designer labels. It is as if the shell-suit fashion disaster has occurred all over again! Instead of the turnstiles being invaded by footballer wannabes, fans now opt for Tommy Hilfiger, Store Island or Ralph Lauren shirts.

Replica shirts are simply not cool any more. Fans have moved towards more aspirational and individualistic brands. This movement away from replica wear has also been associated with constant changes to kits by clubs, the high prices of replica kits and also the poor performance of the England team. Within a short period of time, sales have plummeted by more than 30%. Even Sporty Spice does not wear her Liverpool shirt in public and Oasis have dumped their Manchester City tops.

The only area bucking this trend is the replica kit capital of the world . . . Newcastle, where almost every family of supporters seems to have replicas to suit every occasion!

1 Why has the market for replica shirts changed so dramatically within such a short period of time?

2 How might football clubs have avoided this change in tastes?

3 If you were given the responsibility of launching new products to football fans that related to their changing aspirational needs, what would you do to make them cool?

Marketing penetration

A key objective that many organisations have is to improve their levels of market penetration. This involves making more sales to customers, without changing products in any way. For example, one organisation that has successfully increased the sales of its newspapers and improved its marketing penetration is *The Times*. From a daily circulation low of 385,000 papers in 1992, the paper today has a circulation of over 800,000 daily copies. Improving its level of market penetration sparked off a circulation war amongst the broadsheets which, at one stage, saw a revamped *Times*, sold at 10p, with a variety of offers for its readers.

Better marketing penetration thus helps organisations to improve their market share. In large markets, even a small increase in market share can create significant sales, and studies have shown there is a link between market share and profitability.

Case study: The PIMS study

A study in the USA called 'Profit Impact of Marketing Strategies' (PIMS) attempted to analyse the marketing factors that had the biggest influence on profits. The study identified a close relationship between market share/penetration and profitability (see Figure 12.16).

The PIMS research showed clearly that organisations with a large market share were more likely to be profitable. It also showed that a high market share and increased performance were the results of moving along a 'learning curve', so that the more an organisation learnt about its position through market research, the better it would perform.

Market Share (%)	Profitability (%)
Under 7	9.6
7–14	12.0
14–22	13.5
22–36	17.9
Over 36	30.2

Figure 12.16   The PIMS study

One reason cited for why firms with larger market shares are more profitable is that, with high market share and larger levels of output, they benefit from larger production runs and, when unit costs are reduced, they benefit from increased margins. The PIMS study helped to show that the best competitive strategy for an organisation is to develop a policy designed to increase its market share.

1 Explain why market share is an important marketing objective for many organisations.

2 Why might improving market share be easier in rapidly changing rather than static markets?

3 Provide two examples of organisations that seem to have improved their market share in recent years.

Discussion point	In what circumstances, if any, might small organisations with a small market share be more profitable than large organisations with a large market share?

New product development

A new product may be one that:

* replaces an old product

* opens up a new market

* broadens an existing market.

It may involve an innovation, a technological breakthrough or simply be a line extension based upon a modification. It is often said that only about 10% of new products are really new. In fact, it is often possible to turn old products into new products simply by finding a new market for them.

There are six distinct stages in the development process for new products. These are:

* *Step 1* Ideas.

* *Step 2* Screening of ideas.

* *Step 3* Marketing analysis.

- *Step 4* Product development.
- *Step 5* Testing.
- *Step 6* Launch and commercialisation.

As new products go through each of these stages there is a mortality rate (see Figure 12.17).

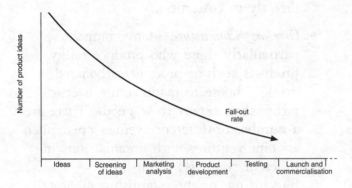

Figure 12.17 Mortality (fall-out) during the new product development process

Step 1 Ideas

All new products start from ideas. These ideas may be completely new or simply be an update of an existing product. Ideas may come from the following sources:

- *Research and development* – product development and market research working together. Technological breakthroughs and innovations from research are very important.

- *Mindstorming* – involving a few people developing ideas from words and concepts.

- *Suggestions box* – working close to customers, the sales force understands their needs and requirements.

- *Forced relationships* – sometimes one or more products can be joined together to form new product concepts. For example, shampoo and conditioner.

- *Competitors* – monitoring the actions of competitors may provide a rich source of new ideas.

Step 2 Screening of ideas

Once ideas have been generated it is important to screen for the ideas likely to be successful and reject the rest. Considerations may include how well the product fits in with others in the product range, the unique elements of any idea that make it competitive, the likely demand for the product and whether or not it could be manufactured economically.

Step 3 Marketing analysis

Once the ideas have been screened, further marketing analysis begins. This involves a thorough analysis of the product's market potential. This type of research helps to identify the market volume (units that could be sold) as well as the value of sales expected. It may also help to identify market potential.

Step 4 Product development

Having come through the test of marketing analysis, it is now time to translate the idea or product concept into a product. Design, innovation and the uses of technology are very important in product development. An assessment of packaging and branding may also be involved.

Step 5 Testing

Testing is a vital stage in the product development process. It may involve identifying valuable information through further market research, which helps to fine-tune the venture. Test marketing may comprise testing one part of a consumer market or trialling the product to ensure it meets the required standards.

Step 6 Launch and commercialisation

The launch is the most important day in the life of a product – it is finally revealed to customers. It may involve rolling from one TV region to another TV region. Today, a common technique is to provide sneak glimpses of new products before they are launched.

Entering new markets

One strategy for either existing or new products is to enter new markets. For example, existing products could be offered to different markets. This may involve an analysis of demographics to see if children, senior consumers, women or specialist groups might be interested in buying the products by targeting a form of distribution that would make the products available to them. The development of the service station shop clearly opened up new market opportunities for many different products, allowing them to enter newly formed markets.

Another alternative would be to consider marketing products more widely through international markets. International marketing involves the marketing of products in two or more countries. There are a number of ways of entering such markets. These might include the following:

- *Indirect exporting.* This may initially be through an *export house* whose main activity is the handling or the financing of international trade. They have links all over the world and will have a key role in providing valuable experience for exporters.

- *Direct exporting.* This involves manufacturers or suppliers shipping their products overseas and selling their wares directly to customers.

- *Overseas manufacture.* Many companies, particularly those who produce bulky products such as beers or carbonated drinks, choose to manufacture overseas rather than export their goods. There are a number of different avenues open, such as joint ventures with organisations in different countries, licensing or franchising, or the establishment of a wholly owned production facility in a different country.

Diversification

This is a strategy for growth that involves developing products or business areas that are outside the organisation's markets. For example, a jeans manufacturer might decide to develop its labels and brand strengths further by going into health foods. Some companies deliberately operate a policy of diversification by always trying to identify the most attractive and rapidly developing industries in which to engage. They feel the best business strategy to guarantee success is to enter attractive and emerging industries, rather than stay in static and slow-developing ones.

Case study: X1 Button radio

From the master of innovation, Sir Clive Sinclair, comes the world's smallest FM radio. It offers the full performance of a VHF radio, yet with its ingenious design it fits discreetly inside your ear!

The Sinclair X1 Button radio fits snugly inside the ear using state-of-the-art circuitry that gives it a specification of top radios many times its size. It is the result of years of research using Sinclair technology. Available only from Sinclair research, the radio is unique and will be available for less than £10.

The X1 is totally hands-free and has virtually no weight. It is possible to run, dance or pedal a bike without fear of the X1 getting in the way. Its sure-grip ear design keeps it snugly in the ear at all times. Users never again have to miss their favourite sports programme. It can be used in the car, train, bus or while at work, without anybody else being aware the user is listening to the radio.

The radio is powered by a lithium cell that will, with normal use, last months. The X1 has push-button autoscans as found on expensive car radios. By pushing the button it simply tunes to the next radio station.

1 Comment briefly on the features and benefits of a radio that fits in the ear.

2 What markets might Sinclair research target for this product?

3 If they were to aim for a high level of market penetration for this radio, briefly suggest a strategy for undertaking a widespread launch for the X1.

Tools for analysing marketing strategies

Alongside any marketing strategy must be some kind of mechanism that enables managers to link their strategies with their marketing objectives. The three different models we discuss here help managers to evaluate the effectiveness of their strategies so that decisions can be made about individual products and services.

The product life-cycle

The life of a product is the period over which it appeals to customers. We can all think of goods that everyone wanted at one time but that have now gone out of fashion. Famous examples from the 1960s include hot-pants and kipper ties!

The sales performance of any product rises from nought (when the product is introduced to the market), reaches a peak

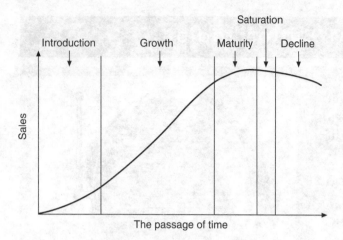

Figure 12.18 Stages in the product life-cycle

and then goes into decline (see Figure 12.18). Most products have a limited life-cycle. Initially the product may flourish and grow, the market will mature and, finally, the product will move towards decline and petrification. At each stage in the product life-cycle there is a close relationship between sales and profits so that, as organisations or brands go into decline, their profitability decreases.

The life-cycle can be broken down into distinct stages. In the *introductory* phase, growth is slow and volume is low because of a limited awareness of the product's existence. Sales then rise rapidly during the period of *growth*. It is during this phase that the profit per unit sold usually reaches a maximum. Towards the end of this phase, competitors enter the market to promote their own products, which reduces the rate of growth of sales of the initial product.

This period is known as *maturity*. Competitive jockeying – such as product differentiation in the form of new flavours, colours, sizes, etc. – will sift out the weaker brands. During *saturation*, some brands will drop out of the market. The product market may eventually *decline* and reach a stage when it becomes unprofitable.

The life-cycle may last for a few months or for hundreds of years. To prolong the life-cycle of a brand or a product, an organisation needs to readjust the ingredients of the marketing mix. Periodic injections of new ideas are needed – product improvements, line extensions or improved promotions. Figure 12.19 illustrates the process of injecting new life into a product.

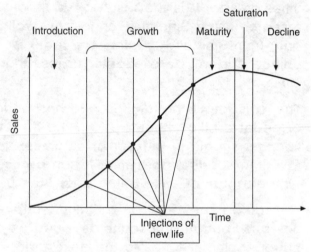

Figure 12.19 Injecting new life into a product

A readjustment of the marketing mix might include the following:

- Changing or modifying the product to keep up with or ahead of the competition.

- Altering distribution patterns to provide a more suitable place for the consumer to make purchases.

- Changing prices to reflect competitive activities.

- Considering carefully the style of promotion.

Most large organisations produce a range of products, each with its own unique life-cycle. By using life-cycles, marketers can plan when to introduce new lines as old products go into decline. The collection of products an organisation produces is known as its *product portfolio* (see Figure 12.20). In Figure 12.20 *T1* represents a point in time. At that point product 1 is in decline, product 2 is in maturity, product 3 is in growth and product 4 has recently been introduced.

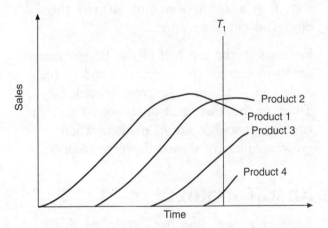

Figure 12.20 A product portfolio

Check your understanding

Look at the portfolio of products or services provided by one large organisation. It may be a car manufacturer who provide different models for different segments of the market. Alternatively, it could be a major retailer who uses different forms of retailing to reach different groups of consumers.

Look at where each of the products or services falls within the product life-cycle. Based upon your analysis. Explain what the organisation's strategies are likely to be in the near future.

The Boston matrix

Examining the life-cycle of a product helps us to appreciate that products go through various phases from infancy to decline. Markets and their structures are changing all the time. In recent years 'niche marketing' has been popular, particularly with the emergence of branding. Today, many organisations have spotted opportunities through the use of the Internet and other technologies to develop their markets.

Market share is important for business organisations. The Boston Consultancy Group have argued that the faster the growth of a particular market the greater the cost necessary to maintain position. In a rapidly growing market, considerable expenditure will be required on investment in product lines and to combat the threat posed by new firms and brands.

The Boston Group developed 'The Boston box' or matrix, which relates closely to product life-cycles. They identify four types of products in an organisation's portfolio (Figure 12.21). *Problem children* are products that have just been launched. This is an appropriate name because many products fail to move beyond this phase. Such products are often referred to as *question marks*. Is it possible to develop these products and turn them into the *stars* and *cash cows* of the future? It might be but,

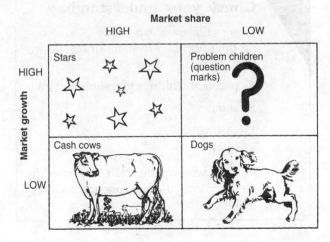

Figure 12.21 The Boston box or matrix

first, they will require a lot of financial support and this will represent a heavy commitment.

Stars are products that have successfully reached the growth stage in the life-cycle. Although these products will also require a great deal of financial support, they will also provide high cash returns. On balance they will provide a neutral cash flow and are good prospects for the future.

Cash cows have reached the maturity stage in their product life-cycle and are now 'yielders'. They have a high market share in markets that are no longer rapidly expanding. Because the market is relatively static, they require few fresh injections of capital; for example, advertising and promotion may be required to inject a little fresh life from time to time. However, the net effect is of a positive cash flow. Cash generated by the cash cows may be used to help the question marks.

Dogs are products in decline. These have a low market share in a low-growing or declining market. As they generate a negative cash flow, they will usually be disposed of.

To maintain an effective portfolio development, it is important to have a balance of products at any one time. An organisation will require a number of cash cows to provide its 'bread and butter'. At the same time, it is important to develop the cash cows of the future by investing in the problem children (question marks). Fortunately, the stars should pay their own way. It is also important to identify the dogs and cut them out.

Products in the top half of the Boston matrix are in the earlier stage of their product life-cycle and so are in high-growth markets. Those in the lower half of the box are in the later stages and so are in markets where growth will have slowed down or stopped.

Ansoff matrix

Another person who has developed this theory further, by outlining a product–market mix, is Igor Ansoff. Ansoff's matrix looks not just at the management of a product portfolio but also widely at market developments and opportunities. The matrix matches existing and new product strategies with existing and new markets (Figure 12.22)

Product / Market	Existing products		New products
Existing markets	Consolidation	Market penetration	Product development
New markets	Market development		Diversification

Figure 12.22 Ansoff's product–market matrix

The matrix suggests five alternative marketing strategies that hinge upon whether the product is new or existing and

Check your understanding

Using your own experience of a product portfolio from an organisation, identify its:

- problem children (question marks)
- stars
- cash cows
- dogs.

In each case explain what evidence you have for drawing the conclusions you make.

whether the market is new or existing. These strategies are as follows:

- *Consolidation* implies a positive and active defence of existing products in existing markets.

- *Market penetration* suggests a further penetration of existing markets with existing products. This will involve a strategy of increasing market share within existing segments and markets.

- *Product development* involves developing new products for existing markets.

- *Market development* entails using existing products and finding new markets for these. Better targeting, market research and further segmentation will identify these new markets.

- *Diversification* will lead to a move away from core activities. This might involve some form of integration of production into related activities.

Chapter 13   Developing strategies to meet customer needs: the marketing mix

Businesses need to combine a set of marketing strategies that fit together in a way that meets customer needs. You need to understand the following marketing strategies, the connections between the different strategies and the need for a coherent mix of strategies:

- Pricing and the techniques of pricing: penetration, skimming, cost plus, the difference between value and price, competitor based.

- Communicating with customers through promotions: branding, advertising, direct mail, public relations, sales promotions, product presentation, direct selling, the Internet.

  The most widely used part of the Internet is the World Wide Web. This has become in itself a mechanism for communication: in addition to being a marketplace offering products and services, it is also a device for displaying a range of published and promotional material for customers and browsers alike.

- Effective logistics and placement in the process of distributing the product to the consumer.

- The conditions required of the physical environment for selling to end-users and other businesses, for example, leisure and retail outlets.

- Effective customer service to support a customer who has bought or is thinking of buying a product or service.

- Well-trained and motivated staff in customer service.

- E-commerce as a means of selling the product/service.

Nearly every financial transaction turns into an electronic process at some stage. The Internet provides an online way for all types of organisations to promote or sell their products. This process has been widely termed 'e-commerce'. It is argued that businesses can gain in terms of control, flexibility and time saving when manual transactions become electronic. The great benefit of e-commerce is that businesses can enlarge their markets and undertake business transactions across the world 24 hours a day, 365 days a year. Not only does e-commerce allow products to be displayed on the Internet, but the use of credit-card transactions means that sales can be made instantly. Another aspect of e-commerce is EDI (Electronic Data Interchange) which enables organisations to exchange information across computer systems securely.

You need to be able to evaluate the marketing strategy for a product or service, applying the principles of marketing outlined in the first section of this unit (Chapter 10).

The marketing mix

The marketing mix provides us with a useful way of looking at the marketing of products. Organisations need to create a successful mix of:

- the right product (or service)
- sold in the right place
- at the right price
- using the most suitable form of promotion.

As you learnt in Chapter 10, this simple mix is often referred to as the four Ps of product, price, place and promotion. This rather straightforward way of looking at what has become an increasingly complex business environment has at times been felt to be a little simplistic and limiting in terms of the real mix and what should be the fullness of our understanding. In recent times, therefore, it has been expanded to include three more Ps to become a seven-P mix. The additional elements are as follows.

People

People are widely recognised as the greatest assets of modern organisations. The governing principle, whether recognised or not, is that everyone who works for an organisation is a customer, either inside (the internal customer) or outside (the 'traditional customer') the company. Both kinds of customer expect to be supplied with the product or service they need, on time and as specified.

This principle holds good for everyone in the company, whatever his or her level of skill and experience, whether his or her 'product' is answering a telephone or masterminding a major new project. It works to everyone's benefit. In doing so it provides the individual with genuine responsibility and scope for initiative, and it virtually guarantees the organisation's performance will be improved.

Provision of customer service

Customer service has become increasingly important in a rapidly changing marketplace. It has become more closely linked with the core product. Customer service is associated with developing bonds with customers in order to create long-term relationships that lead to advantages for all groups.

However, customer service is something that does not just happen. It is a process that involves pre-transaction, transaction and post-transaction considerations. Emphasis upon customer service will change from one product to another. For example, when manufacturing goods such as bread or shampoo, customer service may involve developing strong customer relationships with many of the large retailers. In a pure service industry, such as hairdressing or insurance, there are no tangible goods, and so customers will view nearly all the benefits they get on the basis of the service they receive.

Process management

This involves all the procedures, tasks, mechanisms and activities through which a product or service is delivered to a customer. It is clear that, in a modern organisation, processes are a key part of the marketing mix, involving developing priorities and ways of meeting customer needs. Processes might involve key decisions about customer involvement and employee discretion.

In today's rapidly changing business environment, in order to meet consumer needs more closely it is marketing that should determine the processes that link manufacturing with the customer.

The marketing mix is, therefore, a series of controllable variables an organisation can use in order best to meet customer needs and to ensure an organisation is successful in the markets it serves.

Within this chapter, instead of limiting ourselves to the four-P or seven-P model, we look at a host of mix elements designed to meet customer needs. As we look at each of these mix elements, it is important to relate them to the strategies identified in the previous chapter and also to think closely about the tools and mechanisms for monitoring the progress of such strategies.

Case study: Creating attention-grabbing web sites

Today there are a number of exciting new British-based companies which specialise in designing, hosting and promoting unique attention-grabbing web sites for small businesses. Their expertise is helping companies to market themselves to the world using the Internet.

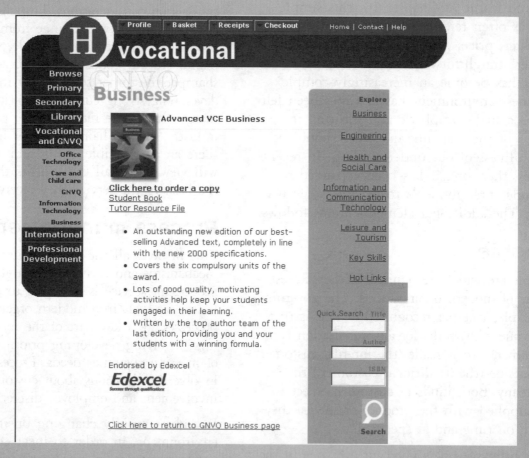

Web sites need to be designed with the user in mind. Well-designed sites load fast, use clean graphics and allow for easy navigation. The web sites need to be designed to ensure the business is marketing in the most effective way through the Internet. The starting process is to consult with customers about what would best suit their audience and then propose solutions to meet their individual needs. The latest design tools are used to make clean-loading graphics, animations, 3D logos, pictures, digital photography, digital video and attention-grabbing animations.

Expert web designers use several web-authoring tools to create the latest in JAVA, shockwave animations, digitised sound and customised applications to fit the needs of their customers. 'Hot link' pages can also be built in for the interests of the site users.

All designs are tested on old and new browsers, and current promotional materials can be used by the web designer to write provocative copy appropriate for Internet marketing. The designer will also provide support for hosting and maintaining the web site, with updates where necessary.

1 There are many fast-growing businesses set up to provide solutions for the technology needs and problems of organisations. The nature of the product they provide is largely described in the case study. Imagine you work for them and then, working in groups, identify how you would develop strategies for the following elements of their marketing mix:

a) The price of the service they provide.
b) The ways in which they communicate with customers and develop customer relationships.
c) The customer service they should provide.
d) Other product elements you would include with the web site design service.

2 Given the rapidly expanding nature of this market and the increasing number of organisations providing similar services, how would you suggest that a company operating in this field should develop their marketing strategy?

Check your understanding

Make a study of consumer choice for a particular type of product that is sold in a supermarket.

How many different types and brands of the product are on sale? How do the types and brands compete against each other? To what extent do consumers benefit from having this choice? Identify the different segments for this type of product. Does variety lead to increased quality? What are the other benefits of variety? What are the drawbacks of having so much choice?

Pricing and the techniques of pricing

The *Oxford English Dictionary* defines prices as the 'sum or consideration or sacrifice for which a thing may be bought or attained'. Price is the only element of the marketing mix that directly generates incomes – other elements of the marketing mix are costs. The importance of price in the marketing mix varies. In low-cost, non-fashion markets price can be critical (for example, in the sale of white emulsion and gloss paint). In fashion markets, such as clothing, it can be one of the least relevant factors. Certain products are designed to suit a particular segment (e.g. economy family cars), while others perform a specific function regardless of price (e.g. sports cars). For consumers with limited budgets, price is a key purchasing criterion while, for those to whom 'money is no object', price is less important.

The first pricing task is to create an overall pricing goal for an organisation that is in line with the marketing strategy and then determine objectives for each of the product lines.

The price charged for a product is associated with a given level of sales. We can illustrate this relationship by means of a demand curve (see Figure 13.1). The curve in Figure 13.1 shows the levels of demand for a floral print dress sold at different market prices. As with most products, customers for floral dresses would be prepared to make more purchases at a lower than a higher price.

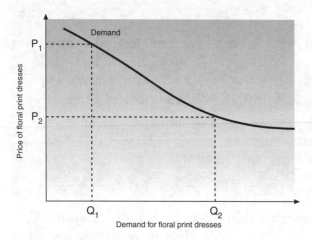

Figure 13.1 Demand curve

The normal way to express customer sensitivity to price changes is through a measure known as *price elasticity of demand*. This is the measure of how quantities purchased will alter in response to given price changes. Demand is said to be *elastic* if the change in quantity demanded is of a greater proportion than the change in price that initiated it. For example, if the price of a particular brand of washing powder fell by 10% and there was an increase in sales of 20%, the demand for the product would be said to be elastic; the change in price led to more than a proportionate response in the quantity demanded:

$$\text{Price elasticity of demand} = \frac{\%\text{ change in quantity demanded}}{\%\text{ change in price}}$$

When a relative change in the quantity sold is less than the relative change in price, demand is said to be *inelastic*. For example, if a price increase of 10% results in a 5% fall in sales, price elasticity will be −0.5.

Price elasticities vary with the level of competition. The more competition in the market, the more likely it is that demand for a particular product line will be elastic. Price elasticity also varies during the product life-cycle. In the early days, when there is little competition, price inelasticity will be the rule within a sensible price range. However, as products mature, elasticity will increase in the competitive price range.

D. Shipley noted the trends shown in Figure 13.2 as among the principal set of pricing objectives of firms. Once pricing objectives have been established, organisations need to establish an appropriate pricing strategy.

Pricing objectives	Percentage of firms
Target profit or return on capital employed	67
Prices fair to firm and customers	13
Prices similar to those of competitors	8
Target sales volume	7
Stable sales volume	5
Target market share	2
Stable prices	2
Other	1

Figure 13.2 Firms' pricing objectives (%)

Penetration pricing

Penetration pricing is appropriate when the seller knows that demand is likely to be elastic. A low price is therefore required to attract consumers to the product. Penetration pricing is normally associated with the launch of a new product for which the market needs to be penetrated (see Figure 13.3). Because a price starts low, even though a product will be developing market share, the product may initially make a loss until consumer awareness is increased.

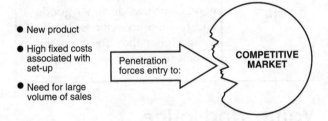

- New product
- High fixed costs associated with set-up
- Need for large volume of sales

Penetration forces entry to: COMPETITIVE MARKET

Figure 13.3 An environment appropriate for penetration pricing

A typical example would be that of a new breakfast cereal or a product being launched in a new overseas market. Initially it would be launched with a relatively low price, coupled with discounts and special offers. As the product penetrates the market, sales and profitability increase. Prices then creep upwards.

Penetration pricing is particularly appropriate for products where economies of scale can be employed to produce large volumes at low unit costs. Products that are produced on a large scale are initially burdened by high fixed costs for research, development and purchases of plant and equipment. It is important to spread these fixed costs quickly over a large volume of output. Penetration pricing is also common when there is a strong possibility of competition from rival products.

Skimming

At the launch of a new product there will frequently be little competition in the market so that demand for the product may be relatively inelastic. Consumers will probably have little knowledge of the product. Skimming involves setting a reasonably high initial price in order to yield high initial returns from those consumers willing to buy the new product. Once the first group of customers has been satisfied, the seller can then lower prices in order to make sales to new groups of customers. This process can be continued until a larger section of the total market has been catered for. By operating in this way, the business removes the risk of underpricing the product. The name 'skimming' comes from the process of skimming the cream from the top of the milk (Figure 13.4).

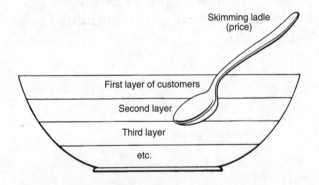

Skimming ladle (price)

First layer of customers
Second layer
Third layer
etc.

Figure 13.4 Skimming

Cost-plus pricing

Any study of organisations in the real world shows that many businesses use no other basis than a *mark-up* on the cost of providing the product or service concerned. Information about costs is usually easier to piece together than information about other variables, such as likely revenue. Firms will often, therefore, simply add a margin to the *unit cost*.

The unit cost is the average cost of each item produced. For example, if an organisation produces 800 units at a total cost of £24,000, the unit cost will be £30. Talk to many owners of small businesses and they will tell you they 'cost out' each hour worked and then add a margin for profits; or they will simply mark up each item sold by a certain percentage. For example, fashion items are frequently marked up by between 100 and 200%.

The process of cost-plus pricing can best be illustrated in relation to large organisations, where *economies of scale* can be spread over a considerable range of output. For a large organisation, unit costs will fall rapidly at first as the overheads are spread over a larger output. It is therefore a relatively simple calculation to add a fixed margin (e.g. 20%) to the unit cost. The organisation is able to select an output to produce and to set a price that will be 20% higher than the unit cost of production (see Figure 13.5).

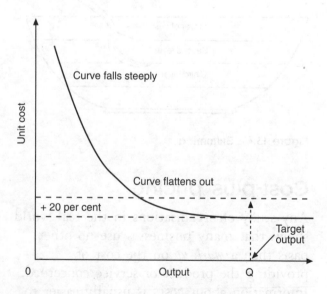

Figure 13.5 Select a target output (0–Q) and add 20% to the unit cost to arrive at the price

Whilst cost-plus pricing is very popular, many dangers are associated with it. If the price is set too high, sales may fall short of expectations; and if the price is set too low, then potential revenue is sacrificed. However, the greatest danger of cost-based pricing is that it indicates a *production-orientated approach to the market*. Emphasis on costs leads to tunnel vision that looks inwards at the company's product rather than outwards at the customers' perceptions of the product.

Discussion point	Why is the margin for luxury goods, such as designer goods and fashion accessories, likely to be higher than for cigarettes or newspapers?

Value and price

There is strong link between value and price. *Delivery of value* is an important ingredient of an exchange. Marketing has been described as 'selling goods that don't come back to people who do'. If the seller does not provide customers with a significant value proposition – whatever the price – goods may be returned or customers will not come back. In the longer term, the success of business organisations (and individuals) will depend on their ability to provide customers with *value for money* through the exchange process.

Most customers compare prices with the perceived quality or value provided by the goods and services they purchase – they are concerned with the value proposition provided by the organisation and its relationship to the price they have paid. For example, some customers are value orientated and want to pay low prices for acceptable quality; some buyers want high quality and are willing to pay more for it.

Many of today's retailers put an emphasis upon 'value' as a form of competition. Instead of focusing simply upon price, they provide customers with a better value package – more for the same price – than other competitors in that segment of the market.

It is therefore important to price according to the nature of customers in the marketplace. On the one hand, you may lose customers by charging too high a price. However, with a low-value proposition customers may feel they are not getting value for money. Potential customers may feel the low price indicates lower quality than they are seeking.

Check your understanding

Compare two products or services for which roughly similar prices are charged. Explain which product or service represents a better value proposition.

Competition-based pricing

In extremely competitive situations, costs have to be treated as a secondary consideration in short-term price determination. This is particularly true when competing products are almost identical, customers are well informed and there are few suppliers.

The nature and extent of the competition are frequently an important influence upon price. If a product is faced by direct competition, it will compete against other very similar products in the marketplace. This will constrain pricing decisions so that price setting will need to be kept closely in line with rivals' actions.

In contrast, when a product is faced with indirect competition (i.e. competition with products in different sectors of the market) there will be more scope to vary price. This opens up the possibility for a number of strategies. For example, a firm might choose a high-price strategy to give a product a 'quality' feel. In contrast, it might charge a low price so consumers see the product as a 'bargain'.

An individual organisation might try to insulate itself against price sensitivity by differentiating its products from those of rivals. Markets are sometimes classified according to the level of competition that applies. For example, an extreme level of competition is termed *perfect competition* (it exists in theory rather than in practice). The other extreme is *monopoly* where a single firm dominates a market. In the real world, most markets lie between these extremes and involve some level of imperfect competition (see Figure 13.6).

Figure 13.6   Competition

If a perfect market could exist there would be no limitations to new firms entering the market, and buyers would know exactly what was on offer and would incur no costs in buying from one seller rather than another. Products would be almost identical. In a monopoly situation, only one firm exists and barriers prevent new firms from entering the market. The seller has considerable powers to control the market.

In imperfect competition, there may be few or many sellers. Products are usually *differentiated* and consumers do not have perfect information about the differences between products.

Where organisations seek to reduce competition and make their products better than their rivals, the development of monopolistic powers enables them to push up prices and make larger profits. The level of competition is thus a key determinant of price. Where there are many close competitors, there is little scope to charge a price that is above the market price. Organisations in such markets are price takers.

In a situation where there is no competition, the seller can often charge a relatively high price. In other words, the seller is a price maker. However, the seller cannot charge more than the consumer is prepared to pay, because consumers can always choose to spend their income on alternative products. Between these two extremes, we find hundreds of different markets. In some the consumer has more power; in others it is the seller.

Communicating with customers

Organisations are the *senders* in the communication process and *consumers* are the *receivers*. A sender will put its information into a form that a receiver can understand. This might involve oral, visual, verbal or written messages to transmit the ideas. This process is called *encoding*. The sender will also choose a particular medium to use to send the message to the receiver (e.g. television, radio, newspapers). If the consumer interprets the message as required, it should have the impact the seller wished for (see Figure 13.7).

Though the message flows to the receiver there is no guarantee the receiver will either receive the full message or understand it. This is because the process may be subject to some form of interference, which affects the flow of information. This is known as

---

Check your understanding

Categorise the following examples into:

- penetration pricing
- skimming
- cost-plus pricing
- value-based competition
- competition-based pricing.

In each instance explain why you have categorised the example in the way in which you have.

1 A new book comes on to the market in hardback form at £25; two months later it comes out in paperback at £15; the following year it comes out in a second edition at £10.

2 In order to improve its competitive position in the high street, a major retailer creates a series of sub-brands designed to improve the ways in which its customers view its products.

3 A breakfast cereal manufacturer introduces a new type of cereal at a low price in order to attract customers to buy the product.

4 A garden centre sets a margin of 30% on all its stock.

5 A company launches a revolutionary piece of software.

6 In a fiercely competitive market, a business simply looks at the price charged by others before setting its own prices.

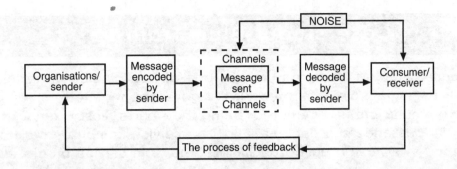

Figure 13.7 The communication process

noise and may lead to the downfall of the message. This takes the form of any barrier that acts as an impediment to the smooth flow of information; for example, one leaflet put through your door may be lost amongst a sea of direct mail from other organisations. Barriers affecting the flow of information between the sender and the receiver may include linguistic and cultural differences.

To increase the chances of a message getting across, an organisation needs to think carefully about the target audience. For example, it is important to channel the message through the most appropriate media. It might also be necessary to repeat the message several times rather than rely on one transmission.

Once the audience has been identified, the communicator also needs to think about the sort of response required. If, for example, the final response required through the communication process is purchase, there may be six phases to the buyer-readiness process (see Figure 13.8)

It is important, therefore, that the promotion mix takes into account each of these stages with different types of promotional activities.

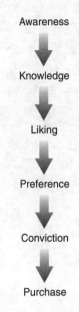

Figure 13.8 Buyer-readiness phases

Check your understanding

Competition in the market for personal computers is fierce. Imagine you work for a small organisation selling machines by mail order and you wish to target 'first-time' purchasers of PCs.

Explain what you would do to build your communication strategy around the purchasing process.

Case study: Blue Train

Virgin have recently revealed plans to purchase one of South Africa's prestigious national assets – the Blue Train. Operated by the government-owned railways, the Blue Train has won many prizes recently for being the world's most luxurious train, accommodating 84 passengers in opulent style. The service comprises two trains that were revamped in 1997 at a cost of £7 million. The train service breaks even.

Each 380-metre-long train has 18 carriages and 27 staff. It travels at a maximum speed of 68 mph. One operates between Pretoria and Cape Town, with guests spending one night on the train; the other travels between Pretoria and Victoria Falls on a trip called the Zimbabwe Spectacular, during which guests spend two nights on board. The latter trip costs £1,100 per person.

Each Blue Train compartment has a bath or shower, a telephone and air-conditioning. A video channel allows guests to watch short documentaries about the area through which the train is travelling. It is in effect a mobile safari. A large screen in the club car provides a driver's eye view of the track ahead, courtesy of a camera mounted on the front of the locomotive. There are also CD players and video machines in the luxury apartments.

1   What would be the arguments: a) for; and b) against buying this brand?

2   Working in groups, describe how the Blue Train brand might be applied across a range of luxury holiday packages or travelling opportunities.

Branding

A *brand* is a particular product or characteristic that identifies a particular producer. However, many mass-produced products are almost identical. For example, most washing powders are similar, as are different types of margarine. These goods tend to be produced by two or three large companies who encourage sales by creating a brand that differentiates the products in the consumers' minds.

The business of creating a brand is a particularly important function of marketing. Often people will buy the brand name as much as the product itself. You will see people in supermarkets pick up an item (which they have not seen before) and say: 'This must be a good one because it is made by . . .'

Large organisations swear by the power of the brand. They will fight tooth and nail to raise the status of their brands and are determined that nothing should affect the power of their brands.

A brand can be a name, a symbol or a design used to identify a specific product and to differentiate it from its competitors. Brand names, designs, trademarks, symbols, slogans and even music can be used to distinguish one product from another and to enable an organisation to distinguish its products from competing ones.

There are three different types of brands:

1 *Manufacturer brands*. Examples of these include Kellogg's cornflakes, Nescafé coffee and Heinz baked beans. These manufacturer brands associate the producer with the specific product, and the producer will be heavily involved with the promotion of the product.

2 *Own-label brands*. Examples of these include Tesco, St Michael (Marks & Spencer), Farm Foods (Asda), Sainsbury's own label, etc. These brands are owned and controlled by retailers and therefore, the producers or manufacturers are not associated with the products, or involved in their promotion.

3 *Generic brands*. Such products are extremely rare in the modern competitive market, and those that exist are usually at the lower end of the market with respect to price and quality. These products have no identifiable name or logo. Examples may include plain T-shirts or bin-liners, if they have no branded packaging or labels attached to them that identify the originator.

Organisations seek to create a portfolio of individual products that supports the image of a brand. Well-known brand names will, therefore, emphasise organisation-wide quality.

Case study: The power of brands

Consumers are hugely more brand literate in the 21st century than they were in the past. As we all become more affluent and there is more and more choice, the brand is one of the few weapons that the marketer has to give a product genuine distinction. People want to bask in the reflected glory of what a marque says about them.

Unfortunately, however, in recent years some old-established British brands have taken quite a knocking. Although companies may be making good products, analysts say, they are not investing in image. Take Rover for example. BMW makes cars for thrusting go-getters – 'The Ultimate Driving Machine'. With Mercedes Benz you get rock-solid engineering and style. But Rover conjures up little that is valued in the public imagination. The same goes for Marks and Spencer versus Gap, or BBC versus Sky Sports, or BA versus budget carriers. It seems that a number of the UK's well-known brands have been neglected and, as a result, old-established businesses are suffering.

1   Why are brands so important to business success?

2   How can you make brands exciting?

3   Can you think of British brands which are doing well and generating real excitement?

A brand that is held in high esteem is worth a great deal of money to an organisation. There is a well-known saying in business that 'an organisation can afford to get rid of its other assets, but not its brand image!'

Check your understanding

Identify two or three brands of products in a particular market. To what extent could these brands be further developed in a way that exemplifies the attributes of each brand?

Advertising

Advertising is a method of communicating with groups in the marketplace in order to achieve certain objectives. Advertisements are messages sent through the media that are intended to inform or persuade (influence) the people who receive them (see Figure 13.9). Advertising can be defined as a *paid-for* type of marketing communication that is *non-personal* but aimed at a specific *target audience* through a *mass media channel*.

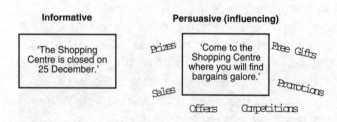

Informative

'The Shopping Centre is closed on 25 December.'

Persuasive (influencing)

Prizes Free Gifts

'Come to the Shopping Centre where you will find bargains galore.'

Sales Promotions

Offers Competitions

Figure 13.9 The difference between informative and persuasive (influencing) advertising

According to the American Marketing Association, advertising is 'any paid form of non-personal presentation and promotion of ideas, goods or services by an identifiable sponsor'.

Advertising must be a communication directed at a targeted market, and should draw attention to the characteristics of a product, that will appeal to the buying motives of potential customers. The ultimate purpose of advertising for an organisation is to enhance buyers' responses to its products by channelling their desires and preferences to the organisation's products ahead of its competitors.

Within this purpose there may be a range of advertising objectives. For example:

- Promoting goods and services. To:

  - Assist with selling.
  - Increase sales.
  - Develop awareness of new products or developments to existing products.
  - Provide information that may assist with buying decisions.
  - Encourage a desire to own a product.
  - Generate enquiries.

- Developing the image of the organisation. To:

  - Provide information for a target audience.
  - Soften attitudes.
  - Assist with public relations activities.
  - Change views.
  - Promote a better external environment.
  - Develop support from a community.

Advertising is often classified under one of three headings:

- *Informative advertising* conveys information and raises consumer awareness of the features and benefits of a product. It is often used in the introductory phase of the product life-cycle, or after modification.

- *Persuasive advertising* is concerned with creating a desire for the product and stimulating purchase. It is used with established and more mature products.

- *Reinforcement advertising* is concerned with reminding consumers about the product, and is used to reinforce the knowledge held by potential consumers about the benefits to be gained from purchase.

The starting point for an advertising campaign is to produce an advertising plan. This will involve allocating a budget to a range of activities designed to meet advertising objectives. There are seven steps in an advertising campaign:

- *Step 1* Identify the target market.
- *Step 2* Define advertising objectives.
- *Step 3* Decide on and create the advertising message.
- *Step 4* Allocate the budget.
- *Step 5* Develop the media plan.
- *Step 6* Execute the campaign.
- *Step 7* Evaluate the effectiveness of the campaign.

Advertising messages may be sent through a variety of media forms, such as TV, radio, cinema, posters, billboards, flyers, transport advertising and the press. For more information about advertising, look at the World Advertising Research Center web site on www.warc.com

Check you understanding

Compare and contrast two advertising campaigns where one is clearly trying to promote goods and services and the other is trying to improve an image by developing public support for its activities.

Comment upon how their approaches to advertising are: **a** similar; and **b** different.

At all stages in the advertising process it is important to assess how effectively advertisements have contributed to the communication process. In order to measure objectives, DAGMAR has become a fundamental part of good advertising practice. This stands for, 'Defining Advertising Goals for Measured Advertising Results'. In other words, before any advertising campaign is started, an organisation must define its communication objectives so that achievements can be measured both during and after the campaign.

Case study: The top six advertisers, 1998

Rank	Company	Total £'000s	Allocation (%)			
			TV	Radio	Press	Other
1	Procter & Gamble	165,895	90.5	0.7	5.9	2.9
2	British Telecom	105,772	59.1	8.1	29.1	3.8
3	Vauxhall Motors	83,323	55.2	3.9	28.7	12.3
4	Ford Motor Co.	80,661	67.8	6.7	19.9	5.6
5	Renault UK	80,298	54.2	6.7	23.0	16.0
6	Kellogg Co. of GB	67,165	76.5	1.3	8.3	13.9

Figure 13.10 The top six advertisers, 1998

Look at the list of the top six advertisers in Figure 13.10 and then use the data provided by the matrix as a basis for answering the following questions:

1 What do the allocations of expenditure tell you about the nature and type of advertising undertaken by each of these advertisers? For example, how does each sector of the media enable them to target appropriate audiences and make maximum use of their advertising budgets?

2 What forms of advertising might fall into the 'other' bracket?

3 Why do you think the six companies have such a large advertising spend?

4 If you were working for one of these companies, how would you evaluate the effectiveness of such a spend?

Printed media

The printed media make up by far the largest group of media in the UK. The group includes all newspapers and magazines, both local and national, as well as the trade press, periodicals and professional journals. There are about 9,000 regular publications in the UK that can be used by advertisers. They allow the advertiser to send a message to several million people through the press or to target magazines of special interest, such as *The Times Educational Supplement*, which allows the advertiser to communicate with people in the teaching profession.

As a result, the media allow for accurate targeting and positioning. For example, Figure 13.11 shows some of the most popular monthly women's magazines. Think of all the hobbies, lifestyles and backgrounds of the readers of these magazines. Customer types are identified by analysing the readership profiles of magazines such as these.

The benefit of the printed media is that long or complex messages can be sent and, as the message is durable, may be read repeatedly. If an advertisement appears in a prestige magazine it may take on the prestige of that particular publication.

Broadcast media

The broadcast media include commercial television and commercial radio. Television is the most powerful medium – reaching 98% of households, and viewing figures for some programmes can exceed 20 million. Television advertisements are expensive, however, and advertising messages are short lived.

Direct mail

Direct mail is personally addressed advertising sent through the post. There has been a massive increase in direct mail in recent years (see Figure 13.12). By using direct mail an organisation establishes a

Magazine	Circulation	Women's readership ('000s)
Prima	508,308	1,381
Candis	460,482	488
Cosmopolitan	430,202	1,665
Marie Claire	406,165	1,426
Good Housekeeping	401,843	1,608

Figure 13.11 Monthly women's magazines (1999)

Year	Consumer items	Business items	Total items
1987	1,161	465	1,626
1990	1,221	545	1,766
1994	2,015	715	2,730
1996	2,436	737	3,173
1998	3,123	891	4,014

Figure 13.12 Direct mail increases: volume of items in £million

direct relationship with is customers. The advertiser supplies promotional literature to

encourage a sale and then tries to cater for the customers' perceived needs.

Check your understanding

Over the period of a week, collect all the direct mail entering your home. Try to explain why your family has been the target of such direct mail.

The ability of direct mail to target precise market segments is cost effective as it eliminates the supply of mailshots to those unlikely to buy. Geo-demographic and

Financial *ACORN Categories	Financial *ACORN Groups	Financial *ACORN Types		CACI's 2000 Pop'n Number	Projections Percent of total
	1 Wealthy Equityholders	1.1	Mature couples & families, extensive financial portfolio	357,649	0.63
		1.2	Professional families, with life assurance, loand & mortgages	295,014	0.5
		1.3	Older families, active in loand & desposit accounts	347,400	0.6
		1.4	Older couples, low on pension pland & high on stocks & shares	443.492	0.7
		1.5	Middle aged couples, making sensible investments, few loans	948,093	1.6
		1.6	Older families with average loans & ample investments	598,787	1.0
		1.7	Mature couples, insurance., life assurance & deposit acciounts	1,261,328	2.2
		1.8	Older couples, equities, pension plans & investments	372,549	0.6
		1.9	Senior citizens with carefully planned savings & investments	491,202	0.8
		1.10	Middle aged, preferring investments in tax exempt savings	518,429	0.9
A Financially sophisticated		1.11	Younger single executives, investing, saving &debit cards	403,777	0.7
		1.12	Professional singles & couples, using credit & debit cards	441,110	0.8
	2 Affluent Mortgage-holders	2.13	Younger couples & families, very active across financial range	366,157	0.6
		2.14	Families with children, credit & debit cards & investing heavily	319,852	0.6
		2.15	Older families, deposit/savings accounts, above average shares	922,301	1.6
		2.16	Young & middle aged couples investing in tax exempt savings	863,922	1.5
		2.17	Young singles & couples, planning ahead, personal pensions	404,992	0.7
		2.18	Families, personal pensions, life assurance, tax exempt savings	362,075	0.6
		2.19	Young couples & families, above av. mortgages & life assurance	804,140	1.4
		2.20	Young adults in couples, settling down with mortgages & loans	501,744	0.9
		2.21	Families & young couples, mortgages but wary of investments	556.375	1.0
	3 Comfortable Investors	3.22	Older couples, wide range of investments, especially in shares	807,832	1.4
		3.23	Middle aged couples with ample personal pensions	286,871	0.5
		3.24	Older couples, av. credit/loans, keen on tax exempt savings	1,167,642	2.0
		3.25	Traditional couples, tax exempt savings & personal pensions	1,156,553	2.0

Financial *ACORN Categories	Financial *ACORN Groups	Financial *ACORN Types		CACI's 2000 Pop'n Number	Projections Percent of total
	4 Better-off Borrowers	4.26	Younger families with children, using loans & mortgages	534,385	0.5
		4.27	Younger families & couples, high spending, new commitments	648.038	1.1
		4.28	Young singles & couples, keen on loans & personal pensions	1,491,438	2.6
		4.29	Families, av. financial activity but above average mortgages	2,956,523	5.1
B Financially involved		4.30	Younger people, setting up home	1,777,093	3.1
		4.31	Family groups, especially younger families, borrowing heavily	145,628	0.3
	5 Prosper-ous Savers	5.32	Older families & couples with careful savings & investments	1,152,928	2.0
		5.33	Mature singles & couples enjoying high share ownership	1,115,445	1.9
		5.34	Older couples, deposit accounts, tax exempt savings, shares	1,576,251	2.7
		5.35	Young, low life assurance but high denationalised stocks	1,218,183	2.1
		5.36	Retired, active in shares, credit cards, deposit accounts	1,294,131	2.2
		5.37	Pensioners, very high share ownership, few loans & mortgages	744,972	1.3
	6 Younger Spenders	6.38	Young adults, very active credit card use & some investments	1,155,413	2.0
		6.39	Younger single people using cash and debit cards, few loans	391,018	0.7
C Financially moderate	7 Settled Pensioners	7.40	Older people, average activity across the financial range	2,671,212	4.6
		7.41	Elderly singles & couples, some savings, generally average	2,670,161	4.6
	8 Working Families	8.42	Younger couples, few children, mortgages & average savings	3,544,104	6.1
		8.43	Families of all ages with children, using above average loans	1,326,281	2.3
	9 Thrifty Singles	9.44	Young adults, average spending & few savings or mortgages	1,094,013	1.9
		9.45	Young singles & couples, low spending & negligible savings	1,341,370	2.3
	10 Middle Aged Assured	10.46	Middle aged & older singles, above average life assurance	2,474,729	4.3
		10.47	Middle aged coupes, above av. life assurance, few investments	594,498	1.0
D Financially inactive	11 Older Cash Users	11.48	Older singles, retired or unemployed, negligible credit	2,896,383	5.0
		11.49	Families & single people, below av. use of financial products	2,723,154	4.7
		12.50	Young families, very low activity in mortgages & credit cards	3,826,028	6.6
		12.51	Families with children, very little savings or spending	1,213,813	2.1
	Unclassified TOTAL			352,569 57,919,047	0.6 100.0

© CACI Information Solutions, 2000. Financial*ACORN is a registered servicemark of CACI Information Solutions. *Source*: ONS © Crown Copyright 1991. All rights reserved.

Figure 13.13 Financial*ACORN PROFILE OF GREAT BRITAIN
The chart shows the Financial*ACORN profile of CACI's 2000 population projections for Great Britain. The table shows the 11 Financial*ACORN groups and 51 Financial*ACORN Types (plus 1 'unclassified') in the Financial*ACORN classification which is derived from the Government's 1991 Census of Great Britain and data from NOP's Financial Research Survery (FRS)

lifestyle systems such as PIN, ACORN (see Figure 13.13) and MOSAIC help the direct-mailer to identify different types of consumer according to where they live and the lifestyle they follow. The majority of mailshots are read, and organisations often use sales promotions such as offers and competitions to encourage a response (Figure 13.14).

Dear Mr Lucky

First of all allow me, on behalf of my colleagues and myself, to offer you our warmest congratulations, because

You really are a winner in our 2001 super prize draw

Yes, you're off to a winning start, since one of our fabulous entry prizes is already yours, and may have even gone one better. If, as I hope, your personal lucky number 20676646 matches our 1st prize, you will also walk away with the prize of prizes, or the car, or £15,000 cash.

Figure 13.14 An inducement to respond to a direct mail shot

If a good impression is made on the consumer, direct mail can provide the opportunity to send a long message and some detailed copy (text). Organisations such as the Automobile Association, Reader's Digest, Consumers' Association and National Geographic are well established in

Discussion point	Direct mail is largely unwanted, environmentally unfriendly and clutters up your hallway. Working in groups, discuss any limitations, if any, you might want to impose upon the increasing amount of direct mail entering your home.

their use of direct mail techniques. It is the easiest form of promotion to measure as it is possible to calculate the number of mailshots sent out, the cost of the campaign, the response rate and the number of sales made.

Public relations

The forces in an organisation's external environment are capable of affecting it in a variety of ways. These forces may be social, economic, political, local or environmental, and might be represented by a variety of groups, such as customers, shareholders, employees and special interest groups. Reacting positively to such forces and influences is very important.

Public relations (PR) is the planned and sustained effort an organisation makes to establish, develop and build relationships with its many publics (see Figure 13.15). The purpose of public relations is therefore to provide an external environment for an organisation in which it is popular and can prosper. Building goodwill requires the organisation to behave in such a way that it takes into account the attitudes of the many people who come across it and its products.

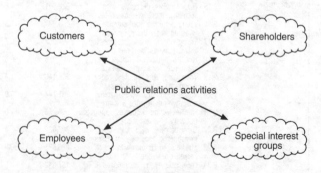

Figure 13.15 Public relations activities

Whereas many of the other promotional methods are *short term*, public relations is long term, as it may take a *long time* for an organisation to improve the way people think more positively about its products and activities. For example, just think about the sort of public relations problems that chemical and oil companies have in a world where consumers have become increasingly environmentally conscious.

The launch of the Millennium Dome in Greenwich at the beginning of 2000 instantly prompted many newspapers to launch an offensive against some of the dome's activities, as they sought to investigate whether the cost of the dome was money well spent. This was a typical public relations problem for those operating the dome, who then had to emphasise its positive attributes. In the political arena, talking positively about activities is sometimes known as 'spin'.

According to Frank Jefkins, PR involves a transfer process that helps to convert the negative feelings of an organisation's many publics into positive ones (see Figure 13.16).

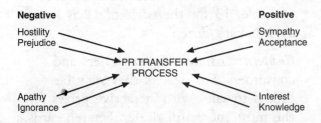

Figure 13.16 The PR transfer process

There are may different types of public relations activities:

- *Charitable donations and community relations* are good for an organisation's image, often provide lots of good publicity and also help to promote and provide for a good cause.

- *Hospitality* at top sporting events is a popular method used by organisations to develop their customer relations. For example, there are opportunities to entertain customers at events such as the FA Cup Final, Wimbledon and the Grand National.

- *Press releases* covering events affecting the organisation – such as news stories, export achievements, policy changes, technical developments and anything that enhances the organisation's image.

- *Visits and open days* are a popular method of inviting people to various events to improve their understanding of what the organisation stands for.

- *Sponsorship* of sporting and cultural events is considered a useful opportunity to associate an image with a particular type of function. For example, the NatWest Trophy and the Embassy World Snooker Championship.

- *Lobbying* of ministers, officials and important people from outside interest groups so that an accurate portrayal can be made of a problem or a case may help to influence these people's views of the organisation.

- *Corporate videotapes* have become an increasingly popular way of providing interested parties with a 'view' of an organisation's activities.

- *Minor product changes*, such as no testing on animals or environmentally friendly products, may provide considerable PR benefits.

Check your understanding

Search the press for a PR problem. Having found the problem, discuss how you would attempt to solve this problem and make a note of the sorts of activities that would help you to do so.

Sales promotions

Sales promotions describes a category of techniques used to encourage customers to make a purchase. These activities are effectively short term and may be used:

- to increase sales

- to help with personal selling

- to respond to the actions of competitors

- as an effective alternative to advertising.

The Institute of Sales Promotion defines sales promotion as follows:

> *Sales promotion is the function of marketing which seeks to achieve given objectives by the adding of intrinsic, tangible value to a product or service.*

The essential feature of a sales promotion is that it is a short-term inducement to encourage customers to react quickly, whereas advertising is usually a process that develops the whole product or brand.

As you walk down a town high street or through a shopping mall, you will see many different examples of sales promotions. Such promotions may serve many different purposes. For example, competitions, vouchers or coupons and trading stamps may be designed to build customer loyalty and perhaps increase the volume purchased by existing customers. Product sampling is a strategy that is often used to introduce new products into the marketplace. Clearance sales of overstocked goods will increase turnover during part of the year in which business might otherwise be slack. Many sales promotions are undertaken in response to the activities of competitors to ensure an organisation remains competitive.

Sales promotions can be divided into two broad areas:

- Promotions assisting with the sale of products to the trade.

- Promotions assisting the trade in selling products to the final consumer.

Selling into the pipeline is an expression used to describe promotions that move products from the manufacturer into the distribution system. Selling out of the pipeline describes promotions that trigger the end-user to make a purchase (see Figure 13.17).

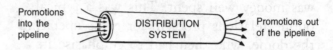

Figure 13.17 Selling into and out of the pipeline

There are many different types of sales promotion:

- *Dealer loaders* are among the inducements to attract orders from retailers and wholesalers. They may include a 'free case' with so many cases bought. For example, 13 for the price of 12 is known as a 'baker's dozen'.

- *Competitions* may interest dealers and consumers. For dealers they may be linked to sales with attractive prizes for the most successful dealer. Scratch cards, free draws and bingo cards are popular promotional methods for consumers.

- *Promotional* gifts, such as bottles of spirits, clocks, watches or diaries, are considered useful bounty for dealers.

- *Price reductions* and *special offers* are usually popular with consumers. They can, however, prove expensive as many consumers would otherwise have been prepared to pay the full price.

- *Premium offers* may offer extra product for the same price. *Coupons* that offer money off or money back may also be attractive incentives to consumers. These may appear in magazines, be distributed door to door or appear on the side of a pack.

- *Charity promotions* can be popular with younger consumers, who collect box tops or coupons and send them to a manufacturer, which then makes a donation to charity.

- *Loyalty incentives* are, today, an increasingly used form of sales promotion. Dealers' loyalty might be rewarded with bigger discounts, competitions and prizes, or even having their names published as stockists in advertisements. For consumers, loyalty incentives, such as loyalty cards and points, may provide 'cash back', free gifts or a variety of other tangible benefits.

Sponsorship

Sponsorship is a good way of increasing brand awareness which, in turn, helps to generate preference and foster brand loyalty. Sponsorship is the material support of an event, activity or organisation by an unrelated donor. A company can reinforce awareness among its target market by sponsoring an event which attracts a similar target market.

Sponsorship involves an arrangement between a sponsor and a sponsee to provide support (either by supplying a product or service or through financial support) for an event or activity of which the sponsee is at the centre. Sponsorship is not an act of charity as far as the sponsor is concerned, and it must show some form of return. Since sponsorship is a business arrangement, standard evaluative criteria should be used to establish the suitability of a proposed event in relation to the sponsor's image and products.

Sponsorship can offer a wide range of benefits for the sponsor. For example, it can be used to raise the image of the organisation as a whole, to promote the virtues of a specific range of products, or can even be used as part of a sales promotion campaign. It can be used as an exercise in corporate hospitality or even, at a local level, can simply be seen as a good community relations initiative.

Before sponsoring an activity, the sponsor must be sure the event will be successful. It is clearly much easier to sponsor an event with a proven track record. Sports sponsorship is the most common form of sponsorship and can range in scale from international and national down to regional and local events.

Product presentation

The form in which a product is presented, and the packaging in which it appears, is an important part of the promotional mix, although its importance is often neglected. In recent years packaging and other forms of product presentation, such as displays and merchandising, have accounted for an increasing amount of the total cost of goods.

The basic function of package is to protect its contents in transit, in storage and in use, and this plays a major part in determining its shape, size and the materials used. However, consumers increasingly see attractive packaging as adding value to products.

Retailers originally carried out the packaging of consumer goods. Today, manufacturers play the major part in

Case study: Sponsoring the Nationwide Football League

In March 1996, Nationwide started its pursuit to sponsor the Football League Championships. When the 1996/7 season kicked off, Nationwide's three-year £5.25 million sponsorship of the game had begun.

In return for its investment, Nationwide receives extensive exposure. More than 60 Nationwide League games, for example, were televised on Sky and ITV in the first season, with an audience of up to 2 million per game. Sponsorship included a shared logo for the Nationwide Football League, with advertising boards at each of the clubs and opportunities to provide Nationwide names and services in every match programme.

Nationwide is a large brand with a high profile. There are Nationwide branches in the area of every team in the League, and many football supporters are Nationwide customers. Sports sponsorship helped the name to be associated with a range of events. It enabled Nationwide to target a key market within a relatively short period of time and build brand awareness through a leisure-time activity.

1 Explain why the Nationwide is committed to sports sponsorship. What benefits does it receive from this process?

2 Describe how sponsorship might help to develop the attributes and values of a brand.

packaging, which enables them to control the image and presentation of their products. Packaging has the following functions. It:

- Identifies and promotes a brand, e.g. the distinctive Coca-Cola bottle.

- Catches the consumer's eye.

- Identifies a line of related products.

- Communicates information on ingredients, quantity and product use.

- Helps with the preservation, storage and safety of the products.

Like packaging, merchandising and display have a major role to play in promoting products to potential customers. *Merchandising* can be regarded, generally, as *presenting stock effectively*, whereas *display* is the specific act of

putting stock in places where it is to be viewed by potential customers. In merchandising, assessment of the customer plays a crucial role, with an assessment of their movement patterns providing an opportunity to work out the best places in which to put stock items. Display materials vary from posters to shelf displays and can inform customers about specific products.

Check your understanding

Explain where you would place the following in a large hypermarket:

- milk
- confectionery
- clothes
- chilled foods.

In each instance, provide an explanation for your response.

Sometimes products are displayed at exhibitions, national shows or regional events for the trade or public. Such exhibitions are an opportunity to demonstrate products, processes and applications to specifiers, customers and opinion formers.

Direct selling

Most days of your life you are involved in some form of selling activity. It might be persuading a friend to come with you to the pictures, or asking a relative to buy something for you. What you are doing is using your relationship to sell your ideas to someone else. Personal or direct selling involves interaction between individuals or groups of individuals. The objective of personal selling is to make a sale, and it is the culmination of all the marketing activities that have taken place beforehand. It involves matching a customer's requirements with the goods or services on offer. The better the match, the more lasting the relationship between the seller and the buyer.

Check your understanding

Make a list of situations in which you have recently been involved in some form of personal selling. Explain how the selling process took place in each instance.

Did you have any responsibilities to the other person(s) involved in the exchange process?

The role of personal selling will vary from business to business. It is a two-way process that can be one of the most expensive areas of the promotional mix. This personal communication element can be very

important, as the final sale might come only as a result of protracted negotiations.

Personal selling is important in both consumer and organisational markets. However, in consumer goods markets, advertising often helps the process and is often the driving force which *pulls* a product through the distribution network. In organisational markets, on the other hand, personal selling may have to work harder to *push* the product through to the market (see Figure 13.18).

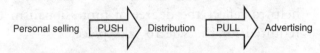

Figure 13.18 The push–pull effect

The main benefit of personal selling is the ability to communicate with, and focus on, customers individually and with precision. For example, if you go into a travel agency and ask for details about a holiday, the sales assistant may explain and point out the features of various packages and any discounts or promotions they might offer. All the other areas of the promotional mix are targeted at groups of people.

Although we have mental stereotypes of the typical salesperson, selling involves special skills. Whereas there is a tendency to downgrade this role in the UK, in many countries (Germany, for example), sales staff require a high degree of technical competence and are generally accepted to be part of the corporate élite. Salespeople are key intermediaries who present information to customers and then provide feedback on customer needs.

Sales staff are representing an organisation and so need to reflect a positive image of that organisation. It is important they do not offend customers by their appearance – the mode of dress should match the nature of the products and the organisation. For example, a sales assistant in a fashion store should wear something up to date, whereas an insurance salesperson should wear more formal clothes. It is often said that the way we look determines the ways others look at us!

Similarly, effective speaking will help to create the appropriate image and situation for the sale to take place. Good grammar, vocabulary, diction and tone of voice may help to reflect the degree of professionalism required for the sale to take place.

Many organisations spend more on personal selling than on any other area of the promotional mix and, within organisations, large number of individuals may find that personal selling forms part of their role. Personal selling may involve individuals developing special skills and using them in many different operational situations. To do so, sales staff need to know their products and be well trained in selling techniques (Figure 13.19).

Figure 13.19 Stages in the selling process

Product knowledge

Communication skills

Point-of-sale service

After-sales service

Sales administration

Customer care

Selling in a highly competitive world means that preparation has never been so important. Though it has been said that salespeople are born and not made, nevertheless skills, knowledge and training can improve performance. Training is designed to build on people's selling skills and to use their personal abilities and understanding to follow the psychological stages of the sales process. Product knowledge is vital as it allows for feedback from the prospective customer's questions about the product's technical specifications, benefits and functions.

Knowing their customers may help to determine how sales staff communicate with them. For example, some customers may prefer to be addressed with the more formal Mr or Mrs while others like to be called by their first name.

Probing is important in the early stage of a sales presentation in order to find out the prospective customer's needs and where his or her priorities might lie. The salesperson can then try to match the product or service with the prospect's requirements. This may involve elaborating on the product's advantages, concentrating on such aspects as savings in costs, design ingredients, performance specifications, after-sales service, etc.

During the presentation, the salesperson must constantly evaluate whether the product is appropriate to the needs of the prospective customer. It is unethical to sell something that is not needed – although this may often happen! The large and more complex the order, the more complex the negotiations over supply. In many different situations it is important to provide a number of services to help with the process. For example, these might include:

- product demonstrations
- performance specifications
- sales literature
- samples
- a meeting to discuss details
- credit facilities
- sales promotions.

The prospective customer may have a variety of objections to the purchase. These objections may be genuine or as a result of a misunderstanding. There might be reluctance to make a commitment at this stage. Logical, well-presented arguments and incentives may overcome such objections.

Timing is crucial to the sale. A salesperson must look for *buying signals* that indicate the prospective customer is close to a decision and almost ready to put a signature on an order form and discuss the contractual arrangements.

It is always important to *follow up the sale with post-sale support*. Promises that might have been made during the negotiations will have to be fulfilled. If the salesperson guarantees delivery by a certain date, that date must be held. Servicing arrangements must be efficiently carried out, and any problems dealt with. Contacting customers to see if they are happy with the product will encourage repeat buying and improve the supplier's concern for its customers.

Check your understanding

Using an example known to you, show how strong after-sales service may help to promote repeat purchasing patterns.

Sales staff may also have a number of other related functions. Communication, for example, is an important role. Sales staff act as an information link between suppliers and their customers. As a result, personal selling involves a boundary role – being at the boundary of a supplying organisation and also in direct and close contact with customers. The role is often not only one of selling but also one of interpreting the activities and policies of each organisation for clients (see Figure 13.20). A considerable amount of administration may also therefore accompany the selling role. For example, reports, schedules and computerised information, such as inventory details, are a part of the daily life for a salesperson.

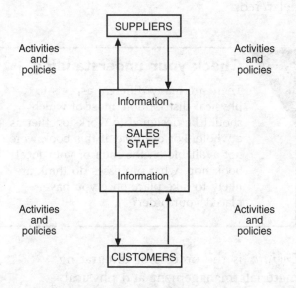

Figure 13.20 The information link between customers and their suppliers

Comprehensive records on customers should be kept and updated after each visit. Keeping sales records enables the salesperson to respond exactly to each customer's individual needs. Knowledge of competitors and their products enables the seller to respond to queries about the relative merits and demerits of products.

Logistics and placement

In simple terms, physical distribution involves getting a product from A to B. Physical distribution management is an important part of the marketing mix. It helps an organisation meet customer needs profitably and efficiently. In doing so it enables manufacturers and distributors to provide goods for customers at the right time, in the right place and in the condition required. It may also reduce the lead-time – from when a customer first makes an order until the time that order is delivered.

> ## Check your understanding
>
> There are many different aspects to physical distribution, most of which should be designed to work together as a whole. For example, if this book were not available on the shelf of your local bookshop, what processes do think are likely to take place once you have placed your order?

Logistics is the process of integrating materials management and physical distribution management, and it involves a whole series of activities from moving raw materials through to manufacturing processes, and moving finished goods to the final consumer.

Physical distribution must balance the need for customer service against the need to minimise costs. On the one hand, to maximise customer service an organisation may need a great deal of stock and warehouse space, efficient staff and rapid transport mechanisms while, on the other, to minimise costs it needs low stock levels, limited storage space, few staff and slower transport. Designing a physical distribution system, therefore, involves trading off costs against service, or inputs against outputs.

Inputs involve all the distribution costs, such as freight costs, inventory costs, warehousing costs and other service costs. It is important to know exactly what each of these costs are and control them in order to minimise waste. This may involve a detailed analysis of labour time, transport time and other factors spent on each product.

Outputs can, primarily, be measured in terms of the value of services provided for customers. Distribution can provide a clear competitive benefit in meeting customer needs, for example, by offering a quick and efficient service. Every business must decide how it is going to use distribution and relate this to its competitive advantage. Weaknesses in distribution would clearly need to be compensated for by strengths in other areas of the marketing mix.

Discussion point	In a market where competition is intense, the physical distribution system is the most important element of the marketing mix.

The physical distribution system an organisation selects will largely depend upon the scale of operations and the size of an organisation's market. A business handling a lot of international mail, for example, might locate near a large airport. Key decisions about physical distribution may include the following:

- *Inventory*. A business that wants to maximise customer service will have the highest inventory costs, because it needs to hold stock to meet all requests. The key inventory decisions are when and how much to order. The danger of keeping too little in stock is that an organisation could lose custom because of dissatisfaction with the quality of service.

- *Warehousing.* A key decision is where to locate warehouses, and how many to have.

- *Load size.* Should units be transported in bulk or broken down into smaller units for delivery? Again, an organisation will have to trade off customer convenience and the cost of distribution.

- *Communications.* It is important to develop an efficient information processing and invoicing system.

Channels are the networks of intermediaries linking the producer to the market. Whereas direct selling methods are *zero-level channels* that do not use an intermediary, indirect selling methods use one or more channels of distribution through which

goods are transferred from the producer to the end-user. These channels consist of one or more individuals or organisations who help to make the products available for the end-user (see Figure 13.21).

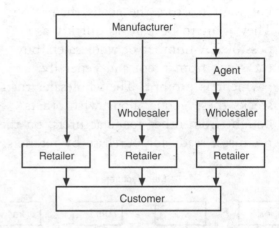

Figure 13.21 Indirect sales channels

Intermediaries, such as *wholesalers,* stock a range of goods from competing manufacturers to sell on to other organisations, such as retailers. Most

Case study: Distribution to Sainsbury's stores

Within the M25 area, Sainsbury's has more than 80 branches, each of which requires several deliveries daily. Average traffic speeds in London have fallen to 11 mph over the last decade as traffic densities have increased.

In order to improve their systems of physical distribution, Sainsbury's have consolidated their supplies into fewer, larger loads for final delivery. Now 38-tonne vehicles enable goods to be delivered in fewer vehicles, reducing delivery costs, carbon dioxide emissions and congestion. As far as possible deliveries are made between 10 pm and 6 am to reduce congestion.

'Just-in-time' scheduling reduces the time goods are held in the warehouse. The requirements of branches are relayed via computer, with many product lines on a 24-hour cycle (ordered one day for delivery the following day), while others are ordered once or twice a week for delivery 48 hours later.

1 What problems might be encountered delivering within the M25 area?

2 How could such problems be overcome?

wholesalers take on the title to the goods and so assume many of the associated risks. These include the following:

- *Breaking bulk*. Manufacturers produce goods in bulk for sale but they might not want to store the goods themselves. They want to be paid as quickly as possible. A number of wholesalers buy the stock from them and generally payment is prompt. The wholesaler then stocks these goods, along with others bought from other manufacturers, on the premises, ready for purchase by retailers.

Manufacturers

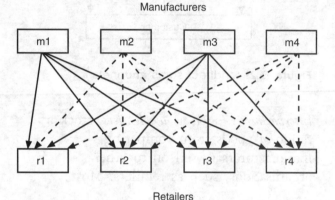

Retailers

Figure 13.22 The distribution chain without the wholesaler

- *Simplifying the distribution process*. The chain of distribution without the wholesaler would look something like Figure 13.22. Manufacturer 1 has to carry out four journeys to supply retailers 1, 2, 3 and 4, and has to send out four sets of business documents, and handle four sets of accounts. The same situation applies to each of the manufacturers, so that in total 16 journeys are made and 16 sets of paperwork are required. This is a simplification because, in the real world, thousands of different transactions might be involved!

An intermediary can simplify costs and processes of distribution by cutting down on journeys, fuel and other costs, as well as cutting down on paperwork such as invoicing and administration.

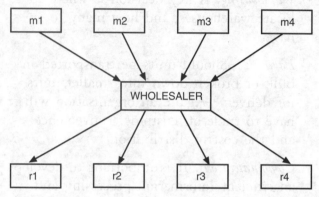

Figure 13.23 The distribution chain with the wholesaler

The chain of distribution with an intermediary (such as a wholesaler) would look something like Figure 13.23. Clearly everything is simplified:

- *Storage*. Most retailers have only a limited amount of storage space. The wholesaler can be looked upon as a cupboard for the retailer. Manufacturers are able to unload finished goods on the wholesaler, which then acts as a conduit to the retailers.

- *Packing and labelling*. The wholesaler will, in some instances, finish off the packaging and labelling of goods, perhaps by putting price tags or brand labels on the goods.

- *Offering advice*. Being in the middle of a chain of distribution, wholesalers have a great deal more information at their fingertips than either the retailer or manufacturer. In particular, wholesalers know which goods are selling well. With this in mind they can advise retailers on what to buy and manufacturers on what to produce.

By contracting out the process of distribution, a company can concentrate on its core functions.

Selling to end-users

The French word *retailler* means *to cut again*. We have already seen that the wholesaler breaks down bulk supplies from the manufacturer. The retailer then cuts the bulk again to sell individual items to customers. In the modern retailing environment, the *physical environment* for selling to end-users has become increasingly complex and in tune with customer focus and needs.

For example, Daewoo is distributing cars in the UK without using a traditional local car dealership network. The use of telephone, modem and fax are also providing the consumer with new ways to view and purchase products. *Telemarketing* is now being used to sell such products as insurance and pensions, which were previously sold by a one-to-one personal interview. The availability of satellite TV channels, has promoted the introduction of *home shopping*, with the American company QVC launching an English-speaking shopping channel within Europe. Simultaneously, the Internet is increasingly being used for *electronic commerce*, selling goods to consumers. This new channel of distribution is being investigated by many other organisations who are already involved in the distribution chain, such as supermarkets (www.tesco.co.uk) and catalogue shops (www.argos.co.uk). These imaginative approaches to distribution are being viewed as a major new opportunity to meet customer needs within a rapidly changing physical environment.

> ### Check your understanding
>
> Discuss: **a** the advantages; and **b** the disadvantages of using the Internet for shopping.

This physical environment for retailing largely depends upon the following:

- *Ownership*. Who owns the retail unit? Does a sole trader independently own it? Is it owned by a large multiple with shareholders? Is it a co-operative or a franchised outlet?

- *Range of merchandise*. Does the retail outlet specialise in a range of goods or does it have a spread of interests? Examples of specialised outlets include ice-cream parlours, furniture stores and fast-food outlets. Woolworths is an example of a more general outlet. Harrods at one time claimed to sell everything from 'a pin to an elephant'.

- *Pricing policy*. Some retail outlets concentrate on the bottom of the price range. They offer discounts and low prices, buying in bulk and selling in large quantities. The early policy of Jack Cohen, founder of Tesco, was 'pile them high, sell them cheap'. In contrast, other retail outlets aim for an upmarket price image. This is true of fashion shops, clothing and jewellery stores.

- *Location*. This has become increasingly important in recent years. Low-price stores frequently choose locations where business rates and other site costs are at a minimum. In contrast, large multiples and department stores need a town-centre location, or a site near a major road. Small 'corner' shops need a healthy volume of custom for their livelihood – their strength is in offering local convenience. The growth of out-of-town centres has provided further opportunities to create a range of retailing environments for customers, including multiplex cinemas and restaurants.

- *Size*. Many variety stores are now over 50,000 sq. ft. in area, but superstores and hypermarkets have areas from 25,000 to 100,000 sq. ft.

Check your understanding

Draw a plan of our local shopping area. Make a list of the different types of retailers in the area.

There are many different ways of meeting customer needs through different forms of distribution. These include the following:

- *Independent traders*. According to the Census of Distribution, an independent trader is a retail organisation with fewer than 10 branches. A typical number is one or two branches. The market share for these has been declining, particularly in food.

- *Multiple chains*. These are usually owned by large companies, with a high degree of control from a head office. Some multiples are classified as specialist stores concentrating on a narrow range of items, while others are variety chains such as Marks & Spencer and Littlewoods. Key features of multiples are:

  - centralised buying
  - concentration on fast-moving lines
  - merchandise is widely known
  - located in busy shopping areas
  - volume sales enable prices to be low
  - shops project a strong corporate image
  - many key functions are centralised.

- *Supermarkets*. A supermarket is defined as a store with at least 2,000 sq. ft. (or about 200 sq. m.) of selling area, using mainly self-service methods and having at least three check-out points. The layout of the store is designed to speed customer flow and reduce the time spent shopping.

- *Hypermarkets*. These are very large supermarkets, usually either out of town or on the fringes of towns or cities. They have a massive selling area and offer a wide range of household goods at discount prices. As well as food and clothing, they stock lines as diverse as DIY equipment, motoring accessories, children's toys and hardware.

- *Department stores*. The definition of a department store, as used by the Census of Distribution, is a store with a large number of departments and employing more than 25 people. They are to be found on 'prime sites' in the centre of most towns and cities. The key feature of a department store is that it is divided into separate departments, providing a range of shopping opportunities within specialised sales areas, so that all shopping can take place under one roof. They have a reputation for selling high-quality branded goods.

- *Discount stores*. Today, specialist companies such as Comet and Curry's concentrate on selling large quantities of consumer durables at discount prices. The aim of these stores is to produce a high level of total profit through fast turnover of stock. Many of these stores offer a range of credit services and other facilities to complement their customer offer.

- *Co-operative retail societies*. There are fewer than 30 co-operative retail societies in various parts of the UK. These aim to provide more than business services; they aim to support the community in a variety of ways.

Check your understanding

Look at the business information pages in a broadsheet newspaper over a two-week period. Collect articles that refer to organisations involved in retailing activity.

Discuss how each article or statement describes recent changes in retailing activities.

- *Catalogue shopping*. Organisations such as Argos and Index publish a catalogue listing all the goods they sell. Customers visit their high-street stores to collect their goods. Goods are not generally on display, with the majority of the store's space allocated to stock. Though the physical environment of these outlets is not particularly attractive for consumers, the low running costs mean consumers benefit from low prices.

- *Home shopping*. There are three main sectors. Agency mail-order catalogues, such as Freeman's and Great Universal Stores, bypass intermediaries. Individuals become agents and either buy for themselves (receiving a commission) or sell goods on to friends and family. Direct mail catalogues, such as Next Directory, have become increasingly popular methods of ordering goods, usually accepting payment by credit card. Interactive television, the Internet and television shopping channels have massive potential to change our shopping habits. As consumers become more confident in using them, they have the potential to serve a range of different needs and requirements.

Check your understanding

Compare and contrast the physical environment of two retailing organisations. Look, for example, at their size, location, number of branches, pricing structure, market position, range of goods, associated services and support for their customers.

Carry out a short shopping survey to find out what type of organisation customers prefer to use for a range of different selected products.

Customer service

Customers are the most important people for any organisation. They are simply the natural resource upon which the success of any organisation depends. When thinking about the importance of customers it is useful to remember the following points:

- Repeat business is the backbone of selling. It helps to provide security and certainty.

- Organisations are dependent upon their customers. If they do not develop customer loyalty and satisfaction, they could lose their customers.
- Without customers the organisation would simply not exist.
- The purpose of the organisation is to fulfil the needs of customers.
- The customer makes it possible to achieve everything the business aims for.

Many argue that all organisations have both *internal* and *external* customers (see Figure 13.24). The belief is that the quality of customer service provided outside the organisation is dependent upon how well employees within the organisation treat each other. For example, if an employee makes an enquiry to personnel or writes out a requisition for some stationery, he or she should expect to be treated with the same respect as a customer outside the organisation. This approach helps to encourage teamwork and customer care, which lead towards total quality management.

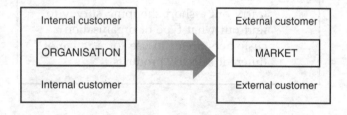

Figure 13.24 Internal and external customers

Many UK companies try to explain the concept of the internal and external customer by referring to the link that starts with the needs of external customers and then includes all the people involved in bringing together resources to satisfy these needs. Everyone has a role in satisfying customers. This process helps to emphasise

that all employees within an organisation are part of a quality chain that is improved with better teamwork, training, employee care and communications procedures.

Though the concept of the internal and external customer is widely used, it has been criticised for focusing an organisation's efforts internally upon itself instead of using resources to satisfy the needs and expectations of external customers. Customer satisfaction is at the heart of the selling process (Figure 13.25). One estimate is that it costs five times as much to attract new customers as it does to keep an existing one. The relationship between the customer and the organisation is, therefore, an important one.

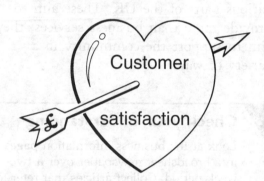

Figure 13.25 Customer satisfaction is at the heart of the selling process

According to Sarah Cook in her book *Customer Care*, customer relationships can be depicted in terms of a loyalty ladder (see Figure 13.26). The willingness of individual customers to ascend the loyalty ladder will depend upon how they are treated when doing business with the organisation. Well-targeted sales methods and efficient personal service will help to convert one-off purchasers to occasional users, then to regular customers and advocates.

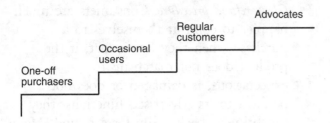

Figure 13.26 The loyalty ladder

In developing a relationship with its customers, an organisation must concentrate on both the selling process and how the relationship between the buyer and seller is managed. This is part of what is widely known as relationship marketing, where an organisation has to develop all its activities in ways that take into account how their activities may affect their relationships with customers. Examples are order times, reputation, the changing of goods or providing of refunds, dealing with faults, correctly addressing letters and the overall efficiency of operations.

In developing suitable ways of meeting the needs of their customers, organisations have to balance their own objectives against the needs of customers (see Figure 13.27). To be able to do this, they need to understand how customers view their organisation as well as what their customers want from their organisation.

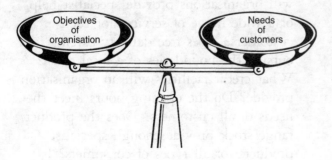

Figure 13.27 Balancing an organisation's objectives against the needs of customers

The starting point in providing customers with appropriate customer service is to identify potential customers and their expectations by listening to their views, so that the organisation can develop suitable service procedures to satisfy their needs. For example, they need to find out:

• what customers want

• how important this is for them

• why they need to have it

• how to provide it in the best possible way.

Check your understanding

On the basis of your own experiences, provide two examples of: **a** good customer service; and **b** poor customer service. In each instance, explain how these affected your repeat-purchasing patterns.

Roderick M. McNealy, in his book *Making Satisfaction Happen*, refers to the 'Making Customer Satisfaction Happen' model (Figure 13.28). This, he claims, is a continuous circular process that provides an

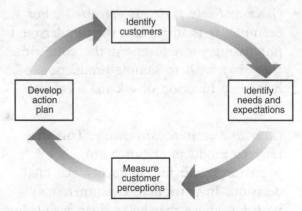

Figure 13.28 The Making Customer Satisfaction Happen model

equation for satisfying customer needs that can then be used as part of an organisation's strategic approach to business.

Avis, the car-hire company, have a customer care balance sheet that takes into account business they may be losing from both customers who complain and from those who are dissatisfied but who do not bother to complain (see Figure 13.29). This emphasises the need to listen to customers and refers to the 'customer care' balance sheet which shows the annual sales lost from customers whose needs have not been met.

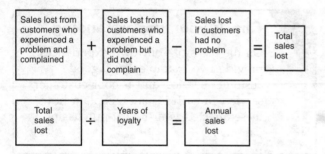

Figure 13.29 Customer care balance sheet

So, what do customers want and how can their expectations be satisfied by the different services and selling methods provided by an organisation? Customers may require the following:

- *Quick and easy purchasing procedures.* For example, it is important they understand purchasing procedures. At the same time they may wish to sample products, see how they function or ask for specialist help.

- *Clear and accurate information.* This may refer to products or purchasing procedures, and may influence the final decision. In particular, consumers may wish for advice that helps them weigh up a range of alternatives.

- *Clear refund procedure.* Consumers are much happier to commit themselves to a purchase when they know that, if the product does not match up to expectations, is damaged or does not perform to its advertised functions, they can bring it back easily for a refund. Many supermarkets have a refund desk at their entrance, and some large organisations, such as Marks & Spencer, have a good reputation for dealing with returns.

- *Easy exchange of goods.* Similarly, exchanging goods if they are not suitable helps to provide a service that closely meets the needs of customers.

- *Complaints procedur.e* There is nothing worse than customers having their complaints passed around from person to person and department to department. This creates a bad impression of the organisation, wastes time and may cause a lot of personal anguish. An efficient customer complaints procedure may help to retain business that might otherwise be lost if the complaint is handled inefficiently.

- *Special services to meet special needs.* Different groups of customers may have different needs. For example, how many stores can cope with wheelchair access or mothers with young children in buggies? Similarly, will organisations provide specialist help or a wide range of services for their customers? Does free delivery extend outside the boundaries of a local town? What credit facilities will an organisation provide? Do the opening hours meet the needs of all customers? Does the product range stock provide enough specialist products for all types of consumers? Is there a customer helpline . . . and do customers know about it? Is the organisation willing to order products on behalf of customers? See Figure 13.30.

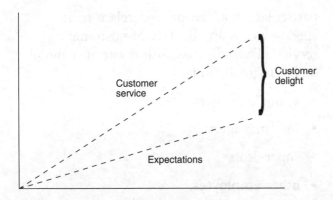

Figure 13.30   Exceeding customer expectations

Figure 13.31   The steps in establishing the need for a new customer service strategy

A *training needs analysis* may be carried out by the personnel department or by someone from outside the organisation. This may take place after a discussion and after interviewing a few members of staff. The needs analysis should identify the dimensions required for a new customer service strategy. It will create a picture of current skills and attitudes towards customer service and identify areas that need to be developed in the future (see Figure 13.32).

> ### Check your understanding
>
> Working in groups, decide what procedures a large retailer of computers should put into place to ensure customers are happy with the service provided.

Training in customer service

It has been said that training is an essential part of any customer service provision. Although the degree of training may depend upon the priorities of a business organisation, it is generally accepted that training in service quality is not just about developing a customer care philosophy but about providing employees with the specific skills and attitude of mind to deal with customer service issues in a retailing workplace.

The first step in assessing the training requirements for customer service is to look at how well employees are already trained in customer service, and then look at what they need to meet the new customer service strategy (Figure 13.31).

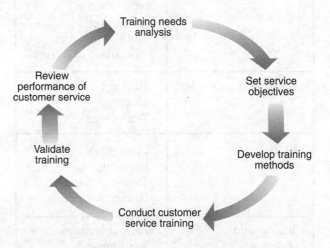

Figure 13.32   Customer service training cycle

> **Discussion point**
>
> Could it be argued that employees learn more about customer service from being in the workplace than from training?

Any training in customer service will prioritise the areas that require training and development most and then determine the methods required to meet these needs. There are a number of different training methods, some of which are shown in Figure 13.33. In developing the most appropriate, it is important to recognise that different employees will have different learning styles. Clearly, developing skills and understanding involves high levels of employee involvement, while telling and showing will require little participation from employees.

Method	Technique
Developing skills and understanding	Role playing Case studies Simulation Mentoring Work experience Workplace exercises
Discussion	Training exercises Meetings Workshops
Knowledge	Programmed learning Training manuals Group instruction
Telling and showing	Formal lectures Reading and booklists Demonstrations

Figure 13.33 Employee training methods

It is argued that most training in customer service is simply common sense. The training may help those who have developed bad habits to get back on track and also improve the attitudes of staff. A typical programme will be unique to a particular organisation and relate to its specific needs in the area of customer service. Training may also occur at a range of levels, to include:

- senior managers
- line managers
- supervisors
- other employees.

A typical workshop for employees might include the following:

1 An explanation of why an organisation is undertaking a customer service strategy.

2 A definition of service quality and customer care, with clear examples.

3 An assessment of current performance.

4 The setting of customer service standards.

5 A customer service action plan to meet such standards.

6 A description of how the process of customer service will continue.

Check your understanding

Working in a team of five or six people, develop a customer service strategy for your school or college, using the guidelines contained within the workshop outline above.

It must be remembered that any form of training aids an employee's personal and professional development as part of his or her career. Once training has taken place, an organisation needs to record each employee's training achievements and use this as a basis for ongoing training and development.

Unit 3 Assessment

You need to produce a marketing strategy for a new or existing product. Your strategy will need to include evidence and information about how it is based on principles of marketing; how you have used sources of primary and secondary information; how you have analysed the impact of the external environment on your appropriate strategy; how you developed a coherent mix of strategies to meet consumer needs; and an evaluation.

A key element in undertaking this assignment is making an appropriate choice of product or service and undertaking the relevant research processes. Remember that it is the output and interpretation of these research processes that help to provide the justification for the strategies you wish to undertake. In a rapidly changing and more competitive environment, making decisions is not just about going with a 'hunch', but more about making measured judgements on the basis of concrete evidence that ensures risks are minimised.

You may wish to base your strategy upon either close knowledge of the market for a product or service or on a period of work placement. Remember to try to talk to as many people as possible about the decisions you intend to take. Your strategy should be extensively supported with research evidence obtained from a range of sources, and sufficiently justified.

To achieve a grade E you must show you can:

- Appropriately identify, collect and use primary and secondary data relevant to the marketing strategy.

- Judge a marketing strategy for a product or service with a clear understanding of the principles of marketing.

- Clearly analyse the external influences affecting the development of the marketing strategy.

- Create a realistic rationale for the development of a coherent marketing mix for the product or service.

- Understand a marketing strategy for a product or service with a clear grasp of the principles of marketing.

- Use presentation skills effectively in explaining one aspect of your marketing strategy to an informed audience.

To achieve a grade C you must also show you can:

- Explain how your understanding of marketing and market research affects your choice of marketing strategy.

- Independently identify, collect and use information relevant to the marketing strategy.

- Identify and explain the links between your analysis of external influences and the development of your marketing strategy.

- Make well-reasoned proposals for your marketing mix, clearly linking the proposals to information generated by your analysis.

To achieve a grade A you must also show you can:

- Evaluate the reliability of different marketing models used.

a Independently identify and collect a range of information relevant to the marketing strategy and apply appropriate methods for checking its validity.

- Use appropriate marketing models and tools to evaluate the likely success of the marketing strategy.

- Evaluate the reliability of the different marketing models used.

• Develop a coherent and well-balanced marketing strategy that reflects appropriate use of marketing models and tools.

Opportunities to develop key skills

As a natural part of carrying out this unit, doing the work set out in the text and through your assessments, you will be developing key skills. Here's how:

Application of number, Level 3

When you are:	You should be able to develop the following key skills evidence:
• Identifying, collecting and using primary and secondary data. This should involve planning and interpreting information from different sources including a large data set of over 50 items. This could be published data rather than data you collect yourself	N3.1 Plan, and interpret information from two different types of sources, including a large data set.

Communication, Level 3

When you are:	You should be able to develop the following key skills evidence:
• Describing your marketing strategy in a group discussion	C3.1a Contribute to a group discussion about a complex subject.
• Presenting part of your strategy in the role of a marketing executive, you must make a persuasive presentation to fellow employees or an agency about one aspect of the marketing strategy you are proposing. You need to understand the importance of presenting information clearly in a well-structured format to suit different audiences	C3.1b Make a presentation about a complex subject, using at least one image to illustrate complex points.
• Researching information for the report	C3.2 Read and synthesise information from two extended documents about a complex subject. One document should include at least one image to illustrate complex points.
• Producing the report	C3.3 Write two different types of documents about complex subjects. One piece of writing should be an extended document and include at least one image.

Information technology, Level 3

When you are:	You should be able to develop the following key skills evidence:

- Identifying and collecting primary data for example, accessing information about marketing, market research reports, and individual business using the Internet and adapting it for your own use

  IT3.1 Plan and use different sources to search for, and select, information required for two different purposes.
  IT3.2 Explore, develop, and exchange information to meet two different purposes.

- Collecting and using primary and secondary data

  IT3.2 Explore, develop, and exchange information and derive new information to meet two different purposes.

- Developing a marketing mix using different data and sets to develop materials

  IT3.3 Present information from different sources for two different purposes and audiences.
  Your work must include at least one example of text, one example of images and one example of numbers.

Problem solving, Level 3

When you are:

You should be able to develop the following key skills evidence:

- Planning the collection of primary and secondary data, you will need to establish how and where the data can be obtained from

  PS3.1 Recognise, explore and describe the problem, and agree the standards for its solution.

- Deciding between different sources of data or between types of secondary data

  PS3.2 Generate and compare at least two options which could be used to solve the problem, and justify the option for taking forward.

- Using the source of data identified, you will review whether it was the right option

  PS3.3 Plan and implement at least one option for solving the problem, and review progress towards its solution.

Working with others, Level 3

When you are:

You should be able to develop the following key skills evidence:

- Selecting information about the product you are investigating, you will need to plan where and from whom, information can be obtained

  WO3.1 Plan the activity with others, agreeing objectives, responsibilities and working arrangements.

- Collecting the information you need from other people and reviewing targets with your tutor

  WO3.2 Work towards achieving the agreed objectives, seeking to establish and maintain co-operative working relationships in meeting your responsibilities.

- Reviewing your work in order to establish that you have collected all the information that you need

WO3.3 Review the activity with others against the agreed objectives and agreed ways of enhancing collaborative work.

Whether you eventually start working for a business or become self-employed, this unit will give you an invaluable insight into how businesses recruit, retain and manage one of their key resources – people. If businesses are to achieve their objectives, they must plan their human resources function so they have the right number of employees with the right kinds of qualifications and training to meet the needs of the business.

You may have part-time working experience and will know first-hand how important it is for a business to keep employees motivated, to monitor their performance and to help them develop continually through additional training.

In this unit you will learn how businesses approach all these different aspects of human resources planning and management. You will have the opportunity to draw on and extend your own experience of this very important aspect of business.

This unit links to the work on how businesses are organised in Unit 1 Business at work and your understanding of the labour market gained in Unit 2 The competitive business environment. Knowledge and skills in this unit will contribute to Unit 6 Business planning. The human resources overview you produce for assessment can also be drawn on for evidence for Unit 6.

This unit is assessed through your portfolio work. The grade on that assessment will be your grade for this unit.

Chapter 14 Human resources planning

Businesses have to plan carefully to ensure they have the right number of suitable employees for their needs. To do this they need a good understanding of the labour market in the areas where they operate. You need to be able to consider the effects of the following labour market factors for human resources planning:

- local employment trends
- local skills shortages
- competition for employees
- availability of labour.

Human resources planning also involves looking at how labour is organised within the business. You need to understand why businesses must take account of a range of factors when making decisions about their internal staffing. The factors include:

- labour turnover (stability index, wastage rate)
- sickness and accident rates
- age, skills and training
- succession.

You need to know how to use statistics to analyse these factors where appropriate.

Human resource management (HRM)

In the last decade of the twentieth century, we saw a transformation in the way companies started dealing with the people who were their employees. Instead of seeking to get the best out of people just for the sake of the business – i.e. to help it achieve its objectives – the new emphasis termed 'human resource management' (HRM) was that people would only work their best for the company if the company gave priority to identifying and seeking to meet the personal needs and objectives of its employees.

This distinction is very subtle – but it is an important distinction to understand (see Figure 14.1).

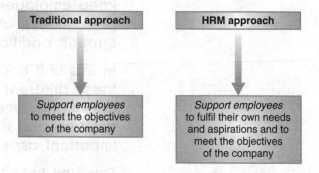

Figure 14.1   The distinction between the traditional and the HRM approach to employees

A second important change in people management in the 1990s was a recognition in many business organisations that 'people work' was not just the responsibility of the 'personnel' department. It is the responsibility of all managers in an organisation – supported by HRM specialists. Increasingly, responsibility for recruitment, selection, appraisal and training in an organisation is carried out by managers who work on an ongoing basis with employees rather than by a specialist in a centralised HRM function.

A third key change in people management was that HRM was given a great deal more status in the organisation. Instead of being something carried on at lower levels of the organisation, HRM is now recognised as a key 'strategic' area of the organisation (i.e. one that needs to be given a high priority in organisational planning involving senior managers).

Many organisations have moved away from 'personnel management' to the new 'human resource management'.

Case study: Contradictions in human resource policy

One of the great ironies of the 1990s was that, while it was the decade of human resource management, it was also the decade that saw one of the greatest restructurings of business in this country, which led to mass unemployment (which only really began to disappear in 1998 and 1999). During the 1990s all the talk in companies was of HRM – that people were the most important resource of an organisation and that people should not be regarded as a cost but as a benefit to the organisation.

The 1990s was the decade in which the information and communications technology revolution began to drive home, leading to mass redundancies in industries such as banking and insurance. The privatisation of industries in the 1980s led to massive downsizing in the newly privatised industries, while major companies like the oil giants Shell and BP shook out thousands of employees. The early years of the 1990s saw organisations strip down their core workforce, increasingly to use contracted-out labour and part-time workers. All this was done in the name of cost-cutting and efficiency in an increasingly competitive global economy.

Meanwhile, the human resource managers were talking about HRM as a strategic function of the organisation, and as the responsibility of all managers. They were saying it was essential to find out what people wanted in the organisation through processes such as appraisal; that people should be empowered through teamworking; and that self-managed teams would lead to greater satisfaction at work.

It is not surprising that, by the late 1990s, many people were cynical about the nature of HRM. Empowerment seemed to apply to those whose jobs were most secure but who had to work hardest to retain their jobs by working longer hours with less job security. Meanwhile, the high level of redundancies in many companies in the first half of the 1990s led to stress and insecurity.

1   Why was it difficult during the 1990s for human resource managers to sell the idea of HRM to employees?

2   Do you think HRM is a good idea?

3   Why might it work better in the first decade of the twenty-first century?

4   Are companies still continuing to downsize? What are the implications for the ongoing success of HRM initiatives?

CHARACTERISTIC EXAMPLES

A reduction in hierarchy and the blurring of the distinction between management and non-management.	The use of quality circles, where employees are part of a team and responsible for their own self-management and regulation. For example, employees in a quality circle in a Jaguar car factory may set their own production targets.
Responsibility for people-management is devolved to line managers. Personnel professionals support and facilitate.	Line managers are responsible for the appraisal of staff and staff development, personnel professionals may offer support through appraisal training for staff and staff managers.
Planning of human resources is part of overall corporate planning.	The mission statements of many organisations today include references to the place of human resources, e.g. – to secure the optimum personal development of company members.
Employees are viewed as individuals with the potential for development, in line with the needs of the organisation.	Many organisations have appraisal systems which focus on the continuing professional development of staff.
Management and non-management are committed to common goals, and have an interest in the success of the organisation.	The increased emphasis on teams in organisations, means that more people are involved in identifying goals and should therefore be more committed to them.

Figure 14.2   The characteristics of HRM

According to Krulis-Randa, a writer on people management, the new HRM has the characteristics as shown in Figure 14.2.

Check your understanding

How has the emphasis on looking after people at work changed in recent years? Is this a good thing?

Human resources planning

Human resources planning is concerned with getting the right people, using them well and developing them in order to meet the goals of the organisation. In order to meet the organisation's aims successfully, it is necessary to identify the means of using people in the most effective way and to identify any problems that are likely to occur (for example in recruiting the best people), and then coming up with solutions to the problems identified.

For example, if a UK-based retailing organisation decides to expand into France and Germany, it will need to identify:

• The skills and competences it will need the new employees to have.

• How many people with these capabilities it will be able to recruit.

• Ways of training and developing people to meet these skill requirements.

Figure 14.3 shows the various stages in the human resource planning process. The top left-hand side of the diagram is concerned with an analysis of the likely future supply of the right sorts of people, while the top

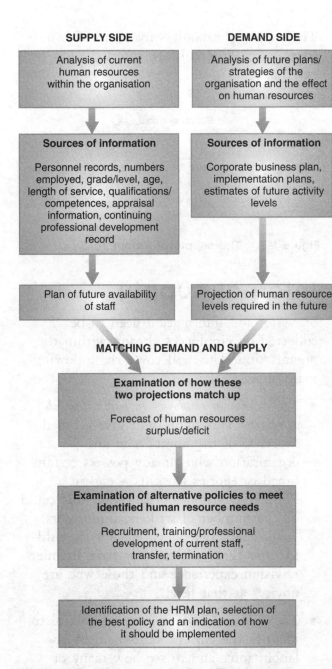

SUPPLY SIDE

Analysis of current human resources within the organisation

⬇

Sources of information

Personnel records, numbers employed, grade/level, age, length of service, qualifications/ competences, appraisal information, continuing professional development record

⬇

Plan of future availability of staff

DEMAND SIDE

Analysis of future plans/ strategies of the organisation and the effect on human resources

⬇

Sources of information

Corporate business plan, implementation plans, estimates of future activity levels

⬇

Projection of human resource levels required in the future

MATCHING DEMAND AND SUPPLY

Examination of how these two projections match up

Forecast of human resources surplus/deficit

⬇

Examination of alternative policies to meet identified human resource needs

Recruitment, training/professional development of current staff, transfer, termination

⬇

Identification of the HRM plan, selection of the best policy and an indication of how it should be implemented

Figure 14.3   The stages in the HRM process

right-hand side looks at the expected future demand for the right sorts of people. The human resources plan is concerned with ways of matching up these two sides.

We will first examine the demand factors that influence human resource planning before going on to look at supply conditions.

Demand side

An organisation's demand for labour will depend on the plans the organisation has for the future, in particular the big plans – what we refer to as 'strategic plans'. For example, in early 2000 Wal-Mart, the new owner of Asda in the UK was seeking to increase its market share quickly in the UK. At the start of 2000, Tesco was the leading supermarket in the UK followed by Sainsbury's. Both these two had nearly twice as many stores as Asda. Wal-Mart, therefore, set out on an expansion programme of opening new stores. This was its strategic plan. In order to support this expansion plan it needed to recruit a great many more employees.

Asda Wal-Mart's expansion in the UK has created many new jobs

Forecasting the demand for human resources

An organisation's demand for human resources must be estimated by analysing its future plans and by estimating the levels of activity within the business. For example, a Premier Division football club's estimates would depend on its projection of where it expects to be in the league in the coming season. If it is seeking to maintain a top position in the UK and to do well in European Championships, it will need to employ more players (including overseas players), it may need a larger training staff, backroom office staff, security staff on match days, more people in the club shop, etc. The demand for staff is related to the demand for the club's goods and services. A hotel complex may have a corporate plan that includes substantial expansion to open a leisure complex. Clearly, these long-term plans will affect the numbers of people which the hotel group employs and the sorts of skills and experience required.

Methods of forecasting demand

Management estimates

Managers may be asked to forecast their staff requirements. They will do this on the basis of past, present and likely future requirements.

Work study techniques

Over the years much work has gone into work study. Work study specialists work out how long various jobs take, using available machinery and equipment. Provided they know what output/sales are likely to be, they can calculate the numbers of employees required and the hours they will need to work.

Supply side

If an organisation is to work out the supply of labour available it must examine the numbers of people available to work, how long they can work for, their ability to do the required jobs, their productivity (output per head) and other factors.

The supply of labour is made up of two sources (see Figure 14.4): internal and external.

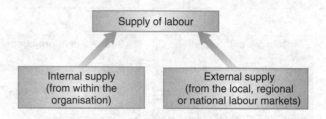

Figure 14.4   The supply of labour

Internal supply

Statistics and information need to be collected on employees already within the organisation. This will cover the following main areas:

- *The number of employees in particular job categories.* This figure will give a broad overview of the numbers in an organisation who already possess certain broad categories of skills – e.g. in a Premier Division football team this could be the number of strikers, midfielders, goalkeepers, defenders, etc. Or it could identify those who already have Premier Division experience and those who are novices at that level.

- *The skills available.* It may be helpful to identify the current skills held by the labour force and to see how many of these are transferable (a skill used in one particular job may be transferable to another job).

- *Skills analysis.* An organisation needs to be sure it has the right number of people available at the right time but also with the right skills. Organisations, therefore, need to assess their present supply of skills across their workforces and to identify the sorts of skills they will require in the future.

A skills inventory of current employees will indicate those who have received recent training and those who will require training. It may be possible to meet the human resource requirements of an organisation by training and developing current staff rather than recruiting externally (this is often a cheaper option and also helps to motivate people who are already working for you).

- *Performance results.* An organisation will want to gather information about the level of performance of various categories of current employees. This sort of information may be collected in a quantitative form (e.g. numbers of items produced of acceptable quality, number of rejected items because of poor quality, etc.). In addition information may be collected that is of a qualitative nature (e.g. information from appraisal interviews).

- *Promotion potential.* Internal promotions will change the availability of existing resources. It is useful to the organisation to know how many employees have the skills and aptitude for promotion to more demanding roles. In addition, it is useful to know how many employees have the potential, with suitable training, for promotion.

- *Age distribution and length of service.* Look at the people who work for an organisation. What impression do you get about the age of the people working there? If there are too many older people then the organisation may be storing up problems for itself: there may be too many people who are soon going to retire, thus leaving the organisation without sufficient experienced workers.

If you find an organisation with too many young people, you may find that people are not staying long enough to make their mark on the organisation. Perhaps promotion prospects are blocked in the organisation so that people are leaving.

It is important, therefore, to be able to plan retirements within the organisation so that you keep a good balance between people who have been in the organisation for a long time and people who are bringing new ideas into the organisation.

- *Staff turnover.* Staff turnover should be analysed in order to help an organisation forecast future losses and to identify the reasons people leave the organisation. A degree of staff turnover may be advantageous to an organization, as fresh staff can be recruited, promotion channels may be opened up and it may allow for natural wastage when an organisation is trying to reduce its workforce. Too high a level of staff turnover will mean that there will be high additional costs of staff replacement and recruitment, additional training costs, and disruption to the quality of service or to production.

Techniques for forecasting internal employee supply: labour turnover

It is possible to measure the rate at which people are leaving (or staying with) an organisation by using two simple methods:

- employee wastage rate
- labour stability rate.

Employee wastage rate

It is possible to calculate the number of staff leaving a business as a percentage of those who could have left:

$$\text{Wastage rate} = \frac{\text{Number of staff leaving in time period}}{\text{Average number of staff employed in time period}} \times 100$$

For example, if a hospital employed a nursing staff of 400 but found that 100 nurses left during the year, the wastage rate would be:

$$\frac{100}{400} \times 100 = 25\%$$

Such information is used to predict likely turnover in the future, to see if there is a need to examine in detail the reasons for the high turnover and to find out if there is need to recruit new staff to replace those leaving.

While the labour turnover index is useful, as with most statistics it needs to be considered alongside other factors. For example, are there particular areas of the organisation where the rate of leavers is high? It would also be useful to identify the leavers' length of service: are the most experienced people leaving, or people with relatively little experience?

Labour stability rate

As well as the wastage rate, some organisations make use of a labour stability index. This provides an indication of the tendency for employees with long service to remain with the organisation, thus linking the leaving rate with the length of service:

$$\text{Stability index} = \frac{\text{Number of staff leaving with more than 1 year's service}}{\text{Number employed 1 year ago}} \times 100$$

If we take the example of a Premier Division football club (first team players only), where the number employed at the start of the 2000–2001 season who had been with the club for over a year was 44, and during the season 11 experienced players

---

Check your understanding

Figure 14.5 shows the numbers of employees in a large advertising agency over a ten-year period.

	1991	1992	1993	1994	1995	1996	1997	1998	1999	2000	2001
Number of employees	120	130	135	140	130	120	136	142	150	176	154
Number leaving	4	4	5	8	15	15	15	12	12	25	40

Figure 14.5 Advertising agency: employees

1 Calculate the wastage rate in each year.

2 What factors might have contributed to the change in the wastage rate over the years?

3 How could you calculate the wastage rate for groups of employees with different levels of experience of working for the company?

Case study: Shelbourne School

Shelbourne School is a small rural comprehensive school. For much of the 1970s and 1980s it retained most of its staff, who were happy to work in a caring and supportive atmosphere. Many staff had children who attended the school and they had confidence in the headteacher. Results were good and parents were happy with performance.

However, during the early 1990s the Conservative government was increasingly putting pressure on schools to produce league tables and to meet performance standards related to students gaining A–C passes at GCSE. Comparisons were made between one school and another. The implication was that while Shelbourne School was above the national average, some people suggested it could do better, including the Chair of the Governors.

Eventually, the existing head felt she was being pushed out and so took early retirement in 1994. A new dynamic head came into the school to drive up standards and to make changes that would raise Shelbourne's GCSE pass rate in the A–C category from 50% of pupils to 60%. The emphasis was to be on putting more staff time into students who might achieve only three or four A–C passes but, with greater staff support, could be pushed into the five A–C grades category.

Figure 14.6 shows the staff wastage rate during the time of transition to the new head (who managed to raise the GCSE pass rate to 55% by the summer of 2000).

	1992	1993	1994	1995	1996	1997	1998	1999	2000
Number of staff employed	100	100	100	100	99	98	97	96	95
Number of staff leaving	1	0	1	1	5	4	10	12	14

Figure 14.6   Shelbourne School: staff wastage rate

1   Calculate the wastage rate in each of the years shown. What has been happening to the wastage rate?

2   What possible explanations could be given for changes in the wastage rate?

3   Do you think the wastage rate reflects well on the school?

were transferred out, then the labour stability index would be:

$$\frac{11}{44} \times 100 = 25\%$$

Knowing about the existing labour force enables an organisation to make the most of the skill and potential already present within the organisation. However, consideration of the availability of people from the local and national labour markets is also vital.

> ### Check your understanding
>
> Work out the labour stability index for your school or college over the last three years. Or work out the labour stability index for your local football team over the same period.
>
> What factors might have led to the changes you have identified in the index over the period covered?

The external labour market

The external labour market for any particular organisation is made up of potential employees, locally, regionally or nationally, who have the skills and experience required at a particular time. There are a range of factors that affect the size and nature of these labour markets.

The national labour market

There are a number of factors to take into consideration when examining the supply of labour in the national market.

Trends in the size/characteristics of the working population

Changes in the age distribution of the UK population will affect the human resource planning of most organisations. The UK has an ageing population, with fewer school-leavers and young workers available for employment. This means that business may need to look to other sectors of the population to meet their human resource requirements. For example, they may need to attract more women back into the workforce or to employ older workers. Some employers actively recruit older workers, e.g. B & Q, the DIY store.

Competition for labour

Where the demand for people with specific skills is high, there will be competition between employers to attract people with those skills. For example, in the first decade of the twenty-first century, employees with information and communications technology skills are at a premium. Employers are therefore continually seeking to offer attractive work packages to ICT graduates in order to attract the best recruits away from rivals.

The overall level of economic activity

Whether the economy is in a boom or a recession will determine the general level of demand for goods and services in the economy and, hence, for employees. In a recovery or boom period, people will generally have more to spend and, therefore, the demand for goods and services will rise. This in turn will lead firms to increase output and therefore increase the demand for labour.

At the start of 2000, unemployment in this country was at a 20-year low. While this is good for the economy, it makes it difficult for human resource planners because of the difficulty of recruiting the right sorts of labour with the right sorts of skills.

Education and training opportunities

The education and training opportunities available to people will affect both the numbers of people coming into the labour market and their overall skill level. In Britain over recent years, there has been an increasing number of young people participating in both further and higher education.

The reasons for this have included more opportunities to stay in education as well as a lack of job opportunities (until 1999/2000). Young people also appreciate the need for higher skill levels in order to compete in the job market.

The effect of government policies

Government legislation can affect the labour market in a number of ways. The government provides incentives to organisations to employ and train people. Where such incentives are available, they will reduce the costs of labour and therefore have implications for human resource planning.

In recent years, the emphasis in this country (and in Europe) on lifelong learning has meant the general skill levels of the working population have been improving. The development of new AVCE (Advanced Certificates in Education) and NVQs (vocational qualifications specifically tied to particular occupations) has led to an increased number of people having the right sorts of skills for the economy.

At the same time there have been increased efforts to make sure the curriculum in schools for all children helps them to fit better into the workforce of the future – e.g. a strong emphasis on numeracy, literacy and information and communications technology skills. All these government initiatives have led to a shift to the right in the supply curve of labour – providing more employees in the labour market (see

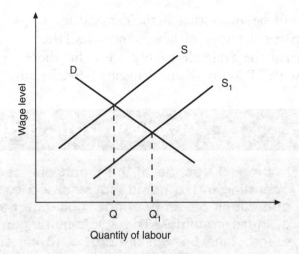

Figure 14.7   Government training initiatives have increased the supply of labour

Figure 14.7). The government's New Deal (providing work for the young and the unemployed by subsidising firms to recruit such employees) has again increased the supply of labour.

In Figure 14.7 the supply of labour shifts to the right showing that through improved training more people with the right skills are available to work at each and every wage level. The net impact is to increase the quantity of labour from Q to Q1 and to reduce wages in occupations where training has been concentrated. (Of course students

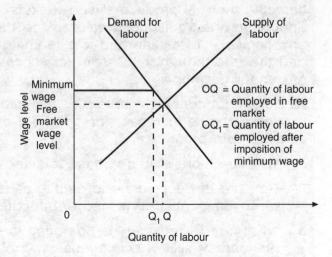

Figure 14.8   The impact of the minimum wage

will be aware that if the demand for a particular type of labour increases faster than the available supply – e.g. for those with IT skills where demand is forecast to outstrip supply by about 350,000 by the year 2003 – wages will increase, rather than fall in those sectors.

Case study: Skills shortage in Asia

In the first decade of the twenty-first century, the number of UK-based businesses operating in the newly industrialised countries of Asia is growing. Staffing these operations presents a real challenge because of a critical skills shortage in several of these countries. The solutions human resource professionals recruiting for these areas come up with are crucial to the success of their organisations.

The boom in Asian economic growth (notwithstanding the 1998 crash) has created a huge, unmatched demand for skilled workers. Malaysia, which produces 5,700 engineers each year, requires almost double that number to satisfy its need for skilled labour. South Korea estimates 340,000 engineers are necessary – 60,000 more than it is graduating. Singapore has turned to other Asian countries for relief. Thirty per cent of its information and communications technology professionals have been imported from India, Australia, the Philippines and China.

Singapore's importation approach is only a short-term solution. Obtaining the necessary government clearance to hire foreign workers can be difficult. Another option, transferring British employees to Asian facilities, is just too expensive, and failure to hire local workers could strain the delicate relationship between UK companies operating in these newly industrialised countries and their host governments.

As a result, companies need to devote more resources to training and developing existing employees (for example, by setting up colleges and training departments in these countries, and perhaps by paying the costs of university courses).

Companies are also co-operating with their host government to develop school curricula that will produce skilled workers. In several Asian countries, secondary education has traditionally emphasised the qualities needed to excel in a factory environment – discipline and rote learning. New curricula that encourage creativity and the free thought necessary for success in the coming era of knowledge work are under development.

As additional countries implement new programmes the number of skilled workers available should increase. Taiwan, India and the Philippines have already made considerable progress.

1   Why are more skilled workers required in southeast Asia?

2   How are the numbers and quality of skilled workers influenced by:
    a) government policy; and b) educational initiatives?

3   What can UK companies operating in southeast Asia do to increase the numbers of skilled employees available?

Other government measures, however, work in the opposite direction. For example, the guarantee of a minimum wage has meant that employers are less keen to employ labour that was previously cheaper to employ, and the creation of increased employment rights, such as the Working Time Directive (setting maximum hours people have to work) and guaranteed holiday entitlements, has acted as a disincentive to some employers (see Figure 14.8).

Local employment

For many companies, the state of the local labour market is as significant as what is happening nationally or regionally. Firms need to know about the supply of labour in the locations where they are operating. They need to know about current and future supply trends. A report published in December 1999 showed that it is a gross simplification to think of the UK simply in terms of a north–south divide. The report showed that a more accurate picture is of a relatively prosperous south with pockets of poverty and a relatively less prosperous north with pockets of prosperity. In the jobs market the gaps between regional unemployment rates in 2000 were lower than they had been for 20 years, but the southeast had far lower unemployment (3.7%) – than the northeast (10.1%). The southeast also had the highest proportion of its working-age population in employment, the lowest proportion of the UK workforce with no qualifications and the lowest proportion claiming benefits.

These sorts of statistics are essential to a business organisation in understanding local supply conditions. Further information is provided by local employment offices and job centres, which hold details of unemployment figures for their particular areas.

Local employers will also want to know about local wage rates and income levels in order to pitch an appropriate wage level to attract the right sort of employees. In January 2000 the average disposable income per head stood at £12,184 in London and £11,859 in the southeast, compared with just £9,600 in Northern Ireland and £10,000 in Scotland.

The sorts of information the organisation will need to know about local employment trends are discussed below.

Local employment trends

Local unemployment levels give an indication of the general availability of labour and suggest whether it will be easy or difficult to recruit. It is also important to find out more about which organisations in a locality have been laying off workers. Often, when a major employer closes down or discards labour, this provides an opportunity for another local company, which may be able to employ the workers who have been made redundant. These employees might have the right sorts

Check your understanding

Collect information from your local newspaper and from your local job centre and unemployment office.

1   What is the current level of unemployment in your area? (This information should be available from your local job centre/unemployment office).

2   Has this figure been rising or falling? What has caused this trend?

3   Which industries/employers have been declining as employers of labour, and which industries/employers have been taking on more employees recently? (This information will be available from the regional office of your employment service – from the Employment Information Unit.)

of occupational skills or transferable skills that could be applied to similar work.

A study of local employment trends will give an idea of whether demand for certain types of work is rising or falling. Where demand increases this will lead to shortages (and also to rising wages).

Local skills shortages

Within any area at any one time, there will be jobs that are going into decline because the skills required for those jobs are becoming redundant. At the same time, new skills and capabilities will be emerging, and demand for these will be rising faster than supply. As a result, skills shortages will arise and these will cause considerable frustration for local employers. The wages of people in the skills shortages areas will be rising, and there will be competition to recruit and retain these scarce employees.

Where a local shortage occurs, employers will often seek to advertise and recruit in other areas – in other regions and from other countries. This is why, for example, there are many doctors from overseas working in both private practice and for the National Health Service the UK.

Organisations need to be aware of local skills shortages so they can develop their own training programmes to make sure there are enough people coming through with the skills required. They will also work together with other local employers in the same industry to support local school, college and university courses that train people in the skills required for these specific industries.

Competition for employees

An organisation will be interested to know whether its competitors are expanding and, therefore, increasing the demand for labour, or whether local redundancies mean labour is more readily available (see Figure 14.9).

Competitors expand	Competitors contract
Demand for labour in the locality increases.	Demand for labour in the locality falls.
Supply of labour contracts.	Supply of labour expands.
Leading to rising wage rates.	Leading to falling wage rates.
Increased difficulty in recruiting the right sort of employees	Easier to recruit the right sort of employees.

Figure 14.9 Competition for employees

Check your understanding

Examine the competition for employees between supermarkets in your area.

How many employees does each supermarket employ? What is the hourly wage rate for different types of employees? Which supermarkets are contracting and which are expanding? What difficulties are the firms that are contracting having in recruiting employees?

Check your understanding

Identify local skills shortages by studying articles from your local press, by interviewing human resource planners in local organisations and by seeking information from the Employment Information Unit of your local employment services.

What actions are local employers taking to deal with these skills shortages (e.g. running their own training courses, recruiting outside the locality, supporting local educational initiatives, etc.)?

Availability of labour

The amount of labour in a particular area depends on the number of people available for work. With modern transport systems it is usually quite easy for people to travel to work, but an organisation may need to develop its own systems to make it easier for people to undertake the journeys – e.g. a works bus. With many modern employers locating on the outskirts of towns, the issue of getting the right numbers of the right sorts of people to work is an important one.

The availability of labour will depend on such factors as the age distribution of the local population (although this tends to follow national patterns), attitudes to women working and the extent to which young people stay on at school, college or go on to higher education.

Check your understanding

Find out from the Employment Information Unit at your regional employment office of the employment service, what is happening to the numbers of people available for work in your area.

What is the trend? What factors have particularly influenced this trend in recent times?

The effectiveness of employee organisation

The effectiveness with which an organisation runs its human resources policies can be measured by the level of employee satisfaction, and this is where stability indexes and wastage rates are so important. If employees are content with their work, they are most likely to turn up for work. Levels of stress and stress-related absenteeism increase when there is a poor human relations atmosphere.

Sickness and accident rates

Most companies will keep a record of the following:

- *Notified absences.* When employees are going to be absent from work (e.g. to attend a funeral, a hospital appointment, a wedding, etc.).

- *Absences due to sickness.* Employees will need to produce a doctor's note so that they are entitled to sickness benefits, etc.

- *Unauthorised absences.* When employees simply do not turn up for work, without telling anyone.

As a result of these records, a firm can record absences as a percentage of the hours/days, etc., that could possibly have been worked. Absence records can be kept for individual employees, groups of employees, and for the workforce as a whole.

Such a detailed statistical analysis enables the organisation to keep an eye on where problems lie – with an individual, with a particular section of workers or with the organisation as a whole. Comparisons can then be made with other workers and with past records (for the individual employee), with other teams/sections (for teams/sections) in the workplace, and with comparable organisations. Breaking down the statistics further highlights whether the problem lies with sickness or with unauthorised absence. And by keeping these records for a number of years, it is possible to establish trends.

Absences should be measured as a percentage of total time. For example, if an employee is due to work for 40 hours in the week but turns up for work for 32 hours only, then his or her absence level is:

$$\frac{8}{40} \times 100 = 20\%$$

If the total hours people in an organisation work in a week is 10,000 but they work only 9,500 of these, the absence rate is:

$$\frac{500}{10,000} \times 100 = 5\%$$

If 250 of the hours not worked were accountable to sickness, the sickness rate is:

$$\frac{250}{10,000} \times 100 = 2.5\%$$

Check your understanding

The XYZ Advertising Agency has 20 employees, each of whom is expected to work a 40-hour week. In the first week of September, only 18 employees work because two are sick for the whole week.

Calculate the sickness rate.

Accident rates are calculated by recording the number of accidents at work. Places of work should have a health and safety committee with the responsibility to:

- Investigate and report on accidents or incidents.

- Examine national health and safety reports and statistics.

- Review health and safety audit reports.

- Draw up works rules and instructions on safe working practices.

- Oversee health and safety training.

- Promote and advise on relevant publicity campaigns.

- Maintain links with external health and safety bodies.

- Recommend updates to the company safety policy.

- Consider and advise on impending legislation.

Part of the health and safety committee's responsibilities will be to ensure accurate records are kept of accidents at work.

The Reporting of Injuries, Diseases and Dangerous Occurrences Regulations 1985 (RIDDOR) set out that injuries resulting from accidents at work where an employee is incapacitated for three or more days must be reported to the authorities within seven days. Injuries involving fatalities must be notified immediately by the most practical means (e.g. by phone). Listed diseases must also be notified.

Organisations will, therefore, keep statistics on both minor accidents at work (i.e. ones however minor that involve some form of first aid) and accidents that have to be reported to the authorities under RIDDOR. Accident statistics relating to particular industries and organisations can then be collected nationally. In addition, organisations will want to keep internal statistics to make sure that undesirable trends do not occur. In the course of time organisations will want to see accident levels falling.

Accident rates can be calculated simply as the number of accidents per year within a chosen unit (team, firm, industry, etc.). In calculating accident rates in a particular industry or firm, the most accurate method is to calculate the statistics according to each employee working in the industry or per hour worked by employees in the industry. This is because some industries employ far more people than others and because the numbers employed change over time.

Check your understanding

Carry out research to find out about accident rates in a particular industry (e.g. agriculture, mining, etc.). How has the accident rate changed over the last ten years? In calculating this figure, try to make sure it accounts for changes in numbers employed in the industry so that meaningful comparisons can be made.

What has happened to the accident rate? Why?

Statistics for age, skills and training

As we have already seen, firms will have a range of employees who have worked for different lengths of time and who have different levels of skills and training. The human resource planner will seek to have a balance of new people entering an organization in order to cover those who are leaving. The human resource planner will also want to make sure that skill levels are rising within the organisation, and that training programmes are devised to make sure people have the skills to meet the firm's job requirements. If all your skilled people are just about to retire, you are quickly going to have to spend money on training to build up a new pool of expertise.

Case study: Age, skills and training at Babcock Engineering

Babcock Engineering is a company that produces items made from pewter, using skilled craftspeople. For example, they make pewter tankards, trays and sports trophies.

The firm employs 100 craft workers. The graphs in Figures 14.10–14.12 show:

• The age profile of employees.

• The skill levels of employees by age (NVQ Engineering).

• The percentage of employees who have received more than two weeks' training in the last year (by age).

1 Comment on the charts for Babcock Engineering in terms of age, skills and training.

2 What problems do you think Babcock Engineering is likely to be faced with in the near future?

3 What should Babcock Engineering be doing to try to counter these difficulties?

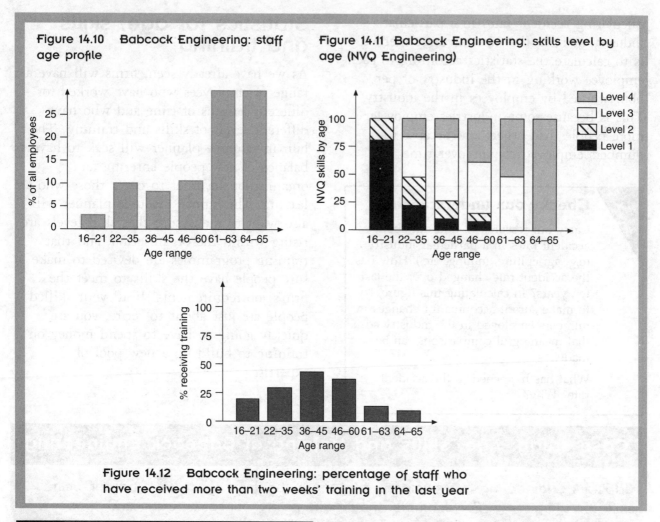

Figure 14.10   Babcock Engineering: staff age profile

Figure 14.11   Babcock Engineering: skills level by age (NVQ Engineering)

Figure 14.12   Babcock Engineering: percentage of staff who have received more than two weeks' training in the last year

Check your understanding

Produce a profile showing the ages, skill levels and amount of training different employees in a particular organisation have been given over a particular period of time. Show this information in a series of charts.

Succession

Succession is the way in which one person follows another person into a particular job or role within an organisation. Every organisation needs to make sure it is

grooming people to take on the responsibilities required. If it does not do this, it will suddenly find itself with a vacuum where it has not developed the people to move into the appropriate positions of responsibility, and the organisation will be missing the right people in key positions to hold the organisation together.

Check your understanding

Show how, in a particular organisation, people are being prepared to succeed others in important positions.

Chapter 15 Recruitment and selection

Businesses recruit staff for a variety of reasons. You need to know why and how decisions to recruit staff are made. These include:

- the growth of the business

- changing job roles within the business

- filling vacancies created by resignation, retirement or dismissal

- internal promotion.

You should understand that the recruitment process can be costly in terms of resources devoted to the process and costs associated with recruiting poor-performing staff. Therefore, it is important to select people accurately for interview. Businesses need to be very clear about the requirements of the job and about the kind of person they are looking for. You need to understand the ways in which they do this through:

- preparing job descriptions and person specifications

- carefully planning how and when to advertise

- identifying the strengths and weaknesses of job applications, curricula vitae and letters of application

- shortlisting candidates.

You need to understand how recruitment interviews are planned, carried out and evaluated.

You should be able to understand the legal and ethical responsibilities relating to equal opportunities, and know the key implications for recruitment of the following legislation:

- Equal Pay Act 1970

- Sex Discrimination Act 1975

- Race Relations Act 1976

- Disability Discrimination Act 1995.

You will also need to identify:

- the appropriate use of different methods of assessment, such as psychometric and aptitude testing

- good interview techniques

- criteria for evaluating the recruitment process.

You should be aware that interviews are also used for performance reviews and for people who are leaving.

You need to understand the importance of recruiting and maintaining a flexible workforce if a business is to remain competitive. You need to know about the different bases for recruiting people for a flexible workforce, including:

- different modes of employment

- different terms and conditions

- core employees

- part-time, temporary and contract labour.

You need to know how contracts of employment that help the business to achieve a flexible workforce are put together. You should understand the key elements of legislation that seeks to protect the rights of employees in relation to employment contracts.

Decisions to recruit staff

Organisations need to recruit staff for a number of reasons.

The growth of the business

When a business grows in size it will usually need more people to carry out:

- existing jobs (e.g. in a tin-box manufacturing company, it may need more production line operators when it moves from running three to four lines); and

- new jobs (e.g. the company may expand its sales operation overseas into France and Germany – so it needs sales staff who can speak French and German).

When existing jobs are being expanded, human resource specialists simply need to copy existing practice on a larger scale (e.g. by interviewing more people, advertising more widely, etc.). In creating new jobs more detailed thought is required, particularly if the jobs are quite different from those that already exist within the company.

Changing job roles within the business

In recent years most British businesses have changed their job structure. In particular, we have seen the decline of many routine, standardised jobs. Increasingly, employers have sought to develop new jobs involving information and communications technology, and which involve ground-level employees taking more responsibility for decision-making – through empowerment. Developing new jobs requires considerable research, often by examining best practice in an industry or by looking at the development of new jobs in other countries, particularly the USA.

Filling vacancies created by resignation, retirement or dismissal

In all organisations people move on. They get older, they hand in their notice or they are dismissed. In most cases it is necessary to replace the employee. However, the manager responsible for recruitment has to decide whether the firm wants a carbon copy of the previous job-holder or whether the job has moved on, requiring new skills and competences.

Internal promotion

In any good organisation there will be opportunities for internal promotion. Internal promotion gives an employee something to aim for in an organization, rather than looking elsewhere. When one person is promoted, it is often necessary to replace him or her.

Check your understanding

Examine new recruitment decisions in the place you work or in the educational institution where you are studying.

Why is the recruitment taking place? How is the recruitment taking place? How do human resource managers plan the recruitment process? Does the method chosen depend on the reason why the recruitment is taking place?

Getting the recruitment process right

The recruitment process can be very costly. It takes a great deal of time to set up an effective recruitment process – involving deciding on what the jobs that are to be recruited for will entail, advertising, sifting through applications, checking which applications best meet the criteria set down for the post, interviewing candidates and, finally, selecting the best candidate for the post.

There is considerable scope along the way for waste and inefficiency. For example, when a job advertisement attracts 100 applicants there is an opportunity for waste

when you reduce the original 100 down to six candidates. If you get your procedures wrong you may eliminate some of the best candidates right from the start and end up with six who are barely satisfactory. If you end up choosing an unsuitable candidate for the job, the company will suffer from having a poorly motivated person, who may make mischief within the organisation before walking out on the job and leaving the company to go through the expense of replacing him or her yet again.

Procedures for attracting and recruiting applicants

An organisation's most valuable resource is its workforce – the people who work for it. Managers therefore need to give careful thought to the needs of employees. An organisation can have all the latest technology and the best physical resources but, unless it looks after its people, it will never thrive and achieve optimum results.

Recruiting individuals to fill particular posts within a business can be done:

- internally, by recruiting within the firm

- externally, by recruiting people from outside.

The advantages of recruiting from within are as follows:

- Considerable savings can be made. Individuals with inside knowledge of how the business operates will need shorter periods of training and time for 'fitting in'.

- The organisation is unlikely to be disrupted by someone who is not used to working with others in the firm.

- Internal promotion acts as an incentive to all staff to work harder within the organisation.

- From the firm's point of view, the personnel staff should already have been able to assess the strengths and weaknesses of an insider. There is always a risk attached to employing an outsider, who may prove to be desirable 'on paper' only.

The disadvantages of recruiting from within are as follows:

- You will have to replace the person who has been promoted.

- An insider may be less likely to make the essential criticisms required to get the company working more effectively.

- Promotion of one person in a company may upset another.

Preparing job descriptions and person specifications

Job descriptions

From the human resource management department's point of view, the purpose of recruitment is to buy in and retain the best available human resources to meet the organisation's needs. Hence the first requirement is to define and set out what is involved in particular jobs.

This can be done by carrying out a job analysis, which leads on to an outline job description. For example, the job of a trainee manager in a supermarket could be described under the following key headings:

- Title of post.
- Supervisory/managerial responsibilities.
- Source(s) of supervision and guidance.
- A simple description of the role and duties of the employee within the organisation.
- Responsibility for assets, materials, etc.

A job description could be used as a job indicator for applicants. Alternatively, it could be used as a guideline for an employee and/or line manager as to his or her role and responsibility within the organisation. (It is not, however, a contract of employment.)

Job descriptions can be used by organisations to provide information for use in drafting a situations vacant advertisement and for briefing interviewers.

Job title

One of the most important parts of a job description is the job title. The job title should give a good indication of what the job entails. For example, you may hear people in organisations make statements such as 'She's supposed to be the Managing Director, let her make the decision' or

'Leave the word processing of letters to the secretary, that's not your job'. I heard a conversation between a lecturer and a porter concerning the carrying of boxes, which ended up with the remark: 'You're supposed to be a porter – get porting!'

When looking through job advertisements the first thing job applicants will look for (apart from the salary) will be the job title.

From time to time, job titles will change, often to give a slightly different feel to some jobs or to confer new status – the Principal of a college may become Chief Executive, a dustbin man may become a 'disposal services officer', etc.

Position within organisational structure

A job description will often establish where an individual stands in a particular organisational structure. This will mean that it can be clearly set out who the post-holder is accountable to, and who is accountable to him or her.

The position within an organisation will also give a clear idea of responsibilities. Job applicants will be interested to locate their position in order to ascertain whether their previous experience will be extensive enough, and to assess the kind of commitment they will be expected to make to the organisation.

Duties and responsibilities

A further important aspect of the job description, will be that which sets out the duties and responsibilities of job-holders. Prior to setting out a job description an organisation may carry out an analysis of the tasks that need to be performed by a job-holder, and of the skills and qualities required.

If this is done carefully, organisational planners will have a clear picture of how particular jobs fit in with all the other jobs carried out in an organisation. It also helps job applicants to get a clear picture of what is expected of them and it helps job-holders to understand the priorities of their work.

Job analysis is very important in creating a clear job description.

Responsibilities for assets and materials

It is also important to set out the range of physical assets and materials the job-holder will be responsible for. He or she will then be sure, and the organisation will be sure, about the accountability of the job-holder for the efficient maintenance of these resources.

Check your understanding

Imagine you are a human resources manager with a large high street retailer. Currently, you do not have enough service assistants to meet the demands of customers, particularly at weekends. There are long queues at the tills and it has become impossible to stack shelves neatly or to price all items accurately.

Set out a job analysis for a shop assistant by answering the following questions:

1 What tasks need to be performed?

2 What skills and qualities are required?

3 How can the skills be acquired?

Alternatively, examine two job descriptions produced by an organisation (perhaps the organisation you work for).

Explain how successful these job descriptions seem to have been in matching applicants with vacancies.

Person specifications

A job specification often goes beyond a simple description of the job by highlighting (specifying) the mental and physical attributes required of the job-holder. For example, a recent Prison Service advertisement specified the following:

'At every level your task will call for a lot more than simple efficiency. It takes humanity, flexibility, enthusiasm, total commitment and, of course, a sense of humour.'

The personnel department may therefore set out, for its own use, a 'person specification', using a layout similar to the one shown in Figure 15.1. The person specification can be used to:

Summary of job			
Attributes	**Essential**	**Desirable**	**How identified**
Physical			
Qualifications			
Experience			
Training			
Special knowledge			
Personal circumstances			
Attitudes			
Practical and intellectual skills			

Figure 15.1   Layout for a person specification

Case study: Details from a person specification

The details in Figure 15.2 (below) appeared in the person specification for a retail assistant in a supermarket.

Attributes	Essential	Desirable	How identified
Physical	Medical certificate from doctor certifying fitness for work, including lifting duties	–	Certificate to be provided at job interview
Qualifications	–	3 GCSEs or equivalent at grade C or above	Examination certificates
Experience	–	Previous experience of working in retail environment	Letter from former employer

1   How useful do you think the details shown in the person specification would be in sifting through candidates for a retailing post?

2   Create a job specification for a job of your choice using the following headings for attributes: physical, qualifications, experience, training, special knowledge, personal circumstances, attitudes, practical and intellectual skills.

- make sure a job advertisement conveys the qualities prospective candidates should have

- check candidates for the job have the right qualities.

Personal attributes and achievements

A person specification is concerned with identifying those people who have the right qualities to fit the jobs you are offering. For example, personal attributes for a member of the Paratroop Regiment might include physical toughness and alertness. The personal attributes of a teacher may include the ability to work well with others and to find out about the learning needs of pupils. The personal attributes of a shop assistant might include punctuality and smartness of appearance.

Personal achievements give a good indication of an individual's existing abilities. For example, someone who has achieved the Duke of Edinburgh Bronze, Silver or Gold Award shows qualities of enterprise and initiative. Personal achievements can be good indicators of qualities such as the ability to work in a team, to help others, to persevere, etc.

Qualifications

Qualifications are another important ingredient in person specifications. For example, when recruiting a new human resources lecturer, it would be essential to appoint someone with formal teaching qualifications and some form of academic qualification, such as a degree in business studies or an Institute of Personnel Management qualification.

Qualifications are a good measure of prior learning. This has been simplified in recent years by the development of NVQs,

GNVQs and AVCEs, which are nationally recognised qualifications. For example, in appointing someone at a managerial level you would be looking for at least NVQ Levels 4 and 5.

The idea of a qualification is that it prepares you to do a particular job or activity. In creating a job specification, organisations will therefore need to consider the level of qualification required by a job-holder.

Experience

There is a well-known saying that there is no substitute for experience. Someone with experience in carrying out a particular post or who has had particular responsibilities should be able to draw on that experience in a new situation. For example, an experienced lecturer has already taught, assessed, administered and carried out a variety of other duties in a college. A new lecturer has not had the same advantages.

We talk about the learning curve that results from experience. The implication is that the good learner will learn at a progressively faster rate as he or she draws on his or her experience. A person specification should therefore set out the required experience for a job-holder.

Competence

Competence is a word that is widely used today. Competence implies that a person has sufficient knowledge or skill to carry out particular tasks or activities. Most people would rather visit a competent than an incompetent doctor or be taught by a competent rather than an incompetent teacher.

Person specifications should set out levels of competence required by a particular job-holder. Modern qualifications, such as

GNVQs, AVCEs and NVQs, are based on a competence model. Hairdressers, for example, need to show competence in a range of performance criteria that make up the elements of hairdressing work.
A hairdresser would be foolish to take on a new stylist for dyeing purposes who had not first exhibited competence in mixing and applying hair dye.

Check your understanding

Examine two person specifications for particular jobs. Write a commentary that explains how successful these have been in matching applicants with vacancies. Show how the person specifications set out the personal attributes and achievements, qualifications, experience and competence required for the specific jobs.

Planning when and how to advertise

Job advertisements form an important part of the recruitment process. An organisation is able to communicate job vacancies to a selected audience by this means. Most job advertisements are written (or at least checked) by the personnel department, a task involving the same skill as marketing a product. Advertisements must reach those people who have the qualities to fill the vacancy.

The nature of the advert will depend on the following:

• Who the target audience is – potential managing director, supervisor, operatives, etc.

• Where the advert will be placed – on a noticeboard in a factory, in *The Financial Times,* at the local job centre, etc.

Job advertisements therefore take many forms, according to current requirements. Good advertisements contain at least the following information (see also Figure 15.3):

New Globe Theatre Company
DIRECTOR
London
Basic £20k + car + bonuses

The New Globe Theatre Company is a new group which will be staging productions in major London theatres. The Director will receive an initial salary of £20 000 but can expect to progress steadily to higher rates as the size of the company increases and the scale of operations expands.

We are looking for someone with extensive experience of theatre production and management who will probably have worked in a similar capacity for at least five years in regional theatre productions.

If you wish to take the opportunity of pioneering this new and exciting venture, please forward a letter of application to:

Director of Personnel,
The New Globe Theatre Company,
1001 The Strand,
London WC2 0NG
Telephone 020 9900 1234

Figure 15.3 A typical job advertisement

- *Job title*. This should form the main heading, possibly in bold print.

- *Job description*. This should highlight the major requirements of the job in a concise format.

- *Organisational activities and marketplace*. There should be a brief description of the environment in which the organisation operates.

- *Location*. Applicants need to know the location of the organisation and the location of the job (which may be different).

- *Salary expectation*. Figures are not always necessary, but an indication of the salary level (or a recognised grade) should always be given.

- *Address and contact*. This should appear, with a telephone number if appropriate.

- *Qualifications*. Certain jobs require a minimum entrance qualification, which should be clearly stated.

- *Experience*. This should be quantified, as it will have a bearing on the expected salary level for the job.

- *Fringe benefits*. The advertiser may wish to mention a company car, a health insurance scheme and so on.

- *Organisational identity*. This may be in the form of a logo (or simply the name of an organisation).

A good job advertisement, while providing prospective candidates with helpful information, also helps to discourage applications from people who do not have the required qualifications for the job.

The presentation of the advertisement is very important as it gives prospective employees a first impression of the organisation.

Job vacancies will need to be advertised in the appropriate media well in advance of the closing date for applications. For example, if a business organisation wants to interview in March, it may place an advert in a national newspaper in early January, stating that the closing date for applications is 8 February.

Check your understanding

1 Cut out three newspaper job advertisements. Mount each separately on a piece of paper or card. On the advert, identify each of the points made above. You could draw arrows indicating job title, job description, location, etc.

   Summarise the strengths and weaknesses of each of the adverts.

2 Think about the features of what you consider would be an ideal job for you. Try to make out a realistic job advertisement to describe this job. You may need to carry out some research to find out such features as a realistic wage and the experience required.

Identify the strengths and weaknesses of job applications: letters of application and curricula vitae

Letters of application

You are now in a position to look at job applications and interviewing from the applicant's point of view. However, before you do this look through the two flowcharts in Figures 15.4 and 15.5, which indicate the selection process for a job (a) from the employer's point of view, and (b) from the applicant's point of view. They present you with a clear picture of this process and one you should be familiar with before you start applying for jobs in earnest.

All students who are following this course will need, at some stage, to produce letters of application for jobs. It is important you get this process right. Over the years we have seen many students applying for jobs.

It is surprising how often there are two students who are almost identical in terms of qualifications, appearance and ability but one is offered many interviews while the other receives only a few. Usually the difference is in the quality of the letters of application.

A letter should have a clear structure, with a beginning, a middle and an ending. It should state:

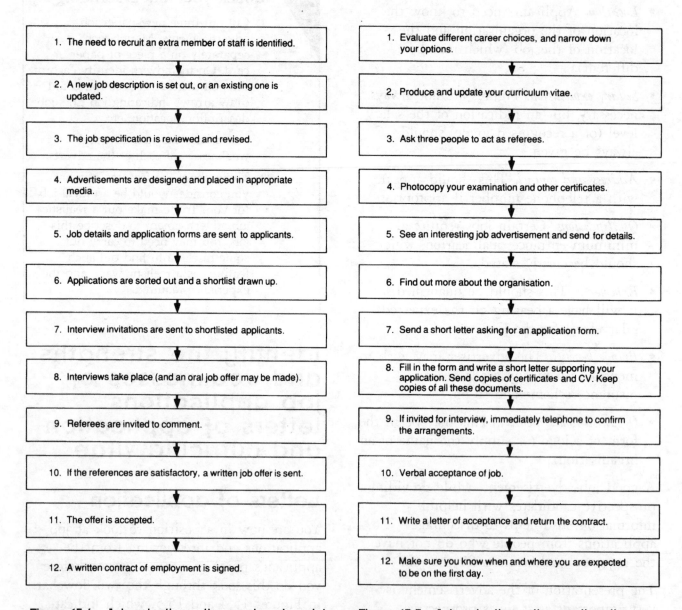

Figure 15.4   Job selection – the employer's point of view

Figure 15.5   Job selection – the applicant's point of view

- your reason for applying for the job

- the contribution you can make to the organisation

- how you have developed your capabilities through training and education

- the skills and knowledge you have acquired that would help you to do the job well.

The letter needs to be interesting – you are writing about (i.e. selling) yourself. It should contain just enough information to support your application form and CV (see Figures 15.6 and 15.7), highlighting the most relevant evidence. You will know you are writing effective letters if they lead to interviews.

Here are some important rules to remember:

- Use good English with accurate spelling. Always check in a dictionary if you are unsure of the spelling of a word.

- Use your own words rather than simply copying those in the advertisement.

- Do not try to be too clever by using long words.

Check your understanding

1 The letter shown in Figure 15.6 was sent by an applicant for the post of trainee accountant with Railtrack. What weaknesses can you spot?

2 Write a letter of application for the post described below:

The position: Trainee Manager at Tesco.

The company: the leading supermarket chain in the UK in 2000 and continuing to grow.

A manager: managers at all levels are expected to show responsibility. The company is looking for people who are tough and talented. They should have a flair for business, know how to sell and be able to work in a team.

The training: the first year's training will introduce the new manager to the stores and to working in a management team. In the second year trainees can specialise in selling or administration.

Salaries: £10,000 – £14,000.

```
                              21 Wade Park Avenue
                                  Market Deeping
                                    Peterborough
                                        PE6 8JL

20th September 2000

Railtrack Finance Manager, Anglia Region
40 Bernard Street
London
WC!n !BY

Dear Sir,

I noticed in my local paper that you have a
job avalable for a junior accountant. I am
very interested in the post because I see it
as presenting a good opportunity. I have
always been very interested in accounts. I am
also studing accounts at collage. I understand
that on your accountancy training scheme there
will be good oppertunities for promotion. I am
also studying an AVCE course in Business. This
is a very interesting course and I have had
good reports from all my tutors on the
course. As part of the course I am studying
accounts. I have found the accounts to be the
most exciting and interesting parts. I am also
interested in train spotting.
    I am working at the Anglia Co-operative
Socety. This is a part time post but it
involves a lot of responsibility. I have to
check the stock and make sure that shelves
are well organised. I also have had my EPOS
training.
    I am currently working on my cv and will
send it to you next week. Many thanks for
your interest in my application.

Yours Sincerely,


Norman Major
```

Figure 15.6   An example of a letter of application

- Keep the paragraphs short.

- Try not to use 'I' too much.

- Word process letters.

- Follow the correct convention of addressing people. A letter beginning 'Dear Sir/Madam' should be ended with 'Yours faithfully', whereas one that begins 'Dear Mr Ramprakash' should be ended with 'Yours sincerely'.

- Keep a copy of what you have written.

Curriculum vitae

A curriculum vitae (usually called simply a CV) is a summary of your career to date. There are three stages you should follow when setting out your CV:

- assemble all the facts about yourself

- draft the CV

- edit the document several times.

Try to create a favourable impression (but always be truthful). Omit negative statements about yourself. Do not be vague. Always use a word processing package with an impressive, yet conservative, font.

Assembling the facts

At this initial stage you are trying to get together as many relevant facts as possible about your career to date. It does not matter if you put down too many to start with – make a list of all your educational, work-based and leisure achievements, as well as training activities and courses you have been on. Make brief notes about each of these as well as about projects and assignments you have been involved in.

Drafting the CV

A CV should be divided into suitable headings and subheadings. For example:

1 Name

2 Date of birth

3 Address

4 Telephone (and email address, if appropriate)

5 Education and training

6 Qualifications

7 Other relevant achievements

8 Interests

9 References.

Remember, the key part of the CV is the career history, so the sections that go before should not be too long. For example, when dealing with training, list only the most important and relevant training course and then, if necessary, include some of the others under 'other information'.

When you set out your responsibilities and achievements, decide whether it is necessary to put some of them under subheadings. It is normal practice to start your career history with your most recent job and work backwards in time, because employers are usually more interested in your recent experience.

If some of your experience is of a technical nature, try to present it in a way that can be read easily by the general reader (rather than by a specialist only).

Try to use dynamic words in your CV. Here are some good examples:

accomplished	expanded	promoted
achieved	finished	redesigned
conducted	generated	reorganised
completed	implemented	set up
created	improved	solved
decided	increased	succeeded
delivered	introduced	trained
developed	launched	widened
designed	modernised	won
directed	performed	work
established	planned	wrote

CURRICULUM VITAE

Name:	Prakesh Patel
Date of birth:	1.3.83
Address:	50 Palmerston Road Reading RG31 9HL
Telephone:	01604 76321
Education and training:	Waingels' Copse School, Reading Sept 1995-July 2000
Qualifications:	GCSE Mathematics (B) GCSE English (C) GCSE Business Studies (A) GCSE French (C) GCSE German (A) GCSE Technology (C) GCSE History (C) All July 2000
Interests and activities:	Captain of school rugby team, house captain and prefect (1999–2000). Venture Scout. Bronze Award for Duke of Edinburgh. Member of Woodley Chess Club.
Work experience:	Assistant in Heelas (Department Store) in Reading on Saturdays
Referees:	Mr I. Marks Waingels' Copse School Denmark Ave Woodley Reading RG3 8SL / Rev. R. Babbage St Jude's Church Street Reading RG4 7QZ

Figure 15.7 An example of a CV

Editing the CV

You may need to alter your CV slightly for each job application so that it concentrates as closely as possible on the requirements of a particular job. Look at the details of the job and ask yourself whether your CV suggests you have the requirements for the post. Imagine yourself in the employer's shoes: what qualities do you think the organisation is looking for?

Shortlisting

Imagine a college has advertised for a new human resource management lecturer.

It has advertised this post in:

- the local newspaper
- the educational section of two national newspapers
- a specialist magazine for teachers and lecturers.

The college wants to secure the best person for the post and is pleased when there are over 50 applicants for the job.

The Head of Business Studies and a lecturer in human resources, together with a member of the college senior management team and an outside governor, sift through the applications. They will discard any

---

Check your understanding

Produce your own up-to-date CV. Ask someone else to evaluate your CV against the following checklist:

1 Have you given a good impression of your skills, knowledge, experience and personality?

2 Are these set out in a concise and readable fashion?

3 Do significant achievements stand out?

4 Have you eliminated confusing terms, jargon and obscure abbreviations?

5 Are all words spelt accurately, have you used correct grammar and is the layout clear and organised?

6 Does the CV have a good 'feel'?

7 Would the person reading it understand it easily?

applications that do not meet certain criteria they are looking for. In this case they want someone who has:

- experience of working in industry in human resource management

- a teaching qualification, plus a minimum of three years' lecturing experience

- an established record of research and published articles.

When they have carried out this process they are left with only 12 candidates. They then decide to reduce this number to a shortlist of eight by looking at the relative strengths of the candidates. Next, they take a more detailed look to reduce the number to five, whom they will call for interviews. The five candidates who make it to the final cut will be notified well in advance so they have plenty of time to prepare themselves for an interview.

Dealing with references

In business, references for employees will usually be taken up by an employer before a contract of employment is agreed. For some posts, prospective employers will send for references as soon as an employee is being considered for a job. This is often the case with fairly routine work. Employers will not even consider the job applicant before they have seen a reference from a school/college or previous employer. This is also often the case in first appointments and for part-time work.

However, a more common practice for many jobs in industry is for the employer to send for references after an interview has taken place. The main reasons for this are as follows.

- It reduces the paperwork involved in the recruitment process. You process only the

papers of the prospective employees you are really interested in.

- Many prospective employees do not want their existing employers to know they are looking for work elsewhere. For every job offer made there will be many candidates who are disappointed. If these people are already employed, sending for references might sour their relationship with existing employers.

When sending for a reference from an employer, it is helpful to set out the key points on which you want to receive comments. References should be relatively brief because they must not be too time-consuming for the writer.

Assessing candidates

A typical job interview

Candidates should be assessed against set criteria for a job. For example, in choosing a lecturer in human resource management, you should be looking for the most knowledgeable candidate, with the best teaching record, the ability to work with others in a team, and the ability to inspire and enthuse students. There will, of course, be other criteria, too. Today it is common practice when selecting lecturers to assess them by asking them to do a presentation that should illustrate their current knowledge of a subject and their ability to teach in a simulated classroom situation.

Recruitment and selection are closely tied. Selection is the process of choosing people to work in an organisation. The selection system should attempt to:

- Get the best people within existing budgets – that is, those with the most appropriate skills, experience and attitudes.

- Select people who will stay with the organisation for a reasonable time.

- Minimise the costs of recruitment and selection relative to returns.

Selection interviews should be well organised. They should be arranged at convenient times and at convenient locations, and should present to candidates a realistic picture of what the job entails and what working for the organisation would be like.

Before selecting candidates for interview, the organisation should have a clear picture of the 'ideal' candidate. As we have seen, it is then a matter of sifting through all the applications to find candidates who best meet the organisation's requirements and then drawing up a shortlist.

As part of the interviews, candidates may be given tasks to complete to test their aptitude. Also, to check whether applicants are likely to stay with the organisation, it is important to ask them about their future intentions and to show them the working environment. While the organisation needs to select suitable employees, it is also important employees select the right organisation.

Interviewer techniques

As part of your Advanced Business course it is very helpful to arrange simulated job

interviews in the classroom. There are a number of benefits to be gained from this.

One benefit is that it provides excellent opportunities to rehearse the key skill of communications, particularly when working with adults in a realistic situation (for example, you might invite personnel officers from local organisations to take part in the interviewing process).

Another benefit is that it helps you to rehearse and practise for the real interviews you will be having shortly when you apply for jobs. The structure and format of a simulated interview will be very similar to the real thing. If you have practised in front of a student audience, you should be better prepared and less nervous in future.

Another very important benefit is that it gives you an insight into the interviewing process. You will gain an idea of what it is like to be in the interviewer's chair, and this will help you to identify the kinds of things the interviewers are looking for. Perhaps groups of students can act as interviewers. What are they looking for? What are the main criteria they are using to judge candidate performance?

It is very helpful to make a video of the job interviews so you can evaluate performance critically. Useful things to look out for are:

- the effective use of body language and eye contact

- the completeness of answers given to questions (rather than answering 'yes' or 'no')

- whether interviewees listened to questions and gave appropriate responses.

Let us first look at some interviewer techniques. By studying these carefully we can get a useful insight into what the interviewer is thinking about and looking for.

Opening the interview

Generally speaking, interviewers should try to make the interviewee feel relaxed. For example, they might ask the interviewee about his or her journey to the interview on that day: 'Where have you come from?' 'Did you find it easy to get here today?', etc.

Of course, there are exceptional times when interviewers deliberately set out to make the interviewees feel uncomfortable to see how they react – for example, by putting them on a wobbly chair or placing them at a lower height than the interviewer's chair. However, the important thing to remember is that modern business organisations are not run like the Gestapo. Generally, they should find some means of making the interviewee feel comfortable so that the interviewee can show his or her best side.

Did you find it easy to get here today?

When there are several interviewers, a starting point might be to introduce the interviewee to each of the panel in turn.

Asking questions

The next stage is to ask the interviewee a set of predetemined questions. The questions asked should relate to the person specification and job description. Remember, you are looking for the candiate who is best able to meet the organisation's requirements. The interviewer will have a copy of the candidate's application form and curriculum vitae. Interviewers will normally want to make notes to check how each interviewee meets the job requirements. For example, they may have a sheet like that shown in Figure 15.8 in front of them. By setting out a score-sheet like this, it is possible to compare candidates' responses to questions and their behaviour in the interview situation.

Post: Shop supervisor		
Candidate name: Melissa Graham		
Requirements	**Score (1–5)**	**Notes**
Tidy appearance	3	Untidy hair.
Intelligence	5	Answered questions quickly, and with good attention to detail.
Punctuality	1	Turned up 2 minutes late for interview.

Figure 15.8 An interviewer's score-sheet

The questions chosen by the interviewer should be carefully thought out in order to ensure they make it possible to draw accurate comparisons. For example, in interviewing lecturers to teach on a Vocational A Level course in business, the interview panel might ask all candidates questions such as the following:

• What can you tell us about the best way to organise the teaching of core units on an advanced business course?

- What do you see as being the strengths of group work?

- What can you tell us about your experience of teaching Advanced VCE students?

- What do you think of the modifications to the Advanced VCE Business course for 2000?

Interviewing also requires a considerable amount of intelligence and inventiveness. When candidates answer your questions you may feel you need to ask them a little bit more in order to get a more complete answer. Follow-on questions are very important here. Some follow-on questions may be planned in advance, while others may need to be developed on the spur of the moment.

For example, when an interviewer talks to someone applying for a job as a shelf stacker in a supermarket, he or she may get the following responses:

Interviewer: Have you had experience of shelf stacking in a supermarket before?

Interviewee: Yes, I worked at Marks & Spencer doing it for three months.

Interviewer: (Follow-up question): Can you tell me exactly what you were responsible for doing in your shelf-stacking job? (And why you left it!)

Without follow-on questions an interview can pass very quickly with little being found out about the true strengths (and weaknesses) of job applicants.

Using body language

People do not just talk to each other through words. They also talk through their body language. An interviewer who wants to draw the best out of candidates for a job will use appropriate body language. The interviewer should be seated at the same height as the interviewee with a good frontal or open posture. The interviewer should not cross his or her arms or make threatening gestures, such as pointing a finger or banging a fist down on the table. He or she should smile and use clear eye contact.

Closing the interview

The usual way of closing an interview is, when the interviewer or interviewing panel have finished their list of questions, they

Case study: Interview for a trainee manager's job at a local supermarket

You are a member of the interviewing panel for a trainee manager's job at a local supermarket. The areas of questioning you have been asked to provide the questions for are about:

- the interviewee's previous experience

- what the interviewee sees as being the chief characteristics of a good manager.

1 Phrase an initial question.

2 Develop some follow-up questions on the same theme to enable the candidates to develop their answers more effectively.

will ask the interviewee if there is anything he or she would like to ask. When this is completed the interviewer will say something like: 'Thank you very much for coming to the interview. I hope you have a safe journey back. You will be hearing from us by . . .' The interviewer will clarify the arrangements through which the interviewee will be informed of arrangements, and explain how any administrative task, such as claiming for expenses, should be done.

Giving feedback

Often, candidates for a post will be given feedback on how they performed in the interview situation. They should be told about their strengths and weaknesses and the reasons why they were or were not chosen for the post. This feedback should be seen as a positive process concerned with the ongoing development of the interviewee.

Interviewee techniques

Interviews can be nerve-racking. In a short space of time the candidate must convince the interviewer he or she is the person the organisation needs.

Preparing

Not only should the interviewer be prepared but, needless to say, so should the candidate as well. The candidate can prepare by practising answers to the questions likely to be asked, possibly with the help of a friend who takes the role of the interviewer.

It must be remembered that interviews are a two-way activity. The candidate has a chance to ask questions and find out if the organisation and the job are suitable. Questions can, for example, be asked about training, promotion prospects and social facilities.

There are all sorts of things you can prepare before an interview. For example, you may want to try out the clothes you will wear to the interview beforehand, perhaps by wearing them to some sort of public occasion. There is nothing worse than feeling uncomfortable in the clothes you have chosen for an interview. Many people like to plan the route they will take to get to the interview, even doing a dummy run beforehand.

You may like to prepare yourself by thinking about the kinds of things interviewers will be looking for in you. The interview assessment form shown in Figure 15.9 gives you some useful indications of

| Factors | \multicolumn{6}{c}{INTERVIEW ASSESSMENT} |
| | \multicolumn{5}{c}{Rating} | Remarks |
	A	B	C	D	E	
Appearance Personality Manner Health						
Intelligence Understanding of questions						
Skills Special skills Work experience						
Interests Hobbies Sports						
Academic						
Motivation						
Circumstances Mobility Hours Limitations						
OVERALL						

A = Exceptional   B = Above average   C = Satisfactory
D = Below average   E = Unsuitable

Figure 15.9   An interview assessment form

the qualities that are looked for in many job applicants. The checklist shown in Figure 15.10 should also be helpful in giving you some useful preparatory advice for interviews.

DO ✔	DON'T ✘
Find out about the firm before the interview	Be late
Dress smartly but comfortably	Smoke unless invited to
Speak clearly and with confidence	Chew gum or eat sweets
Look at the interviewer when speaking	Answer all questions 'yes', 'no', or 'I don't know'
Be positive about yourself	Be afraid to ask for clarification if anything is unclear
Be ready to ask questions	Say things which are obviously untrue or insincere

Figure 15.10   An interview checklist

Showing confidence

It is important for interviewees to appear confident but not over-confident. You should be confident in your own abilities. One of the most important attributes to have in the interview situation is enthusiasm. Candidates who appear hangdog and timid will be viewed in a poor light, particularly for posts that require some degree of responsibility and initiative.

Body language

At an interview it is important for you to adopt the right body language. Look alert and eager. Look the questioner in the eye. Avoid nervous movements, and try not to cross your arms in a defensive position. Try not to threaten the interviewer by pointing your finger or making sudden violent movements. Sit up straight and try to look confident and at ease – not apathetic and too laid back (see Figure 15.11).

Figure 15.11   Appropriate body language

Do not give brief one-line answers, but try to expand on your answers so that the interviewer can see you at your best. Smile and, at all times, try to appear interested and enthusiastic about what is being discussed. You do not have to let yourself be pushed around by an aggressive interviewer – be assertive by standing up for yourself, without taking it to the extreme by becoming heated and argumentative (see Figure 15.12).

Listening to questions

When you are being interviewed, listen carefully to the questions you are asked. If you do not understand a question or have not heard it clearly, it may be helpful to say 'Please could your repeat that question?' If you give an inappropriate answer to a question you have misheard, the interviewers may doubt your intelligence. The golden rule is to concentrate on the question being asked.

Figure 15.12   Inappropriate body language

Responding to questions

When answering questions you will need to expand on points rather than giving a simple yes/no or a short answer. Try to give detailed and clear responses. Remember, the interviewers are judging you against certain criteria. Try to think about what those criteria might be and prepare full answers that enable the interviewers to give you high scores for your answers.

Try to be clear, enthusiastic and interested in the questions. However, don't speak for too long or ramble. This may give the impression you are disorganised. Don't oversell yourself. The person who goes on and on about having wonderful skills is likely to appear both boring and pompous. The interviewing panel will often have to work with you. They won't want to work with an inflated egotist, or someone with verbal diarrhoea.

Asking questions

At the end of the interview you will be given opportunities to ask questions. Try to ask a small number of relevant questions. Don't ask questions that simply involve the repetition of material you have already been told.

If you are not sure whether you want the job or not, ask questions that will enable you to make a more informed choice.

Be clear and concise

Good verbal communication involves asking and answering questions in a clear and concise way. The person who is straightforward, interesting and direct will often sway an interview in a positive way. Remember, the initial impression you give is very important. It is often in the first few minutes of an interview that the panel make up their minds about which candidate to appoint.

Any job interview involves a certain amount of luck and the outcome depends on how you do on the day. A recent study reported that the person who is first on the interviewer's list is three times less likely to be hired than the last name on the list.

Monday is the worst interview day because managers are under pressure on the first day of the week, while Friday offers the distraction of a coming weekend. Early morning interviews are not recommended because managers are too preoccupied, while those after 4 pm are unhelpful because interviewers are anxious to get home.

Check your understanding

In groups, carry out mock interviews for an imaginary post. Before the interviews take place, the interviewing panel will need to establish the qualities they are looking for in the successful applicant. The interviewing panel will also need to establish a set of questions. The same questions need to be asked of each applicant if the interviews are to be fair.

The 'applicants' will each need to produce a CV and a written application. They will also need to research the nature of the organisation and the post.

After the interviews, all interviewers and interviewees should fill in an evaluation sheet containing the following questions:

1 How did you feel about the interview?

2 How did you consider the interview went?

3 What impression do you think you gave?

4 What did you think of the interviewers'/interviewees':

 a planning and organisation

 b preparation for the interview

 c performance at the interview?

Appraising interviewers and interviewees

As part of your AVCE course you will benefit from carrying out mock interviews for a fictitious job or for a real job but in a simulated interview situation.

Carrying out successful mock interviews will involve a considerable amount of planning and preparation. An effective approach would be for one group of students to prepare to interview candidates for a particular post. This group of students will prepare a job advertisement and person specification, and organise the interview schedule. The interviewing team will need to decide what questions to ask, in which order and by whom, and think of follow-on questions. Students will need to make sure the questions they ask are appropriate to the qualities they want to find out about in the job applicant.

The second group of students will play the part of the interviewees. They will need to study the job description and person specification, and should prepare for the interview as if it were the real thing. Issues such as body language, preparation and answering and asking questions should be considered.

Appraising your own performance

Individual students should prepare an appraisal form (see Figure 15.13) for analysing their own strengths and weaknesses in the interview situation. This should be a very helpful process because it encourages you to be objective in your self-criticism. You can then use the form to reflect on your performance. Prepare the form before the interview takes place, either by watching a video showing you interviewing or being interviewed, or simply by recalling your thoughts and feelings.

Aspect of performance	Rating				
	Very good	Good	Fair	Weak	Very weak
Eye contact					
Body language					
Appearing confident					
Answering questions					

Figure 15.13 Appraisal form

The types of things you need to put on the form are shown in Figure 15.13. You can then use another section of the form to identify opportunities for improvement:

Eye contact
I noticed when I watched the video that I did not look the interviewers in the face, and I didn't keep my head still. This is an aspect of my performance I need to concentrate on more in group work.

Body language
I started off the interview sitting up straight but I soon became flustered and crossed my arms in a defensive position. I then became quite aggressive because I was anxious and started pointing in a menacing way.

The purpose of self-assessment is to enable you to improve your performance by being honest about your strengths and weaknesses.

Interaction between participants

For interviews to be successful there will need to be an effective interaction between participants, both in simulations and in the real thing. Interviewees are most likely to be successful if they can generate positive interactions. It is important, therefore, to appraise these interactions.

Once again, all participants in the role play should construct an appraisal form looking at aspects of interactions, as shown in Figure 15.14. More detailed comments will also need to be recorded about each of these aspects.

Aspect of interaction	Rating				
	Very good	Good	Fair	Weak	Very weak
Individuals' support for each other					
Interview conducted in a positive atmosphere					
Clear communication between participants					

Figure 15.14 Interactions appraisal form

Success of the interview

It will be important to appraise the overall success of the interview. One of the key considerations will be whether the interview was an appropriate way of selecting the best candidate for the job (i.e. the one who most closely fitted the person specification and was able to fulfil the job description).

The job interview will need to be carried out in a professional way. This means students should not select candidates on a friendship basis but purely on fitness for the job.

Students will also need to appraise the interview in terms of the way it meets legal and ethical obligations. Recruiters have legal obligations relating to such areas as race relations, sex discrimination, opportunities for disabled people and equal pay (see below). At the same time, staff engaged in the recruitment process need to work to a professional code of ethics embracing concepts of objectivity, confidentiality and honesty (see also below).

Interviews are not only used for people applying for new jobs. They are used frequently for performance reviews (i.e. where a line manager or team leader will discuss with a subordinate or team member his or her performance at work and try to establish new targets for the next time period). Interviews are also carried out with people who are leaving a job – perhaps in some cases to find out why they are moving on, and what their future needs might be. Interviews are particularly important when people are retiring, to help them move safely on to the next phase in their life after (it is hoped) loyal service to the organisation, and to make sure the organisation is meeting all its legal contractual requirements.

Psychometric and aptitude testing

Many jobs today involve some form of psychometric or aptitude testing to find out whether individuals have the right sorts of personalities or dispositions to carry out particular types of work. A psychometric test is a way of assessing an individual's personality, drives and motivations, often by means of a paper and pencil questionnaire.

For example, one of the dimensions the psychometric test might draw out is an individual's willingness or ability to work in a team situation, or to handle stress.

A number of organisations place a great deal of emphasis on these tests because they believe they are reliable indicators of the sociability/personality of individuals, and that they are useful predictors of whether individuals will fit into the organisation and its existing culture.

Check your understanding

Obtain a psychometric test that is used for selection purposes.

Try out the test. What does it claim to show about your personality and disposition? Do you agree?

Legal and ethical responsibilities relating to equal opportunities

Employers are bound both by the law and by the requirement to operate in a moral way (i.e. questions of ethics) in terms of their employment policies. Organisations have to work within the law – failure to comply will lead to court cases, possible fines and adverse publicity. However, it should be expected that businesses will do more than is legally required – they will seek to do what is 'right' (ethical). Organisations that do not operate in an ethical way are likely to be unpopular with employees and other stakeholders, who may then use some of their power to force changes in the organisation.

There are a number of laws businesses and other organisations need to comply with in relation to recruitment:

- The Race Relations Act 1976
- The Sex Discrimination Act 1975
- The Disability Discrimination Act 1995
- The Equal Pay Act 1970

The Race Relations Act 1976 (RRA) and the Sex Discrimination Act 1975 (SDA)

The RRA and SDA have a number of similarities and, because of this, they are often interpreted in the same way by industrial tribunals. The RRA and SDA both protect all employees irrespective of age or status, whether they are full- or part-time workers or have a fixed or temporary contract. They attempt to deal with three sorts of discrimination:

- direct discrimination
- indirect discrimination
- victimisation.

Direct discrimination occurs when one employee or candidate for a job is treated better or more favourably than another because of his or her race or sex. For example, a British Asian applies for a job as a carpenter and he goes for an interview at a building site. He is told there they 'don't tolerate blacks' and he would not fit in. This is a prime example of racial discrimination.

Indirect discrimination takes place when all employees seem to be treated exactly the same on the surface but, when looked at closer, members of a particular racial group or gender are found to be discriminated against. For example, an employer tries to insist that all female staff must wear short skirts. Clearly, this will disadvantage groups whose culture or religion requires that legs should be covered up.

Victimisation occurs when an employee is singled out for unfair treatment because he or she has attempted to exercise rights under the RRA, SDA or Equal Pay Act, or has helped others to enforce their rights. For example, if an employee were to appear as a witness or to support another employee's claim for discrimination and, as a result, was not chosen for promotion within an organisation.

Racial discrimination

The Race Relations Act 1976 states: 'A person discriminates against another if, on racial grounds, he treats another less favourably than he treats, or would treat, another person.' Discrimination on racial grounds is, for the purpose of the RRA, defined as discrimination on the basis of colour, race, nationality, or ethnic or national origin.

Exceptions to the Race Relations Act

The Act recognises that, for certain jobs, being a member of a particular racial group can be a necessary requirement for the particular job. These include entertainers, actors, actresses, artists' and photographers' models, waiters and waitresses (e.g. in a Chinese or French restaurant).

Harassment is another form of direct discrimination. This includes verbal or physical bullying or intimidation and also more subtle forms, such as racist jokes, banter or graffiti. It also includes shunning people, excluding them from conversations or picking on them unnecessarily because of race or colour.

Sex discrimination

The Sex Discrimination Act states that it is unlawful to treat someone else less favourably on the basis of his or her sex: 'A person discriminates against a woman if, on the grounds of her sex, he treats her less favourably than he treats a man.' This applies equally to men and women.

Exceptions to the Sex Discrimination Act

The main exceptions where discrimination is permitted are as follows (see also Figure 15.15):

- Jobs that, for genuine reasons, must be carried out by someone of a particular sex.

- Privacy or decency is required (e.g. a changing-room attendant).

- Single-sex hospitals, prisons or care centres.

- Jobs that involve work in a country whose laws require individuals to be of a certain sex.

SEX DISCRIMINATION ACT 1975

No job advertisement which indicates or can reasonably be understood as indicating an intention to discriminate on ground of sex (eg by inviting applicants only from males or only from females) may be accepted, unless it is exempted from the requirements of the Sex Discrimination Act.

A statement must be made at the time the advertisement is placed saying which of the exceptions in the Act is considered to apply. It is the responsibility of advertisers to ensure that advertisement content does not discriminate under the terms of the Sex Discrimination Act.

Figure 15.15 Sex Discrimination Act 1975: exceptions

The Equal Pay Act 1970 (EPA)

The objective of the EPA was fundamentally to ensure that women receive the same pay as men for the same or broadly similar work. If a woman (or man) wants to claim for pay discrimination, she must ensure that whatever man she compares herself to is in the same employment (i.e. the man has to be employed by the same employer or an associated employer).

Equal Pay Act categories

The purpose of the EPA is to make sure that women are given the same treatment as men:

- Who are engaged in like work in the same employment.

- Whose work is rated as equivalent.

- Whose work is otherwise of equal value.

Pay is defined under the EPA as including:

- fringe benefits or the use of a car

- sick pay

- redundancies or severance payments

- the right to join a pension scheme.

Disability discrimination

The Disability Discrimination Act 1995 (DDA) protects employees who are classified as disabled. Anyone with a physical or mental impairment that has long-term effects upon his or her ability to carry out everyday activities is termed disabled.

The DDA provides that it is unlawful for employers to discriminate against a disabled person in relation to:

Case study: Employee Recruitment Policy Statement for Melton College

Study the following policy statement and outline what you consider to be its major strengths.

1. *Recruitment, Promotion and Training Decisions*
All decisions in relation to the above will be taken, having regard only to the requirements of the job (or of the training proposed). Promotion and training opportunities will be available to all employees, irrespective or race, ethnic origin, religion, sex, marital status or possible family commitments, sexual orientation or disability.

2. *Short Listing, Interview and Appointment Procedures*
Interview and appointment procedures shall be adopted so as to minimise any disadvantage suffered by the handicapped, members of ethnic minority groups or either sex. Accordingly, except in so far as it is necessary for particular appointments, questions will not be asked at interview regarding the following: prospects of marriage, future family plans, religion or sexual orientation.

Application for all posts will be by standard job application forms. A copy of this statement shall accompany every application form issued. All members of interviewing panels should receive appropriate training, be familiar with this policy and be aware of the guidelines to be followed.

3. *Induction*
Induction procedures will include arrangements to ensure that such procedures are clearly understood by everyone. (This particularly applies to instruction and notices in respect of the Health and Safety at Work Policy.) For disabled people with mobility difficulties, special attention will be paid to emergency evacuation procedures.

4. *Other Decisions*
It is implicit in this policy that employees should not be treated more favourably or less favourably in all matters of employment (except where an exception is necessary and is allowed under the law) because of race, ethnic origin, religion, sex, marital status or possible family commitments, sexual orientation or disability. It is possible that discrimination can be implicit (not obvious on the surface) where the employing organisation demands that the employee asks for previous experience or qualifications which are not relevant to the job. Implicit discrimination also exists when employees are asked to go on training courses at times that are not suitable for certain people, e.g. over the weekend.

5. *Monitoring*
Monitoring of this policy in relation to employee recruitment will be by the Senior Management Team together with the Curriculum and Employment Committee of Governors.

* the recruitment process

* promotional opportunities

* dismissal.

Currently, only employers with 20 or more employees are prohibited from discriminating against disabled people. Also the DDA does not apply to operational staff employed in the armed forces, police, prison service, and fire service.

The flexible workforce

During the 1990s many companies adopted flexible labour policies. The term 'labour flexibility' is used to describe a number of aspects of employment, including:

* flexible contracts of employment

* wage or earning flexibility

Check your understanding

Consider the following interview questions from the equal opportunities viewpoint.

Commentary on some of the instances is given in italics. You need to supply your own commentary for the others.

Mrs —, I see you are married. Do you intend to start a family soon?

The question is not relevant to whether the interviewee is capable of doing the job. It also shows direct sex discrimination, because a man is not likely to be asked the question. This question must not be asked.

What will happen when your children are ill or on school holidays? Who will look after them?

This question has no relevance as to whether the interviewee is capable of doing the job.

Your hair is very long, Mr —. If offered the job are you prepared to have it cut?

This question is relevant only if a safety aspect of the job is involved (e.g. use of machinery). Otherwise, the standard of dress expected by the company could be discussed (e.g. the correct image for dealing with customers).

Mr —, as you are 55 do you think it is worth us employing you?

This question may not be relevant because, at this age, it should not stop the person from doing the job. However, if the interviewee is 60 years of age, the company might feel any necessary training would not be worth while.

Miss —, as a woman, do you think you are capable of doing the job?

(Write your own commentary on this one.)

Do you think your disability will affect your performance in the job?

(Write your own commentary on this one.)

How do you feel about working with people from a different ethnic background from yourself?

(Write your own commentary on this one.)

As a woman returner, Mrs —, do you feel you will be able to cope with the new technology in the office?

(Write your own commentary on this one.)

As a man, Mr —, you will be working in a department consisting mainly of women. Are you easily distracted?

(Write your own commentary on this one.)

Miss —, don't you think your skirt is rather short?

(Write your own commentary on this one.)

- subcontracting and outworking
- ability of employees to move from one job to another
- functional flexibility and the breakdown of job demarcations
- flexibility in the place of work

- numerical flexibility
- working-time flexibility.

These changes have been particularly influenced by the new 'round the clock' service industries and the movement to outsource non-core activities.

A major change in production that took place in the 1990s was the growth of contracting out. Before this time there was a tendency for organisations to integrate and to expand. The aim of integration was for an organisation to take control of all stages of the production of a product. For example, the jeans manufacturer would want to control both the retail outlets that sold its jeans and the cloth manufacturers that produced the denim and other cloths used in the production of the jeans (see Figure 15.16).

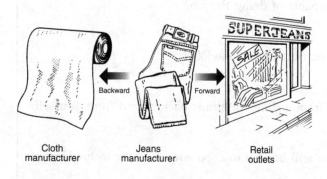

Figure 15.16 Backward and forward integration

There were obvious advantages to this integration in that the organisation took total control over standards. It was in charge of all operations and all activities were focused around the needs of the organisation. It was not just the manufacturing side that would be controlled by the organisation, it was all the services involved in running the business as well –

office administration, public relations, advertising, selling, etc.

Today, the emphasis is far more on the leaner and fitter organisation. Manufacturing and service activities are frequently contracted out to independent suppliers. Organisations concentrate on their core strengths and use contractors to do the rest.

For example, oil companies in the late 1980s typically employed their own people on oil rigs. Today, they award contracts to independent firms to staff the rigs. Car manufacturers may buy in their raw materials and components from many different suppliers, setting out tight contractual schedules for quality and performance.

The emphasis is on an organisation focusing on its core strength and contracting out non-core production and services to independent organisations. Smaller core organisations are much easier to manage and control. They can also impose very tight standards on suppliers (Figure 15.17).

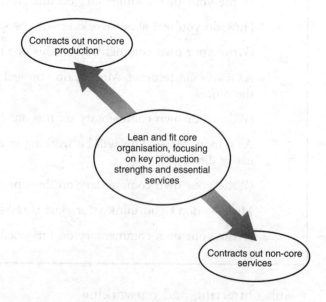

Figure 15.17 Contracting out non-core production and services

Different modes of employment and different terms and conditions

Employees can work full time or part time and on permanent or short-term contracts.

Until recently, full-time core employees had much better terms and conditions than part-timers and temporary workers. They still do, but European social legislation that has been applied in Britain has given much better rights to part-time and temporary workers in relation to sickness and pension rights, and to maternity and holiday pay, etc.

Case study: Mothers' right to part-time work

Despite the rapid growth in flexible working practices, a new survey published by the Institute of Personnel and Development. (html://www.ipd.co.uk) (November 1999) reveals that over a quarter of organisations still do not provide their employees with the option of working part time. What many employers and employees are not aware of is that mothers may have the legal right to insist that their employers explore the option of flexibility. According to the Maternity Alliance, a national charity that works to 'make life better' for all pregnant women and new parents, it is high time they were aware.

The most common perception is that if the boss tells a mother she can't shift from full time to part time, it's too bad. Indeed, the law gave women the right to return to their jobs after maternity leave but not the absolute right to work part time. Nevertheless, the Sex Discrimination Act 1975 states that it counts as indirect discrimination if an employer requires a woman to work particular hours that are not justifiable.

Take the case of Annette Cowley, recently dismissed by her employer, South African Airways, for refusing to work two 16-hour shifts back to back because of childcare responsibilities. She claimed sex discrimination at an employment tribunal and won.

Even if the woman's boss asks her to work eight-hour days, she may have a case. Good reasons for asking to work flexibly are: if the woman cannot find full-time childcare; she cannot afford full-time childcare; she needs to be there when her children come home from school (perhaps because they have special needs); or she suffers severe stress from working long hours (perhaps because her partner cannot share the childcare).

It is not the case, though, that employers automatically have to comply with such requests. Rather, the law requires that they have a good reason for refusing. Refusing even to consider a request would almost certainly be seen as unjustified if the matter went to an industrial tribunal.

1 What do you understand the entitlement to be in law for a woman to move from full-time to part-time work?

2 Why do you think Annette Cowley won her case against South African Airways?

3 Would you suggest any improvements to the laws protecting the rights of women to change to part-time work?

Flexible contracts

One way in which firms achieve greater flexibility is by increasing the use of temporary and part-time contracts, thus reducing job security and reducing the number of employees employed permanently and full time.

Subcontracting and outworking

Some organisations have chosen not to take responsibility for certain activities that were previously carried out internally (e.g. cleaning services and advertising). In the public sector many of the services traditionally provided by local authority employees have been contracted out (e.g. street cleaning).

Ability of employees to move from one job to another

Organisations can gain flexibility within their labour force by having the option of moving employees to different jobs and geographical areas, according to changing economic conditions.

Functional flexibility

This relates to the reduction of job demarcations between occupations in order to allow the more flexible use of labour. Peter Wickens, in a widely read book *The Road to Nissan*, quotes from a company agreement with the trade union the AEU:

To ensure the fullest use of facilities and manpower, there will be complete flexibility and mobility of employees. To ensure such flexibility and change, employees will undertake training for all work as required by the Company.

In the Japanese motor industry many assembly workers, for example, handle routine preventative maintenance and minor breakdowns and will assist the maintenance staff when they arrive. Instead of having a specialist skill, the implication is that people will need to acquire a whole range of skills to allow them to work productively across many tasks.

Flexibility in the workplace

Increasingly, large numbers of people are working away from the traditional workplace (e.g. homeworkers working from their own homes).

Numerical flexibility

The ability of firms to adjust the number of workers or the number of hours worked in line with changes in the level of demand for their goods and services is referred to as numerical flexibility. Typically, firms achieve numerical flexibility through the use of part-time, temporary and self-employed (subcontract) workers.

Working-time flexibility

This relates to changes in the number and timing of hours worked from week to week or day to day, through overtime, short-time working, annual hours contracts and flexitime (start and finish times vary within a broad band).

Check your understanding

Examine one organisation to find out what percentage of its personnel is employed on the following types of contract: full-time; part-time; permanent; and temporary. Interview one person working in each of these contractual conditions to find out what he or she sees as being the advantages and disadvantages of his or her mode of employment.

Case study: Why men and women receive different pay

Institutional and labour market segmentation theories help to explain some of the reasons why men and women receive different levels of pay. These theories start from the assumption that institutions such as trade unions and big organisations play an important role in deciding who is hired, fired and promoted, and how much they are paid. These theories assume that the labour market consists of a number of segments.

The best known of such theories is the dual labour market theory, which distinguishes between a 'primary' and a 'secondary' sector. Jobs in the primary sector are relatively good in terms of pay, security, opportunities for advancement and working conditions (these are what are termed 'core' jobs). Secondary sector jobs tend to be relatively poor as regards pay, chances for promotion and working conditions, and provide little protection or job security (made up of part-time and temporary non-core workers). These two labour markets function independently of each other to a substantial degree.

It is a relatively short step to adapt the concept of the dual labour market to occupational segregation by sex, with one labour market segment comprising 'female' occupations and another 'male' occupations. This segmentation implies relatively low wage rates in 'female' occupations because many women workers are 'overcrowded' into a small number of 'female' occupations. 'Male' occupations, on the other hand, benefit from reduced competition within a wider set of occupations and, consequently, tend to enjoy relatively high wage rates.

The nature of the jobs available in the primary sector would lead one to expect an under-representation of women and, since such jobs are more secure, firms in this sector can be expected to accord a relatively high value to firm-specific experience and low labour turnover. Consequently, given their generally more continuous labour market experience, male workers should tend to be favoured by primary sector employers. Furthermore, since primary sector firms can pay higher wages, they are in a position to cream off the best-qualified workers. This again implies that primary sector firms should tend to prefer men, who be better educated and more experienced than women.

1 How good do you think the theory outlined above is in explaining the difference between male and female earnings?

2 What is missing from the theory?

Core employees, part-time, temporary and contract labour

The flexible firm has become very important in business thinking (Figure 15.18):

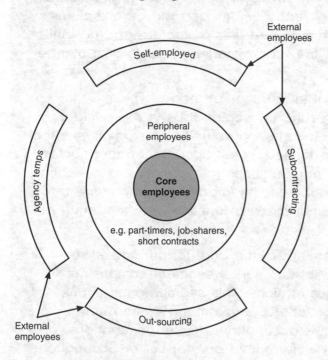

Figure 15.18   The flexible firm

- Core employees are ones who are multi-skilled (i.e. educated and trained to do a variety of job tasks), who work full time and who receive good pay, conditions and benefits.

- Peripheral employees are short-term, temporary and part-time workers, who receive less favourable pay, conditions and benefits.

- External workers are not employees of the firm but are, for example, agency temps, workers in contracted-out services and the self-employed.

The flexible firm, as we have seen, cuts its labour costs by limiting core workers relative to peripheral and external workers. For example, in Xerox's central office, direct wage payments in recent times have accounted for less than one-third of total labour costs. Many former Xerox employees work from their own homes using computer equipment linked to the Xerox network. These independent employees are free to work for other clients apart from Xerox.

Full-time employment

In 1850 the normal working week in the UK was 60 hours, spread over 6 days at 10 hours each. By the early 1960s this had been reduced to 40 hours spread over 5 days. The average full-time working week now lies between 35 and 40 hours, still spread over 5 days.

In reality it is difficult to come up with a hard and fast definition of full-time work. A dictionary definition provides us with 'for the entire time appropriate to an activity'. For example, a full-time teacher would work to the full contractual time established by the school – perhaps from 8.30 am until 4.00 pm each day for 180 days a year. A full-time lecturer in a college may work a set number of contractual hours a year (e.g. 700 hours of contact and preparation time a year).

In its statistical work, the *Labour Force Quarterly Survey* accepts respondents' definitions of whether they are full time or part time. It is interesting to note that, according to respondents' own assessments, the average number of hours worked by full-time employees is about 39 hours (1999).

Part-time employment

Part-time employees are, as the name implies, people who do not 'work for the entire time appropriate to an activity'. Traditionally, jobs that did not require more than a few hours a day to complete, such as school cleaners or dinner supervisors, had been organised on a part-time basis. The number of part-time employees has increased dramatically in recent years and is directly linked to a greater proportion of women in the labour force.

The reasons why employees may choose to work part time are as follows:

- They have greater flexibility in their working hours.

- They can use part-time employment as a supplement to other incomes (e.g. their student grant).

- It enables them to enjoy more leisure time.

- They can regard it as a 'hobby' job, rather than doing nothing during the day.

- Full-time work is not available.

The reasons why employers may want part-time employees are as follows:

- It provides them with a more flexible arrangement. It is easier to recruit part-time staff to work evenings and weekends, for example. This is particularly useful in retailing and bar work.

- Part-time employees are generally lower paid.

- Part-time employees do not have the same legal rights as full-time ones, although the implementation of European Union labour regulations has done much to improve the position of such employees in recent times.

Permanent employment

Permanent employees are those who have a contractual commitment from their employers to continue their employment, irrespective of whether they work full time or part time. A simpler definition is that employees have an open-ended rather than a fixed-term contract.

This open-ended contract can be ended only when either party gives 'notice of termination'. The length of the notice period will depend on the length of time the employee has worked there and the period of notice specified in the contract of employment.

Temporary employment

A temporary employee will have a work contract for a limited period only. They can be employed on a full-time or part-time basis. Many factories, for example, take on temporary packers before Christmas to cope with increased orders.

The reasons why organisations may employ temporary employees are to:

- cover staff sickness or holidays
- assist with exceptionally large orders
- cope with seasonal changes in demand (e.g. in the hotel and tourism industry)
- work on special projects with a limited time-span.
- clear backlogs of work.

Contracted and non-contracted employees

Today, short-term contracts are becoming more and more common. In times of economic uncertainty, employers are finding greater flexibility in giving short-term contracts for one or two years to new employees (e.g. in teaching/lecturing). This gives them the option to renew or not to renew at the end of the period. Computer programming is another example of an area where short-term contracts are commonplace.

The term 'contracted worker' refers either to a fixed-term contract worker, employed for a specific period of time, or to a subcontractor. A subcontractor is hired to do work that someone else has been contracted to do. Subcontractors are very common in the construction industry where builders will contract other companies or individuals to do electrical, plumbing and other work.

A fixed-term contract could be one off or renewed on a periodic basis. Many of the catering staff in schools are on fixed-term contracts that are reviewed annually. Professional footballers usually work on fixed-term contracts.

An evaluation of temporary and flexible working practices

Flexible working patterns have advantages and disadvantages that impact not only on individuals but also on organisations and the economy as a whole.

Although flexible working practices and part-time working provide opportunities for people who may otherwise be excluded from the workplace, individuals can feel insecure in such employment, particularly if they are constantly working on short-term contracts. There is also evidence that part-time or flexible workers receive less training than their full-time counterparts. In these circumstances individuals can feel their contribution is undervalued.

In turn, insecurities and frustrations experienced by part-time staff may affect their job satisfaction and, ultimately, their performance. This then impacts on organisations as they have to manage higher staff turnover rates.

One philosophy that may overcome our sense of personal frustration is suggested by Charles Handy in his book, *The Empty Raincoat*. Handy suggests that, if we think of our lives as 'inside-out doughnuts', with a core in the middle (the essentials of life) and the bounded space on the outside as our opportunities, we can achieve satisfaction in other areas of our lives, even if our jobs are unfulfilling.

On a positive note, there is evidence to suggest that, as individuals have responded to the call for more flexible working practices, this has led to fuller employment in Britain rather than, for example, in Germany and France.

Check your understanding

Set out the arguments for and against an organisation moving towards flexible working practices.

Contracts of employment

Section 1 of the Employment Rights Act 1996 states that employees should receive certain information within the first two months of starting employment. This document is known as a statement of particulars. All contracts of employment should, in theory, provide this information as a minimum.

The statement of particulars should include the following:

- The names of the employer and the employee.

- The name and address of the place of work.

- The date when the employment began.

- The date on which the employee's period of continuous employment began (this is usually calculated from the employee's start date).

- The job title.

- The salary.

- The intervals at which the employee will be paid (e.g. weekly or monthly).

- Any terms and conditions relating to hours of work.

- Any terms and conditions relating to holiday entitlements (including public holidays), holiday and sickness pay and pensions.

- The length of notice required from either party.

- If the employment is temporary, how long it is expected to continue.

- Any disciplinary rules to which the employee may be subject.

If the employer alters any detail of the statement of particulars, the employee must be informed of the change in writing within one month. If it is a significant change the employer should have obtained the employee's agreement.

The employer will agree on a date with the employee for work to start, and the contract of employment becomes binding from this date. The period of notice an employee must be given when being dismissed is stated in the contract, which is a legal document. The contract of employment becomes legally binding once the employee agrees to work for the employer, and the employer agrees to pay the employee a wage or salary.

The contract of employment must set out very clearly whether the employee is full time or part time, permanent or temporary, because this information is used to decide on the employee's rights, particularly should the case go before an industrial tribunal because of a dispute.

Certain entitlements and duties are implied into every contract, written or unwritten, either as a result of conduct (for example, getting paid), by Acts of Parliament (usually referred to as 'statute law'), by legislation or by legal traditions established by court cases (known as 'common law').

Every employee has the right not to be discriminated against on the basis of race, sex or disability. This protection covers every step of the process, from submitting a CV to the job interview and taking up service with an employer.

The Employment Rights Act 1996 provided employees with additional rights, the most important of which were the rights:

- Not to be unfairly dismissed.

- To receive an itemised payslip.

- To receive written reasons for dismissal.

- To receive and give a statutory minimum period of notice.

- To receive statutory maternity pay, take maternity leave and/or maternity absence.

- To receive statutory sick pay.

- To receive a statement of particulars of employment.

Check your understanding

Obtain and compare two contracts of employment – one for a full-time worker and one for a part-time worker.

What significant differences can you see between the two contracts? How do these differences give the firm 'flexibility'?

Chapter 16 Training and development

It is important that you are aware of the important contribution made by training and development to the competitiveness of businesses, and the need for businesses to invest resources in training and development programmes. You need to relate this to the environment within which businesses operate. You should be able to explain and give examples of the following training methods and activities:

- induction training

- mentoring

- coaching

- apprenticeships

- in-house training

- external training.

You should be able to distinguish between on-the-job and off-the-job training and transferable and non-transferable skills developed through training programmes. You should understand how nationally recognised training structures, such as Investors in People and Individual Learning Accounts, and nationally recognised qualifications, including NVQs, GNVQs and AVCEs, can contribute to business training and development programmes.

Training adds to competitiveness

In 1999, stock prices for the hi-tech sector of the economy increased by a large margin.

A major reason for this was the recognition by investors that a key route to competitiveness is through information and communications technology. In modern technology companies, in particular, the new 'knowledge workers are at a premium, using their brain power and intelligence to add value to products. In a 'knowledge economy' training and development take on a greater importance than ever before. The company that trains and develops its people is best placed to add value to products and thus gain competitive advantage. What is true for the individual business is also true for national economies, and this is one reason why recent governments have placed so much importance on education, training and development, particularly on information and communications technology.

In post-industrial Britain, service industries now account for the majority of employment opportunities, and the current strength of the British economy rests upon flexible working practices employed within service and knowledge-based industries (e.g. hospitality, leisure and tourism, media and communications, science and technology). For example, computer software, music, fashion, design, film, broadcasting, publishing and the performing arts are sectors of creativity which, in 1999, accounted for some £50 billion of economic activity and more than a million jobs. (Interestingly, the word 'imagineer' has recently entered the *Oxford Dictionary* along with the term 'knowledge worker'. An imagineer is a person who devises a highly imaginative concept or technology, especially the attractions in Walt Disney theme parks!)

At the beginning of the new millennium, people and human intelligence have been able to reclaim their rightful place as the dominant wealth-creating factors in society. Their role had been usurped by physical capital – buildings and machinery – during the Industrial Age, which saw some of the most destructive (yet highly productive) forces set loose on human relationships – not least of which was the creation of industrial systems. Of course, the remnants of the Industrial Age (Fordism, Taylorism, etc.) are still with us but the influence of top-down mechanistic hierarchies is less prevalent.

Intelligent organisations today recognise that their strength, and the strength of their balance sheets, rests in intellectual capital rather than physical capital. In the Industrial Age, machinery, plant and other items of physical capital drove the industrial process. Today, it is the brain power of people that is at the forefront. It is brain power that enables an organisation to identify customer needs and requirements; it is brain power that enables an organisation to engage in product research and development; it is brain power that enables the organisation to develop the most effective quality systems; and it is brain power that enables the organisation to come up with the most appropriate promotional activities.

Case study: The intelligent organisation takes over

In 1998 the arrival of intelligence as the driving force behind the economy was symbolised by the arrival of Mircrosoft (http.//www.Microsoft.com) as the most valuable company in the USA. On 13 September 1998 Microsoft toppled General Electric as the highest valued company. GE is still overwhelmingly an industrial manufacturer providing big-ticket items such as large domestic appliances (from washing machines to cookers) as well as aircraft engines. The company continues to be successful but not as successful as Microsoft. However, the observant student needs to watch out for future developments – for example, in the first half of 2000 the share price of Microsoft fell considerably as the US law courts began to take action against anti-competitive practices employed by Microsoft in securing unfair advantages for some of its products. In June 2000 the US courts demanded that Microsoft should be split into two parts.

While **GE** represents the Industrial Age, Mircrosoft represents the Information Age, with its dominating presence in providing software systems to personal computers and its success in exploiting the explosion of the Internet. Microsoft is a company that is very much based on the knowledge and expertise of its employees. Training and development programmes lie at the heart of the organisation, because it is recognised that intelligent employees need continually to develop and reinvent their intelligences to stay ahead of the field. The generosity of the company in distributing shares to employees has created no fewer than 4,000 millionaires around its Redmond, Washington, base – the so-called Microsoft Millionaires.

1 To what extent are the new technology companies of the twenty-first century based on education and training?

2 Why is it important for such organisations to invest heavily in training and development?

The training problem

While it is obvious that training is essential to competitive success, it is an area that UK-based companies have not always given high priority to. One reason for this is that many organisations consider it cheaper to hire already skilled workers than to pay the cost of training their own and possibly seeing these employees being poached by other companies.

Another problem is that many UK companies have failed to understand the relationship between training their employees and the return this gives to their profits. The relationship is not one that can be measured easily. However, in the twenty-first century's new knowledge-based economy, more and more employers are waking up to the importance of training and development, supported by a strong government emphasis on becoming competitive through training.

The following chart illustrates the training challenge in this country. The economy is being constantly restructured – old sectors decline, while new sectors develop. This was made blatantly apparent with the major restructuring at the turn of the millennium which saw the arrival of the new .com companies. People suddenly became aware that those with Information Technology and Communications (ICT) skills were at a premium and in big demand. Large companies therefore invested considerably in upskilling their people to develop these skills, and predators were constantly on the lookout to poach skilled ICT professionals

	1999	2000	2001	2002	2003
Demand	1,761,153	1,905,740	2,046,954	2,212,059	2,348,827
Supply	1,605,942	1,685,272	1,782,263	1,914,637	2,019,254
Shortage	155,211	220,468	264,591	297,422	329,573
Shortage (%)	9	12	13	13	14

Figure 16.1 Forcast of IT skills shortages, 1999–2003

from other companies. For example, when in May 2000 the .com clothing company Boo.com became the first major casualty of the new economy, other firms rushed to try to employ the skilled IT workers who lost their jobs with Boo.

Figure 16.1 shows the projected demand for, and supply of, IT professionals over the next few years, and highlights the extent of the training challenge facing many modern businesses.

What is training?

Training includes all forms of planned learning experiences and activities designed to make positive changes to performance and other behaviour (including the acquisition of new knowledge, skills, beliefs, values and attitudes). Learning is generally defined as 'a relatively permanent change in behaviour that occurs as a result of practice or experience'.

Training can be broken down into a number of elements:

- *Traditional training.* Training to promote learning of specific facts and content which enable improvements in job performance, such as technical skills training.

- *Education.* The act or process of acquiring knowledge, skills and understanding, usually in a school, college or university.

- *Vocational education.* Somewhere between educational and traditional training (e.g. apprenticeship training).

- *Management training.* Activities designed to improve managerial competence.

- *Organisational development.* Activities designed to change the way in which individuals operate within an organisation (e.g. to help them to work better with the changing culture of the organisation, perhaps through teamwork development).

What is development?

Development approaches the individual and his or her motivation from a different angle from that of training. While training is typically concerned with enabling the individual to contribute to meeting the objectives of the organisation better, personal development is more concerned with enabling individuals to develop themselves in the way that best suits individual needs. The two, it is hoped, will come together. By helping individuals to develop themselves, they will be more inclined and better able to contribute to helping the organisation meet its objectives (Figure 16.2).

The organisation that just concentrates on its own objectives, without thinking about the needs of its employees, is a selfish organisation. The individual employee who just thinks about his or her own development needs without thinking about how these can support the organisation in

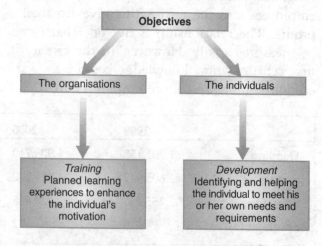

Figure 16.2 Personal development

meeting its own objectives is a selfish employee.

Personal professional development should be the responsibility of the individual concerned: there can be no 'personal' development without an individual taking ownership of his/her own development and choosing how such development will take place.

However, the organisation needs to support the individual in effectively developing him- or herself. The prime opportunity for the organisation to find out about individual development needs is through the appraisal interview. Through appraisal the organisation is able to communicate its objectives to the person being appraised, while the individual employee is able to clarify his or her development needs.

The starting point in the development process should be for each employee to put together a personal development plan (PDP). The personal development plan should include the following:

- The individual's goals and aspirations.

- An outline of the resources, methods and support required to achieve these goals.

- An indication of a time period for achieving these goals.

- An indication of how these goals will be recognised by others.

The personal development plan should be discussed with a line manager or team leader in the organisation so that the individual is able to communicate his or her aspirations to those he or she is working with. The organisation is then best placed to support the individual by providing him or her with the resources, methods and support he or she requires (e.g. the opportunity to go on training courses, opportunities to try out new work, etc.).

The benefits of training

There are a number of major benefits that flow from training:

- Effective training should improve the competitiveness of an organisation, as well as improving its productivity and service to customers.

- Surveys have shows that training costs less in the long run than recruiting fully trained workers from outside the organisation. Recruited, fully trained employees tend to leave much sooner than employees the organisation has trained itself.

- Training creates the 'right attitudes' in employees, and 'attitudes' are often just as important as knowledge and skills.

- The long-term benefits of training outweigh the short-run costs for all sorts of reasons, such as higher morale, higher skill and knowledge levels, lower labour turnover, reduced recruitment costs, etc.

- Improved efficiency results from savings from material costs due to reduced wastage, improved delivery performance, improved quality, reliability and range of products or services to customers, a more flexible workforce, etc.

- Many employees are keen to engage in training because they see it as adding to their own motivation and enjoyment of work.

Check your understanding

Produce a short leaflet outlining the importance of training and development in one industrial sector (e.g. retailing, banking, etc.).

Relating training to the business environment

Training needs to be closely related to the business environment. This is particularly true in organisations where the pace of change is very high. In commerce (buying and selling), for example, there has been a revolution in the development of e-commerce. As a result, many organisations have had to make a great leap forward to ensure large numbers of people are able to work effectively with new Internet-based technologies. Organisations with the right sorts of people to work in this environment have been most successful.

At the same time, there are a number of people in this country who have almost dropped off the bottom of the employability scale in terms of lacking the skills required for the modern economy. Government-funded training schemes have therefore been developed, particularly to enable young people (and others) to develop their information communications technology skills.

Check your understanding

Which sectors of the economy would you identify as being areas in which training initiatives are a key part of competitiveness today?

Training methods and activities
Induction training

Induction is the process of introducing new employees to their place of work, job, new surroundings and the people they will be working with. Induction also provides information to help new employees start work and generally 'fit in'.

As well as following naturally from recruitment and selection, induction should also consider the initial training and development anyone needs either on joining a new organisation or on taking on a new function within it. As well as dealing with the initial knowledge and skills needed to do the job, in the case of a new organisation, it should also deal with the structure, culture and activities of the organisation.

In some large companies, induction training will involve the new employee working in a number of departments for a short period of time to get an overall feel for the organisation before starting in a specific department. This enables the inductee to build up contacts and to obtain a good general overview of the organisation.

Check your understanding

Obtain the induction packs from at least two organisations. Compare and evaluate these to see which gives the better introduction to the organisation.

Typically, induction will involve a talk from a senior member of the organisation, getting to know other new recruits, a corporate video and, often, some activities to break the ice for the new recruit. An important part of induction training will involve an introduction to company regulations and health and safety requirements, etc. The new recruit will usually be given an induction pack that introduces him or her to the organisation.

Mentoring

Mentoring involves a trainee being 'paired' with a more experienced employee. The trainee carries out the job but uses the 'mentor' to discuss problems that may occur and how best to solve them.

This approach is used in many lines of work. For example, it is common practice for trainee teachers to work with a mentor who is responsible for their early training and development. The student teacher will watch the mentor teach before starting his or her own teaching. The mentor will then give ongoing guidance to the student teacher on how best to improve his or her performance. The mentee will take any problems and difficulties he or she is facing to the mentor to seek advice.

Coaching

Coaching involves providing individuals with personal coaches in the workplace. The person who is going to take on the coaching role will need, first, to develop coaching skills and will also need to have the time slots for the coaching to take place. The coach and the individual being coached will need to identify development opportunities they can work on together – ways of tackling jobs, ways of improving performance, etc. The coach will provide continuous feedback on performance and how this is progressing.

Of course, coaching does not just benefit the person being coached; it also aids the coach's own personal development. It is particularly important in a coaching system that:

- The coach wants to coach the person and has the necessary coaching skills.

- The person being coached wants to be coached and has the necessary listening and learning skills.

- Sufficient time is given to the coaching process.

- The organisation places sufficient value on the coaching process.

Some of the best sportspeople in this country have improved their skills and abilities by working closely with a coach they respect.

Check your understanding

Observe a coaching process in action. What makes the coaching successful/unsuccessful? It may be easiest to carry out this activity in relation to sports coaching – but you could apply what you observe to work-based coaching.

Apprenticeships

One of the great strengths of the British industrial system was the existence of a range of apprenticeship schemes, many of which no longer exist. With the apprenticeship scheme, the apprentice learnt by working for a more skilled craftsperson. They learnt on the job by learning from their 'master' or 'master craftsman'. The apprentices had to work for a number of years to master their trades.

Apprenticeships were once widespread in skilled work and, when the apprentices had learnt their trades, they were able to set up on their own and so bring in higher wages, employing apprentices of their own. During the early years of the apprenticeship wages might be quite low, and then rise as the apprentice became more skilled.

The main reasons for the decline of apprenticeships are as follows:

- Replacing skilled labour with skilled machines (factory automation).

- The change from an industrial to a post-industrial society with the development of service industries and, more recently, with the widespread deskilling of many jobs through the use of information and communications technologies.

- The lack of investment in training in this country since the Second World War.

In recent years, the government has developed a Modern Apprenticeship scheme that enables young people to combine learning on the job with college-based courses. These schemes are subsidised by the government, which gives employers a greater incentive to take on apprentices.

In-house training and external training

In-house training is where an organisation has its own training department. External training is where employees are sent on external courses, or are trained in other ways, away from the organisation. In-house training can take place on the job or off the job within the company, but external training always takes place off the job.

On-the-job training

On-the-job training (OJT) takes place when employees are trained while they are carrying out an activity, often at their place of work.

Case study: On-the-job training at Nestlé

On-the-job training (OJT) is the basis of Nestlé's (http://www.nestle.com/) training system. In quantitative terms, it constitutes by far the most important element of training within the group. This form of training, 'at grass roots' or 'on the factory floor', has four distinct advantages:

1 It allows participants to gain a thorough knowledge about the company's infrastructure (i.e. how the company is organised and how it works). This knowledge is not limited to the factory or the Nestlé company concerned but it is designed to get across to participants a feeling of belonging to a larger body by explaining the way Nestlé's different components communicate worldwide.

Nescafé is one of Nestlé's famous brands

2 There can be no substitute for hands-on experience in developing skills.

3 It allows the trainee to engage in productive earnings and it can be carried out without the need for structured, permanent training facilities.

4 OJT is also a useful means of testing a trainee's knowledge and competence for any given task. Since training and work are indivisible, theory immediately relates to practice, thus making the information far more tangible. Furthermore, feedback on performance and understanding can be provided instantly, thus generating a system that also allows for continuous guidance and assessment.

The great thing about on-the-job training is that it makes possible the creation of tailor-made training programmes that are unique to each trainee.

Nestlé provide two kinds of OJT. The first is for trainees. These training sessions are generally short in duration and are geared specifically towards new arrivals or those starting a new job within the company. This kind of OJT is therefore widely used at both national and international levels.

The other is for current employees. Every Nestlé employee continues to receive training throughout his or her time with the company. The process is a constant and systematic communication of knowledge from executive levels down, and includes every level of management. It is so central to Nestlé's training and development programmes that it is regarded as part of the normal duties and responsibilities of management. To ensure this valuable pool of expertise, experience and understanding is used effectively, Nestlé have designed courses aimed specifically at management and for the assessment of management.

Very close attention is also given to the company's first line of supervisors, which could include (among others) middle management in production or district sales managers. The quality of their communication within the company is felt to be particularly vital to the smooth running of the company's infrastructure. Their courses are largely centred on practical management issues. Consequently, training in how to coach – 'to train the trainers' – is given within most of Nestlé's operating companies.

Every Nestlé manager is expected to be a constant mentor to his or her subordinates. This task cannot be delegated, and managers are also evaluated on how well they perform in developing, training and motivating those working under their responsibility.

1 To what extent is Nestlé's OJT concerned with the development of attitudes as well as with skills and knowledge?

2 What do you see as being the disadvantages of OJT?

3 Who is responsible for training at Nestlé?

4 What approaches to training and development are used?

5 Does Nestlé appear to put a great deal of emphasis on training? Why do you think this is?

Off-the-job training

Off-the-job training, as its name suggests, takes place away from the job. This can be either internally within a company or externally using outside trainers. Many large companies will engage in a great deal of internal off-the-job training.

Case study: In-house, off-the-job local and regional training at Nestlé

Throughout the world, all Nestlé operating companies have their own internal training structures. The training courses are held partly at head offices, partly at hotel facilities. In addition to this, five operating companies – France, the UK, Spain, Mexico and Brazil – also have residential training centres that are located near the head office of their national Nestlé company.

The programmes of all these training efforts cover a wide variety of general subjects, such as sales, marketing, finance, data processing, production and human resources. In addition, each operating company offers tailor-made courses geared to the particular needs of the country or countries concerned. It is therefore not surprising to find English language courses on the curricula of most of these courses outside English-speaking countries. Although the official language of the Nestlé Group, due to its history and location, is French (Nestlé is a Swiss company), English is the most widely used language within the company. A good knowledge of English has become indispensable for any Nestlé staff member with international contacts and responsibilities.

Experience has shown that successful local in-house training is directly linked to increased efficiency in local operations. It also fosters a sense of interweaving with the local community by providing employees with information about Nestlé worldwide. Knowledge about Nestlé's worldwide development is useful not only on induction courses but to all employees.

Examples of courses offered include the following:

- The sales force. Because of different degrees of trade development in many countries, as well as language barriers, training is almost always managed at a local level. These courses cover local approaches to selling but within a global context.

- Factory personnel. Since this normally involves either new technologies or new working methods, training is usually carried out on site.

- Management levels. Techniques are changing so rapidly that it is essential to keep management up to date. Courses focus on two main skills: sound team management and supervision change at the operational and strategic level.

- Employee development. A wide variety of courses is available to every employee.

Participation will be the result of a dialogue between the employee and his or her manager. This may take many different forms depending on the individual needs. Among the most popular courses are foreign languages, communication skills, time management, performance objectives and finance for non-specialists.

In addition to local and regional training, Nestlé also have an international training centre at Rive-Reine in Switzerland. This centre not only focuses on developing the sorts of international skills Nestlé's employees need but it also focuses on encouraging employees to develop a deeper understanding of the Nestlé culture, which is based on diversity and teamworking.

1 To what extent is Nestlé's off-the-job training concerned with developing attitudes as well as skills and know-how?

2 What evidence is provided that Nestlé are concerned with employees' individual development, as well as meeting organisational objectives?

3 Why is local and regional off-the-job training carried out by Nestlé?

4 What evidence is there that the training and development programmes are influenced by the dynamic business and competitive environment in which Nestlé operate?

Check your understanding

Identify the on-the-job and off-the-job training opportunities available in either a job you have experienced yourself or a job someone you know has carried out.

Investors in People

INVESTORS IN PEOPLE

® reproduced with permission of Investors in People UK

Many organisations in all sectors now pride themselves in meeting the Investors in People Standard. To achieve the Standard, an organisation needs to show the following:

Commitment – to develop people in order to achieve its aims and objectives

Planning – to be clear on aims and objectives and what people need to do to achieve them

Action – to develop people effectively to improve performance

Evaluation – to understand the impact of investment in people on performance.

Being an Investor in People means that the organisation is likely to be seen more favourably by prospective employees, customers and other stakeholders. To achieve the Standard, an organisation is assessed by an independent assessor who gathers evidence (verbal, written and observed) that all requirements of the Standard are met. The assessor's recommendations are approved by a panel of business peers and the organisation is recognised as an Investor in People.

Check your understanding

Interview someone who has been involved in setting up the systems that have enabled an organisation to gain Investors in People status.

What were the main policies and practices that needed to be put in place?

NVQs, GNVQs and AVCEs

National Vocational Qualifications (NVQs), General National Vocational Qualifications (GNVQs) and Advanced Vocational Certificates in Education (AVCEs) or Vocational A Levels, have played an important part in raising the standards of training and development in recent years. Far more people are engaged in training, education and development than ever before, with over half of young people going on to university. Much of the credit for this goes to the creation of new qualifications young people find enjoyable and worth while.

An NVQ is the expression of a person's ability to do a job satisfactorily and is awarded by a combination of exams and an assessment of competence in the workplace. Standards for NVQs are established by a lead body made up of knowledgeable experts from a given industry, who know what the standards should be to achieve different levels of performance.

It is important for everyone starting work or training to check he or she is being given the opportunity to obtain the relevant NVQ (or similar qualification).

NVQs are well established in service industries and in construction, engineering, office administration jobs, clothing manufacture, retail sales, agriculture and horticulture (and many more sectors).

It is now possible for older people with experience but no qualifications to have their experience assessed. If they are judged to be competent, they will be awarded an appropriate qualification.

Advanced VCEs are a more recent offshoot of NVQs. Advanced VCEs developed in recognition that, in the modern workplace, specific skills related to jobs rapidly become outdated and that it is often more important to have a range of cross-transferable general skills and knowledge suitable for a range of occupational areas (e.g. in the field of business or health and social care).

Advanced VCEs have taken the educational and employment world by storm with their popularity, and the way in which they have effectively won the interest of many students who progress from an Advanced VCE advanced to university or a responsible post in the world of work.

By creating a national framework for qualifications it has been possible to give far greater status to vocational and general vocational qualifications, which are now far more widely understood by employers and the public at large.

Check your understanding

Produce a short leaflet for potential Advanced VCE students explaining why they should do the qualification and how it will help them with their personal development, as well as making them more employable.

The implications for lifetime learning, education and training

As employment becomes less secure, individuals are being urged to develop new transferable skills. Government initiatives are now encouraging individuals to think of education and training as a lifelong process.

Non-transferable and transferable skills

Traditionally, many people have either been trained in or have become adept in specific job-related skills (e.g. a factory operative may have been trained to use a knitting machine). This operative may have become a fast, productive knitting machine operator, but this skill is valued only within the hosiery industry. When an entire industry is in decline, or new technology outdates present skills, the operative's employability will be much diminished.

As individuals are expected to become increasingly flexible in their working patterns, there is a greater need for them to develop generic skills that are transferable, and valuable, to a variety of employers.

Generic skills that are highly regarded today are the key skills of communication (including literacy), problem-solving, teamworking, ICT skills, numeracy and improving one's own learning and performance. A further range of generic skills employers value include: reasoning skills (scheduling work, diagnosing work problems), work process management skills (visualising output, working backwards for planning purposes), and personal values and attitudes (such as motivation, judgement, discipline, leadership and initiative).

In his 1999 Budget address, the Labour Chancellor of the Exchequer, Gordon Brown, said:

Those who are left out of the knowledge revolution will be left behind in the new knowledge economy. The more individual talent we nurture, the more economic growth we will achieve.

The Chancellor then went on to outline proposals to encourage adult learners to build up their basic skills and computer literacy, with the introduction of an 80% discount on basic skills and computer literacy training.

Government initiatives to balance supply and skills demands

In the Department for Education and Employment's *Business Plan* for 1998-99, priorities were listed as follows:

- *Objective 1.* Ensuring all young people reach 16 with the skills, attributes and personal qualities that will give them a secure foundation for lifelong learning, work and citizenship in a rapidly changing world.

- *Objective 2.* Developing in everyone a commitment to lifelong learning so as to enhance their lives, improve their employability in a changing labour market and to create the skills our economy and employers need.

- *Objective 3.* To help people without a job into work.

To meet the first objective the government introduced new measures and targets to improve education in schools, including the introduction of a numeracy and literacy strategy and the creation of Education Action Zones.

Although GCSE attainment standards at grades A–C have risen steadily from 34.5% in 1989–90 to over 50% in 1999–2000, 37% of employers employing young peopled aged between 16 and 19 perceived a skills gap in this particular age group (according to the *Labour Market Skills Trends Survey, 1999*). The skills employers continue to list as lacking are: communication skills, practical skills, customer handling skills and personal skills. These skills are central to AVCEs and, in recognition of their importance, key skills became part of the overall Advanced level framework from 2000.

The *Labour Market Skills Trends Survey* also reported that:

> *the vast majority of young people benefit from work experience placements during their last year in compulsory education. The government is keen to promote work-related learning and to encourage schools to offer higher quality work experience to all pupils.*

The following excerpts taken from press articles emphasise the need for good-quality careers education and work experience to ensure all children have equality of choice and the chance to glimpse the range of opportunities available to them.

On 29 March 1999, *The Times* reported research by the Joseph Rowntree Foundation which indicated that:

> *children become so used to poverty that they are resigned to failure and are not prepared to try to better themselves. Asked what they would like to do when they left school, children from families on income support were more likely than others to want jobs that required little training or few academic qualifications.*

In an article for The Economist's *The World* in 1999, Anthony King observed that:

> *a university degree guarantees nothing. Not having one imposes a serious handicap.*

In addition to the government's initiatives to match education in schools to the needs of employers, considerable emphasis is now being placed on the need to develop a culture of lifelong learning. In 1998, the newly commissioned National Skills Task Force produced its first report, *Towards a National Skills Agenda*. The task force's stated terms of reference included the provision of assistance to the Secretary of State to develop:

> *a National Skills Agenda which will ensure that Britain has the skills needed to sustain high levels of employment, compete in the global market place and provide opportunity for all.*

There is a general view that the current major shortfall in skills is occurring in the sphere of information and communications technology because of the rapid expansion of this area.

Other major government initiatives designed to ensure opportunities for all and to address the skills needs of the economy include the introduction of National Traineeships and Modern Apprenticeships. These will allow young people to combine further education with on-the-job training. National Traineeships assure the provision of education up to Vocational Level 2, whilst Modern Apprenticeships generally support training up to Vocational Level 3.

The New Deal for young people (aged 18–24) is designed to allow the young unemployed a choice of four options:

1 Subsidised employment.

2 Full-time education and training.

3 Working in the voluntary sector.

4 Work with the Environmental Task Force.

Individual Learning Accounts, as outlined in the 1999 Budget, are designed to encourage individuals to save towards the costs of additional training.

Lifelong Learning Partnerships were launched in September 1999. This initiative uses existing structures, such as Training and Enterprise Councils (TECs), to build learning partnerships that will play a key role in regenerating learning in communities and in promoting social inclusion (i.e. involving everyone in the education process).

The University for Industry was launched in 2000 and is designed to be 'the hub of a brand-new learning network' offering improved information to employers and to individuals. For individuals specifically, it aims to overcome complexity, to reduce fear, save time and reduce costs, thus lowering the barriers to learning.

It is foreseen by the government that, in this new century, knowledge is the means by which people escape the trap of low pay. Given the necessity of acquiring skills and qualifications, the important thing now is to develop a society which recognises education as a prize to be valued highly. To do this, the government has to make sure that education is accessible and desirable to individuals from all walks of life.

Case study: Individual Learning Accounts with Lincolnshire TEC

Individual Learning Accounts are part of government policy to encourage everyone to engage in lifelong learning.

The scheme operated by Lincolnshire TEC (which reflects the national picture) is as follows. An individual has to put up the first £25 of his or her own money towards a training or education course. Lincolnshire TEC then puts in £150 of money towards the scheme (from central government funds). The person enrolling on the scheme gets a Smart card which registers the £150 worth of credit. Provided the student/trainee goes to a registered trainer, he or she will be able to deduct fees from the credit card. The scheme is available for anybody in the 18–65 age range who is working or registered for work. The scheme started in 1999 and is currently running to 2002.

1 What do you see as being the advantages of the Individual Learning Accounts scheme?

2 What do you see as being its drawbacks?

3 How could the system be improved?

Check your understanding

Identify a recent development stemming from the government's commitment to competition through education/training and development. Outline the scheme.

Will it add to or decrease the level of flexibility in the labour market?

Chapter 17 Performance management

A business needs to manage the performance of its employees effectively if it is to remain competitive. You need to be able to explain and give examples of the following methods businesses use to manage the performance of their employees:

- performance reviews, including appraisals

- self-evaluation

- peer evaluation

- target-setting for individuals and groups

- measuring individual and group output/production.

You should be aware of how training and development may enhance the performance of individuals and groups of employees. You should also be aware of the need for competitive businesses to link performance reviews and evaluations to training and development.

You need to develop an understanding of the environment within which businesses attempt to manage the performance of their employees. In particular, you should know key aspects of legislation, such as the maximum number of hours employees can work in a week, regulations governing leave arrangements (including maternity and paternity leave) and minimum wage rates.

You should be aware of the importance of employee motivation and the significance of both financial and non-financial incentives. You should be able to identify the influence of the following motivation theories/ideas on the way in which businesses manage their employees:

- Frederick Taylor's 'Principles of Scientific Management'

- Abraham Maslow's 'Hierarchy of Needs'

- Douglas McGregor's 'Theory X and Theory Y'

- Frederick Herzberg's 'Two-factor Theory'.

Managing performance

Organisations have always relied on the performance of the human resource. However, in the twenty-first century this is more true than ever before because the economy is built on intelligence and complex information and communications technology systems. The result of these developments is that most modern employees have to interface directly with customers (they all have an internal customer), and decisions need to be taken by employees at every level within the organisation, rather than waiting to be told what to do. The successful organisation will thus be one that has all its employees firing on all cylinders, working towards helping the organisation to meet its objectives.

Organisations, therefore, have had to develop systems and methods for managing effectively the performance of their employees.

Performance reviews (including appraisals)

In an organisation you want everyone to be pulling in the same direction. Effective organisations will therefore set out a mission statement identifying the overarching aims of the organisation. This will be a brief statement, such as:

Super Airways set out to provide their customers with the best value-for-money air travel combined with unrivalled quality service, while rewarding employees and other stakeholders.

Coupled with this, the organisation will create a values statement, such as:

Super Airways believe in putting service at the forefront of everything we do. We are a caring company that believes in teamwork.

Given the mission and values, the organisation can create objectives at every level within the organisation – right down to personal objectives for individual members of the organisation. It is through these objectives that the success of the organisation can be monitored and evaluated, as well as measuring the performance of individual members of the organization. Figure 17.1 shows an annual results cycle based on an evaluation of these objective.

A well-developed performance management system will include the following:

- A statement outlining the organisation's values.

- A statement of the organisation's objectives.

- Individual objectives, which are linked to the organisation's objectives.

- Regular performance reviews throughout the year.

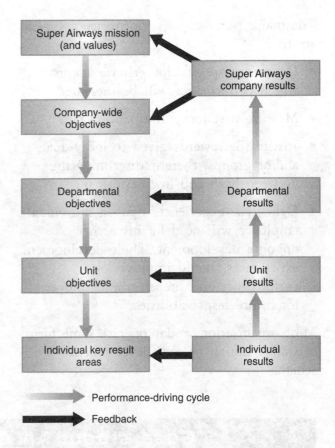

Figure 17.1 Super Airways: annual results cycle

- Performance-related pay.

- Training and counselling.

With such a system in place, it becomes possible to establish for a period of time the key result areas that an individual will be judged against. The results the individual achieves can be judged against expected standards; a reward system can then be tailored to the way in which the individual enables the organisation to achieve its results.

Performance appraisal is a process of evaluating performance systematically and of providing feedback on which performance adjustments can be made. Performance appraisal works on the basis of the following equation:

Desired performance – Actual performance = Need for action

The major purposes of performance appraisal are to:

- Define the specific job criteria against which performance will be measured.

- Measure past job performance accurately.

- Justify the rewards given to individuals and/or groups, thereby discriminating between high and low performance.

- Define the experiences that an individual employee will need for his or her ongoing development. These development experiences should improve job performance and prepare the employee for future responsibilities.

Most organisations today operate some form of staff appraisal or staff development scheme.

Common stages of staff appraisal are as follows:

1 The line manager meets with the job-holder to discuss what is expected. The agreed expectations may be expressed in terms of targets, performance standards or required job behaviours – attributes, skills and attitudes.

2 The outcome of the meeting is recorded and usually signed by both parties.

3 The job-holder performs the job for a period of six months or a year.

4 At the end of the period, the job-holder and line manager or team leader meet again to review and discuss progress made. They draw up new action plans to deal with identified problems and agree targets and standards for the next period.

Case study: An appraisal process

Figures 17.2–17.4 provide information about the appraisal process in a leisure centre that employs 28 full-time members of staff and 40 part-timers.

Full-time staff	100
Part-time staff	52

Figure 17.2 Appraisal interviews completed in 2000 (%)

Nobody is interested in my view	50
Nothing done about previous appraisals	40
Not enough time	20
Other reasons	16

Figure 17.4 Reasons given by staff for not engaging in the appraisal process (% ticking each reason)

For purposes of increasing pay	62
To avoid penalties at work	40
To be able to discuss work-related issues with supervisor	36
To discuss personal development	12
Other issues	20

Figure 17.3 Reasons given by staff for engaging in the appraisal process (% ticking each reason)

1 Given this information, has the appraisal process been effective?

2 Is the appraisal process regarded in a positive or negative light by members of the organisation?

3 What would you do to alter the appraisal process to make it meaningful?

Most people associate appraisal with a top-down appraisal by a supervisor or line manager in an organisation. However, in the modern world of empowered organisations and teamworking there are all sorts of variants.

Figure 17.5 shows some of the possible sources of appraisal for a manager (at the centre of the figure).

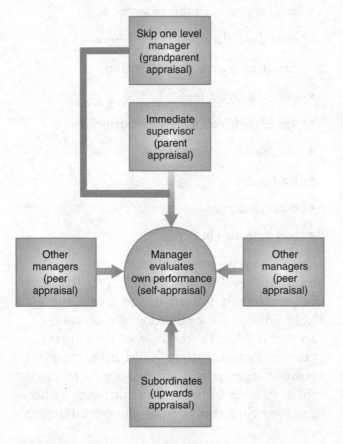

Figure 17.5 Possible sources of appraisal for a manager

Self-evaluation

Self-evaluation is an important part of performance management. Take the example of a student following an Advanced VCE course in business. The student, it is hoped, will increasingly take responsibility for his or her own learning. The student needs to be able to identify the assessment criteria at the start of a particular unit and then identify the best ways of meeting those criteria to get the highest grades. In carrying out work assignments, the student should be able to evaluate his or her own performance against the required standards.

The student who operates in this way is not only learning the skills and content of the course but is also learning how to learn. Once a student becomes effective at managing his or her own performance and evaluating this performance in an accurate way, the student becomes autonomous – he or she does not need regulation (being told what to do): the student can fly on his or her own.

Self-evaluation is therefore very important in the work context. Modern organisations encourage their employees to establish meaningful goals and then to evaluate performance in meeting these goals.

Employees who are given work assignments to do are also often encouraged to evaluate their own performance in carrying out these assignments to the required standard. The benefits of using this approach are as follows:

- The employees take more responsibility for their own work area and for monitoring their own performance in this area. This is clearly motivational.

- The employees may have a greater understanding of their own work area and their job than an external appraiser may have. This is increasingly the case where employees are working in highly creative, individual situations, developing interpersonal relations that are not always easy to scrutinise and measure.

- Self-evaluation is cost effective. It avoids the wasteful expense (including time) of having external evaluators.

- Self-evaluation enables individuals to develop a much clearer picture of exactly what it is they are doing – which makes work definition much better.

> ### Check your understanding
> Identify a situation in which you have been responsible for evaluating your own performance.
>
> How effective is self-evaluation in enabling performance that meets the objectives of an organisation?

Peer evaluation

A process of peer evaluation is sometimes used when students are working on combined projects – working in teams. Without peer evaluation there would be a danger some students do all the work while others sit back and take the rewards. It is therefore possible to devise forms for students to evaluate each other's input – e.g. did they attend meetings? Did they carry out their share of the research? etc. This approach is usually effective because students, as a rule, do not like working with other students who do not pull their weight.

The same sort of approach can be applied to the work situation, where employees are part of a co-operative team or quality circle. Peer group evaluation makes it possible to check on how much team members are contributing to the product of the teamwork (i.e. the work results of the team effort), and to the process of the teamwork (i.e. helping the team to work effectively as a high-performance team).

Peer evaluation can be very effective in that it creates a collaborative approach at work. People don't feel they are being judged

from above. It can lead to a process of critical friendship whereby individuals will help each other to improve performance. There are a number of ingredients that help peer evaluation to be a success:

- respect for each other
- trust in each other
- non-competitive atmosphere
- willingness to take risks
- confidentiality
- listen and give full attention
- say what you feel
- value each other's contribution
- all members participate
- be honest
- don't interrupt
- feel free to challenge.

Unfortunately, peer evaluation can often result in low levels of criticism so that performance is judged in too favourable a light. Also, peer evaluation can create an approach whereby those who work in the peer evaluation system build up a defensive position against the organisation – to justify their own decisions and performance rather than viewing things from the organisation's side.

> ### Check your understanding
> What do you see as being the major strengths and weaknesses of peer appraisal?

Case study: Peer appraisal in an educational setting

It was decided at a college of higher education to introduce a system of peer appraisal rather than top-down appraisal. This meant lecturers were appraised by someone on the same level as them. This approach was welcomed because it supported the collegial structure of the organization, with people seeing themselves as being broadly equal with colleagues and thus sympathetic to their needs and aspirations.

All the lecturing staff were trained in the appraisal process and it was set in motion.

A lecturer would identify a range of targets for the coming year, and look back on performance over the previous year. Meetings were arranged and the results of the interview were carefully recorded. The lecturers taking part in the system felt it worked well because they didn't feel as if they were being judged and could talk freely about their aspirations and the requirements for development in the subsequent year. The process seemed to be effective in that lecturers found a number of their development needs were met through the process, and it led to greater motivation.

However, a new senior executive came into the college and decided the scheme was ineffective in driving home the objectives of the organisation. There was too much emphasis on the needs of the lecturers rather than on focusing them on organisational goals. The system was therefore changed to one where line managers appraised their subordinates. A number of lecturers started to boycott the system. However, the senior managers felt it worked well because it identified those lecturers who most closely supported the senior managers. Also, a number of lecturers who supported the new management team found it helped to improve their own promotion opportunities within the organisation.

1 What do you think would be more effective in the situation described above – peer or top-down evaluation?

2 What do you see as being the chief benefits and drawbacks of each of the two schemes?

Target-setting for individuals and groups

Performance management is a term that is used to describe the process in which employees participate with their superiors in setting their own performance targets. These targets are directly aligned with the stated goals of the teams, units or departments they work for and, hence, with organisational targets.

There are three broad approaches to staff appraisal, based on personal attributes, skills or performance. They are not necessarily mutually exclusive. Schemes may contain elements of each. A large organisation may use different schemes for different groups of employees.

Personal attributes

The designers of the scheme identify the personal attributes that affect job performance. These are used as the basis for appraisal. Some examples are:

- reliability
- judgement
- application
- initiative
- adaptability
- disposition.

There are several criticisms of this approach. For example, the attributes are open to wide interpretation by the many managers undertaking appraisal in different parts of the organisation. The system is also not consistent and, therefore, potentially unjust.

Skills

Appraisal focuses on the employee's proficiency in the skills relevant to the particular job. Depending on the job, these might include technical competence (such as operating particular equipment), communication skills (such as report writing) and the interpersonal skills needed to deal with customers. The person doing the appraisal, usually the manager, observes the employee over a period of time and records his or her judgement of the employee's competence. The standard could be a company's own or it could be the performance standard of a relevant National Vocational Qualification (NVQ).

Performance

The basis of appraisal is the achievement of agreed performance standards or targets. Advocates of this approach point to its objectivity. However, it is difficult in some jobs to find a satisfactory measure of individual performance. The outcome of a nurse's performance is, for example, patient care. One way of assessing the success rate of patient care could be the discharge rate – how soon the patients are fit to go home.

However, there are many variables affecting this outcome: the quality of the resources, the performance of the rest of the team, changes in policy and practice relating to discharge, the home conditions of the patients and so on. To isolate the effects of an individual's performance may be difficult and expensive to achieve and, where close teamwork is desirable, assessment and grading of individual performance could be divisive.

Measuring individual and group output/productivity

Often within organisations there is a considerable amount of dissatisfaction about the way different individuals or groups are rewarded in the system, which may seem to defy logic. Many appraisal schemes include behaviour scales because it is felt that behaviour rather than personality should be appraised and rewarded.

Behaviour scales describe a range of behaviours that contribute, to a greater or lesser degree, to the successful achievement of the cluster of tasks that make up a job. Supervisors carrying out an appraisal are asked to indicate which statements on the specially designed form most accurately describe a subordinate's behaviour. A detailed version of this is the Behaviourally Anchored Rating Scales (BARS). Statements about work behaviour are used to create scales, which must then be tested to confirm their relevance and accuracy.

Today, many organisations use a competency-based approach to measuring performance. Competency is defined as 'an underlying characteristic of an individual which is related to effective or superior performance in a job'. For example, Figure 17.6 illustrates part of a competency list used by managers to evaluate counter staff performance in a fast-food restaurant.

Job evaluation is the process of assessing in an organisation the value of one job in relation to another, without regard to the ability or personality of the individuals currently holding the position. It results in a pay range for each job. An individual's personal worth is recognised by awarding increments within the fixed range for that job.

Merit rating is a system whereby the individual employee is awarded increments or bonuses based on a systematic appraisal of his or her developed skill level and performance. Merit rating usually operates within a job-evaluated pay structure. Job evaluation sets the pay bands while merit rating determines the position of the individual within the band. A typical pattern is as follows:

- *Starter.* Degree of efficiency expected from a learner.

- *Qualified.* Able to perform normal aspects of the job.

- *Experienced.* Able to deal with all circumstances of the job.

- *Superior.* Ready for promotion; equivalent to starter on the next grade.

The merit-rating scheme thus defines and weights the factors against which the manager assesses each employee, usually annually. Typical factors are volume and quality of output, initiative, adaptability,

	Yes (✓)	No (✗)
Greeting the customer		
1 There is a smile?	✓	
2 It is a sincere greeting?	✓	
3 There is eye contact?		✗
Taking the order		
1 The counter person is thoroughly familiar with the menu?	✓	
2 The customer has to give the order only once?	✓	
3 Small orders (four items or less) are memorised rather than written down?	✓	
4 There is suggestive selling?		✗
Assembling the order		
1 The order is assembled in the proper sequence?	✓	
2 Grill slips are handed in first?	✓	
3 Drinks are poured in the proper sequence?	✓	
4 Proper amount of ice?	✓	
5 Cups slanted and finger used to activate?		✗
6 Drinks are filled to the proper level?		✗
7 Drinks are capped?	✓	
8 Clean cups?	✓	
9 Holding times are observed on coffee?		✗
10 Cups are filled to the proper level on the coffee?	✓	
Presenting the order		
1 Is it properly packaged?	✓	
2 The bag is double folded?	✓	
3 Plastic trays are used if eating outside?	✓	
4 A tray liner is used?	✓	
5 The food is handled in the proper manner?	✓	
Asking for and receiving payment		
1 The amount of the order is stated clearly and loud enough to hear?		✗
2 The denomination received is clearly stated?		✗
3 Change is counted out loud?		✗
4 Change is counted efficiently?	✓	
5 Large bills are laid on the till until change is given?	✓	
Thanking the customer and asking for repeat business		
1 Is there always a thank you?	✓	
2 The thank you is sincere?		✗
3 Is there eye contact?		✗
4 Return business is asked for?		✗

Figure 17.6   Counter staff performance in a fast-food restaurant: competency list

attendance and punctuality. Managers need to be trained to use the system.

Merit rating is not without its problems and critics. Such schemes are unpopular with trade unions, which see merit rating as subjective and open to favouritism. From a management point of view, a weakness in most schemes is that an award, once given, is permanent, even if performance drops to a previous level.

Performance-related pay (PRP)

Automatic increases within fixed pay bands have largely disappeared. The trend is towards performance-related pay as the preferred method of deciding non-manual workers' progress through their salary bands. Merit-rating schemes in the past often relied on managers' subjective assessments of employees' personal characteristics. The increments, if awarded, were usually stepped and fixed. PRP schemes use performance and/or competence as the criteria for deciding the size of increments and therefore also the rate of progress through a salary band. The PRP approach is based on a management-by-objectives philosophy of agreeing:

- the key result areas of the job

- clear standards of performance and target levels of competence

- regular, objective reviews of performance and competence.

As a result of the PRP review the manager might, for example, assess an employee as outstanding, superior, standard or developing. The percentage pay increase awarded would then be influenced by the following:

- Typical rates of pay for employees in that industry/occupational grouping at a particular time.

- The financial state of the company.

- The present position of the employee in the salary band.

- Company policy on speed of progress through the salary band.

Guidance to managers might be expressed as in Figure 17.7.

Review grade awarded	Pay increase (per cent)
Outstanding	12
Superior	8
Standard	5
Learning	2

Figure 17.7 Performance-related pay: guidance to managers

The scale of percentage increase might vary according to the employees' current position in the pay scale: larger for those at the bottom end of the scale, smaller for those nearer the top. The reward for those already at the top of their salary band should be promotion. If that is not possible, they might be awarded a lump sum (bonus) that, unlike other increments, is not part of their salary.

Check your understanding

Examine the way in which an organisation you work for (or a relative or friend works for) measures individual and/or group performance.

Linking performance reviews and evaluations to training and development

It is important to stress that the process of appraisal and other forms of evaluation should be closely linked to training and development. This is a two-way process.

If the organisation is to achieve its objectives, it is essential to train and develop its people so they are best able to support the organisation in working towards objectives. At the same time the individual needs to have the opportunity to be able to communicate his or her own personal development needs to the organisation through appraisal or personal development planning schemes.

Check your understanding

Interview someone who has been involved in being appraised to find out the extent to which his or her appraisal was linked to further training and meeting personal development needs.

Legislation affecting performance

It is important to have a broad outline knowledge of how recent legislation affects hours of work, leave arrangements and minimum wages in an organisation.

Maximum hours legislation

The Working Time Regulations 1998 and the Young Workers Directive 1998 provide protection for employees with regard to the hours they can work. These working time regulations now provide that a person's average weekly working time (including overtime) should not have to exceed 48 hours, averaged over a period of 17 weeks. Individuals can agree to be excluded from the maximum working week requirements on a voluntary basis.

Night working should not have to exceed eight hours in each 24-hour period, over 17 weeks.

Adult workers must be permitted to take a rest period of not less than 11 consecutive hours in each 24-hour period, and a weekly rest period of not less than 24 hours in each seven-day period. Young workers are entitled to a daily rest period of 12 consecutive hours, except in unexpected and unpredictable occurrences where compensatory rest may be permitted within three weeks.

Leave arrangements (including maternity and paternity leave)

Maternity and paternity leave has been covered by recent European Union regulations. Employees must have completed one year's service before being entitled to parental leave. They are entitled to 13 weeks' parental leave to care for each child born or adopted after 15 December 1999. This regulation applies to mothers and fathers equally.

Leave can be taken at any time until the child's fifth birthday, or five years after the adoption date. Parents of disabled children can take leave until the child's eighteenth birthday.

Individuals taking maternity or paternity leave are guaranteed the right to return to the same job or similar with the same level or greater pay and benefits.

Minimum wage legislation

In 1998 minimum wage legislation was introduced in this country. The minimum wage is controversial, particularly in respect to the level at which it is set. Those opposed to the minimum wage argue it puts up costs for businesses (particularly businesses that are making low profits) and that it leads to unemployment as firms are forced to shed labour if it becomes too expensive.

The national minimum wage was set at £3.60 an hour for all adults aged 22 or over when it came into force in April 1999.

The legislation included a number of exemptions:

- 18–21-year-old workers had a lower rate of £3 per hour.

- Apprentices under 26 years, au pairs, the armed forces, the self-employed and students on work experience were not covered by the minimum wage.

By February 2000 the government had announced a rise in the standard rate to £3.70 an hour from October 2000. The youth rate was similarly set to rise from £3.00 to £3.20 from June 2000. Many Labour MPs would like to see the minimum wage being increased every year.

The minimum wage regulations are policed by the Inland Revenue's Minimum Wage Enforcement Unit, and offenders are liable to fines and criminal prosecutions. Employment tribunals are also able to demand compensation for victims of illegal underpayment of wages.

Check your understanding

Identify one piece of legislation in the work environment that has been introduced in the last 12 months and that will have an impact on motivation at work.

Describe this legislation and show what its impact is likely to be on motivation.

Case study: Abuse of the minimum wage

The press have reported a number of cases where firms have sought to avoid paying the minimum wage:

- Using ghost workers who are paid in cash who but do not appear in employment records.

- Under-recording working hours to imply an artifically high wage.

- Printing the amount of the minimum wage on wage slips but actually paying less.

- Paying the minimum wage rate but then deducting charges for the supply and cleaning of overalls and work clothes.

1 To what extent are people you know paid at least the minimum wage?

2 What occasions do you know of where the minimum wage has been abused?

Financial and non-financial approaches to employee motivation

There can be no doubt that financial reward is perhaps the most significant factor in persuading people to do jobs. This is why some people will do jobs nobody else will touch. Ask many people why they do their jobs and they will say 'for the money'. However, money is not everything. People stop doing some of the best-paid jobs because they can't stand the people or they can't put up with the conditions or because of other factors that are demotivating them.

What, then, are the non-financial ways of motivating people to work? Approaches such as providing opportunities for personal fulfilment in the workplace provide alternative avenues. The creation of empowered teams creates ways of releasing individual creativity.

The notion that positive experiences lead to motivation is known as *reinforcement theory*. Positive reinforcement involves pleasant experiences, while negative reinforcement involves unpleasant experiences. For example, when a new colleague joins a work team and is praised for all his or her successes, however minor, this is likely to lead to group solidarity and increased motivation.

There are four main kinds of reinforcement:

1 *Positive reinforcement* involves giving pleasurable rewards for desirable behaviour.

2 *Negative reinforcement* involves encouraging people to do things in the desired way in order to avoid negative sanctions and criticism.

3 *Extinction* involves withdrawing reinforcement that was previously employed to encourage certain behaviours. For example, if a supervisor regularly praised employees for good work and then withdrew this praise, the result might be a fall-off in the amount of 'good work' produced.

4 *Punishment* involves sanction and unpleasant consequences as a result of certain actions.

Check your understanding

In what circumstances are non-monetary methods of motivation likely to be more effective than monetary ones?

Motivation theories and ideas

Over the years a number of motivation theories have been put forward that are of interest to us in outlining the sorts of approaches that can be used to motivate people in the workplace. Motivation is the level of commitment individuals have to what they are doing. Workplace motivation is concerned with commitment to an organisation, its objectives and targets.

Much has been written about motivation, and intelligent organisations seek to win the commitment of employees by paying attention to motivation factors in the workplace.

Frederick Taylor's 'Principles of Scientific Management'

F.W. Taylor was associated with an approach entitled 'scientific management'. Scientific managers assumed that people were alike and that their motivations were relatively simple.

They believed that workers' actions could be programmed by their managers. Scientific management is associated with developing 'scientific methods' of organising work.

After dropping out of law school, Taylor took a job as a manual craft apprentice, before moving on to become a gang boss in a lathe department at the Midvale Steel Works, which was one of the most technically advanced steel works in America at the start of the last century.

While working at Midvale, Taylor was determined to stamp out what was referred to as 'systematic soldiering' – an organised attempt by groups of employees to work no harder than was absolutely necessary (e.g. by slowing down the work rate and extending breaks). Taylor sought to cut this out by establishing working practices that made this impossible. He saw that the power of employees to restrict output rested in the fact they usually had a greater understanding than their employers of the tools they worked with and of working practices. They were able to disguise from their employers their real potential to produce more if they worked harder.

Taylor wanted to give control back to employers by developing a science of work in which work would be controlled by the scientific manager. He carried out a series of systematic studies of shopfloor practice with the intention of redesigning jobs so that all knowledge expertise, and hence control of work, rested with management. Jobs were broken down and fragmented to their most basic components in an extreme division of labour.

Taylor also believed monetary reward was an important motivating factor that would

drive the system. Higher rates of pay could be offered as an inducement for increased rates of output. He used workers who were prepared to work hard to set a standard for others: 'rate busters' who would destroy any informal agreements about 'systematic soldiering' established by informal groups of workers.

Taylor set out to discover the single best way of carrying out a job – the scientific approach. He then tried to tempt employees to work hard to do these jobs by paying them higher rates than they could obtain in alternative work.

This form of scientific management dominated management thinking in the early part of the last century and was used by manufacturers such as Henry Ford, who built companies that were like machines, producing standardised parts for motor cars. The employees in these factories hardly had to use their brains because work had been designed in such a way it required minimum thought.

Today, you still find relics of scientific management – for example, in the manufacture of fast foods at MacDonald's where employees don't have to think, they simply have to follow instructions. Another example of scientific management is at the checkout of a supermarket where the till operator simply follows the instructions given by an electronic screen that tells him or her what steps to carry out in processing cheques, etc.

Abraham Maslow's 'Hierarchy of Needs'

Maslow's theories of motivation have been popular since the 1950s and are based on meeting people's needs in the workplace.

The theory suggests that unsatisfied needs can lead to dissatisfaction.

Maslow identified a range of needs that were largely hierarchical in nature:

- *Basic* needs are for reasonable standards of food, shelter and clothing in order to survive. This level of need will typically be met in workplaces by the receipt of money in exchange for work done.

- *Security* needs are also concerned with physical survival. In the workplace these security needs could include physical safety, security of employment, adequate rest periods, pension and sick schemes.

- *Group* needs are concerned with an individual's need for affection and love. Most people want to belong to a group. As organisations grow, individuals can lose their identity, becoming just another number or a face in the crowd. Organisations therefore need to find ways of building individuals into groups and teams.

- *Self-esteem* needs are based on an individual's desire for self-respect and the respect of others. Employees have a need to be recognised as individuals and to feel important. This is where giving status to individuals and recognising their achievements are important.

- *Self-actualisation* needs are concerned with personal development and individual creativity to achieve one's full potential. In order to meet these needs at work, individuals need to be provided with the opportunity to use their creative talents and abilities to the full.

Figure 17.8 presents these needs in diagrammatic form.

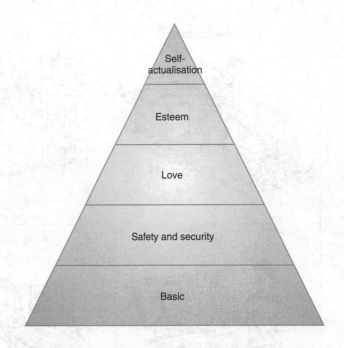

Figure 17.8 Maslow's Hierarchy of Needs

Check your understanding

Study Figure 17.9. According to Maslow's hierarchy, which employee needs does each of the six jobs fulfil? Why?

Douglas McGregor's 'Theory X and Theory Y'

Based on detailed research into managers in action, Douglas McGregor divided managers into two main types. *Theory X* managers tend to have the view that:

- The average person has an inherent dislike of work and so will avoid it if at all possible. Hence management needs to emphasise productivity, incentive schemes and a fair day's work, and to denounce restrictions on output.

- Because people naturally dislike work, most people must be coerced, controlled, directed and/or threatened with

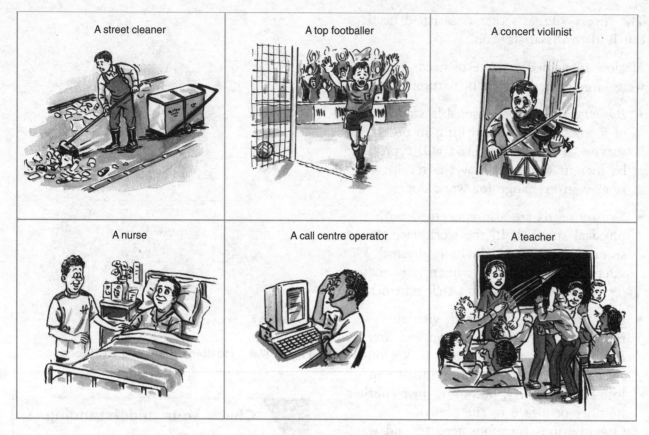

Figure 17.9 At what level are these employees on Maslow's Hierarchy of Needs?

punishment to get them to work towards business objectives.

- The average person likes to be directed, wishes to avoid responsibility, has little ambition and, above all, seeks security.

Against this pessimistic view of human motivation and its implications for the management of an organisation, McGregor proposed an alternative *Theory Y*. The underlying emphasis here is on 'integration' to replace direction and control. The assumptions about human motivation in Theory Y are as follows:

- Physical and mental effort in work are as natural as play or rest. The ordinary person does not dislike work; it all depends on the conditions under which work takes place – these may be enjoyable or not.

- External control is not the only way to get people to work. If they are committed to objectives, they will be motivated to work towards achieving them.

- The most significant reward that will motivate people to work is the satisfaction of an individual's self-actualisation needs. This can be the result of working towards an organisation's objectives.

- The average human being learns, when given the opportunity, to accept and – more importantly – to seek responsibility.

- Many people can contribute to a business's objectives when given the chance.

- The average person's potentialities are currently not being fully used.

Figure 17.10   Theory X and Theory Y managers

Check your understanding

Look at Figure 17.10. Which are Theory X and which Theory Y managers?

McGregor sees the potential to make organisations far more effective by unleashing the people who work for them. Organisations need to see themselves as interacting groups of people enjoying 'supportive relationships' with each other. Ideally, members of an organisation will see the organisation's objectives as being personally significant to them.

Frederick Herzberg's 'Two-factor Theory'

Frederick Herzberg carried out some important research into motivation. He identified a range of *dissatisfiers* associated with the *context* and *satisfiers* associated with the *content* of jobs.

Dissatisfiers include the following:

- Autocratic or arbitrary company policy and administration.

- Low pay.

- Poor working conditions.

- Antagonistic relations between different levels of employees.

- Unfriendly relationships within the hierarchy.

- Unfair management and supervisory practices.

- Unfair treatment of employees.

- Feelings of inadequacy.

- Impossibility of growth and development.

Herzberg suggested that the existence of the above, to any great extent, would cause dissatisfaction which would, in turn, lead to absenteeism, poor levels of output, resistance to change and negativity in the workplace.

In contrast, Herzberg identified a range of *satisfiers* associated with the content of the work that would encourage motivation:

These are:

- Recognition of effort and performance.

- The nature of the job itself – does it provide the employee with the appropriate degree of challenge?

- Sense of achievement.

- Assumption of responsibility.

- Opportunity for promotion and responsibility.

Adams' 'Equity Theory'

Adams' work on 'equity theory' is very important and underpins many approaches to equal opportunities. Equity theory is concerned with how people perceive their treatment as compared with others. To be treated equitably is to be treated in the same way as a similar group or individual.

In simple terms, employees will feel motivated if they are treated equitably and demotivated if they feel they are being treated inequitably.

Adams identified two main types of equity:

- *distributive* equity is concerned with the fairness with which people feel they are being rewarded in comparison to others.

- *procedural* equity is concerned with the employees' views of the fairness of the company's procedures (e.g. in relation to recruitment, selection, job progression, etc.).

Lawler: linking rewards to performance

The work of Lawler and others in the field of motivation suggests it is important to link rewards closely with performance. Successful management involves providing meaningful and valued rewards to employees. Employees need to have the opportunity to engage in 'good performance', and expectations must be clearly communicated to employees. Rewards must be clearly and visibly linked to performance.

Some of Lawler's ideas that have been widely taken up relate to employee involvement (EI) in the workplace. In high-involvement organisations there is the belief that:

- People can be trusted to make important decisions about their work activities.

- People can develop their own knowledge to make important decisions about managing their work activities.

- When people make decisions about the management of their own work, the result is greater organisational effectiveness.

This approach is associated with the term 'empowerment'.

Check your understanding

Which of the theories of motivation do you think is most helpful in providing management with a guide as how best to motivate their employees?

Case study: Theory and practice

In a well-known confectionery plant, an adjustment is made in holiday/rest days in accordance with the rate of absence due to sickness in the plant:

- The calculation excludes authorised absence and absence due to lateness.

- Good sickness absence is defined as below 4.5% and excess sickness absence is defined as above 6.0%.

The absence figure for the whole plant is used to calculate the adjustment to the number of people allowed off on each shift (see Figure 17.11).

Sickness (5)	Number of people allowed off per shift
0	Increased by 2 people
Below 4.5	Increased by 1 person
4.5–6	No change
Above 6	Reduced to 1 person
Above 10	
a) Shift of more than 25	Reduced by 2 people
b) Shift of more than 50	Reduced by 3 people

Figure 17.11   Adjustments to holiday/rest days

1   What do you think Herzberg would have to say about this approach to motivation?

2   What do you think Adams and Lawler would have said about this approach to motivation?

Unit 4 Assessment

You need to produce an analytical report on how one large business manages human resources. You should provide a comprehensive overview of the human resources management, showing its importance to the business, including all four of the following functions and an identification of any possible area of conflict between these areas, and with a focus in depth on one of them:

1 human resources planning

2 recruitment and selection

3 training and development

4 performance management.

To achieve a Grade E you must show you can:

- Accurately describe the responsibilities covered by the human resources function in the business, showing a thorough understanding of the importance of these resources to the business.

- Interpret and use internal staffing information and external labour market information to plan human resources within the business.

- Identify the features of key recruitment documents and describe the factors to be considered when planning to fill a vacancy and carrying out interviews.

- Identify key aspects of the business's training and development programme and explain its importance to the performance of the business.

- Correctly identify any possible areas of conflict between the human resource functions.

- Explain the purpose of performance management and describe how the business's approach may be influenced by motivational theory.

- Explore one human resources function in depth, giving effective examples of how the work is carried out and how its contribution to the activities of the business is evaluated.

To achieve a Grade C you must also show you can:

- Interpret relevant labour market information and compare your interpretation with how the business has used labour market information.

- Analyse the key recruitment documents and evaluate the quality of information in relation to the purpose of each.

- Identify and analyse the relationship between the business's training and development programme and its management of performance, and explain how these two functions may be influenced by different motivational theories.

To achieve a Grade A you must also show you can:

- Analyse how relevant labour market trends relate to the ongoing human resources planning of the business.

- Critically understand the contribution effective human resources management can make to improving the competitiveness of the business and illustrate your points effectively.

- Evaluate the potential conflicts between different human resources management activities within the business.

Opportunities to develop key skills

As a natural part of carrying out this unit and doing the work set out in the text, and through your assessments, you will be developing your key skills. Here's how:

Application of number, Level 3

When you are:

You should be able to develop the following key skills evidence:

- Using external labour market information you may plan and interpret information from different sources, including a large data set

N3.1 Plan and interpret information from two different types of sources, including a large data set.

Communication, Level 3

When you are:

You should be able to develop the following key skills evidence:

- Explaining training and development, recruitment, decision-making, motivational theory

C3.1a Contribute to a group discussion about a subject.

- Researching information for the report

C3.2 Read and synthesise information from two extended documents about a complex subject.

One document should include at least one image to illustrate complex points.

- Producing the report

C3.3 Write two documents about complex subjects. One piece of writing should be an extended document and include at least one image.

Information technology, Level 3

When you are:

You should be able to develop the following key skills evidence:

- Using external labour market information to plan human resources

IT3.1 Plan and use different sources to search for, and select, information required for two market human resources. You may access information about the labour market via the Internet and adapt it for use in your report.

- Using external labour information and derive new information to meet two different purposes

IT3.2 Explore, develop and exchange market information to plan human resources. You may access information about the labour market via the Internet and adapt it for use in your report.

UNIT 4 ASSESSMENT

Working with others, Level 3

When you are:	*You should be able to develop the following key skills evidence:*
• Liaising with staff of the organisation and/or others, agreeing arrangements	*WO3.1* Plan the activity with your tutor when setting objectives, responsibilities and working out to obtain the information you need.
• Collecting the information you need	*WO3.2* Work towards achieving the agreed objectives, seeking to establish and maintain co-operative working relationships in meeting your responsibilities.

Look at the financial pages of any newspaper and you will see the extent to which external confidence in the management of a large business is determined by its financial performance. Shareholders and other external stakeholders keenly await information on financial performance in the business. If you are working for the business, your work will contribute to this financial performance and you may have a role in recording the financial transactions of the business. Even the smallest transaction will be audited so that the final accounts accurately represent what the business has been doing during the year. Public confidence in a business and the confidence of all employees will rely upon good accounts.

In this unit you will find out how businesses manage their finances and about the important indicators of the financial health of the business. You will need to understand the processes of financial monitoring and forecasting and the routine aspects of managing the finances of a business. You will learn how to record financial information and how to interpret this information to make judgements about the effectiveness of a business. You will also find out how important knowledge of financial management is for the effective planning and evaluation of an organisation.

This unit builds on your knowledge and understanding of types of business organisation gained in Unit 1 Business at work (Advanced) and is linked to Unit 6 Business planning (Advanced). It also provides a basis for Unit 12 Financial accounting (Advanced), and Unit 13 Management accounting (Advanced) and Unit 14 Financial services (Advanced).

This unit is assessed through an external assessment. The grade you achieve in that assessment will be your grade for the unit. It also provides some underpinning knowledge for NVQ level 3 in Accounting.

Chapter 18 Recording financial information

You will find out why it is important for a business to create and maintain accurate financial records and to know about the different users of financial information.

Every business has to meet internal and external reporting requirements to show its financial health and to meet legal and other requirements. You need to understand the reasons why the following stakeholders of a business need financial information about the performance of the business:

- *Internal users* – groups within the *organisation*, such as managers.

- External users – groups outside the organisation, such as shareholders and creditors.

You should be aware that financial information has to serve a variety of different purposes depending on the needs of different stakeholders.

You need to be familiar with the range of documents used by business and how and why these are used. The documents you will find out about are:

- purchase order forms
- delivery notes/goods received note
- invoices
- receipts
- credit notes
- statements of account
- remittance advice
- cheques
- paying-in slips
- bank statements.

You need to understand how each contributes to the flow of financial information and how financial data is recorded to construct accounts. You also need to know about the management of these documents and explain their use and importance for stakeholders.

Every business environment is competitive, which, by its very nature, means that in this rapidly changing world in which organisations exist, some will inevitably perform better than others. Where a business does well, there are many rewards and benefits for individuals and organisations affected by its actions. On the other hand, if a business has a bad year or does not do well, there is a similar knock-on effect with a range of consequences for individuals and organisations that may be affected in a range of ways by its poor performance.

Every individual or organisation likely to be affected through the successes, failures or actions of a business will therefore have their own areas of concern. To clarify their concerns, they will have **information needs and requirements**. They will want facts, knowledge and understanding about how the actions of that organisation affect either their own circumstances or the circumstances of the organisation for which they work.

For example, the downturn in fortunes for Marks & Spencer (www.marks-and-spencer. co.uk/) saw an increase in the amount of stock bought from overseas suppliers. This had a dramatic effect upon many businesses within the UK who had developed 'under the wing' of M&S and who had come to depend upon their business over many years. Imagine you work for a business that still supplies M&S. Given all the changes taking place at M&S, you will be concerned that M&S's new business strategies succeed and will be interested in any financial information that tells you they are doing so. You may also want to diversify or develop business strategies that enable you to develop a wider customer base so that all your eggs are not in the one basket!

Different stakeholders in a business will, therefore, have their own areas of concern. In order to clarify their concerns and learn about their 'interests', they will have information needs and requirements.

Accounting and financial records for users of financial information

In order to make judgements about business activities, individuals require accounting

Case study: Putting the sparkle back into Hamleys

Founded in 1760 and with a flagship location in Regent Street, Hamleys have the reputation of the world's most famous toyshop. Given their prestigious name, a visit to Hamleys should have inspired the same delight as a trip to Harrods, Harvey Nichols or Liberty. However, in recent years, Hamleys have gone into decline from their glory days as a result of a series of botched diversification attempts, working their way through four chief executives. A lack of coherent strategy involving the acquisition of Toystack and franchises in Debenhams ended in chaos.

A refurbishment of the Regent Street store, combined with high prices, was also driving customers away. At the start of the millennium, they had reached a point where a profit warning had been issued, dividends had been cut by a third and a pre-tax loss of £2.6 million had been reported.

The new chief executive, Simon Burke, tried to tackle these issues. Reductions took place in the prices of some games and toys, including Furbys by £6 and Flat Eric by £5, and computer games were brought in line with the market average. These changes saw the first-ever sale in Hamleys' history. With new decor, more tills, more products and better customer service, the shop will soon be revolutionised. The aim is to produce the most magical retailing venue in London, so that every child will be awestruck by a unique experience as the revamped store becomes a special destination for those visiting the capital.

1 Which factors might have caused some of the problems experienced by Hamleys in recent years?

2 What individuals and organisations may have been affected by the downturn in their fortunes?

3 Describe some of the decisions taken to revive the business. How might these make Hamleys more competitive?

information from an accounting system. Accounting acts as an information system by processing business data so that those parties either interested in or affected by the business can be provided with the means to find out how well or badly the organisation is performing:

Business data $\rightarrow$ Accounting system $\rightarrow$ Financial information

Business data are the inputs for the accounting system. The output is financial information. Financial information can then be fed to those who require such information.

Accounting information

Accounting information may be used both within and outside an organisation. It involves providing important data that may form the basis for decisions. In order to clarify what we mean by accounting information, it is perhaps best to explain what we mean by accounting:

Accounting is concerned with identifying, measuring, recording and reporting information relating to the activities of an organisation.

We can break each of these activities down into the following:

- *Identifying.* This involves capturing all the financial data within a business related to how it is performing. For example, this would include all information about the sales of goods to customers, data about the payment of expenses (such as wages and rent) and also information about the purchase of any stock, as well as data about the purchase of new vehicles and machinery.

- *Measuring.* Money, in the form of pounds and pence, is used as the form of

measurement of economic transactions. In the future, the form of measurement might change to become euros. For accounting purposes, instead of saying a business had sold 10 cars in a week, which may be meaningless if you do not know the value of the cars, it may be useful to specify the value of the cars. For example, 10 cars valued at £15,000 would mean a turnover during the week of £150,000.

- *Recording.* Accounting data and information must be recorded into either handwritten accounting books or into a suitable computer package, such as a specialised accounting package or a spreadsheet.

- *Communicating.* The reporting of financial information may take a variety of different forms. For example, although some financial information may be required and extracted from the accounts weekly, such as sales totals, there are standard financial statements (such as profit and loss accounts and balance sheets) that have a set format for reporting the activities of organisations.

It is important that, throughout this accounting process, the accounting information is:

- *Reliable* – free from errors and bias.

- *Comparable* – accounting information should be comparable with information from other organisations.

- *Relevant* – accounting information should relate to many of the decisions that have to be made about the business.

- *Understandable* – information should be capable of being understood by those at whom it is targeted.

Financial and management accounting

The process of accounting can be divided into two broad areas:

1 *Financial accounting*. Concerned with the recording of financial transactions and the preparation of financial reports to communicate past financial performance.

2 *Management accounting*. Involves looking to the future using a knowledge of past performance, where relevant, to aid the management of the business.

A number of distinctions can be drawn between these two areas (see Figure 18.1).

It has been said that the number of accountants is increasing so rapidly that, by the end of the twenty-first century, the entire nation will be accountants. To become a qualified accountant, a person must have passed rigorous examinations in order to achieve membership of one of the following accounting bodies:

Check your understanding

Which of the following would fall into the realms of financial accounting and which would be management accounting?

- Recording transactions from source documentation.

- Calculating what the profit is likely to be over a range of outputs for the launch of a new product.

- Producing financial statements to show what has happened to the business during the past year.

- Advising a business on its tax liability.

- Creating a budgetary system to improve control over the costs within a business.

- Setting the prices of products or services.

- The Institute of Chartered Accountants in England and Wales (ICAEW) (www.icaew.co.uk/).

Financial accounting	Management accounting
Subject to accounting regulations to ensure that reports/statements follow a standard approach	Reports are only for internal use so no restrictions are necessary
Provides a broad overview of the whole business using totals	Information extracted relates to parts of the organisation where it is used to help with a particular decision
Provides information to a particular date	Will look at future performance as well as at past perfomance
Produces general statements and reports	Produces reports with a specific decision in mind
Quantifies information in monetary terms and values	May have non-financial information such as stocks

Figure 18.1 Distinctions between financial, and management, accounting

- The Institute of Chartered Accountants in Ireland (ICAI) (www.icai.co.uk/).

- The Institute of Chartered Accountants in Scotland (ICAS) (www.icas.org.uk/).

- The Association of Chartered Certified Accountants (ACCA) (www.acca.co.uk/).

- The Chartered Institute of Management Accountants (CIMA) (www.cima.org.uk/).

- The Chartered Institute of Public Finance and Accountancy (CIPFA) (www.cipfa.org.uk/).

Case study: The Institute of Chartered Accountants in England and Wales (ICAEW)

The ICAEW (www.icaew.co.uk/) is the largest professional accountancy body in Europe, and its qualification allows members to call themselves Chartered Accountants and to use the designatory letters ACA or FCA. This is recognised all over the world as a prestigious qualification.

Established by Royal Charter in 1880, the ICAEW today has a membership of over 115,000 worldwide. Around half its members are employed in industry, finance and commerce, with the other half employed in the 'profession' in firms of auditors, such as Deloitte & Touche and Pricewaterhouse Coopers.

Over recent decades the range of professional activities carried out by chartered accountants has expanded to include financial reporting, taxation, personal finance, corporate finance, financial management and information technology.

Accountants undergo lengthy and rigorous training and must pass examinations to quality for membership of the ICAEW. They are also required to maintain high standards of professional conduct and competence.

The Research Board of the ICAEW is the largest private sector sponsor of accountancy research in the UK. As part of its role it commissions papers for publication and supports conferences on a wide range of accountancy issues.

One of the key areas of the ICAEW is practice regulation. Although it has always given guidance to members on ethical matters and dealt with complaints about members through its professional conduct system, since the mid-1980s the ICAEW has regulated and monitored its members' activities in the areas of investment advice and insolvency licensing.

Twenty-two district society offices provide member support, and the ICAEW's technical enquiry line receives 20,000 individual requests for advice each year. Newsletters and a range of activities are also tailored to the interests of members.

1 Why do 'accountants' need to be members of a professional body?

2 Describe the main purpose of the Institute of Chartered Accountants.

3 How does the ICAEW support its members?

Users of financial information

All businesses differ in one way or another. Some may be very small, such as a corner shop serving a local community as a newsagent, sub-post office and a place to purchase essential groceries. Others may be multinationals, which include famous brand names and which operate all over the world. As a result, many of these types of business will have a different legal structure, with different types of people interested in the sort of financial information they generate.

It is useful at this stage to clarify what is meant by the term 'financial information'. Financial information for you might be your income from a Saturday job, the cost of your bus fares and telephone calls, and the purchase price of a car you may wish to buy. If you were then asked to describe financial information from a business, it would not be vastly different. You might talk about profits, sales, costs, accounting statements (such as balance sheets and profit and loss accounts) or simply the cash within a business. These different examples of financial information help to show that

financial information includes any information on activities within a business that are expressed in some form of monetary term.

There are many different stakeholders both within and outside a business organisation who will have their own needs and requirements as users of accounting information. It is easy to understand that, within a business, financial information is required for record-keeping and decision-making purposes. This is important, as accounting information is useful for those who need to make decisions within a

business. It is also easy to understand that owners of a business, particularly if they take little active part in running it, are going to want information about how the organisation is performing so that they can monitor their investment (see Figure 18.2).

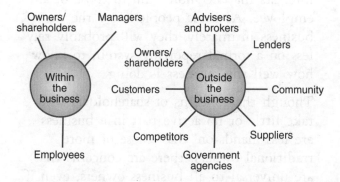

Figure 18.2 A business's internal and external users of information

However, there are other, less obvious, parties who are interested in financial information. For example, in the town of Barnard Castle in County Durham, there is a large Glaxo Wellcome (www.glaxowellcome.com/) factory. It employs many people from the local community and is not just the largest employer in that town but also in that part of County Durham. There are many associated businesses that rely on this factory locally and, if it ever closed, it would be a huge loss to residents in the town. Local residents and the community rely upon the success of this factory and the improving position of Glaxo Wellcome in the world pharmaceutical market. There are therefore many individuals and businesses in that part of Durham who show an interest in the financial information made public by this organisation.

Owners/shareholders

The interests and priorities of business owners are varied. Sole traders and partners are more likely to be involved in the daily management of the business and act as internal stakeholders. In many ways their interests may be more akin to those of an employee. As these people know the business intimately, they will probably rely less on a formal reporting system to know how well the business is doing.

Though the concerns of shareholders who take little or no active part in a business are less 'hands-on' than those of more traditional owners, there are concerns that are universal to all business owners, even if they do not possess informal information channels. For example, they will require information concerning:

- *profitability* – whether the business makes efficient use of resources to provide the desired financial return

- *liquidity* – whether the business has the ability to generate cash to ensure continued trading and to make dividend payments

- *state of financial affairs* – the nature of the business's assets and liabilities

- *financial structure* – the nature and value of the business's loans in relation to the amount invested by the owners

- *future prospects* – an evaluation of the business's future prospects, having regard to the firm's external environment and its adaptability to change.

Managers

At every level of management, from junior managers to directors, managers will be involved with the performance of the organisation. They will be particularly concerned about information relating to their own responsibility, such as management accounting information, which will help them to improve their decision-making capabilities and run their part of the business more efficiently. Financial information is important for the effective management of a business. Information concerning the recent past can be used to monitor and control operations, and financial projections are a vital component of decision-making.

Check your understanding

Choose one of the following roles:

- chief executive
- marketing director
- personnel manager
- purchasing manager
- production director.

Make a list of ten types of financial information the person in your chosen role might require. Briefly explain in each instance how he or she might use that information.

Employees

Employees will be concerned with job security as well as how the business is going to develop so that they can ascertain whether there are opportunities for promotion. Important sources of information for individual employees, as well as employee groups such as trade unions, will be the financial reports that may have been published for public consumption, or be part of employee packs of information. Employees will also want to know about the business's financial solvency so that they can use this to support their wage claims.

Advisers and brokers

These people may require the same sort of information as owners, particularly if they are stockbrokers advising their clients about the nature of their investments. Business analysts may require further information about company performance so that they can advise their clients accurately.

Lenders

The primary concern of lenders is the ability of the organisation to pay interest and make repayments on the loans advanced. Although the information needs of lenders will be similar to those of owners, they will be particularly interested in cash flow, the assets the business owns and the business's ability to pay its debts.

Customers

Customers want to know their supplies are secure, not just in the short term but also in the future. This is particularly important when customers want to develop long-term trading relationships with their suppliers. They may also be interested in the size of the profits their suppliers are making. High profits would be an example of market exploitation. Consumer groups and industry watchdogs may analyse financial information on behalf of customers.

Community

Specific areas depend upon the success of local businesses. If a business is doing well it is helping the local community to prosper, not just by providing employment but also by paying people who spend money in the community, which then provides employment for others. Many organisations also become involved in a wide range of community projects. Individuals local to a business may also be interested in the impact of an organisation's activities upon the environment.

Competitors

These will be interested in the activities of other organisations within their industry. Financial information from companies may be freely available. Other information may be published in the press or be available from data research agencies. Looking at the activities of competitors may help organisations to think ahead and to fine-tune their own strategies.

Check your understanding

Make a list of the sort of financial information that may be useful for a competitor. How might this information be used? Provide examples in each instance.

Suppliers

Suppliers will be concerned about the organisation's ability to pay for materials or services supplied. Before making supplies available on credit terms, a supplier should ensure the customer's business is financially secure and that it generates sufficient cash flow to pay its creditors.

Government agencies

The government requires financial information to assess and collect taxes. The Inland Revenue (www.inlandrevenue.gov.uk/) is concerned about payments to employees and subcontractors, and its taxes on the level of business profits.

Customs and Excise (www.hmce.gov.uk/) monitor the value of sales and purchases that attract VAT. Financial returns are also an important source of information for the compilation of economic statistics that can help the government plan economic and industrial policy.

Reporting requirements

In the UK, regulations influencing the financial reporting of companies to *external stakeholders* come largely from two sources: government legislation and accounting standards.

Government legislation

Government legislation emanates mainly in the form of the Companies Act 1985, as modified by the Companies Act 1989. The Companies Act 1985 lays down requirements concerning financial statements prepared by limited companies. Members of the main accountancy bodies, such as the Institute of Chartered Accountants in England and Wales, are under an obligation to use *best accountancy practice* in the preparation of all accounts intended to give a 'true and fair view' of a business's trading performance and financial position.

As a result, the following information is required within ten months of the end of an accounting period for a private limited company and within seven months for a public limited company:

- Balance sheet.

- Profit and loss account.

- Cash flow statement.

- Notes to the accounts describing the company's accounting policies as well as an analysis of certain items contained in the financial reports.

- Auditor's report confirming that the company's financial reports are consistent with the company's trading records and that they provide a true and fair view of its trading performance and financial affairs.

Discussion point	'Legislation simply creates bureaucracy and makes it more difficult for small and medium-sized businesses to meet their business objectives.'

Accounting standards

Accounting standards are issued by the Accounting Standards Board (www.asb.org.uk/). The 1970s saw the introduction of a number of accounting standards. In 1970, the first *Statement of Standard Accounting Practice* (SSAP) was introduced with the aim of limiting the ability of accountants to use diverse accounting procedures. SSAPs were created by the Accounting Standards Committee, a subcommittee of the Consultative Committee of Accountancy Bodies which linked the six major accounting bodies.

On 1 August 1990 the Accounting Standards Board (ASB) took over the Accounting Standards Committee. Unlike the ASC, which was a joint committee of the six major accounting bodies, the board is independent of the professional institutes and can set accounting standards in its own right. The ASB reports to the Financial Reporting Council (FRC), which oversees the accounting standards process. Its members are appointed by the Governor of the Bank of England, the Secretary of State for Trade and Industry and various interested organisations, including the users and preparers of company accounts.

Whereas the extinct ASC produced SSAPs, the ASB issues accounting standards in the form of *Financial Reporting Statements* (FRSs). Accounting standards indicate current best accounting practice which should be applied to all accounting statements. There is an obligation on the part of members of the main professional accounting bodies to comply with the accounting standards in cases where they prepare accounts or are required to audit them.

Examples of FRSs and SSAPs are as follows:

- *FRS 1 Cash Flow Statements.*
- *FRS 5 Reporting the Substance of Transactions.*
- *SSAP 1 Accounting for the Results of Associated Companies.*
- *SSAP 22 Accounting for Goodwill.*

Case study: Accounting concepts

The Companies Act 1985 specifies that certain basic concepts should be applied when preparing a set of financial reports. *SSAP 2 (Disclosure of Accounting Policies)* provides guidance upon the application of these concepts. The four fundamental concepts are as follows:

a *The going concern concept.* This assumes the business will persist with its business activities in the foreseeable future; therefore, the accountant will not assume there is a desire to cut back on business operations or an intention to liquidate. The significance of this concept is that goods should be valued not at their break-up value but at their net book value, based on the estimation of the cost of depreciation provision.

b *The accruals or matching concept.* This recognises that revenues and costs are incurred when their liability is taken on and not as money is received or paid. Thus, at the end of a trading period, all transactions relating to that period will appear in the accounts whether payments have been made or not. Revenues and profits earned in that period are 'matched' with the costs and expenses associated with these business activities.

c *The consistency concept.* This concept indicates that the accounting treatment of similar items should be consistently applied, with each accounting period and from one period to the next.

d The concept of prudence or conservation. This maintains that businesses should not lay claim to profits unless they are sure they have been earned. Accountants will tend to underestimate profits and overstate losses.

1 Looking at one of the above accounting concepts, explain why you think it was introduced.

2 What might the problems be if such basic concepts were not applied to all accounting processes?

While some of the accounting standards are quite specialised and affect only a few companies, other affect either all or most companies.

Accounting documents

When we buy goods from a shop, there is rarely a need for much documentation. We might pay directly by cash or, if we pay by cheque, credit card or debit card, we will have to sign some form of business document. Organisations, however, require a great deal more documentation to cover the requirements of a transaction. There are a number of reasons for this:

- Most organisations buy goods or services on credit. For example, the good or service is first supplied and then payment is made at a month-end or later. At each stage in the processes involved, documents help to record what is happening.

- Documentation provides the source data for the recording of purchases and sales. It helps to ensure that this process is carried out efficiently and is free from error so that appropriate payments are sent out on time and that mistakes are not made when sending documents to customers.

Check your understanding

If most business transactions involve goods or services being supplied upon credit, what are the risks involved for the supplier?

- Accounts are generated from the documents. These can be used to provide feedback on various transactions. They can also be totalled and summarised to provide an overview of different aspects of the organisation's performance.

- Documents help to create records that meet the legal requirements of such organisations as the Inland Revenue and Customs and Excise. For example, these organisations may wish to know sales figures for the purpose of VAT calculations.

- It is important that parties to a transaction know precisely what they have agreed to, for example, in terms of discounts, amounts and prices. Documentation serves to confirm arrangements, thus helping to create a mutual understanding between the buyer and seller.

- Specific requirements may be met by the use of certain documents, for example, petty cash vouchers and stores requisitions.

- Documents also help to monitor business performance so that information is created for the purpose of internal planning and control.

Check your understanding

Over the period of one month, collect all the business documents you come across. Examine the uses and purposes of each type of document.

Source documents

Source documents are documents that relate first-hand to transactions between customers and organisations. Their importance should never be underestimated. Imagine the sort of confusion that might arise if a source document is mislaid. For example:

- Goods may be sent to the wrong customer.

- The wrong goods may be despatched.

- Payment could be delayed.

- General confusion may arise, leading to complaints and loss of further business.

There are many types of business documents. These capture the details of accounting transactions, are used as proof of business dealings and are a good way of checking goods ordered and received.

Financial information is the end result of a process that may involve the following stages (see Figure 18.3):

- The preparation of source documents.

- The entry of data from source documents into source records.

- The posting of data from source records into a more permanent record of accounting data (called the *ledger*).

- The presentation of accounting reports from ledger information.

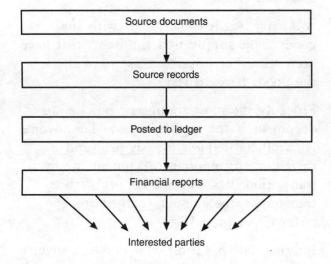

Figure 18.3 Generating financial information

Data flows from source documents are, today (more often than not), channelled through a management system or accounting system. These are used to meet the needs of managers for planning and control. Source documents provide the raw data for such purposes.

Discussion point	In these days of electronic information, why do organisations use documentation systems?

Purchasing documents

The first stage in the purchasing process will be to make decisions about the goods and services required.

A *letter of enquiry* may be sent out by a prospective purchaser to several suppliers to find out what they can offer and so that various details and specifications can be compared. A buyer will wish to find out many things before placing an order – for example, prices, details about the goods, delivery dates and times, and discounts.

In response to the enquiry the potential seller may supply a *quotation* or a *catalogue* with a price list. The buyer will then compare quotations or analyse details from the catalogues. A quotation provides details of availability and of terms being offered. For example, '5% – 30 days' indicates that, if the bill is paid within 30 days, the buyer can deduct a cash discount of 5%.

Discussion point	Does discounting provide large organisations with a competitive advantage over small organisations? How can they deal with this?

Once a buyer has decided upon the best quotation or has scrutinised a series of catalogues, the next step may be the issuing of a *purchase order*. In the example in Figure 18.4, a firm called Customised Caravans of Carlisle is ordering raw materials from J.P.P. Evans & Co. of Dudley.

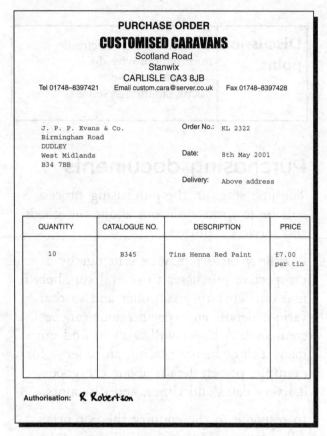

Figure 18.4 A purchase order

When filling in a purchase order, you should include the following information, as has been done in Figure 18.4.

- Order number so that it can be traced easily, and matched against invoices and statements.

- The price, that will have been obtained from a price list, quotation or catalogue.

- The purchaser's name and address. Source documents are usually headed with the name and address of the organisation.

It is possible for the delivery address to be different from this.

- The name and address of the supplier.

- A description of the goods required.

- The catalogue number/reference number of the goods or service required.

- Authorisation, such as the signature and date.

Check your understanding

Look at the specimen purchase order in Figure 18.4. Explain what might happen if:

1 the date was omitted from the order.

2 the reference/catalogue number was missed from the order.

Before despatching the goods the seller may send an *advice note* to say the goods are being sent and that they will arrive shortly. If the goods do not arrive, the buyer can then contact the seller to find out why the delay has arisen.

A *delivery note* is usually sent with the goods. This simply lists the items that have been sent. The buyer can use it to check the goods have arrived.

Probably the most significant purchasing document is the *purchase invoice*. The invoice is an official request for payment and is, therefore, an important document in any transaction. It shows the details of the transaction, the amount charged and the terms (see Figure 18.5).

Information appearing on a purchase invoice may include the following:

- *Order number*. This can be used to check the goods delivered against those ordered.

```
                    INVOICE
        J. P. P. Evans & Co.
              Birmingham Road
                  DUDLEY
               West Midlands
                   B34 7BB

   Tel 0121-378-1666   Email evans@server.co.uk   Fax 0121-379-1676
            VAT Reg 0633 4742 15


   Invoice to:                    Order No:  KL 2322
   Customised Caravans
   Scotland Road                  Date:      12th May 2001
   Stanwix
   CARLISLE                       Account:   PBB33
   CA3 8JB
                                  Invoice No.:
```

Quantity	Cat. no.	Description	Price per unit £	Total £	Discount	Net £
10	B345	Tins Henna Red paint	7.00	70.00	0	70.00
			Total			70.00
			Cash Discount			0.00
						70.00
			VAT			8.75
			Total			78.75

Terms:
Net monthly
E & OE

Figure 18.5 An invoice

- *Terms.* This shows how much time the buyer has to pay for the goods, and the cash discount that may be given for quick payment.

- *Carriage.* If this appears it will show how transport costs should be paid for. 'Carriage paid' means the seller will pay for the transport and 'Carriage forward' means the buyer is expected to pay.

- *E & O E.* This stands for 'errors and omissions excepted', which means the seller can correct any mistake on the invoice at a later date.

- *Trade discount.* This may be given for a variety of reasons. It will be deducted from the invoice price.

- *VAT.* If a good or service is subject to value added tax, this will be added to the amount appearing on the invoice.

- *Invoice number.* This makes it easy for the accounts departments of both the buyer and the seller to identify the invoice quickly.

- *VAT registration number.* Most organisations print their VAT number on their invoices for convenience.

There is so much information on an invoice that they are not always easy to fill in! Remember that the organisation sending sending the invoice is the business that required payment for the goods or services supplied. Don't forget to put all of the other details on the invoice, including the terms, order number, carriage and VAT.

```
                 CREDIT NOTE
        J. P. P. Evans & Co.
              Birmingham Road
                  DUDLEY
               West Midlands
                   B34 7BB

   Tel 0121-378-1666   Email evans@server.co.uk   Fax 0121-379-1676
            VAT Reg 0633 4742 15


   Credit Note to:                Credit Note No: 1478
   Customised Caravans
   Scotland Road                  Date:       21st May 2001
   Stanwix
   CARLISLE                       Account:    PBB33
   CA3 8JB
                                  Invoice No.:
```

Quantity	Cat. no.	Description	Price per unit £	Total £	Discount	Net £
2	B345	Tins Henna Red paint	7.00	14.00	0	14.00
			Total			14.00
			Cash Discount			0.00
						14.00
			VAT			1.75
			Total			15.75

Reason for credit:
2 tins damaged in transit

Figure 18.6 A credit note

If the seller has not transacted any previous business with the buyer, or perhaps if the buyer has been late with payments in the past, the seller might sent the buyer a *pro forma invoice*. This document is sent to the buyer before the goods are delivered and sets out the charges they have to pay in advance. The goods are then delivered after the payments are made.

A *credit note* to the buyer may be sent by the seller to adjust the amount appearing on an invoice (see Figure 18.6). A credit note reduces the invoice price. This price might be reduced because a mistake has been made, because goods have been found to be faulty or damaged, or simply because the wrong goods have been delivered. Information appearing on the credit note may include:

- the original invoice number

- the date

- addresses

- the reasons for the credit being given.

A credit note is sometimes printed in red.

A *goods received note* may be used internally to inform various departments within an organisation about the arrival of orders. For example, copies may be sent to the department that ordered the goods, to purchasing and also to the accounts department where it will be checked against the invoice before the supplier is paid (see Figure 18.7).

Figure 18.7 A goods received note

Check your understanding

Design one purchase document. You may find customised documents within your word processing or 'office' package to assist you.

Having designed the document, explain what it would represent and how it might be used.

Check your understanding

Maureen Coombs, a small sports retailer, deals regularly with a wholesale firm, Suppliers Ltd, and a recent transaction took place as follows:

a Maureen ordered cricket kit worth £3,000 from Suppliers Ltd on 14 April 2001, and the goods were delivered by Suppliers Ltd's own van on 20 April. The kit consisted of £1,700 worth of cricket bats at £100 per bat, £800 of white cricket trousers at £20 per pair and £500 of stumps at £20 per set.

b On 21 April, Maureen found out that 9 sets of stumps were of poor quality and not up to the high requirements she expected. She informed Suppliers Ltd who arranged to collect the faulty goods. Make out the documents you would expect to be used in the transaction, explaining how each would be used.

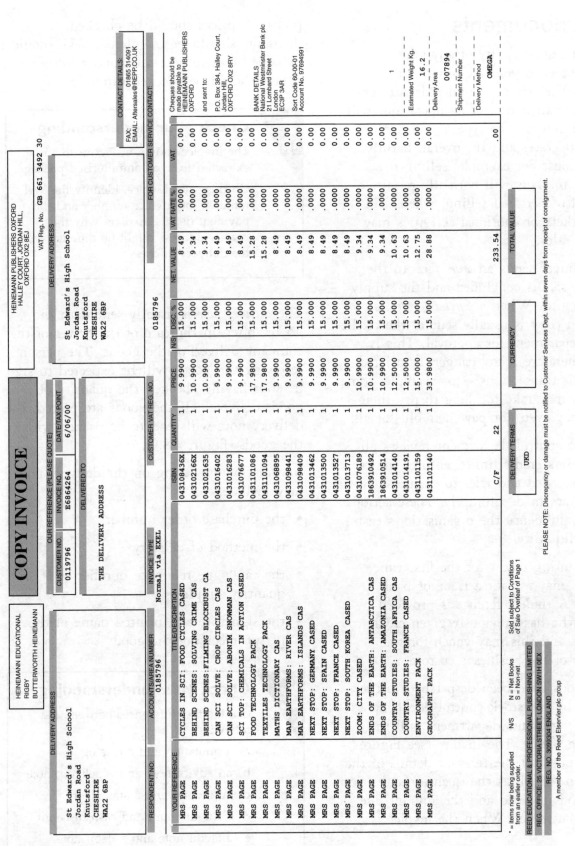

Figure 18.8 A specimen sales invoice

Sales documents

The main responsibility of any sales department is to generate orders for products. The size of the sales department and the overall nature of its operations will depend largely on the type of industry in which it operates and the overall nature of its operations. For example, selling to industrial markets will normally require a great deal of personal selling, whereas in retail markets promotional activities may stimulate sales.

When a buyer sends an *order form* to the seller, the sale is concluded and the supply process begins. When a *purchase order* is received, a copy is usually sent to the credit control department for approval. This is because there are many dangers associated with credit transactions – for example, some customers may take too long to pay their bills or may even not pay their bills at all.

The credit control department reviews all accounts, sets credit limits, ensures limits are not exceeded and tries to ensure payments are made promptly. These actions constantly influence the organisation's cash flow and liquidity.

Before granting credit for the first time, a supplier may ask for a trade or bank reference. A trade reference is provided by a supplier who has previously given credit to a business and this may vouch for the reliability of the business's custom.

When goods have been despatched to the customer by the stock control department, the seller's accounts department will then prepare an *invoice*. The invoice (see Figure 18.8) contains all the relevant details of the transaction – such as the quantity and price of the goods ordered and the amount due from the customer. When the invoice is prepared, prices should be checked, discounts should be calculated, VAT should be added (where necessary) and all other details should be checked carefully.

Check your understanding

The invoice shown in Figure 18.8 is extracted from a computerised package.

On this sales invoice, identify the VAT number, the invoice number and the payment details. Explain why the invoice address might be different from the delivery address.

The *delivery note* is usually sent with the goods, often in the care of the driver of the company delivering the goods. The person receiving the goods will be expected to sign it, after having checked the quantity of goods delivered. If the goods are posted, the delivery note will tend to be packed with the goods (Figure 18.9).

Information appearing on the delivery note may include:

- the purchase order number

- the method of delivery

- the catalogue reference number and quantity supplied

- the signature and printed name of the person receiving the goods.

Check your understanding

Outline the differences between the following:

a a quotation and a catalogue

b an advice note and a delivery note

c an invoice and a statement

d trade discount and cash discount

e a credit note and a debit note.

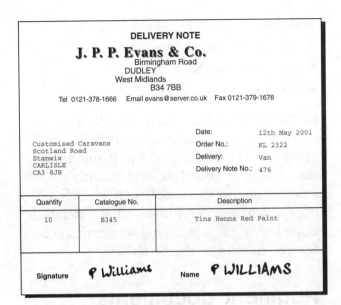

Figure 18.9 A delivery note

Tips for filling in financial documents

1 Look at the top of each document that you have to fill in to find out what type of document it is. For example, is it a purchase order, sales invoice or credit note?

2 Think about the purpose of the document, who you are sending it to, and what other documents refer to it.

3 Make sure that you have all of the information to fill in the document. You may wish to refer to other documents for the information you need.

4 Fill the document in carefully, making sure that each section is filled in.

5 If necessary, use a calculator for some of the arithmetical calculations such as working out the discounts or the VAT.

6 Check your workings after having completed the document.

The seller will send all regular customers a *statement* at the end of every month (Figure 18.10). This is simply a copy of the customer's account in the sales ledger and usually contains a record of all transactions with the customer during the month. The statements will contain details of all invoices that have been issued to each customer, any payments that have been made and any credit notes that have been issued. Information appearing on the statement may include:

- the addresses and customer account number
- the date

Date	Reference		Value £	Outstanding £	Outstanding £
12/5/01	INV	P335	78.75	78.75	78.75
	CN	1478	15.75		
		TOTAL		78.75	78.75

STATEMENT — J. P. P. Evans & Co., Birmingham Road, DUDLEY, West Midlands, B34 7BB. Tel 0121-378-1666 Email evans@server.co.uk Fax 0121-379-1676. VAT Reg 0633 4742 15. Date: 30th May 2001. Account: PBB33. Customised Caravans, Scotland Road, Stanwix, CARLISLE, CA3 8JB.

REMITTANCE ADVICE — J. P. P. Evans & Co., Birmingham Road, DUDLEY, West Midlands, B34 7BB. Account: PBB33.

Figure 18.10 A statement and remittance advice

Check your understanding

Organise yourselves into pairs to work through the following:

a Decide which one of you will be the buyer and which the seller.

b Choose what type of business you are each in. One of you should be the purchaser and the other should be the supplier.

c Using a computer and a basic design package or clip art, design the documentation you would need for a basic transaction between your two businesses.

d Make up documents for four transactions which might happen in your chosen business.

e Present documents for your documents to the rest of the class.

- details of invoices issued
- any credit notes issued
- details of payments made
- the amount outstanding.

In the statement in Figure 18.10, a tear-off slip known as a remittance advice is attached. The buyer can detach this from the statement and then send it with the amount due to the supplier. If a statement does not have a remittance advice attached, buyers may prepare their own remittance advices to send with the cheque.

Payment documents

Business transactions involve a transfer of money from one person or organisation to another. Whereas in the past transactions involved payment in cash, today most involve the use of automated systems that

Case study: Working as an auto-electrician

Caroline Birch recently set up in business as an auto-electrician in York. Her workshop is located in an area that has a large number of garages, many of which have expressed an interest in using her specialist electrical services. Caroline hopes to attract a lot of work from personal customers. She has paid for a regular advert in the *York Advertiser* as well as *Yellow Pages*.

When she started up her business she did not expect to be swamped by the extent of the documentation required in handling the day-to-day running of her business. She has already opened accounts with several suppliers of parts and has received a variety of documentation, including advice notes, delivery notes, invoice and statements.

1 Advise Caroline about the nature and purposes of the documents she has received.

2 Although personal customers will be paying by cash, her garage customers will be allowed to pay by credit. What source documents would you suggest Caroline uses for these transactions?

3 Explain how a computer or some form of information technology might help Caroline with the documentation process.

transfer money directly from one place to another.

The most significant document used for payment and for transferring funds is clearly the *cheque* (see Figure 18.11), which is then issued through the mechanism of the banking system. Although cheques are not legal tender, their use and acceptability is widespread.

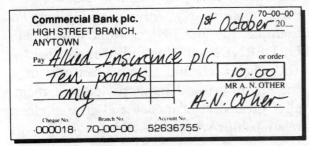

Figure 18.11 A cheque

A cheque is an unconditional order in writing drawn on a bank (and signed by a drawer) that requires a bank to pay on demand a sum of money to the order of a person named or to the bearer.

The various parts of this definition mean:

- *Unconditional.* Payment cannot be dependent upon certain conditions being met.

- *Writing.* A cheque must be in ink or print.

- *Signed.* A cheque must be signed by the drawer, who is the person paying the money.

- *On demand.* The cheque will be paid when presented to the bank.

- *A sum of money.* This must be written on the cheque in words and figures.

- *Named person or to the bearer.* The cheque must be payable to someone by name or

to the bearer (the person in possession of the cheque).

Check your understanding

Write a short booklet entitled *How to Write out a Cheque*. Use a series of illustrations to show the various features of cheques and the points you wish to make.

Another way of transferring money from one account to another is through *credit transfer*. For example, this might involve putting takings into an account for the payment of bills or salaries.

Banking documents act as source documents of entry into an organisation's cash book. It is estimated that more than eight million cheques are processed through the banking system each working day. Dealing with such large volumes of documentation has become an expensive process. As a result, a number of other methods of payment transfer have developed:

- *Standing orders.* Customers can advise their banks to make regular payments on certain dates for fixed amounts. If the amounts or the dates are to be changed, the customer simply advises the bank of such changes.

- *Direct debits.* With this system the customer tells the bank what to pay and when. The receiver provides the documentation requiring payment. This system can deal with variable payments.

- *BACS (Bankers' Automated Clearing System).* This system was set up to deal with bulk electronic clearing for payment purposes. It removes the need to sent vast amounts of paper around the system and is used for standing orders, direct debits and salary credits. The user of the system provides the bank with data in the form of magnetic tape, diskette or disk and this is then sent to the BACS computer centre for processing. If the information is sent through a phone line, it is known as BACSTEL. The input is processed and debits and credits are made to relevant accounts.

- *Credit cards.* Customers are provided with a card and a credit limit and can buy goods up to that limit. Every month a statement is sent to the credit card holder, who may either pay the amount on the statement or pay it at some point in the future.

- *Debit cards.* These allow customers to buy goods and services. The customers' accounts are debited immediately with the cost of the item.

Electronic data interchange (EDI)

In the past, the documents described in here were all on paper. The problem with paper is that it is time-consuming to exchange, inefficient and, with companies transacting all over the globe, it is not easy to handle the vast amount of paper data. Electronic data interchange (EDI) is the exchange of such business transactions as purchases orders, invoices and other documents in a standard computerised form. EDI is, therefore, a form of electronic, paperless contracting between two organisations.

EDI has the objective of speeding up business transactions between suppliers and their customers. It achieves this by allowing data messages or documents to be transferred directly from the computer of one organisation to the computer of another.

Electronic data interchange has many advantages over paper-based systems for handling information. For example, it shortens the 'lead-time' between the sending of an order and its fulfilment. This means orders can be despatched more quickly, companies can hold smaller stock levels and it is easier to plan changes in production. This can be a major saving for a business.

EDI also means that organisations work much more closely with their suppliers. For example, the first EDI network was called ORDERNET and this linked more than 100 wholesalers and 50 manufacturers in the pharmaceutical industry. It saved them all a great deal of money and created closer relationships within the industry.

Another advantage of EDI is that it reduces labour and production costs. A paper-based system requires a considerable amount of manual paper processing. Data has to be keyed into computers, documents need to be stored and then retrieved. EDI is less labour intensive.

Paper-based systems are also prone to error. It is easy for an operator to make a mistake when keying in data. It has been estimated that 70% of data has already been keyed in and checked with EDI, and that the cost of processing an electronic order can be one-tenth of the cost of handling a paper-based equivalent.

Another benefit of EDI is that the trading information that can be extracted from a computer is a useful source of data, which can then be used for both market research and business planning.

When organisations first started using EDI, most communications were directly between trading partners. However, networks, such as the Value Added Network, are now available for direct computer-to-computer communications. EDI networks therefore provide a general communication environment for organisations that use similar or matching transmission speeds and services.

EDT is essentially an electronic post office, receiving electronic messages such as orders and invoices and then posting them into the mailbox of a recipient just like email. Security is a big issue for EDI, and networks such as the Value Added Network have high levels of security with the encryption and decryption of messages. For example, services are password controlled. Only when matching relationships are set up will the network allow transmission and receipt of documents by consenting parties. In recent years the increasing use of the World

Wide Web and other emerging technologies has played a significant role in transforming EDI technologies.

Receipt documents

As well as documents associated with making payments, documents are also used to record receipts. The most basic and common document used to show a receipt of money is simply a *sales receipt*. This is evidence that money has been received and may show the various elements comprising the transaction. For example, Figure 18.12 shows a sales receipt for petrol. Note the VAT number, the date and the total value of the receipt.

One of the most important jobs in a cashier's department is to record incoming

Case study: Developing close supplier relationships

Marks & Spencer (www.marks-and-spencer.co.uk) have a history of buying and dealing directly with their suppliers within the supply chain. This involves Marks & Spencer and their suppliers working together with shared objectives in order to:

- increase sales
- minimise stocks
- minimise commitment
- maximise flexibility.

Communication is therefore an essential part of bringing together all parts of the supply chain to ensure differences between demand from customers and the suppliers' ability to meet such demand can be minimised.

A key element of this is the use of electronic data interchange. Systems transfer information (such as prices, images and product details) between the computers of each organisation. This helps to reduce lead-times and enables all parties to be involved in a much more efficient process of supply, which is much more responsive to customers' needs.

1 What sort of information does Marks & Spencer transfer using EDI?

2 Describe how such information helps all parties to meet the changing requirements of the marketplace.

```
     MANEY SERVICE STN.
    JOCKEY ROAD SUTTON COLDFIELD.
WEST MIDLANDS B73 5PU TEL.0121 354 6808.
       VAT REG.NO.110 7142 27.
  SUN  07-05-00   119990/    0-1 01


 PUMP PRODUCT  LITRES      VALUE(£)
 07 PREMIUM UL  40,63         B
   NETT PRICE        £    41.00

      TOTALS   CHEQUE   £    41.00
 AMT. TEND.             £    41.00
 CHANGE                 £     0.00
     V.A.T. ANALYSIS:-
 RATE   CODE    EXCL   V.A.T.   INCL
 17,50 %   B    34.89   6.11   21.50
               1:44 PM
 THANKYOU FOR CALLING
 PLEASE DRIVE SAFELY.
```

Figure 18.12 A sales receipt

cheques. Cheques are still the most widely accepted form of payment. The various parts of a cheque are illustrated in Figure 18.13.

Cashiers have to make sure that:

- cheques contain current dates

- the amounts in words and figures are the same

- the payee's name is correct

- the cheque is signed

- any alterations are clear and have been signed.

A *paying-in slip* is used when paying cheques and cash into an organisation's bank account (see Figure 18.14). Where a number of cheques are paid in using one slip, they are listed on the reverse side of the slip.

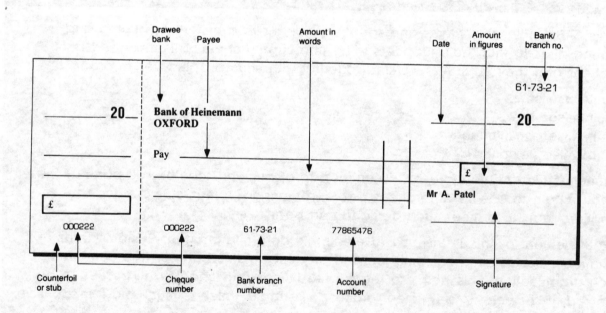

Figure 18.13 The parts of a typical cheque

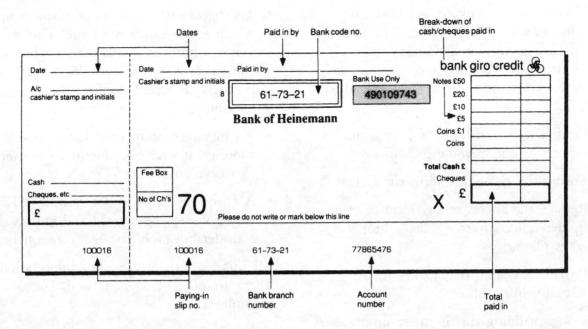

Figure 18.14 A paying-in slip

Check your understanding

Imagine you work in a cashier's department. In the morning post there are a number of remittances. These include:

- a cheque for £8.76
- a cheque for £7.89.

In addition, the following cash payments are received during the day:

- 8 × £10 notes
- 9 × £5 notes
- 8 × £1 coins.

Prepare a paying-in slip for all of the above to be paid into the bank. Make up suitable account and code numbers.

Bank of Heinemann
Oxford Branch

Confidential

Sheet Number

784

Telephone
01865-322222   30th May 2001
Account Number 75283122

Date	Details	Withdrawals	Deposits	Balance (£)
2001				
May 2	Balance from sheet 783			183.45
May 4	Cheque 476124	15.00		168.45
May 5	Cheque 476125	18.50		149.95
May 6	Oxford Council DD	73.85		76.10
May 7	Oxford Telecom credit		956.32	1032.42
May 8	Cheque 476126	149.30		883.12
May 18	Cheque 476129	350.00		533.12
May 25	Cheque 476127	200.00		333.12

Figure 18.15 A bank statement

Banks send *statements* to their customers at regular intervals. The bank statement simply provides a detailed record of all the transactions that have taken place. Information appearing on a bank statement (see Figure 18.15) may include the following:

- A balance that is brought forward from the previous statement.
- Account details.
- A list of deposits paid into the account.
- A list of withdrawals from the account.
- A balance after each transaction.

It is important to ensure that business documents are completed correctly. Internal checks to ensure that day-to-day transactions are correctly recorded will help to detect errors and fraud. They will also help to:

- Limit the responsibility for particular actions to one or more individuals.

- Ensure the records confirm the facts.

- Reduce the effects of any form of error by detecting an error shortly after it takes place.

- Provide a system that makes fraud virtually impossible.

One way of doing this is to set up an *audit trail*. This uses a series of analysis documents that checks all of the steps in the accounting process are error-free, and it also serves to identify errors when they are made.

There are a number of consequences of incorrect completion of source documents (see Figure 18.16). For example, just think about some of the possibilities of the incorrect completion of source documents:

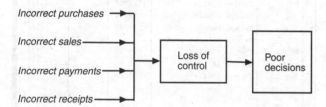

Figure 18.16 The incorrect completion of source documents affects the quality of decision-making

- The organisation fails to send out a large sales invoice or puts a figure on the invoice that is too small (i.e. £1,000 instead of £10,000). This means that profits will be understated.

- The organisation sends out invoices upon which amounts are too large. This will annoy a number of customers, who consequently might consider taking their business elsewhere. Profits will be overstated.

- An incorrect payment is made to a supplier. It may be difficult to recover this payment.

- A cheque is lost and not recorded. This may not even be noticed and will cause considerable problems as a consequence.

All this leads to poor-quality information. There are other dangers as well. For example:

- Not keeping accounting statements that provide a true and fair record of business activity may lead to a breach under the Companies Acts for false accounting.

- A great deal of time that could otherwise be better spent may have to be allocated to finding mistakes and dealing with minor inaccuracies. This costs money.

- Managers may be optimistic about business performance and base their decisions upon the wrong information. In the accounting context, they may feel the business has a strong cash-flow position. If, as a result of errors, this is not so, it could lead to a liquidity crisis.

- If mistakes have been made, information may be permanently lost, which may make it virtually impossible to recover debts.

Check your understanding

Think about your personal financial situation. What would be the worst possible consequence of the incorrect completion of a source document for your bank or other personal account?

There are a number of *security checks* that are necessary for many of the different types of business documents:

- *Orders.* These should be authorised. Copies of the orders should be sent to the receiving department, the stock control department and the accounts department for the checking of prices and discounts. It may be necessary to check that order levels fall within prescribed spending limits (i.e. that members of staff are not exceeding their authority by ordering something of too high a value).

- *Invoices.* These should be checked against the original order to ensure the correct goods have arrived, that prices are correct, that discounts have been correctly calculated and that VAT has been applied correctly. Invoices should also be checked against the goods received note to ensure the details correspond to the goods that have been delivered. Invoices that are incorrect need to be sorted out with the seller. After invoices are checked, they can be authorised for payment.

- *Credit notes.* These should be kept safely and amounts deducted from the prices that appear on invoices.

- *Cheques.* Once invoices have been authorised, eligible cheque signatories may then sanction payment. All organisations will have signed a bank mandate that will set out the names of those employees empowered to sign cheques.

Check your understanding

Explain why every organisation requires a range of security procedures that check documentation.

Find out about the security checks carried out in either the organisation you work for or your school or college.

One list of security checks has been put forward by the Auditing Practices Committee. This list recommended the following checks:

- *Segregation of duties.* This means that job tasks would segregate or break up the roles of those who both record and process a financial transaction. For example, it would not be a good idea for the same person to receive the cash and also be responsible for recording it and taking it to the bank.

- *Physical controls.* These ensure that access to valuable assets within the organisation is restricted through a variety of security measures that involve the use of documentation.

- *Authorisation and approval.* All transactions within the organisation should require authorisation and approval by the person responsible.

- *Management.* Outside the internal controls of the system, managers should be able to use supervisory controls over various procedures.

- *Supervision.* Supervisors should be able to review and oversee the day-to-day recording procedures.

- *Organisation.* Organisations should have a plan that defines the roles of individuals and that comprises a series of controls which include the delegation of authority and responsibility.

- *Arithmetical and accounting.* There should be controls within the organisation which ensure that information is accurately recorded and processed.

- *Personnel.* It is important to ensure that staff have the appropriate personal and professional characteristics to carry out their roles.

Chapter 19 Constructing accounts

You need to understand how the information in financial documents is recorded and used to generate the final accounts. You will need to understand the basic flow of accounting information between the following:

- books of original entry

- general ledger and personal ledger

- trial balance

- final accounts.

You should know how to construct a simple balance sheet and profit and loss account. To do this you will need to be able to distinguish between the following:

- assets

- liabilities

- expenses

- revenues.

You should be able to explain the concept of depreciation in simple terms and how it is calculated. You should also know about the main factors which cause depreciation, including:

- wear and tear

- passing of time

- obsolescence (when things go out of date)

- lack of maintenance.

In the previous chapter we noted that financial accounting involves 'preparing accounting reports from book-keeping records in accordance with acknowledged methods and conventions'. This involves the following:

- *Book-keeping records.* Traditionally, records of accounts have been kept in books or ledgers. These records have been kept in a systematic way. (Today, of course, most book-keeping and accounting procedures are carried out using computers.)

- *Preparing accounting reports.* It is necessary to summarise the entries that appear in book-keeping records in such a way that they can be presented for analysis and examination. Accounting reports summarise the entries that have been made in the books.

- *Acknowledged methods and conventions.* There are set ways of recording accounts that which have been acknowledged over a period of time. Records need to be set out to meet these methods and conventions. This is so that people can look at these records and comparisons can be made between one set of figures and another.

The accounting process, therefore, can be seen as consisting of two parts:

1 Developing and keeping an accurate, full and useful record of the business's financial activities (this part is normally referred to as book-keeping).

2 The interpretation of these records, i.e. the preparation and analysis of accounting reports.

<table>
<tr><td>Discussion point</td><td>How important is it for everybody within a business organisation to have some financial literacy?</td></tr>
</table>

There are a number of stages involved in putting together and keeping a basic accounting system (see Figure 19.1).

In the previous chapter we examined a variety of documents that are used for the trading of goods, including purchase documents, sales documents and payments and receipts documents. These documents provide the raw data for a book-keeping system as book-keepers transfer information from individual documents into accounting records (see Figure 19.2).

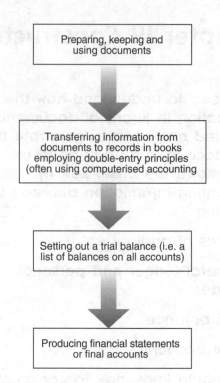

Figure 19.1 The stages involved in putting together and keeping a basic accounting system

Case study: Association of Accounting Technicians

Accounting technicians work alongside professional accountants in a wide range of roles, from accounting clerks and financial managers to credit controllers, where they would manage the accounts of customers. These accounting technicians work in all sectors of the economy, including industry, accountancy practices and the public sector. Some are even self-employed and offer a range of accounting and book-keeping services for the public.

The professional body for accounting technicians is the Association of Accounting Technicians (AAT). The AAT (www.aat.co.uk) has more than 88,000 members and students worldwide. The AAT is unique in being the only accounting body to have its awards accredited by the Qualifications and Curriculum Authority (QCA), and is the only specialist accounting body that awards National Vocational Qualifications (NVQs) and Scottish Vocational Qualifications (SVQs).

1 Why might individuals who work in accounts and book-keeping, and who are *not* qualified accountants from the six professional accounting bodies, want a professional body of their own?

2 What sort of work might AAT members undertake?

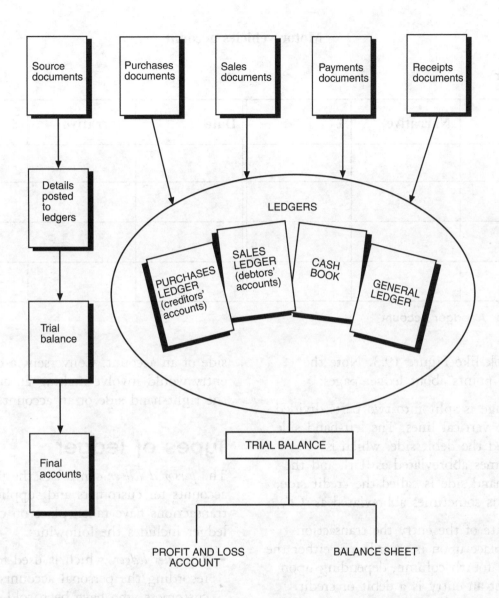

Figure 19.2

Keeping accounting records

In the UK, accounting records have traditionally been kept in *ledgers*. We associate ledgers with clerks toiling long hours in dark and gloomy office conditions writing entries with quill pens into big musty books. Today this picture has long since disappeared and many accounts clerks work in bright and airy offices, with modern computers!

The books in which accounts appear are known as the ledgers. The word 'ledger' really refers to *books of original entry,* as this is the first place book-keeping records are kept. Ledgers are subdivisions of the complete records kept by an organisation. There are a number of ledgers in which accounts appear.

A book-keeping system involves recording transactions in accounts, with each account on a separate page. An account in a ledger

Motor vehicles account

Debit (Dr)   **Credit (Cr)**

Date	Narrative	£	Date	Narrative	£

Figure 19.3 A ledger account

would look like Figure 19.3. Note the following points about ledger pages:

- The page is split into two parts divided by two vertical lines. The left-hand side is called the debit side, which is sometimes abbreviated as 'Dr', and the right-hand side is called the credit side, which is sometimes abbreviated as 'Cr'.

- The date of the entry the transaction takes place upon is recorded in either the first or fourth column, depending upon whether an entry is a debit or credit entry.

- A description of the transaction would be included in the second or fifth column. As we will see shortly, this description will name the *other account* involved in the dual nature of a transaction under the principles of double-entry book-keeping.

- The amounts are entered in the third and sixth columns.

A debit entry into an account would involve making an entry into the left-hand side of an account. Conversely, a credit entry would involve making an entry into the right-hand side of an account.

Types of ledger

The *personal ledger* comprises the personal accounts for customers and suppliers where transactions have taken place on credit. This ledger includes the following:

- *The sales ledger,* which is used for recording the personal accounts of all customers who have been sold goods or provided with services on credit. These accounts are known as the accounts of debtors (i.e. having been supplied with goods/services, they owe the business money).

- *The purchases ledger* is used for keeping the personal records of all the suppliers to whom the organisation owes money. It records all the purchase transactions carried out on credit by the business in purchasing goods or stock to be resold. These accounts are known as the accounts of creditors (i.e. as they are suppliers from whom stock has been received, they are owed money).

The book of original entry used for recording all the cash and bank transactions of the business is known as the *cash book.*

The *general* or *nominal ledger* is used for recording all the other records of an organisation. These may include the following:

- *Asset accounts*, which record the business's assets (such as machinery, motor vehicles and fixtures and fittings).

- *Expenses accounts*, showing all the day-to-day expenses of running a business.

- The owner's *capital account,* showing what the owner(s) has put into the business.

- A *drawings account* listing the amounts drawn out of the business by the owner(s).

Double-entry book-keeping

Double-entry book-keeping has traditionally been accepted as the most efficient way of recording financial transactions. Double-entry is simply what it means. In other words:

> *Every time a transaction takes place it is recorded twice.*

This reflects the dual nature of business transactions. For example, if I pay by cheque for a new motor car, I would need to note I am losing money, which has a negative impact upon the amount in my bank account but on the positive side, I am gaining a motor car. The double-entry system therefore also provides an arithmetic check. What I will have lost in the bank account will be balanced by what I have gained in terms of a motor car.

Each transaction therefore involves:

1 An entry into the debit side of one account.

2 An entry into the credit side of another account.

In ledgers, transactions are recorded using the *double-entry* system whereby, *with each transaction, one account is debited and another is credited* (see Figure 19.4):

A debit entry is made when an account receives something of value, records an asset (something that is owned) or records an expense.

A credit entry is made in an account that gives something of value, records a liability (something that is owed) or records an income item (such as sales).

This means that, for every debit entry into one account, there is always a corresponding credit entry into another account. Such a system assumes all entries into an accounting system reflect a process of exchange. In other words, every transaction involves two entries or two parts, which need to be recorded in the books of account. For example, if we buy equipment for cash we lose cash and have to show this in the cash book, but gain equipment and so have to show this in the equipment account in the general ledger. This dual element is a fundamental principle for recording transactions. It is carried through to the trial balance and then on to the final accounts.

Example

The best way to learn about the principles of double-entry book-keeping is to look at some financial transactions undertaken by a

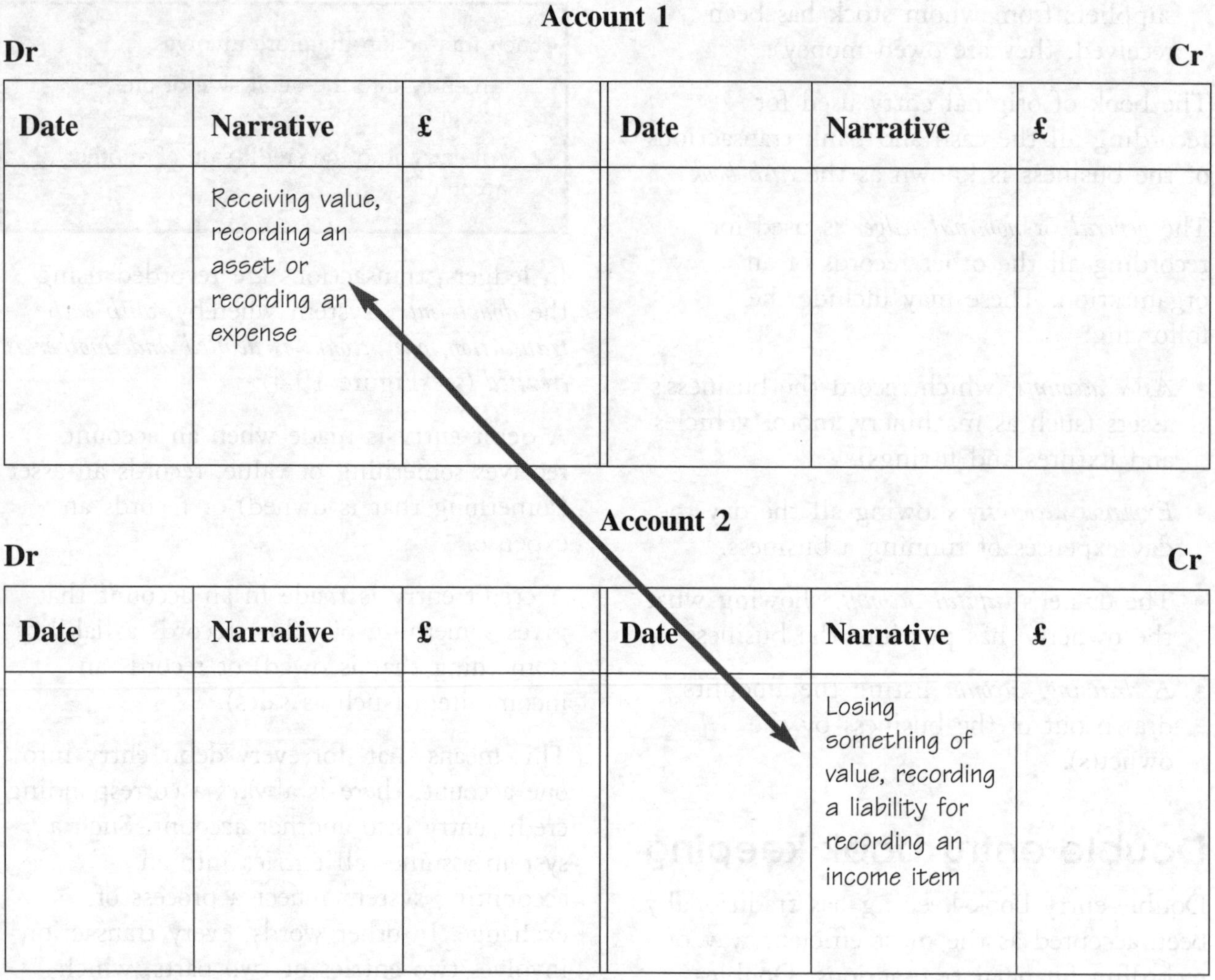

Account 1

Dr					Cr
Date	**Narrative**	**£**	**Date**	**Narrative**	**£**
	Receiving value, recording an asset or recording an expense				

Account 2

Dr					Cr
Date	**Narrative**	**£**	**Date**	**Narrative**	**£**
				Losing something of value, recording a liability for recording an income item	

Figure 19.4 The double-entry system

business and then, of course, *to have a go at some examples yourself.*

Mike Ellis has always wanted to start a market-gardening business and decides to do so on 1 January. The following transactions relate to his business activities in the first half of the year:

Transaction 1 (1 January) Mike starts his business with £20,000 of capital by placing a cheque into his business bank account.

Transaction 2 (15 January) Having negotiated a rental fee of £3,000 per annum

with a local farmer for a substantial plot of land, Mike pays his rent in advance by cheque.

Transaction 3 (4 February) Mike buys tools and equipment for £6,000, paying by cheque.

Transaction 4 (5 February) Mike buys seed by cheque for £1,000.

Transaction 5 (3 March) Mike withdraws money from the bank for his own use by taking £800 out. This is known as drawings.

Transaction 6 (1 April) Mike makes his first sale of seedlings, receiving a cheque for £2,500.

Transaction 7 (3 May) Mike pays advertising expenses £500 by cheque.

Transaction 8 (1 June) In order to expand the business, Mike receives a loan from A Bank plc for £5,000, which is put into his bank account.

Each of these transactions will involve a debit entry into one account and a credit entry into another account. *With each transaction one account is debited and another is credited.*

Transaction 1 Capital is the money invested into an organisation by its owner(s). The amount is then owed by the business to the owner(s). This is the first transaction to be recorded into books of original entry. The entry would be as follows:

- Debit the bank account *in the cash book* as this is receiving £20,000 of value.

- Credit the capital account *in the general ledger* as this is a liability to the business and is what it owes the owner.

Dr			Bank account		Cr
Date	Narrative	£	Date	Narrative	£
1 January	Capital	20,000			

Dr			Capital account		Cr
Date	Narrative	£	Date	Narrative	£
			1 January	Bank	20,000

As we progress from one entry to another, we build up a wider picture of all of the transactions that have been undertaken within the business.

Transaction 2 All business organisations pay expenses. These may include the payment of rent (as in this instance), advertising expenses, vehicle expenses, business rates and so on, many of which are ongoing and paid for in a short period. As a result they are known as *revenue expenditure*. Remember that payment of expenses provides some value (i.e. when rent is paid, it follows that the services accompanying that expense are then to follow). A separate account is usually kept for each main type of expense. The entry for payment of an expense by cheque would be as follows:

- Debit the appropriate expense account *in the general ledger.*

- Credit the bank account *in the cash book* as this account is losing value.

There are now three accounts for the two transactions as one account has had two entries:

Dr			Bank account			Cr
Date	Narrative	£	Date	Narrative	£
1 January	Capital	20,000	15 January	Rent paid	3,000

Dr			Rent paid account		Cr
Date	Narrative	£	Date	Narrative	£
15 January	Bank	3,000			

Dr			Capital account		Cr
Date	Narrative	£	Date	Narrative	£
			1 January	Bank	20,000

Transaction 3 Items purchased by a business organisation for use over a long period of time are known as fixed assets. Common examples might be motor vehicles, property, fixtures and fittings, and machinery. Fixed

assets are particularly important as they are used to support the provision of goods or services by a business. For example, a shop would need fixtures and fittings and a factory would require machinery.

The purchase of such assets incurs *capital expenditure*. So, for example, the purchase of a factory would be capital expenditure but the maintenance of the factory and the expenses incurred in running it would be revenue expenditure. The entries for the purchase of a fixed asset by cheque would be as follows:

- Debit the appropriate fixed asset account *in the general ledger* as this records the receipt of an asset.

- Credit the bank account *in the cash book* as this account is losing value.

There are now four accounts for the three transactions as one account has three entries:

Dr Bank account **Cr**

Date	Narrative	£	Date	Narrative	£
1 January	Capital	20,000	15 January	Rent paid	20,000
			4 February	Tools and equipment	6,000

Dr Tools and equipment account **Cr**

Date	Narrative	£	Date	Narrative	£
4 February	Bank	6,000			

Dr Rent paid account **Cr**

Date	Narrative	£	Date	Narrative	£
15 January	Bank	3,000			

Dr Capital account **Cr**

Date	Narrative	£	Date	Narrative	£
			1 January	Bank	20,000

Transaction 4 Sales and purchases are not recorded into and from a stock or goods account. Instead, where goods are bought to be resold, or converted into a form to be resold, a purchases account is created. Similarly, when sales take place a sales account is used to signify the sale. The entries for the purchase of stock or items to be used and added value to within the business by cheque would be as follows:

- Debit the purchases account *in the general ledger* as value is received.

- Credit the bank account in the *cash book* as this is losing value.

There are now five accounts for the four transactions as one account has four entries:

Dr Bank account **Cr**

Date	Narrative	£	Date	Narrative	£
1 January	Capital	20,000	15 January	Rent paid	3,000
			4 February	Tools and equipment	6,000
			5 February	Purchases	1,000

Dr Purchases account **Cr**

Date	Narrative	£	Date	Narrative	£
5 February	Bank	1,000			

Dr Tools and equipment account **Cr**

Date	Narrative	£	Date	Narrative	£
4 February	Bank	6,000			

Dr Rent paid account **Cr**

Date	Narrative	£	Date	Narrative	£
15 January	Bank	3,000			

Dr Capital account **Cr**

Date	Narrative	£	Date	Narrative	£
			1 January	Bank	20,000

Transaction 5 The term used to describe anything the owner takes out of the business is 'drawings'.

Drawings may not always involve the writing of a cheque from the business bank account. For example, it may include the taking of cash out of the business or the use of goods or services owned by the business. The entries for the withdrawal of money from the bank by cheque would be as follows:

- Debit the drawings account *in the general ledger* to show that the owner of the business has received something of value from the business.

- Credit the bank account *in the cash book* as this is losing value.

There are now six accounts for the five transactions as one account has five entries:

Dr   **Bank account**   **Cr**

Date	Narrative	£	Date	Narrative	£
1 January	Capital	20,000	15 January	Rent paid	3,000
			4 February	Tools and equipment	6,000
			5 February	Purchases	1,000
			3 March	Drawings	800

Dr   **Drawings account**   **Cr**

Date	Narrative	£	Date	Narrative	£
3 March	Bank	800			

Dr   **Purchases account**   **Cr**

Date	Narrative	£	Date	Narrative	£
5 February	Bank	1,000			

Dr   **Tools and equipment account**   **Cr**

Date	Narrative	£	Date	Narrative	£
4 February	Bank	6,000			

Dr   **Rent paid account**   **Cr**

Date	Narrative	£	Date	Narrative	£
15 January	Bank	3,000			

Dr   **Capital account**   **Cr**

Date	Narrative	£	Date	Narrative	£
			1 January	Bank	20,000

Transaction 6 Sales are clearly an important element for every type of business organisation. When sales have taken place, records of such transactions are kept in a sales account which is usually credited to show there is a loss of something of value. The entries, therefore, for the sale of goods by cheque would be as follows:

- Debit the bank account *in the cash book* as this is gaining value.

- Credit the sales account *in the general ledger* to show a loss of value.

There are now seven accounts for six transactions as one account has six entries:

Dr   **Bank account**   **Cr**

Date	Narrative	£	Date	Narrative	£
1 January	Capital	20,000	15 January	Rent paid	3,000
1 April	Sales	2,500	4 February	Tools and equipment	6,000
			5 February	Purchases	1,000
			3 March	Drawings	800

Dr   **Sales account**   **Cr**

Date	Narrative	£	Date	Narrative	£
			1 April	Bank	2,500

Dr   **Drawings account**   **Cr**

Date	Narrative	£	Date	Narrative	£
3 March	Bank	800			

Dr   **Purchases account**   **Cr**

Date	Narrative	£	Date	Narrative	£
5 February	Bank	1,000			

Dr   **Tools and equipment account**   **Cr**

Date	Narrative	£	Date	Narrative	£
4 February	Bank	6,000			

Dr   **Rent paid account**   **Cr**

Date	Narrative	£	Date	Narrative	£
15 January	Bank	3,000			

Dr   **Capital account**   **Cr**

Date	Narrative	£	Date	Narrative	£
			1 January	Bank	20,000

Transaction 7 As we saw earlier, expense accounts are debited as they provide some value. The entries for the payment of advertising expenses by cheque would therefore be as follows:

- Debit the expense account *in the general ledger*.

- Credit the bank account *in the cash book*.

There are now eight accounts for seven transactions as one account has seven entries:

Dr   **Bank account**   **Cr**

Date	Narrative	£	Date	Narrative	£
1 January	Capital	20,000	15 January	Rent paid	3,000
1 April	Sales	2,500	4 February	Tools and equipment	6,000
			5 February	Purchases	1,000
			3 March	Drawings	800
			3 May	Advertising	500

Dr   **Advertising**   **Cr**

Date	Narrative	£	Date	Narrative	£
3 May	Bank	500			

Dr   **Sales account**   **Cr**

Date	Narrative	£	Date	Narrative	£
			1 April	Bank	2,500

Dr   **Drawings account**   **Cr**

Date	Narrative	£	Date	Narrative	£
3 March	Bank	800			

Dr   **Purchases account**   **Cr**

Date	Narrative	£	Date	Narrative	£
5 February	Bank	1,000			

Dr   **Tools and equipment account**   **Cr**

Date	Narrative	£	Date	Narrative	£
4 February	Bank	6,000			

Dr   **Rent paid account**   **Cr**

Date	Narrative	£	Date	Narrative	£
15 January	Bank	3,000			

Dr   **Capital account**   **Cr**

Date	Narrative	£	Date	Narrative	£
			1 January	Bank	20,000

Transaction 8 Receiving a loan will cause the bank account to gain value. The loan becomes a liability and is then owed by the business to the lender. The entries for the receipt of a loan would thus be as follows:

- Debit the bank (or cash) account *in the cash book* as the account is receiving value.

- Credit the loan account *in the general ledger* to show the liability created.

There are now nine accounts for eight transactions as one account has eight entries:

Dr			Bank account		Cr
Date	**Narrative**	**£**	**Date**	**Narrative**	**£**
1 January	Capital	20,000	15 January	Rent paid	3,000
1 April	Sales	2,500	4 February	Tools and equipment	6,000
1 June	Loan: A Bank plc	5,000	5 February	Purchases	1,000
			3 March	Drawings	800
			3 May	Advertising	500

Dr			Loan account: A Bank plc		Cr
Date	**Narrative**	**£**	**Date**	**Narrative**	**£**
			1 June	Bank	5,000

Dr			Advertising		Cr
Date	**Narrative**	**£**	**Date**	**Narrative**	**£**
3 May	Bank	500			

Dr			Sales account		Cr
Date	**Narrative**	**£**	**Date**	**Narrative**	**£**
			1 April	Bank	2,500

Dr			Drawings account		Cr
Date	**Narrative**	**£**	**Date**	**Narrative**	**£**
3 March	Bank	800			

Dr			Purchases account		Cr
Date	**Narrative**	**£**	**Date**	**Narrative**	**£**
5 February	Bank	1,000			

Dr			Tools and equipment account		Cr
Date	**Narrative**	**£**	**Date**	**Narrative**	**£**
4 February	Bank	6,000			

Dr			Rent paid account		Cr
Date	**Narrative**	**£**	**Date**	**Narrative**	**£**
15 January	Bank	3,000			

Dr			Capital account		Cr
Date	**Narrative**	**£**	**Date**	**Narrative**	**£**
			1 January	Bank	20,000

Looking at how all these accounts build up on the basis of simply a few transactions helps you to appreciate why there are a number of books of original entry!

Remember

1 CAPITAL *is recorded as:*
   Debit the bank account if the capital supplied is a cheque.
   Credit the capital account.

2 Recording EXPENSES *will involve:*
   Debiting the expense account.
   Crediting the account paying for the expenses.

3 The purchase of FIXED ASSETS *will be recorded as:*
   Debit the fixed asset account.
   Credit the bank or cash account.

4 The PURCHASE of stock or goods bought by cash or cheque for further work or resale *will involve:*
   Debiting the purchases account.
   Crediting the bank or cash account.

5 DRAWINGS *will involve:*
   Debiting the drawings account.
   Crediting the bank or cash account.

Check your understanding

Derrick Scott has decided to set up in business on 1 June buying and selling model railway engines. The following transactions relate to his business activities:

Transaction 1 (1 June)	Derrick starts his business with £40,000 of capital by placing a cheque into his business bank account.
Transaction 2 (3 July)	Having negotiated a rental fee of £5,000 per annum with a businessperson for a lock-up, Derrick pays his rent in advance by cheque.
Transaction 3 (4 August)	Derrick buys a van for £6,000, paying by cheque.
Transaction 4 (5 August)	Having visited a number of sales, Derrick now buys a range of different types of model engines by cheque for £6,000.
Transaction 5 (3 October)	Derrick withdraws money from the bank for his own use by taking £200 out.
Transaction 6 (8 October)	Visiting a salesroom, Derrick makes his first sale of engines, receiving a cheque for £6,500.
Transaction 7 (9 December)	Derrick pays advertising expenses of £1,000 by cheque.
Transaction 8 (12 December)	In order to expand the business, Derrick receives a loan from A Bank plc for £3,000 which is put into his bank account.

6 SALES for cash or by cheque *will involve*:
Debiting the cash or bank account
Crediting the sales account.

7 Receiving a LOAN *will involve*:
Debiting the bank account.
Crediting the loan account of the lender.

More advanced transactions

Credit transactions So far all the transactions that have taken place have involved payments from a bank account. In business, however, as we saw in the last chapter when we discussed documentation, most transactions are on credit. The sending or receipt of money does not take place until a later point in time. The purpose of the double-entry book-keeping system is, therefore, to record these credit transactions, whether they are credit purchases or credit sales:

1 *Credit purchases* These take place when goods are purchased from a supplier. Payment will then be made at a later date from the purchaser to the supplier. In a credit purchasing transaction the supplier is the purchaser's creditor.

> *Creditors are people or business organisations to whom the purchaser owes money and are, therefore, a liability to the purchaser's business.*

The best way to look at credit purchases is through a simple transaction.

Thompson's Independent Traders made the following transactions during January:

- 1 January   Bought goods on credit from Lillee & Co. for £950.

- 17 January   Paid Lillee & Co. by cheque.

There are clearly two transactions here, which will lead to four entries into the double-entry book-keeping system. On 1 January, when the credit purchase takes place, the entries will be as follows:

- Debit the purchases account *in the general ledger* as this account is receiving value.

- Credit the creditor's account *in the purchases ledger* or *personal ledger* as this account records a liability.

On 17 January payment takes place, and this also has to be shown through the double-entry book-keeping system. The entries are as follows:

- Debit the creditor's account *in the purchases ledger* or *personal ledger* to reduce the amount the business owes them.

- Credit the bank account *in the cash book*, as this is the account recording the payment by cheque.

Dr			Purchases account		Cr
Date	Narrative	£	Date	Narrative	£
1 January	Lillee & Co.	950			

Dr			Lillee & Co. account		Cr
Date	Narrative	£	Date	Narrative	£
17 January	Bank	950	1 January	Purchases	950

Dr			Bank account		Cr
Date	Narrative	£	Date	Narrative	£
			17 January	Lillee & Co.	950

2 *Credit sales* Sales on credit take place when goods are sold to a customer who will then settle their account at a later date. In a credit selling transaction as the customer owes money to the business, they are the business's debtor.

> *Debtors are those individuals or businesses who owe the organisation money.*

As before, the best way to look at a credit selling process is through a simple transaction.

Using the Thompson's Independent Traders business again, they made some other transactions during January.

- 7 January   Sold goods on credit to G. Chappell for £2,300.

- 24 January   G. Chappell paid by cheque.

There are also two transactions here, which lead to four entries into the double-entry book-keeping system. On 7 January, when the credit sale takes place, the entries will be as follows:

- Debit the debtor's account *in the sales ledger* or *personal ledger* as this account is recording an asset.

- Credit the sales account *in the general ledger* as this account records an income item.

On 24 January the debtor makes a payment, and this also has to be shown through the double-entry book-keeping system. The entries are as follows:

- Debit the bank account *in the cash book* as this account records the receipt of a cheque.

- Credit the debtor's account *in the sales ledger* or *personal ledger*, to show the loss in value of the asset.

Dr **Sales account** **Cr**

Date	Narrative	£	Date	Narrative	£
			7 January	G. Chappell	2,300

Dr **G. Chappell account** **Cr**

Date	Narrative	£	Date	Narrative	£
7 January	Sales	2,300	24 January	Bank	2,300

Dr **Bank account** **Cr**

Date	Narrative	£	Date	Narrative	£
24 January	G. Chappell	2,300			

Purchases returns and sales returns Transactions do not always run quite as smoothly as most would like. Occasionally, when goods are bought or sold, returns take place sometimes because the goods are faulty or because the wrong goods have been delivered. There are two types of returns:

1 *Purchases returns*, which are sometimes called *returns outwards,* occur when a business returns goods to a creditor. The book-keeping entries for purchases returns are as follows:

- Debit the creditor's account *in the sales ledger* or *personal ledger,* to reduce the amount of the liability owed to the creditor.

- Credit a returns outwards account *in the general ledger* to show the business is losing something of value.

An example helps to illustrate the process.

Knight & Co. made the following transactions during January:

- 1 January   Bought goods on credit from Piper Ltd for £1,200.

- 5 January   £300 of the goods were faulty and returned outwards/back to Piper Ltd.

Dr **Purchases account** **Cr**

Date	Narrative	£	Date	Narrative	£
1 January	Piper Ltd	1,200			

Dr **Piper Ltd account** **Cr**

Date	Narrative	£	Date	Narrative	£
5 January	Returns outwards	300	1 January	Purchases	1,200

Dr **Returns outwards account** **Cr**

Date	Narrative	£	Date	Narrative	£
			5 January	Piper Ltd	300

2 *Sales returns* are sometimes called *returns inwards* because, having received them, a customer then returns some of them back to the business. The book-keeping entries for sales returns are as follows:

- Debit the returns inwards account *in the general ledger* to show the business is receiving something of value.

- Credit the debtor's account *in the purchases ledger* or *personal ledger* to reduce the value of their debt.

An example to illustrate the process would be as follows:

- 1 June   Sold goods to T. Penney & Co. for £16,000.

- 8 June   £1,400 of the goods sold to T. Penney & Co. have been returned inwards/back to us.

Dr   Sales account   **Cr**

Date	Narrative	£	Date	Narrative	£
			1 June	T. Penny & Co.	16,000

Dr   T. Penny & Co. account   **Cr**

Date	Narrative	£	Date	Narrative	£
1 June	Sales	16,000	8 June	Returns inwards	1,400

Dr   Returns inwards account   **Cr**

Date	Narrative	£	Date	Narrative	£
8 June	T. Penney & Co.	1,400			

Carriage inwards and outwards The cost of transporting goods inwards and outwards when goods are bought or sold is known as 'carriage'. Carriage inwards is where the buyer pays the cost of the purchases, and carriage outwards is where the seller pays the carriage charge. As both of these are *expenses*, as with all expense accounts, they should be debited, with the other half of the transaction coming from the bank or cash account.

Balancing accounts The T or ledger accounts and double-entry book-keeping are an important method of recording business data from all the transactions that take place within the normal business activities of every organisation. Every so often, perhaps every month or half-year, ledger accounts need to be scrutinised so that information can be extracted from them. For example, it would be useful to know:

- How much money is in the bank.

- The amount of sales generated within the last month.

- The amounts owing to each creditor or debtor.

- Total expenses incurred within the business.

In order to do this, accounts have to be balanced. There are a number of stages to balancing accounts:

1 If an account contains entries on either side which are equal to each other, then those entries can simply be underlined twice and the account closed for the financial period (i.e. the account has neither a debit nor credit balance as both sides are equal).

Dr   G. Chappell account   **Cr**

Date	Narrative	£	Date	Narrative	£
7 January	Sales	2,300	24 January	Bank	2,300

2 Where both sides are not equal, a balancing figure is required. Finding out the balancing figure involves adding up both sides of the account. The difference between the two totals is the *balance of the account*.

3 The *balance of the account* is entered on the side of the smaller total on the next line. The date will be the date the balancing process takes place. The balance is described as *Balance c/d* – c/d means 'carried down'.

Dr   Bank account   **Cr**

Date	Narrative	£	Date	Narrative	£
1 January	Capital	20,000	15 January	Rent paid	3,000
1 April	Sales	2,500	4 February	Tools and equipment	6,000
1 June	Loan: A Bank plc	5,000	5 February	Purchases	1,000
			3 March	Advertising	800
			3 May	Advertising	500
			31 May	Balance c/d	16,200
		£27,500			£27,500
1 June	Balance b/d	16,200			

4 Both sides of the account are now totalled so that the totals will be the same on both sides of the account. The totals appear opposite each other on the same line and are double underlined.

5 Double-entry book-keeping involves an opposite entry for the balance, which is then 'brought down' to the other side of the account. The date would be the first day of the new accounting period and *Balance b/d* (meaning 'brought down') would appear in the narrative.

6 The account is now balanced. We can see that the bank account has a debit balance of £16,200. When entries are brought down in the opposite direction they have credit entries. Balances are then transferred to the trial balance.

Check your understanding

Balance the following accounts at the end of January:

Example 1

Dr		Rent paid account			Cr
Date	**Narrative**	**£**	**Date**	**Narrative**	**£**
15 January	Bank	3,000			

Example 2

Dr		Sales account			Cr
Date	**Narrative**	**£**	**Date**	**Narrative**	**£**
			1 January	T. Robinson & Co.	13,000

Example 3

Dr		Bank account			Cr
Date	**Narrative**	**£**	**Date**	**Narrative**	**£**
1 January	Capital	4,300	6 January	Rent paid	2,100
7 January	Loan	5,000	15 January	Motor vehicle	2,300
			21 January	Drawings	700

Computerised accounting

The widespread use of computers by all types of organisations has seen many organisations opt to computerise their book-keeping systems.

> *Computerised accounting systems simply incorporate manual-based theories using customised packages.*

There are a number of advantages of using computerised accounting packages:

- Computers help to improve the control of funds coming into and going out of an organisation and make this control more effective.

- They improve accuracy, particularly where large amounts of data are entering into accounts (i.e. they take away much of the tedium of data entry into double-entry accounts).

- Accounting data is, by its very nature, arithmetical, which is well suited to being recorded and maintained by computer.

- Computerised book-keeping systems can supply reports and account balances much more quickly (such as trial balance, stock valuation, payroll analysis, VAT return, etc.).

- Many reports can be produced quickly and easily in a way that would not be possible in a manual system because of time and cost. For example, it would be easy to go through the sales ledger to find out all the customers (aged debtors) who have not paid their debts and send them reminders to do so.

- They help to provide managers with a readily accessible view of how the business organisation is functioning.

Computer programs for financial accounts usually follow the same system of ledger division into general and personal. In doing so the system provides an element of continuity with past practices. Commercially available accounting software is usually described as an 'integrated package', covering a range of accounting activities. For example, an accounting package would:

- update customer accounts in the sales ledger
- update supplier accounts in the purchases ledger
- record bank receipts and payments
- print out invoices
- make payments to suppliers and for expenses
- adjust records automatically.

Many packages offer more than just the control of each of the ledgers. Some may also provide for payroll, stock control production planning, electronic data interchange (EDI) and financial planning. These can be integrated with the rest of the accounting system.

An *integrated accounting system* means that, when a business transaction takes place and is input into the computer, it is recorded into a range of accounting records at the same time. For example, if a sales invoice is generated for a customer:

- The customer's account will be adjusted with the invoice total.
- The sales account will increase and VAT will be applied.
- Stock records will change.

Case study: Sage Line 50

Sage Line 50 (www.sagesoft.co.uk/) is the UK's best-selling accounting software. It is an integrated package designed to provide users with the opportunity to make best use of their accounting data. The package makes all facts and figures readily available so that managers can quickly analyse their trading situation and solve problems or seize new opportunities. The package handles sales and purchases, stock control and order processing. It also generates invoices, produces statements, creates reports and can be used to create sales letters. There are a number of elements to the system, including the following:

- *Sales Ledger.* This shows who the customers are, what and when they buy and how much they owe and for how long.

- *Purchases Ledger.* This enables the users to get the best value from their suppliers, enabling them to be in a strong position to get better discounts and higher credit levels.

- *Nominal Ledger.* This brings together all the transactions and balances from other ledgers to create a chart of accounts to suit specific user requirements.

- *Financials.* This enables Sage Line 50 to deal with management accounts, VAT returns and budget analysis.

- *Bank*. The system manages accounts as well as transfers between accounts.

- *Fixed Assets Register*. This enables the system to maintain records of all fixed assets and set up depreciation rates.

- *Stock*. Sage Line 50 helps the user to achieve the right balance with reliable and up-to-date information on each stock item.

- *Invoicing*. Prices, discounts and VAT are automatically calculated, with every invoice cross-referenced to ledgers.

- *Order processing*. This provides a window into orders received and placed.

- *Report generator*. This sets templates to allow the users to retrieve, sort and print out all of the information they require.

Sage Line 50 is easy to set up and use. Various forms, such as cheques, bank statements and invoices, are all created on screen and 'Wizards' take the user through various procedures. The real benefit of using this sort of package is speed and efficiency. Sage Line 50 has an automatic backup system, making it easy to spot and amend mistakes, and there is also password security access.

A key benefit of using Sage Line 50 is that it integrates with all other office software. For example, data from the system can be transferred into spreadsheets. Information can also be integrated into mail-merge and marketing databases.

There are single user or network versions of Sage Line 50. The networking option allows more than one user on to the system at any one time.

1 Why does a package such as Sage Line 50 mirror the workings of a double-entry book-keeping system?

2 What are the advantages of using such a package?

Although there are a variety of computerised accounting systems available, there are not many major differences between the packages. This is because all computerised accounting systems adhere to basic accounting concepts and practices (see Figure 19.5).

Check your understanding

Find out if there is a computer package recording financial data within your school or college. Ask a member of the office staff if your group can be shown how the system works. Prepare some questions to ask.

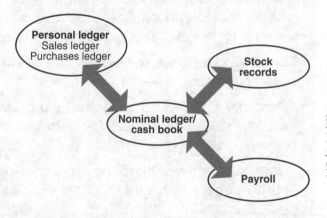

Figure 19.5 A computerised accounting system

The trial balance

As we have seen, at the end of an accounting period (annually, quarterly or monthly), accounts are balanced. These balances are then listed in a trial balance. The trial balance lists all the balances from all the accounts in all the ledgers.

The trial balance is not part of the system of double-entry. It does, however, provide a useful mechanism for checking the accuracy of accounting entries and also provides a list of balances that can then be used to prepare the final accounts.

As we have also seen, ledger accounts have either debit balances or credit balances. The trial balance must be constructed in a way that takes these two types of balances into account. Given that each transaction involves part of a transaction being recorded as a debit and the other parts as a credit, it will follow that when all the accounts are listed together, the total of the debits must equal the total of the credits:

Look at the trial balance opposite. Both sides total to the same amount because, for every debit entry into one ledger account, there is a corresponding credit into another. Note the following:

- The heading for the trial balance gives the date on which the figures were extracted from the book-keeping records.

- The accounts shown above are not numbered. It would be normal practice to have a folio reference number for each account so that entries could be traced.

- The balance for each account is the figure brought down from the balancing process.

- Debit balances include purchases, expenses, returns inwards (sales returns), drawings, fixed asset accounts (such as

Trial balance of Jasbir Sidhu as at 31 December 2000

	Dr £	Cr £
Purchases	15,000	
Returns outwards		1,000
Sales		45,000
Returns inwards	2,500	
Stock 1 January 2000	8,500	
Wages	4,500	
Interest paid	3,200	
Travel expenses	4,000	
Lighting and heating	3,500	
Premises	50,000	
Motor vehicles	15,000	
Plant and machinery	25,000	
Debtors	14,000	
Bank	8,000	
Cash	2,000	
Creditors		16,000
Drawings	10,000	
Bank loan		30,000
Capital		73,200
	165,200	165,200

motor vehicles), debtors, cash and bank. (Note: It is possible for the bank account to have a credit balance if the bank account is overdrawn.)

- Credit balances include sales, returns outwards (purchases returns), capital, bank loan and creditors.

The trial balance includes a stock valuation for the beginning of the year. At the end of the year the stock is valued again and, as we shall see, this figure appears in the trading account as a credit entry and in the balance sheet as an asset.

Note that the trial balance will help to detect certain types of error only – for example, where the debit entry has been made into one ledger account and the credit entry has not been made into another. It must not always be assumed that because the trial balance balances, it is always correct. For example, one error that would not be detected would be if an invoice was misread so that £5,000 was transferred into two accounts instead of £50,000. There are six types of errors that would not be shown by a trial balance:

1 *Errors of omission,* where a business transaction has been completely missed from the accounting records.

2 *Errors of commission,* with an entry posted to the wrong accounts.

3 *Reversal of entries* – making entries into the accounts but on the wrong sides of the two accounts concerned.

4 *Errors of principle,* where a transaction is entered into the wrong type of account.

5 *Errors of original entry,* where the wrong amount has been posted to the accounts, possibly because of a misread invoice.

6 *Compensating error,* where two errors cancel each other out.

Discussion point	Working in groups, discuss what quality control procedures a business might introduce in order to minimise the errors made within its book-keeping system.

As stated earlier, we have not numbered each of the accounts in the illustrated trial balance. Nor have we numbered accounts where we have shown ledger entries. It would be normal practice when managing ledger entries to attribute a *folio reference* number to each account so that entries could be easily traced.

Another way of presenting a trial balance is to list entries in a *single column*. When this is done, debit entries are added and credit entries – which are now shown in brackets – are deducted. The balance at the bottom of the trial balance should then be *zero*:

Trial balance of Jasbir Sidhu as at 31 December 2000

	Dr £	Cr £
Purchases	15,000	
Returns outwards	(1,000)	
Sales	(45,000)	
Returns inwards	2,500	
Stock 1 January 2000	8,500	
Wages	4,500	
Interest paid	3,200	
Travel expenses	4,000	
Lighting and heating	3,500	
Premises	50,000	
Motor vehicles	15,000	
Plant and machinery	25,000	
Debtors	14,000	
Bank	8,000	
Cash	2,000	
Creditors	(16,000)	
Drawings	10,000	
Bank loan	(30,000)	
Capital	(73,200)	
	Zero	

Check your understanding

Example 1 The following balances have been extracted from the books of R. James as at 31 December 2000. Use them to construct both a single-column and a double-column trial balance.

	£
Purchases	12,400
Sales	65,700
Stock 1 January 2000	7,100
Salaries	14,400
Wages	2,500
Returns inwards	3,200
Rent paid	4,000
Light and heating	3,500
Land and buildings	45,000
Machinery	14,000
Motor vehicles	8,000
Debtors	18,000
Bank	7,500
Cash	2,000
Creditors	17,400
Returns outwards	1,000
Drawings	8,000
Bank loan	15,000
Capital	50,500

Example 2 The following balances have been extracted from the books of A. Jenkinson as at 31 December 2000. Use them to construct both a single-column and a double-column trial balance. (Note: Use 'Capital' to balance both trial balances.)

	£
Bank	4,100
Premises	8,400
Fixtures	4,000
Bank loan	6,000
Wages	5,000
Returns inwards	1,000
Advertising	5,000
Rent paid	5,000
Cash	3,000
Debtors	14,000
Creditors	4,000
Purchases	6,000
Sales	17,500
Returns outwards	500
Stock 1 January 2000	4,000
Drawings	5,000
Capital	XXXX

Relationship of the trial balance to final accounts

All entries into the trial balance form the raw data for the final accounts of a business. The **final accounts** of a business are its financial statements that are prepared to meet the needs of various groups of stakeholders. They comprise:

- a trading account
- a profit and loss account
- a balance sheet.

Each entry into the trial balance appears *once* in one of the final accounts.

Remember, the trial balance includes a stock valuation for the beginning of the year. At the end of the year the stock is valued again and, as we shall see, this figure appears in the trading account as a credit entry and in the balance sheet as an asset.

Each item in the trial balance will appear once in the final accounts.

Final accounts

Final accounts are usually produced once a year by a firm of outside auditors or accountants. As well as helping the owners of a business to revise and fine-tune their business strategies, they provide a broad picture of how an organisation is performing and may be presented to the Inland Revenue and lenders of money, such as banks. As we have seen, the starting point for preparing the final accounts is the trial balance (see Figure 19.6).

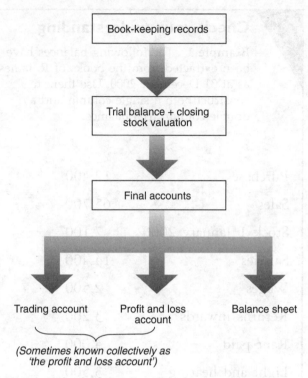

Figure 19.6 **Constructing the final accounts**

The trading account

As the trading account is usually linked together with the profit and loss account, with the trading account appearing above, they are sometimes collectively called 'the profit and loss account'.

The trading account can be likened to a video giving ongoing pictures of an organisation's trading activities. For many business organisations, trading involves buying and selling stock. The difference between the value of the stock sold (sales) and the cost of producing those sales (which may be the production costs of manufactured goods for a manufacturing company, or the cost of purchasing the supplies for a trading company) is known as the gross profit.

The trading account simply shows how gross profit is arrived at:

Net sales – Cost of sales = Gross profit

The trading account *includes only the items in which an organisation trades*. For example, if a small supermarket buys baked beans and sells them to its customers, then the cost of purchasing these and the amounts received from selling them will appear in the trading account. However, if the supermarket's owner decided to sell the business's van, this would not be included in the trading account as he or she is not in the second-hand vehicle business.

Sales

Sales are often described as turnover. As we have seen earlier, sometimes goods which have been sold are returned inwards as sales returns. We obviously do not want to include these in the sales figures because they have come back to us. Net sales, which is the final sales figure, is therefore:

Sales – Returns inwards (sales returns)
= Net sales

Purchases

As with sales, some purchases may have been returned but, in this instance, the returns will have been outwards as purchases returns. Purchases may also include the cost of transporting the goods to the organisation, which must be added to the cost of buying goods, known, as we saw earlier, as carriage inwards. Net purchases, where there is carriage inwards and purchases returns, could therefore be:

Purchases + Carriage inwards
– Returns outward (purchases returns)
= Net purchases

Stocks

The final cost of sales figure must take into account the value of stocks. Opening stock is effectively a purchase as these will be sold in the current trading period. One the other hand, closing stock must be deducted from the purchases as these will be sold next year.

Cost of sales

The calculation for cost of sales taking including a full set of adjustments to purchases and stocks would therefore be:

Opening stock + Purchases
+ Carriage inwards
– Returns outwards (purchases returns)
– Closing stock = Cost of sales

We can show all these with an example:

The trading account of D. Gough for the year ended 31 December 2001

	£	£	£
Sales			21,000
Less: Returns inwards			1,000
Net sales			20,000
Opening stock (1 January 2001)		4,500	
Purchases	12,100		
Carriage inwards	300		
	12,400		
Less: Returns outwards	500		
Net purchases		11,900	
		16,400	
Less: Closing stock (31 December 2001)		3,700	
Cost of sales			12,700
Gross profit			£7,300

Check your understanding

Prepare accounts for each of the following sets of figures:

1 M. Patel on 31 December 2001. His figures are as follows: closing stock 4,100, returns outwards 700, carriage inwards 400, purchases 15,300, returns inwards 500, opening stock 3,900 and sales 34,800.

2 J. Gallian on 31 December 2001. Her figures are as follows: closing stock 3,200, returns outwards 550, carriage inwards 324, purchases 10,125, returns inwards 650, opening stock 4,789 and sales 15,000.

So far, and with all the organisations we have looked at, we have assumed a gross profit is made. This may not always be the case! If the cost of sales is greater than the net sales figure, an organisation may make a gross loss.

The profit and loss account

The profit and loss account may be drawn up beneath the trading account and covers the same period of trading. The gross profit (or gross loss) figure becomes the starting point for the profit and loss account.

Some organisations receive income from sources other than sales. These may be rents received, commission received or profits on the sales of assets. As these are extra income, they are added to the gross profit.

In addition, every organisation incurs expenses and a range of overheads, and these are deducted to show the true net profit (or loss) of the business. These expenses might, for example, include:

- rent of premises
- carriage outwards
- discount allowed
- gas
- electricity
- stationery
- cleaning costs
- insurances
- business rates
- depreciation
- bad debts
- interest on loans
- sundry expenses
- motor expenses
- accountancy and legal fees.

Net profit = Gross profit
+ Income from other sources − Expenses

Net profit is the final profit in the business and will belong to the owner.

The trading and profit and loss account of D. Gough for the year ended 31 December 2001

	£	£	£
Sales			21,000
Less: Returns inwards			1,000
Net sales			20,000
Opening stock (1 January 2001)		4,500	
Purchases	12,100		
Carriage inwards	300		
	12,400		
Less: Returns outwards	500		
Net purchases		11,900	
		16,400	
Less: Closing stock (31 December 2001)		3,700	
Cost of sales			12,700
Gross profit			7,300
Add other income:			
Discount received			2,000
			9,300

	£	£	£
Less expenses:			
Electricity		510	
Stationery		125	
Business rate		756	
Interest on loans		159	
Advertising		745	
Depreciation – motor vehicles		1,000	
Insurances		545	
Sundry expenses		124	
Total expenses			3,964
Net profit			£5,336

It is important to note that trading accounts will apply only to organisations who *trade* in goods or who are involved in the process of manufacturing. Service sector businesses (such as a dentist, estate agent or solicitor) will not require a trading account because they are not buying and selling goods. Instead, their final accounts will consist simply of a profit and loss account and a balance sheet. Instead of starting with gross profit, their profit and loss account will start by listing the various forms of income, such as fees received:

The profit and loss account of U. Afzaal for the year ended 31 December 2001

	£	£
Income from clients		4,100
Add other income:		
Rent received		1,400
		5,500
Less expenses:		
Electricity	412	
Insurances	124	
Sundry expenses	415	
Travel expenses	147	1,098
Net profit		£4,402

The balance sheet

Whereas the trading account provides an ongoing picture, a balance sheet is a snapshot of what an organisation owns and owes on a particular date.

> A balance sheet is a clear statement of the assets, liabilities and capital of a business at a particular moment in time (normally at the end of an accounting period, e.g. quarter, year, etc.).

Looking at the balance sheet can thus provide valuable information because it summarises a business's financial position at that instant in time.

The balance sheet balances because the accounts record every transaction twice. For example, if you lend me £100 we can say that:

- I owe you £100 (a liability or debt).

- I now have £100 (an asset, something I own).

Look at Figure 19.7. As you can see, a balance sheet is represented by a simple formula that underlies all accounting activity:

$$\text{Assets} = \text{Liabilities} + \text{Capital}$$

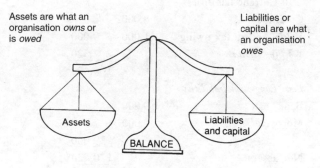

Figure 19.7 Assets equal liabilities plus capital

At the end of a trading period a business will have a number of assets and liabilities. Some of these will be for short periods of time while others will be for longer periods. Whatever the nature of the individual assets and liabilities, the balance sheet will balance.

Check your understanding

Make a list of six probable assets and six probable liabilities of a small corner-shop. Do the same for a public house.

As you work through this section, look at the balance sheet illustrated below:

The balance sheet of D. Bicknell as at 31 December 2001

	£	£	£
Fixed assets			
Land and buildings			80,000
Machinery			13,200
Motor vehicles			8,700
			101,900
Current assets			
Stocks		9,700	
Debtors		3,750	
Bank		2,100	
Cash		970	
		16,520	
Less: Current liabilities			
Creditors	8,000		
Value Added Tax owing	1,000	9,000	
Working capital		7,520	
			109,420
Less: Long-term liabilities			
Bank loan	9,000		
Mortgage	30,000		
		39,000	
Net assets		£70,420	
Financed by:			
Capital		70,000	
Add: Net profit		5,286	
		75,286	
Less: Drawings		4,866	
		£70,420	

Title

Every balance sheet will have a heading containing the name of the organisation as well as the date upon which the snapshot is taken.

Assets

The asset side of a balance sheet is normally set out in what is called an *inverse order of liquidity*. This means items that may be difficult to convert into cash quickly, and are therefore liquid, appear at the top of the list of assets. By looking down the order it is possible to gauge the ease with which successive assets can be converted to cash, until we come to the most liquid asset of all, cash itself.

Check your understanding

Explain what the word 'asset' means.

A small bakery has the following assets. Try to put them into an inverse order of liquidity, with the least liquid at the top and the most liquid at the bottom:

- cash in the tills
- bread in the shops
- a bakery van
- the baker's oven
- supplies of flour
- money in the bakery's bank account
- money owed to the bakery by firms
- the baker's premises.

Assets can be divided into *fixed* assets and *current* assets.

Fixed assets tend to have a life-span of more than one year. They comprise items that are purchased and generally kept for a long period of time. Examples of fixed assets would be premises, machinery and motor vehicles. When a business buys fixed assets it does so by incurring capital expenditure.

Current assets are sometimes called 'circulating assets' because the form they take is constantly changing. Examples of current assets are stocks, debtors, money in the bank and cash in hand.

A manufacturing business holds stocks of finished goods in readiness to satisfy the demands of the market. When a credit transaction takes place, stocks are reduced and the business gains debtors. These debtors have bought goods on credit and therefore owe the business money; after a reasonable credit period payment will be expected. Payments will have to be made on further stocks so that the business has a cash cycle. 'Cash' or 'bank' changes to 'stock' then to 'debtors', back to 'cash' or 'bank' and then to 'stock' again (see Figure 19.8).

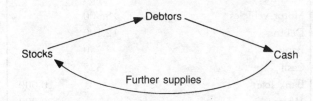

Figure 19.8 The cash cycle

Check your understanding

Identify (with reasons) which of the following items should be considered as a current asset of a newsagent:

- the fixtures and fittings of the shop
- cash in the tills
- money in the bank
- money owed by the newsagent to the suppliers
- money owed by customers for newspaper bills
- the delivery bicycle
- stocks of newspapers in the shop.

Current liabilities

Current liabilities are debts a business needs to repay within a short period of time (normally a year). These liabilities include creditors, who are suppliers of goods on credit for which the business has been invoiced but not yet paid. They may also include a bank overdraft that is arranged up to a limit over a time period and is, technically, repayable on demand. Other current liabilities may include any short-term loans and any taxes owed (see the example above).

Working capital

The balance sheet is set out so as to show working capital because this is always an important calculation for an organisation as it shows how easily the business can pay its short-term debts. Working capital is the ratio of current assets to current liabilities:

Working capital ratio
= current assets:current liabilities

It is important for an organisation to maintain a sensible ratio. The level of ratio depends on the type of business and the likelihood that funds will be required quickly to meet liabilities (e.g. creditors demanding quick repayment). For most businesses a ratio of 2:1 is regarded as a sign of careful management, but some businesses have lower ratios.

Working capital is important because it provides a buffer to 'keep the wolf from the door'. Many businesses have suffered the consequences of having too many of their assets tied up in liquid assets.

Long-term liabilities

A long-term liability is sometimes called a *deferred liability* as it is not due for payment

until some time in the future.
By convention, in a set of accounts this
means longer than one year. Examples for
a sole trader could include a bank loan or
a mortgage.

Capital

As we saw earlier, capital is provided by the
owner of the business and is therefore
deemed to be owed to the owner by the
business. The balance sheet keeps an
updated record of the amount owed by the
business to the owner.

During a year's trading the owner's capital
may be increased by the inflows of profits
(profits for the period) and decreased by
outflows of drawings (money or other assets
taken out of the business for personal use).
Having taken these into consideration, a
new capital figure is calculated at the end
of the year. So the balance sheet shows how
the capital has increased (or decreased!)
since the last balance sheet was prepared.

Most sole traders employ an accountant to
draw up their accounts. Nevertheless, whoever
prepares the accounts, it is the sole trader
who remains responsible for their accuracy
and for correctly declaring the amount of the
profits. The tax authorities will need to be
satisfied that the accounts supplied to them
represent the true results of the business.

It is essential to keep full and accurate
records from the day the business started
trading. Well-kept books make the
preparation of the annual accounts easier,
and save on accountant's time (so keeping
down the fee charged).

Note: In this chapter we consider only the
accounts of a sole trader. In the next
chapter, when we look at how to interpret
financial information, we also look at the
final accounts of limited companies.

Check your understanding

From the following trial balance of
G. Archer, draw up the trading and
profit and loss account for the year
ended 31 December 2001, together with
her balance sheet at that date. The
closing stocks were valued at £10,300.

Trial balance of G. Archer as at 31 December 2001

	£	£
Stock at January 2001	12,700	
Sales		81,250
Purchases	18,325	
Electricity	1,451	
Stationery	1,526	
Business rate	1,845	
Loan interest	3,955	
Advertising	2,150	
Sundry expenses	1,205	
Land and buildings	161,000	
Machinery	4,900	
Motor vehicles	18,300	
Debtors	12,100	
Bank	4,250	
Cash	325	
Bank loan		10,000
Mortgage		20,000
Creditors		4,300
Drawings	9,350	
Capital at January 2001		137,832
	253,382	253,382

Depreciation

One key accounting policy mentioned in
the 'notes to the accounts' accompanying
final accounts is that relating to *depreciation*.

Fixed assets are acquired in order to earn
profits. But although their use is not
limited to a single accounting period, they
do not last for ever. Most businesses have
expectations about the future lifetime of
their assets. They will wish to show a true
asset value in the balance sheet and to

charge the cost of its depreciation to the profit and loss account.

SSAP 12 defines depreciation as:

the measure of the wearing out, consumption or other reduction in the useful life of a fixed asset, whether arising from use, time or obsolescence through technological or market changes.

There are a number of different methods of allowing for depreciation. The most common are:

- the *straight-line* method
- the *reducing balance* method
- the *machine hour* method
- the *sum-of-the-digits* method.

Straight-line method

The most frequently used method is the straight-line or equal-instalment method of depreciation. This charges an equal amount of depreciation to each accounting period for the life of an asset. The instalment is calculated by:

$$\frac{\text{Cost of asset} - \text{Residual value}}{\text{Expected useful life of asset}}$$

For example, a machine that is expected to last five years costs £20,000; at the end of that time its residual value will be £5,000:

$$\text{Depreciation charge} = \frac{£20,000 - £5,000}{5 \text{ years}}$$

$$= £3,000$$

	Year 1 £	Year 2 £	Year 3 £	Year 4 £	Year 5 £
Cost	20,000	20,000	20,000	20,000	20,000
Accumulated depreciation	3,000	6,000	9,000	12,000	15,000
Net book value	17,000	14,000	11,000	8,000	5,000

Reducing balance method

The reducing balance method calculates the depreciation charge as a fixed percentage of net book value from the previous period. This method allocates higher depreciation costs to the earlier years of an asset. It can be argued that this system is more realistic, as it caters for the increased expense of repairs and running costs as machinery becomes older.

For example, a machine is purchased by a business for £20,000 and its expected useful life is three years. The business anticipates a residual value of £4,320 and thus wishes to depreciate it at 40%:

	Accumulated depreciation £	£
Machine at cost	20,000	
Depreciation year 1	8,000	8,000
Net book value	12,000	
Depreciation year 2	4,800	12,800
Net book value	7,200	
Depreciation year 3	2,880	15,680
Residual value	4,320	

Machine hour method

The machine hour method relates depreciation to use rather than time. Therefore, depreciation is calculated on the basis of the number of hours a machine has been worked. The depreciation charge per hour is calculated by:

$$\frac{\text{Cost of asset} - \text{Residual value}}{\text{Expected lifetime of asset in machine hours}}$$

For example, a machine is purchased for £34,000 with an estimated life of 10,000 machine hours and a residual value of £4,000. The depreciation rate would be:

$$\frac{34,000 - 4,000}{10,000} = \text{£3 per machine hour}$$

Therefore, if the machine was used for 2,000 hours in year 1, 3,000 hours in year 2 and 1,000 hours in year 3, depreciation would be charged as follows:

	Depre-ciation charge £	Accumulated depreciation £	Cost of asset £	Net book value £
Year 1:				
2,000 × £3	6,000	6,000	34,000	28,000
Year 2:				
3,000 × £3	9,000	15,000	34,000	19,000
Year 3:				
1,000 × £3	3,000	18,000	34,000	16,000

Sum-of-the-digits method

The sum-of-the-digits method is similar to the reducing balance method in that higher levels of depreciation are charged in earlier years. However, it uses digits rather than percentages as a simplified way of working out the depreciation charge. Digits are allocated in a descending order to each year of the life of an asset, and a charge is worked out for each digit used.

For example, a machine is purchased for £15,000 and is expected to last for three years, after which it will be sold for £3,000:

Year	Digits
1	3
2	2
3	1

Sum-of-the-digits = 6

A weighted charge is then calculated as follows:

$$\frac{\text{Cost of asset} - \text{Residual value}}{\text{Sum-of-the-digits}}$$

$$\frac{15,000 - 3,000}{6} = \text{£2,000 per digit}$$

	Digits	Depreciation charge £	Accumulated depreciation £
Year 1	3 × 2,000	6,000	6,000
Year 2	2 × 2,000	4,000	10,000
Year 3	1 × 2,000	2,000	12,000

Depreciation and book-keeping entries

Once the amounts for depreciation have been calculated using any of the above methods, they will be recorded within the double-entry book-keeping system.

Looking at the earlier example, we saw that a machine that is expected to last five years costs £20,000 and at the end of that time its residual value will be £5,000. Using the straight-line method the instalment is calculated by:

$$\frac{\text{Cost of asset} - \text{Residual value}}{\text{Expected useful life of asset}}$$

$$\text{Depreciation charge} = \frac{£20,000 - £5,000}{5 \text{ years}}$$

$$= £3,000$$

Entries in the book-keeping system would be as follows:

Dr				Machinery account	Cr
Date	Narrative	£	Date	Narrative	£
1 January	Bank	20,000			

The account balance is £20,000 and this remains the balance. However, the provision for depreciation account increases each year by the value of the depreciation. To find out the net book value of the asset, you simply have to take away the provision for depreciation balance from that of the machinery account:

Dr			Provision for depreciation account – machinery		Cr
Date	Narrative	£	Date	Narrative	£
31 Dec 2000	Balance c/d	3,000	31 Dec 2000	Profit and loss account	3,000
31 Dec 2001	Balance c/d	6,000	1 Jan 2001	Balance b/d	3,000
			31 Dec 2001	Profit and loss account	3,000
		6,000			6,000
31 Dec 2002	Balance c/d	9,000	1 Jan 2002	Balance b/d	6,000
			31 Dec 2002	Profit and loss account	3,000
		9,000			9,000
31 Dec 2003	Balance c/d	12,000	1 Jan 2003	Balance b/d	9,000
			31 Dec 2003	Profit and loss account	3,000
		12,000			12,000
31 Dec 2004	Balance c/d	15,000	1 Jan 2004	Balance b/d	12,000
			31 Dec 2004	Profit and loss account	3,000
		15,000			15,000

Depreciation and final accounts

There are two entries made for depreciation in the final accounts. These are as follows:

1 *The profit and loss account* The amount of depreciation for each asset is an expense charged to the profit and loss account. As we can see above, this involves:

- Crediting the provision for depreciation account with the amount to be charged to the profit and loss account.

- Debiting the profit and loss account with the amount allocated as an expense.

The amount of the 'provision for depreciation' for each asset is therefore simply added to the expenses after balancing the provision for depreciation account. So, for example, for machinery above in December 2000, the entry would simply be:

Less: Expenses

Electricity	510
Stationery	125
Provision for depreciation:	
machinery	3,000
Rent paid	500
Etc.	

2 *The balance sheet* In the balance sheet each type of fixed asset is shown at:

Cost price
Less: Depreciation to date
= Net book value

It is usually set out in the following way:

The balance sheet of S. Brown as at 31 December 2001

	Cost	Depreciation to date	Net book value
Fixed assets			
Machinery	20,000	3,000	17,000
	20,000	3,000	17,000

Chapter 20 Interpreting financial information

The information provided by profit and loss accounts and balance sheets can be interpreted in a variety of ways. You need to understand how different stakeholders use financial ratios to assist them in interpreting accounts and in making judgements about the effectiveness of a business. You need to be able to calculate and use ratios relating to:

- performance
- solvency
- profitability.

The ratios you need to know are:

- return on capital employed
- profit margin ratios
- asset turnover
- stock turnover
- selling and debt collection period
- current ratio
- acid test ratio.

You need to be able to identify and compare past and present data for a business. You also need to understand the limitations of using ratios to make judgements about the effectiveness of businesses.

Financial performance is also measured using other indicators. You need to be able to understand and explain how the following indicators can be used to show the performance of a public limited company:

- share prices
- dividends
- price earnings ratios.

There are a number of important reasons for interpreting financial information from a business organisation.

Monitoring performance

Monitoring financial performance creates a number of invaluable indicators that can be used to improve future performance. For example, by monitoring performance it would be possible to identify which debtors are taking longer to pay than others. Incentives could be introduced for early payment and penalties for late payment. Financial planners may set targets for financial performance. For example, targets may include a given return. Monitoring of actual performance then makes it possible to identify what areas are performing well or badly.

The accounts of an organisation may also be monitored in order to make sure it has an adequate supply of finance to meet its trading and investment requirements, its cash flow, and can meet commitments to other areas of the business. For example, financial managers may wish to seek answers to such questions as:

- 'When is finance going to come in?'
- 'What is it needed for?'
- 'Do we have enough finance to meet current requirements?'
- 'Do we have enough finance to meet future requirements?'

For example, a manufacturing business may need to replace machinery at regular intervals. Therefore, it needs to make sure it puts finance aside or acquires fresh finance to meet this requirement. A trading organisation must generate enough cash to purchase fresh stocks. It needs to be sure it can generate sufficient cash or be able to buy new stocks on credit. Studying accounting information enables managers to gain a picture of how well placed they are to maintain finance.

Another reason for monitoring performance is to meet the requirements of the taxation authorities. Taxation rules change from time to time and business organisations will employ professional accountants so that the tax due can be calculated in a particular way. Value Added Tax (VAT) will be calculated according to the rules set out by Customs and Excise (www.hmce.gov.uk/) at a particular time. Inland Revenue (www.inlandrevenue.gov.uk/) will want to use the profit calculation as a basis for calculating the tax assessment. Corporation Tax is the tax charged on a company's profit.

Solvency

The word 'solvency' means 'to be able to meet financial obligations'. A business becomes 'technically insolvent' when it has sufficient assets to meet all its financial obligations, but insufficient time to convert these assets into cash. It is 'legally insolvent' if it is in a situation of permanent cash shortage.

A number of users of accounting information will want to check regularly on the solvency of business organisations. For example, owners and shareholders will want to know their money is 'safe'. In this respect they will want to look at the distribution of assets and liabilities a company has. The company may have money coming in at 'some time in the

future'. However, unless it has money coming in now, tomorrow, and the next day, it may face cash flow problems so that it becomes 'technically insolvent'.

Lenders of money to organisations want to know their loans will be repaid and that interest will be paid at regular intervals. Employees and other stakeholders in organisations will want the security of knowing the organisation is solvent.

Managers will want to know the extent of solvency so that they can restructure assets and liabilities into an appropriate form. Solvency is a base-line for ongoing business operations.

When auditors carry out a periodic audit of an organisation's accounts, one of the key areas they would need to emphasise would be how solvent the organisation is.

Profitability

Following the financial reports in any newspaper will reveal that one of the key newsworthy areas constantly emphasised by the press is that of profits. For example, 'M&S rocked by profit warnings' or 'Somerfield to retreat to the high street'. Profits are a key indicator when judging business performance. It is the first point of reference for many organisational stakeholders.

It is all very well saying that sales have risen, productivity is soaring and the organisation is growing. However, shareholders and providers of capital will always ask the question: 'But, have you been making a profit?'

As we saw in the previous chapter, profits are calculated through the profit and loss account.

Check your understanding

Identify four stakeholder groups to an organisation. Describe the sort of information they might require or want to extract from a set of final accounts.

Final accounts of a limited company

So far, our analysis of accounts has centred on those of a sole trader. Before looking further at how to interpret and analyse financial information, we are going to look at another type of business organisation, that of a company. Accounts of a company are prepared on a similar basis to those for a sole trader, but there are some important differences in the appropriation of profit and in the organisation's capital structure.

As we have seen in earlier chapters, a limited company has:

- A legal identity separate from that of its owners.
- Owners who are known as shareholders and who have limited liability.

Case study: Deloitte & Touche (www.drrus.com/)

The Industrial Revolution saw the birth of new types of organisations that raised capital by selling equity in the form of shares to the public. The Great Western Railway (GWR), a British company founded in 1835, was one of the most famous of these early 'joint stock companies'. When its share price slumped in 1849, GWR turned to an independent public accountant, William Welch Deloitte, to audit the company's accounts. The experience was so valuable that the directors of GWR felt this form of independent auditing ought to be made compulsory. Though this recommendation was gradually implemented in England over the following decades, it was 84 years before the USA adopted this practice.

The boom in joint stock companies led to a demand for people skilled at understanding the financial problems of these types of businesses. George A. Touche, a Scotsman, was a financial adviser with a background in accounting and investment trusts, which he used to establish a London-based accounting company in 1898. Two years later, he followed the flow of British capital to the USA establishing the first US office of Touche, Niven & Company.

The two firms founded in part by Deloitte and Touche joined forces in 1989 to become a global leader in the provision of accounting services.

1 Explain why the process of external auditing developed.

2 Why is it important for auditors to be independent?

- A management that is delegated to a board of directors, who may or may not be shareholders.

- A commitment to pay Corporation Tax on any profits made.

Companies must comply with the Companies Acts, and the Companies Registration Office controls their formation. There are two types of limited companies:

- *Public*, which have their shares traded on the Stock Exchange,

- *Private*, for which there are restrictions on the trading in their shares.

Registering a company

To set up a limited company, it is necessary to go through a number of legal procedures. This mainly involves the presentation of various documents to the Registrar of Companies (*www.companies-house.gov.uk/*). All limited companies must produce a *Memorandum of Association* and *Articles of Association* to receive a *Certificate of Incorporation*.

The *Memorandum of Association* spells out the nature of the company when viewed from the outside. Someone reading the memorandum should be able to gain a general idea of what the company is and the business with which it is concerned. The memorandum sets out:

- the name of the company

- its address

- its objectives (i.e. what types of activities it will engage in)

- its capital.

The *Articles of Association* spell out the rules that govern the inside working of the company. In particular, they set out the details of how accounts will be kept and recorded.

Once a private company has lodged these documents with the registrar and had them accepted, it can start to trade. The *Certificate of Incorporation* sets up the company as a legal body in its own right. The company (not the individual shareholders) enters into contracts and can sue or be sued in a court of law.

A public company, however, must take further steps before being granted a certificate. A prospectus has to be issued and shares have to be allotted.

One clause of the *Memorandum of Association* states the share capital of the company and indicates how it is to be divided into separate shares. Authorised share capital is the amount the shareholders have authorised the directors to issue. Issued share capital is the amount that has actually been issued by the directors.

Shares

There are a number of types of securities (www.londonstockexchange.com/). These may include:

- *Ordinary shares* – dividends/profits for these are normally expressed as a percentage of the nominal value of the shares or as a monetary value per share.

- *Preference shares* – these carry a preferential right to receive a dividend.

- *Debentures* – these are split into units in the same way as shares but are, in effect, loans to the company that may be secured on specific assets.

A company's capital is split into shares that are recorded at a *nominal value*. Nominal values might be at 5p, 10p, 25p, 50p or £1. For example, a company with 10,000 shares issued at a nominal value of £0.50 has a share capital of £5,000, and this would be disclosed in the capital section of the balance sheet. The difference between the issue price paid by the shareholder and the nominal value is called the share premium.

Reserves

Limited companies rarely distribute all their profits. A proportion is usually retained in the form of reserves. There are two forms of reserves:

- *Revenue reserves* Sometimes known as distributable reserves, these are left as the balance of the 'profit and loss account' or 'retained profits'. To give shareholders confidence in the funding of the business, directors may decide to transfer some of the profit and loss account balance into a general reserve. In doing this, directors are communicating their intention not to use those funds for dividends. As this reserve is created out of distributable profits and can be used for dividends, it is still a revenue reserve.

- *Capital reserves* These cannot be used to fund dividend payments. They may include revaluation reserves that occur when property is revalued and also share premium, the value of the higher amount than the nominal value.

The trading/profit and loss accounts

The trading account of a limited company is similar to the trading account of any other type of organisation. However, in the profit and loss account:

- Directors' fees or salaries may be included, because these people are employed by the company and their fees and salaries are an expense.

- Debenture payments, being the same as loan interest, may also appear as an expense.

The appropriation account

Beneath the profit and loss account of a company will appear the appropriation account. This is designed to show what happens to any profit and how it is divided (see Figure 20.1).

	£	£
Net profit		250,000
Less: Corporation Tax		100,000
Profit after taxation		150,000
Less: Proposed dividends		
Ordinary shares	70,000	
Preference shares	20,000	90,000
		60,000
Less: Transfer to general reserve		40,000
		20,000
Add: Retained profit from previous year		30,000
Balance of retained profit carried forward		50,000

Figure 20.1 An appropriation account for a company with a net profit of £250,000

Corporation Tax

Corporation Tax is the first charge on profits and has to be paid to the Inland Revenue. Proposed dividends are the portion of the profits paid to the shareholders. After dividends have been paid, it is possible to allocate profits to reserves. Any profit left over at the end of the year, after taxes and shareholders of all kinds have been paid, is added to the balance of profit from the previous year to give the new retained profit:

Balance of profit at end of year
= Net profit from current year
+ Retained profits from previous years
− Corporation Tax − Transfers to reserves
− Dividends

Check your understanding

Workhard Ltd has just announced a net profit of £300,000. Prepare the appropriation account for the end of December 2001 from the following details:

- The taxation rate is 25%.
- There are 500,000 ordinary shares of £1 each.
- A dividend of 10% is proposed.
- There are 300,000 10% preference shares of £1 each, fully paid. The 10% dividend is to be paid.
- £50,000 is to be transferred to the general reserve.
- Retained profit from the previous year was £125,000.

The balance sheet

In the balance sheet of a company, the fixed and current assets are presented in the same way as in any other balance sheet.

Current liabilities

The current liabilities are the liabilities due to be paid within 12 months of the date of the balance sheet. In addition to those which normally appear in this section, limited companies also have to show Corporation Tax that is due to be paid during the next 12 months, as well as ordinary and preference share dividends to be paid. Long-term liabilities may include debentures.

Capital

At the beginning of the 'Financed by:' section of the balance sheet, details will appear of the authorised capital, specifying the type, value and number of shares the company is authorised to issue. These are in the balance sheet for interest only and their value is excluded from the totals. Issued capital contains details of the classes and numbers of shares that have been issued (obviously, the issued share capital cannot exceed the authorised).

Reserves are shown beneath the capital. Reserves and retained profits are the amounts the directors and shareholders decide to keep within the company. Shareholders' funds comprise the total of share capital plus reserves.

Example

From the trial balance of Wargrave Ltd and the notes below, we can prepare the trading account, the profit and loss account, the appropriation account and the balance sheet for the year ended 31 December 2001. The following notes are attached:

- The closing stock is £12,250.
- Corporation Tax is charged at 25% of profits.
- There is a 6% dividend on ordinary shares.
- The 10% preference dividend is to be paid.
- £2,000 is to be allocated to the general reserve.
- Authorised share capital is 400,000

Trial balance of Wargrave Ltd as at 31 December 2001

	Dr £	Cr £
Stock at 1 January 2001	21,300	
Sales		118,100
Purchases	35,000	
Electricity	8,000	
Stationery	5,000	
Business rate	1,300	
Loan interest paid	1,000	
Debenture interest paid	800	
Advertising	3,200	
Sundry expenses	1,350	
Directors' salaries	12,000	
Land and buildings	320,000	
Machinery	24,000	
Motor vehicles	12,000	
Debtors	7,100	
Bank	23,200	
Cash	500	
Bank loan		10,000
10% debentures		8,000
Creditors		500
General reserve		4,000
Retained profit at 31 December		35,150
Issued share capital:		
200,000 ordinary £1 shares		200,000
100,000 10% £1 preference shares		100,000
	475,750	475,750

ordinary shares of £1 each and 100,000 10% preference shares of £1 each.

The trading, profit and loss and appropriation account of Wargrave Ltd for the year ended 31 December 2001

	£	£
Sales		118,100
Opening stock	21,300	
Purchases	35,000	
	56,300	
Less: Closing stock	12,250	
Cost of sales		44,050
Gross profit		74,050
Less: Expenses		
Electricity	8,000	
Stationery	5,000	
Business rate	1,300	
Loan interest paid	1,000	
Debenture interest paid	800	
Advertising	3,200	
Sundry expenses	1,350	
Directors' salaries	12,000	
		32,650
Net profit		41,400
Less: Corporation Tax		10,350
Profit after taxation		31,050
Less: Proposed dividends		
Ordinary shares	12,000	
Preference shares	10,000	22,000
		9,050
Less: Transfer to general reserve		2,000
		7,050
Add: retained profit from previous year		35,150
Balance of retained profit carried forward		42,200

The balance sheet of Wargrave Ltd as at 31 December 2001

	£	£	£
Fixed assets			
Land and buildings			320,000
Machinery			24,000
Motor vehicles			12,000
			356,000
Current assets			
Stocks		12,250	
Debtors		7,100	
Bank		23,200	
Cash		500	
		43,050	
Less: **Current liabilities**			
Creditors	500		
Proposed dividends:			
Ordinary shares	12,000		
Preference shares	10,000		
Corporation Tax	10,350	32,850	
Working capital			10,200
			366,200
Less: **Long-term liabilities**			
Bank loan		10,000	
10% debentures		8,000	
			18,000
Net assets			348,200
Financed by			
Authorised share capital			
400,000 ordinary shares of £1			400,000
100,000 10% preference shares of £1			100,000
			500,000
Issued share capital			
200,000 ordinary shares of £1			
fully paid		200,000	
100,000 10% preference			
shares of £1 fully paid		100,000	
			300,000
Reserves			
General reserve		6,000	
Balance of retained profit		42,200	
			48,200
Shareholders' funds			348,200

Check your understanding

From the following trial balance of Twyford Ltd and the attached notes, prepare the trading account, profit and loss appropriation account and balance sheet for the year ended 31 December 2001:

Trial Balance of Twyford Ltd as at 31 December 2001

	£	£
Stock at 1 January 2001	7,300	
Sales		123,400
Purchases	12,500	
Electricity	4,100	
Advertising	3,200	
Business rate	800	
Salaries	16,000	
Directors' salaries	18,000	
Loan interest paid	4,400	
Debenture interest paid	1,000	
Land and buildings	124,000	
Motor vehicles	16,000	
Debtors	7,000	
Bank	15,000	
Cash	1,000	
Bank loan		25,000
10% debentures		10,000
Creditors		4,000
General reserve		3,000
Retained profit at 31 December 2000		4,900
Issued share capital:		
50,000 ordinary shares (£)		50,000
10,000 10% preference shares (£)		10,000
	230,300	230,300

You have been informed that:

- The closing stock has been valued at £3,400.
- Corporation Tax will be charged at 25% of profits.
- The 10% share dividends are to be paid.
- £3,000 is to be allocated to the general reserve.
- Authorised share capital is the same as issued share capital.

Using financial ratios

A great deal can be discovered about an organisation simply by reading its annual report and by comparing the current year's results with those of the previous year. However, a more scientific and measured approach is to use financial ratios. Accounting ratios provide the users with a number of benchmarks against which they can measure performance.

Organisations are not equal. When using accounting ratios it is important to think about them in the context of the organisation to which they apply. An accounting ratio compares the value of one item with that of another. For example, a retailer who buys an item for £25 and then sells it for £50 enjoys a gross profit to sales ratio of 50% (£25/£50) on that product line. This gross profit per cent can be evaluated by comparison with appropriate benchmarks. For example, these ratios might relate to:

- A *previous period* – so that it is possible to assess whether performance is improving or deteriorating.

- A *budget* – to compare actual performance with expected performance.

- A *similar business* – to show relative performance.

- *Different divisions of the same firm* – to show responsibility for performance.

- *Different product lines or different markets of the same firm* – to identify the most lucrative activities in which to deploy financial resources.

Accounting ratios are not simply the domain of the accountant. There are many users of accounts who will use a range of accounting ratios to make judgements and to influence decisions related to the business. For example:

- *Lenders of money* will want to use the ratios to find out how well the business can meet its repayments.

- *Managers* within the business will want to use the ratios to improve the way in which they manage the business and make decisions that affect the future.

- *Customers* will want to be sure that supplies will be sustained in the future, and that their suppliers can meet their commitments.

- *Creditors* will want to know that the business they supply to can meet their payments. They might also want to know more about how long they will expect to wait for payment.

- *Employees and their representatives* have a key vested interest within the business. They want to know about the financial strength of the organisation, whether there is a likelihood of redundancies and what the long-term future is for the business.

- *Government departments* will wish to find out about the tax liabilities of the business.

- *Shareholders* will want to know not just that their investment is secure but what the returns are likely to be on that investment for the near and distant future.

Performance ratios

Performance ratios help to measure how successfully an organisation is being run and/or how well management is handling different aspects of the business. As with all accounting ratios, these ratios need to be compared with previous periods or with similar types of organisations. There are a number of different ratios.

Stock turnover

Stock turnover is a very important measure of the number of days' stock that is held on average. The value of the stock is related to sales revenues to find the number of times it has been 'turned over' during the period. It can be measured in two ways:

$$\frac{\text{Stock turnover}}{\text{(times per year)}} = \frac{\text{Cost of sales}}{\text{Average stock}}$$

Where:

$$\frac{\text{Average}}{\text{stock}} = \frac{\text{Opening stock} + \text{Closing stock}}{2}$$

For example, a stock turnover of 26 times per year would mean that two weeks' stock is held. Stock turnover refers, therefore, to the average time an item of stock is held in stores before it is used or sold. The adequacy of this ratio depends heavily upon the type of business sector within which an organisation is operating. For example, a greengrocer would expect a much higher stock turnover than a furniture business.

In order to improve their efficiency and performance, many organisations today hold smaller stock levels than in the past. Remember that high stock levels soak up investment with assets that are not performing for the business. Some organisations operate a 'just-in-time' policy by having just enough stock to meet current demand. As a consequence they would have a higher stock turnover:

$$\frac{\text{Number of days' stock held}}{\text{on average}} = \frac{\text{Average stock}}{\text{Cost of sales}} \times 365 \text{ days}$$

Check your understanding

Work out the stock turnover figures for a business from the following figures:

	2000	2001	2002
Average stock	260	380	500
Cost of sales	1,200	1,600	1,900

Explain the implications of the changes in stock turnover during this period.

Debtors' collection period

This is calculated by using the formula:

$$\frac{\text{Debtors' collection}}{\text{period}} = \frac{\text{Debtors}}{\text{Average daily sales}}$$

Average daily sales are calculated by dividing sales over the year by 365. This ratio shows the average number of days it takes for debtors to pay for the goods sold to them by the organisation. Although there is considerable variation and this is often dependent upon the industry, the normally accepted debt collection period is between 30 and 60 days.

It may be possible to improve the efficiency and performance of the business by reducing this period. Customers who are late in paying their debts are receiving free finance for their business.

This ratio indicates the average number of days of credit received by customers before they provide a payment. Comparisons are usually made from one year to another.

Check your understanding

In the group profit and loss account for The Boots Company (www.boots-plc.com/) for the 12 months up to 31 March 1999, turnover was £5,044.6 million. At that time the group balance sheet showed debtors of £402.2 million. Net assets at that time were £1,780.6 million, ordinary shareholders' funds were £1,780.2 million and tangible assets were £1,788.6 million. Calculate:

- The average number of days it takes for the debtors of The Boots Company to make their payments.

- The asset turnover performance for The Boots Company over this period.

- The proprietary ratio.

Comment upon how this ratio might help managers to make decisions about how to improve the financial performance of the company.

Of course, it is helpful to remember the basics of good debtor control, namely:

- *Invoice quickly.* As soon as the goods have been delivered and accepted, invoice!

- *Invoice correctly.* If your customers want you to attach a copy of the purchase order, or quote the order number, make sure you do. Ensure your invoice is clear and well laid out.

- *Check creditworthiness.* Find out whether your customers are able to pay and their reliability. If you agree to a level of credit, keep to it.

Check your understanding

Interview a business manager with some responsibility for accounts to find out the debt collection period in his or her organisation, and ask how he or she seek to reduce it.

Creditors' payment period

This ratio measures the speed the organisation takes to pay its creditors. It is calculated using the formula:

$$\text{Creditors' payment period} = \frac{\text{Creditors}}{\text{Average daily purchases}}$$

Average daily purchases are calculated by dividing purchases for the year by 365. This ratio is particularly useful for businesses that constantly buy and sell goods. These types of business organisations would prefer a longer creditors' payment period than debtors' collection period, as this provides the organisation with leeway to collect money before it pays its creditors.

Asset utilisation

This ratio indicates how efficiently fixed assets are being used to generate sales. It is measured by:

$$\text{Asset utilization} = \frac{\text{Sales}}{\text{Fixed assets}}$$

Asset turnover performance

A more appropriate ratio than asset utilisation is considered to be that of asset turnover. This ratio measures the efficiency of net assets in generating sales. It is calculated by:

$$\text{Asset turnover performance} = \frac{\text{Sales}}{\text{Net assets}}$$

Net assets for the purpose of ratio analysis is:

Fixed assets + Current assets − Current liabilities.

The ratio examines the efficiency of the organisation and helps managers to understand how well they are using net assets for running the business. The ratio will depend upon the type of business concerned and the sector within which it operates. For example, a fast-food retailer with high turnover and few assets will have a higher figure than a heavy engineering business that has large capital assets.

Proprietary ratio

This shows the proportion of owners' funds to the tangible assets of an organisation. The tangible assets of an organisation are the tangible fixed assets plus the current assets. The formula is calculated by:

$$\text{Proprietary ratio} = \frac{\text{Ordinary shareholders' funds}}{\text{Tangible assets}}$$

Tangible assets are those assets with material substance and would not include patents and goodwill, as these would have less value if the business was sold. It would be usual to have a minimum ratio of around 0.5:1.

Solvency ratios

Solvency ratios are sometimes known as *liquidity ratios*. This refers (a) to the ability of an organisation to convert short-term or current assets into cash to cover payments as and when they arise; and (b) to the liquidity of long-term areas within the balance, such as the ease with which interest can be paid or the relationship of long-term loans to capital. In the short term, stocks are the least liquid of the current assets because they must first be sold (usually on credit) and the customer is then provided with a payment period before payment is made. As a result, there is a time lag before stocks can be converted to cash. There are a number of different ratios.

Working capital

Working capital is required to finance an organisation's everyday activities. It is calculated by:

$$\text{Working capital} = \text{Current assets} - \text{Current liabilities}$$

Managing working capital involves making sure a business has sufficient stocks to meet the needs of customers, enables such customers to become debtors and has liquid funds which give it the ability to pay creditors.

Working capital ratio or current ratio

The current ratio is an important way of measuring an organisation's ability to settle current liabilities (short-term debts). It is measured using the formula:

$$\text{Current ratio} = \frac{\text{Current assets}}{\text{Current liabilities}}$$

Clearly, some current assets are more liquid than others, and the time factor involved in transferring them to cash is something an experienced manager should be able to estimate. A prudent ratio is sometimes 2:1. This may not be the case if stocks form the bulk of the value of current assets.

Companies have to be aware that bank overdrafts are repayable on demand and that figures extracted from a balance sheet, while reflecting the position of current assets and liabilities at a moment in time, do not reflect the current assets:current liabilities ratio at other times. In practice, most businesses operate with a ratio slightly lower than 2:1.

Case study: Calculating the current ratio

The following figures reflect the current assets and current liabilities of a small business:

	£	£	£
Current assets			
Stocks			
Raw materials	500		
Work-in-progress	300		
Finished goods	800	1,600	
Debtors		1,000	
Cash/bank		400	
		3,000	
Less: **Current liabilities**			
Trade creditors	500		
Tax due	300		
Loan interest due	200	1,000	
Working capital			2,000

1 What is the working capital ratio of this business?

2 If trade creditors increased by 1,500, what action should the business take?

Acid test ratio

The acid test ratio is sometimes known as the quick ratio or liquidity ratio. One major problem for some businesses is that they are not able to convert stocks rapidly into cash. Organisations, therefore, often use a more severe ratio to test whether they have the ability to meet current liabilities. This is called the 'acid test ratio' and does not include stock in the liquid assets of the business. The acid test ratio is measured by:

$$\text{Acid test ratio} = \frac{\text{Current assets} - \text{Stocks}}{\text{Current liabilities}}$$

The acid test ratio is sometimes referred to as the Plimsoll line of a business. The Plimsoll line is a line drawn on a ship's hull. If the ship sinks below this line in the water, it is danger of sinking (see Figure 20.2).

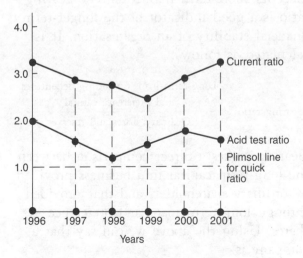

Figure 20.2 Solvency ratios

We have gone below the Plimsoll line. It looks like we are going to sink!

CURRENT LIABILITIES

LIQUID ASSETS

- low-geared if the gearing is less than 100%

- high-geared if the gearing is more than 100%.

The higher the gearing the less secure is the investment of ordinary shareholders. For example, it is said that gearing of more than 100% is not good for a business organisation. This is because debt adds to the expenses of the business and its ability to meet all its commitments.

Interest cover

This ratio is clearly closely linked to the gearing of a business. Managers within an organisation that is highly geared must think closely about how easily they can make interest payments and what margins of safety they have built into the business, particularly if interest rates change. Interest cover is calculated as follows:

$$\text{Interest cover} = \frac{\text{Profit before interest and tax}}{\text{Interest paid in the year}}$$

If the ratio is 1 or 2, the business is not earning enough to more than cover interest charges. For example, if the business made profit before interest and tax of £50,000 and interest paid was £25,000, the ratio would be 2 (which is low). The higher the interest cover, the easier an organisation will find it to meet its commitments to its debts. A ratio of 3 would provide the minimum level of safety required.

Profitability ratios

Although business organisations have a range of business objectives, for most the main objective is to make a profit. The profitability of an organisation should be studied by looking at the general

---

Check your understanding

Look at the final accounts of any business by extracting this information from a balance sheet. Find out the current ratio and acid test ratio of the organisation. Comment upon the figures you extract. Discuss the positioning of the Plimsoll line of this business.

Gearing ratio

Working capital and gearing ratios help us to understand how well an organisation can meet its short-term liabilities. The gearing ratio is a good indicator of the longer-term financial stability of an organisation. It is calculated as follows:

$$\text{Gearing ratio} = \frac{\text{Long-term loans (including debentures and preference capital}}{\text{Ordinary shares and reserves}}$$

Gearing makes a direct comparison between the long-term capital in a business provided by ordinary shareholders and that provided through long-term loans and preference shares. Using the above we can say that a company is:

profitability of an investment made or by looking at the profits the business makes on its sales, based upon information supplied through the profit and loss account.

Gross profit percentage

Sometimes known as the gross profit ratio or profit percentage, this ratio is extracted from information within the trading account. It simply relates gross profit to sales revenue. For example, if the ratio is 35% it means that for every £1,000 of sales, 35% of these sales will be gross profit. It is calculated by:

$$\text{Gross profit percentage} = \frac{\text{Gross profit}}{\text{Sales}} \times \frac{100}{1}$$

The gross profit percentage should be relatively consistent and should be calculated at regular intervals. If it suddenly rises or falls, the reason should be investigated. For example, if the percentage falls it could mean stock is being stolen or damaged. Alternatively, it could mean the cost of stock is rising and that the increase has not been passed on to the consumer through rising prices.

Net profit percentage

This ratio indicates the net profit as a percentage of sales. As with the gross profit percentage, the net profit percentage should remain consistent from year to year. It should also be possible to compare the net profit percentage of organisations within the same type of industry. It is calculated by:

$$\text{Net profit percentage} = \frac{\text{Net profit}}{\text{Sales}} \times \frac{100}{1}$$

If the gross profit percentage is consistent, any changes in the net profit percentage could indicate an increase in overheads as a proportion of sales, and a need to make economies or cut costs.

Operating profit percentage

The net profit percentage is charged after interest has been paid on loans. It can be argued that, therefore, when making comparisons between businesses, it is difficult to do so because one might be highly geared and financed with a considerable amount of loans, while another might be financed with capital from the owner. This is calculated by:

$$\frac{\text{Operating profit}}{\text{percentage}} = \frac{\text{Profit before interest and tax}}{\text{Sales}}$$

Return on equity

Whenever one is investing in a business, it is important that the investor thinks about alternative investments and other uses for the money. For example, what would be the point of investing in a business that provides a 2% return, when a building society would provide less risk and a higher return? Return on equity is calculated by:

$$\text{Return on equity} = \frac{\text{Net profit (after tax and preference dividend)}}{\text{Ordinary share capital and reserves}} \times \frac{100}{1}$$

Return on equity (sometimes known as ROE) indicates how well a business has used its financial resources in the interests of ordinary shareholders.

Return on capital employed

Whereas ROE takes into account only ordinary shareholders' investments, the return on capital employed (sometimes known as ROCE) adopts a wider measure of the methods for financing a business by taking into consideration preference shares and debentures. Capital employed is thus:

Ordinary share capital
add
Reserves
equals
Equity
add
Preference shares
add
Debentures
equals
Capital employed

It is calculated by:

$$\text{Return on capital employed} = \frac{\text{Net profit + Interest on debentures}}{\text{Ordinary share + Reserves + Preference shares + Debentures}} \times \frac{100}{1}$$

There are many reasons for adopting this wider definition. In particular, a business has use of these resources and so it is, therefore, a better measure to take these into account when working out profitability.

Dividend yield

A number of ratios are much more specially aligned to the needs of larger companies, particularly those quoted on the London Stock Exchange as public limited companies. The dividend yield relates the shareholders' dividend to the market price of the share. It is calculated by:

$$\text{Dividend yield} = \frac{\text{Ordinary share dividend}}{\text{Market price per share}} \times \frac{100}{1}$$

Dividend yield can be obtained by looking at the information about shares in the financial press. It provides an investor or a potential investor with a good guide to the annual percentage return paid on a share. Dividend yield as a raw measure, however, ignores wider profits or earnings (such as retained profits) that give investors more capital growth than increased income.

Earnings per share

Earnings per share (or EPS) measures the amount of profit made by each share, after tax and preference dividends have been paid. This is an important determinant of the value of each share. It is calculated by:

$$\text{Earnings per share} = \frac{\text{Net profit after tax and preference dividends}}{\text{Number of ordinary shares}}$$

This provides the ordinary shareholder with key information about the earning capacity of each share and enables comparisons to be made with previous years in order to develop a good understanding of performance.

Earnings/dividend yield

This relates the shareholders' dividend to the market price of the shares. It is calculated by:

$$\text{Earnings/dividend yield} = \frac{\text{Earnings per ordinary share}}{\text{Market price per share}} \times \frac{100}{1}$$

This shows the return earned by the company on each share and this includes not just the part paid to investors but also the amount kept within the company to increase the value of the capital owned by ordinary shareholders.

Price/earnings ratio

This is sometimes called the P/E ratio. The P/E ratio compares the current market value of a share with the earnings per share. It shows the amount that each share is earning and provides the ordinary shareholder with key information about the earning capacity of each share. It is calculated by:

$$\text{Price/earnings ratio} = \frac{\text{Market price per share}}{\text{Earnings per share}}$$

If a share has a market price of £8.00 and the earnings per share in one year are £1.60, the P/E ratio would be 5. The person owning the share would have a share value 5 times that of its earnings. A low P/E ratio would indicate investors would not be experiencing much growth in the near future.

Dividend cover

This ratio illustrates the difference between an organisation's margin of safety and the amount it has to pay out in dividends. It is calculated by:

$$\text{Dividend cover} = \frac{\text{Net profit after tax and dividends}}{\text{Ordinary dividends}}$$

Case study: BT's (www.bt.com/) nine-month results to 31 December 1999

BT's nine-month results to 31 December 1999 can be summarised as follows:

	Third quarter		Nine months	
	1999 £m	1998 £m	1999 £m	1998 £m
Total turnover	5,585	4,684	15,901	13,326
Profit before taxation	651	858	2,313	3,459
Profit after taxation	453	592	1,608	2,425
Earnings per share	7.0p	9.2p	24.9p	37.5p

According to Iain Vallance, Chairman of BT:

As I indicated in my half-year report, growth prospects in the UK and internationally remain good but we face increasing competition as the globalisation of our industry continues. In this quarter, competitive pressures have adversely affected our operating margins in the UK fixed voice telephony market. The results also reflect the costs of meeting increased customer demand and of growing new areas of business.

The results for the nine months were 24.9p compared with 37.5p in the comparable period of the previous year. The reduction in earnings in the third quarter were due to reduced call prices, lower margins and the cost of developing new products for customers. At the same time, turnover over the nine months increased by 19.3%

1 What stakeholder groups would be interested in the above figures?

2 Comment upon their significance.

3 How would shareholders feel about the figures, and what other questions might they wish to ask?

This is a useful ratio to work out how easily a company can pay dividends to its ordinary shareholders. A ratio of between 5 and 10 would provide a secure margin of safety, with profit exceeding dividends of more than 5 times.

Check your understanding

Over the next week of your course, try to learn as many of the following ratios as you can. Test yourself by writing down the ratio names and trying to remember the ratio itself.

Performance ratios

1 Stock turnover (times per year) = $\dfrac{\text{Cost of sales}}{\text{Average stock}}$

Where:

Average stock = $\dfrac{\text{Opening stock} + \text{Closing stock}}{2}$

Number of days' stock held on average = $\dfrac{\text{Average stock}}{\text{Cost of sales}} \times 365$ days

2 Debtors' collection period = $\dfrac{\text{Debtors}}{\text{Average daily sales}}$

3 Creditors' payment period = $\dfrac{\text{Creditors}}{\text{Average daily purchases}}$

4 Asset utilisation = $\dfrac{\text{Sales}}{\text{Fixed assets}}$

5 Asset turnover performance = $\dfrac{\text{Sales}}{\text{Net assets}}$

Net assets for the purpose of ratio analysis is:

Fixed assets + Current assets – Current liabilities

6 Proprietary ratio = $\dfrac{\text{Ordinary shareholders' funds}}{\text{Tangible assets}}$

Solvency ratios

1 Working capital = Current assets – Current liabilities

2 Current ratio = $\dfrac{\text{Current assets}}{\text{Current liabilities}}$

3 Acid test ratio = $\dfrac{\text{Current assets} - \text{Stocks}}{\text{Current liabilities}}$

4   Gearing ratio $= \dfrac{\text{Long-term loans (including debentures and preference capital)}}{\text{Ordinary shares and reserves}}$

5   Interest cover $= \dfrac{\text{Profit before interest and tax}}{\text{Interest paid in the year}}$

Profitability ratios

1   Gross profit percentage $= \dfrac{\text{Gross profit}}{\text{Sales}} \times \dfrac{100}{1}$

2   Net profit percentage $= \dfrac{\text{Net profit}}{\text{Sales}} \times \dfrac{100}{1}$

3   Operating profit percentage $= \dfrac{\text{Profit before interest and tax}}{\text{Sales}}$

4   Return on equity $= \dfrac{\text{Net profit (after tax and preference dividend)}}{\text{Sales}} \times \dfrac{100}{1}$

5   Return on capital employed $= \dfrac{\text{Net profit + Interest on debentures}}{\text{Ordinary shares + Reserves + Preference shares + Debentures}} \times \dfrac{100}{1}$

6   Dividend yield $= \dfrac{\text{Ordinary share dividend}}{\text{Market price per share}} \times \dfrac{100}{1}$

7   Earnings per share $= \dfrac{\text{Net profit after tax and preference dividend}}{\text{Number of ordinary shares}}$

8   Earnings/dividend yield $= \dfrac{\text{Earnings per ordinary share}}{\text{Market price per share}} \times \dfrac{100}{1}$

9   Price/earnings ratio $= \dfrac{\text{Market price per share}}{\text{Earnings per share}}$

10   Dividend cover $= \dfrac{\text{Net profit after tax and dividends}}{\text{Ordinary dividends}}$

Case study: Comparing the performance of two organisations

The financial statements below are the latest results of two companies, Alpha Ltd and Beta Ltd. One of these companies is a food retailer, while the other is an engineering firm.

The trading and profit and loss and appropriation account of Alpha and Beta for the year ended 31 December 2001

	Alpha ('000) £	Beta ('000) £
Sales	1,200	1,300
Cost of sales	930	600
Gross profit	270	700
Distribution costs	80	200
Administration expenses	40	200
Profit before taxation	150	300
Taxation	50	100
Profit after tax	100	200
Dividends	50	75
Retained profit	50	125

The balance sheets of Alpha and Beta as at 31 December 2001

	Alpha ('000) £	Beta ('000) £
Fixed assets	250	325
Current assets		
Stocks	60	120
Trade debtors	5	210
Cash	10	20
	75	350
Current liabilities		
Creditors	50	90
Net assets	275	585
Financed by		
Share capital	100	200
Profit and loss account	175	385
	275	585

1 Use a range of ratios to analyse the performance, solvency and profitability of each of these businesses.

2 Comment upon the data presented by each of these ratios.

3 On the basis of your analysis, which of the two businesses is more likely to be the food retailer and which is more likely to be the engineering company?

Monitoring a business

When monitoring a business, we can make comparisons both with the business's performance in past years and with the performance of similar firms.

For example, let us assume a business has set itself a budgeted target of making £100 million in profits before tax in 2003. This is intended to improve on its 2002 performance of £90 million. In the event, it makes a profit of only £90 million but this can be explained by a downturn in the economy leading to a lack of demand. In fact the performance is regarded as quite good because the firm's nearest rival (which is almost exactly the same size and similar in every respect) performed less well. Its profit before tax was £90 million in 2002, but had fallen to £82 million in 2003. We can set out these comparisons in a table (see Figure 20.3). Clearly, comparisons will need to be made using a range of factors.

It is always a good indicator to compare a business's performance with its achievement in previous years. Of course, the business will change and so too will its external environment. Over a period of time we are able to build up a picture of how the business is doing.

Comparisons of profits with previous year	Comparisons of budgeted profit with actual profit	Comparison with nearest rival's profit
2003 = £90 million	Budgeted = £100 million	Rival 2003 = £82 million
2002 = £90 million	Actual = £90 million	Rival 2002 = £90 million

Figure 20.3 Monitoring a business's performance

Past information

Studying past information helps to provide a good picture of change within an organisation. This also shows how the organisation is performing. For example, by looking at past balance sheets it would be possible to identify changes in the following:

Case study: A fresh face leading Boots

The Boots (www.boots-plc.com/) Company embraces businesses operating principally in retailing, the manufacture and marketing of health and personal care products throughout the world, and the development and management of retail property. Its objective is to maximise the value of the company for the benefit of its shareholders. For years, Boots was one of the acknowledged leaders of retailing, but in recent times it has fallen out of fashion with the City. As the former chairman of Boots stepped down in 1999, the final phase of his office was characterised by a plummeting Boots share price and questions about the prospects for the business.

The job of revitalising Boots' share price and its street-cred in the City has fallen to Steve Russell, who took over as chief executive in April 2000. Russell is well aware of the market perception that Boots needs to change. He is aware that Boots needs to be perceived as aggressive and dynamic and needs to develop opportunities for long-term growth and profits. He is aware that he has to deliver growth that will reverse the share price decline and warn off predators.

1 Why might Boots have fallen out of fashion with the City?

2 What will investors in the City be looking for, as Boots changes under the leadership of its new chief executive?

- The size of the fixed capital base of the organization.

- The asset structure.

- The relationship between assets and liabilities.

- The dependence of the organisation on outside finance.

- The extent of the debtors and creditors to the organisation.

Similarly, by looking at the profit and loss account it is possible to see changes in:

- The sales made by the organization.

- The expenditures of the organization.

- The net profit or losses made by the business.

It is also possible to study previous years' figures to gain information on changes in the speed at which the organisation is having debts repaid or at which it is paying creditors, etc.

Variances

In planning financial activities it is important to have a target or standard to achieve. For example, if you intend profits to be £100 million and they are only £65 million, an organisation would have a 'negative variance' of £35 million.

In planning and monitoring financial performance, assessing variances can be used as a way of checking and then (if possible) making corrections or amendments to business activities in order to put the business back on track to achieve standards.

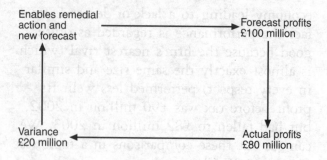

Figure 20.4 Planning and monitoring financial performance

Of course, the remedial action required may be to create a more accurate forecast (see Figure 20.4).

Variance analysis can thus be used to measure the difference between budgeted (intended) and actual outcomes. Feedback from such analysis can be used to inform decision-making in the next accounting period.

Variance analysis makes it possible to detect problems and it enables managers to take speedy decisions to improve performance and profitability. It also gives managers greater control over managing performance.

Interfirm comparisons

Another way of monitoring financial performance is to use interfirm comparisons. The purpose of comparing two businesses or two sets of data is to identify differences between them (variances) and then to interpret these variances in order to improve business performance. Interfirm comparison enables you to compare two businesses in the same industry.

Check your understanding

Compare the performance of two businesses in the same business sector. For example, you might wish to use the web to compare the performance of Nationwide (www.nationwide.com/)
* and Bradford & Bingley (www.bradford-bingley.co.uk/).

In particular, business people will want to compare their own performance with that of rival firms. Businesses will want to know how their market share has changed and compare this with that of rivals (e.g. pre-tax profits, return on capital employed, sales, etc.). Visit any board meeting that is looking at financial performance and you will see that much discussion is on how their business is doing in comparison to their rivals.

Of course, if you want a representative indicator of how well a business is doing, it is often best to compare it with a business

of a similar size operating in similar market segments and using similar technologies.

Forecasts

It is also important to forecast what the balance sheet, profit and loss account and cash flow will look like during the next accounting period.

In forecasting it is essential to focus plans upon likely events and transactions in the current accounting period, which will normally be for the next year. By setting out the organisation's intentions it is possible to produce a set of figures showing what the targets are. This will involve anticipating incomes and expenditures through the profit and loss account, perhaps on a monthly basis, and then using this to forecast the next annual profit and loss account. A simplified form of this is set out in Figure 20.5.

	Forecast for month 1		Forecast for month 12	Annual forecast
Income:				
Sales				
Other income				
Total income				
Expenditures:				
Materials				
etc.				
etc.				
Total expenditure				
Net profit or loss				
Cumulative profit or loss				

Figure 20.5 Forecasting the profit and loss account

	January			Total	
	Forecast	Actual		Forecast	Actual
Income					
Expenditures					
Net profit or loss					
Cumulative profit or loss					

	January			December	
	Forecast	Actual		Forecast	Actual
Receipts					
Payments					
Net cash flow					

	January			Total	
	Forecast	Actual		Forecast	Actual
Income					
Expenditures					
Net profit or loss					
Cumulative profit or loss					

Figure 20.6 Cash flow forecast

It is also possible to use this with a cash flow forecast (a simplified model is set out in Figure 20.6). It is also possible to draw up a forecast balance sheet based upon these expected activities during the year, including the purchase, sale and depreciation of fixed assets.

Dividends

Dividends are the profits allocated to shareholders in proportion to their shares. Where there are different classes of share,

there are priorities in allocating dividends. For example, preference shareholders receive priority over ordinary shareholders for receiving their dividends. These dividends are usually recommended by directors in their annual report and are declared by shareholders at the annual general meeting. Sometimes interim dividends are allocated on the basis of profits to date.

Dividends are important for shareholders as they provide them with a regular return in the form of profits upon their investment. However, it is argued that dividends and the profits they yield are a crude way of evaluating an investment, as what matters is not just the dividends but also the share price and all that the price represents in capital growth. One element an investor will look for is dividend growth. The prospect of dividend growth can improve the valuation of shares. Useful ratios that show how well dividends can be paid are dividend cover, gearing, dividend yield, earnings per share, earnings/dividend yield and price/earnings ratio.

Share prices

Shares are long-term investments by shareholders. One of the old-fashioned notions of an investor is someone who buys shares at a low price in a relatively small company that one day turns into an IBM (www.ibm.com/) or a Glaxo (www.glaxowellcome.co.uk/), with massive growth in the share price. An acorn has suddenly grown into a massive oak.

Growth industries in recent years have included those involved with new technologies, particular computers and media. Many of these share prices have risen quickly whenever prices begin to rise within the stock market. The price/earnings ratio on growth stocks is usually a good indicator, as it is well above the market average. There is always a danger, however, that when stock prices begin to fall, the share prices of stocks that have grown rapidly begin to fall faster than others.

The price of shares is something shareholders will constantly be scanning. They will be looking for both sales and earnings of their chosen investments to rise quickly, with good profit margins and prospects for growth.

Chapter 21 Cash flow management and budgeting

As well as recording financial information and making judgements about the effectiveness of the information, businesses need to manage their finances. The two main elements of financial management are budgeting and cash flow.

Budgets help businesses to plan, set targets and control expenditure. To understand how budgets are used you need to know what they are, how they work and their particular purposes. You will need to be able to identify and interpret variance and explain the benefits of budgeting to businesses.

Businesses need to control their working capital. To understand how they can do this you need to know what working capital is and how businesses manage their cash. You also need to know that businesses may have cash flow problems and that they need to be solved. This involves examining credit control and other methods businesses use to maintain their working capital.

Financial planning involves defining objectives and then developing ways to achieve them. To be able to do this, a financial manager must have a realistic understanding of what is happening and what is likely to happen within the organisation – for example, when is money going to come in, what is it needed for and would it be possible to use some of it for expansion and development? In the 'money-go-round' (see Figure 21.1), capital and sales revenue come into a business, but is there enough left over, after paying all the costs, for expansion and development?

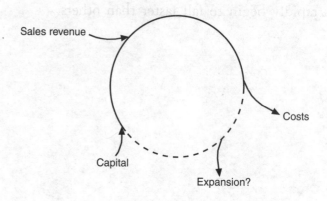

Figure 21.1 The money-go-round

Budgets

Looking into their future helps all organisations to plan their activities so that what they anticipate and want to happen can actually happen. This process of financial planning is known as budgeting. It is considered to be a system of *responsibility accounting* because it puts an onus on budgeted areas to perform in a way that has been outlined for them, and its success will depend upon the quality of information provided. Businesses that do not budget may not be pleased when they view their final accounts. Budgeting helps the financial manager to develop an understanding of how the business is likely to perform in the future.

Budgeting and people

We all budget to a greater or lesser extent. Our short-term budget may relate to how we are going to get through the coming week and do all the things we want to do. Our slightly longer-term budget may

Case study: The Society of Practitioners of Insolvency (www.spi.org.uk/)

The Society of Practitioners of Insolvency has recently changed its name to the Association of Business Recovery Professionals. The organisation is the leading organisation for licensed insolvency practitioners. Its main objectives are to promote higher standards within the insolvency profession as well as an understanding of insolvency within the community at large.

Recent surveys by the association have revealed that the main reasons behind insolvency are poor management and financial constraints upon business activity. Its research has shown this problem is far more prevalent amongst smaller companies. Indeed, large companies are far more likely to respond to treatment and be able to pay their remaining creditors.

To help businesses the association has recently published *The Ostrich's Guide to Business Survival* (www.r3.org.uk/ostrich/index2.cfm). The guide emphasises that any business can have a financial crisis and that no business is free from the forces around it. Survivors, however, are organisations that know where they are going, think about the problems they face and have plans to deal with them. The guide poses the following questions for small businesses:

- Do you have a current business plan?
- Do you review costs and overheads as well as sales?
- Was your last set of audited accounts more than 12 months ago?
- Do you prepare regular management accounts?
- Do you prepare annual projections and cashflow forecasts?
- Is actual performance regularly reviewed against plan?
- Do you prepare and use aged debtor and creditor lists?
- Do you and your co-directors meet regularly to formally review progress? Or, if your are on your own, do you set aside time just to understand your financial position?

'If you are doing all these things, then you are likely to be in a position to notice the signs of impending crisis, if they occur.'

1 Use an example to explain why poor management and financial constraints seem to be the main reasons behind insolvency.

2 Why do small businesses need *The Ostrich's Guide to Business Survival*?

3 Look at the questions posed for small businesses. What do these questions imply about the need to manage cash?

involve being able to afford Christmas presents in two months' time. Our longest-term budget could involve the planning necessary to afford the car tax, MOT and motor insurance, which all fall due in ten months from now. Also, when can we afford in the longer term to replace the car?

Check your understanding

Identify a range of activities in which you participate that you think could be helped by some form of budgeting. For example, these may include your personal finances, or some club responsibility. Explain how in each instance.

In exactly the same way, businesses try to see far into the future. The problem is that, the further one looks into the future, the more difficult it is to see it accurately.

A budget is a financial plan developed for the future. Many businesses appoint a budget controller whose sole task is to co-ordinate budgetary activities. A short-term budget would be for up to one year, a medium-term budget would be for anything from one year to five years and a budget for a longer period than this would be a long-term budget (see Figure 21.2).

Wherever budgeting takes place, it is important to draw upon the collective experience of people throughout the

business. A budgeting team might consist of representatives from various areas of activity. The team will consider the objectives of the budgeting process, obtain and provide relevant information, make decisions, prepare budgets and then use these budgets to help to control the business (see Figure 21.3).

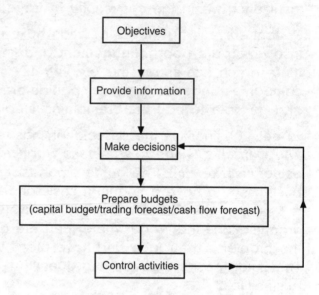

Figure 21.3 The budgetary process

Benefits of budgeting

Budgeting provides a valuable benchmark against which to measure and judge the actual performance of key areas of business activity. There are therefore many benefits of budgeting:

* It helps to predict what the organisation thinks will happen. Given the experience within the organisation, budgets help to show what is likely to take place in the future.

* Budgets create opportunities to *appraise alternative courses of action*. Information created for budgeting purposes forms the basis of decisions that have to be taken. The research necessary for budgeting will

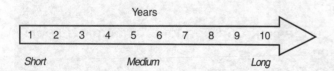

Figure 21.2 Budgetary periods

look at alternative ways of achieving the organisation's objectives.

- Budgets set *targets*. If communicated to people throughout the organisation, the budgets will help them to work towards the targets that have been set.

- They help to *monitor and control performance*. This can be done by studying actual results, comparing these to budgeted results and then finding out why differences (known as *variances*) may have occurred. Sometimes variances are bad, while at other times they may be good. Whatever the causes of the variances, they are a useful starting point for dealing with issues within the business.

- Budgets are fundamental to the process of *business planning*. They provide a series of quantitative guidelines that can be used for co-ordination and then followed in order to achieve the organisation's business objectives.

- They can be used as a source of *motivation*. As part of the consultation process, budgets help to keep people involved. They also help to create *goal congruence*, so that the aims and objectives of the individual are the same as those for the organisation.

- Budgets are a form of communication. They enable employees from across the organisation to be aware of performance expectations with regard to their individual work area.

Budgeting may also have some useful spin-offs. Every year the business is reviewed and this gives members of the various departments a better understanding of the working of the organisation as a whole. In fact, by participating in the budgetary process they feel their experience is contributing to policy decisions.

It also increases co-operation between departments and lowers departmental barriers. In this way members of one department can become aware of the difficulties facing another department. By being involved in the budgetary process, non-accountants also appreciate the importance of costs.

In reality, budgeting may take place in almost all parts of an organisation. Budgeting should also be viewed as something that is going on all the time and as a source of useful information and guidance for managers.

The process of budget setting

The process of setting budgets has to be seen within the context of the longer-term objectives and strategies at the highest level of management of any organisation. The administration of the budgeting process will usually be the responsibility of the accounts department. Many organisations set up a budget committee to oversee the process.

The budgetary process is usually governed by a formal budget timetable. This helps to link the budget in with all other aspects of business planning (see Figure 21.4).

The accounts department is involved at all stages of the budgeting process, and an effective accounts team will provide a range of advice to managers as the exercise develops. Spreadsheets are an effective 'what-if' tool that are often used to help within the budgeting process.

Setting up a system of 'responsibility accounting' such as budgeting involves

Date	Narrative	Responsibility
Budget timetable for year 1 April 2001 to 31 March 2002		
1 Sept	Board of directors to review long-term objectives and strategies and specify short-tem goals for the year	Directors
22 Sept	Budget guidelines and standard forms issued to line managers	Accounts
6 Oct	Actual results for year are issued to line management, so that comparisons can be made with current budget and last year's actual results	Accounts
20 Oct	Budget submissions are made to the management accountant	Line management
27 Oct	First draft of the master budget is issued	Accounts
3 Nov	First draft of the budget is reviewed for results and consistency – line managers to justify their submissions	MD and individual directors
6 Nov	New assumptions and guidelines issued to line management	Accounts
10 Nov	Budgets revised and resubmitted	Line management
20 Nov	Second draft of master budget issued	Accounts
27 Nov	Final review of the draft budget	Managing director and financial director
1 Dec	Final amendments	Accounts
11 Dec	Submission to the board for their approval	Financial director

Figure 21.4 A budget timetable

breaking down an organisation into a series of 'control centres'. Each individual manager then has the responsibility for managing the budget relating to his or her particular control centre.

Budgetary reports, therefore, reflect the assigned responsibility at each level of the organisation. As all organisations have a structure of control, it is important the budgetary system fits around this. The reports should be designed to reflect the different levels within the organisation and the responsibilities of each of the managers concerned.

If the budgeting process reflects the different levels of control, managers will be kept informed not just of their own performance but also of that of other budget holders for whom they are responsible. They will also know that managers above them will be assessing their performance. This system can be reviewed regularly at meetings attended by all the individual managers concerned (see Figure 21.5).

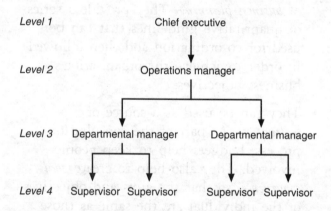

Figure 21.5 A reporting hierarchy

Check your understanding

Find out more about the budgeting process within your school or college. For example, how are budgets set, what processes take place and who are the budget holders? What happens if budget holders overspend?

Although it could be claimed that they are mechanistic, budget models formalise the inter-relationships between departments and provide a basic understanding of work flows within business organisations.

The overall budget as a plan will have real value only if the performance levels set through the budget are realistic. Budgets based upon *ideal* conditions are unlikely to be met and will result in departments failing to meet their targets. For example, the sales department may fail to achieve their sales budget, which may result in goods remaining unsold. Budgets can be motivating only if they are pitched at a realistic level.

There are two approaches to budget setting. The top-down approach involves senior managers specifying what the best performance indicators are for the business across all departments and budgeted areas. The bottom-up approach builds up the organisational *master budget* on the basis of the submissions of individual line managers and supervisors, based upon their own views of their requirements. In practice most organisations use a mixture of both methods (see Figure 21.6).

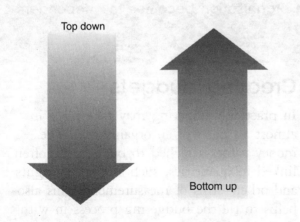

Figure 21.6 Approaches to budget setting

Budget setting should be based upon realistic predictions of future sales and costs. Many organisations base future predictions solely on past figures, with adjustments for forecast growth and inflation rates. Although the main advantage of this approach is that budgets are based upon actual data, future conditions may not mirror past ones.

One of the dangers of budgeting is that, if actual results are dramatically different from the budgeting ones, the process could lose its credibility as a means of control. Following a budget too rigidly may also restrict a business's activities. For example, if the budget for entertainment has been exceeded and subsequent visiting customers are not treated with the usual hospitality, orders may be lost. On the other hand, if managers realise that towards the end of the year a department has underspent, they may decide to go on a spending spree.

Budgeting is a routine annual event for many different types of organisations. The process may start in the middle of the financial year, with a revision of the current year's budget and with first drafts of the budget for the coming year. Some organisations plan further ahead with an outline plan for 3–5 years.

Budgets provide an opportunity for everyone to play a part in either the strategic or tactical development of the organisation. As the activities following the budgetary process unfold, they provide a benchmark against which actual performance can be measured and judged.

As a result, an essential feature of the budgetary control system is the feedback of actual results. The process of measuring the difference between budgeted (intended) and actual outcomes is known as *variance analysis*. Variance analysis makes it possible

Case study: Spreadware Budgeting (http://spreadware.com/finfiles/005.html)

Spreadware Budgeting is designed to help the budget creation process. It is also designed to consolidate a budgeting process and enable multiple budgets to be created easily and quickly.

The great benefit of using this type of software is that revisions of budgets can be made easily and at any time. Budgets can be analysed as soon as actual data becomes available, which quickly allows variances to be detected and also whether departmental objectives are being met. There is also a forecast option that allows for projected results based upon actual data.

Spreadware Budgeting is interactive, which makes it easy to use. It can also be set up within both large and small organisations. The benefits of the system are as follows:

- An unlimited number of budget periods can be applied to an unlimited number of cost centres.

- It is possible to compare the actual cost, versus the budget, for the period.

- A forecast option allows projections to be developed based upon early actual data.

- Budgets can be based upon actual numbers, growth rates and previous reporting periods.

- There is an unlimited number of budget models.

1 What are the advantages of using computer software for budgeting purposes?

2 How important is it for a manager to be able to: a identify variances; and b make forecasts?

3 What sort of problems could develop if an organisation becomes too dependent on this type of budgeted data?

to detect problems. Reasons can be sought for variances and speedy action can be taken to improve performance.

Budgeting should be viewed as something that is going on all the time and as a source of useful information and guidance for managers.

Creating budgets

In practice, budgeting may take place in almost all parts of an organisation. The money values attached to budgets are often linked to quantities, such as units, weights and other forms of measurement. This also helps to tie the budgeting process in with operational activities so that the budget can be used as a management tool. We shall discuss three key areas of budgetary forecasts:

- *The capital budget* The word 'capital' refers to the buying of fixed assets. Do we plan now for the money we will need in the future to buy another machine? The capital budget is a simple statement of intent or forecast, which specifies the planned purchase of assets, the date of intended purchase and the expected cost of purchase.

- *The cash budget or cash flow forecast* This forecast looks at the cash coming in to the organisation as well as the cash going out. It is a prediction by a business of how much money it thinks it will receive and how much it thinks it will pay out over a specified time. By forecasting cash flow, managers will know what their future financial requirements will be and will be able to take action beforehand if they need an overdraft or some form of loan.

- *Subsidiary budgets and the master budget* Functional budgets for different business activities and budgets for individual balance sheet items are called subsidiary budgets. The exact nature of subsidiary budgets will depend on the organisational structure and the operational processes of an organisation. The term 'master budget' includes the budgeted profit and loss account, balance sheet and cash budget.

The capital budget

Capital expenditure refers to the acquisition of fixed assets. Capital budgets are prepared to plan for the purchase of fixed assets.

The capital budget is prepared after reviewing fixed asset needs for the budget period. This will be done in the light of business objectives and planned strategy for the next budget period. The next step is to consider the condition and capacity of existing fixed assets. For example, a planned expansion into new markets will require a review of existing assets to ensure sufficient business capacity is available. Capital expenditure may also be required to renew existing assets, such as worn-out equipment. In recognising that more fixed assets are required, it is necessary to plan their purchase, including the time and cost of acquisition.

It follows from the nature of this type of expenditure that some years will require more capital expenditure than others. Together with the fact that, for many businesses, the value of fixed assets used is significant, it is important capital budgets are prepared to ensure adequate finance is planned.

Classifications of capital expenditure will follow those you are already familiar with from constructing the fixed assets section of the balance sheet. Typically they include:

- land and buildings
- factory plant and machinery
- office fixtures and fittings
- computer equipment
- motor vehicles.

Expenditure may be further analysed into assets required for:

- expansion of existing product ranges
- expansion into new products
- replacement of existing assets
- satisfying health and safety requirements.

In this way information is provided as to whether the business is expanding or just maintaining its productive capacity. It may also indicate whether items of capital expenditure are essential or merely desirable.

	Jan. £	Feb. £	March £	April £	May £	June £	July £	Aug. £	Sept. £	Oct. £	Nov. £	Dec. £	Total £
Replacement													
CNC machine						50,000							50,000
2 motor vans								20,000					20,000
Computer			5,500										5,500
Expansion													
Building extension									50,000				50,000
Production line										40,000			40,000
Health and Safety													
Air conditioning		9,500											9,500
Total	0	9,500	5,500	0	0	50,000	0	20,000	50,000	40,000	0	0	175,000

Figure 21.7 A budget timetable

Look at the capital budget of Jason Robards (see Figure 21.7). The forecast shows that, over the year, £50,000 is needed for a CNC machine, £20,000 for two motor vans, £5,500 for a new computer, £50,000 for a new building extension, £40,000 for improving the production line and £9,500 for installing a new air conditioning system. The capital budget quickly provides an indication that £175,000 is needed for capital purchases for the year and then itemises amounts required month by month.

When evaluating expenditure on capital items, the business managers will consider the likely returns on making the investment and the associated risk of not reaping the hoped-for benefits. The cost of purchasing assets should be evaluated against a range of benefits such as increased sales or reduced costs. In many cases it is necessary to perform a cost–benefit analysis to recognise the more qualitative aspects of the proposal. For example, expenditure on welfare facilities (such as employee social clubs and catering facilities) will be evaluated for the goodwill and lower staff turnover such facilities may encourage.

Check your understanding

Whitehills Leisure Centre provides customers with a gym, swimming pool and team sports hall. The centre's management is reviewing capital expenditure needs for 2002. They intend to expand facilities during the year with four squash courts and more equipment for the gym. The squash courts will be built in May at a cost of £75,000. The additional gym equipment will comprise three exercise bikes costing £1,000 in March, a rowing machine costing £1,200 in July and weight-lifting equipment costing £2,000 in November.

The receptionist has been complaining about the number of repair visits required recently for the computerised cash till, and so it has been decided to replace this in January at a cost of £1,600.

The floor surface around the swimming pool is too slippery when wet and so the management have decided this should be replaced in January at a cost of £5,000 to minimise the risk of accidents. It has also been decided to refurbish the changing rooms. New lockers and benches will cost £5,000 in June.

Prepare a capital budget for Whitehills Leisure Centre for the year ended 31 December 2002, with separate sections for expansion, replacement and health and safety.

Remember that, even though we are looking at the capital budget and the cash budget individually, all budgets are linked to the master budget. Once prepared, the details from the capital budget are incorporated into the cash budget.

The cash budget/cash flow forecast

Whereas profit is a *surplus* from trading activities, cash is a liquid asset that enables an organisation to buy the goods and services it requires in order to add value to them, trade and make profits. It is therefore possible for an organisation to be profitable while, at the same time, creditors have not been paid and liquid resources have not been properly accounted for.

On the other hand, an organisation must look carefully to see that its use of cash is to its best advantage. For example, if it holds too much cash in the bank, it might be sacrificing the potential to earn greater income.

An organisation must therefore ensure it has sufficient cash to carry out its plans, and that the cash coming in is sufficient to cover the cash going out. At the same time it must take into account any cash surpluses it might have in the bank.

Looking carefully at the availability of liquid funds is essential to the smooth running of any organisation. With cash planning or budgeting it is possible to forecast the flows into and out of an organisation's bank account so that any surpluses or deficits can be highlighted and any necessary action can be taken promptly. For example, overdraft facilities may be arranged in good time so funds are available when required.

Case study: Planware (www.planware.org/)

Planware is a trademark property of Invest-Tech Ltd. One of its products is a financial planner called Exl-Plan (for Excel), a planning or budgeting tool that enables users to compile 3–5-year cash flow projections by month for the first year, by quarter for the next two years and annually for the final two years.

This mathematical model helps to prepare cash flow projections that enable organisations to identify their short-term financial projections and banking requirements. They claim that there are a number of advantages of using this type of computer-based model. For example:

- It reduces the tedium of carrying out numerous repetitive calculations.
- It presents a range of results that can be used for estimating banking requirements.
- The computer-based model can assess the consequences of alternative strategies.
- Assumptions can be altered to meet different scenarios.

1 How does using computers, and spreadsheet packages in particular, help with forecasting processes?

2 Who might require this information, and how would they use it?

The cash flow forecast is an extremely important tool within an organisation and has a number of clear purposes. For example:

- The forecast can be used to *highlight the timing consequences* of the capital budget and different elements of subsidiary budgets and the master budget. For example, the capital budget may point to when machinery needs to be replaced and this can then be included in the cash flow forecast. Similarly, the trading forecast may have various expenses, such as business and water rates, which may be paid quarterly or half-yearly. These can again be included in the cash flow forecast.

- The cash flow forecast (see example in Figure 21.9) is an essential document for the compilation of the *business plan*. It will help to show whether the organisation is capable of achieving the objectives it sets. This is very important if the business applies for finance, where the lender will almost certainly want to know about the ability of the applicant to keep on top of the cash flow and meet the proposed payment schedules.

- The cash flow forecast will help to boost the *lender's confidence* and the *owner's confidence*. By looking into the future it will provide them with the reassurance they require that their plans are going according to schedule.

- It will also help with the *monitoring of performance*. The cash flow forecast sets benchmarks against which the business is expected to perform. If the organisation actually performs differently from these benchmarks, the cash flow forecast may have highlighted an area for investigation. As we have seen, investigating differences between forecast

figures and actual figures is known as variance analysis.

To prepare a cash flow forecast you need to know what receipts and payments are likely to take place in the future and exactly when they will occur. It is important to know the length of the lead-time between incurring an expense and paying for it, as well as the time lag between making a sale and collecting the money from debtors. The art of successful forecasting is being able to calculate receipts and expenditures accurately.

Most business transactions take place on credit and, as we have discussed earlier in this book, most payments are made either weeks or months after documentation has been sent. For example, assume goods are paid for three months after a sale. This means that in April the cash will be received for sales in January, in May the cash will be received from February and so on. From the other viewpoint, if you have been given three months' credit you would pay for goods bought in January during April and so on (see Figure 21.8).

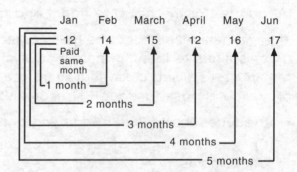

Figure 21.8 Payments made on credit

When working though a cash flow forecast, it is important to look carefully at the timing of every entry.

Example

A cash flow forecast for the six months ended 31 December 2001 can be drafted from the following information:

1 Cash balance 1 July 2001: £4,500.

2 Sales are £15 per unit and cash is received three months after the sale. For the period in question the sale of units is:

2001

Mar	Apr	May	June	Jul	Aug
60	60	75	90	55	140

2002

Sept	Oct	Nov	Dec	Jan	Feb
130	150	150	160	170	150

3 Production in units:

2001

Mar	Apr	May	June	Jul	Aug
40	50	80	70	80	130

2002

Sept	Oct	Nov	Dec	Jan	Feb
130	150	145	160	170	160

4 Raw materials cost £4 per unit and these are paid for two months *before* being used in production.

5 Wages are £5 per unit and this is paid for in the same month as the unit produced.

6 Running costs are £4 per unit. 50% of the cost is paid in the month of production, while the other 50% is paid for in the month after production.

7 Sundry expenses of £50 are paid monthly.

Receipts from sales

		£
July	60 (April) × 15 =	900
August	75 (May) × 15 =	1,125
September	90 (June) × 15 =	1,350
October	55 (July) × 15 =	825
November	140 (Aug) × 15 =	2,100
December	130 (Sept) × 15 =	1,950

Payments per month

July

		£
Raw materials	130 (Sept) × 4 =	520
Wages	80 (July) × 5 =	400
Running costs	80 (July) × 2 =	160
	70 (June) × 2 =	140
Sundry expenses	=	50
		£1,270

August

		£
Raw materials	150 (Oct) × 4 =	600
Wages	130 (Aug) × 5 =	650
Running costs	130 (Aug) × 2 =	260
	80 (July) × 2 =	160
Sundry expenses	=	50
		£1,720

September

		£
Raw materials	145 (Nov) × 4 =	580
Wages	130 (Sept) × 5 =	650
Running costs	130 (Sept) × 2 =	260
	130 (Aug) × 2 =	260
Sundry expenses	=	50
		£1,800

October			£
Raw materials	160 (Dec)	× 4 =	640
Wages	150 (Oct)	× 5 =	750
Running costs	150 (Oct)	× 2 =	300
	130 (Sept)	× 2 =	260
Sundry expenses		=	50
			£2,000

November			£
Raw materials	170 (Jan)	× 4 =	680
Wages	145 (Nov)	× 5 =	725
Running costs	145 (Nov)	× 2 =	290
	150 (Oct)	× 2 =	300
Sundry expenses		=	50
			£2,045

December			£
Raw materials	160 (Feb)	× 4 =	640
Wages	160 (Dec)	× 5 =	800
Running costs	160 (Dec)	× 2 =	320
	145 (Nov)	× 2 =	290
Sundry expenses		=	50
			£2,100

VAT

VAT is charged by many businesses on the goods and services they provide. Customs and Excise administer the VAT system and ensure businesses comply with the regulations. To forecast the cash flows of a business accurately, it is important you have some knowledge of VAT regulations:

- VAT is charged as an addition to the selling price of a business's goods or services.

- Businesses have to pay the VAT they receive from customers to Customs and Excise.

- The standard rate of VAT is set by Parliament and is currently at 17.5%.

- Like private individuals, businesses that are registered also pay VAT on goods and services provided by other VAT-registered businesses. However, businesses that are registered for VAT can claim back the VAT they have paid by deducting it from the amount they have to pay to Customs and Excise.

	July	Aug	Sept	Oct	Nov	Dec
Receipts						
Sales	900	1,125	1,350	825	2,100	1,950
Total receipts	900	1,125	1,350	825	2,100	1,950
Payments						
Raw materials	520	600	580	640	680	640
Direct labour	400	650	650	750	725	800
Variable expenses	300	420	520	560	590	610
Fixed expenses	50	50	50	50	50	50
Total payments	1,270	1,720	1,800	2,000	2,045	2,100
Receipts – payments	(370)	(595)	(450)	(1,175)	55	(150)
Balance b/f	4,500	4,130	3,535	3,085	1,910	1,965
Balance c/f	4,130	3,535	3,085	1,910	1,965	1,815

Figure 21.9 Example: cash flow chart

- Businesses have to register for VAT and charge it on their sales if annual turnover is more than £51,000 (1999/2000).

- VAT is usually accounted for in three-monthly periods (tax quarters).

- VAT has to be charged if three conditions are satisfied:

1 The goods or services are classified as a taxable supply.

2 The supply of goods or services is in the UK.

3 The supply is made by a VAT-registered business, whether it is a sole trader, partnership or company.

As Figure 21.10 shows, many things a business buys and sells are classified as a taxable supply, but some items are specifically excluded.

Taxable at standard rate – 17.5%	VAT is not charged on
Most items not specified as being non-taxable, e.g. Petrol Maintenance and repairs Materials Factory and office equipment Stationery	Food Water and sewerage Books and periodicals Certain supplies to charities Public transport Transactions in land and buildings including rent Financial services Insurance Postal services by Post Office Betting and gaming Wages paid to employees Drawings Dividends

Figure 21.10 The classification of financial transactions for VAT purposes

When preparing a cash flow statement we must include the VAT that is added to taxable sales and purchases. In addition, we must also remember to plan for the VAT payment to Customs and Excise:

$$\text{VAT payable} = \text{VAT on sales} - \text{VAT on purchases}$$

The difference between the VAT charged to customers and the VAT paid on supplies has to be paid to Customs and Excise by the end of the month following the VAT quarter. Let us look at a business that has a VAT quarter at the end of February (see Figure 21.11). The net payable of £2,000 must be paid to Customs and Excise by 31 March.

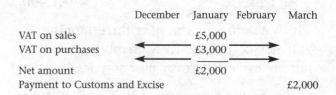

	December	January	February	March
VAT on sales		£5,000		
VAT on purchases		£3,000		
Net amount		£2,000		
Payment to Customs and Excise				£2,000

Figure 21.11 A VAT quarter at the end of February

Example

Jane Covey is preparing a cash forecast for her first six months of trading to August. She will start with a cash balance of £1,000 and will purchase equipment for £1,000 during that month. There will be no credit transactions and forecast figures each month are: sales £5,000, wages £2,000, rent £500, materials £2,000. The equipment, sales and materials are subject to VAT at 17.5%. Jane's VAT quarters end on May and August.

Care should be taken to ensure VAT is calculated only on those items that are subject to tax:

- The VAT on sales will be £5,000 × 17.5% = £875 per month.

- The VAT on purchases will be based on payments for equipment and materials. Rent and wages do not attract VAT.

The VAT to be paid to Customs and Excise is payable in the month following the VAT quarter, in this case June. (VAT is charged and paid only on equipment and materials in this instance.) It is made up as follows:

- VAT on sales for the quarter:

  (£875 + £875 + £875)   = £2,625

- VAT on purchases for
  the quarter   = £1,225

- VAT payable to Customs
  and Excise   = £1,400

The VAT due for the next three months will not be paid until September, so will not appear in the cash flow statement.

If the business pays more VAT in a quarter than the VAT it charges customers, the difference can be reclaimed from Customs and Excise in the form of a refund. If this situation arises, an additional 'VAT refund' line should be inserted in the receipts section of the cash flow statement (see Figure 21.12).

> ## Check your understanding
>
> Dallington Roofing requires you to prepare a cash flow forecast for the six months to June. All transactions are on a cash-only basis. The following figures are forecast for each month: sales £7,000, materials £1,600, wages £3,500, rent £1,000. The difference between VAT charged to customers and claimed on purchases for the quarter to December of the previous year amounted to £1,500. This will have to be paid in January. It is also forecast that the business will buy additional equipment in March for £2,000 plus VAT. The company will have £3,000 in its bank account at 31 December.

Cash flow headings

Cash flow headings may vary according to the nature of the business and the complexity of the exercise, as well as according to the range of possible inflows and outflows it is possible for a business organisation to have (see Figure 21.13).

	March	April	May	June	July	August	Total
Receipts							
Sales	5,000	5,000	5,000	5,000	5,000	5,000	30,000
VAT on sales	875	875	875	875	875	875	5,250
Total	5,875	5,875	5,875	5,875	5,875	5,875	35,250
Payments							
Equipment	1,000						1,000
Rent	500	500	500	500	500	500	3,000
Wages	2,000	2,000	2,000	2,000	2,000	2,000	12,000
Materials	2,000	2,000	2,000	2,000	2,000	2,000	12,000
VAT on payments	525	350	350	350	350	350	2,275
VAT paid to C&E				1,400			1,400
Total	6,025	4,850	4,850	6,250	4,850	4,850	31,675
Receipts – payments	(150)	1 025	1,025	(375)	1,025	1,025	3,575
Balance b/f	1,000	850	1,875	2,900	2,525	3,550	1,000
Balance c/f	850	1,875	2,900	2,525	3,550	4,575	4,575

Figure 21.12 Jane Covey: cash flow statement for the six months to August

	Jan £	Feb £	March £	April £	May £	June £
Cash inflows { **Receipts**						
Start-up capital						
Loan receipts						
Miscellaneous receipts						
Sales receipts						
VAT recoveries						
Total						
Cash outflows { **Payments**						
Assets						
Raw materials						
Expenses						
Interest payments						
Loan repayments						
VAT payments						
Receipts less payments for each column { *Total*						
Receipts – payments						
Running cash balance { *Balance b/f*						
Balance c/f						

Figure 21.13 Cash flow headings

Some of the more likely cash inflow headings are as follows:

- *Start-up capital.* This would be the capital put into the business when trading activities begin.

- *Loan receipts.* If a business receives monies from a loan it would appear as a receipt.

- *Miscellaneous receipts.* A business organisation may have a number of miscellaneous receipts which could inject finance into the cash flow forecast (for example, rent received and income from the sale of an asset).

- *Sales receipts.* Clearly the most common form of receipt; this is simply income from sales.

- *VAT recoveries* If more VAT is paid on purchases than is received on sales, then

the VAT recovered from Customs and Excise would be an inflow. (Note: This is likely to happen very often.)

Some of the more likely cash outflow headings include the following:

- *Payments for assets.* Asset purchase will be predictable through the capital budget, and the amounts used for each purchase will be deducted through the cash flow forecast.

- *Raw materials.* This is likely to be a regular outflow, which may relate to a production schedule or the volume of sales.

- *Expenses.* These might include water rates, telephone bills as well as many other running costs. They will *not* include depreciation as this is not a movement of funds.

- *Interest payments/loan repayments.* Where these appear they are regular payments for the use of capital.

- *VAT payments.* As we have seen, VAT is usually charged for three-monthly periods.

Check your understanding

1 C. Moon Ltd has £500 in the bank on 1 January. The owner, Christine Moon, anticipates that her receipts over the next six months are likely to be:

Jan	Feb	March	April	May	June
£2,300	£1,400	£5,300	£6,100	£4,700	£1,400

She has also worked out what her payments are likely to be over the next six months:

Jan	Feb	March	April	May	June
£1,400	£4,100	£5,600	£5,000	£3,100	£900

Christine Moon is concerned about whether she needs an overdraft facility and, if so, when she is likely to use it. Construct a cash flow forecast and advise her on her financial requirements.

2 Prepare the cash flow forecast of S. Huang Ltd. The business has £250 in the bank and the owner anticipates his receipts over the next six months are likely to be as follows:

Jan	Feb	March	April	May	June
£1,400	£1,600	£1,500	£1,000	£900	£700

He has also worked out his payments and expects these to be:

Jan	Feb	March	April	May	June
£1,100	£700	£900	£1,400	£1,000	£900

Prepare S. Huang Ltd's cash flow forecast for the six months.

3 Following their recent fashion revival, Andrew Nut sets up in business as a manufacturer of string vests by putting £28,500 into a business bank account on 1 January. For the first six months of the year he anticipates or budgets for the following situations:

- His forecasts for the purchase of raw materials and sales receipts for finished goods, based upon extensive market research, are as follows:

	Purchases (£)	Sales (£)
January	6,500	5,500
February	7,000	7,100
March	7,300	8,000
April	7,500	14,000
May	6,100	17,000
June	6,500	14,300

- Andrew Nut has arranged one month's credit from suppliers, so raw materials purchased in January will have to be paid for in February.
- He expects one half of sales to be for cash and the other half on credit. He anticipates two months on average to be taken by credit customers (i.e. sales made in January on credit will not be settled until March).
- Wages are expected to be £1,000 per month, paid in the same month.
- Machinery must be purchased for £15,500 on 1 January and must be paid for in the same month.
- Rent for his factory is £6,000 per annum, payable in equal instalments at the start of each month.
- Other costs (overheads) are £1,500 per month, and these are assumed to be paid in the month following that in which they are incurred.
- In April, Andrew Nut expects to receive an inheritance from his Aunt Kitty of £8,000, which he will put straight into the business bank account.

Prepare Andrew Nut's cash flow forecast for the first six months.

4 Albert Spanner sets up as a manufacturer of machine tools by putting £17,400 into the business bank account on 1 January. For the first six months of the year he anticipates or budgets for the following:

- His forecast for the purchase of raw materials and sales receipts for finished goods, based upon market research, are as follows:

	Purchases (£)	Sales (£)
January	3,200	2,000
February	3,350	4,000
March	4,185	6,200
April	5,500	7,000
May	5,700	8,200
June	5,900	8,400

- Albert Spanner has arranged two months' credit from suppliers.
- He expects one quarter of sales to be for cash and the other three quarters to be on credit. He anticipates two months' credit on average to be taken by credit customers.
- Wages are expected to be £800 per month, paid in the same month.
- Machinery is to be purchased in January for £2,500 and in April for £3,500. On both occasions the owner anticipates making payments in the month following purchase.
- Rent for his factory is £3,000 per annum, payable in equal instalments at the start of each month.
- Other overheads are £1,000 per month, to be paid in the month following that in which they are incurred.

- In May, Albert Spanner will take out a loan for £4,000, which he intends to put straight into the business bank account.

Prepare A. Spanner's cash-flow forecast for the first six months of the year.

5 Anna Djurkovic sets up a business on 1 January by putting £1,000 capital into the business bank account. (Assume a nil bank balance on 1 January.) Her projected income and expenditures are as follows:

Receipts

- From clients: January £3,000, February £3,400, March £3,300, April £3,500, May £3,300, June £3,800.
- Loan in February: £8,000.

Payments

- Purchase of motor car March £7,000.
- Salary £1,000 per month.
- Raw materials £1,200 per month paid in the month following.
- Loan repayment from February £250 per month.
- Loan interest £15 per month.
- Electricity £50 payable in March and June.
- Telephone £80 payable in May.
- Water rates £300 payable in June.
- Vehicle expenses £50 per month payable from the month in which the car is purchased.
- Post £90 per month.
- Rent £1,000 per annum payable quarterly.

Draw up the cash flow forecast for the first six months.

6 Robin Chilton sets up in business as a joiner on 1 January. His transactions are on a cash-only basis. He forecasts the amount his business charges for work completed will be £8,000 per month. VAT is to be charged on sales and is paid for raw materials and equipment only at the current rate. He expects to pay £10,000 for equipment in January and £3,500 for raw materials each month. Expenses include rent £100 each month, water rates £50 every 3 months, wages £2,500 per month, VAT should be paid in April. Robin had £1,350 in his bank account on 1 January. Prepare his cash flow forecast.

Subsidiary budgets and the master budget

Subsidiary budgets include all parts of a business organisations. When put together they are used to produce the master budget, which includes the profit and loss account, balance sheet and cash budget, all of which help to map the future of a business organisation for the next accounting period.

Example

Randle & Hopkins manufacture and sell one design of filing cabinet. It is the start of 2002 and the company wishes to budget for the coming year.

You have been given the following information from which to draw up a budget:

- The company anticipates selling 8,800 cabinets at a price of £50.

- Each cabinet requires 10 m^2 of materials costing £0.75 per m^2 and 3 hours of direct labour at £4 per hour.

- Other factory costs include variable indirect labour of £0.50 per unit and expenses (including power and paint) at £1.00 per unit. Fixed overheads comprise £40,000 and depreciation on plant is calculated at 10% of cost.

- Halfway through 2002, the partners intend to purchase additional plant at a cost of £20,000.

- Stock levels at the end of 2001 were 300 finished cabinets and 7,000 m^2 of raw materials.

- Stock levels at the end of 2002 are forecast to be 500 finished cabinets and 5,000 m^2 of raw materials. Finished goods stock is valued to include the cost of direct labour and materials and factory overheads.

- Each cabinet incurs distribution costs of £2 and salesperson's commission of £3. Selling and distribution fixed costs are forecast at £40,000.

- Administration costs are forecast at £54,000 for salaries, £8,000 for stationery and telephone, and £20,000 for other expenses.

- Trade debtors are currently historically low, so Randle suggests it might be prudent to assume they will increase by £10,000 over the coming year.

- Trade creditors are forecast to end the year at one month's worth of raw materials purchases. Unless otherwise stated, all other transactions are on a cash basis.

- The balance sheet for 2001 is as follows:

The balance sheet of Randle & Hopkins as at 31 December 2001

	Cost £	Depreciation £	Net £
Fixed assets			
Plant	100,000	50,000	50,000
Current assets			
Raw materials stock		5,250	
Finished goods stock		7,380	
Debtors		65,000	
		77,630	
Less: **Current liabilities**			
Creditors	12,000		
Bank	10,000	22,000	
Working capital			55,630
Net assets			105,630
Financed by:			
Capital			95,000
Net profit			10,630
			105,630

You are required to prepare the following budget statements for 2002:

1 Sales budget
2 Production budget
3 Raw materials usage budget
4 Raw materials purchases budget
5 Direct labour budget
6 Factory overhead budget
7 Selling and distribution budget
8 Administration budget
9 Debtors budget
10 Creditors budget
11 Cash budget
12 Budget profit and loss account
13 Budgeted balance sheet.

1 *Sales budget*

Forecast number of units	8,800
Selling price (£)	50
Sales turnover (£)	440,000

2 Production and finished goods budget

Stocks of finished goods are budgeted to increase by 200 units. Production therefore has to be in excess of sales:

	Units
Forecast sales units	8,800
Add: Required closing stock to start the next year	500
	9,300
Less: Opening stock from this year	300
Production required	9,000

3 Raw materials usage budget

	m^2
Forecast production units	9,000
Material per unit	× 10
Total	90,000
Price per m^2	£0.75
Total value	£67,500

4 Raw materials purchases budget

Stocks of raw materials are budgeted to fall over the coming year, so purchases will be less than production requirements. We know the opening and closing balances and the production requirements, so by deduction we can arrive at purchases:

	m^2	£
Opening stock	7,000	5,250
Add: Purchases at 75p	88,000	66,000
Less: Production usage	90,000	67,500
Closing stock	5,000	3,750

5 Direct labour budget

Forecast production units	9,000	
Direct labour hours per cabinet	3	
Total direct hours	27,000	
Wage rate per hour	£4	
Total wages	£108,000	

6 Factory overhead budget

For factory overheads we need to identify expenses that will vary with the level of business activity and those that are fixed costs:

Variable overhead per unit	£
Labour	0.50
Expenses – power and paint	1.00
Total variable overhead per unit	1.50
Forecast production units	9,000
Total variable overhead	13,500

Fixed overhead	
Depreciation	11,000
Other	40,000
Total fixed overhead	51,000
Total factory overhead	64,500

7 Selling and distribution budget

As with the production overhead budget, we have to identify both fixed and variable elements of the various indirect expenses charged to the profit and loss account:

	£
Variable costs	2
Distribution per cabinet	3
Commission per cabinet	5
Total variable costs for 8,800 cabinets	44,000
Total fixed costs	40,000
Total selling and distribution costs	84,000

8 Administration budget

	£
Salaries	54,000
Stationery and telephone	8,000
Other	20,000
	82,000

9 *Debtors budget*

Debtors are forecast to increase over the year, so we know the amounts received from customers will be less than the level of sales included in the profit and loss account:

	£
Opening debtors balance	65,000
Sales	440,000
Cash received (balancing figures)	430,000
Closing debtors balance	75,000

10 *Creditors budget*

As with debtors, if we know the level of creditors at the beginning and end of the year, together with the purchase figure, we can calculate the amount to be paid to suppliers in the year:

	£
Opening creditors balance	12,000
Purchases	66,000
Cash payments (balancing figure)	72,500
Closing creditors balance (£66,000/12)	5,500

11 *Cash flow forecast/cash budget*

In the subsidiary budgets we have identified all the cash to be received and paid out, so we are in a position to prepare the cash budget:

Randle & Hopkins cash budget for the year ended 31 December 2002

	£
Receipts	
Sales	430,000
Payments	
Raw material suppliers	72,500
Direct labour	108,000
Factory overhead	53,500
Selling and distribution	84,000
Administration	82,000
New machinery	20,000
Total payments	420,000
Receipts – payments	10,000
Opening cash balance	–10,000
Closing cash balance	0

Remember that when preparing cash flow statements we are interested only in items that relate to actual cash transactions. The factory overhead budget included a depreciation charge of £11,000, which is not a cash flow item so should be excluded from the cash flow forecast (£64,000 – £11,000 = £53,000). The cash flow forecast shows the bank overdraft has been paid off by the end of 2002.

12 *Budget profit and loss account and balance sheet*

The budgeted trading and profit and loss account of Randle & Hopkins for the year ended 31 December 2002

	Units	£	£
Sales	8,800		440,000
Opening stock	300	7,380	
Raw material usage	9,000	67,500	
Direct wages		108,000	
Factory overheads		64,500	
	9,300		247,380
Closing stock at £26.60 per unit (£247,380/9,300)	500	13,300	
Cost of sales	8,800		234,080
Gross profit			205,920
Less: expenses			
Selling and distribution		84,000	
Administration		82,000	
			166,000
Net profit			39,920

The budgeted balance sheet of Randle & Hopkins as at 31 December 2002

	£ Cost	£ Depreciation	£ Net
Fixed assets			
Plant	120,000	61,000	59,000
Current assets			
Stocks			
Raw materials		3,750	
Finished goods		13,300	
Debtors		75,000	
Bank		–	
		92,050	
Less: **Current liabilities**			
Creditors		5,500	
Working capital			86,550
Net assets			145,550
Financed by:			
Capital			105,630
Net profit			39,920
			145,550

Check your understanding

The Premier Christmas Pudding Co. require you to prepare their budget statements for the seven months to January 2002. You have been given the following information:

- The sales forecast for 1 kg puddings is as follows:

July	Aug	Sept	Oct	Nov	Dec	Total
100	100	500	1,300	10,000	20,000	32,000

- No sales of puddings have been made in the previous six months.
- Each 1 kg pudding sells for £2.50.
- Customers are mainly retailers and wholesalers who take one month to pay for puddings received.
- It is company policy to hold a minimum stock of puddings each month that is equivalent to the next month's forecast sales. After December, sales are not forecast until July of the next year. The requisite minimum stock would be held at the end of June, valued at £1.20 per pudding.
- Sufficient dry fruits are held in stock to cover the next month's forecast production. Other ingredients are purchased in the month of use.
- All suppliers are paid on delivery.
- Production capacity is limited to 10,000 kg per month.
- Direct labour is employed on a piece-work rate of £0.20 per kg of pudding.
- Costs for a 100 kg batch are as follows:

	kg	£
Dried fruit	50	60
Other	50	30
Packaging	10	
Distribution	20	

- The whole period's packaging materials will be received from the printers at the beginning of July. The packaging is of a special design to celebrate the firm's 50th anniversary. In case sales exceed forecast, sufficient packaging for 35,000 puddings has been ordered. Excess packaging is to be disposed of in December.
- Administration overhead is fixed at £3,000 per month and is payable up to the end of January 2002.
- The bank balance at the end of June 2001 is forecast to be £15,930.
- No losses are assumed in the production process.

For each of the seven months up to 31 January 2002, prepare:

1 The sales budget
2 The finished stock and production budget
3 The raw materials stock and purchases budget (separate for mixed fruit, packaging and other)
4 The direct labour budget
5 The cash budget
6 The forecast trading and profit and loss account.

Budgets and control

A key feature of the budgeting process is the feedback it provides for individuals and groups throughout an organisation. Feedback should reflect the information needs of each level of the organisation, with each level of reporting being inter-related with levels above and below. For example, a budget holder will wish to be informed of his or her own performance as well as that of the budget holders for whom he or she is responsible.

Variance analysis

Earlier in this chapter we looked at the construction of budgets related to functional aspects of an organisation for the control and monitoring of performance. The key benefit of the budgeting process is to analyse how closely actual performance relates to budgeted performance. Wherever actual differs from budgeted performance a **variance** takes place. The process of analysing the difference between actual performance and budgeted performance is called **variance analysis**.

Variances are recorded as being either **adverse (A)** or **favourable (F)**, depending upon whether actual expenditure is more or less than budget. For example, if actual expenditure is *less* than budgeted expenditure, the variance would be favourable. On the other hand, if actual expenditure is *more* than budgeted expenditure, the variance is adverse.

Figure 21.14 shows that managers cannot be answerable for cost over-runs if they occur in areas where they have no control. For example, whereas expenditure on machine maintenance may be controlled, this is not true of depreciation, which is outside the manager's control.

Machine shop overhead report for October 2001

	Budget £	Actual £	Variance £	
Controllable				
Indirect wages	8,000	8,200	200	A
Machine maintenance	2,250	1,900	350	F
Consumable materials	500	550	50	A
Total controllable costs	10,750	10,650	100	F
Uncontrollable				
Depreciation	5,700	6,000	300	A
Property cost apportionment	8,500	9,000	500	A
Total uncontrollable costs	14,200	15,000	800	A
Total cost centre overhead	24,950	25,650	700	A

A = Adverse
F = Favourable

Figure 21.14 Controllable and uncontrollable costs

Understanding variances

Variances may arise for a number of reasons. These include:

- *Random deviations* which are uncontrollable. As we saw above, these are outside the control of individual managers.

- *An incorrectly set budget*. This may require further research and management action.

- *Failure to meet an agreed budget*. This would be because a manager has failed to meet the appropriate figures and deadlines.

Problems of the budgetary process

Budgetary and control systems vary from one organisation to another. They are found both in the private sector and the public sector, and in all sorts of organisations from the very small to the very large. Given the different aims of organisations, budgetary systems reflect the context in which they are put to use. There are, however, certain problems associated with budgeting processes that have to be recognised.

First, reliance upon budgeting and its processes is no substitute for good management. Budgeting should simply be viewed as one tool among many for managers to use. If forecasting is poor or inadequate allowances are made, the process may create unnecessary pressure upon managers to perform in a particular way. This may be stressful and cause antagonism and resentment within the organisation.

The creation of rigid financial plans that are 'cast in stone' may cause inertia in certain parts of a business and reduce its ability to adapt to change. Budgets may also not reflect the realities of the business environment and act simply as a straitjacket upon the performance of managers and decision-makers. It has also been argued that delays and time lags can make it difficult to compare budgeted and actual results.

Check your understanding

Which of the following costs could be controlled by a marketing manager? Give reasons for your answers:

- depreciation of furniture
- insurance of the building
- wages paid to staff
- advertising
- stationery
- office redecorations
- training costs.

Standard costing

Standard costing is a key method for budgetary control. Standard costing establishes predetermined estimates of costs and sales and then compares them with actual costs and sales achieved. The predetermined costs are known as *standard costs*. As we have already seen, the difference between standard and actual costs is known as a variance.

There are a number objectives of standard costing. To:

- Control costs by establishing a range of standards from which variances can be analysed.

- Assist with the setting of budgets.

- Provide a basis for measuring performance.

- Assist with the process of responsibility accounting.

- Motivate staff and managers.

- Provide a basis for evaluating and improving upon current performances.

According to Lucey in *Management Information Systems*, standard cost can be defined as:

> A *standard expressed in money. It is built up from an assessment of the value of cost elements. Its main uses are providing a basis for performance measurement, control by exception reporting, valuing stock and establishing selling prices.*

Based on this interpretation, a standard must be set at a planned cost per unit from whatever is being costed. A standard cost may include use of materials, the price or other standard upon which cost is based, the planned hours to be worked and the hourly labour rate as well as the overheads incurred.

Setting standards is the critical part of the standard costing process. Line managers are clearly involved here, assisted by work study staff, engineering specialists, accountants and many other specialists, all of whom can provide an input into the standard-setting process.

The four key elements in the standard costing process are:

1 materials

2 labour

3 overheads

4 sales price and margin.

Materials

Standards are set for the quality and the quantity of materials used for a specific volume of production and the price to be paid per unit of direct material. The amount of materials used for a product will be derived from some form of bill of materials, based upon the specifications for the assembly or provision of a product. Standard quantities should make an allowance for losses in production, returns and breakages. The purchasing department has a responsibility for material prices. Costs will be based upon expected forecast costs for the budgeted period.

Labour

It is sometimes difficult to set standard labour times, although work study and work measurements help to provide a basis upon which a standard can be developed. Labour standard costs will specify the grades of labour, the direct labour hours and the standard rate per hour. The standard rate per hour will be the quantity of work that can be achieved at standard performance over the hourly period.

Overheads

It is difficult to associate overheads with a given product in the same way as labour and materials. Instead, an *overhead absorption rate* can be used to create the standards for overheads for each cost centre. This usually involves developing a rate based upon the estimated overheads for the cost centre and the expected number of direct labour hours or machine hours needed in order for a product to be completed.

Overheads are analysed into *fixed* and *variable* rates:

- Standard variable overhead rate:

$$\frac{\text{Budgeted variable overheads for the cost centre}}{\text{Budgeted standard labour hours for the cost centre}}$$

- Standard fixed overhead rate:

$$\frac{\text{Budgeted fixed overheads for the cost centre}}{\text{Budgeted standard labour hours for the cost centre}}$$

Sales price and margin

The setting of a selling price involves a number of factors. Once a selling price has been set, this becomes the *standard selling price*. The *standard sales margin* is the difference between the standard cost and the standard selling price. Normally, where total standard cost is identified, cost-plus absorption principles are involved. These incoporate a unit fixed and variable cost, to which the margin is added to achieve the price.

The net effect of developing standard costs for materials, labour and overheads is the setting of a standard cost for each product, which may be recorded on a standard cost card (see Figure 21.15).

Part no. G459 per 100	Description Ball joint	Work study ref. B345		
Cost type/quantity	Standard price/rate	Dept 3 £	Dept 6 £	Total £
Direct materials				
2 kg P10	£10 kg		20.00	20.00
Direct labour				
Machine operation 3 hrs	£4.50 hr	13.50		13.50
Assembly 4 hrs	£3.50 hr		14.00	14.00
Overheads				
Machine hour rate	£10 hr (× 3 hrs)	30.00		30.00
Assembly rate	£9 hr (× 4 hrs)		36.00	36.00
		43.50	70.00	113.50
Standard cost summary	£			
Direct materials	20.00			
Direct labour	27.50			
Overheads	66.00			
Standard cost per 100	113.50			

Figure 21.15 A standard cost card

Case study: MBB Tools Ltd

MBB Tools Ltd recently appointed a young accountant, with a brief to set up a budgetary control system that could be used to co-ordinate activities across the business. Budgets were drawn up for all departments based upon actual results over the last five years.

Shortly after the system started, it was noted that total expenditure was considerably higher than expected. Certain departments, such as production and marketing, had expenditure higher than planned, while other departments, such as personnel and administration, had favourable variances.

On receiving the results, the chief executive threatened to dismiss the managers of the production and marketing departments for exceeding their budgeted costs. The production manager resigned and has since joined a competitor.

1 What problems arose at MBB Tools?

2 How could these problems have been avoided?

Managing working capital

In the last chapter we saw that working capital is the difference between current assets and current liabilities. Current assets are either in the form of cash or in a form that can soon lead to cash, and current liabilities will soon have to be paid for with cash. As we saw, a prudent ratio of current assets to current liabilities is considered to be 2:1, although most businesses operate with a slightly lower ratio than this. The working capital ratio will usually depend to some extent upon the type of business and the nature of its operations.

Working capital is often considered to be the portion of the capital that 'oils the wheels' of business. It provides the stocks from which the fixed assets help to produce the finished goods. It allows the salesforce to offer attractive credit and terms to customers, which creates debtors.

Organisations that do not have sufficient working capital lack the funds to buy stocks and to produce and create debtors.

The *operating cycle* expresses this connection between working capital and the movements of cash. It can measure the period of time between:

- The purchase of raw materials and the receipt of cash from debtors.

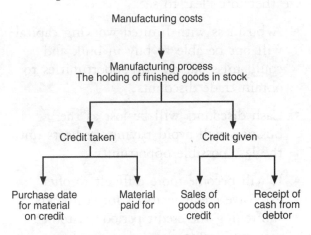

Figure 21.16 The operating cycle

- The time when cash is paid out for raw materials and the time when cash is received from sales (see Figure 21.16).

Example

A business buys raw materials on two months' credit and holds them in stock for half a month before issuing them to the production department from which they emerge as finished goods. These are held on average for one and a half months before sale. Debtors take three months to pay. The cash cycle would be:

	Months
Raw materials credit from suppliers	(2.0)
Turnover of stock of raw materials	0.5
Turnover of stock of finished goods	1.5
Debtors' payment period	3.0
Cash cycle	5.0

Not only does this cycle show the time ingredient but it also shows that income from debtors should be more than enough to cover any manufacturing costs and overheads encountered.

The dangers of insufficient working capital are therefore clear to see:

- A business with limited working capital will not be able to buy in bulk and could miss out on any opportunities to obtain trade discounts.

- Cash discounts will be lost as the business will avoid paying creditors until the last possible opportunity.

- It will become more difficult to offer extensive credit facilities for customers. By shortening the credit period, customers may well go to alternative suppliers.

- The business will be unable to innovate. Limited finances will hinder its ability to develop new products or improve production techniques.

- The business's financial reputation as a good payer may be lost.

- Creditors may well take action. As capital becomes squeezed, a business will be forced to finance its activities by overdrafts and trade credit. A point could well be reached where its future is dependent upon the actions of creditors.

- Overtrading could take place. This is where a larger volume of production or orders take place, without sufficient working capital to support it. This then leads to a complete imbalance in the working capital ratio.

As a result of problems with working capital, there are a number of options. These may include the following:

- Reducing the period between the time cash is paid out for raw materials and the time cash is received from sales. This helps to provide funds for regeneration. However, although the improved efficiency of the cash cycle may improve working capital, actions taken may be unpopular with creditors.

- Fixed assets (such as land and buildings) may not be fully utilised, or space may be used for unprofitable purposes. Space could be rented, sold or allowed to house a more profitable operation so that cash flow could be improved. A business's cash flow might be improved by selling assets and leasing them back, although this may commit an organisation to heavy leasing fees.

- A company could review its stock levels to see if these could be subject to economy measures. If the stock of raw materials is divided by the average weekly issue, the number of weeks' raw materials held in stock can be calculated. The problem with this is the business might then lose out on trade discounts or have problems obtaining supplies.

- Many businesses employ a credit controller to manage cash flow and control the debtors. A credit controller will vet new customers and set them a credit limit, ensure that credit limits are not exceeded and encourage debtors to pay on time. Credit controllers are often caught in a conflict with sales staff, who wish to offer attractive credit terms, and the accounts department, who want debtors to pay quickly and so increase their working capital.

- As we have seen, the use of cash budgets can be an important control mechanism that can be used to predict the effects of future transactions on the cash balance of a company. Cash flow forecasting or cash budgeting can help an organisation to take actions to ensure cash is available when required.

- A number of short-term solutions are available to increase working capital. Companies might extend their overdraft or bring in a factoring company to buy some of their debtors and so provide them with instant finance. It might be possible to delay the payment of bills, although this obviously displeases creditors.

When a business can no longer pay its debts it may go into *liquidation*. This may be ordered by a court, usually on behalf of a creditor. This may then be followed by *receivership*, where independent accountants supervise the sale of the different parts of the business. But, sometimes, while struggling to survive and meet the demands of creditors, a *white knight* appears on the scene to launch a rescue bid and save the business.

Unit 5 Assessment

This unit is assessed through an external assessment. The grade on that assessment will be your grade for the unit.

In your external assessment you will be expected to apply your knowledge and understanding of the unit to answer questions on specific business situations. The questions may cover the following:

- The need to keep accurate records.
- Stakeholders' interests in financial information.
- Identification and completion of business documents.
- Financial documents and financial information flows.
- Differences between assets, liabilities, expenses and revenues.
- Calculation and identification of appropriate accounting ratios.
- Cash flow and budgeting.

To achieve a Grade E you must show you can:

- Identify why businesses need to keep accurate financial records.
- Identify different stakeholders and explain their interests in gaining financial information about businesses.
- Recognise and complete simple business documents.
- Identify the links between financial documents and how financial information flows through the accounting system.
- Distinguish between assets, liabilities, expenses and revenues.
- Identify appropriate financial information and use it to calculate performance, solvency and profitability ratios.
- Identify elements of cash flow and budgeting.

To achieve a Grade C you must also show you can:

- Explain the consequences of inaccurate record-keeping.
- Explain why different groups of stakeholders may interpret data about the financial performance of a business in different ways.
- Interpret simple business documents and explain the importance of these documents to stakeholders.
- Explain the links between financial documents and how financial information flows through the accounting system.
- Create final accounts from given data.
- Explain how financial ratios are used by different groups of stakeholders to interpret financial data.
- Compare and evaluate ratios in different businesses over time.
- Explain how businesses manage their working capital.

To achieve a Grade A you must also show you can:

- Evaluate the consequences of inaccurate recording of financial data.
- Recognise, complete and interpret complex business documents and understand their inter-relationships.
- Evaluate the significance of the final accounts to different groups of stakeholders.
- Explain why ratios change over time and how this affects different groups of stakeholders.
- Draw conclusions about the financial performance of the business based on your use and understanding of a range of financial data.
- Justify changes to business practices to achieve required cash flow and budget requirements.

Opportunities to develop key skills

As a natural part of carrying out this unit and doing the work set out in the text and through your assessments you will be developing key skills. Here's how:

Application of number, Level 3

When you are:

You should be able to develop the following key skills evidence:

- Extracting information from balance sheets and profit and loss accounts

N3.1 Plan and interpret information from two different types of sources, including a large data set.

- Completing different ratios and financial documents, calculating revenue and profits and checking calculations and correcting errors

N3.2 Carry out multi-stage calculations to do with:
a amounts and sizes
b scales and proportion
c handling statistics
d rearranging and using formulae.

You should work with a large data set on at least one occasion.

N3.3 Interpret results of your calculations, present findings and justify your methods. You must use at least one graph, one chart and one diagram.

Communication, Level 3

When you are:

You should be able to develop the following key skills evidence:

- Discussing the use of financial information and the performance of a business in a group

C3.1a Contribute to a group discussion about a complex subject.

- Identifying the limitations of the financial data in an annual report and using financial commentaries in newspapers

C3.2 Read and synthesise information from two extended documents about a complex subject. One document should include at least one image to illustrate complex points.

Information Technology Level 3

When you are:

You should be able to develop the following key skills evidence:

- Identifying appropriate financial information

IT3.1 Plan and use different sources to search for, and select, information required for two different purposes.

- Creating or completing accounts using a computer spreadsheet or other financial software. You may enter numbers, use

IT3.2 Explore, develop and exchange information and derive new information to meet two different purposes.

formulae, and
generate charts and
graphs. These skills
are particularly
useful for business
planning in Unit 6

Problem solving, Level 3

When you are:

You should be able to develop the following key skills evidence:

- Tackling an accounting problem such as interpretation of accounts of a business

PS3.1 Recognise, explore and describe the problem, and agree the standards for its solution.

- Deciding on the financial position of a given company

PS3.2 Generate and compare at least two options which could be used to solve the problem, and justify the option for taking it forward.

Central to the work of any business, large or small, existing or newly established, is its business plan. Without an effective plan there is no way of judging whether or not the business is likely to succeed in meeting its objectives. Anyone who tries to get start-up funds from a bank for his or her business without a plan will be quickly disappointed because a clear plan is the most effective way of seeing whether or not the owner or directors can translate their objectives into actions. Business planning is part of developing entrepreneurial skills, and can provide you with a firm basis for bringing your creative idea into a reality.

In this unit you will produce a business plan for an enterprise you are establishing. You will find out about the market for your product or service and produce a marketing plan in line with your findings. This will involve you predicting the potential demand for your product or service by understanding and analysing the market within which your business will operate. You will consider the production of your product or service and relate this to the financial and marketing elements of the overall business plan. You will take account of the resource requirements of producing and marketing your product or service and build your findings into your plan as a whole. You will also investigate financial aspects of your business and prepare a financial plan for your product or service. This will help you to understand the importance of financial management in the effective planning of an organisation. Look out for the 'In your business plan' boxes which are to be found throughout this unit: they pose questions which will help you prepare your own business plan.

This unit builds on knowledge and understanding you have developed in other compulsory units. This unit is linked to Unit 7 Marketing and promotional strategies (Advanced), Unit 8 Marketing research (Advanced) and Unit 17 Management and enterprise (Advanced).

This unit is assessed through your portfolio work. The grade on that assessment will be your grade for the unit.

Chapter 22 Market analysis and marketing planning

To make informed judgements about the likely sales levels of your product or service you will need to identify and analyse carefully the market it will be sold in. To do this you will need to understand the following:

- the use of primary data in market research
- the use of secondary data in market research
- the factors affecting demand for your product or service
- methods of identifying and analysing competition.

Your marketing plan should build on the findings of your market analysis. You must be able to identify your target consumers and demonstrate why they will be prepared to purchase your product or service. You should also be able to identify potential competitors and demonstrate why consumers may purchase your product in preference to those marketed by competitors.

Based on your market analysis, your marketing plan should describe and explain the following:

- your choice of product or service and its distinctive features
- the price(s) of your product or service
- the methods you will use to promote your product or service
- how your product or service will be distributed to consumers.

No business organisation will be able to sell anything unless there is someone or an organisation out there willing to buy what it is offering. Market research and analysis, therefore, provide the basis upon which a marketing plan can be developed. For example, market research will constantly be seeking to find out 'is there anyone out there wanting to buy the goods or services on offer?' A first task always, therefore, is for organisations to look at their market and constantly monitor whether there is enough demand to generate the business they require.

For many organisations, making decisions and building plans on the basis of marketing analysis involves matching their intentions to the realities of the business environment. All organisations have to make decisions about whether to go ahead with their plan or not. There are three main factors involved in this:

1 *Suitability* is concerned with whether plans or solutions fit the situation. For example, it would be unlikely to be suitable for an organisation to aim for expansion in a period of contracting markets. It would be unsuitable for a relatively small firm producing a fairly homogeneous product to try to undercut the prices of a large rival enjoying extensive economies of scale.

2 *Acceptability* is concerned with whether a plan will be acceptable to the organisation and to those with a significant interest in it (the stakeholders). For example, is the level of risk acceptable, and are shareholders and other stakeholders prepared to agree to

the plans? They may have reservations based on what they consider to be risky, ethical, fair or reasonable.

3 *Feasibility* is concerned with whether plans can work in practice and, primarily, whether the organisation has adequate resources to carry our particular plans. For example, are funds available, will the organisation be able to sustain the required level of output, will the organisation be able to deal with the level of competition it generates and will it be able to meet the required market share?

Jane Brown's letter (see below) to her bank has failed to answer a number of questions, such as the following:

- *Why will people buy her product?* Some market research would have answered this crucial question. She might have found, for example, most of her potential customers know very little about how PCs work. It might also have found out about the nature and type of software problems people encounter. Market research would have indicated the benefits different groups of consumers were looking for. This would have put Jane in a better position to provide these benefits.

- *Who will buy her product?* Market research would have indicated the main groups wanting her product. She might then have been able to target benefits at specific groups.

Case study: Personal computer repairs

Jane Brown is seeking financial support from her bank to finance a PC repair service. She also wants to be able to provide simple solutions to software problems her customers might encounter. She has provided her bank with a short letter:

> I have decided to move into repairing PCs and helping people with software problems because I have always been interested in problem-solving. I have built PCs in the past and have helped friends repair their machines. Although I cannot solve all types of problems, people have always been happy with my efforts and generally satisfied with my work. I have decided to charge £15 per hour for my labour, and will also charge for parts and petrol. I think there is a huge demand out there for people like myself who can provide this kind of service. With a bit of luck I will take the market by storm and be employing several other people. This business idea is a winner. I just know I am going to succeed. I expect the market to grow rapidly as more and more people own PCs and want a local business to service and repair their machines.

It would appear Jane has not produced either a business plan or a marketing plan. Staff at the bank are impressed with her ideas, but they want more.

1 What sort of information should Jane have supplied to the bank?

2 How might she have obtained this data?

3 What questions should she be seeking answers to, and what should she be spelling out in her analysis?

- *How much will her customers buy?* Jane needs to know how often her customers require her services. Finding out about how often PCs need to be repaired would give her a clear idea of the quantity of business she could expect. This information would have been vital in planning targets and in seeking financial support for her business.

- *Who are her competitors?* Research into the competition would have enabled Jane to find out what benefits they were offering and whether she would have been able to compete with them. She would need to find out the strengths and weaknesses of her competitors. She could then concentrate on those benefits her customers required but which the competition was weak at supplying, and make sure she was effective in supplying the benefits in which competitors were strong.

- *What will her market share be?* The calculation of market share is important in any business plan. For example, if the total market value for PC repairs in a small town was £100,000 a year, and Jane expected to take 5% of this, she would have a turnover of only £5,000. However, if she expected to take 50%, she would have a turnover of £50,000.

- *When will her customers buy?* Jane needs to identify the peak periods of the year (i.e. when customers would be using PCs most). For example, there might be a lull during summer months. She can then tailor her business activities to meet customer requirements.

- *What price will consumers be willing to pay?* Market research might indicate that £15 per hour is too high a price. It will also indicate the quantities that can be sold at different prices. Jane can then work out ways of maximising revenues.

- *Is the market growing or contracting?* Jane would need to provide hard evidence that people are keeping PCs as they get older rather than simply replacing them. Perhaps newer models will be more reliable and require fewer repairs. She also needs to find out how many people take out extended warranties when they buy their PCs. She might be able to look at published sources of consumer trends. If she can show her market is growing by 10% a year, she can start to quantify her likely sales in future years.

The case of Jane Brown shows the importance of basing a marketing plan upon careful research.

Check your understanding

Jill runs a business supplying sandwiches to business premises. In 2001 she calculated the value of the delivered sandwich market in her home town was worth £50,000. She expected to be able to win 40% of this market. The market is expected to grow at 10% a year. Calculate Jill's sales revenue for 2002.

Vikram is a freelance graphics artist producing business stationery and posters. The market in which he operates is currently worth £400,000. Vikram estimates the market will increase in value by £50,000 next year. However, economic forecasts suggest the value of the market is likely to fall by between 10% and 20% next year. Vikram is likely to win 10% of the total market. He is seeking a bank loan but because of recent experience the bank is taking a pessimistic view. What value would the bank place on Vikram's likely sales next year?

Market analysis

> A market exists when buyers and sellers come into contact.

In some markets the buyer and the seller may meet face to face. In others, they may rarely meet and simply contact each other using some form of external business communications, such as letter, phone or fax.

Discussion point	Given the developing electronic marketplace in which we now live, how is this likely to change the nature of 'relationships' between sellers and buyers of goods and services?

Organisations tend to be classified according to the goods or services they supply. The markets for these goods or services are known either as *consumer* markets or *organisational* markets (see Figure 22.1).

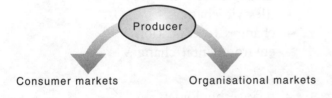

Figure 22.1 Types of markets

Consumer markets are made up of individuals who purchase items for personal or domestic consumption. Consumers typically buy from retailers and their transactions tend of be of low value. These markets include the following:

- Rapid-turnover consumer goods with a short shelf-life, manufactured for immediate consumption (e.g. foods or confectionery).

- Durable consumer goods with a much longer life that are bought less frequently, such as cars, personal computers and houses.

Industrial or *organisational* markets consist of buyers who purchase goods and services to use towards the production of other goods or services. They include the following:

- Industrial consumption goods that have a frequent purchase pattern but a limited life – such as chemicals and lubricants.

- Industrial durable goods that have a longer life – such as machinery and equipment.

Some organisations sell products in both consumer and organisational markets. For example, a motor manufacturer may produce cars for individuals to buy as well as commercial vehicles for manufacturers to use.

Every organisation needs to know how it stands in the marketplace in relation to its customers. It is important for marketers within an organisation to ask the following questions:

- *Who are the customers?* In doing so they should ask what their key characteristics are and what differentiates them from other members of the population.

- *What are their needs and wants?* They need to find out what they expect the product to do and what their special requirements and perceptions are.

- *What do they think of the organisation and its products or services?* For example, what are their attitudes towards products and how will this influence their buying behaviour?

In order to find out more about the market, an organisation has to undertake a *marketing audit*. A marketing audit is the starting point in marketing planning (see Figure 22.2).

Market audit and analysis

Plan

Implementation

Figure 22.2 The auditing process

The marketing audit helps an organisation to examine the market and evaluate how well it can meet its objectives in serving a market.

External audit

The *external* analysis of a market might involve identifying the following:

- Total market size, growth and trends (volume and value).
- Market characteristics and developments and trends.
- Products/prices of competitors.
- Physical distribution channels.
- Customers/consumers.
- Communication industry practices.
- Competition.
- Major competitors and their strategies.
- Market shares.
- Size.
- Marketing standing and reputation.
- Production capabilities.

- Distribution policies.
- Marketing methods.
- Extent of diversification.
- Human resource issues.
- International links.
- Profitability.
- Key strengths and weaknesses.

Marketers within an organisation may use the PEST framework so that they can identify all the external factors to an organisation that are in a state of change and that may have an influence upon the organisation in the coming months or years:

- *P Political/legal/fiscal*
  - privatisation
  - taxation
  - duties/levies
  - change of government

- *E Economic*
  - inflation
  - budget
  - energy prices
  - unemployment

- *S Social/cultural*
  - demographic changes
  - lifestyle changes
  - changes to education
  - environmental changes

- *T Technical*
  - new technologies
  - changing material technologies
  - new products
  - energy-saving substitutes.

Forces outside an organisation are rarely stable and many can alter quickly and dramatically. PEST analysis helps to recognise that, while some of these are clearly harmful to marketing efforts, others help to create new opportunities. By constantly scanning the marketing environment it is possible to identify new opportunities that can be built upon by changing the marketing mix. Marketing should therefore be seen as a matching process, matching the marketing mix to the business environment (see Figure 22.3).

Figure 22.3 Matching the marketing mix to customer needs

Today, nearly all organisations operate in competitive markets. Even managers of schools and hospitals have to operate within market-focused sectors and have to compete for pupils and for funds. In effect, this means all organisations need to involve themselves in marketing analysis and planning. They all need to carry out a range of different analyses, such as PEST analysis, and use a range of research data before making key decisions about the marketing plan.

Internal audit

To meet the needs of the market and serve the interests of its customers, a business needs to have the capability to achieve the objectives it sets. The marketing audit will also *internally* assess the following:

- Sales (total, by geographical location, by industrial type, by customer, by product).

- Market shares.

- Profit margins.

- Costs.

- Marketing information research.

- The variables within the marketing mix.

An internal audit seeks to evaluate the strengths and weaknesses of marketing objectives, the organisation of marketing, the personnel involved and the operating procedures involved. For example, it would analyse the following:

- *The appropriateness of marketing objectives.* For example, do they incorporate areas where markets are likely to result in profitable growth, or is the organisation still tied to producing low-profit lines because of past history?

- *The appropriateness of the structure of the marketing organisation.* Key areas of interest would be the openness of communication channels between those involved in the marketing process, the strength of the marketing focus of the organisation (is it still fully in touch with consumers?), and how effective the marketing system is in managing new product and existing product development.

- *The appropriateness of the marketing mix.* Is the organisation offering the best possible marketing mix in different marketing programmes? How well do product lines fit with the segments in which they operate? How effective is distribution? How effective is pricing policy? How well do promotions work? (see Figure 22.4).

Figure 22.4 The internal audit

Case study: Soft drinks

A soft drinks manufacturer has two main lines: orange and lemon fizzy drinks. It sells these in the UK and Europe and, over the past ten years, it has been making healthy profits and has built up reserves for expansion. In addition, it has won the confidence of financial institutions and of shareholders. Marketing intelligence has revealed the world market for soft drinks is expanding at a fast pace as real incomes rise for consumers in newly emerging markets such as China, Vietnam and Poland.

The soft drinks manufacturer has already been successful in developing marketing systems, activities and distribution channels for its products in Eastern Europe and China. Market research indicates a number of other soft drinks manufacturers are increasingly expanding and moving into new markets, and there is a threat overseas soft drinks manufacturers will encroach upon the domestic market. If the organisation moves into the global marketplace, there will be considerable resourcing implications in terms of investment in new plant and the development of the supply chain.

The strategic choice involves a number of options:

- Do nothing.
- Concentrate resources on protecting the domestic market.
- Continue to develop distribution outlets in new markets.
- Develop production capacity in new markets by setting up joint ventures.

1 Working in groups, decide what further information you would require before making any of these decisions.

2 What are the dangers involved in rushing into a decision?

3 If the information emphasised a range of profitable business opportunities, what decision would you opt for?

Using primary and secondary data

As we saw in Chapter 11, any information commissioned by an organisation for its own use is called *primary* data. As it is obtained by research conducted by or on behalf of an organisation, such data is specific to its needs. As well as using primary data, organisations may use *secondary* data. Secondary data may be obtained from internal sources, such as accounting records, stock records or sales records, and this is often described as 'desk research', or it may come from other published sources not specifically researched for them (e.g. from government publications, trade associations, the media and directories).

The value of this research for market analysis and planning has to be defined in relation to its objectives. For example, how important and potentially valuable is the data generated through the research process? How should the data be handled and then used? What decisions will be influenced by such data?

All the information collected through both the primary and secondary market research process needs to be co-ordinated and managed so that it is used properly. In order to do this, marketers need to set up some form of *marketing information system*.

A well-constructed marketing information system should, ideally, be able to identify sales levels, together with stock and output figures, and then analyse these together with market share details, trend data and information on profitability. For example, the system should regularly generate:

- *Internal* weekly or monthly operating data, such as sales trends, price information, production targets and budgets.

- *External* data, such as sales performances in the market, information on consumer behaviour, lifestyles and attitudes, and consumer needs for products.

The marketing information system helps an organisation to develop in response to its research objectives, and provides information in a usable form for a range of management purposes. This *database* of knowledge and supporting statistical analysis will then help managers to ensure they supply goods and services effectively for their customers.

Check your understanding

Robin Lee is a project manager for a large international company responsible for introducing and developing his company's market for body spray in various countries around the world. Competition within the UK market is fierce and dominated by four large companies with major brands.

At the end of 1999, the penetration within the UK market of users per week aged between 11 and 74 years was 23.2%. Of these users, 17.0% were men and 29.4% women. The projected population for the UK is set to rise from 59,616 million in 2001 to 60,929 million in 2011 and 62,244 million in 2021.

Use of body spray has risen annually over the past five years. Robin has been asked by his American company to produce a report that comments upon whether there is potential for a new company to introduce body spray within the UK.

Other than the information above, what else might Robin require to help him to compile his market research report? For example, what further information might he require about brands, competitors, market shares, products, etc.? How might he want to present this information?

As his company does not currently market any products within the UK, what barriers or problems might he expect if his company makes a decision to enter the UK market?

In your business plan:

Will you use primary and secondary research to find out whether there is a market for your product?

Once statistical market research data has been obtained from all sources, it needs to be broken down and presented in such a way that its significance can be easily appreciated. Information can be displayed as text, tables, charts and graphs.

Tables

A table is just a matrix of rows and columns defining the relationships between variables; it summarises information into a form that is clear and easy to read. With suitable computer software, a table can be shown on a screen in the form of a *spreadsheet* – a grid of columns across the screen and rows going down the screen (see Figure 22.5). It can also be manipulated through a series of calculations to show what would happen if alterations were made to any of the figures. As a result, one of the great benefits of spreadsheets is that they allow 'what if' questions to be asked and answered quickly.

OUTPUT	FIXED COSTS	VARIABLE COSTS	TOTAL COSTS	AVERAGE COSTS
10	300	20	320	32
20	300	120	420	21
30	300	200	500	16.6666667
40	300	260	560	14
50	300	300	600	12
60	300	320	620	10.3333333
70	300	390	690	9.85714286
80	300	460	760	9.5
90	300	620	920	10.2222222

Figure 22.5 A spreadsheet

Check your understanding

Make up a spreadsheet containing the sort of data that might be useful for a marketing department. Explain how your spreadsheet might be used or interpreted for making decisions.

Pictograms

Pictograms are eye-catching and enable information to be presented in a form that can be readily understood. Items represented may be supported by a key (Figure 22.6).

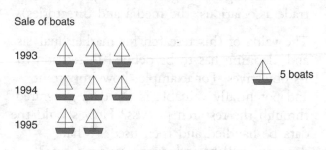

Thompson's Boat Yard

Sale of boats

1993

1994

1995

5 boats

Figure 22.6 A pictogram

Pie charts

In a pie chart, each slice of the pie represents a component's contribution to the total amount. A circle is divided up in proportion to the figures obtained and, in order to draw the segments accurately, a protractor is necessary to mark off the pieces. Alternatively, the pie chart can be developed electronically from a spreadsheet. If not, the following formula can be used to find the angle (in degrees) for each segment:

$$\text{Angle for segment A} = \frac{\text{Amount of A}}{\text{Total}} \times 360°$$

Check your understanding

A company's sales are made up from the statistics shown in Figure 22.7.

	Sales (million)
Home	15
USA	4
Australia	3
EU	8
Middle East	10
Total	40

Figure 22.7 Company sales (£ million)

Draw an accurate pie chart to present these sales figures. Label the chart.

Bar charts

In bar charts, the areas for comparison are represented by bars, which can be drawn either vertically or horizontally. The lengths of the bars indicate the relative importance of the data.

Graphs

Graphs are another way of displaying data. They show the relationship between two variables either in the form of a straight line or in the form of a curve. In particular, a graph shows how the value of one variable changes given a shift in the value of another. A graph, for example, may be constructed to show:

- sales over a period of time

- the way the total cost of production varies according to the units of output produced.

As with the pie chart, computers are an important tool for helping users to take figures from spreadsheets using programs, such as Excel, and then presenting that information in the form of a range of images (see Figure 22.9).

Although information may be presented in a variety of attractive forms, it also needs to be interpreted. Statistical analysis of the hard-won information enables forecasting to take place. Decision-making techniques applied to the data allow decisions to be taken with a greater degree of precision and probability of success. Statistics are, therefore, a tool of management that tells managers what has happened in the past, what is happening now, and thus providing a more secure base for direction in the future.

One way of analysing market research information based upon a collection of values is through the use of *central tendency* – middle values. When we talk about middle values in everyday speech we

Check your understanding

Look at the bar chart in Figure 22.8, which shows the proportion of men and women in each job category in the marketing industry. Comment upon:

- the nature of the information
- the form of presentation.

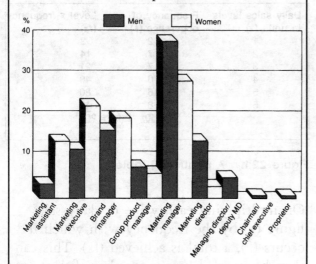

Figure 22.8 Proportion of men and women in marketing by job category

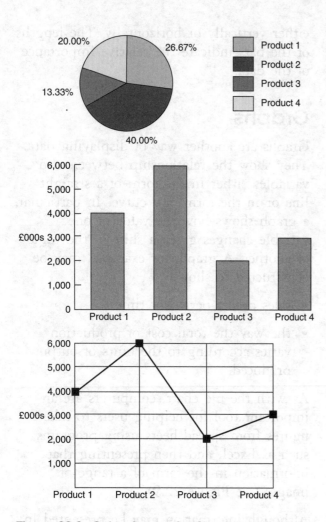

Figure 22.9 Sales figures for four products shown as a pie chart, a bar graph and a graph

normally think of an 'average'. This average is more correctly called the *arithmetic mean*. Two other measures of average or central tendency are the *median* and the *mode*.

The mean is quite simply the sum of a set of numbers divided by the number of items. For example, if sales figures (in pounds) over a six-day week were 165, 190, 185, 190, 180 and 170, the mean would be:

$$\frac{165 + 190 + 185 + 190 + 180 + 170}{6} = \frac{1080}{6}$$

$$= £180$$

Therefore we can say that:

$$\text{Arithmetic mean} = \frac{\text{Sum of observations}}{\text{Number of observations}}$$

If data (such as daily sales figures) is collected over a long period, adding up all the levels and dividing by the number of days may be time-consuming and prone to error. In these circumstances it could be useful to derive a *frequency distribution table*. For example, assume that a business's sales figures (in units) over 50 days are as shown in Figure 22.10.

5	6	2	6	5	2	6	4	6	5
5	6	4	5	3	5	6	5	6	5
6	5	3	3	2	4	3	2	3	5
4	3	5	2	1	4	2	5	1	4
5	4	4	4	5	3	5	2	4	5

Figure 22.10 Sales figures (in units) over 50 days

These can be put into a frequency table (see Figure 22.11). (In the table, the Greek letter sigma Σ stands for 'sum of'.)

Daily sales levels in units (*x*)	Frequency of occurence (*f*)	Level x frequency (*fx*)
1	2	2
2	7	14
3	7	21
4	10	40
5	16	80
6	8	48
	$\Sigma f = 50$	$E(fx) = 205$

Figure 22.11 A frequency table

On multiplying each value or daily sales figure (x) by the frequency with which it occurs (f), a total is achieved (fx). This can then be divided by the number of days to derive the arithmetic mean. The arithmetic mean is usually shown by $\bar{x}$ and the formula by which it is calculated is:

$$\bar{x} = \frac{\sum (fx)}{\sum f}$$

In our example, the arithmetic mean is 205/50, or 4.1 units per day.

The *mode* is simply the value that occurs more frequently than any other value. If sales levels over four days were 15, 12, 15 and 17, the mode would be 15 because that number had occurred more than any other value in this period. If two or more frequencies occur the same number of times, there is clearly more than one mode, and the distribution is *multimodal*. When there is only one mode the distribution is *unimodal*.

The *median* is the middle number in a distribution or array of figures. When figures are arranged into numerical order, the median is the one in the middle. For example, data ordered into the array 2, 7, 9, 12 and 15 would have the number 9 in the middle and so 9 would be the median value.

When calculating the median for a frequency distribution it is usual to say the middle value is $(n + 1)/2$ if the total frequency (n) is an odd number.

In our earlier example of daily sales figures, there was an even number of figures (50). If n is an even number, the median is taken to be halfway between the $(n/2)$th value and the $(n/2 + 1)$th value. In this example both the 25th and 26th values are 4, so the median reflects a daily sales figure of 4 units.

Check your understanding

Conduct an interview of 50 people to find out what brands of computers they use. Use the mean, median and mode to help with your analysis of the results.

Time series

Another way of analysing market research data using a measure of central tendency is by using time series. A time series is the name given to a set of figures recorded as they occur through time. The series may be plotted daily, weekly or monthly and it is usual for the horizontal axis to be used to denote the time dimension. If there is a clear trend, these historical figures can be used to predict what will happen in the near future.

Figure 22.12 is an example of a graph showing a time series. Here the sales figures vary month by month, with troughs and peaks. The movement from trough to trough and peak to peak is called a *cycle*. However, what we need to know is whether

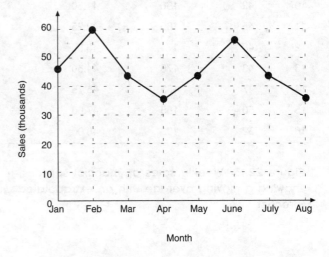

Figure 22.12 A time series showing monthly sales

the sales, while fluctuating, are steadily increasing in the longer term. Somehow, we need to decide how to distinguish the trend from the short-term fluctuations.

To separate out a trend from a cycle we can use a statistical technique known as a *moving average*. Imagine a business that sells financial services wants to keep a weekly moving average of sales in order to identify a trend. Its sales tend to peak every four weeks. The moving average smoothes out the peaks so the underlying trend can be followed. The table in Figure 22.13 shows how this is done.

Week	Sales (thousands)	Four-week moving totals	Four-week moving averages
1	25		
2	28		
3	33		
4	38	124	31.00
5	34	133	33.25
6	37	142	35.50
7	42	151	37.75
8	43	156	39.00
9	39	161	40.25
10	42	166	41.50
11	45	169	42.25
12	48	174	43.50
13	43	178	44.50
14	47	183	45.75
15	50	188	47.00
16	52	192	48.00

Figure 22.13 Weekly sales of financial services, showing a moving average with an extrapolated forecast

The moving average is calculated in three stages:

Stage 1   Calculate the four-week moving totals using the sales figures from the second column. For example:

$$25 + 28 + 33 + 38 = 124$$

The total then moves by deleting the first week and adding the following (fifth) week. The second total is:

$$28 + 33 + 38 + 34 = 133$$

Stage 2 Calculate the four-week moving averages by dividing the four-week moving totals by 4. For example, 124 divided by 4 is 31, 133 divided by 4 is 33.25, etc.

Stage 3 The four-week moving averages show the trend. If the trend line is drawn on a graph and extended to the right, this is known as a process of *extrapolation,* and it will help to provide a forecast of sales activity in the coming weeks.

Factors affecting demand for products or services

The process of supplying a good or a service for customers is not quite as simple as it seems. People or organisations do not just go to their supplier without thinking carefully about what they want, and every business environment is constantly changing. Wherever there is a choice consumers make decisions, and such decisions may be influenced by complex motives.

Economists refer to the group of factors that affect consumer behaviour as the *economic determinants of consumer demand.* These include the following:

- The real disposable incomes available to consumers to spend on goods and services. An increase in real incomes will generally increase the demand for goods and services unless a commodity is perceived as an inferior one (unbranded clothing).

- The relative price of substitute products whose purchases might be preferred or seen as better value for money.

- Population size or composition. For example, if the birth rate increases, Mothercare products could be in greater demand.

- Government influences in areas such as credit regulations and safety requirements. These could influence demand for a host of commodities.

- Tastes, fashions and habits, which constantly influence the pattern of demand for goods and services (DVDs instead of videos).

For example, consumers want to make purchases in order to satisfy their needs and wants both today and for the future. We all regularly make decisions about our purchases. Sometimes these decisions are made quickly, while in other circumstances, we may spend a great deal of time weighing up the alternatives. These alternatives can be broken into three different categories:

1 *Routine response behaviour*. This describes what happens when we frequently buy items of low value that require very little thought. For example, we might go into the newsagent to buy *The Times* every weekday morning.

2 *Limited decision-making*. Some thought might be necessary if an unfamiliar brand comes to the market. For example, if a new chocolate brand is launched in competition with a well-known brand, the consumer might try to find out more information before making a purchase.

In your business plan:
What factors will determine the demand for your product or service?

Case study: Cream teas over the web

As the use of the Internet continues to develop, many consumers are using it to buy food online. For example, many use it to purchase pizzas, sandwiches and ready-made meals. Recently cream teas have come online from The Thin End Patisserie (www.thin-end.co.uk).

Based in Cornwall, one of the traditional homes of cream teas, the site shows cakes photographed on a background resembling a green chequered tablecloth. The goodies are sent by special delivery and take a day to arrive. A cream tea consists of two homemade scones, a pot of strawberry conserve, a tub of Rodda's clotted cream and a selection of teas.

1 Identify the various influences upon the purchasing behaviour of consumers across the web.

2 Describe how each of these influences could affect the success of The Thin End Patisserie.

3 *Extensive decision-making.* Some products are durables purchased less frequently. The buyer will need to think about the benefits of different products and will require further information.

Discussion point	To what extent do the types of decisions people make depend upon their levels of income? Does your answer imply that incomes determine how people think when making decisions?

Prominent marketers often refer to the consumer's mind as a 'black box' (see Figure 22.14). In the black box, the decision-making process takes place – and the response will be a decision about a product, brand, dealer and the timing or size of the purchase.

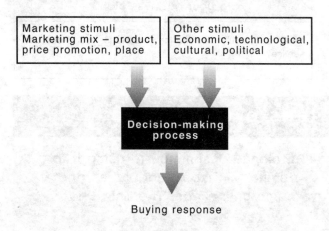

Figure 22.14 The black box

Another frequently used model of the consumer process recognises five distinct stages:

1 *Problem or opportunity recognition.* This stage starts when the consumer becomes aware there is a difference between his or her existing state of affairs and a desired state of affairs.

2 *Information search.* After recognising the problem, the consumer will gather information that will help him or her to achieve the desired state of affairs.

3 *Evaluation of alternatives.* The buyer now has to evaluate the alternatives identified from the information search.

4 *Purchase decision and act.* At the end of the research and evaluation process, the consumer will make a purchase decision and carry out the act of purchase.

5 *Post-purchase evaluation.* The act of purchase creates either satisfaction, which removes the difference between the actual and desired state of affairs, or creates a dissatisfaction which may still leave a discrepancy. When consumers do not feel they have made the correct decision, they may experience *cognitive dissonance*. This means they are worried or are guilty about the decision they have made.

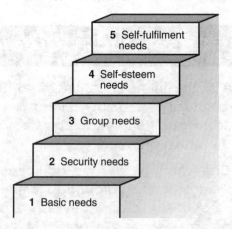

Figure 22.15 Maslow's Hierarchy of Needs

It is argued that, in order to think about what this 'desired state of affairs' might be, marketers must understand consumer needs.

It was Abraham Maslow who suggested that although it is difficult to analyse individual needs, it is possible to develop a plan that can be split into five broad categories (see Figure 22.15):

1 *Basic needs* are concerned with acquiring food, shelter and clothing.

2 *Security needs* are concerned with physical well-being and the need to provide protection, perhaps with a house in a safe trouble-free environment, with protected and reliable items within it.

3 *Group needs* centre on the desire for acceptance, the need for affiliation and purchases associated with belonging to a community.

4 *Self-esteem needs* stem from one's desire for status, for a sense of achievement and for respect for one's accomplishments. This might lead to the possession of prestigious items (living a lavish lifestyle) or self-esteem generated, for example, through making donations to charities.

5 *Self-fulfilment* is concerned with full personal development and individual creativity. To achieve this level, individuals try to ensure their individual skills and capacities are being fully utilised.

The implications of Maslow's hierarchy are easy to perceive, as different products and services are related to different needs. For example, life assurances and pensions are rooted in a desire for safety, a Mercedes is related to self-esteem needs and so on.

Discussion point	How might an understanding of Maslow's hierarchy enable a marketer to select appropriate marketing messages?

Methods of identifying and analysing competition

Once an organisation has established whom it is selling to, it is important to identify the total size of the market as well as who their competitors are. It can sometimes be difficult to find out who are either the biggest or most direct competitors.

For example, if we were to think about who the competitors of Coca-Cola would be, we would start with Pepsi Cola and then progress to Virgin Cola, supermarkets' own brands and then budget brands, such as Panda Cola. But this would not show the whole picture, as there could be other competition. For example, this may include the following:

- Other carbonated drink brands (7-Up, Irn-Bru, Lucozade and makers of lemonades, orangeades, etc.).

- Bottled water manufacturers (Perrier, Evian, Buxton Water or Highland Spring).

- Other soft drink manufacturers (Robinson's cordials, Ribena, Nesquik milk shakes, energy drinks, soda, ginger ale, tonic waters).

- Fruit juice manufacturers.

- Tea and coffee manufacturers.

- Manufacturers of other social drinks, such as beers, wines and spirits.

- Manufacturers of alco-pops.

- We might also include any other firms competing for the same customer's money. Coca-Cola is principally a young person's drink so, in this case, it might include fast-food establishments, night clubs, sporting events, CD and clothing manufacturers.

Establishing the identity of competition may not be obvious, therefore, and marketers should open their minds to possibilities. Once this has been established, firms should examine the product mixes offered by each of the leading competitors. In doing so, they should seek to outline:

- How many competitors there are.

- What types of products are produced by each firm.

- The sales of each product.

- The market share enjoyed by each.

- The quality of the products.

- New products being developed or recently launched.

- The impact on the market of new products.

- The range of brands produced by each firm.

- The degree of brand loyalty enjoyed by the competitors.

There may be many different competitor characteristics and strategies. A larger market, for example, could be divided into three distinct strategy groups:

1 *Budget brands*, offering an adequate product at a low price, such as Falcon lager and low-priced supermarket brands.

2 *Mid-price brands*, offering a good product at a reasonable cost, such as standard off-licence lagers.

3 *Premium price brands*, offering higher-quality products such as Budweiser.

Research should also seek to outline answers to the following questions:

- Are the competitors innovators – producing new ideas?

- Are they followers, waiting for other firms to come up with new ideas and then copying them?

- Do they respond swiftly and positively to moves by competitors?

- Are they working under their capacity, or using their resources efficiently?

- What are the key objectives of each competitor? Are they looking to increase their market share? Do they show a desire to dominate the market? Do they try to force out new competitors? Or are they simply ensuring they survive?

- Which suppliers do they use?

- What outlets do they use?

- How vertically integrated are the competitors?

- What degree of concentration is there within the industry?

Check your understanding

Over a three-week period, use each of the above questions to analyse the behaviour of one competitor within a market of your choice.

In your business plan:

Who are the main competitors for your good or service?

Case study: Competition between the 'majors' in petrol retailing

Oil companies today compete in an increasingly competitive market. As a result of the increase in competition there has been a steady erosion of the big three's market share.

Hypermarkets have been particularly influential in creating cut-price competition between service stations, mainly because they do not set out to make more than a token profit on their petrol retailing operations.

The costs of entry into and exit from the petrol retailing market are quite low, so there are always organisations entering the market whenever profits are being made, while at other times, organisations leave when profit margins are squeezed. However, the majors have to be there through thick and thin; they have to price accordingly, which makes the market highly competitive.

For 90% of the country, in each 10 km^2 there is on average a choice of 19 stations and eight different brands (Figure 22.16). In urban areas the choice is even greater, with 75 stations in every 10 km^2 and with 14 brands on offer (Figure 22.17).

Research shows that about one-third of motorists will always go for the cheapest price, even if it is a little out of the way. Another one-third balance price against other factors, such as facilities and convenience. The remaining third tend to rely

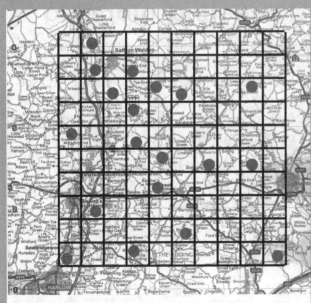

Figure 22.16 Average number of petrol stations per 10 km^2 in 90% of the country

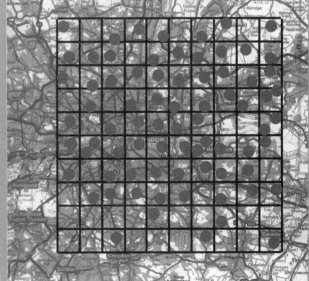

Figure 22.17 Average number of petrol stations per 10 km^2 in urban areas

exclusively on convenience and prefer sites with a full range of modern facilities, even if the petrol costs slightly more.

1 Find out who the main competitors are in the petrol retailing market.

2 Describe six ways in which they compete.

3 How can a particular company seek to gain a competitive edge? How is it possible to differentiate one product from another?

4 What factors are likely to: a) encourage; and b) discourage competition in the petrol market?

An organisation may also need to assess whether or not it should fear the opposition. Obtaining appropriate information may involve extensive research into competing businesses, examining their performance over time and looking at their strategies. This may involve studying their reports and accounts as well as other secondary sources, such as *Key Note Reports*. An assessment of competitors' strengths and weaknesses should seek to outline:

- The cost structures of each competitor.

- Levels of profits and profit margins achieved by each.

- The quality of the staff employed.

- The financial stability of each firm.

- Levels of cash held by each firm.

- The sizes of their respective customer bases.

- Pricing policies.

- The quality of sales and marketing teams.

- Levels of diversity.

- New or impending legislation that will affect the competitors.

- Whether strategic planning is taking place.

- The growth potential in the market.

- Potential threats from foreign competitors.

- The image of products and brands.

- Whether the market is expanding, static or contracting.

Marketing planning

Marketing planning is concerned with identifying objectives and then setting out how these objectives can be achieved (see Figure 22.18). Marketing objectives need to be built into the organisation's strategy and tactical thinking. It is thus concerned with:

- Establishing objectives and goals, allocating resources to meet these and setting out a clear plan of action.

- Setting out ways of evaluating performance against marketing targets.

Marketing objectives ➡ Marketing strategy and tactics

Figure 22.18 Marketing planning

- Assessing the position and performance of the organisations in the various markets in which it operates, and their strengths and weaknesses.

Check your understanding

A useful directory of more than 2,000 restaurants in London is www.londoneats.com. The site enables users to search for restaurants by area, name or type of food. Make a list of marketing objectives the owners of such a site would have.

There are many different parts to this process. Marketing planning will bring together many elements within an organisation. For example, it:

- Helps to place value upon market research by using the information obtained to understand markets and trends within markets, as well as the needs of a whole range of customers and potential customers.

- Enables an organisation to evaluate its strengths and weaknesses and provides a clear pathway for it to confront its competitors.

- Provides a mechanism for focus, through the establishment of clear objectives from which strategies can be developed.

- Enables the organisation to evaluate each element of the marketing mix in relation to such objectives.

- Provides the organisation with balance and focus for the mix.

- Translates objectives into actions for members of the organisation.

- Helps an organisation to develop competitive products and services.

- Moves the organisation forward by carefully positioning its activities so that marketing objectives can be achieved through marketing strategies.

Marketing planning is an essential ingredient for corporate strategy and provides a focus for all business activities.

Check your understanding

Using a number of examples, explain how a marketing plan could affect all parts of a business.

Planning also makes it possible for management to evaluate performance. Without evaluation there is no control. Of course, plans are unlikely to be met in every detail, but they establish guidelines against which performance can be checked and then modified.

There are many different models of marketing plans. One model is to start out by establishing objectives, then clarify the planning assumptions that are being made, collect and sort useful data, evaluate alternative courses of action, select an appropriate course of action, re-evaluate the chosen course and, finally, to modify planning in the light of the results (see Figure 22.19).

Another way of approaching planning involves the following (see also Figure 22.20):

- *Diagnosis* Where are we and why? This usually involves some form of audit of company performance, which will then be analysed.

- *Prognosis* Where are we going? This involves looking at possible future scenarios in the light of present performance and trends.

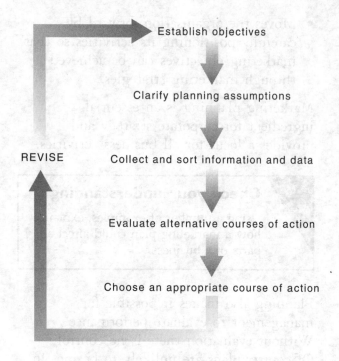

Figure 22.19 A model for planning

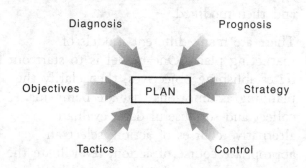

Figure 22.20 A further model for planning

- *Objectives* Where do we want to go? What is important?

- *Strategy* What is the best way of achieving our objectives?

- *Tactics* What specific actions will enable us to meet day-to-day targets?

- *Control* How far have we progressed? An organisation will need to establish performance indicators against which it can measure its success.

A more practical model might include the following:

- *Executive summary.* This would provide a synopsis of current influences, followed by a description of objectives, strategies, tactics and financial expectations.

- *Background.* This part of the plan would analyse the historic background of the market, citing changes in market activity, sales, costs and profits and technology, as well as market circumstances. There may also be changes in the regulatory environment.

- *Situation analysis.* By evaluating market, industry, environment and sales factors, it is possible to find the answers to key questions relating to customers.

- *Competitor analysis.* It is important to think about the competitors' strategies. For example, what are their strengths and weaknesses and how are these likely to change?

- *Marketing objectives.* Marketing objectives have to fit wider corporate objectives. For each marketing objective there may be a rationale as well as a time frame, direction and quantifiable ways of assessing how it is being met.

- *Marketing strategy.* This would look at how the core strategy meets the objectives through the strategic direction chosen.

- *Marketing programmes.* This would refer to the more specific ingredients of the marketing mix, such as pricing, distribution and communication.

- *Financial documents.* A plan must be supported with a means of ensuring or evaluating the financial outcomes, as well as taking into account the cost of implementing the plan. This would look at budgets allocated for each activity, as well as forecasting revenues and profit expectations.

- *Monitors and controls.* Specific information may relate to how the plan is to be managed and monitored.

- *Contingency plans.* It is important to consider what might go wrong and, if it does, what the organisation should do. Contingency plans should consider alternative strategies in case they become necessary.

Within a total marketing plan (see Figure 22.21), marketing and financial objectives will be brought together. The financial objectives are usually tied in with the strategic objectives, which may, for example, be described in terms of profit-making and growth, although there are many possible objectives depending on the vision and relative strengths of coalitions of stakeholders.

Figure 22.21 A total marketing plan

Choosing the product or service

Many organisations set out to produce products, while others set out to provide services. For example, in your town or locality, you will find young people who have set up their own enterprises producing goods such as a sandwich-making and delivery service, making pizzas, or making clothes or engineering parts, as well as ones who have concentrated on services such as hairdressing, financial services and running their own shops.

These individuals may have a range of marketing objectives for their products or services. For example, a group of young people with a mini-enterprise making gingerbread may want to:

- Produce and sell gingerbread.

- Trade under the name Simply Super Gingerbread.

- Purchase ingredients in bulk at trade prices.

- Produce gingerbread on the morning it is sold.

- Create gingerbread products that are consistently better and more attractive to customers than those sold by competitors.

- Sell gingerbread from a market stall on Saturday morning.

- Build up a supply of regular customers.

- Sell gingerbread at prices 10% below those charged by other sellers of gingerbread.

- Set production and sales targets, and monitor these targets at regular intervals.

- Review these trading and marketing objectives at regular intervals.

Products have a range of features. On the surface there are tangible benefits – things that you can touch and see. Tangible features of products include:

Check your understanding

Identify a local business within your community. Find out as much about that business as possible.

Although it is likely the owners of the business will not tell you their marketing objectives, use your investigation to guess what these objectives might be.

- shape
- colour
- size
- design
- packaging
- taste.

The intangible features may not be quite so obvious. These include the reputation of the business or the corporate brand or image.

There are also extra features to be considered, such as:

- after-sales service
- availability of spare parts
- customer care policy
- guarantees.

A product is made up of a range of distinctive features that serve to meet customer requirements. For example, a customer buying a new car may not just want a family saloon. Additional requirements could include:

- a blue door
- four doors
- a well-known name
- a long guarantee
- credit facilities
- free after-sales servicing

Case study: Flower selling

Anil and Aisha have just left school and they would like to set up in business selling flowers from a market stall. They will be able to hire a small stall for £20 a day and a larger stall for £40 a day. The market is open each day from Monday to Saturday from 9 am to 5 pm except for Thursday, when there is half-day closing.

Anil and Aisha will be able to purchase stocks of flowers and plants from a local grower. Prices vary according to the season. However, Anil and Aisha have found out that, as a 'rule of thumb', they can mark up flowers by 300% in winter and 200% in summer.

They have decided to carry out some market research before finally deciding to set up in business.

1 How can Anil and Aisha research their market?

2 What questions should they ask in their market research?

3 Whom should they ask?

4 How can they obtain accurate predictions of what the future demand for their product is likely to be?

- low petrol consumption

- a proven safety record.

Check your understanding

Choose a product or service. Identify the tangible and intangible benefits and features of this product or service. Explain how such features help to distinguish it from its competitors.

Another interpretation of a product and the various elements that emphasise its distinctive features is provided by Kotler and Armstrong. They perceive three different levels of a product that can be used for planning purposes (see Figure 22.22).

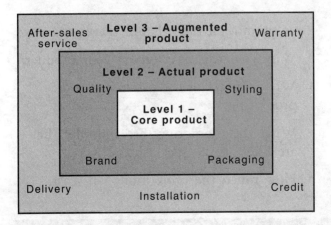

Figure 22.22 Product levels

- *Level 1 The core product.* This consists of benefits customers are provided with when they purchase and use a good or service. For example, the core benefit of purchasing a car would relate to how it works.

- *Level 2 The actual product.* This consists of five elements, including the brand, quality, styling, features and packaging.

- *Level 3 The augmented product.* A number of support issues, which are important to the customer, help to take the product and the benefits it offers one stage further. For example, for a car, this may be after-sales service and extended warranty conditions, as well as the provision of credit and free delivery.

In your business plan:

What product or service will you provide? What will be its distinctive features?

The price of the product or service

Setting the right price is one of the most critical decisions to be taken in the marketing mix. Various pricing strategies were discussed in Chapter 13. The importance of price within the marketing mix varies from one market to another and between different segments in the same market. Certain products are designed to suit a particular price segment and there are a host of influences upon the pricing decision. Some of these may be internal, while others will be external to the organisation.

Internal influences on price may include the following:

- The objectives of the organisation.

- The pattern of costs.

- Existing prices of similar and other products produced by the company.

- Existing ideas about price-setting in the organisation.

- The organisation's knowledge of the market.

- Pressures or feedback from salespeople and other members of the organisation.

- Levels of research and development and the pace of new product development.

External influences on price may include the following:

- The strength and behaviour of competitors.

- The attitudes and influences of other groups involved in the chain of production and distribution (e.g. what size margin do distributors want, and how much power do they have?).

- Pressures from suppliers of raw materials and components used in the product.

- Elasticity of demand for the product.

- Customer motivations.

- Existing and anticipated government policies.

- General conditions in different markets.

In your business plan:
What price will you charge? How did you come up with that figure?

Promoting a product or service

When you start a new business you need to tell customers of your existence through advertising and promotion. You then need to get people to try out your product, possibly by giving away free samples or by sending out special offers or invitations to view. The next step will be to persuade people to buy, and you want customers to come back for more.

Discussion point	To what extent could it be argued that advertising reduces the ability of consumers to make rational and measured decisions about their purchases?

Your promotion plan should therefore show:

- Why you need to promote your product.

- What aspects of the product you are promoting.

- What the promotions are and why they are likely to be successful.

- How much the promotions will cost.

Case study: Cricket 2000

EA Sports recently launched Cricket 2000 for the PlayStation with a pricing point of £29.99. The exciting graphics and match simulation recreate the excitement of cricket, with commentary provided by Richie Benaud and David Gower.

In order to bat, the user picks the direction he or she wants to hit the ball after taking note of the bowler placement target, waits for the power meter to reach the optimum target and then attempts to belt the ball. The bowling mechanism allows for a high degree of intuitive flexibility.

1 Describe the product features of these types of computer games.

2 What factors will have influenced setting the price at £29.99?

- How much profit the promotions will generate.

- Ways of evaluating the effectiveness of promotions.

There are many different ways of reaching different audiences, with technology opening up new forms of advertising such as that on the Internet. Advertising may take place through the following:

- *Printed materials.* These make up by far the largest group of media in the UK and include all newspapers and magazines, both national and local, as well as the trade press, periodicals and professional journals.

- *Broadcast media.* These include both publicly owned and commercial television

and radio. They also include electronic forms of media, such as the Internet.

- *Outdoor media.* Fixed posters, hoardings, advertising on buses, taxis, underground trains and other forms of transport provide opportunities for advertisers to generate specific messages.

- *Direct mail.* This is personally addressed advertising sent through the post.

- *Cinema.* There has been a resurgence in cinema attendance. Certain films attract narrowly defined types of audience.

In your business plan:
How will you promote your product or service?

Case study: Targeting working women

The modern woman can be a household's main income holder, managing the family budget, buying pension plans or making family decisions. She might be a housewife, a working mum, a single parent, a successful businesswomen or a senior executive. Given all these, and many more, roles, advertisers have to consider how to communicate their message to reach the intended recipient, as well as how to ensure their message makes the right impact.

No advertiser would want to reach every woman. The changing dynamics of the female population have meant advertisers have to choose their media opportunities carefully. Traditional indicators, such as demographic trends, social class and age, have become less important. Frequently, in order to platform their message, advertisers try to target women through magazines.

The range of magazines on offer for women is vast. The weekly *Take A Break* has a circulation of more than one million. The range of magazines varies from specialist bi-monthlies, such as *Weight Watchers* and *Wedding & Home*, to upmarket magazines, such as *Vogue*.

1 How do magazines help advertisers to target certain categories of women?

2 How might an advertiser determine whether or not the intended advertising message is achieving its objectives?

Distributing products and services

In looking at distribution, a marketing plan will need to show how goods or services are going to reach or be supplied to consumers. Market research will reveal important information about consumer preferences for distribution. The distribution plan additionally needs to indicate plans for getting goods to consumers in the right place, and the costs stemming from such operations.

A number of different factors will influence the choice of distribution:

- The image of the product and how this image may be projected by the chosen distributor.

- The size, nature and quality of the sales force.

- The ability to provide after-sales support.

- The financial standing of the intermediary.

- The use of specialist support and equipment.

- The strategy of competitors in reaching their customers.

Check your understanding

Compare and contrast how two products or services have been developed to reach consumers.

In your business plan:

How will you distribute your product or service?

Chapter 23 Production and resource requirements

As well as considering the features of your product or service, you will need to determine the process by which it will be produced. This will involve you considering the following aspects of the production process:

- the quantity to be produced
- the plant, machinery and equipment required
- quality levels required and means of assuring targeted quality
- the different stages of the production for the product or service
- the timing of production to meet customer needs.

It will be important for you to relate your production decisions to aspects of your marketing plan.

You will need to judge the resource requirements of all aspects of the production and marketing of your product or service. You should consider the following resource requirements:

- financial
- physical
- human
- time.

You should also be aware of any legal, financial, social, environmental or technological constraint you need to take into account when making decisions about producing and marketing your product.

Every organisation from the multinational news companies such as News International, public corporations such as the British Broadcasting Corporation (BBC), to the small local free paper, exists to satisfy the needs and wants of customers. It is thus through operations that organisations are able to satisfy consumer needs and wants.

Operations means the processes and acts an organisation performs (often of a practical nature) to satisfy customers. It is sometimes called 'production' and is used to cover all the processes of *adding value* by the private and public sectors in the provision of goods and services to consumers and customers.

The notion of value added lies at the heart of business practice. We can illustrate the process of adding value by means of an example. The following is a list of some of the ingredients that go into making a typical car:

- *Raw materials*: steel, iron work, aluminium, other non-ferrous metals, paint and solvents, textiles and leather, plastics.

- *Finished products*: windows, tyres, engines.

- *Fuels*: gas, electricity, oils.

If the car producer purchases during a year £70 million worth of raw materials and finished products, and makes 30,000 cars that are sold for £10,000 each, the firm receives £300 million for its cars. The value added in the process of production is therefore £230 million:

Revenue from selling cars	£300 million
Cost of buying components and materials	£70 million
Value added	£230 million

The business will seek to operate in the most effective way to add value to its inputs. It will then sell its finished products in the marketplace.

Success in business is concerned with adding the most value. Figure 23.1 indicates what a firm can do with the value it adds. The left-hand side shows the value of sales to customers. We must deduct from this the value of goods and services bought from other firms. This gives us a figure for the gross value added by the business organisation. We can then deduct money that needs to be set aside for paying back debts from the past, finally arriving at a figure for the net added value created by the business in a particular time period.

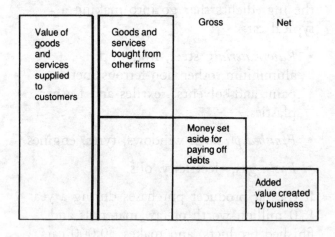

Figure 23.1 The creation of added value

We can next look at how this added value is distributed. Some will go the government in taxes, some in dividends to shareholders, some in interest to investors. Usually the largest chunk (often as much as 70%) will go in wages and salaries. The remainder can be retained as profits by the business. This profit is kept in the business and is very important because it can go into expanding or consolidating the business in the next year.

One of the key things you should learn from a business course is the importance of adding value. Value can be added to products by making them more desirable so more people are prepared to buy them and at higher prices. For example, value is added to motor cars by creating desirable features, such as side-impact airbags, dashboard computers, route finders and economic fuel consumption.

One of the most important ways of adding value to products in today's competitive market conditions is through service – personal attention to customers' requirements, friendly relationships with customers, etc.

The value added by a business to its input materials is thus more than simply physical improvement: it also involves non-tangible considerations such as service and 'image'. There is also an essential human dimension. A business has to benefit not only the people who buy the products and services but also its own employees, its suppliers and the community at large.

Benefits, whether tangible in the form of scientifically measurable product differences, or intangible in the form of 'image' or service, are comparatively easy to add. However, the key is to add benefits that go above and beyond those being offered by competitors.

Check your understanding

Identify the added benefits which persuade you to purchase one organisation's products rather than alternatives. For example, what extra added value does your hairdresser provide compared with rivals?

Case study: Adding value in the airline business

When you travel with a major airline, like British Airways (www.british-airways.com/ecp_no_dhtml.shtml), you have a choice of where you want to sit and hence the price you want to pay for tickets. Passengers can travel ordinary standard class, business class or first/club class. There are a range of benefits associated with each class but, essentially, the level and quality of benefit rise with the amount passengers are prepared to pay.

When staff are trained at British Airways they will progressively develop skills that enable them to earn higher pay. The most highly paid staff will be those who serve first-class passengers. They will be able to use their skills to pamper the passengers and thus add value through the service they offer.

By travelling first class, passengers will have much more leg room, and more spacious and comfortable chairs so they feel as if they are in a large hotel lounge with access to newspapers and magazines. They will also have far more privacy and room to sleep. Throughout the journey their every need will be met by smiling staff who are always helpful. These passengers received the most value.

Business-class passengers will also have their needs met regularly in the form of drinks, food and access to facilities. However, they won't have quite as much space as first-class passengers. These passengers receive the second most value.

Finally, standard-class passengers will receive a good service, but will not benefit from as many services or from such highly trained staff as the other passengers. Their seats and accommodation are less comfortable.

Of course, British Airway's ability to create value for each class of passenger is important. The success of British Airways will rest with their value position when compared to rival companies – and, of course, price will be part of the equation. Passengers choosing to travel by a particular airline weigh up the benefits they receive in relation to the price they pay. The more value organisations can add to their service, the more competitive they are. It is not surprising, therefore, that organisations pay such attention to staff training and development.

1 Within the context of this study, what does the term 'value added' mean?

2 How does an airline add value in the process of production?

3 Explain how this element of added value is used to differentiate one type of service or product from another.

Studying operations management is useful because similar organisations face similar problems. By studying how one organisation manages its operations you can learn how to manage your own operations better.

There are a variety of different types of producers. In each category there will be a number of common threads to the production process. Some organisations are mainly goods producers, other focus upon service and a third group combine the two. For example:

- *Mainly goods producers* would include chemical installations, engineering works, oil drilling and refinery installations.

- *Mainly service producers* would include schools and colleges, banks and management consultants. These institutions primarily focus upon providing a service.

- *Mixed producers* include insurance companies and fast-food outlets that mix production with a service. Manufacturing organisations often sell guarantees and provide repairs and after-sales service.

Discussion point	To what extent could it be argued that all organisations are in some way 'mixed producers'?

Operations involves converting inputs into finished outputs. Figure 23.2 shows how operations management involves successfully transforming inputs into desired goods and services. (Note there needs to be a feedback loop to ensure that, if outputs do not conform with the required standards, changes can be made to inputs and or operations.)

We can make a distinction between transforming resources and transformed

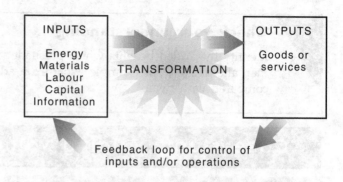

Figure 23.2 Transforming inputs into desired goods and services

resources. Managers, employees, machinery and equipment are transforming resources. The resources they transform are the materials and the information they process.

In developing a *process* of operations that is geared to the needs of customers, organisations need to consider the six Os:

1 *Occupants* Who makes up the market? For example, is the business concerned with a limited market for a small band of customers (e.g. left-handed golfers or Braille readers), or is it concerned with a mass market, such as those for the utilities like household gas or water?

2 *Object* A business must be concerned with answering the questions 'what do consumers wish to buy?' and 'what benefits are they looking for?'

3 *Occasions* The question to be answered here is: 'When will consumers purchase the product?' Will it be every week, every month, once a year? 'What time of the day are they most likely to make a purchase?' By finding the answers to these questions, the organisation should be able to provide goods at the right time for customers.

4 *Organisations* The question here is: 'Who is involved in the decision to purchase?'

An organisation that is selling goods needs to aim its sales pitch at the purchasers. For example, in selling carpets to a department store you need to target the person in that organisation who makes the decisions about carpet buying. In dealing with a large organisation you need to identify the part of the organisation that makes these decisions.

5 *Objectives* A key question is: 'Why do consumers buy particular goods or services?' In other words, you are trying to focus on the benefits they are seeking. If you can find out why people make a purchasing decision, you will be best placed to provide a solution to their buying problem.

6 *Operations* This is concerned with 'How do consumers buy products and services?' For example, do they pay cash or use some form of credit? If you know their preferred method, you can make it easier for them to make a purchase. If you know people are most likely to buy a car in hire-purchase instalments over three years, you can make sure the right credit terms are available.

The quantity to be produced

One of the most important decisions an organisation has to make is to identify the most appropriate scale of production to provide goods or services for its customers. Organisations can gain many operational benefits from producing goods on a large scale. Whereas bridges and submarines will never be mass produced, the vast majority of everyday consumer goods can be.

The scale or size of production is usually measured by the number of units produced over a period of time. If the scale of production increases, average unit costs over most production ranges are likely to fall because the company will benefit from economies of scale (the advantages of being larger). All businesses will aim for the scale of production that suits their line of work best, and this will be achieved when unit costs are at their lowest for the output produced. Beyond this point a company will start to find inefficiencies push average costs up, and diseconomies of scale (i.e. the problems of growing too large) set in.

If output increases faster than the rate of inputs, average unit costs will be falling and a company is said to be benefiting from increased returns to scale. Beyond the point at which average unit costs are at their lowest, the increase in output will be less than the increase in input so that average unit costs are pushed up and the company is suffering from decreasing returns to scale (Figure 23.3).

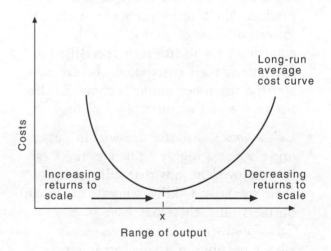

Figure 23.3 Returns to scale

If as the organisation becomes larger it manages to organise its production more efficiently, it is benefiting from internal economies of scale. If the company is a member of an industry that is growing, benefits will be felt outside the individual organisation (i.e. by all the companies in an industry), and these are known as external economies of scale.

Discussion point	In recent years there has been a move away from very large-scale organisations. Instead, there has been a move towards leaner and more flexible organisations. Does this mean that 'small is beautiful?'

There are a number of *internal economies:*

- *Technical economies* Large organisations use techniques and equipment that cannot be adopted by small-scale producers. For example, a company might have four machines each producing 1,000 units per week at a unit cost of £2; as the company becomes larger, these could be replaced by one machine that can produce 5,000 units per week at the lower unit cost of £1.75. If small companies try to use such specialised machinery, their costs would be excessive and the machines might become obsolete before the end of their physical life.

- *Labour and managerial economies* In larger organisations, highly skilled workers can be employed in jobs that fully utilise their specialised skills, whereas in a small business unit, they may have to be 'jacks-of-all-trades'. The division of labour possible in a large organisation therefore avoids the time-wasting element caused by the constant need to switch from one type of job to another. In the same way, a larger company can employ a number of highly specialised members on its management team, such as accountants, marketing managers and

personnel managers, in the hope that the improved quality of work and of decisions made by this more qualified workforce will reduce overall unit costs.

- *Commercial economies* Larger organisations obtain considerable benefits in the commercial world. They can gain enormously be devoting more resources to market research and the development of new products. Raw materials can be purchased in bulk, so large discounts and extended credit periods can be negotiated. Larger companies may be able to organise their retail outlets or to have a financial stake in their suppliers, and thus can collect profit at the various stages of production. Overheads, such as rent and rates, can be spread over a larger output. Goods can be distributed via a network of warehouses rather than at one central store, and carefully targeted advertising can be spread over a wider marketplace.

- *Financial economies* As larger companies tend to present a more secure investment, they find it easier to raise finance, are frequently treated more favourably by the banks and are in a better position to negotiate loans with preferential interest rates. For example, larger companies have the ability to raise capital by issuing new shares on the Stock Exchange.

There are also a number of *external economies.* In many industries, the reduction of average unit costs and the benefits of internal economies of scale will depend upon a company's ability to increase the length of production runs, to introduce mass production and standardisation techniques, and to increase the output capacity of the industry as a whole. This could lead to the following economies of scale:

- *Concentration* A concentration of special benefits builds up as companies within an industry concentrate in a particular area. These benefits may include: a skilled workforce, the reputation of an area for high-quality work, local college courses tailored to the needs of that particular industry and better social amenities.

- *Information* Larger industries often set up information services designed to benefit all producers in that industry, such as the Motor Industry Research Association.

- *Disintegration* Companies producing components or supplying specialist machinery might well be attracted to areas of specialised industries, along with companies that are able to help with maintenance and processes.

There are two main ways in which organisations can grow and take advantage of economies of scale. These are:

1 *Organic growth* Organisations can obtain the benefits of economies of scale through a gradual build-up of their business, through acquiring assets, developing products and/or expanding sales. Organic growth of this kind, however, is often a slow process.

2 *Mergers or take-overs* A quicker and more dynamic form of growth is through mergers or take-overs, which involve the integration of a number of business units under a single umbrella organisation. In addition to enjoying the benefits of being larger, the new organisation will have a larger market share, will probably be more competitive in export markets and, depending on the type of merger, could be in a position to control raw material supplies or the sales of finished products. Sometimes the easiest way to achieve large-scale production is to

Case study: British Book Printers plc

In recent years, British Book Printers plc has grown through a rapid expansion programme to become one of the biggest book printers in London and southeast England. The statistics shown in Figure 23.4 have been extracted from the most recent financial statements.

	1998	1999	2000	2001
Yearly output ('000)	300.00	450.00	525.00	615.00
Number of machines	8.00	10.00	12.00	13.00
Number of employees	175.00	182.00	190.00	194.00
Number of products	14.00	27.00	38.00	51.00
Cost of manufacture per publication (£)	3.20	3.10	2.90	2.00

Figure 23.4 British Book Printers plc: growth in recent years

1 To what extent do these figures illustrate economies of scale?

2 What sort of economies do are likely to have taken place within this company?

merge. This may bring financial and marketing economies of scale.

A *horizontal* merger takes place when two companies producing goods of a similar type at the same stage of production join together. A *vertical* merger takes place when two companies producing goods of a similar type at different stages of production join together. *Backward vertical integration* involves the take-over of a supplier, and *forward vertical integration* involves joining with a company at a later stage of production.

Check your understanding

Study the business pages of newspapers and professional business magazines. Make a list of some of the recent mergers and acquisitions of larger companies. Find out about the main trading activities of the companies involved, and comment on whether the mergers were horizontal, vertical or lateral.

What motivations would you expect to lie behind each merger?

Discussion point	It is a fact that one of the major failings of many businesses is overtrading. In other words, they try to get too big too quickly. In doing so they often take on too many orders and run into cash flow problems. Why, therefore, do many entrepreneurs try to expand their businesses?

One of the dangers companies face when they become large is that the optimum size for the business could be exceeded. Large organisations are considerably more difficult to manage, and these inefficiencies are known as *diseconomies of scale*. Diseconomies include the following:

- *Human relations* Larger numbers of employees are always more difficult to organise. It can be difficult to communicate information, and instructions that need to be passed down long chains of command reduce the personal contact between decision-makers and staff. This can lead to a low level of morale, lack of motivation and, ultimately, industrial relations problems. Larger organisations tend to have more industrial disputes than smaller organisations.

- *Decisions and co-ordination* The sheer scale of production may limit the management's ability to respond to change and make good decisions. With a large hierarchy, both the quality of the information reaching the decision-maker and the quality of the instructions passed on could be affected. Difficulties arising from discussions could involve considerable paperwork and many meetings.

- *External diseconomies* In recent years, many consumers have become more discerning about both the quality of product they purchase and the activities of certain organisations. Public displeasure can ultimately lead to some form of consumer boycott.

Not only is the existence of small businesses necessary because of diseconomies of scale, but they also obtain many separate and vital economic advantages. Small businesses have the flexibility to respond quickly to market opportunities. Small companies often specialise and so contribute towards division of labour within the wider productive process.

Clearly, some industries will suit a larger-scale organisation better than others. A business needs to look carefully at the effects of size upon its cost structure before deciding on the most appropriate scale. There may be little scope for economies of scale because of limited demand (the corner shop, for example, may cater for a very local demand); or the product may be highly specialised, as in the case of the market for 'customised' motor bikes.

No matter what scale an organisation chooses, it will always be difficult to predict what changes will take place, or the demands of the marketplace of the future. Today, we live in a highly uncertain environment with millions of organisations developing products and new ideas in competition with each other. The impact of these changes often revolutionises the ways in which other products are made, and has considerable significance for production decisions.

In order to cater for these changes, organisations have to plan and control their operations carefully. These plans will depend upon the level of operations and the time period. Much of production planning and control will be concerned with an organisation's ambitions and will need to be carefully co-ordinated with marketing policy.

Discussion point	Explain why production decisions about the quantity to produce should be carefully co-ordinated with marketing information.

Production planning and control involves finding the answers to questions such as:

- How many should we produce?
- How close are we to completion?
- How do we resource our production requirements?

Programming

Programming is concerned with timetabling all the resources used by the production department. Production managers set dates for the delivery of resources and part-finished products, and allocate production services accordingly.

Purchasing

Purchasing is another key function. Procuring materials is a key management function for any type of business. The importance of its role can be appreciated when one takes into account that an average manufacturing company spends about half its income on supplies for raw materials and services.

The purchasing department aims to provide an organisation with a steady flow of materials and services whilst, at the same time, ensuring the continuity of supplies. It aims to obtain the best value for money. *Value analysis* often makes it possible for considerable savings to be made, though a particular danger is that quality could be sacrificed to cost considerations.

Just-in-time involves finished goods being produced just in time for them to be sold, rather than weeks or months ahead. It involves the parts that go into a finished product arriving just in time to be put together to make the final product, rather than being stored (at some cost) in a warehouse.

Intelligent systems have recently been developed for the purchasing function. These systems can analyse a problem (decide on economic ordering levels based upon predictions of demand) and can make a choice from a selection of suppliers.

In an ideal world, where businesses would know their demand well in advance and suppliers would always meet delivery dates, there would be no problem with deciding stock levels. In practice, however, predicting quantities is difficult as demand varies, and suppliers are often late with deliveries, so stocks act as a protection against unpredictable events.

Organisations hold stocks in a variety of forms such as:

- raw materials

- work-in-progress

- finished goods

- consumables

- plant and machinery spares.

The aim of a stock control system is to provide stocks that cater for uncertainties but are at minimum levels, thereby ensuring costs are kept low.

Problems of low stocks:
- It may be difficult to satisfy your consumer demand.

- It can lead to a loss of business.

- It can lead to a loss of goodwill.

- Ordering needs to be frequent and so handling costs are higher.

Problems of high stocks:
- There is an increased risk of a stocked item becoming obsolete and therefore unusable.

- The risk of stock losses is increased (e.g. through theft or damage).

- The costs of storage are too high.

- Stocks can tie up a company's working capital.

Buffer stocks can be built up as a preventative measure against running out owing to unexpected variations in demand. A minimum level should be set below which stocks should not fall, and this level will depend on the *lead-time* between placing an order and its receipt.

Figure 23.5 represents an ideal situation in which stocks never fall below the set minimum level or go above the set maximum stock level. Stocks are replenished just at the point at which the minimum stock level is about to be breached.

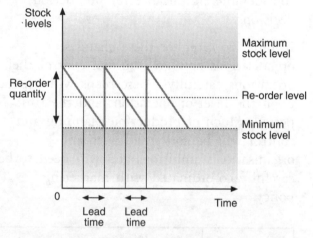

Figure 23.5 Managing stock levels

Forecasting

A key area used to make decisions about the quantity to produce is that of *forecasting*. A forecast is a statement that looks into the future and uses past information to help to make predictions. For example, some supermarket chains decide on the next day's staffing on the basis of the present day's sales figures. In some organisations, cash flow forecasting is used to assess how much cash will be available in the near future.

Every organisation will have useful internal sources of data (such as management accounts and budgetary information) that can help in preparing forecasts. These forecasts include costing and sales figures for individual products, breakdowns of overheads, sales results for staff and performance data for operating units. Reports are frequently prepared showing the potential of different projects, options for development and the time periods concerned.

Forecasting resource requirements is a key aspect in order to meet customer demands. Accurate forecasting reduces uncertainty and increases confidence in the way resources are used. However, forecasting is not easy, as trends can alter and shocks do occur.

Many management decisions depend heavily on software packages. Decision-supporting software uses static forecasting techniques. These base decisions upon a data set that holds past data.

In your business plan:
What quantity of your good or service will you provide?

Plant, machinery and equipment
The five Ps of production

Production activities vary considerably depending upon the product, but there are a number of components common to all forms of production. Together these make up the so-called 'five Ps of production':

1 product
2 plant
3 people
4 process
5 programme.

The *product* is essential to provide a good or service that clearly meets consumer needs and that can be provided for them at the right place, at the right time and for the most attractive price.

To add value to a product or service, organisations nearly always need some form of *plant* or base.

Case study: Tactician maps and analyses

Tactician 4 (www.orsoc.org.uk/about/topic/tactic.htm) is the latest version of an advanced mapping and analysis system available for business users. This software uses data and mapping capabilities to generate patterns, trends and meanings behind sales territories, sites and customer databases. Wherever information is held with reference to geography, this application helps to analyse, interrogate and plan sales and marketing activity.

1 How might such software help production planners?

2 What sort of information would this system require?

The location, size, design, safety and layout of the plant are all very important. Managers need to think carefully how parts and materials are to be delivered, and how finished goods will be transported away from the plant. The layout should make it easy to co-ordinate the various activities that will take place there. Times and costs involved in transferring goods, materials, information and people should be kept to a minimum.

Managers must also make sure plant and equipment are properly maintained. A maintenance department may include electricians, plumbers and joiners, as well as many other skilled workers. The effectiveness of the maintenance department can be judged by the number of breakdowns and accidents. Safety is vitally important.

The success of any production process will depend upon the *people* involved. And the quality of people depends upon how much is invested in them. Training and development are vital.

The *process* is also important. Different organisations will have different sets of operations depending on the nature of the product they make, the type of plant and equipment employed and many other factors. Process management sets out to:

- Identify the key processes of business activity. If these are carried out properly, it will be possible to maximise customer satisfaction, thus leading to better financial performance.

- Develop a detailed understanding of how processes work.

- Identify who in the organisation is involved in these processes.

- Seek ongoing improvements in the management of these processes.

- Set in motion an ongoing cycle of continuous process improvement.

Programming is mainly concerned with timetabling the use of resources. To meet orders successfully, the organisation will need to plan and control activities carefully. Successful programming involves purchasing, stock control and quality control.

Location

One of the most important decisions affecting an organisation's success, apart from the five Ps, is its location. For example:

- Local businesses need to decide on the best location within a particular town or area.

- National businesses need to decide on the best spot in a country.

- International companies often search the world for the right location.

The location of an organisation and its plants will undoubtedly have a major effect on its performance. The problems of location are long term and, clearly, decisions taken today have implications for tomorrow. For many smaller businesses, the problem is not so much one of location but of finding a site. For example, an owner who lives in one area may not wish to set up a business away from that locality: the local area may provide the entire market for a small local business, such as that of a plumber, electrician or fast-food retailer. In contrast, large companies may have the world as their market, and numerous factors (when taken together) are capable of influencing any decision.

Whatever the type of business, the aim will be to locate in an area where the difference between the benefits and costs is maximised. Important considerations will be the minimising of unit costs and the maximising of outputs from given quantities of resources. Some of the important factors influencing the choice of location are considered below.

Transport costs

In situations where raw materials or finished goods are bulky, the transport costs are more significant. If the output of an industry is more expensive to transport than its input, it is a *bulk-increasing industry*, and is more likely to locate near to the market. For example, brewing tends to take place close to the market because of the expense of transporting the finished product.

However, if the raw materials are bulky and expensive to transport and the industry is a *bulk-decreasing industry*, it would be beneficial to locate near raw materials. For example, historically, the steel industry has located near sources of coal, iron ore and limestone. In practice, decisions are not as clear cut as theory would indicate. Markets tend to be spread out and raw materials tend to come from a number of suppliers. The type of industry, the spread of the market, the availability of raw materials and their influence upon the costs of transport all have to be weighed against each other.

Integration with group companies

To 'integrate' means to join together. A large organisation will wish to locate a factory where its work can be integrated with the work of other units in the same group. The ease with which it can integrate will influence its location. For example, if a large company is thinking about taking over a supplier of raw materials, it is far more likely to integrate with a supplier to which it is connected by fast and effective transport links than one that is remote and inaccessible.

Labour/housing

Labour and skills are more readily available in some areas than others. Providing labour with incentives to move can be expensive and has had little success. Variations in house costs may also inhibit the mobility of labour. Often, an organisation will find it easier to move work to the workers than to try to encourage workers to move to the work.

Amenities

There are five standard amenities to be considered:

1 gas
2 electricity
3 water
4 waste disposal
5 drainage.

For example, certain industries use considerable reserves of water, such as for food preparation, metal plating and paper making; their use of water could exert considerable pressures on a local system. In the same way, the disposal of waste can be an expensive business. An assessment must be made of all these requirements, as underestimating the cost of amenities can cause a problem.

Land

Land costs will vary from area to area. In some circumstances the geology of the area needs to be considered (e.g. whether the land can support heavy buildings and plant). Climate may also affect the manufacturing process. For example, it is not always easy to produce chocolate in hot climates.

Local regulations may also affect certain types of activity and may need to be checked. Moreover, it would be unwise to build a factory that used up all the land available on a given site with no room for expansion. A large employer will also require parking spaces and will have investigated access to land.

Regional advantages

Locating in an area that contains similar businesses, suppliers and markets may be a considerable advantage. Local research facilities and commercial expertise may be of some use.

Safety requirements

Certain types of industry may be considered

to be a danger or a nuisance to the local environment (e.g. nuclear power stations, munitions factories or chemical plants). Locating such plants away from high-density population levels may be considered desirable.

Communications

Accessibility of ports, airports and motorways has become an increasingly important factor over recent years. A good infrastructure will encourage industry to move to a region.

Government influences

High levels of unemployment in certain areas of the country have been a feature of the last ten years or so. Governments look towards balanced economic growth and provide incentives for organisations to move to identified areas.

Case study: Electronic Miniature Products Ltd (EMPL)

EMPL is a company in the electrical components industry that is in the process of reviewing its present location at site D in Figure 23.6. A, B and C are three possible alternative locations for an electrical components factory.

The management at EMPL understands the need to take many factors into consideration when deciding on the most appropriate location. These factors include the following:

Figure 23.6 Electronic Miniature Products Ltd: relocation options

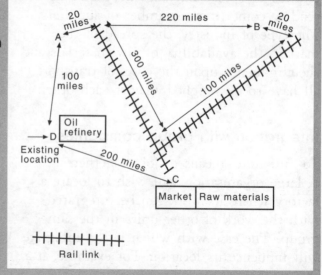

- Cost of transporting finished goods to the market.
- Cost of transporting raw materials and oil supplies to the plant.
- Grants and other inducements available from the government.
- Labour costs.
- Removal costs.

The company will locate its plant at the point where all these costs are minimised. Production costs are constant wherever the factory is located. EMPL management needs to compare the costs involved, and then provide a recommendation. This can be done by calculating the costs of providing electrical components at each of the three alternative locations and comparing these with the costs of staying at the existing location. The preferred location will be the one with the lowest costs.

The market for components exists at location C, and locations A and B are eligible for government grants. For each 1,000 electrical components:

- Transporting oil costs £2 per mile by road and 50p per mile by rail.
- Transporting raw materials from C costs £4 per mile by road and 70p per mile by rail.
- Labour costs are £1,300 at A, £1,400 at B, £1,300 at C and £1,500 at D.
- Transporting finished goods to the market at C costs £5 per mile by road and £1 per mile by rail.
- Removal costs would be spread over 10 years and would be £1,000 per 1,000 units per annum.
- Government grants reduce costs by 20%.

1 Work out the costs by copying out and filling in the table shown in Figure 23.7.

2 Find the lowest cost location.

3 Production is forecast at 492,000 units for the next year. How much would moving to the lowest cost location save in the first 12 months?

4 What additional information do you think would help the company in making a location decision?

5 What factors might alter and upset the calculations you have made?

	A	B	C	D
Oil transport costs				
Raw material transport costs				
Labour costs				
Finished goods transport costs				
Removal costs				
Effects of government grants				
Total cost per 1,000 units				

Figure 23.7 Electronic Miniature Products Ltd: relocation costs

Layout

Having decided upon the location of plant, an important factor is its organisation within its location. The plant's design and the positioning of equipment should enable it to function smoothly. Although designing the layout is normally a work-study problem, it needs to be carried out with specialist engineers who are concerned with factors such as the structure of the plant, power availability, maintenance requirements and so on.

Plant layout tends to follow one of a number of basic designs. But whatever techniques are used in setting up a layout, the aim must be to maximise flexibility and ease of co-ordination so process time and costs will be minimised.

With *product* or *line* layout, plant is laid out according to the requirements of the product in a line of production. Products 'flow' from one machine or stage to another. Control is simplified as paperwork, material handling and inspection procedures are reduced (Figure 23.8).

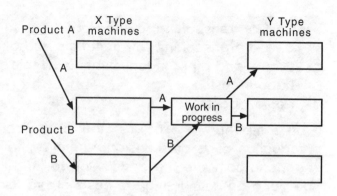

Figure 23.9 Function or process layout

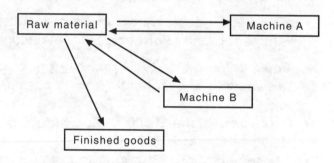

Figure 23.10 Layout by fixed position

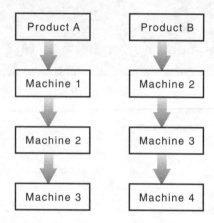

Figure 23.8 Product or line layout

With *function* or *process* layout, all operations of the same type are performed in the same area; for example, spot welding may be in one location, riveting in another and stapling in a third. This is rather like the provision of a centralised print service or word processing pool. Although this system is flexible, considerable preproduction planning is necessary to ensure machines are neither overloaded nor idle (Figure 23.9).

Layout by fixed position involves materials or part-finished goods returning to a fixed position after each process (Figure 23.10).

The justification for expenditure on new plant, machinery and equipment is that it contributes towards the quality of goods

and services being provided. Before equipment is bought, the general effects upon the organisation have to be evaluated and standard capital appraisal techniques have to be applied to find out if such changes will be worth while.

It is the duty of an employer to remove all possible causes of accidents. Accidents can cause time to be lost by the unfortunate employees and supervisory staff. An accident can damage equipment, interfere with production schedules and lead to compensation payments. Employers need to anticipate circumstances likely to lead to such accidents, to try to eliminate hazards and to train staff in good production practices.

In your business plan:
What plant, machinery and equipment will be required by your business?

Quality levels

Tim Hannagan has suggested that quality can be defined as: 'continually meeting agreed customer needs' or 'what it takes to satisfy the customer' or simply 'fitness for purpose'.

In his widely acclaimed book, *Thriving on Chaos*, Tom Peters argued that consumers' perception of the quality of a product or service is the most important factor in determining its success.

Quality (as defined by the consumer), he argued, is more important than price in determining demand for most goods and services. Consumers will be prepared to pay for the best value. Value is thus added by creating those quality standards required by consumers.

Discussion point	To what extent would most consumers prefer lower prices rather than higher quality?

Figure 23.11 shows what is meant by quality from the consumer's point of view.

Figure 23.11 The consumer's quality standards

Check your understanding

Identify three familiar products you feel are of high quality and three that are of poor quality.

In taking quality to new heights, it is generally recognised there are three stages in the development of quality:

1 *Quality control* This is an old idea. It is concerned with detecting and cutting out components or final products which fall below set standards. This process takes place after these products have been produced. It may involve considerable waste as defect products are scrapped. Quality control is carried out by quality control inspectors. Inspection and testing are the most common methods of carrying out quality control.

2 *Quality assurance* Quality assurance occurs both during and after the event, and is concerned with trying to stop faults from happening in the first place. Quality assurance is concerned to make sure products are produced to predetermined standards. The aim is to produce goods with 'zero defects'.

Quality assurance is the responsibility of the workforce, working in cells or teams, rather than an inspector (although inspection will take place). Quality standards should be maintained by following steps in a quality assurance system.

3 *Total quality management (TQM)* Total quality management goes beyond quality assurance. It is concerned with creating a quality culture so that every employee will seek to delight customers. The

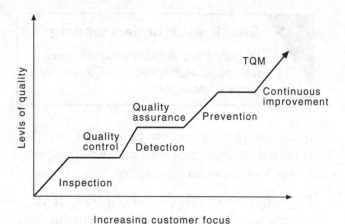

Figure 23.12 The move towards total quality management

customer is at the centre of the production process. Figure 23.12 shows the move along the path to total quality management.

Total quality management (TQM)

In a total quality system, TQM takes place at every stage of an organisation's operations and is the responsibility of all employees. It is therefore a business philosophy as well as a set of guiding principles.

Emphasis is placed on quality chains (i.e. links between groups and individuals involved in operations). Quality chains exist both within an organisation and between the organisation and other stages in the value chain.

The concept of 'customer' extends to include the *internal* customer. Internal customers are people inside the business receiving products (usually unfinished) or services from their colleagues also in the company. This extended concept is useful for several reasons:

- It enables people inside the company to realise the importance of what they are doing.

- It makes the point that the quality of the products and services sold to the external customer depends on the quality of products and services provided by the business.

- It helps people to realise their own significance.

There are a number of benefits to be reaped from TQM:

- It enables an organisation to focus on the customer.

- It enables the organisation to focus on quality.

- The emphasis is placed on continuous improvement.

- All operations and activities are thoroughly scrutinised on an ongoing basis to identify scope for improvement.

- Teamwork is emphasised.

- Team members feel they have ownership over the improvement process.

- TQM can lead to the motivation of all concerned. They are trusted and empowered.

- The system builds in control mechanisms and accountability.

- TQM is a total system involving everyone in the consumption and production of products.

The disadvantages of TQM are as follows:

- The system requires considerable planning and organisation, and is initially costly to introduce (e.g. training costs can be high).

- TQM requires a commitment from all those involved in the process.

- Setting up quality systems involves considerable paperwork and bureaucracy.

- Stress may arise from establishing TQM processes.

- At times, TQM is based more on rhetoric rather than on practice.

Quality circles

Quality circles are made up of small groups of employees engaged on any sort of problem affecting their working environment, (e.g. safety, quality assurance and efficiency). They are a means for employees to improve their working life by putting forward their points of view on day-to-day issues. They are therefore a form of indirect consultation designed to meet

Case study: Murphy Company

Murphy Company (www.murphynet.com/) define QUALITY QUEST as an ongoing structured approach to providing one hundred per cent customer satisfaction via error-free, waste-free and accident-free operation. QUALITY QUEST is both a philosophy and a set of guiding principles that represent the foundation of a continuously improving organisation.

To establish this quality process, management staff attend 6 four-hour sessions on total quality management and 4 two-hour sessions on leadership. Within the company, a quality improvement team meets weekly to lead and monitor the quality process.

The company implements improvement cycles by asking the following questions:

- What needs to be done and how?
- How well are we doing?
- Are we meeting expectations?
- What changes are necessary?

The four keys to QUALITY QUEST are:

1 meeting customer requirements
2 prevention of defects
3 an attitude to satisfy the customer all the time
4 measurement to verify the process is meeting requirements.

Murphy Company are total committed to TQM, which means developing a continuous commitment to improving methods of doing business.

1 What is QUALITY QUEST and whom will it involve?
2 Explain how this process helps to improve customer satisfaction.

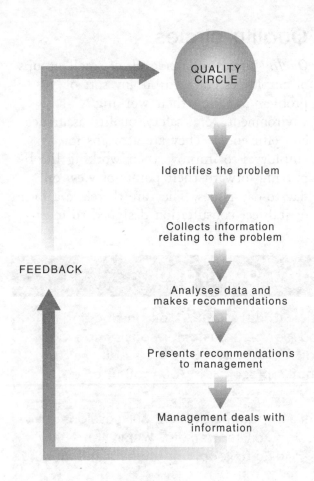

QUALITY
CIRCLE

Identifies the problem

Collects information
relating to the problem

FEEDBACK

Analyses data and
makes recommendations

Presents recommendations
to management

Management deals with
information

Figure 23.13   The functions of a quality circle

both employee and management needs (see Figure 23.13).

Check your understanding

Organise a quality circle with a group of class members. Prepare an agenda for the meeting. The purpose of the meeting is to improve the quality of your course. Make recommendations to your course tutor.

Continuous improvement

Kaizen is a term much used in the area of quality. It is a Japanese word that, when translated, simply means 'continuous

improvement'. The improvement is gained by slow and steady change, and once achieved it is maintained at that level until such time as the next improvement step takes place. *Kaizen* is one way in which employees may participate in issues that affect the workforce. The *kaizen* philosophy may be applied anywhere at one time. Everyone is encouraged to participate in the activity and, as a member of a team, everyone learns how to analyse situations logically and efficiently.

Quality standards

Quality standards are another important feature of quality systems. Today, more and more businesses are creating quality standards that match ISO 9000 specifications. BS 5750 was introduced in 1979 and has been updated to become ISO 9000, which brings it into line with European and international standards. It is made up of a series of national standards that can be used by any organisation, whether it employs 10 or 10,000 people.

Achieving ISO standards may take an organisation between one and two years, and the costs to the organisation will vary.

Check your understanding

Explain how ISO 9000 would be useful to an organisation with which you are familiar.

What drawbacks can you see facing an organisation going for ISO 9000?

Benchmarking

Benchmarking is an approach that has become increasingly popular in recent times for organisations to improve the quality of their goods and services. Benchmarking involves identifying 'best practice' in a particular sector, industry or group of firms and then seeking to employ this practice within your own organisation. Benchmarking, therefore, involves looking either inside or outside your own organisation to ensure it utilises best current practice. Once best practice is found, the organisation should attempt to exceed it in order to lead the field.

In your business plan:

What quality levels will be required in your business and how will you ensure this quality?

Different stages of production

New products change our lives. Create a brilliant breakthrough and you should be able to generate an excellent business from it.

Some new ideas are simple and some are extraordinarily complex. Major breakthroughs include the development of non-stick frying pans, 'cat's-eyes' on roads, cordless kettles and DVDs. At any given time huge numbers of people will be putting time and effort into finding new ways of taking a product a little bit further.

There is a very close link between research and development and marketing. A great deal of planning needs to take place before a good or service is developed. This involves knowing the market and the way it is changing. At the same time, research and development should take place alongside marketing processes. R&D is a very important business process that relies heavily on market research information.

Setting up a production line can be very expensive. Organisations, therefore, need to

be sure the product is right before going into production on a large scale. Careful

STARTERS

New ideas for the future that have to be researched

New ideas that are being researched both through market and product research

Prototypes that are ready to be trialled and test marketed

Products that are just being launched

Products for which consumer awareness is growing and sales are rising

Products that are becoming increasingly popular and that are being produced and sold on a larger scale at lower unit cost

Products that are booming and are very popular – perhaps becoming market leaders

Products that need a face-lift, relaunch or injection of new life to keep up their momentum

Products that are starting to go into decline

Products that have become outdated and are just about to be wound up

Products that are no longer made and that begin to appear in industrial museums

FINISHERS

Figure 23.14 The product stream

work in the early stages will help to ensure that the launch will be successful and that consumers get the benefits they want (see Figure 23.14).

Once it has been established that there is a suitable market for the product, research and development must find out the best way of meeting demand. The design needs to be attractive to consumers and meet their needs. Designers need to bear in mind the treatment their products will receive (e.g. garden tools must be weather-resistant, while kitchen appliances need to be safe and easy to clean).

Designers often build in 'planned obsolescence' so that the product will need replacing after a particular period. Many cars are built to last only a limited number of years and, today, we even have throw-away cameras. Product designers will also want to incorporate certain features into their products, particularly if it provides some form of status or helps to give a good image of the organisation.

Once a design has been developed, the researchers will either build a prototype that can be tested or will trial the service on offer. Many prototypes will be tried and later discarded, while others may be altered and improved.

It is essential to look at the likely profits a new product is going to generate. This involves estimating how many units it is likely to sell in a given period and how much costs will be.

Sometimes a test market is set up, where the product or prototypes are tested with a sample of consumers. This provides useful feedback that reduces the risk of failure at the time of the launch.

The launch is the final stage and involves presenting the product to the real market for the first time.

Production methods

There are a number of different production options for organisations as they develop processes and products.

Job production

Job or 'make complete' production is the manufacture of single individual items by either one operative or a team of workers. Ships and bridges are built this way. It is possible for a number of identical units to be produced in parallel under job production (e.g. several ships of the same type). Smaller jobs may also be viewed as job production (e.g. writing this book, hand-knitting a sweater, rewiring a house, etc). Job production is unique in that the project is considered to be a single operation that requires the complete attention of the operative before he or she passes on to the next job.

The benefits of job production are that each job is a unique project that exactly matches the requirements of the customer; supervision and inspection work are relatively simple; specifications for the job can change during the course of production; and working on a single job provides employees with a sense of purpose. There are, however, a number of problems. Labour, plant and machinery have to be versatile to adjust to a range of specialised tasks. As job production is unique, costing is based on uncertain predictions of future costs, and unit costs tend to be high as there are fewer economies of scale.

Batch production

The term 'batch' refers to a specific group of components which go through a production process together. As one batch finishes, the next one starts. For example, on Monday machine A produces Type 1 engine part (for an aircraft engine), on Tuesday it produces a Type 2 engine part, on Wednesday a Type 3 engine part and so on. All engine parts will then go forward for the final assembly of different categories of engine parts.

Batches are continually processed through each machine before moving on to the next operation. This method is sometimes referred to as 'intermittent production', as different types of jobs are held as work-in-progress between the various stages of production.

Batch production is particularly suitable for a wide range of nearly similar goods that can use the same machinery on different settings. It also enables organisations to respond quickly to customer orders by moving buffer stocks or work-in-progress through the final production stages.

There are, however, considerable organisational difficulties associated with batch production – for example, sequencing batches from one job to another to avoid building up excessive or idle stocks of work-in-progress. There is also a time lag between the initial investment in material and its eventual transfer into cash upon the sale of a product.

Flow production

Batch production is characterised by irregularity. If the rest period in batch production disappeared, it would then become flow production. Flow production is a continuous process of parts passing on from one stage to another until completion. Units are worked on in each operation and then passed straight on to the next work stage without waiting for the batch to be completed. To make sure the production line can work smoothly, each operation must be of equal length and there should be no movements or leakages from the line (e.g. hold-ups to work-in-progress).

For flow production to be successful, there needs to be a continuity of demand. If demand is varied this will lead to a constant overstocking of finished goods (or periodic shortages). Achieving a smooth flow of production requires considerable preproduction planning to ensure traw materials are purchased and delivered on time, that sufficient labour is employed, that inspection procedures take place and that all operations take the required time (Figure 23.15).

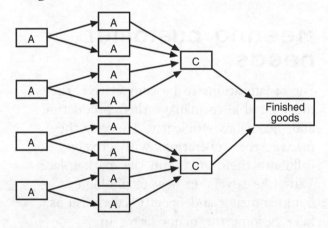

Figure 23.15 Flows in the production process

Check your understanding

Think about the traffic situation within your local town or city. Try to identify roads or traffic areas that are processed by: **a** batch; and **b** flow.

What factors influence the ways in which traffic is processed and how could the situation be improved?

Lean production

With lean production, the emphasis is upon getting more from less and cutting down on waste. Much of this approach draws on the experience of Japanese business organisations, such as Toyota. The starting point is to focus upon what the customer needs 'at a specific price at a specific time'.

Having decided that, lean production involves thinking about 'value'. By identifying the value stream or set of actions required to bring a product from concept to completion, it is possible to discover all sorts of *muda* (waste). Once *muda* is cut out, the next step is to get the value steps to flow together and focused upon the customer. When companies have all these steps in action, there is no end to the process of reducing effort, time, space, costs and mistakes.

Meeting customer needs

For organisations to be competitive, they must be able to manage their production and operations efficiently. The way they manage their operations will actively influence their success in the marketplace. With the advent of new technologies, manufacturing and operational decisions have become the major factor in determining a company's competitiveness. The organisation that delivers high-quality products at the right time at reasonable cost will quickly eliminate less successful rivals.

To manage production, there are three distinct phases of production and operations. These are:

1 Planning the operations process.

2 Starting up the operations process.

3 Controlling or running the operations process.

Much has been said about the factory of the future. Numerical-controlled (NC) machines and computer numerical-controlled (CNC) machines have been around since the 1960s. More recently, we have seen:

- *Computer-aided design (CAD).* This assists the designer with the use of computer graphics and computer-based structural analysis. It helps design to be responsive to changing specifications.

- *Computer-aided manufacture (CAM).* This converts the CAD design into instructions for manufacturing equipment. As CAM follows CAD, the result is often called CADCAM.

- *Computer-aided engineering (CAE).* This involves using sophisticated computer equipment to aid engineers. Though for many organisations this is still experimental, the aim of CAE is to provide rapid engineering solutions and responses to problems.

Another key element of timing to meet customer needs is the notion of *flexibility*. The word 'flexibility' is often used in operations management. In the operations context, it is really about *responsiveness* and how well an organisation is able to meet changing needs. Perhaps the best way to understand it as a concept is to think of a small factory. To explore how flexible the factory is, the following questions would be relevant:

- How many products do we make and how many do we promote in our catalogue?

- How quickly can we change from making one type of product to making another?

- How soon could we make a product that is not in our catalogue, but is required by our customers?

Though these questions relate to output for the customer, they are also about the organisation's internal ability to change in order to meet customer requirements.

At present, there are two leading concepts that are associated with flexibility:

1 *Flexible manufacturing systems (FMS).* FMS systems apply computer technology to drive machines to produce high-quality goods and services at low cost. The basic elements of FMS are computer-driven work stations that are operated entirely through remote entry terminals. The transfer of work between work stations is also computerised. There is a hierarchy of groupings of equipment, starting with numerical-controlled machines. Several NC machines are grouped together with an automatic transfer system between them. The result is an FMS cell.

2 *Computer-integrated manufacture (CIM).* Whereas FMS may simply consist of a few machines that are linked together, CIM looks at a manufacturing system as an entity. CIM involves co-ordinating people with their machines, computers and design for the process of manufacture. It involves integrating all parts of an organisation.

Increased flexibility enables smaller-scale organisations to compete with larger businesses. Short delivery times better service customer needs and enable closer contacts to be established with customers.

In your business plan:
What will be the key stages in the production of your good or service? How will you time production to meet customer needs?

Case study: Falling productivity

In 1982, the US Department of Labor reported that 42 of 69 industries surveyed experienced a fall in productivity. The American Productivity Institute suggested that:

- Falling productivity results in rising labour costs.
- Unit labour costs increases lead to higher prices.
- Higher prices lead to declining sales volumes.
- Declining sales volumes lead to reduced employment and reduced plant capacity.
- Reducing capital utilisation leads to lower productivity.
- Lower productivity leads to reduced competitive ability.

A number of other sources and reasons for the slow-down in productivity were identified:

- Insufficient capital investment.
- Slow-down in research and development.
- Growth in government regulation.
- Labour and management inattention.

- Ageing industrial plant.
- Increases in energy costs.
- Growth of the service sector.
- The age mix of the workforce.

1   What lessons could we draw from this survey?
2   What are the implications for resource requirements?
3   In what way does falling productivity lead to a downward spiral?

Resource requirements and efficiency

The last century saw many dramatic changes in our way of life. The production of food, clothing, shelter, housing, communications and durable goods is now achieved through highly developed technological systems. In fact, there are few places today, even in the developing world, where production processes remain in the hands of artisans.

In an increasingly complex world, the concept of *productivity* (the measure of a country's efficiency in converting inputs to outputs) is crucial. Over recent years, a great deal of attention has been focused upon why some people, organisations and countries are better at producing certain goods or services than others.

A key aspect in improving the use of resources is through *cost leverage*. The price charged for goods or services must either be equal to or exceed the costs of producing the goods or providing the services. Therefore, costs form a base upon which all price structures are built and upon which productive systems can be analysed.

The design of a productive system must be developed in a way that minimises costs and avoids unnecessary expenses. If an organisation fails to minimise costs in designing its production system, it provides cost leverage for its competitors. Cost leverage accrues to organisations that are sharp enough in developing their systems to identify low-cost opportunities.

There are many different strategies that can be employed by UK businesses to improve their competitiveness:

- organisational structure
- human resourcing
- marketing
- scale of production
- finance
- time.

Organisational structure

An organisation needs to operate in such a way as to give it a competitive edge. In today's competitive markets, organisations must respond quickly to dynamic change, so they will need to have loose and flexible arrangements that *empower* people to make appropriate decisions in diverse markets.

A great deal of emphasis is given to creating the architecture for business success. Professor John Kay of the London Business School defines the 'architecture' as the 'network or relational contracts within, or around, the firm'. All too often, however, businesses are limited because an effective organisational architecture is not put into place. Members of an organisation should feel proud to belong to it. Frequently they do not, and this is a severe limitation to competitiveness.

Maintaining morale implies both motivating people effectively and creating an organisational structure tailored to the needs of the business concerned. The quest for efficiency often leads businesses to change the nature of their management structure. This can improve morale but it can also be destructive of an individual's sense of well-being.

People

People are the most important resource of organisations. It is necessary to ensure the commitment of individuals to the success of an organisation. Human resource management involves seeking to develop individuals to the best of their potential.

Individual development is best for the organisation and for the individual because it encourages commitment. Individuals also need to be encouraged to become decision-makers in their own right. This helps to create a thinking organisation rather than one in which decisions are simply passed downwards.

Marketing

Weak marketing may mean potential demand has not been effectively identified. Effective marketing involves identifying consumers' requirements and meeting them to make a profit. Ineffective marketing involves failing to identify and meet consumer requirements at a profit.

The ability to extend a product life-cycle is often essential if firms are to continue to grow.

The *spotlight technique* is a useful way of analysing a business's strengths and weaknesses. It employs four spotlights:

1 *Market penetration* This spotlight helps an organisation to test how well it is selling to its chosen market. Improvements could be made by increasing sales to current customers or attracting new ones in the same sector.

2 *Market development* This lights up new markets for products and services.

3 *Product development* This illuminates products that can be developed or changed so that the most can be made of current markets.

4 *Diversification* This spotlight sheds new light on possibilities for developing new products and/or services in order to open up new markets.

Check your understanding

Interview a local business manager. Find out how he or she uses marketing to take advantage of new opportunities.

Can you relate his or her marketing to the spotlight approach?

Scale of production

The scale of production is a major factor in giving a competitive edge for nearly all products for which there is a high demand. Coca-Cola and Mars are prime examples of organisations being able to spread their fixed costs over very large outputs. The way to achieve large-scale production is to sell successfully into a large market. Increasing the scale of production can lead to greater productivity.

Finance

Finance is one of the biggest stumbling blocks to business expansion. It is not just a case of having enough finance, but it must also be of the right type. In particular, there must be sufficient cash flow to meet day-to-day trading needs.

Businesses must be careful not to borrow too much. Every organisation needs to structure its financing carefully so as to meet its key objectives – whether these are to retain a liquid position or to provide funds for investment projects.

Financial control is also an important element of business activity. It is essential businesses control the costs of labour, production and marketing carefully in order to retain a competitive edge.

Time

It is important to measure productivity trends over a period to see whether an organisation is becoming more or less efficient. Clearly, if a company increases workforce training, increases the automation of its plant or successfully reorganises the production process, it will expect to see an increasing productivity ratio. This can be tracked over time. Value is thus added through increasing productivity because revenues can be added to at a quicker rate than costs rise:

$$\text{Productivity index} = \frac{\text{Productivity ratio in time period}}{\text{Productivity ratio in base year}} \times 100$$

The productivity of a system is the amount of output that can be produced from a given set of inputs:

$$\text{Productivity} = \frac{\text{Output}}{\text{Input}} \quad or \quad \frac{\text{Results achieved}}{\text{Resources consumed}}$$

This productivity ratio therefore measures how efficient a system is in converting inputs of resource into useful outputs.

In your business plan:
What key resources will you need to build into your business plan? Consider the following kinds of resource: • financial   • physical   • human   • time.

Chapter 24 Financial analysis and planning

You will find out about and use financial information to assess the viability of your idea. To do this you will need to produce a financial plan consisting of:

- **sources of finance**
- **budgets, including estimates of start-up and working capital**
- **break-even forecasts**
- **simple cash flow forecasts**
- **projected profit and loss accounts**
- **start-up balance sheets.**

You will be able to use IT, such as a spreadsheet, to present your financial projections effectively.

Your financial planning should allow you to clarify, identify and justify the legal status of your business.

All organisations require resources. These may be tangible (such as property, equipment and materials), or less tangible (such as human resources). Using any of these resources requires financial planning. The management and planning of financial arrangements are therefore inseparable from the management of every organisation as a whole and an integral part of strategy building.

For example, a company whose objective is to become a national supermarket operator may decide to adopt a strategy of smaller company acquisitions. The financial plan for the company, therefore, has to consider all the financial resources required to buy these smaller companies, as well as the sort of financial performance that would justify such a strategy to different stakeholders, such as the following:

- *The organisation's owners* These will want to know how the business is performing given this new strategy. They will want to know how much profit they are making now and are likely to make in the future. They will want to know about the value of assets they acquire as well as the debts they will incur.

- *Managers* Given all the changes in the business, managers will want information that enables them to be 'on top' of handling the business. For example, they will need to keep a regular update on the cash flow position as well as other information that helps them to generate profits. They will want immediate information about any improvement or deterioration in performance.

- *Providers of finance* Any providers of finance, either now or in the future, will want to know how secure their loans are, when they are likely to be repaid and at what rate of interest. For example, a bank that has lent money to the organisation may not be too pleased to find the organisation might be increasing its borrowing and the risks involved to such an extent that it might not be able to pay back its loans.

- *Tax authorities* Tax authorities (such as the Inland Revenue and Customs and Excise) will want financial information to find out how much they are due in tax.

- *The general public* The general public will also have an interest in accounting information. For example, some may be customers of the supermarket while others may be thinking about becoming shareholders.

- *Employees* Employees have a right to know how well a company is performing. For example, if the business is improving its profitability, they may feel they deserve better rewards. If it is increasing its debts, although there may be more job opportunities, clearly there is greater risk in working there.

The accounting system will provide the financial data to justify such a strategy. A financial plan is often based on a model of the business that can be used to test strategic proposals.

For example, a business currently selling 500 units per annum at a price of £100 each is considering a price reduction of 10% that may increase volume by 15%. What are the financial implications if there was a variable cost of £50 per unit?

	Current (£)		Proposed (£)
Sales 500 × £100	50,000	575 × £90	51,750
Variable cost 500 × £50	25,000	575 × £50	28,750
	25,000		23,000

Check your understanding

Looking at the information in the above example, what decision might you make? Is there any other information you might require before making this decision? What are the assumptions behind this model?

A planning model may consist of thousands of calculations and underlying assumptions. Many businesses construct their financial plan with the aid of a forecasting model or a *spreadsheet* that can recalculate profit, cash flow and the balance sheet after every change in basic assumptions.

One of the basic concepts of financial planning is that it relates to a *time period*.

This could be as short as six months or one year, or as long as five years. The period chosen will depend upon the needs of the business and its ability to make predictions about the future.

When planning for the future, the biggest uncertainty arises from any changes in the *external environment* of the business. Porter, the management theorist, identifies five forces acting upon an organisation that could affect any forecasts about its future:

1 Threats from new entrants.

2 The bargaining power of suppliers.

3 The bargaining power of customers.

4 The threat of substitute products.

5 The extent of competitive pressures.

As we saw earlier, in Chapter 11, a PEST analysis is another way of looking at factors that could influence the planning process. These might include:

- Political influences, such as changes in legislation.

- Economic influences, such as interest rates, growth rates and economic cycles.

- Social changes, such as population changes.

- Technological change, such as the use of the Internet.

All these changes make forecasting and planning difficult. Most of these external influences will be known with some certainty for the short term, but forecasts are less certain over the longer period (Figure 24.1).

Every plan will require certain assumptions. However, if the assumptions on which the plan is based are poorly evaluated, the plan will become meaningless. The financial

Figure 24.1 Forecasting

planning process will highlight critical uncertainties. These may need further research or more thought.

Long-term financial planning (see Figure 24.2) should:

- Provide an opportunity to examine the organisation's objectives.

- Provide long-term direction that enables managers to focus beyond current issues.

- Provide a framework upon which budgeting decisions can be made.

- Enable long-term decisions to be made about investments and borrowing.

Case study: A changing industry

In the new millennium, public houses are having to change or gradually die. This is happening at a time when regulators are dismantling old brewery empires to allow greater competition. But while many large operators are sprucing up the George & Dragon or Red Lion, new operators have become increasingly popular with different groups of customers.

Surrey Free Inns have created a chain of concept superpubs called The Litton Tree. These use town-centre sites vacated by retailers who have headed for the out-of-town retail parks. The Litton Tree pubs are large and appeal to a wide range of people, depending on the time of day. During the day they offer food and drink to town-centre workers and shoppers; at night, the young flock because of the entertainment and music.

A slightly more established newcomer is J. D. Wetherspoon, which convert well-positioned properties, such as old banks, into pubs. Another operator, Regent Inns, have gone public and spread their format fast from their London base into the Midlands and the north of England. Their formula is for large outlets where young singles like to meet and drink. Irish pubs have also developed with successful brands such as O'Neills, and town and city centres have seen the birth and development of wine and café bars. With the spit-and-sawdust image rapidly disappearing, the industry is having to respond to higher customer expectations.

1 What are the main external influences that have caused the changes to the pub sector?

2 Describe the pubs that are flourishing within your own area.

3 What strategic initiatives are required by pub operators over the next few years?

4 What are the variables that might influence any forecasting for pubs?

5 How difficult is it to plan as a pub operator?

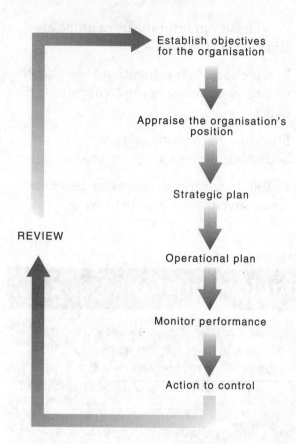

Establish objectives
for the organisation

Appraise the organisation's
position

Strategic plan

REVIEW

Operational plan

Monitor performance

Action to control

Figure 24.2 Long-term financial planning

- Establish a benchmark of success against which performance can be monitored and controlled.

The problem, however, with planning is that the process can be time-consuming and there might be a failure to respond to unforeseen circumstances that have not been included in the plan.

Sources of finance

Every modern organisation needs to draw upon sources of finance. It needs to have funds to carry out its activities. The financial problem for an organisation is similar to that of an individual. If I want to visit the cinema, I will need to have cash in my pocket. If I want to buy a relatively expensive item such as a DVD player, I will

probably need to be able to draw on my bank account using a cheque book or 'hole in the wall'. At other times I buy goods on credit, such as borrowing money to purchase a car.

Sources of finance are the people and organisations that provide finance for an individual or an organisation. Methods of finance are the form in which the funds are provided.

Check your understanding

Think about the methods of finance your household draws upon. Rank these in order of the length of time these funds are required for.

Why is it that some methods of finance are required for longer periods than others? What are the sources of finance used within your household?

Organisations have available to them a number of sources of finance:

- individuals
- organisations providing venture capital
- banks and other financial institutions
- suppliers
- government
- profits retained by the business.

By drawing on these sources of finance, organisations have a number of methods of raising money. In choosing what type of finance to draw upon, they may consider the following:

- The length of time for which they need the finance.

	Sole traders	Partnerships	Private limited companies	Public limited companies	Non-profit organisations
Personal funds	✓	✓	✓	✓	✓
Shares			✓	✓	
Mortgage	✓	✓	✓	✓	
Grants	✓	✓	✓	✓	✓
Gifts					✓
Loans	✓	✓	✓	✓	✓
Profit retention	✓	✓	✓	✓	✓
Trade credit	✓	✓	✓	✓	✓
Overdraft	✓	✓	✓	✓	✓
Leasing and hire purchase	✓	✓	✓	✓	✓
Trade credit	✓	✓	✓	✓	✓
Factoring	✓	✓	✓	✓	✓

Figure 24.3 Methods of finance used by different types of organisations

- The cost of raising the finance in one way rather than another.

- The flexibility of the finance (i.e. how easy is it to change from one form of finance to another, for example, by transferring a long-term loan into a short-term one).

Methods of finance (see Figure 24.3) can be ranked in order of the length of the term they are typically used for. Going from the shortest term to the longest term we have: trade creditors, overdraft, leasing and hiring, borrowing (loans), profit retention and capital.

Owner's capital

The business owners are the ultimate risk-takers as they provide the business with capital and expect a return only if the business proves to be profitable. Providers of owner's capital benefit most when the firm is successful, but stand to lose the most if it fails. The form these funds take depends on the business's legal form.

Unincorporated businesses are made up of individuals acting as sole traders and groups of individuals who set up in partnership. Their businesses are simple to set up but are not recognised by the law as being separate from the owners. The assets (what the business owns or is owed) and liabilities (what the business owes) of the business belong directly to the owners or partners. This means, therefore, that when a partner leaves or joins the business, the inconvenient situation arises of one partnership ceasing or another partnership commencing. In addition, the owner may be forced to transfer more personal wealth into the firm if the business cannot generate enough funds to pay its debts. Generally speaking, unincorporated businesses are relatively small and are able to raise only limited amounts of capital. However, there are some very big partnerships that have access to vast sums of capital, such as accountancy partnerships and major city law firms.

Unlike sole traders and partnerships, companies are legal identities quite separate from that of their owners. This enables easier exit for investors who wish to tie up their money for only a limited period of time, as the company's ability to trade is unaffected by changes in its ownership. The capital contributed by the owners of the business is divided into shares. Hence an owner is called a *shareholder*.

Shareholders enjoy limited liability as the maximum amount they can lose in the business venture is the amount they paid for the shares they hold. Shareholders receive benefits from profits earned in the form of cash dividends and an increase in the value of their shares.

A private limited company is one that restricts the rights of members to transfer their shares and that limits the ability of the public to subscribe for its shares. Membership of the Alternative Investment Market (AIM) is often seen as a halfway stage between a small company and a fully listed company on the London Stock Exchange.

A fully listed company on the London Stock Exchange has almost limitless opportunities to raise fresh capital from the market, as long as it abides by its rules. For example, a public company has a number of methods open to it for the issue of shares:

- It can create a public issue by prospectus. An issuing house will organise the issue by compiling a prospectus, accompanied by an advertisement and an invitation to buy shares. This can be an expensive method, and up to 7% of the money raised by the issue can go to meet the costs.

- An offer for sale exists where a public company issues shares directly to an issuing house which then offers them for sale at a fixed price. This is also an expensive method and is best used when the size of the issue is too small to need a public issue by prospectus.

- A rights issue is a cheaper method, whereby existing shareholders are offered further shares at an advantageous price.

- A placing avoids the expense of going to the market by placing shares with a number of investors through an intermediary. Since this method avoids the market, the Stock Exchange keeps an eye on these transactions.

- With an offer by tender, an offer is made to the public but the company states a minimum price below which shares will not be offered. Buyers then have to indicate the price they are willing to offer for the shares.

Most capital is normally raised through the issue of *ordinary shares*, which are commonly called *equities*. An ordinary share is a fixed unit of ownership giving the holder the opportunity to share in the profits or losses. Ordinary shares carry voting rights at shareholders' meetings. Shareholders elect the board of a company and can sanction the level of dividends proposed. *Authorised capital* is the amount of share capital a company is empowered by its shareholders to issue. *Issued capital* is the actual amount of share capital that has been issued. In other words, a company may hold back part of its authorised capital to issue at a later date.

Deferred shares are sometimes called *founders' shares*. These are issued to the people who originally set up the business. Sometimes these shares have superior voting rights relative to other shares to ensure that the founders keep a substantial part of the power and influence within a company.

Preference shares are a less flexible class of share. Owners of these shares are not, strictly speaking, owners of the company. Their exact rights are set out in the company articles of association. Holders of these shares have preferential rights to receive dividends if profits exist and, in the event of a company going into liquidation, will receive the face value of their shares before the ordinary shareholders are paid. However, dividends on preference shares are limited to a fixed percentage of par value (the face value of the share).

Some companies issue *cumulative preference shares* and this avoids the difficulty of having to pay preference shareholders if profits are too small. The holder of a cumulative preference share will receive arrears of dividends accumulated from the part in later years. With *redeemable preference shares,* the company can buy back the shares from the shareholders. Redemption can be made from profits or reserves, or it may be financed by a fresh issue of shares. *Participating preference shares* receive dividends above the fixed rate when ordinary shareholders have been paid if the company has done well in a particular year.

There are many advantages of using risk capital instead of alternative sources of finance, including the following:

- If the business has had a bad year, the company is under no legal obligation to pay shareholders.

- Unlike loans, whereby the principal has to be returned at the end of a period on a contracted date, the company does not have to pay the share capital back.

- Interest on loan capital is an overhead that reduces profits, whereas share capital does not create overheads.

However, there are several disadvantages of issuing risk capital. For example:

- It can be expensive to issue shares.

- Companies have to undergo the rigorous

financial requirements of the London Stock Exchange to be listed, and demands for shares are subject to the uncertainties of the marketplace.

- The creation of more shareholders may dilute the influence of the company's founders and thus affect their ability to make decisions.

Discussion point	In a world where it is easier for large firms rather than small businesses to raise finance, why do small businesses continue to exist?

Venture capital

Another form of capital for a business is venture capital. Venture capital companies provide finance in return for an equity (ordinary) shareholding in the company and an element of control. 3i is the largest venture capital company of this type. In recent years, the law has changed to allow companies to buy back their capital if certain safeguards have been met.

Profit retention

One of the most important sources of finance for business are profits that have been ploughed back. Initially, profits are subject to corporation tax, payable to the Inland Revenue. Then a proportion of what is left over is allocated to shareholders as dividends. The directors will recommend how much profit should be distributed in this way. The board needs to satisfy shareholders while, at the same time, ensuring sufficient funds are available for reinvestment.

Case study: The birth of The Body Shop

The presentation of a business plan can be just as important as the facts and figures contained within it. This was a lesson learnt by Anita Roddick when she approached her bank manager for the start-up capital to open her first Body Shop.

She came up with the name after finding her first premises between two funeral parlours in Brighton. She had a good idea and a well-developed business plan, so in 1976 she went to see her bank manager in her Bob Dylan T-shirt, with her two small children in tow. She thought her enthusiasm and energy would convince the bank manager to believe in her. Sadly, she was turned down. So, next time she went she decided to 'dress up like a bloke' in pinstripes and leave the kids behind. After walking into the bank, she came out with a £4,000 loan.

Today, the company has a market value of more than £200 million, operates in 47 countries around the world and makes 400 products.

1 What lesson did Anita Roddick learn about approaching her suppliers of finance?

2 Describe the sort of information she would have included in her business plan.

Borrowing

Borrowing is an important part of business activity. The charge for borrowing is interest, and a crucial element in calculating the interest charge is the amount of risk involved with the loan. For example, longer-term loans tend to carry higher rates, as will loans made to small businesses with an unproven track record.

Bank loans

Bank loans are taken out for a fixed period, repayment being either in instalments or in full at the end of the term. Banks generally provide funds on a short- to medium-term basis, with relatively few loans over more than ten years' duration. The details of bank loans are as follows:

- *Source*: main clearing banks and merchant banks.

- *Cost*: in addition to interest charges levied at so many percentage points over base rate (e.g. 3% over base), there may be arrangement fees and a security fee.

- *Limit*: banks are unlikely to lend more than the owners are putting into the business. In particular, the banks need to be convinced of the owners' commitment to the enterprise before they will pledge their own funds.

Debentures

Large, publicly quoted organisations may borrow money by issuing debentures. A debenture is a certificate issued by a company acknowledging a debt. The debt is paid at a fixed rate of interest and the certificate states the terms of repayment at the end of the period of debt. It is thus a long-term loan that can be traded on the Stock Exchange (i.e. the holder of a debenture can sell it on to someone else). A debenture holder is not a shareholder but a creditor. This means interest payments are an expense to the company and are allowable against profits.

Although holding debentures is much less risky than holding shares, their value in the marketplace will vary according to interest rates. For example, a debenture that pays a 10% rate of interest will be worth 10/8 or 1.25% of its face value when interest rates are 8%. If interest rates rise to 15% it would be worth only 10/15 or 0.66% of its face value. Thus, if interest rates rise the value of the loan falls and *vice versa*.

Bank overdrafts

An overdraft is the most frequently used form of short-term bank finance and is used to ease cash flow problems. Arrangements are made between the customer and the bank to include an agreed limit on an account beyond which the customer will not draw. Interest is calculated on the level of the overdraft on a daily basis. Often a bank will make a special charge for arranging an overdraft and committing the bank's money, whether the withdrawal facilities are used or not. After an agreed period, the bank will examine the account and make a decision about whether to revise or reinstate the limit.

Whereas the account of a personal customer will show a regular input of income per month and a regular pattern of expenditure, this does not happen to a business customer, who is dependent upon debtors paying their bills. As a result, it is easy to understand why business customers often slip into an overdraft situation and need this flexible form of short-term finance (see Figure 24.4).

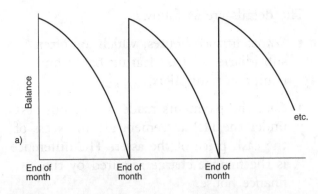

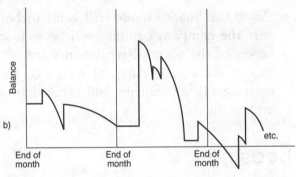

Figure 24.4 Bank accounts: a) personal; b) business

> ## Check your understanding
>
> Make a list of the advantages and disadvantages of arranging for an overdraft facility.

Hire purchase

Hire purchase (HP) allows the business to use an asset without having to find the money immediately. A finance house buys the asset from the supplier and retains ownership of it during the period of the hire-purchase agreement. The business pays a deposit and then further payments to the finance house, as stipulated in the agreement. At the end of the agreement, ownership of the asset is passed to the business.

The details are as follows:

- *Source*: finance houses, which are often subsidiaries of the clearing banks and equipment suppliers.

- *Cost*: the payments made by the business under the HP agreement are in excess of the cash price of the asset. The difference is the finance charge required by the finance house.

- *Limit*: the finance house will want to be sure the company's profits will be well in excess of the planned repayments and that it has a good payment record on the existing HP agreements and other debt arrangements.

Leasing

Leasing an asset provides similar benefits to hire purchase in that a leasing agreement with a finance house (lessor) allows the business (lessee) to use an asset without having to buy it outright. The real distinction between the two forms of finance is that leasing does not confer an automatic right to eventual ownership of the asset. It is a very popular form of finance for company vehicles, office equipment and factory machinery.

The benefits of leasing are that:

- It enables a business to have complete use of an asset without having to use risk or loan capital to finance it.

- Leasing payments are an expense and are charged to the profit and loss account before tax is assessed.

- Leasing enables businesses to change their equipment more often and thereby keep up to date with modern technology.

- Tax allowances can be claimed by the lessor and be filtered through to the lessee in lower lease payments.

Case study: RealCall float

RealCall (www.realcall.net/index.ihtml), the Internet callback service, has recently gone public in a flotation valued at around £300 million. RealCall has three main products – RealCall Alert, Telebanner and TVCall. RealCall Alert links a company's web site to its call centre or any telephone so it can talk to potential customers while their interest is still fresh. Telebanner is a version of RealCall Alert that sites on an online banner advert, and TVCall is a service that allows users to contact call centres by clicking directly on Internet adverts.

Before going public, they announced they had gained £8 million of venture capital funding from Advent Venture Partners and ACT Venture Capital as a prelude to the float. Under the terms of the venture capital deal, Advent and ACT are providing cash for investment in RealCall infrastructure in Britain, America and Germany.

The float will make millionaires of the three RealCall directors, who will own around 40% of the company at the time of the listing.

1 Explain why RealCall required investment capital.
2 How did they obtain funding for their expansion?
3 What alternative sources of finance could they have used?

Although leasing enables the lessee to manage expenditure more easily, the lessee does not own the equipment. If income falters, lease payments may impose a considerable burden on a business; furthermore, loans cannot be secured on assets that are leased.

Factoring

Trade debts mean that money can often be tied up for as much as six months. For a business requiring cash quickly, this can be a real problem. A factoring company may offer immediate payment of part of the amount owed to a business (normally around 80%), with the balance being paid when the debt is settled. This provides an immediate way for a business to improve its cash flow. In return, the factoring company will charge a fee that includes interest and administration charges.

Commercial mortgages

A mortgage is a loan secured on land and buildings and can be used either to finance the purchase of the property or to provide security for a loan applied to some other purpose. It is a long-term financing arrangement of typically 10–30 years. The details are as follows:

- *Source*: financial institutions, such as insurance companies and pension funds as well as the banks.

- *Cost*: interest on amount outstanding.

- *Limit*: values of the property and income are the basis for determining the maximum mortgage permissible.

Sale and lease-back

This involves a business selling its freehold property to an investment company and then leasing it back over a long period of time. This releases funds for other purposes in the business.

Loan Guarantee Scheme

The government guarantees the repayment of 70–85% of a medium-term bank loan (2–7 years) in return for a 2.5% annual premium. The scheme enables banks to lend money to businesses of less than 200 employees for projects that would otherwise be thought too risky.

Suppliers

Suppliers are a valuable source of finance for many businesses. Just as the business may give credit to its own customers, the firm may be able to negotiate credit terms with its suppliers. Credit terms are typically 30 days from date of supply or the end of the month following the month of delivery (i.e. 30–60 days).

Public private partnerships (PPPs)

Over recent years the government has forced its departments and local authorities to look for finance for capital projects. By doing this it has created a new industry – public private partnerships, which used to be known as private finance initiatives (PFIs). The aim of public private initiatives is to use the private sector to manage and run projects or institutions that have been traditionally associated with the public sector. Others have criticised the initiative because they feel it is a smoke screen behind which the government reduces the amount it makes available for a capital project by encouraging the private sector to take on more responsibility.

For example, a public private initiative might be to build and run a new school. Instead of the local authority paying for the building, under the public private partnership it would be built by the private sector and then leased back. One issue would be how much influence the private investor would have over the running and maintenance of the school. The Channel Tunnel rail link is a public private partnership and is set for completion in 2003. It is claimed that public private partnerships provide an alternative way of looking at investments in the public sector, with opportunities existing for new prisons, hospitals, colleges and public buildings, as well as for roads, light-rail systems and bridges.

The European Union

The EU provides a range of finance for businesses, such as loans or loan guarantees for investment projects.

In your business plan:
What source of finance will you draw on in your business?

Budgets, start-up and working capital

In Chapter 21 we saw that budgets help organisations to look into and plan for the future. The aim of budgeting is, therefore, to provide a system of control that enables the organisation to work towards its objectives. In fact, it has been said that

Check your understanding

Identify the most relevant sources of finance for each of the following organisations:

- A school wishes to replace its existing photocopier with a more elaborate version, which they want to pay for over a period of time.
- The Queens' Medical Centre wishes to build a new hospital wing on vacant land close to its existing site.
- Prakesh Patel needs a new computer system costing £5,000 for his business.
- A medium-sized company wants to expand its factory building. The cost will be £500,000.
- A small firm is having temporary problems with its cash flow.

'the preparation of a budget depends critically upon its purpose.' In fact, there are two kinds of purposes for budgets. To:

1 Provide a 'map' of an organisation and all the parts of the organisation which go into that map.

2 Form the basis for financial management and control.

A budget can be defined as a 'quantitative economic plan for a period of time'. Let us look at these terms more closely:

- *Quantitative* A budget involves values expressed as quantities. An organisation may produce a number of household brand names. It would only be through quantification that a worth could be attributed to these brands.

- *Economic* A budget is expressed in economic terms. Though a business may be a market leader, its budgets are expressed in financial rather than market terms.

- *Plan* A budget is a plan designed to achieve a range of objectives. It is not a forecast in the sense of a prediction, but an intention (i.e. something which is intended to happen).

- *Time* Budgets have to be expressed over a specific time period.

For organisations to operate effectively and plan for the future, they need to pay for the use of resources. For example, start-up capital for a business would have to include the following:

- *Fixed assets* These are relatively permanent items the business owns and operates, such as premises, equipment, plant and machinery, motor vehicles, furniture and other tangible items.

- *Capital expenditure* is the form of expenditure that relates mainly to fixed assets. This is because expenditure upon some assets lasts longer than one year.

- *Working capital* This is more usually defined as current assets minus current liabilities. Working capital provides the short-term funds that enable the organisation to operate – for example, paying for stocks of raw materials and paying the running costs of the business.

- *Revenue expenditure* relates mainly to the shorter-term running costs of the organisation because it is on items that last less than one year.

Check your understanding

Within the educational establishment you attend, think of five examples of relatively long-term assets that are fixed and five examples of items that are short term and that will have been sourced by working capital.

In your business plan:

Create a budget for your business and include estimates of start-up costs and working capital.

Break-even forecasts

The *break-even point* is the point at which sales levels are high enough not to make a loss, but not high enough to make a profit.

The concept of break-even is a development from the principles of *marginal costing*. Marginal costing is a commonly employed technique that uses costs to forecast profits from the production and sales levels expected in future periods. The great benefit of marginal costing over other costing methods is that it overcomes the problem of allocating fixed costs – only variable costs are allocated, as we shall see.

The difference between an item's selling price and the variable costs needed to produce that item is known as *contribution* (that is, its contribution to the whole profit):

Contribution = Selling price per unit
less Variable costs per unit

By producing and selling enough units to produce a total contribution that is in excess of the *fixed costs*, an organisation will make a profit.

For example, Penzance Toys Ltd manufactures plastic train sets for young children. They anticipate that next year they will sell 8,000 units at £12 per unit. Their variable costs are £5 per unit and their fixed costs are £9,000. From the above formula we can deduce that the contribution is £12 minus £5, which is £7 per unit. Therefore, for each unit made,

	(£)
Sales revenue (8000 × £12)	96,000
Less: Marginal costs (8000 × £5)	40,000
Total contribution	56,000
Less: Fixed costs	9,000
Net profit	47,000

Figure 24.5 Penzance Toys Ltd: profit statement

£7 will go towards paying fixed costs. We can also see this using totals to show how much profit will be made if the company sells 8,000 units (Figure 24.5). The problem can also be looked at by constructing a table, as in Figure 24.6.

Check your understanding

Rovers Medallions Ltd produce a standard-size trophy for sports shops and clubs. They hope to sell 2,000 trophies next year at £9 per unit. Their variable costs are £5 per unit and their fixed costs are £4,000.

Draw up a profit statement to show how much profit they will make in the year. Also construct a table to show how much profit they will make at each 500 units of production up to 3,000 units.

Marginal costing is particularly useful for making short-term decisions – for example, helping to set the selling price of a product, or deciding whether or not to accept an order. It might also help an organisation to decide whether to buy in a component or whether to produce it themselves.

Break-even analysis is a concept that is central to the process of marginal costing. Breaking even is the unique point at which an organisation makes neither profit nor loss. If sales go beyond the break-even point, profits are made, and if they are below the break-even point, losses are made. In marginal costing it is the *point at which the contribution equals the fixed costs.*

To calculate the break-even point there are two stages:

1 Calculate the unit contribution (selling price less variable costs).

2 Divide the fixed costs by the unit contribution:

$$\text{Break-even point} = \frac{\text{Fixed costs}}{\text{Unit contribution}}$$

Units of production	Fixed costs (£)	Variable costs (£)	Total costs (£)	Revenue (£)	Profit (loss) (£)
1,000	9,000	15,000	14,000	12,000	(2,000)
2,000	9,000	10,000	19,000	24,000	5,000
3,000	9,000	15,000	24,000	36,000	12,000
4,000	9,000	20,000	29,000	48,000	19,000
5,000	9,000	25,000	34,000	60,000	26,000
6,000	9,000	30,000	39,000	72,000	33,000
7,000	9,000	35,000	44,000	84,000	40,000
8,000	9,000	40,000	49,000	96,000	47,000
9,000	9,000	45,000	54,000	108,000	54,000
10,000	9,000	50,000	59,000	120,000	61,000

Figure 24.6 Penzance Toys Ltd: profit table

For example, in Penzance Toys Ltd (see above) the contribution per unit is £7 and the fixed costs are £9,000. The break-even point would therefore be:

$$\frac{9,000}{7} = 1,286 \text{ units (to nearest unit)}$$

The *sales value* at the break-even point can be calculated by multiplying the number of units by the selling price per unit. For Penzance Toys this would be:

$$1,286 \times £12 = £15,432$$

Penzance Toys have covered their costs (fixed and variable) and broken even with a sales value of £15,432. Anything sold in excess of this will provide them with profits.

If an organisation has a *profit target* or selected operating point to aim at, break-even analysis can be used to calculate the number of units that need to be sold and the value of sales required to achieve that target.

For example, we can imagine that Penzance Toys wish to achieve a target of £15,000 profit. By adding this £15,000 to the fixed costs and dividing by the contribution, the number of units can be found that need to be sold to meet this target. Thus:

$$\frac{£9,000 + £15,000}{£7} = 3,429 \text{ units (to nearest unit)}$$

The difference between the break-even point and the selected level of activity designed to achieve the profit target is known as the *margin of safety*.

A break-even chart can be used to show changes in the relationship between costs, production volumes and various levels of sales activity. The following is the procedure to construct a break-even chart

Check your understanding

B. Hive Beehives Ltd are a small business selling hives to local keepers. Each hive is sold for £25. Fixed costs are £18,000 and variable costs are £13 per unit. The company wishes to achieve a profit of £18,000.

Calculate the break-even point in both units and sales value. Calculate both the units and sales value necessary to achieve the selected operating profit.

(you may find it useful to look at Figure 24.7 as you read these procedures):

- Label the horizontal axis for units of production and sales.

- Label the vertical axis to represent the values of sales and costs.

- Plot fixed costs. Fixed costs will remain the same over all levels of production, so plot this as a straight line parallel to the horizontal axis.

- Plot the total costs (variable costs and fixed costs). This will be a line rising from where the fixed cost line touches the vertical axis. It is plotted by

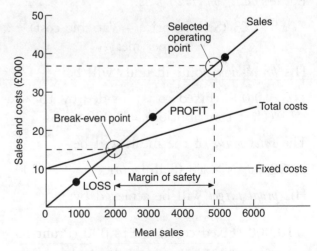

Figure 24.7 Eddie Bowen's break-even chart

calculating the total costs at two or three random levels of production.

- Sales are plotted by taking two or three random levels of turnover. The line will rise from the intersection of the two axes.

The break-even point will be where the total cost line and sales line intersect. The area to the *left* of the break-even point between the sales and total cost lines will represent *losses*, and the area to the *right* of the break-even point between these lines will represent *profit*.

As always, an example will make this clearer. Eddie Bowen plans to set up a small restaurant. In doing so he knows he will immediately incur annual fixed costs of £10,000. He is concerned about how many meals he will have to sell to break even. Extensive market research indicates a typical customer will pay £8 for a meal, and Eddie knows that variable costs (such as cooking ingredients and the costs of serving customers) will amount to about £3. Eddie has set himself a profit target of £14,000 for the first year of operation. Our task is to advise Eddie on the number of meals he has to sell and to indicate to him his margin of safety.

Eddie's *unit contribution* is:

£8 − £3 (Selling price − Variable cost)
= £5 per meal

His *break-even* point in units will be:

£10,000 (Fixed costs) divided by £5
(Unit contribution) = 2,000 meals

The *sales value* of the meals will be:

2,000 meals × £8 (Selling price) = £16,000

His *profit target* will be achieved by:

$$\frac{£10,000 \text{ (Fixed costs)} + £14,000 \text{ (Profit target)}}{£5 \text{ (Unit contribution)}} = 4,800 \text{ meals}$$

Check your understanding

Make up an example of a business selling a product of your choice. Construct a break-even chart and then comment how the chart could be used for planning and making key decisions within the organisation.

The *margin of safety* will be the difference between the selected level of activity and the break-even point. It will be between 4,800 meals with a turnover of £38,400 and 2,000 meals with a turnover of £16,000.

The three random levels of variable costs and sales chosen for the purpose of plotting the break-even chart at 1,000 meals, 3,000 meals and 5,000 meals are:

	1,000 meals £	3,000 meals £	5,000 meals £
Variable costs (£3/meal)	3,000	9,000	15,000
Fixed costs	10,000	10,000	10,000
Total costs	13,000	19,000	25,000
Sales	8,000	24,000	40,000

We can now plot the break-even chart (Figure 24.7) which shows graphically the break-even point of 2,000 meals with a sales revenue of £16,000. The margin of safety can be seen on the chart if we identify the selected level of profit (at 4,800 meals) and the targeted turnover (of £38,400), and compare this point with the break-even point.

The break-even chart is a simple visual tool enabling managers to anticipate the effects of changes in production and sales upon the profitability of an organisation's activities. It emphasises the importance of earning revenue and is particularly helpful for those who are unused to interpreting accounting information.

The break-even chart can be used to explore changes in a number of key variables. These may include:

- *Sales volume and value* By looking at the chart it is possible to predict the effects of any changes in sales trends. For example, a sudden fall in sales may lead to a loss and a sudden increase may improve profitability.

- *Profits or losses at a given level of production* The break-even chart enables a business to monitor levels of production. By

doing this, important decisions can be made if changes take place.

- *Prices* It is possible to use the break-even chart to analyse different business scenarios. For example, given market research information, what would happen if we reduced price by £2?

- *Costs* The effects of any sudden changes in costs can be plotted on the break-even chart.

Any of the above may affect an organisation's ability to achieve its selected operating point and margin of safety. The break-even chart is a useful management technique upon which to base action that enables an organisation to achieve its plans.

Task 1

John Smith had a visit from an aged relative who wanted advice. For many years she had run a small hotel in a market town in the Thames valley. After careful consideration she had decided to 'call it a day' and retire, but she was keen to see the business continue and wished to retain her ownership in it.

John is interested in a proposition she has put forward, which involves running the hotel on her behalf. The hotel has been allowed to deteriorate over the years and, in John's opinion, it is obvious that extensive refurbishment is necessary before he could realistically consider her proposal. The hotel is, however, in a prime spot, was extensively used little more than ten years ago, and John feels that, with hard work, it has the potential to become successful again.

He arranged for a number of quotations to be made for the building work. The most favourable received was for £180,000, which involved extensive interior redecoration and refurbishment as well as completely reorganising the reception and kitchen areas.

John's intention is that the finance for the building work should come from a five-year bank loan with a fixed annual interest rate of 10%, payable each calendar month, and based upon the original sum. The loan principal would be paid back in five equal annual instalments.

He has estimated the following fixed and variable costs:

Fixed

Annual loan repayment	£36,000
Annual interest on loan	£18,000
Business rate and water rates	£7,000 per annum
Insurance	£4,500 per annum
Electricity	£1,300 per quarter
Staff salaries	£37,000 per annum

Variable

These include direct labour (such as cleaners and bar staff), as well as the cost of food, bar stocks, etc. After careful research John has estimated these to be £2,000 for each 100 customers who visit the hotel.

John has had a local agency conduct an extensive market research survey and feels confident the hotel will attract about 100 customers per week, who will each spend on average (including accommodation, food and drinks) about £70 in the hotel.

1 Work out the break-even point for the hotel in both numbers of customers and value.

2 Work out the numbers of customers required to make a gross profit of £35,000.

3 Draw a break-even chart showing the break-even point, the profit target and the margin of safety.

4 What other information might John Smith require before deciding to go ahead with the project?

Task 2

Theme Holidays Ltd are a private company that specialise in providing holidays for adults and children alike who require a unique form of entertainment. All their holidays involve overseas packages based upon a theme. With the opening of Disneyland Paris they are finding that half the packages they now provide are based on this one resort, while the other half are to theme destinations in the USA.

Theme Holidays are currently reviewing their profitability for 2002. They anticipate their fixed overheads will be £450,000 for the year. With the Disneyland Paris packages, a quarter of the variable costs go in travel costs, at an average of £30 per package. They anticipate selling packages at an average of £160 per holiday in 2002.

The American holidays are sold at an average price of £650 per holiday. Travel costs of £200 for the American holidays comprise half the variable costs of the holiday.

Market research has revealed that, during 2002, Theme Holidays expect to sell 400 holidays.

1 Work out the contribution for both the European and American holidays.
2 Calculate the company's profit for the year before tax and interest.
3 Market research also revealed that, if Theme Holidays reduced their prices by 10%, they could sell 300 more holidays per year. Calculate how this would affect profitability and advise accordingly.
4 Theme Holidays are aware of the size of their fixed overheads. How would a 10% reduction in fixed overheads through cost-cutting measures affect both the above?

Task 3

Insolvency specialists, it seems, are not the only type of business to flourish during a recession. As many companies drive to improve efficiency and cut costs without compromising quality, many have turned to contracted business services in an effort to hive off non-core activities.

CleanEasy has benefited enormously from this process. They claim that conditions are booming as many companies wake up to the benefits of utilising professionally managed external support services. CleanEasy have noted the rapid growth of the contracted services sector with pleasure and feel confident this area will continue to grow. They have responded rapidly to this growth by undertaking an expansion programme that has resulted in an increase in their fixed costs so that they are now as follows:

	£
Loan repayments and interest	230,000
Rent and rates	95,000
Insurance	980
Staff salaries	325,000
Other fixed overheads	100,000
Promotion	5,000

The average contract size for CleanEasy is £24,000 per annum and they currently expect to increase their number of contracts for the forthcoming year to 130. Each contract will cost them at least £12,000 in direct labour and at least £4,000 in direct materials. Other variable overheads will be about £1,000.

1 Work out the break-even point for CleanEasy in terms of value and volume (to the nearest contract).
2 Draw a break-even chart to illustrate the above.

3 How much profit will they make with 130 contracts?

4 Given the nature of their investment, CleanEasy wish to make £300,000 profit for the year. How many contracts would they require to achieve this?

5 One strategy CleanEasy are proposing to adopt is to increase their promotion budget. If they increase the budget to £50,000, research has indicated they will achieve at least 35 more contracts. How will this affect profitability?

6 Another strategy they are considering is to decrease price. Further research has revealed that, if the average contract price fell to £22,000, they could expect to gain at least 45 new contracts. How will this affect profitability?

Break-even analysis is often considered to oversimplify organisational behaviour by reducing it to an equation: how to generate sufficient contribution to cover fixed costs and provide a surplus (profits).

The limitations are as follows:

- It can be argued that, in real situations, fixed costs actually vary with different activity levels, and so a stepped fixed cost line would provide a more accurate guide.

- Many organisations fail to break even because of a limiting factor restricting their ability to do so (e.g. a shortage of space, labour or orders).

- The variable cost and sales lines are unlikely to be linear (i.e. straight). Discounts, special contracts and overtime payments mean the cost line is more likely to be a curve.

- Break-even charts depict short-term relationships, and forecasts are therefore unrealistic when the proposals cover a number of years.

- Break-even analysis is (like all other methods) dependent upon the accuracy of forecasts made about costs and revenues. Changes in the market and in the cost of raw materials could affect the success of the technique.

Task 4

Competition in the air travel business is fierce – witness the price competition between carriers on transatlantic flights.

One such airline is Richard Branson's Virgin Atlantic. This operates on the busiest international routes only, where it can fill most of the seats on its planes. It is the only way a small airline can compete with companies like British Airways.

Although Virgin are competitive on price, Branson knows his firm cannot compete on this alone. Bigger airlines benefit from economies of scale. So Virgin attempt to provide a better service for a lower fare than their rivals.

Virgin launched a new service in recent years called 'mid class' for the full price of an economy ticket. By reducing the number of economy-class cabins, there are fewer seats on a plane, but Branson thinks Virgin gains in two ways. By:

1 Filling a greater proportion of seats as flights rarely operate at full capacity.

2 Encouraging more early bookings and less need for last-minute price discounting.

The rationale behind this move was that customers who are prepared to pay the full price of an economy ticket would prefer to travel with Virgin if they received a better service for their money.

The following are some illustrative costs and revenues for a full-capacity return flight operation to North America:

	£
Depreciation of plane	25,000
Fuel	27,000
Flight crew costs	3,000
Cabin crew costs	6,000
Food	4,000
Selling costs and administration	10,000
Landing fees	15,000
Maintenance	10,000
Total cost for identical mid class and economy class	100,000

A plane with large economy class can carry 375 passengers with an average revenue per passenger of £350. A plane with mid class can carry 325 passengers with an average revenue per passenger of £425.

1 Analyse and then comment on the fixed costs and variable costs in this operation.

2 Identify the break-even point for a standard economy-class plane with the new mid class (draw a break-even chart for each level of service and identify the break-even point for each).

3 If 80% of seats were filled, how much profit would each type of service make?

4 Some airlines sell tickets at £100 each. How can last-minute discounting make sense?

5 Evaluate Richard Branson's decision to introduce mid class.

In your business plan:
Set out a break-even chart for your business.

Cash flow forecasts

In Chapter 21 we looked at simple cash flow forecasts. As managers within organisations plan ahead they have to ask key questions, such as:

- Can we afford X?

- Are we going to be able to pay the wages bill this month?

- Why, when the business is making profits, do we not seem to have enough cash?

- If we borrow money to buy a new machine, can we meet the repayments?

To answer such questions and make critical decisions, an organisation has to engage in financial planning, which involves using present knowledge of the business to plan ahead.

To plan ahead, a financial manager must have a realistic understanding of what is happening within the organisation – for example, when is money going to come in, what is it needed for, and would it be possible to use some of it for expansion and development?

Check your understanding

Explain how cash differs from profit. Draw up a simple cash flow forecast for a small organisation. Describe where the information would come from to form the basis of the cash flow forecast.

In your business plan:

Set out a simple cash flow forecast for your business.

Projected profit and loss accounts, and start-up balance sheets

Using the outline shown below, it is possible to set out a projected profit and loss account. In each month target figures for income and expenditure can be placed. Do this for a fictitious business over a twelve-month period using a *spreadsheet*:

The forecast trading, profit and loss account for the year ended . . .

	£	£	£	£
	Month 1	Month 2	Month 3	Month 4
Sales				
Opening stock				
Purchases				
Less: Closing stock				
Cost of sales				
Gross profit				
Less: Expenses				
Electricity				
Stationery				
Business rate				
Loan interest paid				
Depreciation				
Marketing expenses				
Training				
Debenture interest paid				
Advertising				
Sundry expenses				
Directors' salaries				
Net profit or loss				

The following notes may help you:

- *Sales*. Remember to allow for seasonal fluctuations, and break sales down by product groups. Choose the groups according to the markets you have targeted and the sales patterns that characterise each. (For example, if you were selling ice-creams and hot dogs, you might expect the sales of ice-creams to rise in the summer and fall in the winter, and the reverse situation to apply to hot dogs!)

- *Expenses*. This is the reverse side of income, so be accurate! Even if some overheads (e.g. rent), are paid quarterly, spread the amounts over the whole period.

- *Depreciation*. This figure is the part of your profits set aside to pay for replacement assets when the ones you have wear out or become unsuitable.

- *Net profit or loss*. Where you make a loss, put this in brackets.

Before proceeding to produce a balance sheet for your business, you should review the notes on balance sheets on page 513 in Chapter 19.

A balance sheet is a list of all the assets (what the firm owns) and liabilities (what the firm owes). These assets may be:

- Fixed assets (e.g. land and buildings, plant and machinery, fixtures and fittings).

- Current assets (such as stocks, debtors, cash and bank).

- Intangible assets (e.g. relationships with customers, business and technical know-how, which have a value but no physical existence).

On the liabilities side we have investors' capital, because the firm owes it to the investors. Similarly, the business is, in effect, being funded by money owned by the firm to the Inland Revenue and other creditors' as well as money owed to the bank. Set out your balance sheet like the one shown in Figure 24.8.

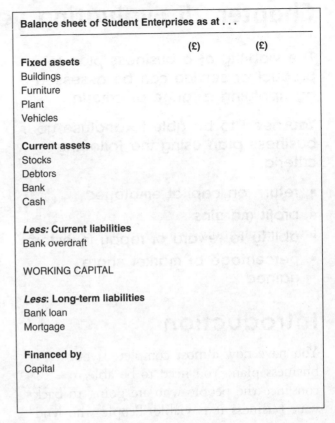

Balance sheet of Student Enterprises as at . . .

	(£)	(£)
Fixed assets		
Buildings		
Furniture		
Plant		
Vehicles		
Current assets		
Stocks		
Debtors		
Bank		
Cash		
Less: **Current liabilities**		
Bank overdraft		
WORKING CAPITAL		
Less: **Long-term liabilities**		
Bank loan		
Mortgage		
Financed by		
Capital		

Figure 24.8 Sample balance sheet

In your business plan:

Set out a projected profit and loss account and start-up balance sheet for your business.

Chapter 25 Evaluating your business plan

The viability of a business plan for a product or service can be assessed by applying a range of criteria.

You need to be able to analyse your business plan using the following criteria:

- return on capital employed
- profit margins
- ability to reward or repay investors
- percentage of market share gained.

Introduction

You have now almost completed your business plan. You need to be able to convince the people who are going to back your business it is viable. People who lend you money, or who are willing to become part owners of your business (e.g. partners and shareholders), will want to know their money is safe. They will want to know that, by putting their money into your business, they will receive at least as high a return on their capital investment as they would from the next best alternative use of that money. You therefore need to evaluate your business plan to show it is viable.

Who will be involved in evaluating the plan?

(see Figure 25.1)

To make it easy for the business plan to be analysed and evaluated, it needs to have the following characteristics:

THE BUSINESS PLAN

Internal scrutineers
The owners of the business (e.g. the sole owner, partners, shareholders)

External scrutineers
People who have lent money to the company (e.g. banks, debenture holders, etc.)

Figure 25.1 The people involved in evaluating the business plan

- *Clearly set out and attractive to the eye.* A modern business plan should look good, and the reader should be able to find his or her way around the various sections of the plan with ease. The plan, therefore, needs to use state-of-the-art desktop publishing techniques, including spreadsheets, tables and charts.

- *Systematically organised.* The plan should be set out in clear sections that include all the relevant information. There should be a table of contents at the start of the work, and related pieces of information should be grouped together (e.g. financial information, marketing information, etc.).

- *It should not be too long.* Readers of a business plan want to find their way round quickly – and check that the relevant information is set out in a convincing way. The reader who cannot quickly track down the market research information, the cash flow projection, profit projections, etc., will become frustrated and may even begin to wonder if the sheer volume of information may be masking real weaknesses in the business.

People who lend businesses money, or who become involved as part owners, tend to take a pretty hard-nosed view of whether to get involved with a specific business or not.

The sorts of questions they will be seeking the answers to when they invest in or lend money to a business are as follows:

- Will the business use my capital in an efficient way – so that there is a good rate of return on it relative to alternative investment opportunities?

- Will the business make a healthy profit margin indicating the business plan is sound?

- Will the business reward us adequately for the risk we are taking in tying up

funds with it – as well as being able to repay the initial investment if the need arises?

- How large a share of the market will the organisation be able to command? The larger the market share, the more opportunity the organisation may have to develop competitive advantage over its rivals.

Of course, anyone lending money to or putting money into a business should be aware of the risks involved. A business plan is simply that – a plan. A well-thought-out plan enables a business to step out with confidence. It does not, and can never, guarantee business success.

Case study: Investing in the new economy

The recent history of new Internet-based companies in this country shows us just how uncertain the world of business is at a time when everyone knows someone who is thinking of, or is in the process of, setting up a web page designing business.

In the last quarter of 1999 and the first quarter of 2000, we saw the rise of the .com companies (i.e. new companies that were based on the Internet). For example, one of the best known of these .com businesses was Lastminute.com – a company specialising in last-minute deals (traded through the medium of the Internet). For example, if you are looking for a holiday on the Costa Brava this weekend you will probably be able to book it through Lastminute.com, or if you want to hire a car tomorrow or to book a hotel in Exeter at 24 hours' notice.

Another company that caught the eye was Studentnet.com – an Internet company set up by four students at the Nottingham Trent University providing a range of online information for students nationally.

These and many other Internet companies captured the imagination of the investing public in late 1999/early 2000. At the time, many of these companies

were making losses rather than profits. However, what appealed to investors was the potential of these ideas to generate future profits. For example, Studentnet was snapped up by a larger American company for £10 million making the student entrepreneurs millionaires overnight.

Increasingly, shares in Internet companies were being bought through online trading. Internet surfers who were enthusiastic about the power of the Internet were buying shares using this medium. All this led to a wave of excitement about these new companies.

However, as with any period in which new companies are rapidly appearing, it is not always easy to tell which ones will be successful and which have little substance to them. Many investors rushed to put money into the new companies, not fully understanding what the return on their investment might be.

A number of commentators likened this rapid development of new companies to that of the railway age of the nineteenth century, when thousands of miles of railways were built in this country. Of course, during the railway age many of the railway companies were spectacular failures, going down with huge debts.

In the second quarter of 2000, the share price of many of the new Internet companies took a tumble. One of the triggers to this fall was the rapid decline in the share price of Microsoft (www.microsoft.com) – the world's largest information and communications technology company. The law courts in the USA were contemplating the breakup of Microsoft because of the way in which they had restricted competition in the ICT industry. If even the mighty Microsoft could slip from their pedestal, there was no certainty that the new .com companies would secure safe profits for the future.

From the second quarter of 2000, investors began to become more realistic about the future of the .com companies. In a fast-changing business environment, it is best not to be too optimistic about profit forecasts for Internet-based companies – where it is all too easy to copy a good idea and in which 'better' ideas are always coming to the fore.

In setting out profit forecasts, it always pays to be realistic.

1 Identify one .com company that has recently been in the news.
2 What is the product or service of that company?
3 What has been happening to the share price of the company? Why?
4 Assess the long-term prospects of the company.
5 If you were going to evaluate the business plan of a new .com company, what would you be particularly looking for in the plan that might persuade you to lend money to or invest in the company?

Good idea

One of the first things to look for in evaluating a business plan is the extent to which plan is based on a 'good idea'. Sometimes, good ideas are completely original ones. For example, William Bartfield (an inventor from Leeds) was the first person to invent a chip-making machine (Figure 25.2). Mr Bartfield spent ten years researching production of the machine. His Prize Frize company, backed by investors, spent £5 million on research and development. Mr Bartfield first found a company that produced reconstituted potato for the armed forces and then began to develop a machine that would turn out hot, fresh chips within seconds of coins being deposited.

The machines cut the potato concentrate into 33 chips, then a conveyor moves them to a fryer for a 15-second fry in vegetable oil. They drop into a second cooking basket for 30 seconds and, finally, fall into a paper carton. The consumer deposits his or her coins in the machine and waits 45 seconds for the chips.

Mr Bartfield is just one of a long line of people with bright ideas who have been able to create business ideas – people such as Akio Morita, the former Chairman of Sony, who invented the Sony Walkman, and Laszlo Biro, who invented the ballpoint pen.

However, a good idea is not necessarily a novel idea no one has thought of before. Many of the best business ideas are simply copies of good ideas that have been tried elsewhere. Indeed, Heinz are already creating their own chip-making machines, and there are many producers of 'walkmans', 'diskmans' and ballpoint pens.

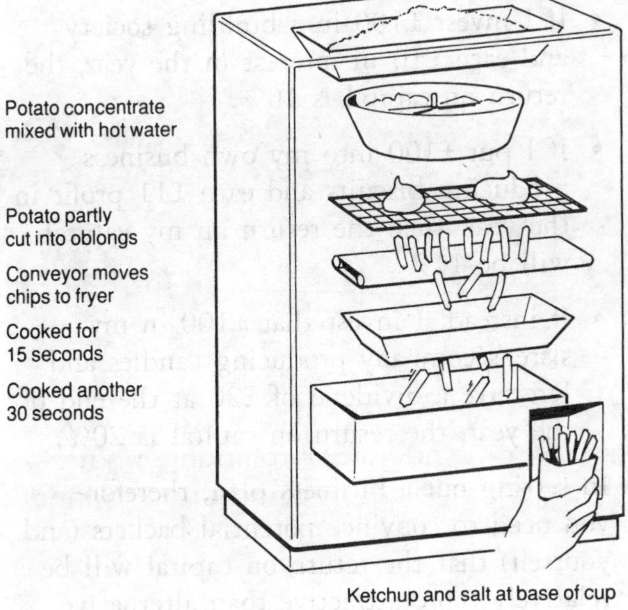

Attention to detail

Just as important in the creation of a business plan as the idea itself is the attention to detail that goes into the planning process. Far too many businesses fail because the business plan has been rushed.

A good business plan will not only show careful attention to the product but also to the market and to financial aspects. Throughout this text we have been emphasising the importance of understanding your market. Market research provides the sort of security that enables a business to proceed, knowing there is a demand for the product. Market research reveals exactly what it is consumers are seeking in a new product. In evaluating a business plan, it is important to ask: 'Does the entrepreneur understand their market?' 'Do they really understand what consumers are looking for?' And, of course: 'Is the market large enough to sustain the business?'

Potato concentrate mixed with hot water

Potato partly cut into oblongs

Conveyor moves chips to fryer

Cooked for 15 seconds

Cooked another 30 seconds

Ketchup and salt at base of cup

Figure 25.2 The chip-vending machine

In addition, it is important to show attention to detail in doing the financial calculations. For example, in setting out projected cash flows, you need to get only one or two figures wrong to go seriously adrift. Robert Maxwell, one of the best-known business figures of the twentieth century, failed to anticipate changes in interest rates that were to create an impossible burden of debt for his business. He secretly 'borrowed' money from the pension fund of one of his companies to support other parts of his business empire. When this borrowing proved insufficient to cover outgoings, Maxwell disappeared over the side of his yacht. The exact circumstances of what happened will never be known.

Organisation

Coupled with attention to detail, an effective business plan will be based on highly detailed organisation. Jack Cohen, the businessman who created the Tesco organisation, started up as a market trader before moving on to set up a chain of supermarkets. In the early days, he bought cheap and sold cheap. Tesco was a low-price store. In the first half of the twentieth century, this proved to be a successful formula. However, Cohen was not tremendously well organised. He tended to keep figures and plans in his head rather than on paper. He was fortunate enough, though, to employ a professional accountant and, later, professional managers, who were able to make detailed plans for Tesco in an organised way.

While there is a great deal of room in business for flair and risk-taking, this is only likely to be successful in the medium to longer term when built on a platform of detailed organisation.

In evaluating a business plan, therefore, you should look to see if it is:

- Based on a good idea.

- Based on attention to detail.

- Clearly organised and has a clear pattern.

Having satisfied yourself with these attributes, you can go on to weigh up some key financial and marketing criteria in relation to the plan.

Return on capital employed

One way of evaluating the success of a business plan is to look at the return on the capital employed (ROCE) in the business. The figure for capital employed is usually taken as that at the start of the year, as this is the capital that generated the profit in the following year.

The best way to think about the percentage return on capital is to compare it with other investments. For example:

- If I invest £100 in a building society and earn £10 in interest in the year, the return on capital is 10%.

- If I put £100 into my own business producing biscuits and earn £11 profit in the year, then the return on my capital will be 11%.

- If instead, I invest that £100 in my sister's company producing candles and I receive a dividend of £20 at the end of the year, the return on capital is 20%.

In setting out a business plan, therefore, you need to convince potential backers (and yourself) that the return on capital will be relatively more attractive than alternative investment opportunities. Of course, another ingredient is the reliability of the return.

If people reading your business plan feel your figures are just 'pie in the sky', they will not risk their money with you.

Return on capital employed (ROCE) can be measured using the following formula:

$$\text{ROCE} = \frac{\text{Profit before interest and tax}}{\text{Capital employed}} \times 100$$

(*Note*: Capital employed = Net assets before deduction of long-term debt.)

In your business plan:

Outline the expected return on capital employed that your business will generate. Justify why this return will be appropriate, given alternative ways of using that capital.

Profit margins

If you follow the financial reports in any newspaper, one of the key aspects they will headline will be profits:

- 'First quarter results yesterday confirmed that Nestlé is firmly on track to meet projected full-year profits of £2bn by 2006'.

- 'Life is getting tougher in the insurance business – but no one seems to have told Sun Alliance. Its pre-tax profits beat City expectations by jumping 62% to £206m in the March quarter of 2000.'

Profits are a key indicator when judging business performance. It is the first point of reference for many organisational stakeholders. It is all very well saying sales have risen, productivity is soaring and the organisation is growing. However, shareholders and providers of capital will always ask the question: 'But have you made a profit?'

In creating a business plan, the entrepreneur should set out a projected profit and loss account. This account will set out a number of profitability targets. For example:

Profitability targets

	January	February	March
Income			
Sales	3,000	4,000	5,000
Purchases	2,000	2,000	2,000
Gross profit	1,000	2,000	3,000
Gross profit (%)	33	50	60
Expenditures	1,000	1,000	1,000
Net profit	0	1,000	2,000
Net profit (%)	0	25	40

Useful ways of calculating profit are gross profit and net profit margins. In the above example, you can see the person who created the business plan anticipated gross profit percentages would quickly rise from 33% to 60% in the first quarter of the year, while net profit percentages would rise from 0% to 40% over the same period.

r, the reality for most businesses is that, for the first few months of running a business, losses will be made:

- Because it takes time to publicise a business and its products to generate sales.

- The start-up costs of a business usually outweigh early sales.

In evaluating the success of the business, it is important to examine the scale of profits and losses and to identify the point at which the business will break even. The *gross profit margin* shows the gross profit made on sales:

$$\text{Gross profit margin} = \frac{\text{Gross profit}}{\text{Turnover (sales)}} \times 100$$

For example, if your business made £200 gross profit on sales of £1,000, the gross profit margin would be 20%.

In evaluating whether 20% is a suitable gross profit margin, you would need to compare it with returns on similar businesses. For example, if students in a class create business plans involving similar amounts of start-up capital, it may be reasonable to compare profit margins (although it would also be important to compare timescales – some start-up

businesses may take time to make good profit margins, while others break even almost immediately).

Higher profit margins are better than lower ones and, as a general rule, the quicker the turnover the lower the gross profit margin.

The *net profit margin* shows the net profit expressed as a percentage of turnover. It is a measure of the business owners' ability to control indirect costs, as net profit equals gross profit minus overheads:

$$\text{Net profit margin} = \frac{\text{Net profit}}{\text{Turnover}} \times 100$$

Again, higher net profit margins are more desirable than lower ones, and comparisons can be made between business plans by comparing net profit margins. A business that has been planned well will prove to yield higher net profit margins than ones where the planning has been weak.

Check your understanding

In your business plan, outline the intended gross and net profit margins. Explain how these profit margins will be appropriate when compared with similar businesses.

Case study: The growth in Tesco's operating profits

Since the early 1990s Tesco have undergone considerable growth, particularly in market share, which has risen from 10.4% in 1992–93 to 15.2% in 1997–98. The changes in key profit figures are shown in Figure 25.3.

Evaluate the success of Tesco in terms of profit margins.

Year	Turnover (£m)	Operating profit (£m)	Market share %
1992–93	7,581	496	10.4
1993–94	8,600	521	10.7
1994–95	10,101	617	12.0
1995–96	12,094	724	13.7
1996–97	13,887	774	14.5
1997–98	17,400	817	15.2

Figure 25.3 Tesco: changes in profit figures, 1992–98

Case study: Tesco share earnings in the late 1990s

Figure 25.4 shows earnings per share and dividends per share at Tesco. Earnings per share is the profits divided by the number of shares. Dividends per share is the profit distributed to shareholders divided by the number of shares.

Why might an investor be pleased to have put money into Tesco?

Year	Earnings per share (pence)	Dividends per share (pence)
1992–93	18.3	7.10
1993–94	18.8	7.75
1994–95	20.1	8.60
1995–96	21.9	9.60
1996–97	23.5	10.35
1997–98	26.6	11.60

Figure 25.4 Tesco: earnings per share and dividends per share, 1992–98

Ability to reward or repay investors

The prime motive investors have for investing in a business is to gain a return on their investment that is at least equal to what they can make from similar investments.

In setting out your business plan you need to show the rewards your investors will receive in terms of earnings per share or dividends per share – if you are selling shares in your business. You will also need to be able to show the potential investor the rewards they will earn will be comparable to those of similar businesses operating in the same business sector as yourself.

In your business plan:

In your business plan you must make it clear how potential investors in your business will be rewarded, by setting out a forecast of returns you will be making to shareholders (where appropriate). Clearly, if you are not offering shares, this will not be appropriate.

Percentage of market share gained

Much of the success of Tesco during the 1990s was based on the organisation's ability to increase market share. Tesco's market share rose in the following way:

Market share (%)

1992–93	10.4
1993–94	10.7
1994–95	12.0
1995–96	13.7
1996–97	14.5
1997–98	15.2

Being able to win an increasing market share is an important part of business success.

A good business plan will tell the reader about market share. The plan should set out the size of the total market, and what percentage of the market the business will gain. If these figures are well researched, it is possible to make an accurate assessment of likely turnover and profit potential.

Case study: Estimating market share

This case study shows you how you can set out an accurate picture of market share and thus of likely income streams for a business. It is part of a business plan for a New York-based company that uses the Internet to enable people looking for roommates to find people wanting to share accommodation. Note that the projection uses actual figures for the numbers of people living in cities in the USA in the appropriate segment, then projects the number of customers who are likely to use 'Roommates' (in New York City) in order to calculate market share:

> According to the Bureau of Census, Roommates Central's target market segment of people 18–35 years of age represent 25% of the population or 68 million people, with over 80% (54 million) of these living in metropolitan areas. The largest metropolitan area, New York City, represents almost 4.3% or 2,322,000 of these individuals and is growing at a rate of 3.4% annually. Additionally, the Census estimates that 15 million people currently share residences in non-family households. One-third (33%) of this number is estimated to move each year – using classifieds, word of mouth, brokers, agencies, listing services, bulletin boards, billboards, fliers or Internet postings. Within the group, we are looking to achieve a 10% market penetration, representing $50 million in annual income, within our first five years of operations.

This case provides you with a good model for calculating your market share.

1 Find published figures showing the total size of the market you are targeting. Alternatively, carry out some market research to find this out.

2 Identify the segment of the overall market you will be targeting. What is the size of this segment?

3 What percentage of this segment is it realistic for you to be able to win?

4 What, then, will be the total value of the sales you are able to make to this market segment?

Using this approach will provide a useful indicator of the value of sales you can make.

In your business plan:

Identify the effectiveness of your business plan in:
- Identifying the target market.
- Calculating the size of the total market.
- Calculating the size of the market segment targeted.
- Identifying the proportion of this market that can be won.
- Identifying the value of this market share.

Unit 6 Assessment

You need to produce a business plan for a new product or service. The business plan should be wide ranging and should include:

- A market analysis for the product or service you choose.

- A marketing plan.

- A production and quality assurance plan.

- A financial plan, including a spreadsheet or similar document produced using IT.

- An evaluation of all components of the plan.

The entrepreneurs of all new businesses have to plan ahead, often within an uncertain business environment. Although planning will not eliminate risk, it will help to reduce it. Producing a business plan is a key skill in business and one many find it difficult to acquire. If a business requires finance, particularly from a bank or other large creditor, it is essential that a well-researched business plan is developed beforehand.

You may wish to construct your plan based upon a business you have first-hand experience of, or it could simply be fictitious.

To achieve a Grade E you must show you can:

- Effectively use primary and secondary market research data and a competition analysis to complete the market analysis.

- In the marketing plan, describe and explain your choice of product/service, the price(s) of the product/service, the promotional methods for the product/service and how the product/service will be distributed/provided for customers.

- Describe the production process for the product/service, including quality assurance.

- Effectively base the financial plan on a market analysis that identifies sources of finance and includes a budget, break-even analysis, cash flow forecast, projected profit and loss account, and a start-up balance sheet.

- Make a basic judgement about the viability of your business plan.

- Describe and justify the approach you took to constructing your business plan.

To achieve a Grade C you must also show you can:

- Use marketing and financial concepts accurately in your market analysis and marketing and financial plans.

- Make a realistic and detailed judgement about the financial viability of your financial plan.

- Evaluate the business plan accurately using appropriate evaluation tools.

- Describe and justify the approach taken to constructing the business plan and indicate the alternative approaches you considered.

To achieve a Grade A you must also show you can:

- Effectively link the marketing, production and financial elements of your marketing plan.

- Include viable marketing, production and financial alternatives in your assessment of your business plan, based on your understanding of the financial information generated by your evaluation.

- Consider fully the relevant advantages and disadvantages in a detailed justification of the approach taken to constructing your business plan.

Opportunities to develop key skills

As a natural part of carrying out this unit and doing the work set in the text you, will be developing your key skills. Here's how:

Application of number, Level 3

When you are:

You should be able to develop the following key skills evidence:

- Drawing on and interpreting complex numerical data for marketing, production and finance

  N3.1 Plan and interpret information from two different types of sources, including a large data set.

- Interpreting their financial calculations

  N3.3 Interpret results of calculations, present your findings and justify your methods. You must use at least one graph, one chart and one diagram.

Communication, Level 3

When you are:

You should be able to develop the following key skills evidence:

- Making decisions in the planning process for marketing, production, QA and finance

  C3.1a Contribute to a group discussion about a complex subject.

- Reading and synthesising information on the different components of the plan, showing how these components fit together

  C3.2 Read and synthesise information from two extended document about a complex subject. One document should include at least one image to illustrate complex points.

Information technology, Level 3

When you are:

You should be able to develop the following key skills evidence:

- Using data or formats for planning from commercial IT resources, such as those provided by banks and building societies, or via the Internet

  IT3.1 Plan and use different sources to search for and select information required for two different purposes.

- Drawing on data, such as market research data or financial information that you develop and present in new formats to suit the context of the overall plan

  IT3.2 Explore, develop and exchange information and derive new information to meet two different purposes.

- Using different kinds of data and information to create text, a spreadsheet showing your

  IT3.3 Present information from different sources for two different purposes and audiences.

calculations, and images such as graphs or tables appropriate to your analysis

Your work must include at least one example of text, one example of images and one example of number.

Problem solving, Level 3

When you are:

You should be able to develop the following key skills evidence:

- Compiling your plan and considering alternative strategies

- Compiling your plan, producing two alternative cash flow statements

PS3.1 Recognise, explore and describe the problem, and agree the standards for its solution.

PS3.2 Generate and compare at least two options which could be used to solve the problem, and justify the option for taking them forward.

Working with others, Level 3

When you are:

You should be able to develop the following key skills evidence:

- Beginning to draw up your plan you will need to liaise with others and will need to set targets producing the plan

- Compiling your plan, you will need to monitor progress and liaise with your tutor

- Reviewing your plan with your tutor and/or business advisers

WO3.1 Plan the activity with others, agreeing objectives, responsibilities and working arrangements.

WO3.2 Work towards achieving the agreed objectives, seeking to establish and maintain co-operative working relationships in meeting your responsibilities.

WO3.3 Review the activity with others against the agreed objectives and agree ways of enhancing collaborative work.

Index

...BUT HAVE YOU BEEN MAKING A PROFIT?